The Advanced HTML Companion

Second Edition

The Advanced HTML Companion

Second Edition

Keith Schengili-Roberts
Kim Silk-Copeland

AP PROFESSIONAL
AP PROFESSIONAL is a Division of Academic Press, Inc.

San Diego London Boston
New York Sydney Tokyo Toronto

ACADEMIC PRESS
a division of Harcourt Brace & Company
525 B Street, Suite 1900, San Diego, CA 92101-4495
http://www.apnet.com

ACADEMIC PRESS
24-28 Oval Road, London NW1 1DX
http://www.hbuk.co.uk/ap/

Library of Congress Cataloging-in-Publication Data

Schengili-Roberts, Keith.
The advanced HTML companion / Keith Schengili-Roberts, Kim Silk-Copeland, — 2nd ed.
p. cm.
Includes index.
ISBN 0-12-623542-2 (paperback)
1. HTML (Document markup language) I. Silk-Copeland Kim,
II. Title.
QA76.76.H94S257 1998
005.7'2—dc21 98-3866
CIP

Printed in the United States of America
98 99 00 01 02 1P 9 8 7 6 5 4 3 2 1

To the memory of my late father, A. Henry Roberts

Keith J. Schengili-Roberts

To Dr. Sue Wasun, who sent me an email in 1993 asking,
"have you heard about this Mosaic thing?"; to Paul Kaliciak,
a great friend and mentor; and to my mom and family and friends,
for everything. Without their love and support and good humour,
this book would not be a reality.

Kim Silk-Copeland

Contents

Foreword

Welcome to the second edition of The Advanced HTML Companion. When the first edition was written back in late 1996, relative upstart Internet Explorer was just beginning to make serious inroads into a browser marketplace dominated by Netscape Navigator. The World Wide Web Consortium, the standard-setters for HTML, had just issued their HTML 3.2 specification, bringing "official" HTML more in line with what the Web community was actually using. The first book came out at the right time, bringing a no-nonsense approach to HTML when much of what was available was either too technically challenging for the beginner or not concrete enough for the more advanced user. HTML is the core of any Web page, and HTML was the focus of the first edition. But as Keith said in the first edition "the Web does not wait for publications to catch up with it—it pushes on, developing new standards and

programs." It's been just over a year since that line was written, hence the need for a second edition.

Plenty of developments have happened to HTML in the past year: the HTML 4.0 standard, Internet Explorer and Netscape Navigator 4.0, Cascading Style Sheets, XML, and plenty more. HTML has increasingly migrated from the Web to the desktop, appearing in such things as Channels and HTML Help. The Web has become increasingly popular both on the Internet and on many corporate intranets, and is transforming our culture and the way we do business.

This book looks at what are essentially three different types of HTML that currently exist today: the accepted "official" HTML 3.2 standard, the HTML 4.0 specification that exists but whose elements have not yet been fully incorporated, and the HTML tags and features specific to the two most popular browsers, Netscape Navigator and Microsoft Internet Explorer. This book aims to provide you with a working knowledge of the current state of HTML of what's usable, what's not, and what's soon to come.

Whether you are creating your first Web page or need a handy reference while working on your corporate Web site, we hope you find this book suited to your needs.

Keith Schengili-Roberts and Kim Silk-Copeland
Toronto, Ontario
April 2 1998

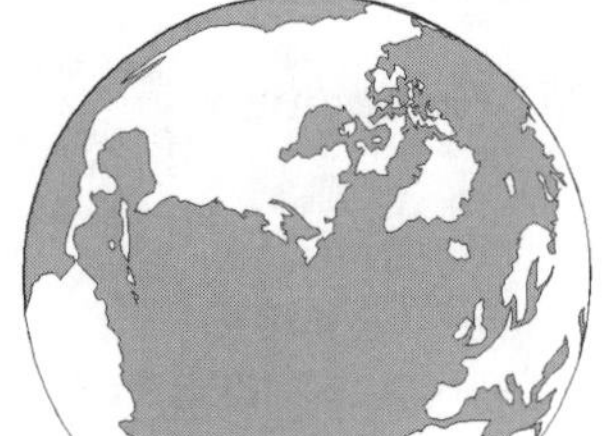

CHAPTER 1

The Beginnings of HTML and the Web

The Origins of HTML and the Web

Think back a few years. It seems like it wasn't long ago when nobody knew about the Internet. Now, the World Wide Web seems to be almost ubiquitous; Web addresses for corporate sites are pasted onto billboards and splashed across TV screens, feature articles about the Internet appear in the national news magazines, and there doesn't seem to be a day that goes by without some story about it appearing on television. The Internet and the Web seem to be everywhere.

But the Internet is over a quarter-century old. During much of its existence, access to it was limited to a relatively small number of people working in academia, government agencies, and in a select few research firms. So why all the interest in the Internet now?

The Internet, and especially the Web, have become popular because of a number of factors that came together at roughly the same time in the early 1990s.

The Founding of the Internet

The Internet began as a network of computers used by military and academic researchers in the United States. At this time, these two groups were among the very few people who had access to large computer systems of any type, and collectively they had the most computers and the most experience with them, though they were increasingly being introduced to the business world.

It has been ironically observed that the creative anarchy that is the Internet and the World Wide Web was ultimately inspired by an idea born out of the U.S. Military during the heyday of the Cold War in the 1960s. As computers became faster and more could be done with them, they were increasingly seen as an important line of communications. The U.S. Military realized they required a networked computing system that was completely reliable, and could function even if some systems in the network became unavailable. With this in mind, they began to scout about for the ways in which this plan could be implemented.

Nuking the Net?

A legend has grown about the U.S. Military's original specification for the network that would one day become the Internet. The military required a networked computer system that was completely reliable, even in the event that some of the computers in the network became unavailable, which has led many people to believe that a nuclear war strategy lay behind the idea. The popular thought has grown that the military devised this strategy because they thought that the main reason why a computer might become "unavailable" would be because it had been vaporized by a nuclear bomb. While this was a worst-case scenario, the truth is less explosive. This specification was a practical solution in the days when computers were often up and running as much as they were down. Computers have become much more reliable over the years, but they still occasionally go down. Thanks to the initial design for the Internet, it is increasingly rare that any large geographic area is without access to the Internet.

In 1962, RAND Corporation researcher Paul Baran came up with an idea that would eventually become the winning design for this proto-Internet. His idea was to build a network that had no central point of control and which used a messaging system that

could route itself through a network, even if there were outages in a section of that network. The "packet-switching" scheme that Baran devised meant that messages sent along this decentralized network would be broken up into little pieces, called *packets*, which not only contained a piece of the whole message, but information as to its destination. When a message is sent, an individual computer receiving the message reads the addressing information, and then it determines the best route.

The packet-switching concept works like this: say you want to send a message from your computer (computer A) to somebody at a distant computer (computer B). There is no direct connection between point A and point B, but there is a third computer (called C) that links to both A and B. The message you send is broken down into small packets, and then sent from your computer, which determines that the best way of getting the message to B is to send it through C. C then takes the message, and then routes it to B.

But what happens if C crashes as you send the message? As your computer sends the message to C, it soon realizes that C is unresponsive, so it tries an alternate route, sending the remainder of the message to another computer (D). Computer D then sends the message to the intended recipient at B. The computer at B reassembles all of the parts that comprise the message, puts them in order, and then delivers the message to the intended recipient. This is the essence of Paul Baran's packet-switching scheme, which was eventually adopted by the U.S. Military for its computer network, and is still used today by the Internet. In fact, whenever you receive email, download a file through FTP, or view a Web page, chances are that the individual packets of information that comprise the message, file, or Web page data have passed though several computers before getting to you (see Figure 1.1).

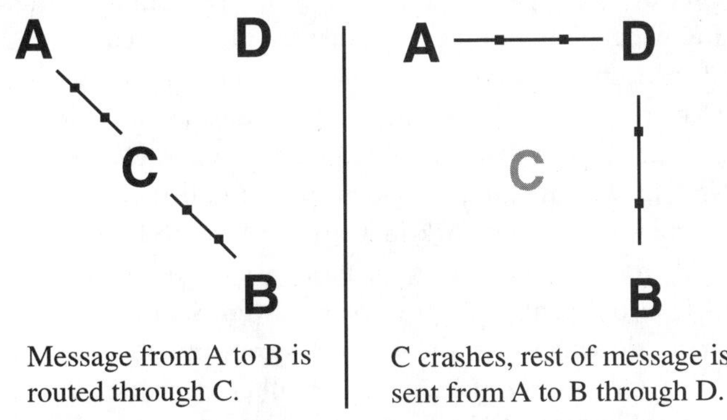
A
D
C
B
Message from A to B is routed through C.
A
D
C
B
C crashes, rest of message is sent from A to B through D.

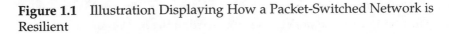

Figure 1.1 Illustration Displaying How a Packet-Switched Network is Resilient

The agency that funded the development of this networked computer concept was The Advanced Research Projects Agency (ARPA) of the U.S. Department of Defense. The result, which was launched in 1969, was called the ARPANET, and was composed of computers (called *nodes*) located at four different universities and research institutes.

The First Email

The first Internet message was sent sometime in early September 1969 (the exact date was not recorded, but it is generally thought to have been on Labor Day). It was sent from the University of California to the other three nodes of the ARPANET. The message was: "Are you receiving this?"
(Thankfully, it was.)

Though not intended solely as a messaging network, researchers quickly made use of the email program that could be operated and used over the ARPANET. The ARPANET was designed primarily to transfer data between computers to maximize computer processing time over the network, and not for sending and receiving email between researchers. In fact, email capability was thrown in as an afterthought. Email rapidly became the dominant form of communication on the ARPANET, as researchers realized the benefits of contacting and spreading information to other researchers in their field.

As the benefits of being part of the ARPANET to communicate to other researchers became widely known in the academic and research communities, more universities and institutes joined the network. As more nodes were added to the network, the network as a whole became more stable, as more nodes meant more ways a message could be successfully routed from point A to point B.

The ARPANET grew, extending its nodes located in different countries, and the traffic between nodes on the network increased. More nodes on the network not only meant that there were more ways for messages to successfully travel between two points, but it also meant that more people were sending data and messages across the network, slowing down the network's transmission as a whole.

In part to alleviate this problem, and for other concerns, in 1983 the U.S. Military decided to split the ARPANET in two. The military nodes of the network became MILNET, and the rest of the nodes were called the "Internet." This only temporarily slowed down the amount of traffic between nodes, and only a year after the split, over a thousand nodes were connected to the newly minted Internet.

In 1984, the National Science Foundation (NSF) stepped in and proposed that a special, high-bandwidth backbone network be added to the Internet to make it more reliable. By 1986 the NSF had established a high-speed backbone connecting five major super-computing facilities of the Internet that ran at 56 kbps. This backbone network, known as the NSFNET, sped up the data flow on the Internet tremendously, and spurred the growth for the Internet. Universities around the world began to join the Internet en masse. By the end of the decade, the number of nodes had increased to over 100,000.

The rise of the personal computer in the early 1980s saw a parallel growth in the use of computers that could "speak" to each other, and the birth of both private and nonprofit networks. Bulletin Board Systems (BBSes) popped up in the major urban centers of North America, which allowed people to send email to other people at the BBS, or to transfer files to one another. As the number of BBSes grew, many BBS operators began to transfer email from other BBSes, so it became possible for anyone with a modem to send email over a distance. However, the system used was not fool-proof, and soon small networks roughly based on the design structure of the Internet began to emerge. At this point it just made sense for BBSes to tap into the Internet, resulting, in 1985, with the first major cross-over between the academic and general computing communities, as the members of the Whole Earth 'Lectronic Link (WELL) BBS could now communicate across the Internet.

Since the backbone of the Internet (the NSFNET) was funded through taxpayer's dollars, it was suggested that access to the Internet should be made available freely. This idea was at the heart of the first "Freenet," which was established in 1986 in Cleveland, Ohio, where local residents equipped with a computer and modem could hook up to the Internet for free. The Freenet concept spread, and increasingly the general public had access to a network formerly reserved for academia and major institutions.

Link: Want to see if a local Freenet exists near you? Freenets exists far and wide, and if you live in a major urban center in North America, your chances are good that one is located a local phone call away from you. A good place to start is Yahoo!'s listing of Freenets at http://www.yahoo.com/Business_and_Economy/Companies/Computers/ Networking/Online_Services/Free_Nets/ (see Figure 1.2).

Despite the rapid growth of the Internet in the 1980s, it was not an easy place to navigate. Even sending something as simple as an email often required a working-knowledge of the notoriously user-unfriendly Unix operating system. This technological barrier kept a lot of people from using the Internet. It would take the

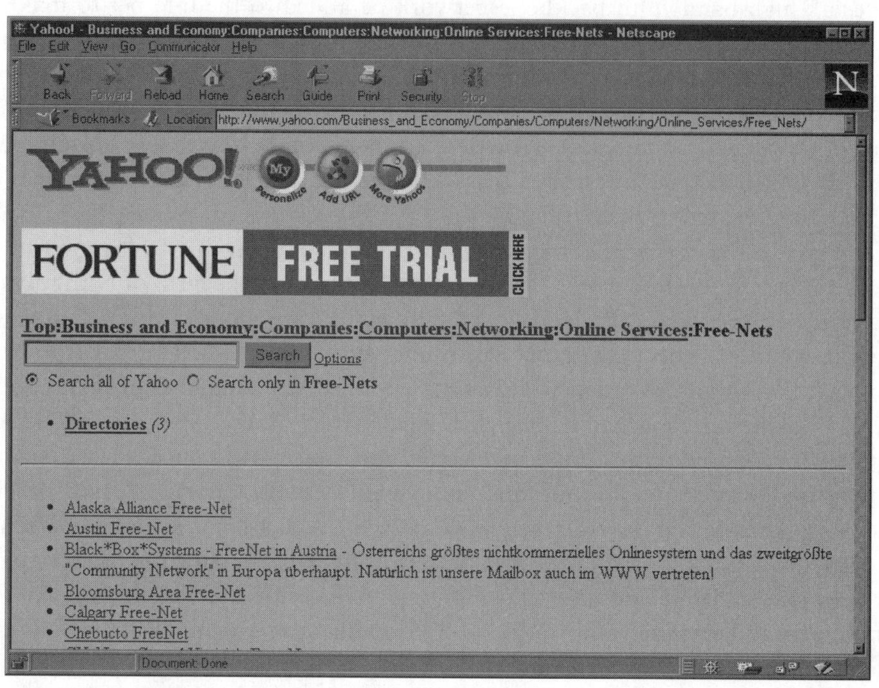

Figure 1.2 Listing of Freenets Found on the Yahoo! Search Engine

graphical user interface of the World Wide Web to make it widely usable, eventually bringing the Internet to attention of the general public.

Link: For a good synopsis of the events that led to the development of the Internet, see "A Brief History of the Internet" at http://info.isoc.org/internet-history/ (see Figure 1.3).

Hypertext and the Web

Although the concept of the World Wide Web and hypertext seems like a new one, most people are surprised to find out how old these concepts actually are.

Hypertext differs from the linear reading style accustomed with typical book reading by adding connections (called *links*) between different parts of the same

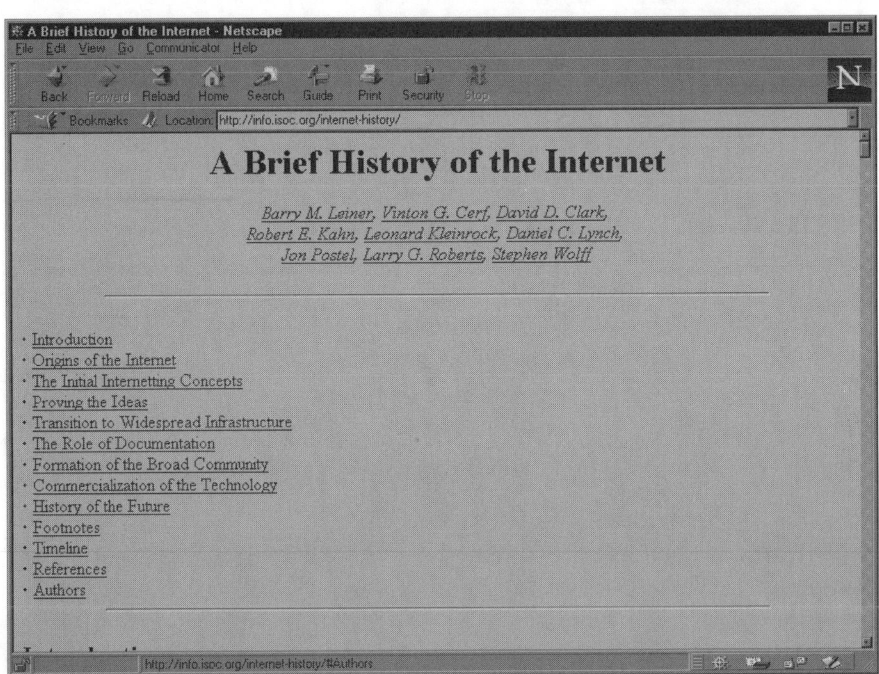

Figure 1.3 Brief History of the Internet Web Page

text, or to different texts entirely. Hypermedia takes this idea a step further by introducing images, sound, and video within a hypertext document.

The idea of hypertext came from an idea by MIT Professor Vannevar Bush. He was a former science advisor to President Roosevelt, and had worked on building one of the first mechanical computers back in the 1930s. He had always been fascinated by how the mind processes information, and in the July 1945 issue of Atlantic Monthly he published an article called "As We May Think," which talked about his concerns about a world increasingly facing information overload, and his solution to this problem (see figure 1.4). His work experience taught him that as the amount of scientific literature in a field grew, the harder it became for individual researchers to find the information they were looking for. His solution to this problem was an idea for a machine he called the "Memex," a device that could store vast amounts of textual information and images on microfilm. It differed from a typical microfiche reader in its ability to use keywords that contained associated links to other documents. This concept came from Bush's idea that because the

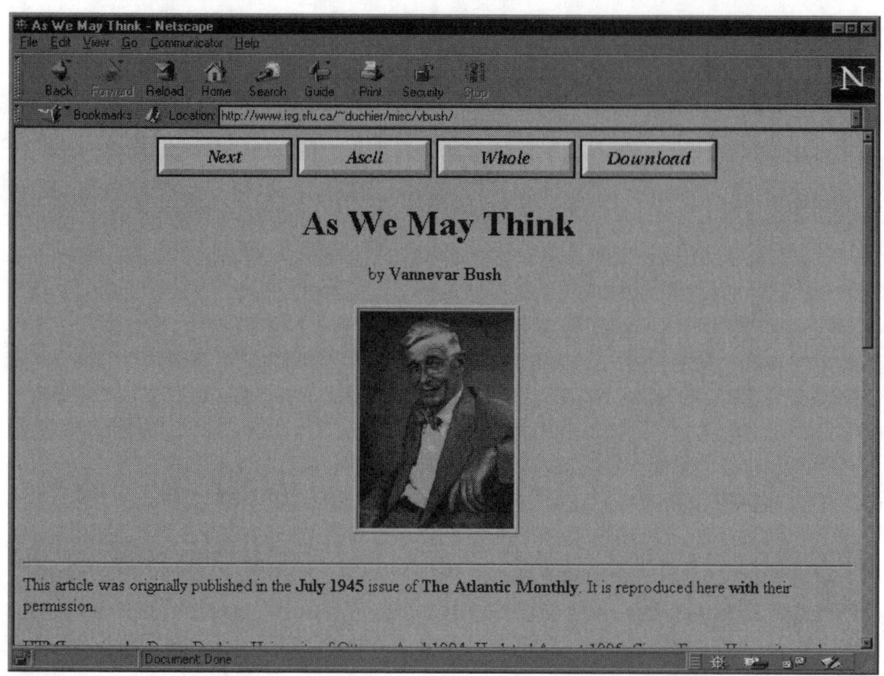

Figure 1.4 The "As We May Think" Article on the Web

human mind works in an associative fashion, that information is best laid out in a similarly nonlinear fashion. Though the Memex was never built, the idea was revolutionary, and influenced the thinking of many who followed.

Link: If you are interested in reading the original "As We May Think" article by Vannevar Bush, you can find it on the Web at http://www.isq.sfu.ca/~duchier/misc/vbush/.

In 1965, researcher Ted Nelson followed up on Bush's original ideas by inventing the first hypermedia system, and coming up with the terms *hypertext* and *hypermedia*. Nelson conceived and began work on the first hypertext system, called Xanadu, at Brown University. In its conception, Xanadu was much like Bush's Memex, but was digitally based rather than being limited to microfilm, and could include all types of media, not just text and images. Other computer scientists would come up with inventive schemes that would make Vannevar Bush's idea of the Memex come true, and many hypertext and hypermedia systems have been devised over the years. But it would be the demands of technical writers that would lead to the basis of the Hypertext Markup Language (HTML) that is the basis of the Web.

SGML and HTML

Prior to the introduction of computers, technical manuals had to be done as typeset, limited-edition print runs. As computers were increasingly introduced to the workplace, technical writers picked up the possibilities of doing their work on computers, using simple publishing programs. In the 1970s, most computers were proprietary systems unable to communicate directly with one another. So what would happen was that a publication that had been typeset on one computer would have to be completely redone on a different computer.

This situation led to efforts to find a common language and formatting style that could be read by all computer systems. The Standardized Markup Language (SGML) was the result, developed over a couple of decades and spearheaded by a group of researchers at IBM. SGML is based on two major rules:

- The markup should reflect the structure of a document rather than its physical layout
- The markup should be in a format that could be understandable to both computers and to humans

These two simple rules lie at the root of SGML, and are also at the core of HTML.

The emphasis on structure rather than physical layout means that a writer is not restricted to the layout characteristics of a particular computing system. The markup structure adopted within SGML was one of *tags* that control and contain the logical structure of a document. This tag structure generally involved surrounding text with markers that modify the text. The start form of the tag indicates where a particular attribute begins, and the end tag indicates when it finishes.

Most computers are able to understand ASCII, a computer standard for the characters used in the English language. It was readily adopted as the base language for SGML, and would later be adopted within the first HTML standard. SGML was adopted as a standard by the International Standards Organization in 1986, and has been widely adopted within many large firms and organizations.

SGML is the progenitor language of HTML, and many—though not all—of SGML's tags and rules apply to HTML. Anyone serious about learning HTML will benefit from learning a bit about the structure and organization of SGML.

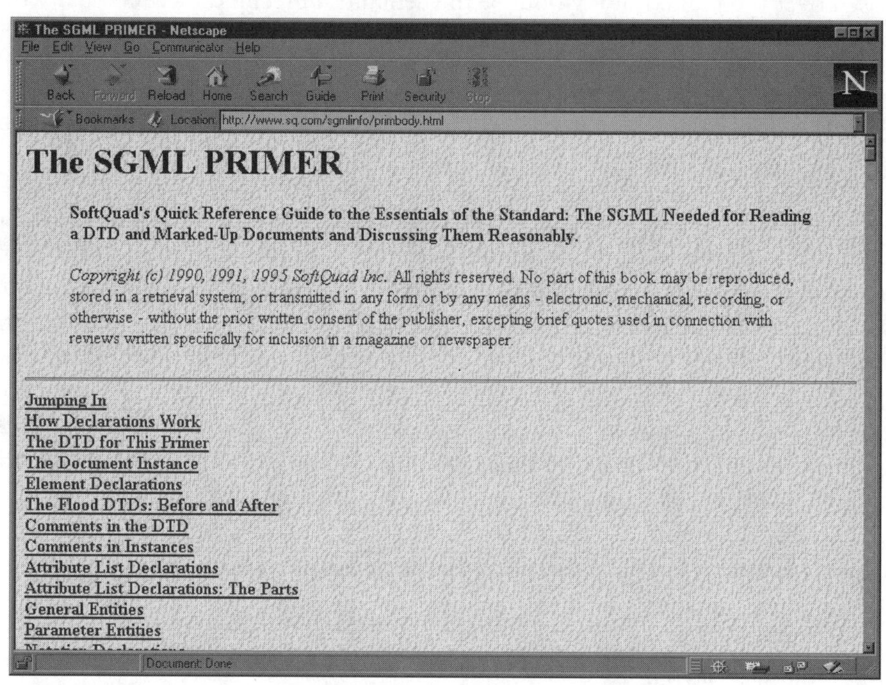

Figure 1.5 The "SGML Primer" on the Web

Link: If you are interested in learning more about SGML, a good tutorial worth checking out is SoftQuad's "SGML Primer" at http://www.sq.com/sgmlinfo/primbody.html (see Figure 1.5).

One place that adopted SGML within its internal computing network was CERN, an internal center for particle physics whose enormous particle accelerator ring is located on the borders of Switzerland and France near Geneva. CERN used many different types of computers in its facilities. It was often at the forefront of many different computing technologies, and its computer scientists were often innovators by necessity. As a result CERN became a major center of the concept of "distributed computing," where computers are linked to each other and share data and processing time. It was one of the first places in Europe to sponsor a major link to the Internet, and it would become the birth-place of the Web (shown in Figure 1.6).

One of the computer scientists at CERN was Tim Berners-Lee, a young Oxford

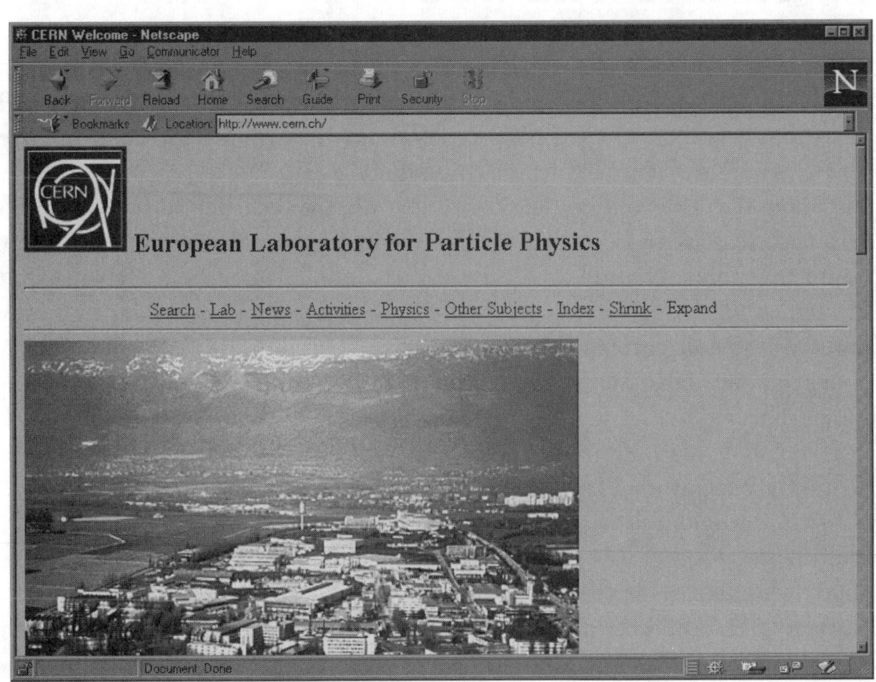

Figure 1.6 CERN, the Birthplace of the Web, whose Home Page can be Found at http://www.cern.ch/

graduate who had been working with the basic concept of hypertext for many years. In 1989 Berners-Lee was given a project by his employers at CERN to devise a mechanism to distribute research information across CERN's computer network. The specifications included the idea that the program should use a single interface that would be capable of displaying such things as images and documents. To this Berners-Lee brought in his own idea of incorporating hypertext to navigate within this information environment. Not only could links be made within a document, but to other documents as well. CERN adopted the idea and gave it the name "World Wide Web."

CERN set the standards for the new hypertext language, based largely on SGML, and called it the Hypertext Markup Language. This was the first HTML standard, called HTML 1.0. This was followed shortly thereafter by the first Web browser, a simple command-line program that could not view images directly.

Thus in 1991 the World Wide Web and HTML were both born.

HTML AND THE BROWSER WARS

Interest in the World Wide Web exploded in the academic world. It caught the attention of some people working at the National Center for Supercomputing Applications (NCSA). One of NCSA's many goals is to develop noncommercial software to aid the scientific research community. Realizing the potential of the Web to distribute scientific and academic information, they decided to fund an internal program to create a graphical browser that could run on multiple operating systems. Up until this point the only Web browser, (the one released by CERN), operated solely under the Unix operating system. This greatly limited its audience—even within the academic community, where most such machines were found only in the computer science labs. With the goal of creating a graphically driven browser in mind, NCSA employed a number of computer science students at the University of Illinois in Champaign, Illinois, to develop a Web browser that could work equally well on PCs, Macintoshes, and X-Window Unix computers. The resulting program was NCSA Mosaic, released early in 1993 (see Figure 1.7). It was free, it had a graphical interface that was extremely easy to use, it could view images directly, and anybody who had an Internet connection could get it.

Interest in the Internet and the Web surged with the release of Mosaic. Within a year of its release, over two million people were using Mosaic, and people were learning HTML in droves, creating thousands of Web sites in the process. Around this time, the possibility of using the Internet for commercial purposes was opened up.

When the National Science Foundation laid the background network for the NSFNET, part of the guidelines for using it included an "Acceptable Use Policy," which stated the purposes the network could be used for. It stressed that NSFNET's purpose was to support research and education among academic institutions. It also excluded use of the network for profitable activities, or use by private businesses. This policy effectively prohibited commercial activity on the Internet, because if you used the Internet, you inevitably used the NSFNET backbone.

In 1991, NSF lifted these restrictions, and it became possible to make money through the use of the Internet. This was when the first of the commercial Internet Service Providers (ISPs) began to appear across North America, allowing people access to the Internet for a fee. The commercial possibilities of the Internet were not lost to commercial software companies either. The majority of the programs that enable users to do things on the Internet, such as sending email, downloading files, or surfing the Web were free. However, though the price may have been right for a lot of people, these programs were generally considered, inferior to the quality of other programs that people were familiar with, such as word processors or BBS communications software. The rush was on to create better programs for the

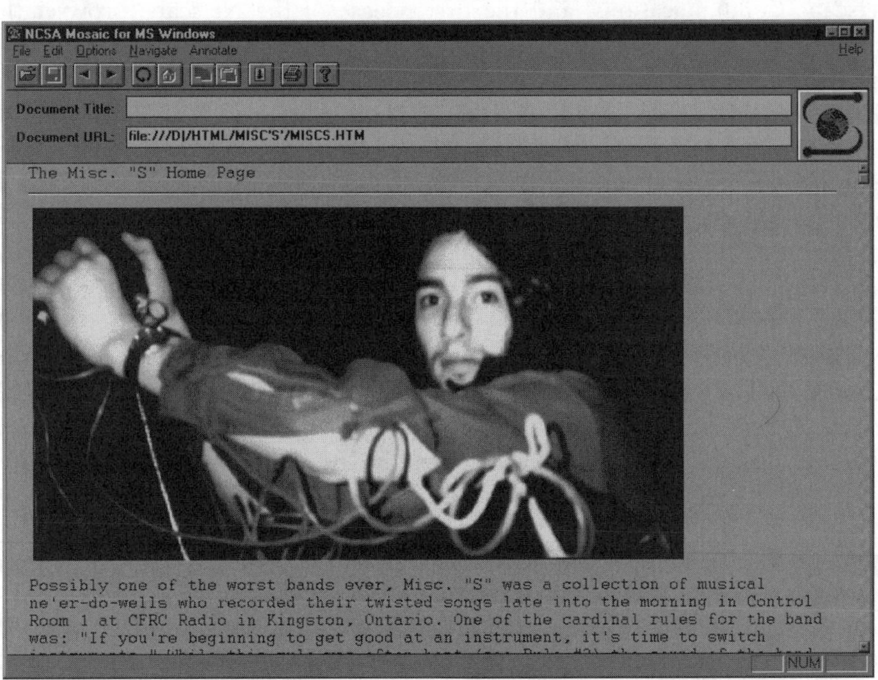

Figure 1.7 Early Views of the Web: The First Mosaic Web Browser

Internet. The Holy Grail of Internet applications was to create a much-improved Web browser, as it became obvious to many that the Web would prove to be the most popular application on the Internet. Soon dozens of firms started making Web browsers that boasted minor enhancements over NCSA's Mosaic.

The first to make the big breakthrough was a browser called Netscape. People familiar with the early versions of Mosaic will remember that you often had to wait a long time for anything to appear on your screen. The initial version of Mosaic worked by downloading *everything* from a Web page first, displaying the full page only when everything had been downloaded. If a Web page contained a number of graphics and you had a slow connection, you could go and get a coffee and maybe by the time you were back you could view the Web page you were trying to see. Marc Andreessen, who was one of the original developers of Mosaic back at the NCSA, had an idea about how to solve the problem of having to wait for all of the images on a Web page to load before you read the text on the page.

In March 1994 he and six of the other developers of Mosaic left the NCSA to

form Mosaic Communications Corporation. The name was later changed to Netscape Communications, and the first release of the Netscape browser (later called "Netscape Navigator") was available by the fall of 1994. The main advantage it had over Mosaic was its ability to do "continuous document streaming," which meant that users could read the text contained on a Web page while they were still waiting for the images to download fully. This single significant improvement made people switch from Mosaic to Netscape in droves, and soon Netscape became the Web browser of choice (see Figure 1.8).

In the face of increasing competition, Netscape took a decidedly different route to making their Web browser stand out—creating new HTML tags that Web authors could use whose effects could be viewed only within their own Web browser. Subsequent releases of Netscape have introduced a number of innovative features, such as the addition of tables, frames, and Java. If you were a Web author designing Web pages for Netscape, you had a number of extra tags and enhancements you could add to Web pages that couldn't be seen within any other browser. Using this strategy, Netscape Corporation quickly grabbed much of the Web

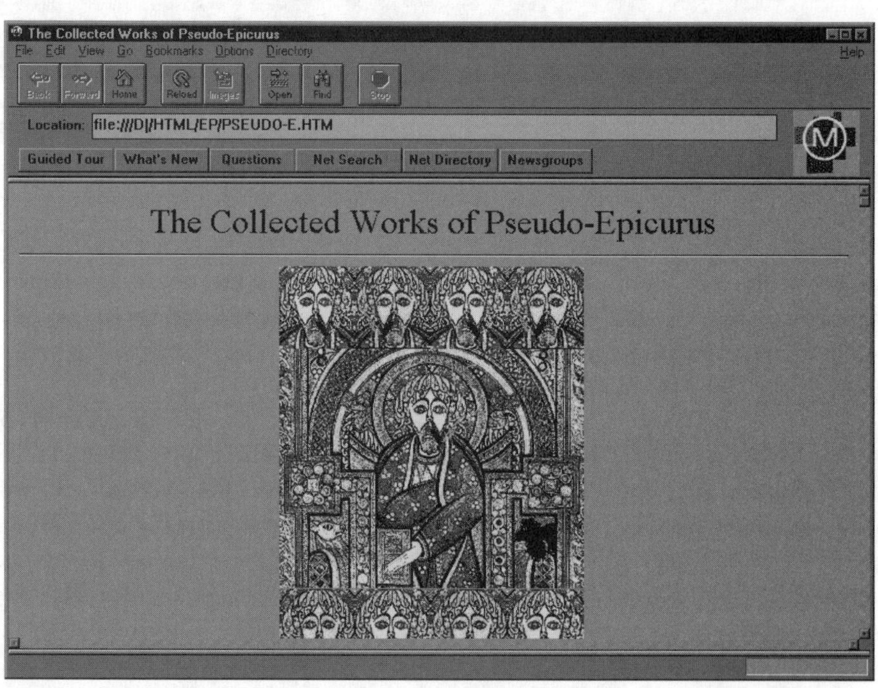

Figure 1.8 Another early view of the Web: The first Netscape browser

browser market, and to this day more users still view Web pages with Netscape than with any other browser.

However, browser development did not end with Netscape. For a while the competition was quite furious for "mind-share" of Internet users who surfed the Web. At one point there were dozens and dozens of different browsers available to choose from, most now used by only a handful of people, if they are used at all. But competition is far from dead—Netscape's biggest rival in the browser market is Microsoft, whose Internet Explorer is currently the second most-used browser on the Web.

Internet Explorer was originally based on code licensed from Spyglass, a company that made its own commercial version of the Mosaic browser. As Microsoft Chairman Bill Gates realized the important role the Internet and the Web is likely to make on the near-future of computing, he devoted more and more resources to improving Internet Explorer. The latest version of Internet Explorer is freely available, and boasts a feature-set at least as rich (and some would say more so) than Netscape's latest.

The ongoing battles between Netscape and Microsoft to dominate the Web browser market has resulted in what has often been called the "browser wars." Depending on whom you listen to, this war has either been a boon or a detriment to the HTML authoring community. The abundance of new tags has provided HTML authors with the tools to create better-looking Web sites containing more and more features. However, the plethora of new HTML tags, many of them unreadable by other browsers, meant that there was confusion as to the standards that should be used when creating Web pages. Should they be viewable by all browsers? Should they be enhanced for Netscape? Or should they be enhanced for Internet Explorer?

All through this period the HTML standards body has not been asleep—though it is not always given the respect it deserves. As commercial interests came to the fore in Web development, the standards bodies came increasingly under attack. The main standard body for HTML is currently trying to regulate and stabilize the unruly nature of HTML standards.

CERN initiated the initial standards for HTML 1.0 and its successor, HTML 2.0. But in 1994 CERN abdicated its role as the standards-setting body for HTML, passing this responsibility to a new body, called the World Wide Web Consortium (often simply called W3C). The W3C (Figure 1.9) is a collaborative effort between the Massachusetts Institute of Technology and the European Commission's Institut National pour la Recherche en Informatique et Automatique (INRIA). These two founding institutes have more recently been joined by Keio University in Japan, which represents Asian concerns over HTML standards.

Soon after its founding, development at W3C soon began work on a successor standard for HTML 2.0. In March 1995, the official HTML 3.0 specification was launched. It included a number of enhancements over the old standard, but it did not

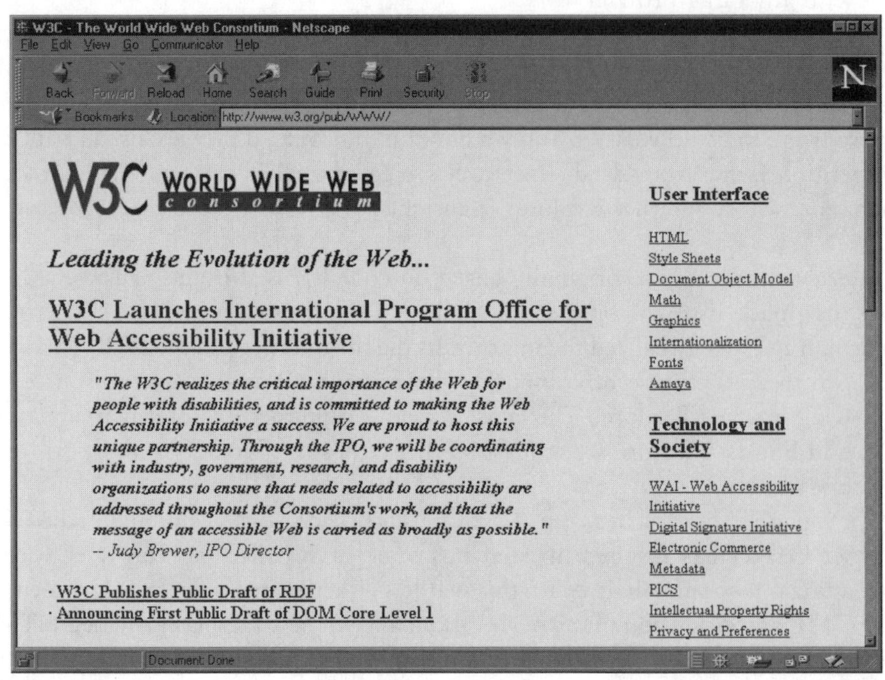

Figure 1.9 The World Wide Web Consortium (W3C) on the Web at http://www.w3.org/pub/WWW/

reflect the reality of Web design at that time. At this time a number of "Netscape-isms" had been adopted wholesale by the Web authoring community, such as tables, frames, background image files and many other HTML enhancements. Microsoft's Internet Explorer included many of these Netscape-isms, and added many additional ones of its own, such as the ability to add sound, control font faces, and scroll marquees. The HTML 3.0 standard was essentially ignored. By the time the HTML 3.0 specification was made official, it was effectively obsolete.

Realizing that it had to be relevant to have any pull on the fast-growing Web authoring community, the W3C dropped the HTML 3.0 standard and in May 1996 started work on a new, interim standard that better reflected the reality of Web design, called HTML 3.2. The Consortium has managed to sign up both Netscape Communications and Microsoft, along with other major software firms, including IBM, Novell, Spyglass, Sun Microsystems and many more, as members of this standards body. This arrangement provides the software firms with a line of communication both to other member firms and to a body recognized as having a lot of experience with devising and setting a workable standard for HTML. The W3C is designed to be a neutral meeting ground where competing companies can come together to define common goals.

As of January 1996, W3C officially recommended that the HTML 3.2 specification (code named "Wilbur" after Wilbur Wright, the first man to fly) be adopted. The new specification includes things like tables, and adds new elements, such as cascading style sheets. Work then commenced on the successor specification HTML 4.0, code named "Cougar." This new specification adds such things as an officially recognized structure for recognizing Framed Web pages, Dynamic HTML, and much more.

Link: For more information on the HTML 4.0 standard, see the official HTML 4.0 Specification Web page from the W3C at http://www.w3.org/TR/WD-htm140/ (Figure 1.10).

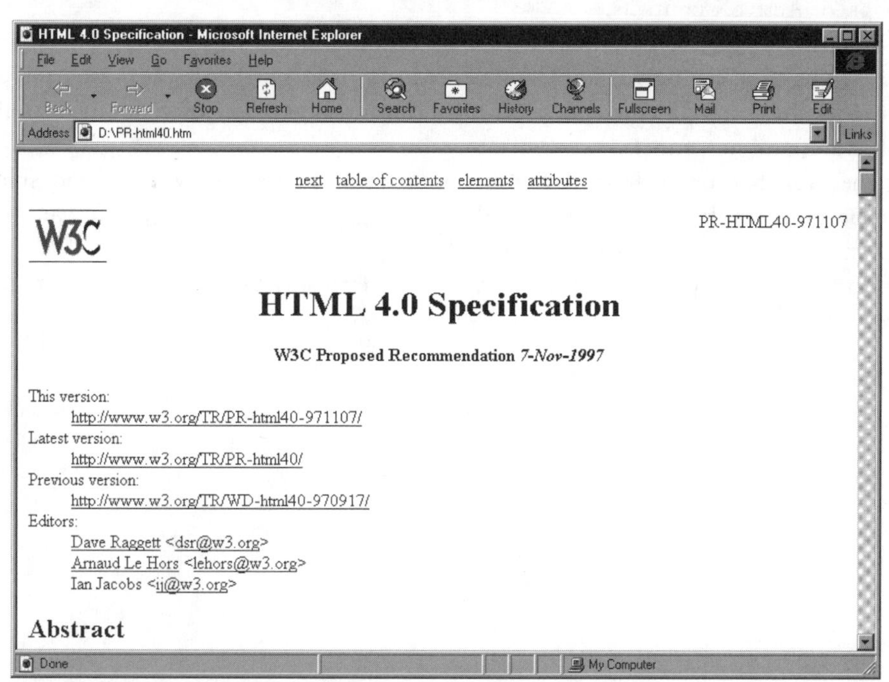

Figure 1.10 The HTML 4.0 Standard on the Web

One general trend in the development of HTML standards is a movement away from the strict logically structured approach of SGML to a model that is centered around page layout. The Web is still evolving, and the stakes have been raised as the Web and HTML are increasingly being seen as the basis of a new computing model that will extend and encompass such diverse subjects as operating systems, messaging services, online commerce, and software development. Both Netscape and Microsoft are in the middle of a new war for control of the desktop, the environment in which users work and play on their computers but are always a mouse-click away from accessing information stored anywhere in the world.

The potential of the Java programming language, designed specifically for the Web, is now being brought directly to the desktop as well, and will likely be incorporated into future operating systems. In the near future you may not know (or care) if you are running a program from your hard drive or from the Internet. More and more firms are going online to provide new or enhanced services to customers, often reaching a worldwide audience for a cost cheaper than most print or television ad campaigns. Software developers are increasingly looking towards Web-centric models of computing, writing new applications and programs using such Web-friendly computing models as the Java programming language, JavaScript, or ActiveX controls.

HTML and the Web are increasingly becoming a part of computing in general, and not just the online world. The proliferation of intranet (which is an internal, corporate Internet) promises to be as big—if not a bigger—market for Web tools, hardware, and personnel.

The Web has opened up new job opportunities, too: Many large and small corporations employ Web masters, and there are an increasing amount of want-ads looking for people with experience in HTML.

No matter how you look at it, the Web is here to stay. And the excitement ain't over yet.

CHAPTER 2

Introduction to HTML

All Web pages are created using Hypertext Markup Language (HTML). HTML uses a set of *tags* to describe how text, pictures, and other elements are arranged on a page. These tags indicate where text should appear in bold, where a paragraph break occurs, hypertext links to other pages, and more. HTML elements define the way Web pages are presented. Web browsers interpret individual HTML elements and then display them on your computer screen. These *elements* are HTML tags.

HTML tags are very limited in their ability to manipulate the appearance of the content of your Web pages. HTML tags should not be confused with the page layout tags common to many desktop publishing programs. Desktop publishing programs often use tags to determine the layout of text and graphics on a page. The key difference with tags in HTML is that they determine the appearance, but not necessarily the precise placement, of text and graphics when interpreted by a

Web browser. One of primary goals behind the initial design of HTML is to provide the logical structure of a document, rather than its layout. This structure provides the flexibility to construct and view Web pages so that they will appear the same across a variety of different browsers working under different operating systems. This trade-off means that while just about anybody will be able to view your Web pages, you will not be able to produce the type of text or graphic layout anything like the printed pages you are reading now.

Tags are delineated by angle brackets (< >) that surround the text of the tag. There are two basic forms of tags: container tags and empty tags. Either of these two types of tags can be further modified by an attribute specific to that tag.

Container Tags

Most HTML tags are container tags, which have a start tag and an end tag. These tags enclose (or "contain") text or other elements in a Web page. The start tags tell the Web browser where a particular HTML element begins, and the end tag marks its finish. End tags are differentiated from start tags by using a forward slash (/). The following is an example of a standard container HTML tag:

```
This text is normal, and <B> this appears in bold. </B>
```

It is then up to the Web browser to determine how the enclosed content is displayed on screen. When viewed through a Web browser, the words "this appears in bold" are displayed in the manner described by the bold (<B>) HTML tag (as seen in Figure 2.1).

Empty Tags

Some HTML tags are empty tags. This does not imply that they do not do anything. They are stand-alone tags that do not require an end tag, so they do not contain

This text is normal, and **this appears in bold.**

Figure 2.1 The Bold Tag as Displayed in a Web Browser

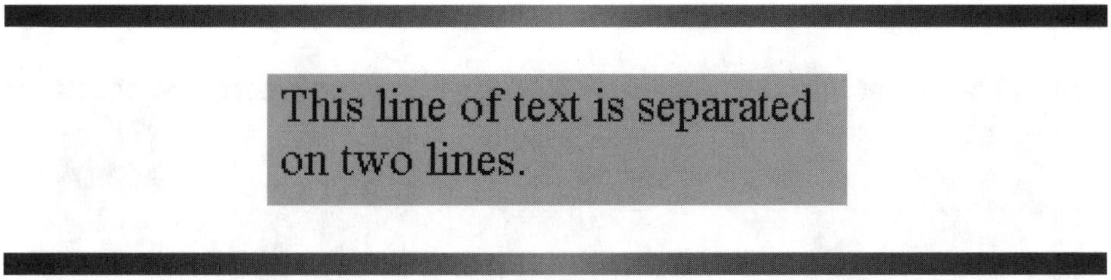

This line of text is separated
on two lines.

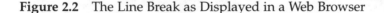

Figure 2.2 The Line Break as Displayed in a Web Browser

any content on a Web page. They mark where particular formatting actions should appear. A typical example of an empty tag is the line-break tag (<BR>), which tells a Web browser where a carriage return should appear in a line of text. The following example uses this tag in a line of text:

```
This line of text is separated <BR> on two lines.
```

When interpreted by a Web browser, this line of text appears with a carriage return after the word "separated" (as shown in Figure 2.2).

Tag Attributes

Some tags can be modified by attributes, which refine properties specific to a tag. In many cases this modifies a tag that can also be used without an attribute. For example, the level-1 header tag (<H1>) can appear as is, as in the following example:

```
<H1>This is a Level - 1 Heading</H1>
```

or it can be modified by an attribute specific to that tag, so you can have the following:

```
<H1 ALIGN="CENTER">This Level-1 Heading is
Centered</H1>
```

The difference in the appearance of both of these examples can be seen in Figure 2.3.

In some cases, the tag is always modified by an attribute. For example, the anchor tag (<A>) always appears with a modifying attribute. It is often used to set hypertext links, as in the following example:

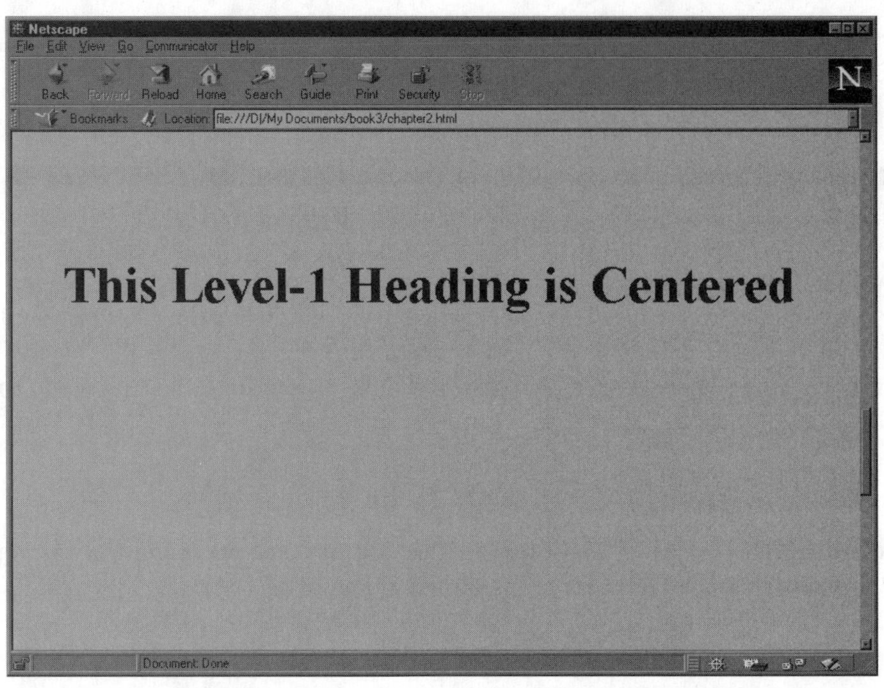

Figure 2.3 An Example of How the ALIGN=CENTER Attribute Modifies the Appearance of a Header

```
<A HREF=≅www.yahoo.com≅>Yahoo! </A> is a good place
to find information.
```

or it can be used to mark an endpoint for a hypertext reference within a document, as in the following example:

```
<A NAME="Naomi">Naomi's </A>Words of Wisdom
```

The end tag is never used to modify an attribute; it merely ends the container.

STRUCTURAL RULES

HTML also has rules determining its structure. This means that there are places where tags can and cannot go. It follows a logical structure, determining which tags can work together. For example, the level-1 header tag (<H1>) can contain only a limited number of other tags. You can place line breaks and emphasized text with the header, but not much else. The following HTML code sample is invalid, because the level-1 header tag cannot contain a level-3 header, and there is no logical reason why you would want to do this in the first place.

```
<H1><H3> This is a mixed-up header. </H3></H1>
```

Another structural rule is that elements cannot overlap, so container tags must be nested within each other to function properly. The following HTML code example shows how to insert italicized text correctly using the italics (<I>) tag into a level-1 header:

```
<H1> This is a <I>header</I></H1>
```

and this is incorrect:

```
<H1> This is a <I>header</I></H1>
```

Each container tag must begin and end within any other container tag it resides in.

There are a number of other small rules to remember when writing HTML code. Remember that HTML tags are not case-sensitive. They can be written in uppercase, lowercase or a mix of cases. The following HTML code is displayed in exactly the same way in a browser, as seen in Figure 2.4. Much of the examples of HTML code in this book are displayed in uppercase. This is purely a stylistic issue, as many HTML authors find it easier to distinguish the HTML code from the content of the Web page.

```
Go to the <A HREF="www.yoyodyne.com">Yoyodyne</A> home
page. <BR>
Go to the <a href="www.yoyodyne.com">Yoyodyne</a> home
page. <BR>
```

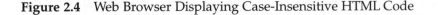

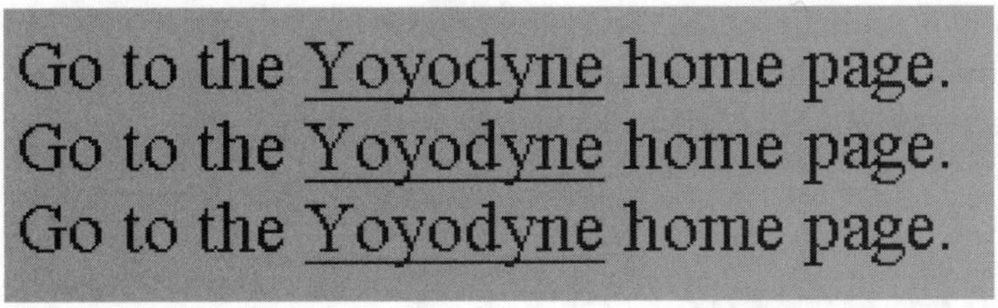

Go to the Yoyodyne home page.
Go to the Yoyodyne home page.
Go to the Yoyodyne home page.

Figure 2.4 Web Browser Displaying Case-Insensitive HTML Code

```
Go to the <a HrEf="www.yoyodyne.com">Yoyodyne</A> home
page.
```

It is also worth remembering that the same tag can be displayed in different ways by different browsers, and that some tags work only within specific browsers. Differences in the display characteristics of a tag are indicated in the description of a tag's function in this book. Browser-specific tags are also indicated.

Things To Know Before Starting To Write Web Pages

Before you actually start constructing your own Web pages, make sure your Internet Service Provider (ISP) will permit you to place one on their site. Many Commercial ISPs provide a certain allotment of disk space (usually a few megabytes) to a user when you get an Internet account. If you plan on putting up lots of pictures, sound, or video files, the more disk space you have available the better. Many people use this space to store files, and the ISP does not always want this space used for home pages. Although popular Web pages often provide free publicity for an ISP's services, large numbers of people accessing a Web site at once can overwhelm an ISP and can impair the speed of its services to all users or shut it down altogether.

If you access the Web from a university or from a noncommercial account, check what policies are in place about putting up your own Web pages. If you are unable to put up your own home page and are still interested in learning about the processes behind it, check with the system administrator as to whether you can help with any Web-related projects they may be doing.

It is always a good idea to check with the ISP's system administrator or with somebody who has already put up a Web page on the system you use about any procedures or people to notify about activating your home page Web site. In many cases a "switch" has to be thrown or a directory structure has to be created to enable people outside of your ISP to access your Web pages.

For information on how to upload files to your Web server, and how to manage your Web server, see Chapter 17, "Working with the Server."

Copyright Issues

It is wrong to assume that because the contents of a Web page are freely available to all, that you have the right to use the same text, image, sound file, or other content of someone else's Web page within your own Web page. In most countries, copyright for an author is assumed even if a copyright symbol does not appear on a page—this applies equally to the printed as well as virtual Web pages.

Several legal arguments may come into play when constructing Web pages using information derived from other sources. One of these is the doctrine of "fair use." The fair use doctrine is well-defined in U.S. law, and many of its ideas hold under principles of Common Law in the British Commonwealth. Under the right circumstances it allows people to copy and distribute material without permission of the copyright holder.

The problem is, there is no clear-cut line in determining what falls under the idea of fair use. This is a particular problem of this digital age, where seemingly anything and everything can be encoded using a digital format.

One of the deciding factors in determining fair use includes the way and for what purpose the copyrighted material is used. Material used for commercial purposes tend not to fall under the idea of fair use, but nonprofit or educational purposes may qualify. Therefore schools may be able to use material from another Web site for educational purposes, or rock fans may incorporate small snippets of songs on their Web pages. Keep in mind that the fair use doctrine is not universal, and what may be considered valid use of copyrighted material in one country may be considered copyright infringement in another.

Link: A good place to find out about copyright issues relating directly to the Web can be found at the "10 Big Myths about copyright explained" Web page at: http://www.clari.net/brad/copymyths.html.

A related factor is whether copyrighted material is being used for a new purpose, transforming the nature of the copyrighted content. Simply converting pictures or sounds to a computer-compatible format doesn't count, but if you incorporate the material in new way, it may qualify. Downloading a picture of a Picasso painting and using it on your Web site may constitute infringement of copyright, but using an altered version of the same painting could be construed as a new work of your own creation.

Another factor is the amount of a copyrighted work that is being used without permission. This rule is not always clear-cut. A case where musician Biz Markie digitally sampled three words out of a song was considered an infringement of copyright, but people are allowed to copy entire movies on videocassette for personal use.

Whenever you are in doubt whether you may be infringing somebody else's copyright, it is always best to seek permission to use the material first.

Elvis Has Left the Web

Andrea Berman created an Elvis home page back in the summer of 1994. While on a tour to Graceland with her mother, the idea hit her to do a virtual tour of the mansion, based on some postcards she bought while there. Soon, people with a Web browser could contact the site and take a "Cyber-Graceland Tour," download Elvis software, and listen to sound-clips from the "King." It fast became a popular site, playing host to virtual tourists from around the world.

That was until Ms. Berman got a letter from the lawyers for Elvis Presley Enterprises, Inc. A fairly typical cease-and-desist letter, it asked Ms. Berman to drop the "Cyber-Graceland Tour" featured on her Web pages, along with the sound clips. The letter claimed copyright infringement, and it threatened legal action if the pictures and sound files were not immediately pulled from the Web. Not willing to be a martyr for the Web, Andrea duly pulled the images the next day, and replaced the original Elvis home page with a note explaining what had happened.

The site still exists (Figure 2.5) at http://sunsite.unc.edu/elvis/elvishom.html), and the Cyber-Graceland Tour was finally resurrected using images given to Andrea by an independent photographer, but it was an early example of how copyright can affect the content of the Web.

WRITING HTML

If you take a look at the HTML code behind any Web page you will see that many different tags define the structure of the Web page. One of the best ways of learning how to use HTML tags is to find Web pages you like, and then view the code to examine how it works. In many Web browsers there is a function that lets you download the contents of the Web page you are currently viewing, and/or displays the source code. Reading and comparing the HTML code to what you see in your Web browser is probably one of the best ways to start learning how HTML works. (Keep in mind while doing this the warning about copying the content of other people's Web pages—it applies equally to HTML code.)

Link: For a listing of available HTML editors, go the following site at the Yahoo! search engine: http://www.yahoo.com/Computers_and_Internet/Internet/World_Wide_Web/HTML_Editors/.

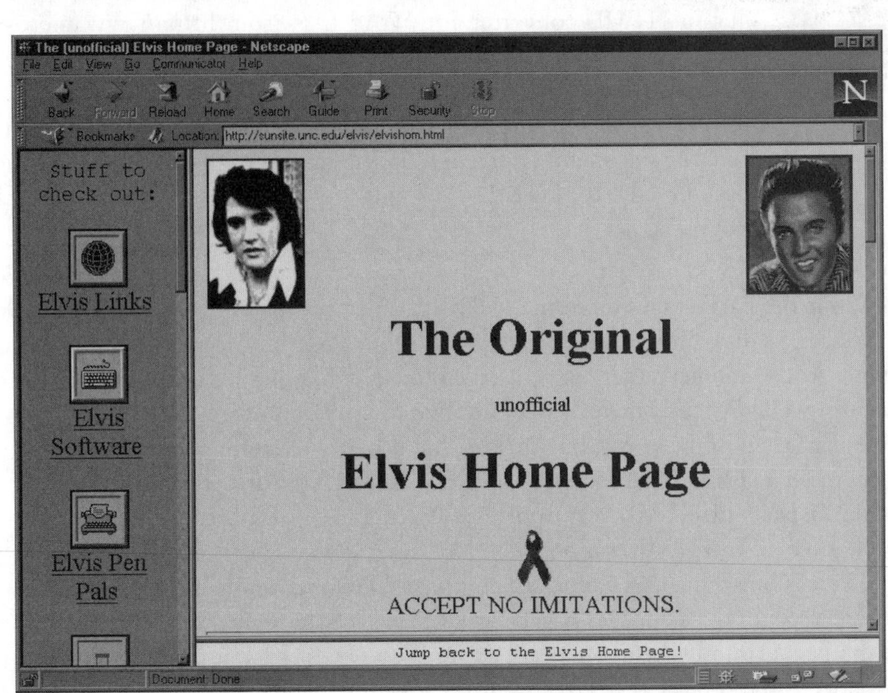

Figure 2.5 The Unofficial Elvis Home Page

You can use any basic text editor to write HTML. There are two basic types of HTML editors: Tag editors and Representational editors. Tag editors provide the Web author with direct control over the tags that go into a Web page. Their main advantage is that they are flexible—you can insert a tag anywhere you want within a Web page. Their main disadvantage is that you already have to know at least some HTML to get any use out of them, and that creating individual Web pages using this method is slow and labor-intensive. Representation editors present a display that is a rough equivalent of the text and other elements that would be displayed by a Web browser. These types of editors can be add-ons to existing word processing programs like Microsoft Word or Corel WordPerfect. Their main advantage is speed, because they can produce a lot of HTML pages quickly. Their main disadvantage is they tend to be inflexible, and may not allow you to add new tag types easily within an HTML document.

Tip: If you are using Microsoft Word 6.0 or 7.0, you can download a plug-in HTML converter for Word files from http://www.microsoft.com/ie/. Note that you must access this site using Internet Explorer. If you are using Word 97, the ability to convert your documents to HTML is built into the program. Try using the Save as HTML feature from the File menu to give it a try. Increasingly, the ability to save your files directly to HTML is a part of the latest versions of many programs.

While the battle rages on in the HTML Usenet groups as to which type of editor is best, in reality, most professional Web authors use both types of editor in their work. At the moment there is no one editor that handles all types of HTML jobs equally well. Instead, there are a number of individual HTML editors that are exceptional in some areas but lacking in others. Therefore, most Web authors acquire an HTML Toolbox over time, containing favorite programs that do particular aspects of HTML very well. See Chapter 18 for a listing of programs that make up a good HTML toolbox.

There is one thing that cannot be emphasized enough: proofread your Web pages before uploading them. It is a very good idea to have your Web browser running in the background when you are creating Web pages. Link it to the document you are creating and click the refresh button (or equivalent) on your Web browser to see the result. If you have access to more than one Web browser, view your Web pages through each of them and notice how each browser formats (or does not format) your HTML code.

The Two HTML Paradigms: Logical and Physical Tags

When it was originally conceived, the Hypertext Markup Language (HTML) was based on the two main principles built into the Standardized Generalized Markup Language (SGML). The first is that markup should reflect the logical structure of a document rather than its physical layout, and the second is that it should also be in a format that could be understandable to both computers and to humans.

Though the latter of these two principles still holds, recent trends in HTML development are pushing it away from its roots in the logical formatting structure outlined in the SGML standard, and more towards describing the physical layout of a document.

For example, you can italicize text using two different tags, as illustrated here:

```
<I>This text is italicized</I> while this text is not.
<EM>This text is italicized</EM> while this text is
not.
```

The <I> and </I> tags are physical because the "I" stands for italics. The <EM> and </EM> tags are logical because "emphasis" describes logical formatting rather than physical.

HTML's formal design philosophy is that tag markup should indicate the logical structure of a document rather than describing it using visual layout principles. This is in keeping with the SGML principles from which HTML was derived. For that reason, the creators of HTML maintain that logical tags are generally preferred over the physical tags.

In contrast, physical tags are preferred by many Web authors over their logical equivalents. Part of the reason is historic—when the tag standards were first set, browsers were generally incapable of displaying all of the different characteristics required in the specification. Compromises were made by browser designers, and so the logical set of tags had functional equivalents in the physical set of tags. Whether or not you used the <EM> or <I> tags, the result was always the same: italicized text was displayed. The simple and descriptive nature of the physical tags made them that much easier to use than their logical equivalents.

There are other matters to consider when deciding which tags to use when constructing Web pages. If you are using a program (like a Web index) that understands how to use the logical or header tags, it is to your advantage to use them. Using the logical structure format also ensures that the information in a Web page can be properly interpreted across multiple delivery formats. A good example of this is the "speaking browser," which reads the content of Web pages aloud to the blind. If you write your code strictly to the HTML 2.0 specification, it can be read by the vast majority of browsers. However, the many extensions provided by Web browsers like Internet Explorer and Netscape Navigator enable Web authors to vastly extend the capabilities of their Web pages. Keep in mind the type of audience you want to reach when you construct a Web page. If the priority is universal access, it is hard to go wrong keeping to the HTML 2.0 specification and using logical tags wherever possible. If you are more concerned about the appearance of your Web page, then tag extensions and the physical tags are the way to go.

Link: To get a better understanding of how other browsers interpret HTML code, check out the "Dehanced for Lynx" Web page at http://world.std.com/~adamg/dehanced.html.

No matter which format you use to construct your Web pages, the best two pieces of advice are:

- Be consistent in your coding style
- Write code so that it can be understood easily at a later date

If you decide to go for a physical formatting style, be consistent in its application to your Web pages. When you write your HTML code, space things out to make your beginning and end tags easy to locate. There is always the possibility that you or somebody else will have to rewrite your original HTML code for a Web page. The easier it is to decipher, the easier it will be to edit.

The World Wide Web opens up a number of possibilities for the prospective writer. Learning HTML could improve your marketable skills, as businesses that go online are beginning to hire people experienced in HTML. But whether or not you want to improve your skills, create your own online business, or simply post information on your favorite rock band on the Web, it is here to stay. It is easy to learn the basics of HTML, so if you've got an Internet account, why not try putting up your own personal billboards on the Information SuperHighway.

Web Document Structure Tags

HTML 4.0 is the current standard at the time of this writing, and is the standard on which the following tags are based. HTML is a living language so by the time this book goes to print there could very well be an HTML 4.X standard, or greater. As a Web author you must be prepared to be aware of new HTML developments constantly, and apply them according to your design and technical requirements.

There are four basic parts to every HTML 4.0 document:

- The DOCTYPE tag defines the document as HTML 4.0-compliant
- The HTML tag encloses the entire document
- The HEAD tag encloses header information describing the document
- The BODY tag encloses the content of the Web page

Though Web pages may differ a great deal in content and design, they all have the preceding four parts in common. It is important to note that the DOCTYPE tag was introduced into the HTML 3.2 specification. HTML documents that do not include the DOCTYPE tag are still functional, but cannot be labeled as compliant with the HTML 3.2 (or higher) standard as defined by the World Wide Web Consortium.

The <!DOCTYPE> Tag—Declaring HTML Compliance

The <!DOCTYPE> tag is an empty tag that is used to define your HTML document as being SGML compliant. The <!DOCTYPE> tag should be the first thing to appear at the top of your HTML document. SGML (Standard Generalized Markup Language) is a markup language that is similar to HTML, but much more complex and powerful. As electronic documents become more mainstream, the <!DOCTYPE> tag will indicate to SGML tools that your document should use the HTML 3.2 (or higher) document type definition (DTD).

<!DOCTYPE>

Element Name: Document type definition tag.

Description: Identifies to the Web browser what kind of HTML document it is about to display.

Attributes: None.

Associated Tags: None.

Sample:

```
<!DOCTYPE HTML PUBLIC "-//W3C//DTD HTML 3.2 Final//EN">
```

Although your Web page will function properly without the <!DOCTYPE> tag, the HTML 3.2 specification requires that it be present, and that it is the first tag in a Web document.

The <HTML> Tag—Defining Your HTML Document

The HTML tag is a container tag whose start and end tags define the beginning and end of your HTML document. All tags, except for the <!DOCTYPE> tag, must appear within the HTML container tag.

<HTML> . . .</HTML>

Element Name: HTML tag.

Description: Declares the beginning and the end of an HTML document. This is the tag that must appear immediately after the <!DOCTYPE> tag, and its ending tag (</HTML>) must appear at the end of the document.

Attributes: None.

Associated Tags: All other HTML tags.

Sample:

```
<!DOCTYPE HTML PUBLIC "-//W3C//DTD HTML 3.2 Final//EN">
<HTML>
<HEAD>
<TITLE>Kim's Web Page</TITLE>
</HEAD>
<BODY>
All other tags, and the content of your HTML page belong
here.
</BODY>
</HTML>
```

Although your Web page will display properly without the <HTML> tags, to omit them is considered bad form.

The <HEAD> Tag—Document Header Information

The <HEAD> tag is a container tag that holds header information about your HTML document. This must at least include a <TITLE>, and may also include other tags such as <BASE>, <ISINDEX>, <LINK>, <META>, <STYLE>, and <SCRIPT>.

<HEAD> . . .</HEAD>

Element Name: Header tag.

Description: Contains information about the Web page, and must include the <TITLE> tag.

Attributes: None.

Associated Tags: <BASE>, <ISINDEX>, <LINK>, <META>, <STYLE>, <SCRIPT>, <TITLE>.

Sample:

```
<HEAD>
This text does not display on the Web page.
</HEAD>
```

The HEAD tag does not appear by itself; it encloses at least the <TITLE> tag, and can also contain the other aforementioned tags. The seven associated tags can appear only within the <HEAD> tag. They are described next.

<BASE>

Element Name: Base tag.

Description: Identifies the HTML file's current location.

Attributes: HREF=URL. Use the HREF tag to specify the full Web address of the source Web page.

Sample:

```
<HEAD>
<TITLE>HTML 3.2 Reference Specification</TITLE>
<BASE HREF="http://www.w3.org/pub/WWW/TR/REC-html32.html">
</HEAD>
```

The <BASE> tag is an empty tag that must appear within the <HEAD> tag. This tag is needed when your HTML document is being read from a site other than where its original source is stored. It is a good idea to always use this tag so that the original source can be found. This tag is also useful in that you can use relative path names in the body of the Web document, for example for images, and they will always be located relative to the URL stated in <BASE>.

<ISINDEX>

Element Name: Is Indexed tag.

Description: Indicates that the HTML document is indexed and part of a searchable directory of Web pages. This tag is no longer commonly used.

Attributes: None.

Sample:

```
<HEAD>
<ISINDEX>
</HEAD>
```

The <ISINDEX> tag is an empty tag that must appear within the <HEAD> tag. The <ISINDEX> tag does not automatically make your Web page searchable, but is a label that indicates that the Web site that the document is a part of offers a local search engine. This tag is no longer commonly used.

<LINK>

Element Name: Link tag.

Description: Indicates where a Web document fits into the hierarchy of the Web site.

Attributes:
REL = *URL*
Indicates the URL of a subdocument.
REV = *URL*
Indicates the URL of a parent document.

Sample:

```
<HEAD>
<TITLE>Kim's Web Page</TITLE>
<LINK REL="sub-document"
HREF="http://www.interlog.com/~ksc/burgundy.htm">
<LINK REV="parent document"
HREF="http://www.interlog.com/~ksc/winegeneral.htm">
</HEAD>
```

The <LINK> tag is used to show how the information in the document is related to other Web documents within the Web site. For instance a Web page explaining the qualities of red wine may be related to several subdocuments that examine red wines from specific regions. Conversely, the generic document discussing red wines is the parent of the several documents discussing specific wine regions.

<META>

Element Name: Meta tag.

Description: Provides details about the HTML document that are not covered by the other tags within the <HEAD> tags.

Attributes:
NAME= *text*
Indicates a name that a Web search engine would understand.
CONTENT= *text*
Indicates the content of a Web page; a string that will be recorded by a search engine.
HTTP-EQUIV= "refresh"
Used to perform a "client pull": the Web browser will refresh to display a specified URL after a specified number of seconds. These values are specified in the CONTENT attribute.

Sample:

```
<HEAD>
<TITLE>Kim's Web Page</TITLE>
<META NAME="description" CONTENT="Kim Silk-Copeland's Web
Page">
<META NAME="keywords" CONTENT="Kim, Silk, Copeland, fun,
HTML, Discovery, EXN">
<META HTTP-EQUIV="refresh" CONTENT="3;
http://www.fis.utoronto.ca/~silk/">
</HEAD>
```

The <META> tag can be defined to provide any kind of extra information about your Web page. Many search engines look for a <META> tag and use that information to index your Web page in their database.

<SCRIPT> and <STYLE>

The <SCRIPT> and <STYLE> tags provide information regarding style sheets and client-side scripts. The HTML 3.2 specification left placeholders for these tags, and they are well-defined for HTML 4.0. For detailed information on using the <STYLE> and <SCRIPT> tags, please see Chapter 11, "Cascading Style Sheets" and Chapter 13 "Dynamic Documents."

<TITLE>...</TITLE>

Element Name: Title tag.

Description: Defines the title of your HTML document.

Attributes: None.

Sample:

```
<HEAD>
<TITLE>Kim's Web Page</TITLE>
</HEAD>
```

The text you enclose in the TITLE tags appears in the top menu bar area of most browsers, not in the HTML document body itself. Text browsers such as Lynx do not display the title tag. The title is the text that will be displayed in the Web browser's bookmark list when a user bookmarks your page. It is also the caption used in search engine results.

The <BODY> tag—The Content Begins

The <BODY> tag is a required container tag marking the beginning of the main content area of your Web page. All tags and text contained within the <BODY> tags are displayed in the Web browser window. The majority of HTML tags occur within the <BODY> tags. In HTML 2.0, the <BODY> tag had no attributes, but the HTML 3.2 specification officially sanctioned the following attributes for the <BODY> tag: ALINK, BACKGROUND, BGCOLOR, LINK, TEXT, and VLINK. With the introduction of cascading style sheets, the attributes of the <BODY> tag have been deprecated for HTML 4.0. However, many Web authors still these attributes if the author chooses not to use style sheets. For more information on style sheets, see Chapter 11 "Cascading Style Sheets."

<BODY> . . .</BODY>

Element Name: Body tag.

Description: Contains all other HTML tags and the entire content of your Web page. The <BODY> tag is mandatory.

Attributes:

ALINK= *colorname* or *colorvalue*
Defines the color of a hypertext link as the user clicks on it. The color is defined using RBG values.

BACKGROUND= *colorname* or *colorvalue*
Defines the image for the background of your Web page. This image must be in GIF or JPEG format. See Chapter 6 "Color, Images, and Imagemaps" for more information on images.

BGCOLOR= *colorname* or *colorvalue*
Defines the color of the background of your Web page. The color is defined using RBG values.

LINK= *colorname* or *colorvalue*
Defines the color of a hypertext link before the user clicks on it. The color is defined using RBG values.

TEXT= *colorname* or *colorvalue*
Defines the default color of the text in your document. The color is defined using RBG values.

VLINK= *colorname* or *colorvalue*
Defines the color of a hypertext link after the user clicks on it. The color is defined using RBG values.

Associated Tags: All other tags occur within the <BODY> tag.

Sample:

```
<BODY BGCOLOR="#FFFFFF" LINK="#23238E" ALINK="#FF0000"
VLINK="#215E21" TEXT="#000000">
```

The attributes defining color are usually RBG values. See Appendix D for a list of colors and their RBG values. Note that either the BGCOLOR or the BACKGROUND attribute can appear in the <BODY> tag, not both at once. Keep in mind that your color decisions will greatly affect the appearance of your Web page. Too much color can be much worse than no color at all.

MIME Types

There are many file types used on the Internet. In addition to the basic HTML file, there are files for conveying sound, video, still images and different document types. Your browser has to be able to recognize these types of files properly to be able to deal with them. Many browsers can recognize the common file types without any problems, but in some cases a bit of extra help is necessary.

That's why MIME was created. MIME is an acronym for Multipurpose Internet Mail Extensions, originally designed to enable users to send nontext media via email. Traditionally, many email programs did not deliver nontext media files very well, and since there is no standard for email client software, media files were easily corrupted when users sent and received them. MIME was introduced as a standard that email clients could use to ensure that media files could travel between different email clients and remain uncorrupted. This has been extended to the Web as well, enabling Web authors to specify the exact type of file the user may be downloading to ensure its proper delivery to the user.

MIME is designed to extend to any new kinds of media that are developed in the future. Current basic MIME types include text, image, audio, video, and application. By specifying the type of file contained within a Web page (say, within a hypertext link), you explicitly tell the user's browser what to expect, giving it a better chance to deal with the file type. Here's a short list of the most common MIME types, as defined by the W3C: text/html, image/png, image/gif, video/mpeg, audio/basic, text/tcl, text/javascript, and text/vbscript.

SUMMARY

Now that you've read about the conventions of HTML and have learned about the structure of an HTML document, and the types of files that can be inserted into a Web page, you are ready to learn more about the guts of a Web page. The next chapter will show you the HTML tags you'll use to build the visible content area of your Web page.

CHAPTER 3

Displayed Elements

Formatting elements are composed of those tags whose sole purpose is to change or in some way alter the way text is displayed on a Web page. Many different types of text formatting tags are available, though they tend to fall into two different categories: logical tags and physical tags. Logical tags are designed to assist in the structure of a Web page by defining the types of elements they enclose. Classic examples of logical text formatting tags include <ADDRESS>, <BLOCKQUOTE>, and <DFN> tags. Many more, like the <BLINK>, <CENTER>, or <MARQUEE> tags are used purely for physical purposes, often adding "spice" to a Web page.

The best advice on using these tags is to use them effectively—never add gratuitous HTML to a Web page, because it almost invariably makes it appear "busy." Not that a Web page needs to be sparse—far from it; but make sure that your Web page does not overuse many of the tags described in this section. Remember that

HTML tags are designed to convey information in an effective manner to a viewer; if it doesn't do that, you have failed as a Web author to get your point across.

By the same token, it is good to experiment with how tags work, because that is the only way people truly learn how to use them. It is highly recommended that you try out the tags described in this chapter on your Web pages, and observe their effects before placing your Web page on your Web server. Some elements will enhance your message, some will detract from it—the only way to find out is to try them out.

The Address Tag

The <ADDRESS> tag is used to contain addressing information. The details about the tag follow.

<ADDRESS> . . .</ADDRESS>

Name: Address tag.

Description: Contains address information.

Attributes: None.

Associated Tags: <BODY>, any other formatting element.

Sample Code:

```
<ADDRESS>
AP Professional
6277 Sea Harbor Drive
Orlando, FL
32821-9816
</ADDRESS>
```

The <ADDRESS> tag is a container tag designed to enclose addressing or contact information, like a firm or person's name and mailing address, telephone number, and related information. It is a classic logical style of tag, in that it exactly describes the contents of what it is supposed to contain, so it is hard to mix-up an <ADDRESS> tag for use with any other sort of text on a Web page. Browsers typically render the contents of an <ADDRESS> tag in an italic font.

The <ADDRESS> tag does not automatically retain the line spacing information contained within the original text. It will render all of the text it contains on a single line. This mean that the <ADDRESS> tag is typically used in conjunction with other text formatting tags. The following code example shows how <ADDRESS> is more typically used, in this case in conjunction with the line break (<BR>) tag.

```
<ADDRESS>
K.R. Croeckquo, Empressario<BR>
Croeckquo Emporium Unlimited<BR>
3001 Vanessa Blvd.<BR>
Whoville, YK<BR>
980191<BR>
</ADDRESS>
```

Figure 3.1 shows the difference between the two forms in which the <ADDRESS> tag is typically formatted.

More information on the break (<BR>) tag can be found later in this chapter.

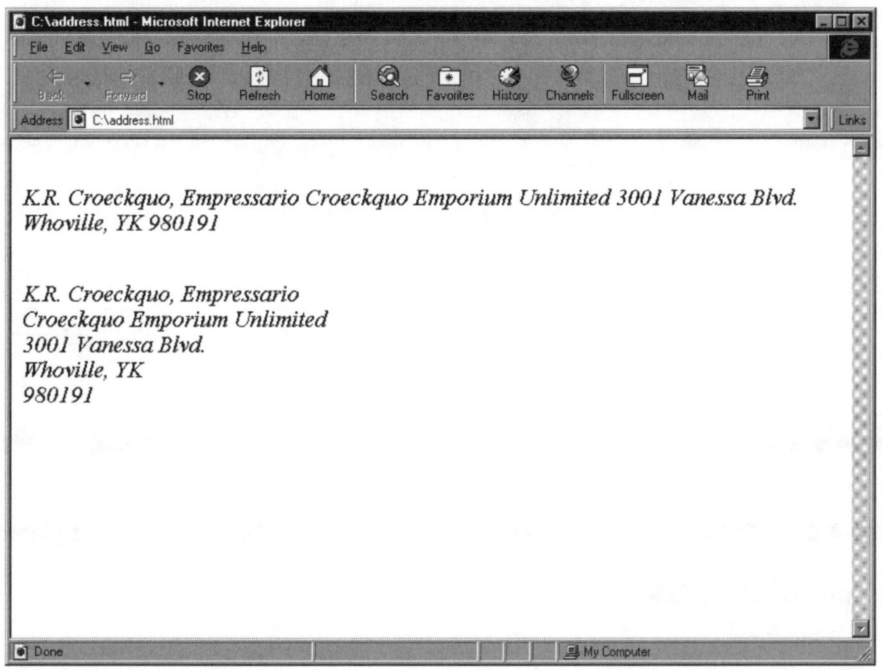

Figure 3.1 The <ADDRESS> Tag without and with Additional Formatting Elements

The Basefont and Font Tags

Many text characteristics can be set using the <BASEFONT> and <FONT> tags, which can alter the size, color, and type of font used to display text on a Web page.

Note: The <BASEFONT> and <FONT> tags are deprecated for HTML 4.0, but are still commonly used and are recognized by Web browsers.

Though they do not have to be used together, when the <BASEFONT> tag is used, the <FONT> tag will generally also be found on the same Web page, so they are both discussed in this section.

The following are the specifications for the <BASEFONT> and <FONT> tags.

<BASEFONT> . . .</BASEFONT>

Element Name: Basefont tag.

Description: Specifies the base font value(s) for the text to be displayed on a Web page.

Attributes: COLOR= *colorname* or *colorvalue*
Specifies the color of the font to be displayed.
FACE= *fontname*
Specifies the type of font to be displayed.
SIZE= *number*
Specifies the base font size. Valid ranges are between 1–7 (smallest to largest).

Associated Tags: <FONT>, <BODY>, any other formatting element.

<FONT> . . .<FONT>

Element Name: Font tag.

Description: Specifies the specific font to be displayed on a Web page.

Attributes: COLOR= *colorname* or *colorvalue*
Specifies the color of the font to be displayed.

FACE= *fontname*
Specifies the type of font to be displayed.
POINT-SIZE= *number*
Specifies the specific font size to be displayed.
SIZE= *number*
Specifies the base font size. Valid ranges are between 1–7 (smallest to largest).

Associated Tags: <BASEFONT>, <BODY>, any other formatting element.

Sample:

```
<BASEFONT=2>
This text is set to a BASEFONT value of 2
<P>
<FONT SIZE=+1>This text has been incremented by
one.</FONT>
<P>
<FONT SIZE=+2>This text has been incremented by two over
the original, &lt;BASEFONT&gt; value.</FONT>
<P>
<FONT FACE=ARIAL COLOR=RED>Other characteristics, such as
color and the font type can also be changed</FONT>
```

As you can see, <BASEFONT> and <FONT> share many of the same characteristics. There are two ways in which the <BASEFONT> and <FONT> tags are used: they are either used together, or the <FONT> tag is used separately.

Here's how the <BASEFONT>/<FONT> tags are used in combination: the <BASEFONT> tag is used to set the initial characteristics of the font used on a Web page, and the <FONT> tag is then used to modify those base characteristics within specific sections of the Web page. Using the sample code displayed earlier, Figure 3.2 shows off the effect of using the <BASEFONT> and <FONT> tags together.

The <FONT> tag can also be used by itself on a Web page to set specific font characteristics on a Web page. Instead of altering font characteristics in relation to a specified base font, it changes font characteristics in relation to the unspecified base font used by the viewer's browser. It has many characteristics, the majority of which are supported by both Internet Explorer and Netscape Navigator, and for this reason it tends to be used solo rather than in conjunction with the <BASEFONT> tag.

Here's some sample code that shows how the <FONT> tag can be used.

```
<B>Changing the Font Face</B><BR>
<FONT FACE=ARIAL>This text has been set to the Arial
font.</FONT><BR>
<FONT FACE=COURIER>This text has been set to the
Courier font.</FONT><BR>
```

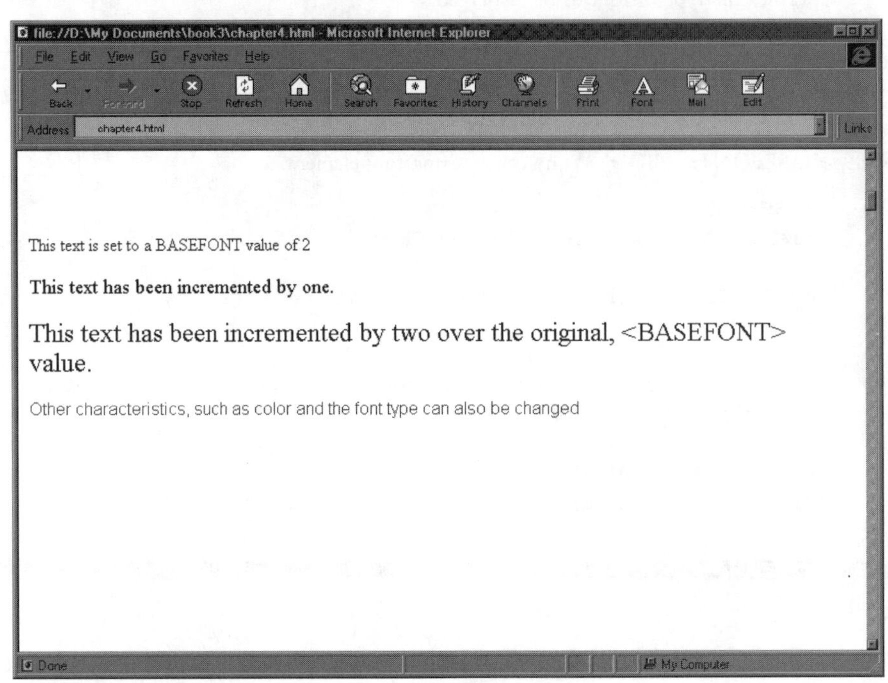

Figure 3.2 The <BASEFONT> and <FONT> Tags Used Together within a Web Page

```
<FONT FACE=ALGERIAN>This text has been set to the
Algerian font.</FONT><BR>
<P>
<B>Changing the Font Color</B><BR>
<FONT FACE=RED>This text is displayed in
red.</FONT><BR>
<FONT COLOR=GREEN>This text is displayed in
green.</FONT><BR>
<FONT COLOR=0000FF>This text is displayed in
blue.</FONT><BR>
<P>
<B>Changing Font Size</B><BR>
<FONT SIZE=1>Size=1<FONT>,
<FONT SIZE=2>Size=2</FONT>,
<FONT SIZE=3>Size=3</FONT>,
<FONT SIZE=4>Size=4</FONT>,
```

```
<FONT SIZE=5>Size=5</FONT>,
<FONT SIZE=6>Size=6</FONT>,
<FONT SIZE=7>Size=7</FONT>.
<P>
<B>Several Font Modifying Characteristics
Combined</B><BR>
<FONT SIZE=5 COLOR=TEAL FACE=DESDEMONA>FONT SIZE=5
COLOR=TEAL FACE=DESDEMONA</FONT>
```

Figure 3.3 shows how the same code is displayed within a Web browser.

NOTE: The <BASEFONT> and <FONT> tags are deprecated for HTML 4.0, but are still commonly used and are recognized by Web browsers.

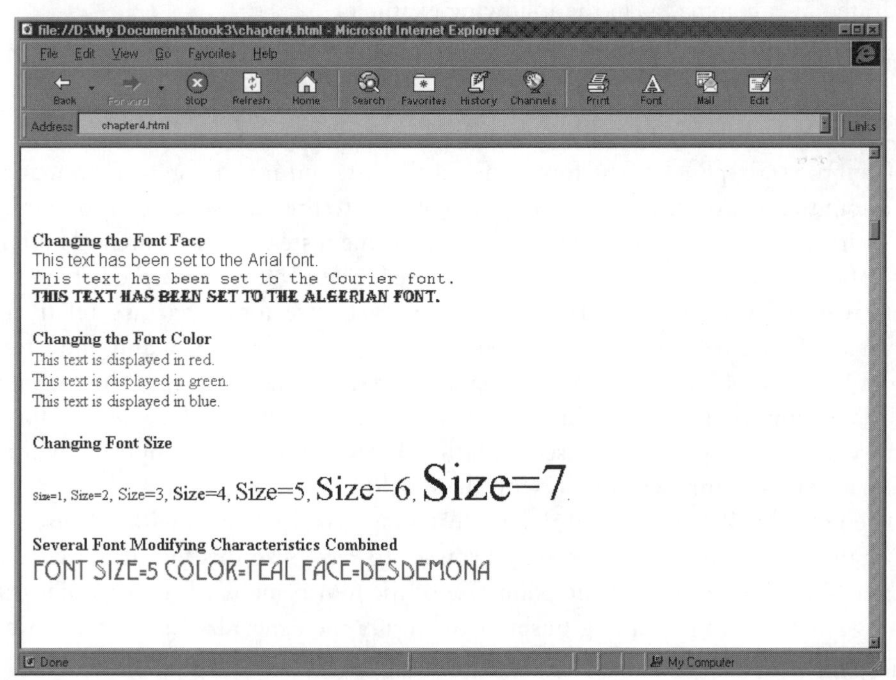

Figure 3.3 The Various Font-Modifying Characteristics of the <FONT> Tag Displayed

Now that you've had a sample of how some of the attributes of the <BASEFONT> and the <FONT> tag are used, here are more of the details of how they are used.

The COLOR attribute sets the color of the font to be displayed. It can take either a colorname (like RED, GREEN, or BLUE) or a hexadecimal color value (like FF0000, 00FF00, or 0000FF, the hexadecimal equivalents of red, green, and blue). See Appendix D, "Listing of Common Color Values/Colornames" for a listing of color values and names that can be used. This attribute is supported by both Internet Explorer and Netscape Navigator when used with the <FONT> tag, but is supported within Internet Explorer only when used with the <BASEFONT> tag.

The FACE attribute sets the type of font to be used and displayed by the browser. This attribute was first added within Internet Explorer 1.0, and was later adopted within Netscape Navigator 3.0. It takes as a value the name of the font to be used, such as Arial, Helvetica, or Courier. Any font can be specified, but it will be displayed only if it matches the name of a font used on the viewer's system. Since there is no way you can automatically determine what types of fonts are available on a viewer's system, you are able to "cascade" several font names together, separated by a comma, as in the following example.

```
<FONT FACE="ARIAL, HELVETICA, GARAMOND">Some
text.</FONT>
```

The browser reads the first font name in the list, and if it doesn't find a match for a font that exists on the viewer's system, it goes to the next specified font name, and if it exists on the viewer's system, uses that one instead. If no match is found, the default font of the viewer's browser is used. Since you cannot predict which fonts will be available, it is a good idea to try to use fonts that are relatively universal. There are about five different font types that are reasonably universal across Windows, Macintosh, and Unix systems: Arial, Times Roman, Courier, Sans Serif, and WingDings. The FACE attribute is supported by both Internet Explorer and Netscape Navigator when used with the <FONT> tag, but is supported within Internet Explorer only when used with the <BASEFONT> tag.

The POINT-SIZE attribute of the <FONT> tag was first added within Netscape Navigator 4.0, and so far is the only browser to recognize this tag. It allows the HTML author to set the specific point-size of the font being used. *Point-size* is the expression used in the printing business to specify the exact size of the font to be displayed. When used within Netscape Navigator, it will display only the font sizes that are available to it—this is important to remember because many systems use noncontinuous fonts that do not portray a continual level of point-sizes, so you may be able to specify only a small range of point-sizes. The following code portrays how the POINT-SIZE attribute can be used.

```
<B>Using the default browser font (Times Roman)</B><BR>
<FONT POINT-SIZE=8>POINT-SIZE=8</FONT>,
<FONT POINT-SIZE=10>POINT-SIZE=10</FONT>,
<FONT POINT-SIZE=12>POINT-SIZE=12</FONT>,
<FONT POINT-SIZE=14>POINT-SIZE=14</FONT>,
<FONT POINT-SIZE=16>POINT-SIZE=16</FONT>,
<FONT POINT-SIZE=18>POINT-SIZE=18</FONT>,
<FONT POINT-SIZE=20>POINT-SIZE=20</FONT>,
<FONT POINT-SIZE=24>POINT-SIZE=24</FONT>,
<FONT POINT-SIZE=36>POINT-SIZE=36</FONT>.
<P>
<BR>
<P>
<B>Using a different font (Arial)</B><BR>
<FONT FACE=ARIAL POINT-SIZE=8>POINT-SIZE=8</FONT>,
<FONT FACE=ARIAL POINT-SIZE=10>POINT-SIZE=10</FONT>,
<FONT FACE=ARIAL POINT-SIZE=12>POINT-SIZE=12</FONT>,
<FONT FACE=ARIAL POINT-SIZE=14>POINT-SIZE=14</FONT>,
<FONT FACE=ARIAL POINT-SIZE=16>POINT-SIZE=16</FONT>,
<FONT FACE=ARIAL POINT-SIZE=18>POINT-SIZE=18</FONT>,
<FONT FACE=ARIAL POINT-SIZE=20>POINT-SIZE=20</FONT>,
<FONT FACE=ARIAL POINT-SIZE=24>POINT-SIZE=24</FONT>,
<FONT FACE=ARIAL POINT-SIZE=36>POINT-SIZE=36</FONT>.
```

Figure 3.4 shows how this code is displayed within Netscape Navigator 4.0.

It is worth noting that this attribute is not included in the HTML 4.0 specification, and is recognized only by Netscape Navigator 4.0.

The SIZE attribute is a universally usable attribute for both the <FONT> and <BASEFONT> tags. It is used to specify a specific font size. When used with <BASEFONT>, it sets the base font to be displayed by the browser, which can then be altered by using the <FONT> tag with the SIZE attribute, with either a positive or negative value, as in the following example.

```
<BASEFONT SIZE=2>
This text is displayed with the "base" font value.
<FONT SIZE=+2>This text is 2 sizes larger than the
"base" font value.</FONT>
<FONT SIZE=-2>This text is 2 sizes smaller than the
"base" font value.</FONT>
```

When used with the <FONT> tag alone, it takes a straight numerical value, as in the following code example.

```
<FONT SIZE=2>This text is set to FONT SIZE=2.</FONT>
<FONT SIZE=6>This text is set to FONT SIZE=6.</FONT>
```

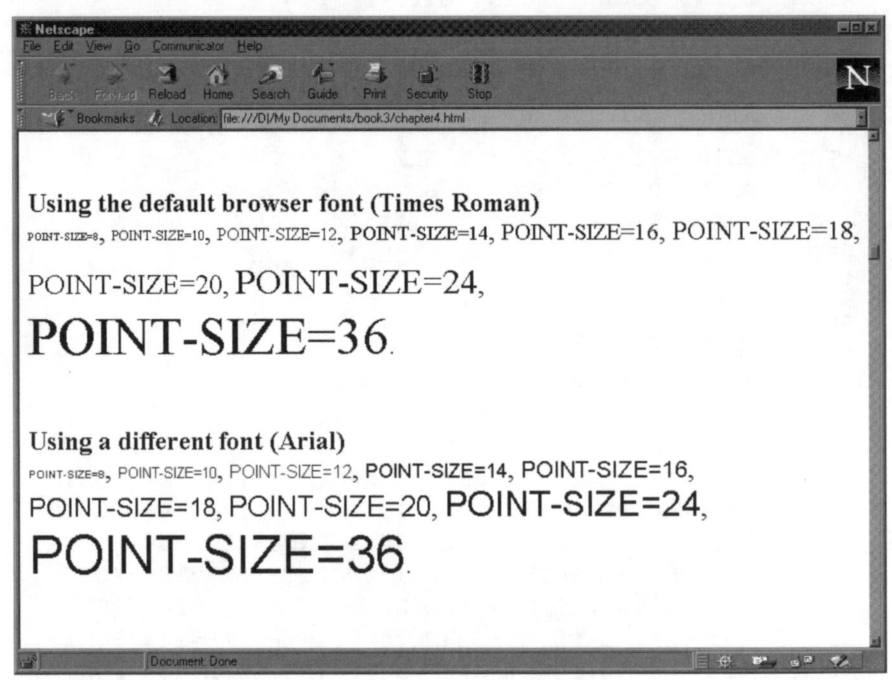

Figure 3.4 The POINT-SIZE Attribute Sample Code Displayed

The valid range for the SIZE attribute is between 1–7 (smallest to largest). It works in a similar fashion to the header (i.e., <H1>) tags, but is more intuitive—larger SIZE numbers display larger font sizes, which is exactly the opposite of the header tags. Also, unlike the header tags, no extra spacing is added above or below the text that is displayed. (The header tags are explored in more depth later in this section.) If the SIZE and POINT-SIZE attributes are used together and viewed through Netscape Navigator 4.0 and higher, the POINT-SIZE attribute is used by the browser in preference to the SIZE attribute.

It is also possible to nest particular font attributes within a Web page. If you want to set various <FONT> attributes in different sections of a Web page, this is possible by simply nesting different <FONT> attributes one within the other. So when you add a terminating font end tag (i.e., </FONT>) with a list of nested <FONT> tags in a Web page, only the innermost <FONT> attribute is turned off, and not all of them. The following example code shows how this can be accomplished.

```
<FONT FACE=ARIAL>Hello there <FONT SIZE=4>and welcome
</FONT> to my Web page.</FONT>
```

In this case the browser displays the Arial font throughout the whole of this sentence—it does not end when it meets the first of the two </FONT> tags. The words "and welcome" are rendered in an Arial font set to SIZE=4, this font attribute ending at the first </FONT> tag.

As a final note, it is worth pointing out that the <BASEFONT> and <FONT> tags are deprecated (i.e., not recommended) for use within the HTML 4.0 specification. Instead, the W3C is trying to drive Web authors to use cascading style sheets to achieve the same effects. It is retained within the HTML 4.0 specification because it is in such wide use, and because it is also much easier for beginning Web authors to deal with than their cascading style sheet equivalent. Cascading style sheets are covered in detail in Chapter 11.

The Blink Tag

This much-reviled tag in the Web authoring community is used to make the text it encloses flash, or "blink" on and off in the browser display. It is recognized only by Netscape Navigator.

The specifications for the <BLINK> tag follow.

<BLINK> . . .</BLINK>

Element Name: Blink tag.

Description: Makes the text it encloses flash on and off.

Attributes: None.

Associated Tags: <BODY>, any other formatting element.

Sample:

```
<BLINK>
This text will blink uncontrollably forever! And you have
no control over how it is displayed. Ha ha ha!
</BLINK>
```

The blink tag is designed to draw the viewer's attention to a particular piece of text. Although it does have this effect, since there is no way for either the Web author or the user to control the blinking behavior, it gets annoying very quickly.

Keep in mind that this tag works only within Netscape Navigator, so its effects are not universal. It also only alters the display of text and related elements—it will not flash things like images or objects contained within a Web page on and off (though this characteristic is arguably undesirable). It is also quite possible for a user to scroll past a page containing blinking text when it is off, thereby defeating the whole purpose of the blink tag in the first place. Use this tag sparingly, if at all, in your Web pages.

THE BLOCKQUOTE AND QUOTE TAGS

The blockquote tags and quote tags are used to display quotations within a Web page.

The specifications for the <BLOCKQUOTE> tag follow.

<BLOCKQUOTE> . . .</BLOCKQUOTE>

Element Name: Blockquote tag.
Description: Used to contain a large quotation.

Attributes: CITE= *URL*
Specifies an URL that points to the source of the quotation.

Associated Tags: <BODY>, any other formatting element.

Sample:

```
Sample quotation:
<BLOCKQUOTE>
A cloud lay over Asgaard. Not in the sky, for the sun
shone clear in the soft blue heaven; nor on the earth,
for the flowers starred the meadows with their gay
blossoms and birds sang in the whispering groves.
<P>
The gloom was in the hearts of the &Aelig; and Asynjar,
for Baldur, their darling, the Shining God, was sad.
</BLOCKQUOTE>
```

<Q> . . .</Q>

Element Name: Quote tag.

Description: Used to contain a short quotation.

Attributes: CITE= *URL*
Specifies an URL that points to the source of the quotation.

Associated Tags: <BODY>, any other formatting element.

Sample:

```
Edmund Burke said that one must <Q>"guard against the
treasure of our liberty, not only from invasion, but from
decay and corruption".</Q>
```

Rather like the <ADDRESS> tag, the <BLOCKQUOTE> is a logical tag that encloses the type of text it describes: a quotation. It is designed to enclose lengthy quotations that are several lines in length. Web browsers render the text contained within a <BLOCKQUOTE> with indentations to the left and right sides of the quote—usually by about five character spaces from the margin of the browser window. Though it is supposed to be used purely for quotations, its indenting abilities are often used by Web page authors for nonquotation text.

The optional CITE attribute has been added under the HTML 4.0 specification, which is designed to point the reader to an original source document from which the quote is derived.

Figure 3.5 represents sample code depicted earlier. Note how an extra line is added both above and below the quotation.

Like the <BLOCKQUOTE> and <ADDRESS> tags, the quote (<Q>) container tag is a logical tag that encloses the type of text it describes: a quotation. It differs from the <BLOCKQUOTE> tag in design because it is supposed to enclose short quotations that are less than a couple of lines long. It does not indent the text it contains. The <Q> tag does insert the quotation marks around text it contains.

The CITE attribute is an option designed to point the reader to an original source document from which the quote is derived. The quote tag itself is new for the HTML 4.0 specification, and will likely be recognized by the major browsers shortly.

It is worth noting that a previous HTML specification (HTML 3.0) recom-

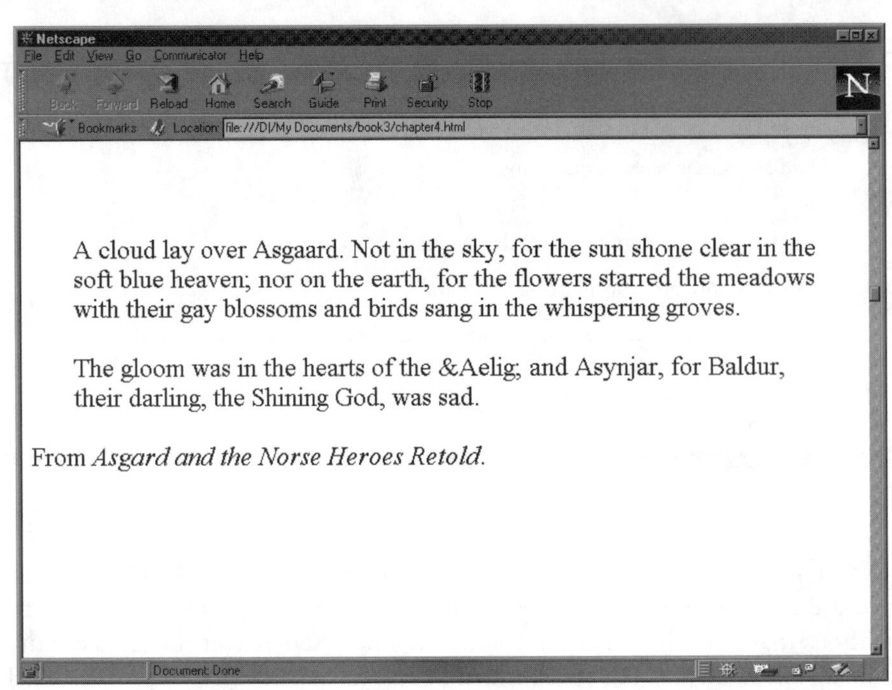

Figure 3.5 A Quotation Contained within the <BLOCKQUOTE> Tag Displayed

mended replacing the <BLOCKQUOTE> tag with the more concise <BQ> tag, which would work in an identical fashion. It was never adopted for use within either Internet Explorer or Netscape Navigator.

The Break, Nobreak, and Word Break Tags

The break tag is used to add a line break to a line of text. The nobreak tag works in the opposite fashion—if you do not want artificial line breaks inserted within text, this tag is used to prevent this from occurring. The word break tag tells the browser where a break in a line is allowed.

The characteristics for the break tag follow.

Element Name: Break tag.

Description: Used to add line breaks at the end of line of text.

Attributes: CLEAR= *NONE | LEFT | RIGHT | ALL*
Used whenever a floating element exists on a Web page, to break the line and start the text that appears after it in the next clear margin.

Associated Tags: <BODY>, any other formatting element.

Sample:

```
This is a continuous line of text.
<P>
This line of text<BR> is broken up<BR> and spread over
several lines.
```

The break tag is an empty tag used to put in line breaks with a line or lines of text within a Web page.

Its sole attribute, CLEAR, should be used whenever a floating element (such as images, spacers, or tables) existing on a Web page breaks the line and starts the text that appears after it in the next clear margin. By default, the value of <BR> is NONE. LEFT breaks the line and moves down vertically until there is a clear left margin, RIGHT breaks the line and moves down vertically until there is a clear right margin, and ALL breaks the line and moves down vertically until both margins are clear of floating elements.

The following sample code and figure 3.6 show the effects just described.

```
<IMG SRC="crosleyD25.jpg" ALIGN=LEFT>
<B>&lt;BR&gt;</B>: This text appears to the right of
the image.
<BR>This text appears underneath the first line of
text.
<P>
```

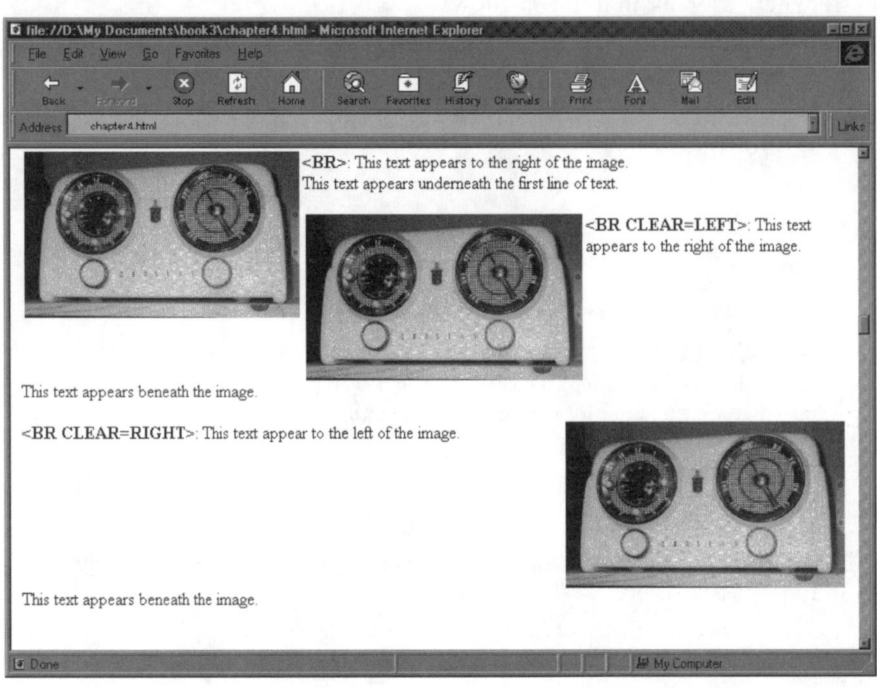

Figure 3.6 Illustration Depicting the Function of Several Values of the CLEAR Attribute when Used in Conjunction with an Image on a Web Page

```
<IMG SRC="crosleyD25.jpg" ALIGN=LEFT>
<B>&lt;BR CLEAR=LEFT&gt;</B>: This text appears to the
right of the image.
<BR CLEAR=LEFT> This text appears beneath the image.
<P>
<IMG SRC="crosleyD25.jpg" ALIGN=RIGHT>
<B>&lt;BR CLEAR=RIGHT&gt;</B>: This text appear to the
left of the image.
<BR CLEAR=RIGHT>This text appears beneath the image.
```

The nobreak (<NOBR>) container tag works in the opposite fashion to the break tag—it ensures that the browser does not insert an artificial line break in a long line of text.

Here are the specifications for this tag:

<NOBR> . . .</NOBR> (Internet Explorer only)

Element Name: Nobreak tag.

Description: Designed to prevent the browser from inserting an artificial line break within a long line of text.

Attributes: None.

Associated Tags: <BODY>, any other formatting element (other than <BR>).

Sample:

```
<NOBR>This is a long-ish line of text that will not be
broken up into separate lines by the browser</NOBR>
```

This tag is best used when it is crucial that information be contained on the same line. In practice, there are rare occasions where there is demand for it. The only real-life case occurs when you have a long hyphenated word that you do not want to be broken by the browser if it appears at the end of a line of text on the browser. Do not overuse this tag—it can result in some very messy looking Web pages.

This tag was first introduced within Internet Explorer 3.0, and has only recently appeared for use within Netscape Navigator 4.0. It is considered a nonstandard tag, and is not part of the HTML 4.0 specification. Instead, the W3C recommends that you use the nonbreaking space entity (or) between words in a sentence to achieve the same effect. This technique even works for words that contain a natural word-break (i.e., a hyphen) within them.

<WBR>

Element Name: Word break tag.

Description: Tells the browser where a line break can occur in a sentence. It is designed to be used in conjunction with the <NOBR> tag.

Attributes: None.

Associated Tags: <BODY>, <NOBR>, any other formatting element.

Sample:

```
<NOBR>
```

```
This is a really, really, really, really, really,
really,<WBR> really, really, really, long sentence that
can be broken after the sixth "really". Really.
</NOBR>
```

The word break tag is designed for use in conjunction with the <NOBR> tag, and is inserted into a sentence to tell the browser where a line of text can be broken. This adds a little bit of flexibility to the usage of the nobreak tag.

THE CENTER TAG

The center tag is used to align an element horizontally on a Web page. This tag has been deprecated in the HTML 4.0 specification; however, the major browsers continue to recognize it.

The specification for the tag follows.

<CENTER> . . .</CENTER>

Element Name: Center tag.

Description: Used to align any element of the viewer's browser window horizontally.

Attributes: None.

Associated Tags: <BODY>, any other formatting element (other than <BR>).

Sample:

```
<CENTER>This plain text is centered on the Web
page.</CENTER>
<P>
<CENTER><H2>This level-2 header is centered on the Web
page.</H2></CENTER>
<P>
<CENTER>This image<BR> <IMG SRC="philco jnr.jpg"><BR> and
text is centered on the Web page.</CENTER>
```

The center tag is a formatting tag that allows the Web author to center just about *any* element on a Web page. It can be used to center text, images, tables, and many other elements on a Web page, as Figure 3.7 shows.

This tag was first introduced within Netscape Navigator 1.0, was later adopted when the Internet Explorer 1.0 was released some time later, and was finally adopted within the official HTML 3.2 specification.

There are other ways in which text and other elements can be horizontally centered on a Web page. In Figure 3.7, note how the following line of code produces the same effect as using the center tag on a line of text.

```
<P ALIGN=CENTER>This plain text uses &lt;P
ALIGN=CENTER&gt; to be centered on the Web page
instead.</P>
```

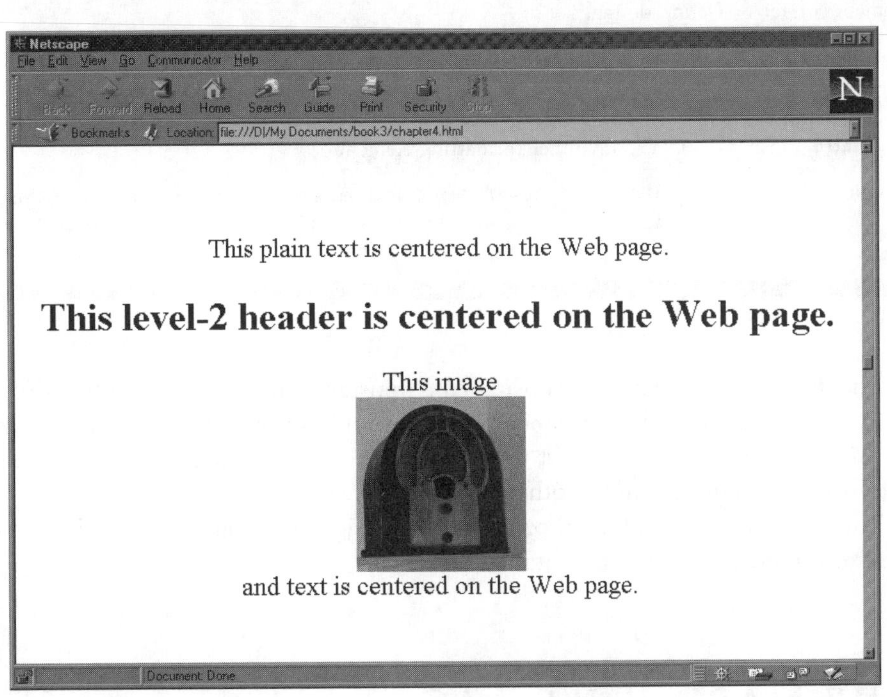

Figure 3.7 Illustration Depicting How Text and Images Can Be Centered Using the <CENTER> Tag

The ALIGN attribute has been added to many different tags, and CENTER is a common value that can be used with ALIGN. The center tag is easier to remember however, and cuts down on the amount of times you need to add ALIGN=CENTER to the tags contained on a Web page.

THE DEFINITION TAG

The definition tag is used to enclose some text that describes a definition.

<DFN> . . .</DFN>

Element Name: Definition tag.

Description: Contains a definition of a term.

Attributes: None.

Associated Tags: <BODY>, any other formatting element.

Sample:

```
The definition of an isosceles triangle is: <DFN>a
triangle that has two sides of equal length</DFN>.
```

The definition tag was once considered a nonstandard tag, though it has always been supported in both Netscape Navigator and Internet Explorer since their respective inceptions. It was first made part of the HTML 3.2 specification, and over time is gaining ground in other browsers as well.

The definition tag is a logical container tag designed to contain the definition of a term. It renders the text in an italic font.

THE HARD RULE TAG

The hard rule tag is used to insert a horizontal line in a Web page. It is used to differentiate and separate elements visually on a Web page.

The following is the specification for the tag.

<HR>

Element Name: Hard rule tag.

Description: Designed to insert a horizontal rule line in a Web page.

Attributes:
ALIGN= *LEFT | CENTER | RIGHT*
Aligns the hard rule on the Web page.
COLOR= *colorname* or *colorvalue (Internet Explorer only)*
Specifies a particular color for the hard rule line.
NOSHADE
Specifies that the hard rule should be a solid line, with no shade effects.
SIZE= *# pixels | % of browser window*
Sets the vertical size of the hard rule line in pixels, or as a percentage of the browser window's width.
WIDTH= *# pixels | % of browser window*
Sets the horizontal size of the hard rule in pixels, or as a percentage of the browser window's width.

Associated Tags: <BODY>, any other formatting element.

Sample:

```
Here is some text that appears above a horizontal hard
rule.<BR>
<HR>
This text appears beneath the hard rule.<BR>
```

The ALIGN attribute works like it does with most other tags: it positions the hard rule according to the specified value. The default value for ALIGN is CENTER. It makes no sense to use this attribute unless you intend to use the WIDTH attribute as well, since by default a straight, horizontal line is drawn across the entire Web browser's window, so there would be nothing to align.

Note: All the attributes for <HR> have been deprecated in the HTML 4.0 specification.

Here's some sample code that shows how it can be specified.

```
Aligning a hard rule (WIDTH=50%).<BR>
ALIGN=LEFT<BR>
<HR ALIGN=LEFT WIDTH=50%>
```

```
ALIGN=CENTER
<HR ALIGN=CENTER WIDTH=50%>
ALIGN=RIGHT
<HR ALIGN=RIGHT WIDTH=50%>
```

The results are shown in Figure 3.8.

If you are authoring Web pages for use in Internet Explorer, you can also add color to your hard rule lines. This attribute is supported within Internet Explorer only—it is not recognized by other browsers, nor is it part of the HTML 4.0 specification.

It can either take a colorname or color value, as shown in the following sample code.

```
COLOR=RED<BR>
<HR COLOR=RED>
COLOR=GREEN<BR>
```

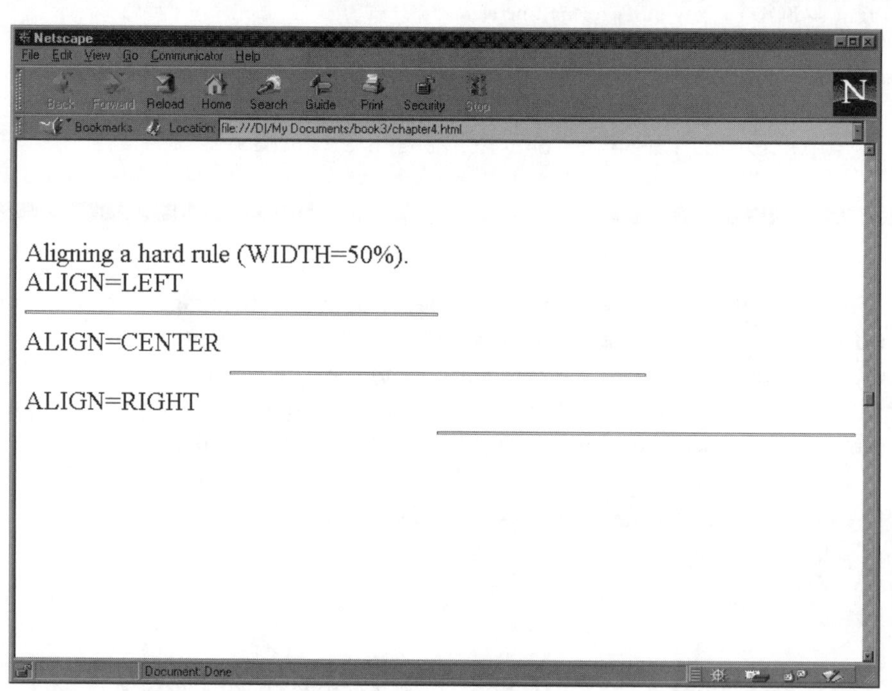

Figure 3.8 An Illustration Depicting the Effects of the ALIGN Attributes of the Hard Rule Tag

```
<HR COLOR=GREEN>
COLOR=0000FF (blue) <BR>
<HR COLOR=0000FF>
```

The results of this code can be seen in Figure 3.9. See Appendix D, "Listing of Common Color Values/Colornames" for a listing of color values and names that can be used with a hard rule line.

The NOSHADE stand-alone attribute tells the browser to display the hard rule as a solid line, rather than as a raised line with shading, its default display characteristics.

The following code sample shows how it is used.

```
<HR NOSHADE>
```

Figure 3.9 depicts these attributes as displayed within Internet Explorer.

The SIZE attribute sets the vertical size of the hard rule line in pixels, or as a

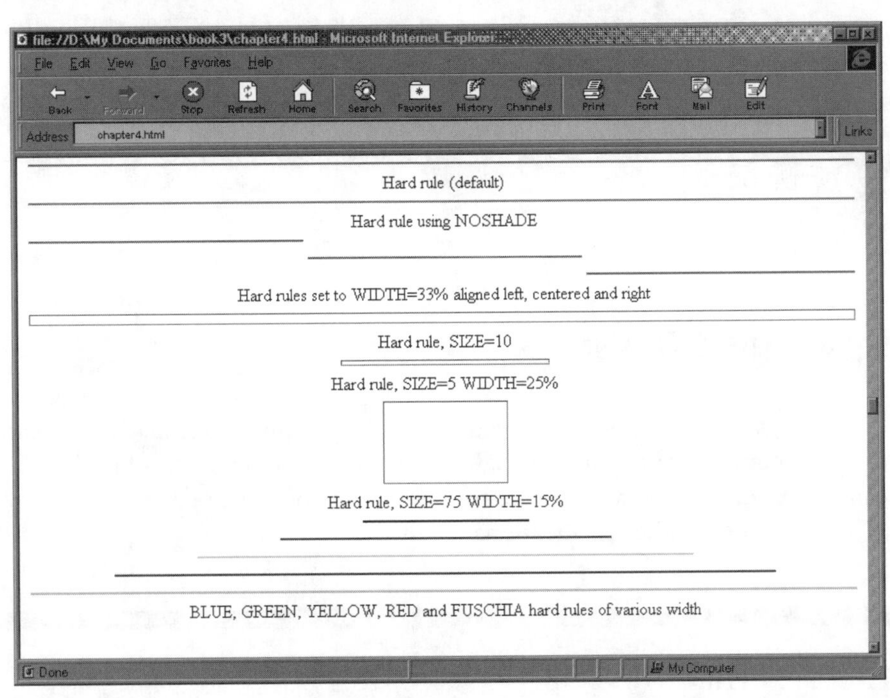

Figure 3.9 An Illustration Depicting the Effects of the NOSHADE, SIZE, and WIDTH Attributes of the Hard Rule Tag

percentage of the browser window's width. It essentially makes the line look thicker. It is highly recommended that a pixel value be specified for this attribute, as you cannot easily predict the vertical size of either the Web page or the vertical dimensions of the viewer's browser window.

The following code sample (whose results can be seen in Figure 3.9) shows how it can be used.

```
A hard rule that is 10 pixels in depth (SIZE=10).<BR>
<HR SIZE=10>
A hard rule that is 50 pixels in depth (SIZE=50).<BR>
<HR SIZE=50>
```

The WIDTH attribute works in a similar way, and sets the horizontal size of the hard rule in pixels, or as a percentage of the browser window's width. Although you still cannot predict the overall size of the viewer's browser window, it is much safer to use a percentage value with the WIDTH attribute.

The following code sample (whose results can also be seen in Figure 3.9) shows how it can be used.

```
A hard rule that is 10 pixels in width (WIDTH=10).<BR>
<HR SIZE=10>
A hard rule that is 50 pixels in width (WIDTH=50).<BR>
<HR SIZE=50>
A hard rule that is 25% of the browser window's width
(WIDTH=25%).<BR>
<HR SIZE=25%>
```

HEADING TAGS

Heading tags are designed to provide the Web author a means of indicating different section headings. It is a logical tag, in that different heading levels are meant to provide a natural structure to the contents of a Web page.

The following are the specifications for the tag.

<Hn> . . .</Hn>

Element Name: Heading tag.

Description: Specifies a topic heading.

Attributes: ALIGN= *LEFT* | *CENTER* | *RIGHT* | *JUSTIFY* (Netscape 4.0 and Internet Explorer 4.0 only).

Associated Tags: <BODY>, any other formatting element.

Sample:

```
<H1>Level-1 Heading</H1>
<H2>Level-2 Heading</H2>
<H3>Level-3 Heading</H3>
<H4>Level-4 Heading</H4>
<H5>Level-5 Heading</H5>
<H6>Level-6 Heading</H6>
```

There are six heading levels, and each is specified by using a number immediately after the "H" in the tag (i.e., <H1>–<H6>). A level-one heading (<H1>) is rendered as the largest of the six headings, and all subsequent headings are rendered in progressively smaller sizes. Web authors should use headers in a logical order, with an <H1> heading the "top" heading of the greatest importance, going down to the <H6>, which is a topic of the lowest importance or order in a document.

Heading tags have only one attribute—ALIGN—and it can be used within Netscape Navigator and Internet Explorer only. It takes one of four values: LEFT, CENTER, RIGHT, and JUSTIFY. LEFT is the default value for ALIGN, and places the heading against the left margin of the browser window. Similarly the CENTER and RIGHT values align the heading in the center and right margin of a Web page, respectively. JUSTIFY is recognized by version 4.0 of the Netscape and Internet Explorer browsers.

The following code shows how ALIGN can be used.

```
<H1 ALIGN=CENTER> This Level-1 heading is centered</H1>
```

Figure 3.10 depicts all of the heading levels, and a centered level-1 heading.

Note how the header tags automatically insert some vertical spacing both above and below the header. If you do not desire this characteristic, you may want to use the <FONT> tag with a large SIZE value instead.

The Marquee Tag

The marquee tag is used to display a horizontal line of scrolling text on a Web page. It is recognized only within Internet Explorer 2.0 and higher.

Here are the specifications for the marquee container tag.

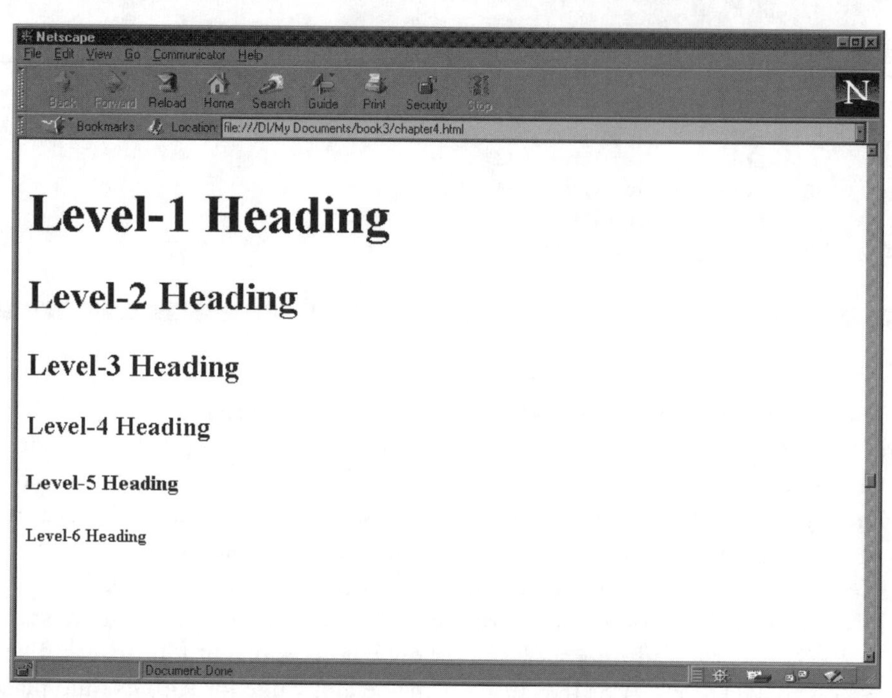

Figure 3.10 Heading Levels Displayed within Netscape Navigator

<MARQUEE> . . .</MARQUEE>

Element Name: Marquee tag.

Description: Produces a horizontal line of scrolling text within a Web page.

Attributes:

ALIGN= *TOP* | *MIDDLE* | *BOTTOM*
Specifies where the text should appear within the marquee space.
BEHAVIOR= *SCROLL* | *SLIDE* | *ALTERNATE*
Specifies how the text in the marquee should behave.
BGCOLOR= *colorname* or *colorvalue*
Specifies a color for the background of the marquee space.
DIRECTION= *LEFT* | *RIGHT*
Specifies the direction in which the marquee text should scroll.

HEIGHT= # *pixels* | % *of browser window*
Specifies the height of the marquee display as either a fixed pixel value or as a percentage of the browser window.
HSPACE= # *pixels*
Specifies the horizontal (left and right) spacing margins for the outside of the marquee.
LOOP= *number* | *INFINITE*
Specifies the number of times the text in the marquee should cycle.
SCROLLAMOUNT= # *pixels*
Specifies the amount of space in pixels that is between the display of the end of a line and the beginning of the next successive draw of the text.
SCROLLDELAY= # *milliseconds*
Specifies the amount of milliseconds the marquee should wait between drawing successive displays of the text.
VSPACE= # *pixels*
Specifies the vertical (right and left) spacing margins for the outside of the marquee.
WIDTH= # *pixels* | % *of browser window*
Specifies the width of the marquee display as either a fixed pixel value or as a percentage of the browser window.

Associated Tags: <BODY>, any other formatting element.

Sample:

```
<MARQUEE>
This text will scroll across the screen.
</MARQUEE>
```

Many different attributes are available to the marquee tag to change its behavior and appearance. Two areas of the marquee whose appearance can be altered are the text itself and the background banner upon which text will scroll.

Many of the display attributes of the MARQUEE tags should be familiar to experienced HTML authors. The ALIGN tag tells the browser where to appear within the marquee banner space. It takes one of three possible values: TOP, MIDDLE (the default), and BOTTOM. The BGCOLOR attribute adds a color to the background of the marquee banner space, and takes either a colorname or color value. The HEIGHT and WIDTH attributes specify the height and width of the marquee display, respectively, as either a fixed pixel value or as a percentage of the browser window. The HSPACE and VSPACE attributes sets horizontal (left and right) spacing and vertical (top and bottom) margins, respectively, for the outside of the marquee, setting it off from the other elements on a Web page.

The behavioral elements of the marquee tag are pretty much unique to the marquee tag. The BEHAVIOR attribute takes one of three possible values: SCROLL (the default), SLIDE, and ALTERNATE. SCROLL simply moves the text

from left to right across the marquee; SLIDE similarly moves the text from left to right, but once it reaches the left margin, it stops. Finally, ALTERNATE moves the text from left to right across the screen, and when it reaches the left margin, begins moving back to the right. The DIRECTION attribute specifies the direction from which the marquee text should begin scrolling. It takes two possible values, LEFT (default) or RIGHT. LOOP tells Internet Explorer how many times the text in the marquee should cycle through its actions. It either takes a straight numerical value, or can be set to the INFINITE value (a numerical value of –1 is similarly considered infinite). SCROLLAMOUNT and SCROLLDELAY achieve similar aims through different means—they both set a delay between the time the text in a marquee is displayed once the line of text has finished. SCROLLAMOUNT takes a numerical pixel value that specifies the amount of space in pixels between the display of the end of a line and the beginning of the next successive draw of the text. SCROLLDELAY takes a numerical value that sets the number of milliseconds the browser should wait between drawing successive displays of the text in the marquee space.

The following code shows off some of the attributes of the marquee tag, which is then displayed in Figure 3.11.

A basic, no frills marquee:

```
<MARQUEE>
This text will scroll across the screen.
</MARQUEE>
<P>
MARQUEE ALIGN=TOP HEIGHT=75 BGCOLOR=RED
DIRECTION=RIGHT<BR>
<MARQUEE ALIGN=TOP HEIGHT=75 BGCOLOR=RED
DIRECTION=RIGHT>
This text will scroll across the screen.
</MARQUEE>
<P>
MARQUEE BEHAVIOR=SLIDE WIDTH=50% HSPACE=5 <BR>
<MARQUEE BEHAVIOR=SLIDE WIDTH=50% HSPACE=5>
This text will slide across the screen and stop.
</MARQUEE>
<P>
MARQUEE BEHAVIOR=ALTERNATE BGCOLOR=YELLOW
SCROLLDELAY=100 LOOP=INFINITE
<MARQUEE BEHAVIOR=ALTERNATE BGCOLOR=YELLOW
SCROLLDELAY=100 LOOP=INFINITE>
This text will bounce across the screen infinitely.
</MARQUEE>
```

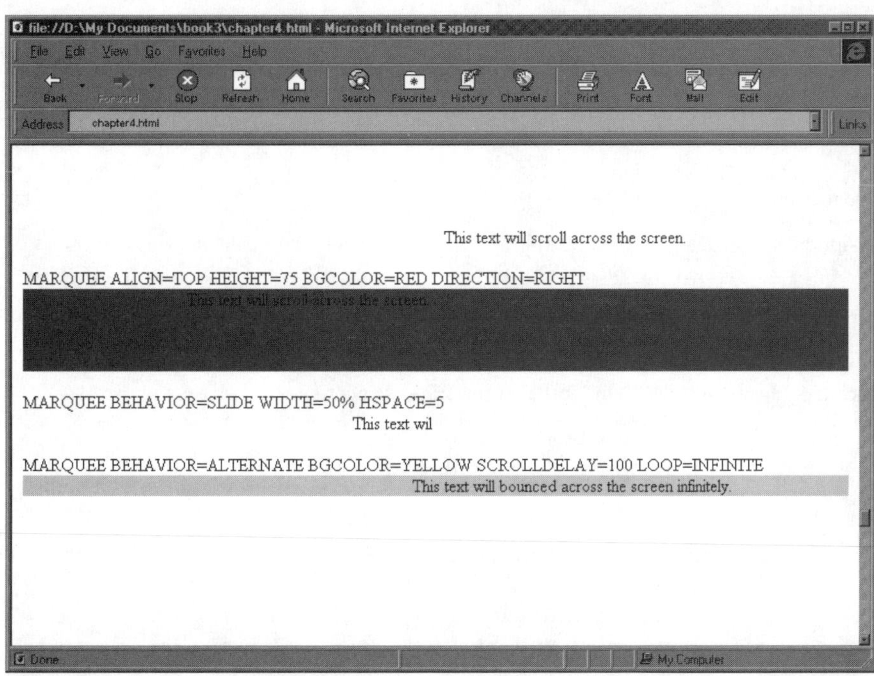

Figure 3.11 Web Page Showing Off Some of the Various Display and Behavioral Attributes of the <MARQUEE> Tag

As with any moving or animated display, it is generally a good idea not to go overboard, and to keep marquee displays relatively discrete, not making them too flashy, as they can get annoying rather quickly.

Since they can be seen within Internet Explorer only, it is a good idea not to include any critical information about the Web site in a marquee, so that you do not exclude users of other browsers.

The Paragraph Tag

The paragraph tag is one of the basic layout tags available to Web authors, and is easily one of the most commonly used tags.

Its characteristics are as follows.

<P> (. . .</P>)

Element Name: Paragraph tag.

Description: Defines a paragraph of text by inserting a vertical space between lines of text, or other elements on a Web page.

Attributes: ALIGN = *LEFT* | *CENTER* | *RIGHT*
Aligns the text in the browser window.

Associated Tags: <BODY>, any other formatting element.

Sample:

```
<P ALIGN=LEFT>
This paragraph is aligned to the left.
</P>
<P ALIGN=RIGHT>
This paragraph is aligned to the right.
</P>
<P ALIGN=CENTER>
This paragraph is centered.
</P>
```

The paragraph tag essentially adds a single vertical space between lines of text or other elements on a Web page. The paragraph tag is something of an oddball—it is both an empty and a container tag. When it was originally specified, the end paragraph tag (</P>) was specified, but if a new beginning paragraph tag appeared without an end tag, the end tag was "assumed" by the browser. Over time, many Web authors have dropped the use of the end form of the paragraph tag, though it can still be used.

The paragraph tag is a logical tag, and was designed to separate text logically on a Web page. For that reason, putting two paragraph tags together (i.e., <P><P>) does not create two vertical line spaces. It is not logical to have a paragraph end if it does not contain any text—it can't be a paragraph then, can it? Instead, to create multiple vertical lines, you need to insert another element, like the break tag. The following code inserts two vertical lines between elements on a Web page.

```
<P>
<BR>
<P>
```

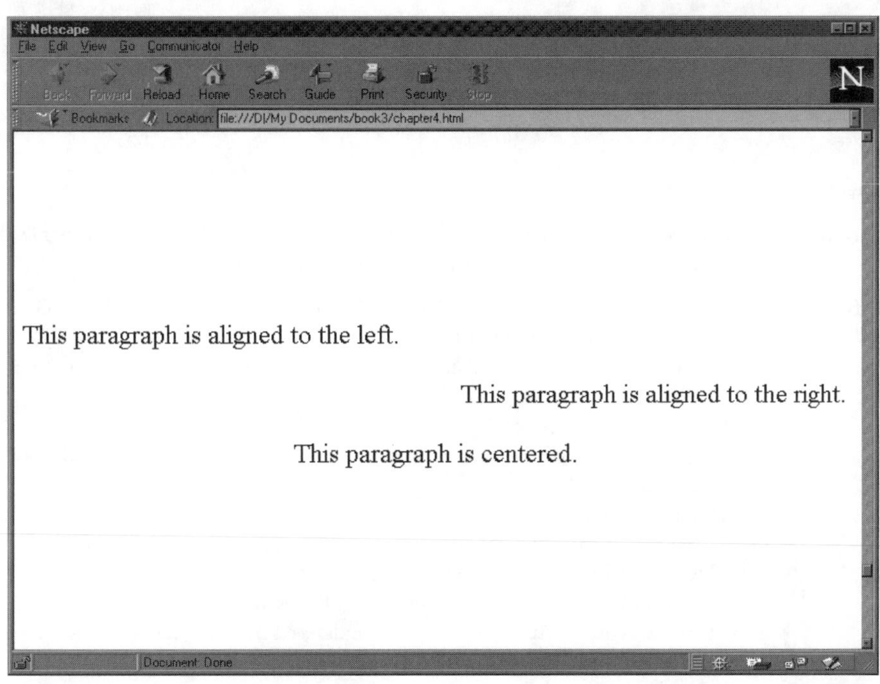

Figure 3.12 The Various Attributes of the <P> Tag Displayed

The paragraph tag takes a single attribute: ALIGN. It has three values: LEFT, RIGHT, and CENTER. LEFT (the default) aligns the text it contains to the left of the browser, RIGHT aligns the text it contains to the right of the browser, and CENTER places the text in the horizontal middle of the browser display. Using the sample code shown previously, Figure 3.12 displays the effects of all of the ALIGN attributes on a short line of text.

THE SPACER TAG

The spacer tag is another innovation first introduced within Netscape Navigator 3.0. Using the spacer tag, the Web author can control horizontal spacing, vertical spacing, or block spacing (both vertical and horizontal spacing) of elements on a Web page.

The specification for the empty spacer tag follows.

<SPACER>

Element Name: Spacer Tag.

Description: Adds whitespace between elements on a Web page. This tag is recognized by Netscape Navigator only, and is not part of the HTML 4.0 specification.

Attributes:
ALIGN= *LEFT* | *RIGHT* | *TOP* | *TEXTTOP* | *MIDDLE* | *ABSMIDDLE* | *BASELINE* | *BOTTOM* | *ABSBOTTOM*
Controls the alignment of text surrounding the spacing block. Can be used only when TYPE=BLOCK.
HEIGHT= # *pixels*
Sets the height of the spacing block as a pixel value. Can be used only when TYPE=BLOCK.
SIZE= # *pixels*
Controls the pixel height or width of a spacing element. Can be used only when TYPE=HORIZONTAL or TYPE=VERTICAL.
TYPE= HORIZONTAL | VERTICAL | BLOCK
Sets the type of whitespace area to be defined by the other spacing attributes.
WIDTH= # *pixels*
Sets the height of the spacing block as a pixel value. Can be used only when TYPE=BLOCK.

Associated Tags: <BODY>, any other formatting element.

Sample:

```
<SPACER TYPE=HORIZONTAL SIZE=100>
This text is indented by a horizontal &lt;SPACER&gt; tag
set to 100 pixels in depth.
<SPACER TYPE=VERTICAL SIZE=100>
This text is separated by the one above it by a vertical
&lt;SPACER&gt; tag set to 100 pixels.
<BR>
This text has a &lt;SPACER&gt; tag in the middle <SPACER
TYPE=BLOCK HEIGHT=100 WIDTH=50> of it. It contains a
discrete white-space block that is 50 pixels in width and
100 pixels in height.
```

There are essentially two different types of whitespace that you can define: a spacing block that can be set to a specific height and width, or a horizontal/vertical spacing block set to a specific size. For this reason, the attributes can be used only with certain combinations.

To set a whitespace block, you set TYPE=BLOCK. This allows you to specify two other attributes for the spacing block: HEIGHT and WIDTH. Both the HEIGHT and WIDTH attributes take a pixel value.

To set a vertical or horizontal whitespace, you set TYPE= to VERTICAL or HORIZONTAL, respectively. You then use the SIZE attribute to set the size of the whitespace as a pixel value.

The sample code, showing both types of spacing behavior, can be seen in Figure 3.13.

The block spacing element can take an additional attribute: ALIGN. It comes with a number of values. It controls the alignment of text relative to the whitespace specified. LEFT and RIGHT align the text to the left and right of the whitespace, respectively. TOP and TEXTTOP both align the text to the top of the spacing element, MIDDLE and ABSMIDDLE align it to the horizontal middle of the spacing element, and BASELINE, BOTTOM, and ABSBOTTOM all align the text to the bottom of the whitespace specified.

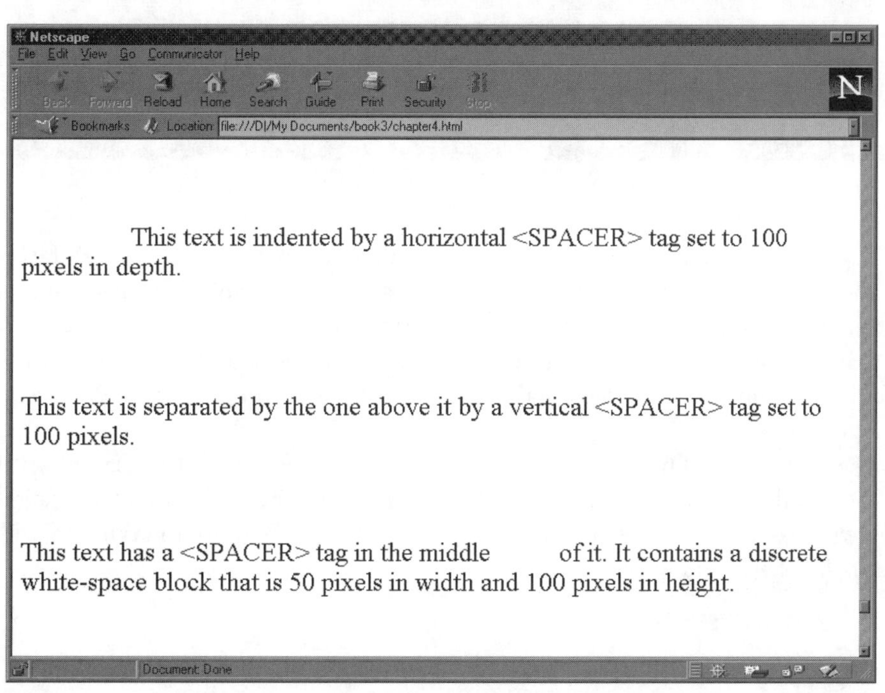

Figure 3.13 Various Spacing Elements Displayed

The Preformatted Tag

The preformatted tag is designed to display large amounts of text in a fixed-width font.

Here are the characteristics for the preformatted tag.

<PRE> . . .</PRE>

Element Name: Preformatted tag.

Description: Used to display text in a fixed-width font.

Attributes: WIDTH= # *characters*
Specifies the maximum numbers of characters that can appear on a line.

Associated Tags: <BODY>, any other text formatting element.

Sample:

```
<PRE>
This text is not quite rendered in an <B>as is</B>
fashion by the browser.
</PRE>
```

Text that is placed within a <PRE> tag is rendered in almost an "as is" fashion by the browser; it does display the effects of any other formatting tags contained within the text (such as the bold tags inserted in the previous sample code). It displays the text using a fixed-width font (usually Courier), and retains the original length of the line and any line breaks that naturally occur in the text, as can be seen in Figure 3.14.

The preformatted tag does have a single attribute: WIDTH. It is used to set the defined width of the preformatted display as a number of characters. So, the following code example would set the preformatted display to a maximum width that is 80 characters wide.

```
<PRE WIDTH=80>
Text.
</PRE>
```

Note, however, that this attribute is not supported in either Netscape Navigator or Internet Explorer.

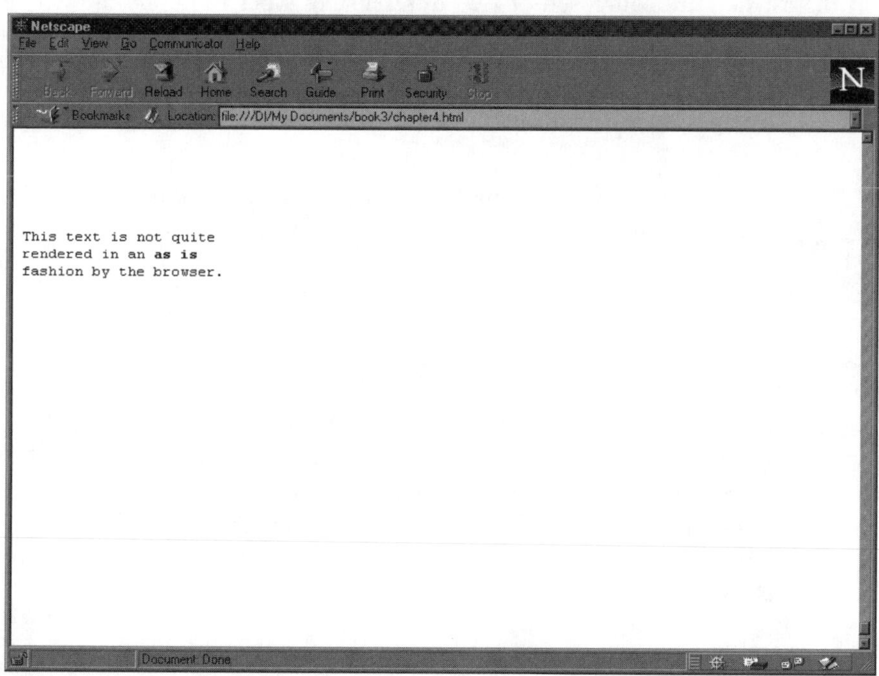

Figure 3.14 The Effects of the <PRE> Tag Displayed

It is worth noting that several other types of tags were used to display text in a similar fashion to the preformatted tag: <LISTING>, <PLAINTEXT>, and <XMP>. All three were dropped from the official HTML 2.0 specification and are considered obsolete. They should not be used because there is no longer any guarantee that they will work within all modern browsers.

List Tags

Lists give Web authors the ability to arrange a number of similar items in a convenient point form. Graphically speaking, lists stand out on a Web page, and provide a convenient way of arranging and ordering information on a Web page.

HTML supports many different list formats. You can use five different types of lists in your Web pages: ordered or numbered, unordered or bulleted, directory,

menu, and definition or glossary lists. With the exception of the definition list type, all of the list tags are composed of two different tag types to define the whole of the list. The type of list and its boundaries (i.e., beginning and end) are set by the defining list tag, and the individual elements in the list are marked by list item (<LI>) tags.

Note: Directory and menu lists have been deprecated in the HTML 4.0 specification.

You may have noticed by now that HTML code can become quite messy looking, and you'll find that lists can increase the chaos since so many tags are used. To improve the readability of your HTML code, arrange your list code so that each list tag has its own line, and that each new list item has a line to itself. Bunching all your list code together can look pretty confusing, like this:

```
<ol><li>Item 1<li>Item2<li>Item3</ol>
```

whereas keeping list tags each on its own line makes the code much easier to read:

```
<ol>
<li>Item 1
<li>Item 2
<li>Item 3
</ol>
```

Both examples create the same output in a browser window; the difference is that the second example is much easier for Web authors to read, edit, and debug.

The HTML definitions for the various types of list tags make them very flexible, and it is easy to combine and nest most tags within other list tags. If you are designing Web pages specifically for Netscape, you have the option of specifying the types of symbols that precede the list elements in a few of the list tag types.

The Ordered and Unordered List Tags

The ordered (numbered) list (<OL>), and unordered (bulleted) list (<UL>) tag types are the most commonly used list tags found on Web pages. They are generic in nature, simple to use, and their effects are easy to manipulate.

<UL> . . .</UL>

Element Name: Unordered list tag.

Description: Used to display a number of unordered items in a list.

Attributes: TYPE= *DISC | CIRCLE | SQUARE*
Tells the browser to display the bullet as a solid circle, a hollow circle, or a solid square.
COMPACT
Tells the browser to display the list in a compact form. The space between list items is lessened, making the list appear more compact.

Associated Tags: <LI> — Always used with the list element (<LI>) tag, which denotes the individual elements within the list. Each new list item requires its own <LI> tag.
Can be contained within:
<BLOCKQUOTE>, <BODY>, <DD>, <FORM>, <LI>.

Sample:

```
<UL>
<LI>guitars
<LI>banjos
<LI>ukeleles
<UL TYPE=SQUARE>
<LI>violins
<LI>viols
<LI>double-bass
</UL>
</UL>
```

<LI> (. . .</LI>)

Element Name: List item tag.

Description: Used immediately prior to individual items within directory, menu, ordered, or unordered lists. Some HTML editors add an end tag (</LI>) for each list item, but its use is optional.

Attributes: None.

Associated Tags: <UL>, <OL>, <DIR>, <MENU>.
Can contain:
text, text markup tag, <A>, <BLOCKQUOTE>, <BR>, <DIR>, <DL>, <FORM>, <IMG>, <MENU>, <P>, <PRE>.

Sample:

```
<OL>
<LI>Item #1
<LI>Item #2
<LI>Item #3
</OL>
```

The unordered list tag (<UL>) is a container tag that defines the beginning and end of an unordered list. Both the start and end tags are required; not using the end tag will make your list go on forever!

Individual elements within an unordered list are defined by the list item (<LI>) tag, which is typically used as an empty tag, but can also be used as a container tag. The assumption made by the designers of the HTML specification was that the next instance of an <LI> tag not only begins the next list element, but also automatically denotes the end of the previous list element. The following two examples of code are both correct forms of using the <LI> tag, and are displayed in exactly the same way by Web browsers.

```
<UL>
<LI>Budgies
<LI>Canaries
<LI>Toucans
<UL>
<UL>
<LI>Budgies</LI>
<LI>Canaries</LI>
<LI>Toucans</LI>
<UL>
```

Whenever an unordered list is nested within another list, the nested list is indented. When viewed through Netscape Navigator and Internet Explorer, the bullet type that precedes the element in a nested list changes. The initial bullet type is a solid, round bullet. A nested list element appears as an empty round bullet, and a list element nested one level deeper is a square filled bullet. Further nesting always produces the same square filled bullets, though each nested list element is indented further. The following code example, which contains a number of nested lists, demonstrates this effect. Figure 3.15 shows how Netscape Navigator and Internet Explorer display this list code.

```
<UL>
<LI>This is a regular list element.
<UL>
<LI>This list element is nested.
```

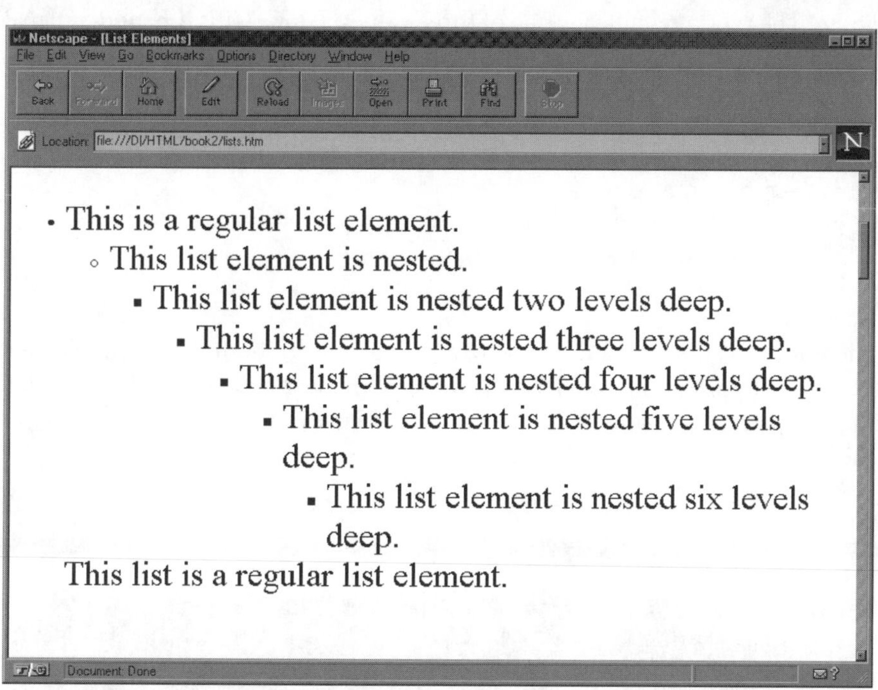

Figure 3.15 Nested Bullets as Displayed within Netscape Navigator

```
<UL>
<LI>This list element is nested two levels deep.
<UL>
<LI>This list element is nested three levels deep.
<UL>
<LI>This list element is nested four levels deep.
<UL>
<LI>This list element is nested five levels deep.
<UL>
<LI>This list element is nested six levels deep.
</UL>
</UL>
</UL>
</UL>
</UL>
</UL>This list is a regular list element.
</UL>
```

It is possible to specify the type of bullet that appears directly by using the TYPE attribute. The type attribute has one of three values: DISC, CIRCLE, and SQUARE. To set an unordered list that begins with a square instead of a disc (the default) you would use the following code:

```
<UL TYPE=SQUARE>
<LI>One squares.
<LI>Two Squares.
<LI>Three Squares in a list.
</UL>
```

The effects of the TYPE attribute are recognized by both Netscape Navigator and Internet Explorer. Figure 3.16 shows how the last code example is displayed within Netscape Navigator. Internet Explorer displays the code in a similar way.

Table 3.1 illustrates the different list types available for unordered lists.

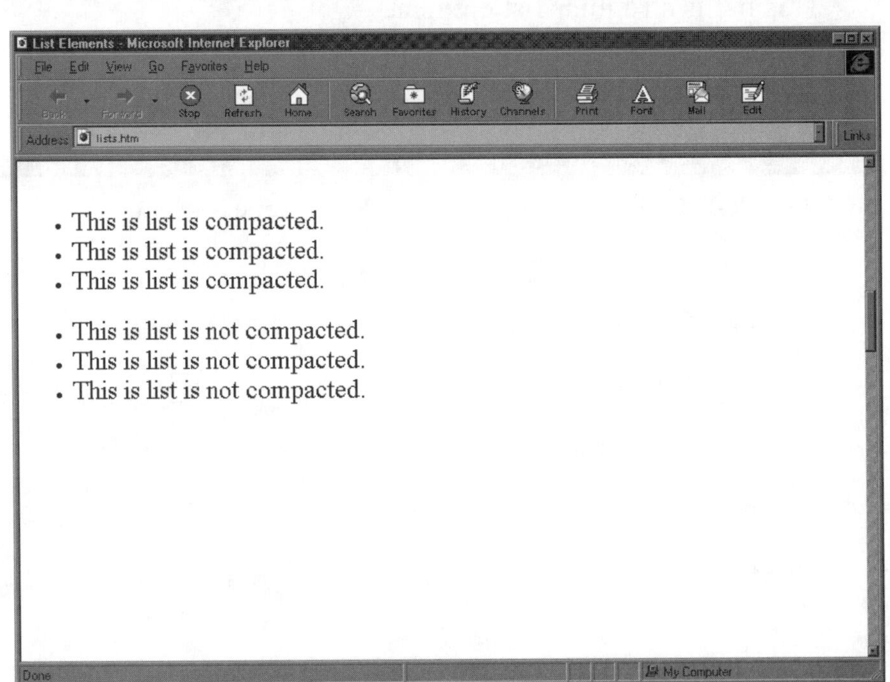

Figure 3.16 The Effects of the TYPE Attributable on the <UL> Tag Viewed through Netscape Navigator

Table 3.1 Different unordered list types

TYPE Attribute:	*List item preceded by:*
TYPE=DISC (default)	Solid round bullet
TYPE=CIRCLE	Hollow round bullet
TYPE=SQUARE	Solid square bullet

The COMPACT attribute instructs the browser to reduce the horizontal space between items on a list, making the list as a whole appear more compact on the Web page. The COMPACT attribute (which can be added to any type of list tag) was officially sanctioned for use in the HTML 3.2 specification, but it has only recently been incorporated into Internet Explorer 4.0 and Netscape Navigator 4.0. Here's some sample code that demonstrates how it can be used.

```
<UL COMPACT>
<LI>This is list is compacted.</LI>
<LI>This is list is compacted.</LI>
<LI>This is list is compacted.</LI>
</UL>
<UL>
<LI>This is list is not compacted.
<LI>This is list is not compacted.
<LI>This is list is not compacted.
</UL>
```

The effects of this code can be seen in Figure 3.17.

<OL> . . .</OL>

Element Name: Ordered list tag.

Description: Displays a number of ordered items in a list.

Attributes: TYPE= A
List items are preceded by uppercase letters (i.e., A, B, C).
TYPE= a
List items are preceded by lowercase letters (i.e., a, b, c).
TYPE= I
List items are preceded by uppercase Roman numerals (i.e., I, II, III).
TYPE= i

List items are preceded by lowercase Roman numerals (i.e., i, ii, iii).
TYPE= 1
List items are preceded by numbers (i.e., 1, 2, 3).
COMPACT
Tells the browser to display the list in a compact form. The horizontal space between list items is reduced, causing the list to appear more compact.

Can contain: <LI>
Can be contained within:
<BLOCKQUOTE>, <BODY>, <DD>, <FORM>, <LI>.

Sample:

```
<OL>
<LI>The First item.
<LI>The Second item.
<LI>The Third item.
</OL>
```

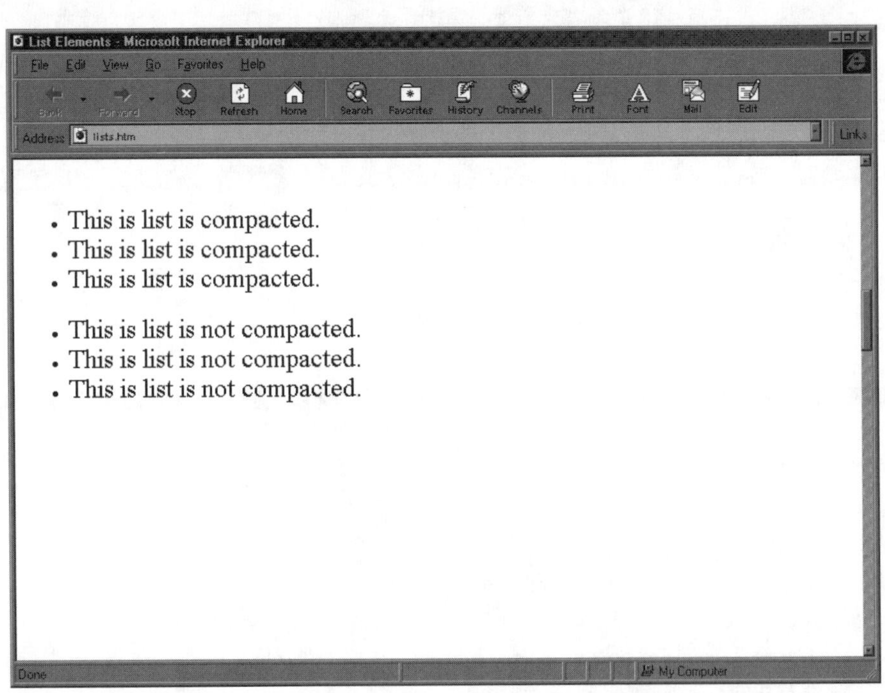

Figure 3.17 The Effects of the TYPE Attribute on the <UL> Tag Viewed through Netscape Navigator

The ordered list tag (<OL>) works in exactly the same way as the unordered list tag, but instead of being preceded by a bullet, each list element is preceded by a number. For obvious reasons, the TYPE extension works in a different way. Instead of specifying different bullet types, within an ordered list the TYPE tag defines the type of number that appears before the list element. There are five different variations of the type tag that are generally recognized: TYPE=1 (the default) places an arabic numeral before the list element, TYPE=A places a capital letter before the list element, TYPE=a places a small letter before the list element, TYPE=I places a capital Roman numeral before the list element, and TYPE=i places a small Roman numeral before the list element. These five types of ordered lists are created by the following code example, whose results are displayed in Figure 3.18.

```
<P>
<OL TYPE=1>
<LI>List element preceded by a number.
<OL TYPE=A>
```

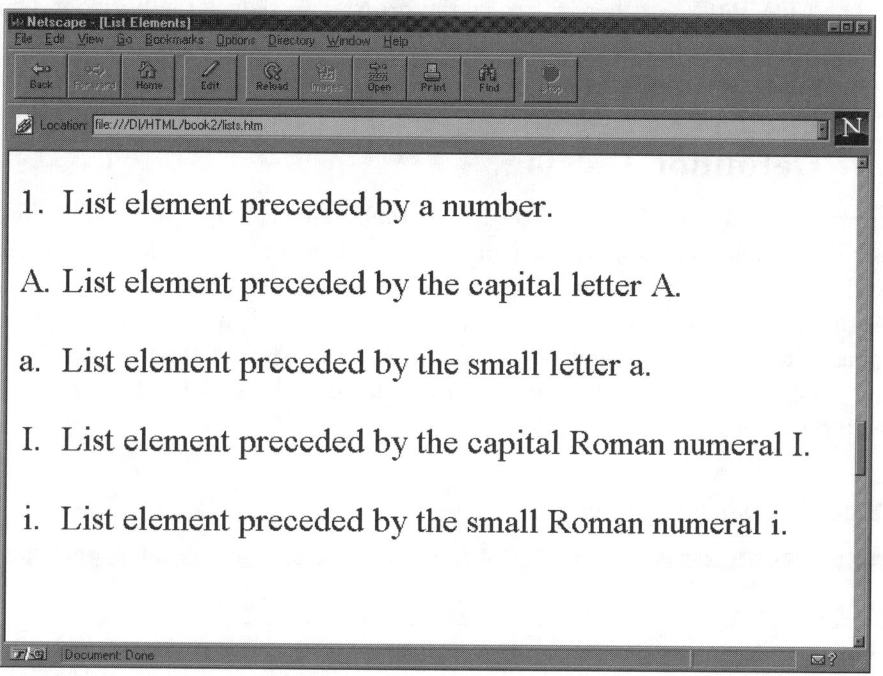

Figure 3.18 The Effects of the TYPE Attribute on the <OL> Tag as Viewed through Netscape Navigator

```
<LI>List element preceded by the capital letter A.
<OL TYPE=a>
<LI>List element preceded by the small letter a.
<OL TYPE=I>
<LI>List element preceded by the capital Roman numeral
I.
<OL TYPE=i>
<LI>List element preceded by the small Roman numeral i.
</OL>
</OL>
</OL>
</OL>
</OL>
```

Table 3.2 illustrates the different list types available for ordered lists.

A sixth type allows the Web author to specify the specific arabic numeral that starts a new sequence. The idea would allow Web authors to specify the number at which an ordered list starts. This feature is not implemented within either Netscape Navigator or Internet Explorer.

The COMPACT attribute instructs the browser to reduce the horizontal space between items on a list, making the list as a whole appear more compact on the Web page.

The Definition List Tag

A very different type of list tag is the definition list tag (<DL>), also called a glossary list. Each definition is composed of three separate parts: the definition list tag (<DL>), which defines the boundaries of the list; the definition term (<DT>); and the definition itself (<DD>). Each definition term is left-aligned, and each definition appears indented to the right of the definition term. Though the <DT> and <DD> tags do not require end tags, some HTML editors include them. Browsers display them the same either way.

Table 3.2 Different Ordered List Types

TYPE Attribute:	*List item preceded by:*
TYPE=A	A, B, C
TYPE=a	a, b, c
TYPE=I	I, II, III
TYPE=i	i, ii, iii
TYPE=1 (default)	1, 2, 3

<DL> . . .</DL>

Element Name: Definition list tag.

Description: Creates a list of definitions, composed of a list of terms and their corresponding definitions.

Attributes: COMPACT
Tells the browser to display the list in a compact form.

Can contain:
, <DD>, <DT>.

Can be contained within: <BODY>, <BLOCKQUOTE>, <DD>, <FORM>, <LI>.

Associated Tags: <DD>, <DL>.

<DT> (. . .</DT>)

Element Name: Definition term tag.

Description: Defines an individual term within a definition list. The end tag can be used but is not required. The <DT> tag is typically followed by a definition (<DD>).

Attributes: COMPACT
Tells the browser to display the list in a compact form.

Can contain: Text, text markup, <A>, <IMG>.

Associated Tags: <DL>, <DD>.

<DD> (. . .</DD>)

Element Name: Definition tag.

Description: Defines the definition for the preceding the definition term (<DT>) within a definition list (<DL>). The end tag can be used but is not required.

Attributes: COMPACT
Tells the browser to display the list in a compact form.

Can contain: Text, text markup, <A>, <IMG>.

Associated Tags: <DL>, <DD>.

Sample:

```
<DL>
<DT>Cardinal<DD>A colorful North American bird. The male
is a deep red.
<DT>Blue Jay<DD>A raucous, intelligent bird.
</DL>
```

The idea behind the design of these tags was to provide an easy way to provide a list of definitions or a glossary of terms. The definition term (<DT>) and the definition (<DD>) are by strict definition container tags, but most Web browsers assume the beginning of a new line when they meet the next sequential element in the series, much like the <LI> tag. Even though the use of the <DT> and <DD> tags require the use of the definition list (<DL>) tags, both tags are considered optional within the actual definition list. In other words, you can create a definition list that does not have to contain both terms and definitions; this arrangement provides the HTML author with some flexibility.

You don't necessarily have to restrict the use of a definition list to glossaries and the like; you can use it anywhere an indented list would be useful or appropriate.

When the tags are all used, the definition term is set flush right, and the definition is indented and displayed one line down from the definition term. When only the <DD> tags are used within a definition list, the definitions are displayed as indented without any preceding definition term. When only the <DT> tags are used within a definition list, only the definition terms are displayed. The following example, whose results are shown in Figure 3.19, show the possible code variations of the set of definition tags.

```
<DL>
<DT>Apples<DD>A tasty red fruit.
<DT>Oranges<DD>A tasty orange fruit.
</DL>
<DL>
<DT>Apples
<DT>Oranges
</DL>
<DL>
<DD>Apples
<DD>Oranges
</DL>
```

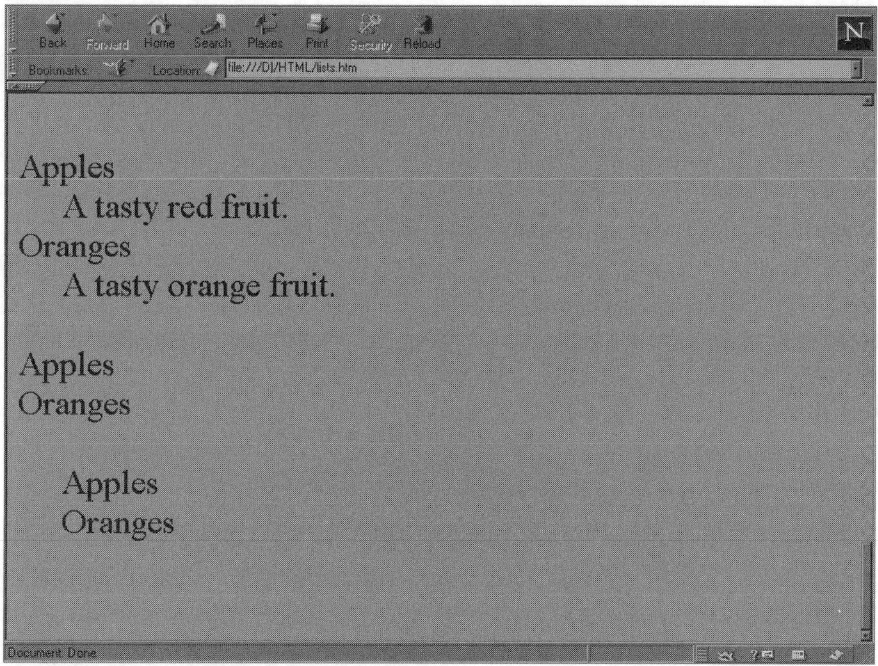

Figure 3.19 Three Combinations of Definition List Tags as Displayed within Netscape Navigator

Though it is also possible to use the <DL> tags without using the <DT> or <DD> tags, it does not visually modify the text it contains.

The COMPACT attribute instructs the browser to reduce the horizontal space between items on a list, making the list as a whole appear more compact on the Web page.

Although it is considered bad HTML, the indenting feature of the <DD> is often used by Web authors to indent sections of text designed to draw a reader's attention.

The following HTML code example provides a sample nonstandard use for the definition list tags.

```
<DL>
<DT><B>Note:</B><DD>Here is an important message
designed specifically for you to notice.
</DL>
```

The Menu and Directory List Tags

Although originally defined in the HTML 2.0 specification, both the menu (<MENU>) and director list (<DIR>) tags are rarely implemented within browsers in the manner they were originally designed. Both <DIR> and <MENU> have been deprecated in HTML 4.0. They are little used in the Web authoring community and are generally considered obsolete. When they are displayed within a browser, the <DIR> and <MENU> tags tend to be displayed with bullets preceding the list items, in exactly the same way as the unordered list (<UL>) tag.

<MENU> . . .</MENU>

Element Name: Menu tag.

Description: Displays lists of items containing no more than a single line per item. Bullets precede each list item.

Attributes: None.

Can contain: <LI>.

Can be contained within: <BLOCKQUOTE>, <BODY>, <DD>, <FORM>, <LI>.

Sample:

```
<MENU>
<LI>Clam Chowder
<LI>Chicken Soup
<LI>Cream of Mushroom
</MENU>
```

The menu tag is a container tag designed to contain a number of unordered elements, displayed as single column menu lists. Individual elements within the list are defined by the list item (LI) tag, an empty tag. Using the </LI> end tag is not required. It differs from the design of the unordered list tag in that it is supposed to be rendered in a more compact format. The design of the menu tag in the original HTML specification states that it cannot contain nested lists. These rules are ignored by most browsers, and a menu list is usually displayed in an identical manner to an unordered list (<UL>). Its use is generally discouraged within the Web authoring community.

<DIR> . . .</DIR>

The <DIR> tag is a container tag designed to display lists of items in a multicolumn directory list.

Element Name: Directory list tag.

Description: Displays a number of directory items in a columnar format, but is rarely implemented and little used. Each list item is preceded by a bullet.

Attributes: None.

Can contain: <LI>.

Can be contained within: <BLOCKQUOTE>, <BODY>, <DD>, <FORM>, <LI>.

Associated Tags: <LI>.

Sample Code:

```
<DIR>
<LI>A
<LI>B
<LI>C
<LI>D
<LI>E
<LI>F
</DIR>
```

As with the ordered list and unordered list tags, each item contained within a directory listing must be preceded by an <LI> tag. Each definition listing is designed to hold no more than 20 characters of text. Nested <DIR> tags are disallowed, so it is not possible to nest directories within other directories.

This tag is not widely implemented according to the original HTML 2.0 specification it was first specified within, and is generally avoided by most Web authors due to its unwieldy structure and poor to nonexistent implementation within many browsers. Many Web browsers render the contents of the <DIR> tag as if it were an unordered list. Both Internet Explorer and Netscape Navigator display the tag in this fashion, with bullets preceding the list items. Its use is not recommended.

Examples of how the <MENU> and <DIR> tags are rendered within Netscape Navigator are shown in Figure 3.20.

Lists have proven to be a favorite of Web authors, since they display information so well. Their ability to be customized to have different kinds of bullets and numbers give authors a lot of flexibility, and nested lists can display hierarchies clearly and

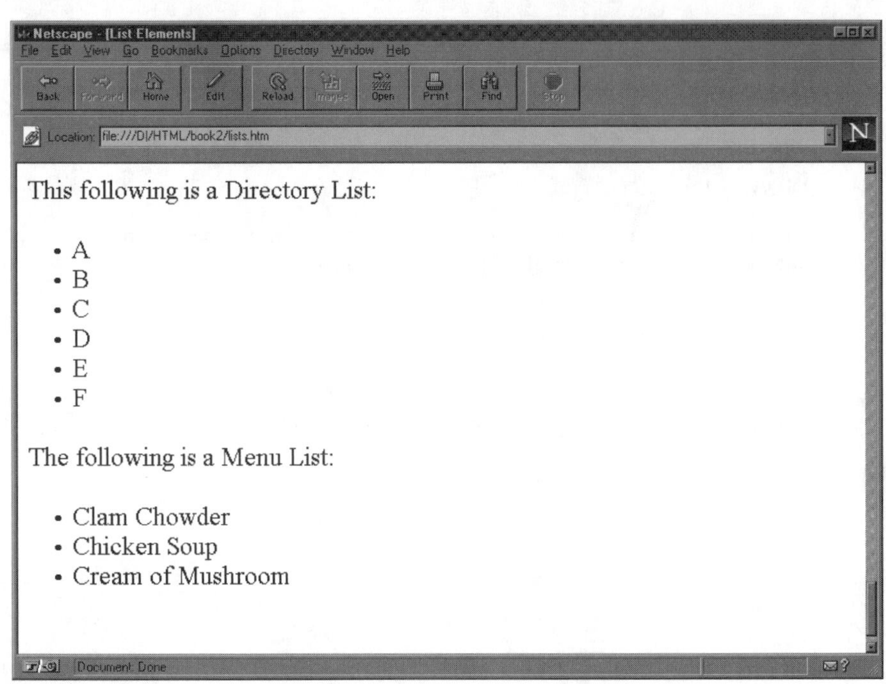

Figure 3.20 The <DIR> and <MENU> Tags as Displayed within Netscape Navigator

efficiently. Though lists do not allow for creating multiple columns horizontally across a page, Web authors can create a table and then place the lists inside the table cells. With table borders turned off, the Web page displays information in multiple columns. For further information on tables, see Chapter 8, "Tables."

If you plan to use imagemaps on your Web page, consider including a list of the same information for users who are not using a graphical browser, or have chosen to turn images off. In short, take great advantage of the list tag; it may prove to be one of the most valuable elements of the HTML language.

Character Formatting Elements

Character formatting is used to enhance the look of the text that makes up your Web page. Most character formatting tags are container tags, requiring both a start

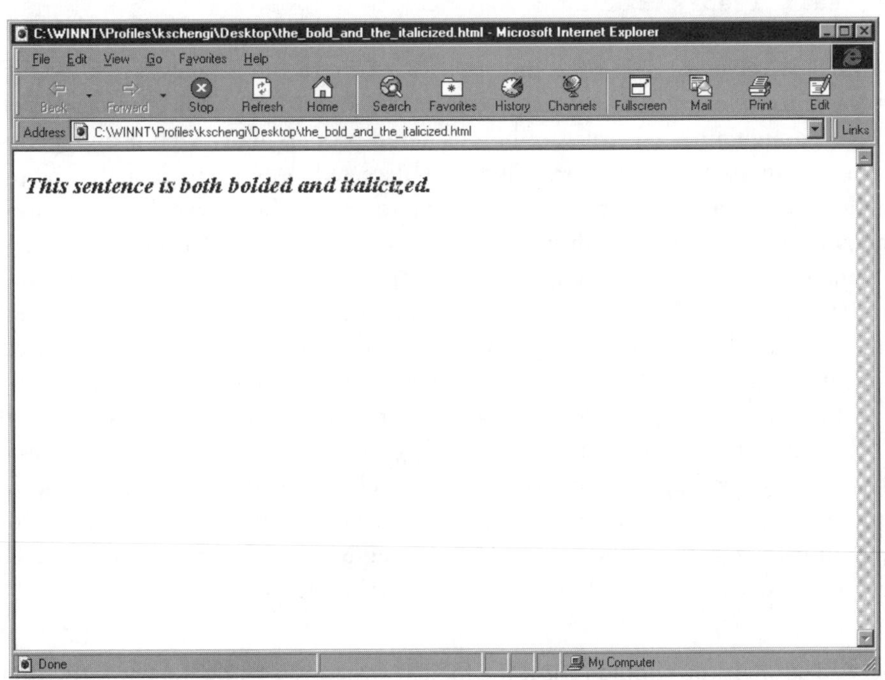

Figure 3.21 An Example of Text that Uses Nested Bold and Italics Tags

and end tag to define where the formatting should begin and end in your text. Remember that the definition of a container tag is that it contains the text it modifies—anything outside of the container (i.e., outside of the formatting tags) is not modified. Multiple formatting tags should be nested, which means that beginning and end tags should appear in the same order, with one set of beginning and end tags contained (or nested) within another set of beginning and end tags. The following example (shown in Figure 3.21) displays a tag that contains nested italic and bold tags.

```
<B><I>This sentence is both bolded and
italicized.</I></B>
```

If the agreement of the start and end tags do not correspond to each other in the correct manner, your formatting may not work. Tags should reside within each other. To explain this point further, the same sentence could be formatted the following way, with the bold and italics tags in the wrong order:

```
<B><I>This sentence is both bolded and
italicized.</B></I>
```

Note how the end-bold (</B>) tag appears before the end-italics tag (</I>). This arrangement no longer follows the proper nested structure, and is considered poor HTML. Though a nested structure is considered proper, many Web browsers now recognize unnested tag structures like that depicted previously. Years of sloppy HTML coding has led software developers to make their Web browsers more responsive to these types of editing mistakes, so most will render the above line in the same manner as the correctly formatted example. Unnested tag structures are considered sloppy HTML not only because some browsers are unable to properly decode how to display the text, but because it also makes it much harder to edit the resulting code at a later date. By properly nesting tags, you do not have to search through a Web page looking for stray end tags located who-knows-where. HTML supports two kinds of formatting: logical and physical. The two types of formatting tags go back to the original design characteristics of HTML, and are worth mentioning here. HTML was based on the two main principles derived from its parent language, the Standardized Generalized Markup Language (SGML). The two main goals of SGML reflected in the original design of HTML were:

- That markup should reflect the logical structure of a document rather than its physical layout,
- That it should also be in a format that could be read and understood easily by both computers and humans.

Logical tags were developed so that people could format Web documents following a specific document structure, describing the *type* of text it contains. An alternate set of physical formatting tags were also added to HTML so that people could add formatting elements more in keeping with such things as word processing and desktop publishing programs. As a result, there were often two (or more) ways you could format the text on a page using either logical or physical tags.

Both kinds often have the same result; the difference lies in how character formatting is approached. The logical tags, including <CITE>, <CODE>, <EM>, <KBD>, <SAMP>, and <VAR> format the text in terms of logical structure. The physical tags, including <B>, <I>, and <U>, format the text in terms of physical layout. Using logical or physical tags, or a combination of both, will not affect the look of your Web page, as most browsers recognize both kinds of tags.

In many cases, there are a number of tags that are functionally equivalent, which means that many browsers render dissimilar logical and physical formatting tags—like the <EM> and <I> tags, or the <STRONG> and <B> tags—in exactly the same way. The original design for HTML tags specified that many of the logical and physical tags should be formatted in a slightly different manner than each other, but in the early days of Web browsers, it was simpler to display tags that were supposed to be rendered slightly differently on-screen in the same manner.

Table 3.3 contains a list of the logical and physical formatting tags described in the rest of this chapter.

Although both types of tagging styles are still used, the general trend in HTML development is to move towards and emphasize the physical formatting tags over that of logical formatting tags. As a result, more and more physical formatting tags are being introduced into HTML standards than logical tags. The choice of which tags to use when formatting a Web page are up to the designer of the Web page—neither is inherently more correct than the other these days, though some HTML purists would argue otherwise.

Probably the best measure to use when deciding what format to choose in a Web page is how it will look and read when you have to go back and edit the code. Many people prefer to use as many logical formatting codes as possible, so they can easily keep track of what and where certain elements of a Web page are. For example, listing a citation within a pair of <CITE> tags tells you much more about *what* it is. If you enclose the citation within a pair of <I> tags, which renders the text in the exact same manner, this information is lost, making it harder to search for any citation listed within a page. The obverse of this argument is that the more types of tags you use in a page, the more complicated it is to read and edit later. The simple and descriptive nature of the physical tags often makes them much easier to use than their logical equivalents. Despite how logical many of the logical tags are, on the whole they are harder to remember than their physical equivalents.

Table 3.3 A Listing of Logical and Physical Tag Types

Logical Tags	*Physical Tags*
<STRONG>	<B>
<CITE>	<BIG>
<EM>	<I>
<SAMP>	<SMALL>
<VAR>	<SUB>
<CODE>	<SUP>
<KBD>	<TT>
	<U>
	<BLINK>

Whether or not you used the <EM> or <I> tags to surround a section of text on a Web page, the result is always the same: italicized text is displayed.

In short, use whatever method suits you the best, and stick with it.

Comments Welcome

Though it doesn't really fit as either a true logical-style tag—it doesn't actually *format* the tag it encloses, because no text is actually displayed—the comment tag can be considered a type of logical tag. It is used by Web designers to add a comment within the body of a Web page.

The comment tag is a container tag. Text occuring within the beginning (<!—) and end (—>) delimiters is not displayed by the Web browser. An unlimited number of characters and lines can appear within the comment tag. Note that you must end the text with the end —> delimiter; otherwise the text it encloses will be displayed within the browser.

This tag is useful for putting document information, such as the date the Web page was last updated or defining different sections within the body of a Web page—all the while keeping this housekeeping type information from the eyes of users viewing the page in their browser. (Note however that it *will* appear if the user views the HTML source of the document.) Comments cannot be nested.

Element Name: Comment Tag.

Description: Text enclosed between the <!— and —> delimiters is not displayed by graphical Web browsers. Lynx browsers will display the commented text.

Attributes: None.

Sample:

```
<!-- This commented text will not display in a graphical
Web browser -->
```

You can add several lines of commentary text within a comment tag, and you do not have to add new tags to each line—just make sure you end the comment sentence(s) with the end —> delimiter, as in the following example code.

```
<!-- Here is my long-winded comment about comments that
goes on and on and on and on and on and so on and so
forth, illustrating the fact that a comment can go on for
several lines, but that it has to end with the proper
end-comment delimiter -->
```

The comment tag has also been adopted for use within some programs for inserting information—like JavaScript or VBScript code—within a Web page that you need but do not want displayed by the browser. For example, the following HTML depicts some JavaScript code inserted within a Web page in such a way that older browsers that do not understand the relatively recent <SCRIPT> tag not display it.

```
<HTML>
<HEAD>
<SCRIPT LANGUAGE="JavaScript">
<!-- Beginning of JavaScript Applet
/*
   Scoller: Scroll some Text in the statuswindow.
   This script is a freescript and can be used and
   modified at will.
   If you use it, you do it at your own risk. I take no
   responsibility
   whatsoever. If it doesn't work, don't blame
   me . . .
   Comments and enhancements are welcome.
   Stephan Mohr <stephan.mohr@uni-tuebingen.de>

 */
var timerid = 0;
var scrollOn = false;
var waitfor=100;
var maxspc=150;
var msg = "";

function scroll stop()
{
  if (scrollOn) {
    clearTimeout (timerid);
    scrollOn = false;
  }
}

function scroll start ()
{
  var i=0;
  scroll stop ();
  msg="Here's some text that will scroll";
  msg+="along the bottom of the browser window.";
  for (i=0;<maxspc;i+) msg=""+msg;
```

```
    scrollOn=true;
    timerid=window.setTimeout ("scroller(0)",waitfor);
  }
  function scroller (pos)
  {
    var out = "";
    scrollOn=false;
    if (pos < msg.length) window.status = msg.substring
    (pos, msg.length);
    else pos=-1;
    ++pos;
    scrollOn=true;
    timerid=window.setTimeout ("scroller("+pos+")",
    waitfor);
  }
  // -- End of JavaScript code -->
  </SCRIPT>
  </HEAD>
  <BODY onLoad="scroll start();" on Unload="scroll
  stop();"
  This Web page contains a JavaScript that scrolls the
  text contained in the in the "msg" field in the
  browser's status bar.
  </BODY>
  </HTML>
```

(More information on JavaScript can be found later in the book.)

The comment tag is a very useful tag and it is worth using by any serious Web sïte designer.

Logical Formatting Tags

As mentioned earlier in this section, logical formatting tags describe the logical structure of a document rather than its physical layout. Logical formatting tags were developed so Web authors could format Web documents following a specific document structure, describing the *type* of text it contains rather than how they should *look*. Using these tags, Web authors could easily format the parts of a Web page that contain things like citations, code listings, or variables.

Many of the following tags render the text on-screen in the same way as do many physical tags. The choice in using either the logical or physical forms of tags depends on the Web author—there is no correct way with these tags. If you find that logical formatting tags help you keep better track of the placement of various types of content in your Web pages, then use them.

<CITE> . . .</CITE>

Element Name: Citation tag.

Description: Indicates that the text is a citation. It is usually displayed in italic text.

Attributes: None.

Sample:

```
<CITE>The Last Voyage of Somebody the Sailor</CITE> by
John Barth.
```

The <CITE> tag is useful for indicating citations within a Web page. It is functionally equivalent to the physical <I> (italic) tag, covered later in this section.

<CODE> . . .</CODE>

Element Name: Code tag.

Description: Indicates that the text is a source code sample. It is displayed in a fixed-width font.

Attributes: None.

Sample:

```
To begin the solitaire game, type <CODE>sol.exe</CODE> on
the command line.
```

The <CODE> tag is useful for separating code text from the body of your document. It is displayed in fixed-width font, and is functionally equivalent to the physical <TT> (teletype) tag. To display more than one line of code without the text wrapping, use the <PRE> (preformatted text) tag, as described elsewhere in this chapter.

<EM> . . .</EM>

Element Name: Emphasized text tag.

Description: Indicates that the text is displayed with an emphasized font, usually rendered by Web browsers as italicized text.

Attributes: None.

Sample:

```
<EM>Keep Out!!</EM>
```

The <EM> tag emphasizes the text it encloses. It is functionally equivalent in most browsers as the physical <I> (italic) tag. Note that this depends on the browser—though the vast majority of browsers render the text contained within an <EM> tag as italicized text, some browsers have been known to take a different approach and instead bold the text. Emphasized text is rendered in the same fashion within Netscape Navigator as within Internet Explorer.

<KBD> . . .</KBD>

Element Name: Keyboard tag.

Description: Indicates that the text is displayed in typewriter, or fixed-width, font.

Attributes: None.

Sample:

```
<KBD>This is keyboard font,</KBD> and this regular font.
```

The <KBD> tag is used to display keyboard input. It is functionally the same as the physical <TT> (teletype) tag.

The original design specification for the <KBD> tag was that it should be displayed in a slightly different fashion than the <CODE> tag, so users could visually distinguish between the code that should be entered into a program, and the resulting code that is displayed within a program-editor program. However, this fine distinction in display was never widely adopted, and it is displayed in exactly the same manner within Netscape Navigator as in Internet Explorer.

<SAMP> . . .</SAMP>

Element Name: Sample tag.

Description: Indicates that the text is a sample statement, and is displayed in fixed-width font.

Attributes: None.

Sample:

```
<SAMP>This text is enclosed in sample tags.</SAMP> This
text is not.
```

The <SAMP> tag displays text in a fixed-width font. It is functionally the same as the physical <TT> (teletype) tag. The idea behind the <SAMP> tag was to display text that is to provide a sample of how a procedure is done that is not code.

<STRONG> . . .</STRONG>

Element Name: Strong text tag.

Description: Indicates that the text is displayed with a strong font, usually in bold face.

Attributes: None.

Sample:
```
<STRONG>Caution:</STRONG> The Internet can become
addictive!
```

The <STRONG> tag indicates text that needs to be strongly emphasized. Most browsers display text enclosed in <STRONG> tags as functionally equivalent to the physical <B> (bold) tag. The logical structure behind the <STRONG> tag is that it is intended to render text that should be emphasized more strongly than that emphasized by the <EM> (emphasis) tag.

<VAR> . . .</VAR>

Element Name: Variable tag.

Description: Indicates text that is a variable name.

Attributes: None.

Sample:
```
<VAR>a</VAR> plus <VAR>b</VAR> equals <VAR>c</VAR>
```

The <VAR> tag is used to indicate variable names. <VAR> text is usually rendered in a functionally equivalent manner as the physical <I> (italics) tag within most Web browsers.

One of the problems you may have noticed from some of the preceding descriptions is that some browsers may render the same logical tags in a different manner than another browser would. This is a risk when using logical rather than physical tags, but for the most part both Internet Explorer and Netscape Navigator render these tags in a similar, if not always identical, fashion (see Figure 3.22).

Physical Formatting Tags

Physical formatting tags were added to HTML so Web authors could easily add formatting elements common to such programs as word processing and desktop publishing programs. This approach to formatting has become very popular, and on the whole these tags tend to be used more often than the physical tags that

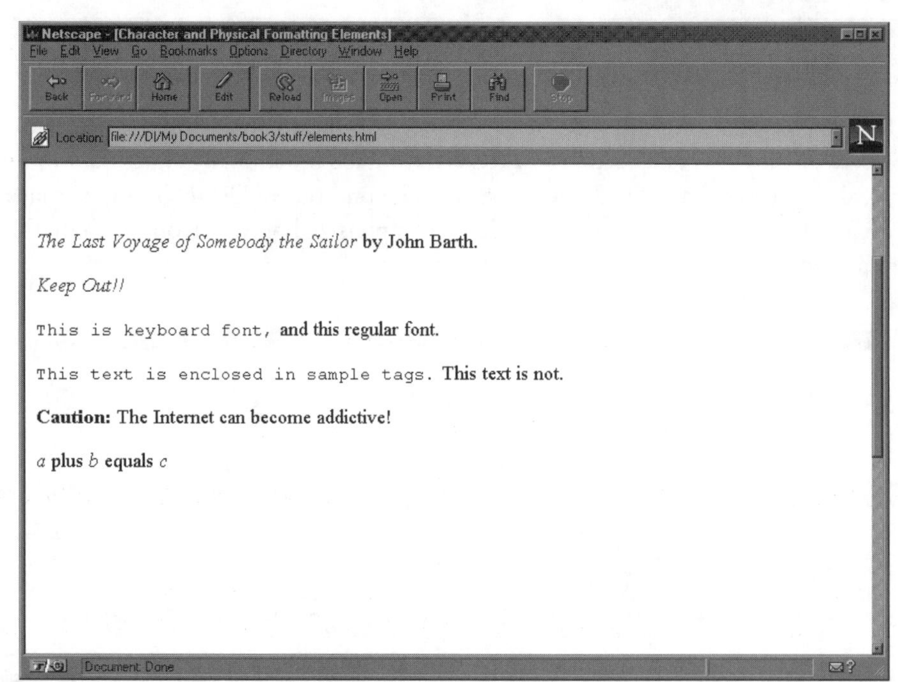

Figure 3.22 A Web Page Displaying the Logical Tag Code Examples Covered in This Section

produce the same results—sometimes in cases where a physical tag may be more directly applicable. A logical tag might be more suitable in some situations, but physical tags are easier to remember, and yield more consistent formatting of text on a Web page.

<B> . . .</B>

Element Name: Bold tag.

Description: Indicates text displayed in bold font.

Attributes: None.

Sample: `<B>This text is bold,</B> while this text is more demure.`

The <B> container tag displays text in bold font. It is functionally equivalent to the logical <STRONG> tag.

<BIG> . . .</BIG>

Element Name: Big font tag.

Description: Indicates text displayed in a larger font than regular font size.

Attributes: None.

Sample: `<BIG>This text is bigger</BIG> than this text.`

The <BIG> tag, along with the <SMALL> tag, was first introduced in HTML 3.0 to create text that was a larger font size than regular text font. Since the introduction of the <FONT> tag in the official HTML 3.2 specification, it is not used as frequently since the exact font size cannot be defined. However, it is a handy way of quickly boosting the text up a font size without having to keep track of what the current size of the text specified by <FONT> is.

The <FONT> tag is discussed in detail earlier in this chapter.

<I> . . .</I>

Element Name: Italic tag.

Description: Indicates text displayed in italic font.

Attributes: None.

Sample:

```
<I>This text is italicized,</I> while this text is not.
```

The <I> tag displays text in italicized font. It is functionally equivalent to the logical <EM> (emphasis) tag.

<SMALL> . . .</SMALL>

Element Name: Small font tag.

Description: Indicates text displayed in a smaller font than regular font size.

Attributes: None.

Sample:

```
<SMALL>This text is smaller</SMALL> than this text.
```

The <SMALL> tag, along with the <BIG> tag, was first introduced in HTML 3.0 to create text that was a smaller font size than regular text font. Since the introduction of the <FONT> tag in HTML 3.2, it is not used as frequently since the exact font size cannot be defined. However, just like the <BIG> tag, <SMALL> is a handy way of quickly reducing the text by one font size without having to keep track of what the current size of the text specified by <FONT> is.

The <FONT> tag is discussed in detail earlier in this chapter.

<STRIKE> . . .</STRIKE> and <S> . . .</S>

Element Name: Strike tag.

Description: Indicates a line of text with a horizontal line through it.

Attributes: None.

Sample:

```
<STRIKE>This sentence has a strike through it.</STRIKE>
```

The <STRIKE> (and the twin <S>) tag was proposed for HTML 2.0 but was not approved until the HTML 3.2 specification. Both are now depreciated in the HTML 4.0 specification. They are designed to display text that has a line running through it—the idea is to convey text that has been struck out. In other words, it is supposed to display text that has been deleted by the writer in a previous edit, but is shown to display the changes in the text that have occurred.

<STRIKE> was first added by the introduction of Netscape Navigator 2.0. The twin <S> tag was first added within Internet Explorer 2.0. By version 3.0 of each browser, both <STRIKE> and <S> were recognized by both browsers, and both browsers render struck-out text in exactly the same way.

_{. . .} and ^{. .}

Element Names: Subscript and Superscript tags.

Description: The text enclosed within the <SUB> tags is displayed in subscript font, and the text enclosed within the <SUP> tags is displayed in superscript font.

Attributes: None.

Sample:

```
Subscript is useful for formulas like H<SUB>2</SUB>0.<BR>
Superscript is useful for trademarks like
This<SUP>TM</SUP>.
```

The <SUB> and <SUP> tags were introduced in HTML 3.0, and are gaining popularity in many browsers. The <SUB> tag displays text that the browser should render as subscript, and the <SUP> text tag displays text that the browser should render as superscript.

Both tags were first implemented within Netscape Navigator 2.0, and they were first adopted for use within Internet Explorer 3.0.

These tags tend to be used for displaying things like mathematical figures (i.e., displaying a number that has been squared or cubed) or for special typographical symbols (such as the trademark symbol).

<TT> . . .</TT>

Element Name: Teletype tag.

Description: Indicates text that is displayed in fixed-width font.

Attributes: None.

Sample:
```
<TT>This text looks like output from a teletype.</TT>
```

The <TT> tag displays text in fixed-width font. Its functional equivalents are the logical <CODE> and <KBD> tags.

Though little-seen these days since the advent of fax machines, email, and the World Wide Web, teletype machines were used to transmit text messages across telephone lines. They printed text in a fashion similar to a typewriter, and often used the same machinery to produce the text—the only difference is that the original text may have been typed by somebody at a different machine at the other end of the country. It was often used for such things as printed telegrams or for transmitting important messages, hence its deployment as a type of physical HTML tag.

<U> . . .</U>

Element Name: Underline tag.

Description: Indicates text that is underlined by a horizontal line.

Attributes: None.

Sample:
```
<U>This text is underlined.</U>
```

The <U> tag was first proposed in the HTML 2.0 draft, and is now recognized by most browsers. It has been deprecated in the HTML 4.0 specification.

Keep in mind when using this tag that most Web browsers usually render

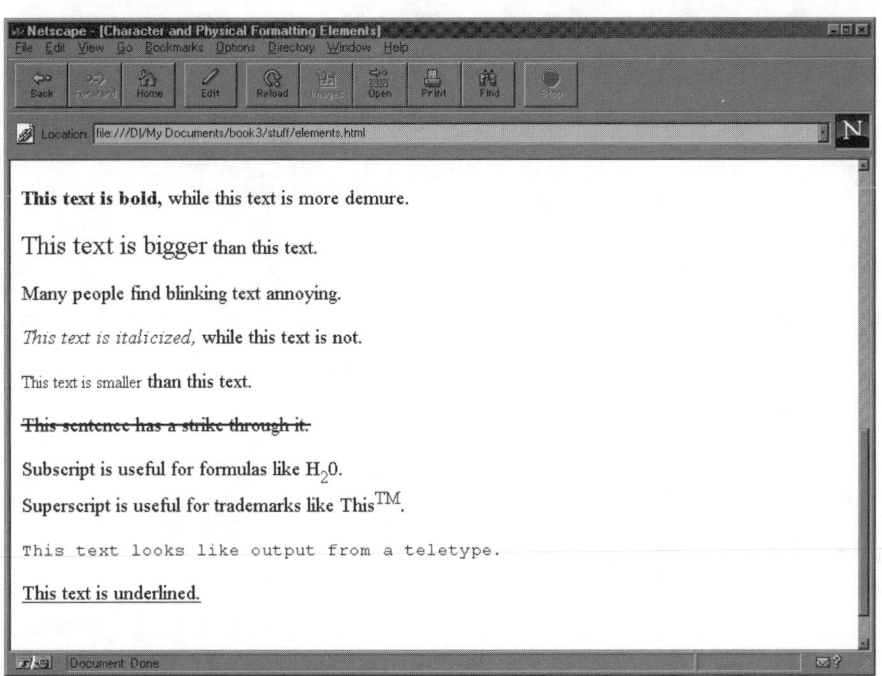

Figure 3.23 A Web Page Displaying the Physical Tag Code Examples Covered in this Section

hypertext links as underlined, and that underlining other text that is not a hyperlink will cause confusion. It is best to use other types of character formatting if at all possible.

Figure 3.23 shows the physical tag codes described in this section.

CHAPTER 4

Hypertext Anchors

Hypertext anchors, also referred to as hypertext links or hot links, are used to allow the user to travel from one hypertext document to another, either within the same Web site or across the World Wide Web at large. Anchors can also be used to travel to specific points within the same document.

The <A> Tag—Creating Hypertext Anchors

The anchor tag is a container tag that defines what Web page will be displayed when the user clicks on the text contained within the anchor tag. The text that

appears within the anchor start and end tags is displayed as the hypertext link itself, and can appear underlined and in a different font color depending on the text properties you have set, and also on the display properties the user has set in their Web browser. For more information on changing font colors, see the information on the <FONT> tag and on the <BODY> tag in Chapter 3, "Displayed Elements."

<A> . . .</A>

Element Name: Anchor tag.

Description: Creates hypertext links. This tag always needs either the HREF or the NAME attribute to define what Web page will be downloaded when the user clicks on the text contained within the anchor tags.

Attributes:

ACCESSKEY= *key*
Specifies the keyboard key associated with the legend.
CHARSET= *ISO-#*
Indicates the international character coding used for the hyperlink.
COORDS= *x,y*
Sets the x,y coordinates of the hotspot area.
HREF= *URL*
A hypertext reference that points to the URL of another Web page, or to a specific point within another Web page when used with the NAME attribute. The URL that follows the HREF can be either a path NAME to indicate a link to another Web page on the same Web server, or a full URL to indicate a link to a Web page on an external Web server on the World Wide Web. The URL must be enclosed in quotes.
HREFLANG= *text*
Specifies the base language of the resource indicated in the HREF attribute.
NAME= *text*
Used to NAME a specific part of a Web document so that it can be a TARGET for a hypertext link within the same document, or at a specific point within a Web page.
REL= *URL*
Indicates the URL of a subdocument. This attribute is not commonly used.
REV= *URL*
Indicates the URL of a parent document. This attribute is not commonly used.
SHAPE= *CIRCLE | POLYGON | RECT*
Specifies the type of hotspot shape. RECT is the default.

- CIRCLE: "center x, center y, radius" values
- POLYGON: the successive x1, y1, x2, y2, etc. points of the polygon
- RECT (default): "left, top, right, bottom" values.

TABINDEX= *number*
Specifies the order in which an individual item can be selected from a group of items by using the TAB keyboard key.

TARGET = *target_name*
Used to specify a specific frame within a Web page. For more information on frames, see Chapter 9 "Frames, Multiple Columns and Layers."

TITLE = *text*
Used to provide a TITLE for the URL the hypertext link is referencing. Some browsers, such as Microsoft Internet Explorer, display the text specified in the TITLE attribute when the mouse is moved over the hypertext link.

TYPE = *MIME type*
Specifies the MIME type of the file type the hypertext anchor points to.

Associated Tags: None.

Sample:

```
<A HREF=http://www.exn.net>This hypertext link takes you
to the Exploration Network Web site.</A>
```

This sample code appears on a Web page as shown in Figure 4.1.

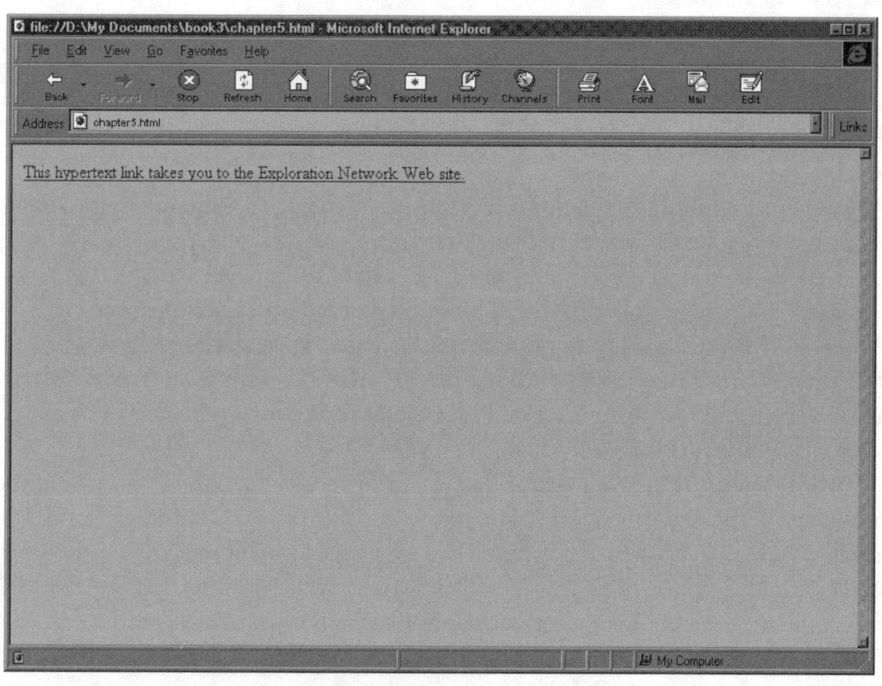

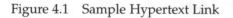

Figure 4.1 Sample Hypertext Link

Hypertext anchors can be used in several different ways, depending on where you want the hypertext link to take the user. If you are linking to another Web page, either within your own Web site or anywhere on the World Wide Web, then using the HREF attribute is appropriate, as demonstrated in the preceding sample code.

However, if you want to link to a specific part of a document within your own Web site, you must use both the HREF and NAME attributes to mark where the hypertext link should be, and where the link should take the user.

First you must decide where you want the hypertext link to take the user, and mark that part of the page with the NAME attribute. Then, mark the text that will become the hypertext link with the HREF attribute. The sample code follows.

```
<!DOCTYPE HTML PUBLIC "-//W3C//DTD HTML 3.2 Final//EN">
<HTML>
<HEAD>
<TITLE>Kim's Web Page</TITLE>
</HEAD>
<BODY>
<A HREF="testpage.htm#bottom" >This hypertext link
takes you to the bottom of the Web page.</A>
<p>
Lots more text and paragraphs and pictures can go here.
<p>
<A NAME=bottom>This is the bottom of the page.
</BODY>
</HTML>
```

The pound symbol (#) must appear after the Web page's filename to indicate that the string that follows is a named anchor within the Web page; the </A> end tag is not needed. If you are linking within the same Web page, the filename is not necessary; you can simply provide the pound symbol and anchor name.

Browsers do not display hypertext links created with the NAME attribute any differently from those created with the HREF attribute. Using the NAME attribute can be very useful for bringing the user exactly to the information you want them to see.

The little-used CHARSET attribute is used to specify the international character coding used for the hyperlink. The default value is the standard Latin-1 ISO standard, which is used by most European languages (including English). Alternate character sets can be specified. The TYPE attribute is used to specify the MIME type of the file type the hypertext anchor points to. For more information on MIME types, see Chapter 2. The obscure HREFLANG attribute sets the base language of the resource that is being linked to.

If you are making a link that is represented by an image, you can turn it into a simple client-side image map by using the COORDS and SHAPE attributes. For a full explanation of these attributes, see the "Creating and Using Imagemaps" section in Chapter 6.

There are also some attributes which have been specified but are not as yet used within any major browser. With the ACCESSKEY attribute you can specify a keyboard key to be associated with the link. For example, say you have three links in a list, like the following:

```
<UL>
<LI><A HREF="apples.html" ACCESKEY=A>Apples
<LI><A HREF="bananas.html" ACCESKEY=B>Bananas
<LI><A HREF="cucumbers.html" ACCESKEY=A>Cucumbers
</UL>
```

To choose a link, a user can click on the link, or the user can click the letter on the keyboard corresponding to the link, which selects the corresponding link. In the previous example, if the user selects B, the bananas.html page is fetched by the browser.

The TABINDEX attribute works in a similar manner, but uses the TAP key to select between different links on a page. If you want to let a user select between the links on a page, you can specify the order of selection associating a number with the TABINDEX attribute. In the following example, when a user repeatedly hits the tab key, they would go to Link #1, then Link #3, then Link #2.

```
<A HREF="link1.html" TABINDEX=1>Link #1<BR>
<A HREF="link2.html" TABINDEX=3>Link #2<BR>
<A HREF="link3.html" TABINDEX=2>Link #3<BR>
```

Unfortunately, at the time of this writing, neither of these attributes are currently supported within the major browsers.

Directory Structures

When you are using hypertext anchors or inserting images within a Web page and you want to refer to other pages or images located on your Web site, you are not restricted to simply keeping all of your files in a single directory. In fact it is a much better idea to keep all of your Web files sorted into different directories so that you can keep easy track of them. For example, let's say you have an online storefront and you have many items for sale. You might want to keep the many diverse items in your inventory separate from each other and stored away in different directories so that it is easier for you to immediately see the images and Web pages you have devoted to a particular product.

You have two options when you want to refer to items stored in different

directories on your Web site. You can either use an "absolute link" or a "relative link." An objective link spells out the full URL of your Web site along with the full directory structure in which you have placed the Web file. So for example if you have a Web page at /bigproduct/index.html and your Web host name is www.yoyodyne.com, you could reference the Web page in this way:

```
<A
HREF="http://www.yoyodyne.com/bigproduct/index.html">Cli
ck Here!</A>
```

You can do the same thing with an image file—you can even specify an image already in use on another's Web site by specifying the exact URL of the image, as in the following example:

```
<IMG
SRC="http://www.anotherfirmswebsite.com/images/funkyimag
e.gif">
```

The alternative is to use a relative path to specify the Web page or image file. This is done by specifying the page or image file relative to the location of the Web page you are at. For this reason, the path you specify to a single file will often be quite different depending on where you are in the Web site. For example, let's say we are trying to reference the Web page thispage.html from different places within your Web site. If the Web page you are specifying can be found in the same directory as the current Web page—in other words if are both contained within the same directory—you can point to it using the following code:

```
<A HREF="thispage.html">Click Me!</A>
```

To reference a page or file that is contained in a directory level immediately above the one you are currently in, use a ../ before the hypertext reference, as in the following example:

```
<A HREF="../thispage.html">Click Me!</A>
```

By specifying ../, it references a directory structure immediately above the one you are currently in. Use combinations of these along with directory names to move easily between directories.

Now let's say that the target file is contained within a directory called /SomePages. If you want to specify the target file from a directory immediately above this directory, you would use the following code:

```
<A HREF="SomePages/thispage.html">Click Me!</A>
```

If you are in a directory that is parallel to the one that contains the target file, you would specify the Web page in the following manner:

```
<A HREF=" . ./SomePages/thispage.html">Click Me!</A>
```

All of these examples are represented in Figure 4.2, which represents all of the example codes relative to the directory structure in which they are contained.

Tip: Make sure that when you specify a file or image on your Web site that you use the same case used by the path and file. In the preceding example we reference a file called thispage.html in a directory called /SomePages. If you referenced the file from another directory and used a different case for either the path or the filename (like /somePAGES/This-Page.html) the Web browser will likely not find the page. Most Web servers run on the Unix operating system which is case-sensitive, and will not be able to distinguish correctly the slight (to us) difference between files called THISPAGE.HTML, ThisPage.html, or THIS-page.HTML from the correct thispage.html. This is a common reason for many broken links found on Web sites.

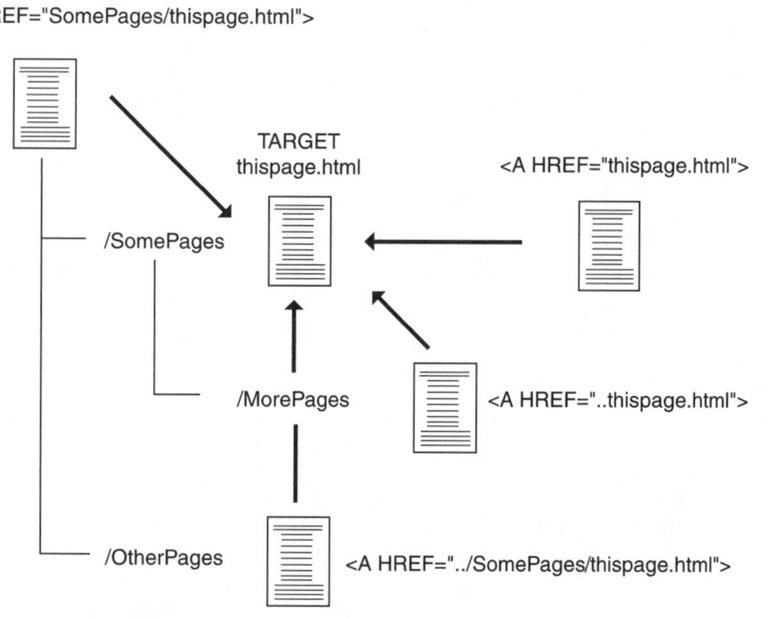

Figure 4.2 Illustration Depicting How To Specify Relative Path to thispage.html from Different Locations in a Web Site

CHAPTER 5

Entity Characters

Back in 1986, the International Standards Organization (ISO) devised a standard for representing the most commonly used characters of the various European languages on computer systems. These characters include all of the upper- and lowercase letters used in the English language, and included most (though not all) of the characters used in many other European languages.

This initial standard formalized for use on the Web was the ISO 8859-1 Latin-1 character standard, which had already been widely adopted for use within many computing systems. When the HTML standards were originally devised, this standard was incorporated into the HTML specification, as it allowed browsers to represent characters and symbols outside of the English alphabet, and to display characters normally reserved for use within HTML documents. The release of the HTML 4.0 standard, once fully adopted within the popular browsers, will soon enable people to use an extended range of characters. With all of these characters

an HTML writer can insert international letters, mathematical symbols, spacing characters, and much more into a Web page.

THE ISO 8859-1 LATIN-1 CHARACTER STANDARD

The ISO 8859-1 Latin-1 character standard used an 8-bit encoding scheme, which was common to computer systems at that time. This placed an upper limit on the characters that could be specified—up to a maximum of 256 different characters could be represented under this encoding scheme. In addition to the standard English characters, it also specifies many numerical and symbolic characters (such as the one-half fraction or the character for the Japanese Yen) and many accented characters (those European characters that include acute, grave, umlaut, and other accent forms). This set of characters is fully implemented and can be viewed within all modern browsers.

It was natural to include these entity characters within HTML—for the most part, they were already incorporated into most of the operating systems commonly used for surfing the Web. Since these characters were already part of many of the computing systems being used, it could simply be referenced by the browser instead of having to create and display these characters from scratch. In essence the ISO 8859-1 Latin-1 character standard "came for free."

Not all of the 256 reserved spaces for encoding display characters could be used however. Many of the initial characters were already widely used for encoding information necessary for transmitting messages and system commands; for example, the seventh character space was reserved for creating a system sound. This left much less than 256 characters that could be specified. To economize and to keep things as compatible between different computing systems, the initial 128 characters were derived from the US-ASCII standard, which specifies all of the English characters.

There are two ways these characters can be specified within a Web page: either by their numeric references, or by their character references. These terms are known as *numeric entities* and *character entities*. For example, the numeric reference for the less-than sign is 60, and its equivalent character reference is lt. However, you cannot simply specify 60 or lt within the HTML code for a Web page and have it displayed as a less-than sign. To display the numeric or character entities within a Web document, the browser has to be told that a special character is being used. To do this, the ampersand symbol (&) is used to specify that what follows is a special character, and terminates with a semicolon (;). To display the less-than sign as a numeric entity, < is used, and to specify it using its character equivalent, < is used. Note that the hash symbol (#) is used in conjunction with the ampersand to define a numeric entity. These characters can be used to display entity characters on Web pages.

There are four distinct divisions in the ISO 8859-1 Latin-1 character standard:

1–32 Control characters

33–127 Basic Latin characters (English letters and symbols)

128–159 Extended control characters

160–255 Latin (accented letters and symbols)

The first 32 characters and those specified between 128–159 are reserved as control or extended control characters for computer use, and are not supposed to be used for encoding display characters.

In addition to these entity characters, the HTML 4.0 standard introduced a number of new symbols. These are discussed later in the chapter.

NUMERIC ENTITIES

To specify a numeric entity within the text of a Web page, simply use the form displayed in the first column of Table 5.1. For example, if you wanted to display a copyright symbol beside some text, you'd enter the following:

```
Copyright&#169; Capt.Mondo Productions, 1998.
```

A copyright symbol is displayed in place of the © inserted into the text of the Web page.

Table 5.1 contains a list of all possible numeric entities, followed by a description of the entity and what (if anything) is displayed by the browser.

On the whole, numeric entities are more universally recognized than their character entity equivalents. Although a character entity may be easier to remember and specify than its numeric equivalent, whenever possible, try to use the numeric entity instead.

As new standards are beginning to emerge, Microsoft's Internet Explorer now allows Web authors to specify numeric entities that are more than three characters long. For example, it is valid within Internet Explorer to specify the high, right single quote mark ('), normally rendered as ’, as ’.

Table 5.1 A Listing of All Numeric Entities (Latin-1)

Numeric Entity	*Description*	*What's Displayed*
�	NUL Null	Nothing is displayed
	SOH Start of heading	Nothing is displayed
	STX Start of text	Nothing is displayed
	ETX End of text	Nothing is displayed
	EOT End of transmission	Nothing is displayed
	ENQ Enquiry	Nothing is displayed
	ACK Acknowledge	Nothing is displayed
	BEL System bell	Nothing is displayed
	BS Backspace	Nothing is displayed
	HT Horizontal tab	Nothing is displayed
NL New line	Nothing is displayed
	VT Vertical tab	Nothing is displayed
	NP New page	Nothing is displayed
CR Carriage return	Nothing is displayed
	SO Shift out	Nothing is displayed
	SI Shift in	Nothing is displayed
	DLE Data link escape	Nothing is displayed
	DC1 Device control 1	Nothing is displayed
	DC2 Device control 2	Nothing is displayed
	DC3 Device control 3	Nothing is displayed
	DC4 Device control 4	Nothing is displayed
	NAK Negative acknowledgment	Nothing is displayed
	SYN Synchronous	Nothing is displayed
	ETB End of transmission block	Nothing is displayed
	CAN Cancel	Nothing is displayed
	EM End of medium	Nothing is displayed
	SUB Substitute	Nothing is displayed
	ESC Escape	Nothing is displayed
	FS File separator	Nothing is displayed
	GS Group separator	Nothing is displayed
	RS Record separator	Nothing is displayed
	US Unit separator	Nothing is displayed
	Space	(Space character)
!	Exclamation mark	!
"	Double quote mark	"
#	Number (hash) symbol	#
$	Dollar symbol	$
%	Percentage symbol	%
&	Ampersand	&
'	Apostrophe	'
(	Left parenthesis	(
)	Right parenthesis	)
*	Asterisk	*

Table 5.1 *Continued*

Numeric Entity	*Description*	*What's Displayed*
+	Plus symbol	+
,	Comma	,
-	Minus symbol (hypen)	-
.	Period	.
/	Forward slash (solidus)	/
0	Zero	0
1	One	1
2	Two	2
3	Three	3
4	Four	4
5	Five	5
6	Six	6
7	Seven	7
8	Eight	8
9	Nine	9
:	Colon	:
;	Semicolon	;
<	Left angle bracket	<
=	Equal symbol	=
>	Right angle bracket	>
?	Question mark	?
@	At symbol	@
A	Uppercase A	A
B	Uppercase B	B
C	Uppercase C	C
D	Uppercase D	D
E	Uppercase E	E
F	Uppercase F	F
G	Uppercase G	G
H	Uppercase H	H
I	Uppercase I	I
J	Uppercase J	J
K	Uppercase K	K
L	Uppercase L	L
M	Uppercase M	M
N	Uppercase N	N
O	Uppercase O	O
P	Uppercase P	P
Q	Uppercase Q	Q
R	Uppercase R	R
S	Uppercase S	S
T	Uppercase T	T
U	Uppercase U	U
V	Uppercase V	V

Table 5.1 *Continued*

Numeric Entity	*Description*	*What's Displayed*
W	Uppercase W	W
X	Uppercase X	X
Y	Uppercase Y	Y
Z	Uppercase Z	Z
[	Left square bracket	[
\	Backslash (backwards solidus)	/
]	Right square bracket	]
^	Caret (circumflex)	^
_	Underline (underscore)	_
`	Grave accent	`
a	Lowercase a	a
b	Lowercase b	b
c	Lowercase c	c
d	Lowercase d	d
e	Lowercase e	e
f	Lowercase f	f
g	Lowercase g	g
h	Lowercase h	h
i	Lowercase i	i
j	Lowercase j	j
k	Lowercase k	k
l	Lowercase l	l
m	Lowercase m	m
n	Lowercase n	n
o	Lowercase o	o
p	Lowercase p	p
q	Lowercase q	q
r	Lowercase r	r
s	Lowercase s	s
t	Lowercase t	t
u	Lowercase u	u
v	Lowercase v	v
w	Lowercase w	w
x	Lowercase x	x
y	Lowercase y	y
z	Lowercase z	z
{	Left curly bracket	{
		Vertical bar	|
}	Right curly bracket	}
~	Tilde	~
	DEL Delete control character	Nothing is displayed
€	Not assigned	Nothing is displayed
	Not assigned	Nothing is displayed
‚	Rising low left single quote*	‘

Table 5.1 *Continued*

Numeric Entity	*Description*	*What's Displayed*
ƒ	Function symbol (function of)*	*f*
„	Rising low left double quote*	“
…	Low horizontal ellipsis*	...
†	Dagger mark*	†
‡	Double dagger mark*	‡
ˆ	Letter modifying circumflex*	^
‰	Per thousand (mille) sign*	‰
Š	Uppercase S caron or hacek*	Š
‹	Left single angle quote mark*	‹
Œ	Uppercase OE ligature*	Œ
	Not assigned	Nothing is displayed
Ž	Not assigned	Nothing is displayed
	Not assigned	Nothing is displayed
	Not assigned	Nothing is displayed
‘	Left single quotation mark *	‘
’	(High) right single quote mark *	’
“	Left double quotation mark *	“
”	(High) right double quote mark *	”
•	Round filled bullet *	•
–	En-dash *	–
—	Em-dash *	—
˜	Spacing tilde accent *	˜
™	Trademark symbol *	™
š	Lowercase s caron or hacek *	š
›	Right single angle quote mark *	›
œ	Lowercase oe ligature *	œ
	Not assigned	Nothing is displayed
ž	Not assigned	Nothing is displayed
Ÿ	Uppercase Y umlaut*	Ÿ
	Nonbreaking space	(Nonbreaking space character)
¡	Inverted exclamation mark	¡
¢	Cent sign	¢
£	Pound sterling sign	£
¤	General currency sign	¤
¥	Yen sign	¥
¦	Broken (vertical) bar	|
§	Section sign	§
¨	Umlaut (dieresis)	¨
©	Copyright symbol	©
ª	Ordinal indicator, feminine	ª
«	Angle quotation mark, left	«
¬	Not sign	≠
	Soft hypen	-

Table 5.1 *Continued*

Numeric Entity	*Description*	*What's Displayed*
®	Registered sign	®
¯	Macron	¯
°	Degree sign	°
±	Plus-or-minus sign	±
²	Superscript two	²
³	Superscript three	³
´	Acute accent	´
µ	Micro sign	µ
¶	Pilcrow (paragraph sign)	¶
·	Middle dot	·
¸	Cedilla	¸
¹	Superscript one	¹
º	Ordinal indicator, masculine	º
»	Angle quotation mark, right	»
¼	Fraction one-quarter	¶
½	Fraction one-half	©
¾	Fraction three-quarters	®
¿	Inverted question mark	¿
À	Uppercase A, grave accent	À
Á	Uppercase A, acute accent	Á
Â	Uppercase A, circumflex accent	Â
Ã	Uppercase A, tilde	Ã
Ä	Uppercase A, dieresis or umlaut mark	Ä
Å	Uppercase A, ring	Å
Æ	Uppercase Ae diphthong (ligature)	Æ
Ç	Uppercase C, cedilla	Ç
È	Uppercase e, grave accent	È
É	Uppercase E, acute accent	É
Ê	Uppercase E, circumflex accent	Ê
Ë	Uppercase E, dieresis or umlaut mark	Ë
Ì	Uppercase I, grace accent	Ì
Í	Uppercase I, acute accent	Í
Î	Uppercase I, circumflex accent	Î
Ï	Uppercase I, dieresis or umlaut mark	Ï
Ð	Uppercase Eth, Icelandic	Ð
Ñ	Uppercase N, tilde	Ñ
Ò	Uppercase O, grave accent	Ò
Ó	Uppercase O, acute accent	Ó
Ô	Uppercase O, circumflex accent	Ô
Õ	Uppercase O, tilde	Õ
Ö	Uppercase O, dieresis or umlaut mark	Ö
×	Multiple sign	x
Ø	Uppercase O, slash	Ø
Ù	Uppercase U, grave accenta	Ù

Table 5.1 *Continued*

Numeric Entity	*Description*	*What's Displayed*
Ú	Uppercase U, acute accent	Ú
Û	Uppercase U, circumflex accent	Û
Ü	Uppercase U, dieresis or umlaut mark	Ü
Ý	Uppercase Y, acute accent	Ý
Þ	Uppercase THORN, Icelandic	Þ
ß	Lowercase sharp s, German (sz ligature)	ß
à	Lowercase a, grave accent	à
á	Lowercase a, acute accent	á
â	Lowercase a, circumflex accent	â
ã	Lowercase a, tilde	ã
ä	Lowercase a, dieresis or umlaut mark	ä
å	Lowercase a, ring	å
æ	Lowercase ae diphthong (ligature)	æ
ç	Lowercase c, cedilla	ç
è	Lowercase e, grave accent	è
é	Lowercase e, acute accent	é
ê	Lowercase e, circumflex accent	ê
ë	Lowercase e, dieresis or umlaut mark	ë
ì	Lowercase i, grave accent	ì
í	Lowercase i, acute accent	í
î	Lowercase i, circumflex accent	î
ï	Lowercase i, dieresis or umlaut mark	ï
ð	Lowercase eth, Icelandic	ð
ñ	Lowercase n, tilde	ñ
ò	Lowercase o, grave accent	ò
ó	Lowercase o, acute accent	ó
ô	Lowercase o, circumflex accent	ô
õ	Lowercase o, tilde	õ
ö	Lowercase o, dieresis or umlaut mark	ö
÷	Division sign	÷
ø	Lowercase o, slash	ø
ù	Lowercase u, grave accent	ù
ú	Lowercase u, acute accent	ú
û	Lowercase u, circumflex accent	û
ü	Lowercase u, dieresis or umlaut mark	ü
ý	Lowercase y, acute accent	ý
þ	Lowercase thorn, Icelandic	þ
ÿ	Lowercase y, dieresis or umlaut mark	ÿ

* May be displayed within an MS-Windows-based browser. See "Windows-Only Entities" later in this section for more information.

Character Entities

To specify a character entity within the text of a Web page, simply use the form displayed in the first column of the following table. For example, if you wanted to display a © symbol using a character entity, you'd enter the following:

```
I give this movie 4&half; stars.
```

A © symbol is displayed in the place of the ½ inserted into the text of the Web page.

Note that character entities are case-sensitive. If you want a lower case acute accent e, you type é. To get an uppercase e acute, you type É.

Table 5.2 lists of all possible character entities, followed by a description of the entity and what (if anything) is displayed by the browser.

Table 5.2 A Listing of All Common Character Entities (Latin-1)

Character Entity	*Description*	*What's Displayed*
&sp;	Space	(Space character)
!	Exclamation mark	!
"	Double quote mark	"
#	Number (hash) symbol	#
$	Dollar symbol	$
%	Percentage symbol	%
&	Ampersand	&
'	Apostrophe	'
(	Left parenthesis	(
)	Right parenthesis	)
*	Asterisk	*
+	Plus symbol	+
,	Comma	,
−	Minus symbol (hyphen)	-
.	Period	.
/	Forward slash (solidus)	/
:	Colon	:
;	Semicolon	;
<	Left angle bracket	<
=	Equal symbol	=
>	Right angle bracket	>
?	Question mark	?
@	At symbol	@
[	Left square bracket	[
\	Backslash (backwards solidus)	/
]	Right square bracket	]

Table 5.2 *Continued*

Character Entity	*Description*	*What's Displayed*
ˆ	Caret (circumflex)	^
_	Underline (underscore)	_
`	Grave accent	´
{	Left curly bracket	{
		Vertical bar	|
}	Right curly bracket	}
˜	Tilde	~
‚	Rising low left single quote*	‘
ƒ	Function symbol (function of)*	á
‚	Rising low left double quote*	"
&hellip	Low horizontal ellipsis*	...
†	Dagger mark*	†
‡	Double dagger mark*	‡
ˆ	Letter-modifying circumflex	^
‰	Per thousand (mille) sign*	‰
Š	Uppercase S caron or hacek*	Š
‹	Left single angle quote mark*	‹
&Oelig;	Uppercase OE ligature*	Œ
‘	Left single quotation mark*	‘
’	(High) right single quote mark*	’
“	Left double quotation mark*	“
”	(High) right double quote mark*	”
•	Round filled bullet*	•
–	En-dash*	–
—	Em-dash*	—
˜	Spacing tilde accent	~
™	Trademark symbol*	™
š	Lowercase s caron or hacek*	š
›	Right single angle quote mark*	›
œ	Lowercase oe ligature*	œ
Ÿ	Uppercase Y umlaut*	Ÿ
	Nonbreaking space	(Nonbreaking space character)
¡	Inverted exclamation mark	¡
¢	Cent sign	¢
£	Pound sterling sign	£
¤	General currency sign	¤
¥	Yen sign	¥
¦	Broken (vertical) bar	¦
§	Section sign	§
¨ or ¨	Umlaut (dieresis)	¨
©	Copyright symbol	©
ª	Ordinal indicator, feminine	ª
«	Angle quotation mark, left	«
¬	Not sign	≠

Table 5.2 *Continued*

Character Entity	*Description*	*What's Displayed*
	Soft hyphen	-
®	Registered sign	®
¯ or &hibar;	Macron	¯
°	Degree sign	°
±	Plus-or-minus sign	±
²	Superscript two	^{2}
³	Superscript three	^{3}
´	Acute accent	´
µ	Micro sign	µ
¶	Pilcrow (paragraph symbol)	¶
·	Middle dot	·
¸	Cedilla	¸
¹	Superscript one	^{1}
º	Ordinal indicator, masculine	º
»	Angle quotation mark, right	»
¼	Fraction one-quarter	¼
½ or ½	Fraction one-half	½
¾	Fraction three-quarters	¾
¿	Inverted question mark	¿
À	Uppercase A, grave accent	À
Á	Uppercase A, acute accent	Á
Â	Uppercase A, circumflex accent	Â
Ã	Uppercase A, tilde	Ã
Ä	Uppercase A, dieresis or umlaut mark	Ä
Å	Uppercase A, ring	Å
&Aelig;	Uppercase AE diphthong (ligature)	Æ
Ç	Uppercase C, cedilla	Ç
È	Uppercase E, grave accent	È
É	Uppercase E, acute accent	É
Ê	Uppercase E, circumflex accent	Ê
Ë	Uppercase E, dieresis or umlaut mark	Ë
Ì	Uppercase I, grave accent	Ì
Í	Uppercase I, acute accent	Í
Î	Uppercase I, circumflex accent	Î
Ï	Uppercase I, dieresis or umlaut mark	Ï
Ð or Đ	Uppercase Eth, Icelandic	Đ
¿	Uppercase N, tilde	Ñ
Ò	Uppercase O, grave accent	Ò
Ó	Uppercase O, acute accent	Ó
Ô	Uppercase O, circumflex accent	Ô
Õ	Uppercase O, tilde	Õ
Ö	Uppercase O, dieresis or umlaut mark	Ö

Table 5.2 *Continued*

Character Entity	*Description*	*What's Displayed*
&Oring;	Multiply sign	x
&Oelig;	Uppercase O, slash	Ø
Ù	Uppercase U, grave accent	Ù
Ú	Uppercase U, acute accent	Ú
Û	Uppercase U, circumflex accent	Û
Ü	Uppercase U, dieresis or umlaut mark	Ü
Ý	Uppercase Y, acute accent	Ý
Þ	Uppercase THORN, Icelandic	Þ
ß	Lowercase sharp s, German (sz ligature)	ß
à	Lowercase a, grave accent	à
á	Lowercase a, acute accent	á
â	Lowercase a, circumflex accent	â
ã	Lowercase a, tilde	ã
ä	Lowercase a, dieresis or umlaut mark	ä
å	Lowercase a, ring	å
æ	Lowercase ae diphthong (ligature)	æ
ç	Lowercase c, cedilla	ç
è	Lowercase e, grave accent	è
é	Lowercase e, acute accent	é
ê	Lowercase e, circumflex accent	ê
ë	Lowercase e, dieresis or umlaut mark	ë
ì	Lowercase i, grave accent	ì
í	Lowercase i, acute accent	í
î	Lowercase i, circumflex accent	î
ï	Lowercase i, dieresis or umlaut mark	ï
ð	Lowercase eth, Icelandic	ð
ñ	Lowercase n, tilde	ñ
ò	Lowercase o, grave accent	ò
ó	Lowercase o, acute accent	ó
ô	Lowercase o, circumflex accent	ô
õ	Lowercase o, tilde	õ
ö	Lowercase o, dieresis or umlaut mark	ö
÷	Division sign	÷
ø	Lowercase o, slash	ø
ù	Lowercase u, grave accent	ù
ú	Lowercase u, acute accent	ú
û	Lowercase u, circumflex accent	û
ü	Lowercase u, dieresis or umlaut mark	ü
ý	Lowercase y, acute accent	ý
þ	Lowercase thorn, Icelandic	þ
ÿ	Lowercase y, dieresis or umlaut mark	ÿ

*May be displayed within an MS-Windows-based browser. See "Windows-Only Entities" later in this section for more information.

Windows-Only Entities

These characters are part of the Windows operating system when they are specified by either their numeric or character entity name, they may appear within a Windows-based browser. The range of characters used (130–159) lie within the range of Extended Control Characters (128–159), which normally display nothing under most operating systems.

It is really best to avoid using these characters unless you are in an environment (such as a local, small corporate intranet) where you can reasonably expect that your viewers will be viewing your Web pages only through Windows-based browsers. In other words, use these characters only if you can use them in reasonable safety, without having the content of your page misinterpreted by people viewing them under circumstances you can't predict.

In an effort to conform more closely to the recognized HTML 3.2 specification, Netscape Navigator 4.0 no longer recognizes and displays these characters, though earlier versions of Netscape Navigator did. Internet Explorer 3.01 for Windows does recognize these tags, and they have been dropped from Internet Explorer 4.0.

Many of the characters in Table 5.3 are now specified within the latest HTML 4.0 specification, and it is recommended that they be used instead (see "HTML 4.0 Special Characters" near the end of this chapter for more information).

Using Nonbreaking Spaces

In addition to the ability to insert characters from non-English languages in a Web page, many of these entity characters have other uses. For example, there are two types of spacing characters specified within the ISO Latin-1 standard: a regular space (and &sp;), and a nonbreaking space (and). The former works like any space you may add in an HTML files—all but the first space in a line of characters is ignored. However, the latter works in a different way;—if you add a number of nonbreaking spaces together, you get a long horizontal space on a line. Adding about five nonbreaking space characters, as demonstrated in the following line of code, is a good substitute to a tab space.

```
     This line is indented
from the left margin by five spaces.
```

The effect of this code can be seen in Figure 5.1.

Note that this can also be accomplished using Netscape's <SPACER> tag; however, since <SPACER> is, as yet, only implemented within Netscape Navigator,

Table 5.3 A Listing of All Windows-Only Special Characters

Numerical Entity	*Character Entity*	*Description*	*What's Displayed*
‚	‚	Rising low left single quote*	'
ƒ	ƒ	Function symbol (function of)*	*f*
„	‚	Rising low left double quote*	"
…	…	Low horizontal ellipsis*	...
†	†	Dagger mark*	†
‡	‡	Double dagger mark *	‡
ˆ	ˆ	Letter modifying circumflex *	^
‰	‰	Per thousand (mile) sign *	‰
Š	Š	Uppercase S caron or hacek *	Š
‹	‹	Left single angle quote mark *	‹
Œ	&Oelig;	Uppercase OE ligature *	Œ
‘	‘	Left single quotation mark *	'
’	’	(High) right single quote mark *	'
“	“	Left double quotation mark *	"
”	”	(High) right double quote mark *	"
•	•	Round filled bullet *	•
–	–	En-dash *	–
—	—	Em-dash *	—
˜	˜	Spacing tilde accent *	~
™	™	Trademark symbol *	™
š	š	Lowercase s caron or hacek *	š
›	›	Right single angle quote mark *	›
œ	œ	Lowercase oe ligature *	œ
Ÿ	Ÿ	Uppercase Y umlaut*	Ÿ

the numeric and character entities are more widely recognized. Whenever possible, use the numeric ( ) version of the nonbreaking space entity over that of its character equivalent ( ). It is worth noting that the character entity for the nonbreaking space is not specified in HTML 3.2, apparently an oversight made when finalizing the specification.

The nonbreaking space character has another use—keeping words together on a line. If you have a situation where you need to keep some words on the same line without the line of words being broken by the browser, simply insert a nonbreaking space entity between them, as in the following example:

```
<H1>Welcome to Keith 's Web 
Page</H1>
```

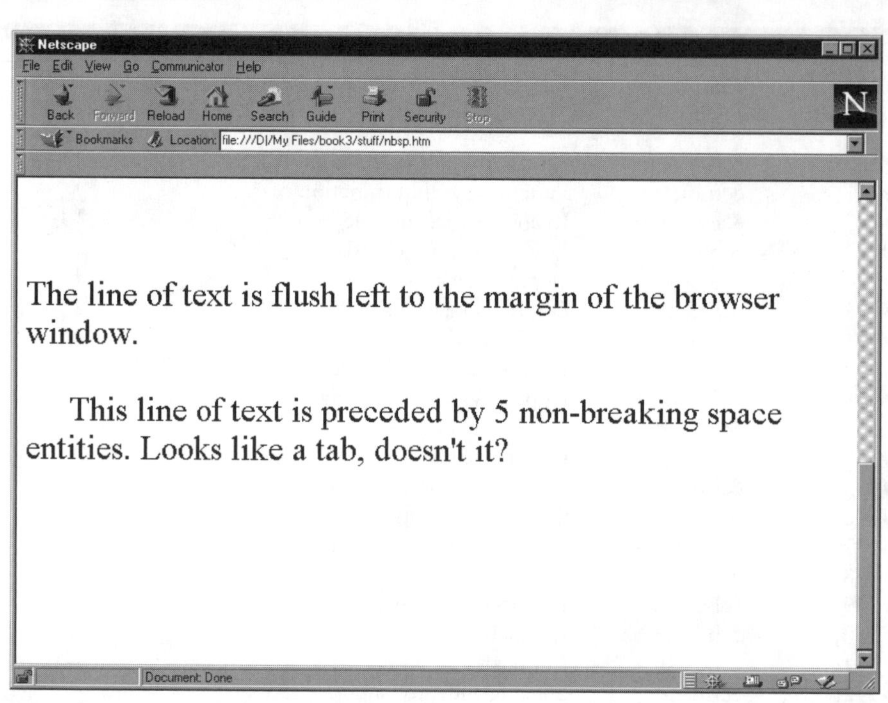

Figure 5.1 The Effects of Five Nonbreaking Spaces Added to the Beginning of a Line of Text

No matter how the browser window is sized by the user, this line of text will never have an artificial line break inserted, and will always remain on the same line.

Again, much the same effect can be achieved by using the <NOBR> tag, but this tag was first introduced with Internet Explorer 3.0, and has only recently been adopted within Netscape Navigator 4.0. Using an entity is still the preferred method.

Special Characters Introduced under the HTML 4.0 Standard

The HTML 4.0 standard introduces a number of new useful characters that many Web authors have been asking for. Though at the time of this writing they were not fully implemented within the most popular browsers, you can expect them to be implemented shortly.

These characters are all derived from the Unicode standard, (ISO 10646-1). This specification is more robust, and the whole Unicode standard enables you to specify many, many more characters than is possible in Latin-1—over 30,000 characters in total. This number makes it capable of representing most (though incredibly, not all) of the characters of all living languages.

The HTML 4.0 specification does not cover the whole of the Unicode standard, but instead contains a subset of it. The HTML 4.0 specification contains the characters sets for representing Greek characters, general symbols, letter-like symbols, arrows, mathematical symbols, miscellaneous technical symbols, punctuation symbols, and more.

The Greek characters are aimed primarily at people who need these symbols for mathematical purposes, not really for people who want to display Web pages in modern Greek. There are many other symbols here that will be useful for many other purposes, including such things as the trademark symbol, card suit symbols, and much of the ligature characters and spacing characters that were formerly available only to MS-Windows users.

At the time of this writing, many of the characters in Tables 5.4 through 5.14 are already supported in Internet Explorer 4.0, whereas few are supported in the latest release of Netscape Navigator. Descriptions of which characters are and are not supported can be found at the end of each table.

All of the characters in Table 5.4 are supported with Internet Explorer 4.0 with the exception of the last three (Greek small theta symbol, upsilon with hook symbol, and pi symbol). None are supported within Netscape Navigator 4.0.

All of the characters in Table 5.5 are supported within Internet Explorer 4.0. Only the numeric entity version of the bullet and horizontal ellipsis are supported within Netscape Navigator 4.0.

Only the trademark symbol, in Table 5.6 is supported within Internet Explorer 4.0 and Netscape Navigator 4.0.

The first five arrow characters in Table 5.7 are supported within Internet Explorer 4.0. None are supported within Netscape Navigator 4.0.

The symbols in Table 5.8 that can be seen in Internet Explorer 4.0 are: partial differential, n-ary product, n-ary sumation, minus sign, square root, infinity, intersection, integral, almost equal to, not equal to, identical to, less-than or equal to, and greater-than or equal to. None of these are supported within Netscape Navigator 4.0.

None of the symbols in Table 5.9 are currently supported within either Internet Explorer 4.0 or Netscape Navigator 4.0.

The character in Table 5.10 is not currently supported within either Internet Explorer 4.0 or Netscape Navigator 4.0.

Table 5.4 Greek Characters

Character Entity	*Numerical Entity*	*Description*	*What's Displayed*
Α	Α	Greek capital alpha	Α
Β	Β	Greek capital beta	Β
Γ	Γ	Greek capital gamma	Γ
Δ	Δ	Greek capital delta	Δ
Ε	Ε	Greek capital epsilon	Ε
Ζ	Ζ	Greek capital zeta	Ζ
Η	Η	Greek capital eta	Η
Θ	Θ	Greek capital theta	Θ
Ι	Ι	Greek capital iota	Ι
Κ	Κ	Greek capital kappa	Κ
Λ	Λ	Greek capital lambda	Λ
Μ	Μ	Greek capital mu	Μ
Ν	Ν	Greek capital nu	Ν
Ξ	Ξ	Greek capital xi	Ξ
Ο	Ο	Greek capital omicron	Ο
Π	Π	Greek capital pi	Π
Ρ	Ρ	Greek capital rho	Ρ
Σ	Σ	Greek capital sigma	Σ
Τ	Τ	Greek capital tau	τ
Υ	Υ	Greek capital upsilon	υ
Φ	Φ	Greek capital phi	Φ
Χ	Χ	Greek capital chi	Χ
Ψ	Ψ	Greek capital psi	Ψ
Ω	Ω	Greek capital omega	Ω
α	α	Greek small alpha	α
β	β	Greek small beta	β
γ	γ	Greek small gamma	γ
δ	δ	Greek small delta	δ
Ε	ε	Greek small epsilon	ε
ζ	ζ	Greek small zeta	ζ
η	η	Greek small eta	η
θ	θ	Greek small theta	θ
ι	ι	Greek small iota	ι
κ	κ	Greek small kappa	κ
λ	λ	Greek small lambda	λ
μ	μ	Greek small mu	μ
ν	ν	Greek small nu	ν
ξ	ξ	Greek small xi	ξ
ο	ο	Greek small omicron	ο
π	π	Greek small pi	π
ρ	ρ	Greek small rho	ρ
ς	ς	Greek small final sigma	ς

Table 5.4 *Continued*

Character Entity	*Numerical Entity*	*Description*	*What's Displayed*
σ	σ	Greek small sigma	σ
τ	τ	Greek small tau	τ
υ	υ	Greek small upsilon	υ
φ	φ	Greek small phi	φ
χ	χ	Greek small chi	χ
ψ	ψ	Greek small psi	ψ
ω	ω	Greek small omega	ω
ϑ	ϑ	Greek small theta symbol	θ
ϒ	ϒ	Greek upsilon with hook symbol	ἐ
ϖ	ϖ	Greek pi symbol	π

Table 5.5 General Symbols

Character Entity	*Numerical Entity*	*Description*	*What's Displayed*
•	•	Bullet	•
…	…	Horizontal ellipsis	...
′	′	Prime	'
″	″	Double prime	"
‾	‾	Overline	‾
⁄	⁄	Fraction slash	/

Table 5.6 Letterlike Symbols

Character Entity	*Numerical Entity*	*Description*	*What's Displayed*
℘	℘	Script capital P	𝔓
ℑ	ℑ	Blackletter capital I	ℑ
ℜ	ℜ	Blackletter Capital R	ℜ
™	™	Trademark sign	™
ℵ	ℵ	Alef symbol	ℵ

Table 5.7 Arrows

Character Entity	*Numerical Entity*	*Description*	*What's Displayed*
←	←	Leftwards arrow	←
↑	↑	Upwards arrow	↑
→	→	Rightwards arrow	→
↓	↓	Downwards arrow	↓
↔	↔	Left-right arrow	↔
↵	↵	Downwards arrow with corner leftwards	↵
⇐	⇐	Leftwards double arrow	⇐
⇑	⇑	Upwards double arrow	⇑
⇒	⇓	Downwards double arrow	⇒
⇓	⇓	Downwards double arrow	⇓
⇔	⇔	Left-right double arrow	⇔

Table 5.8 Mathematical Symbols

Character Entity	*Numerical Entity*	*Description*	*What's Displayed*
∀	∀	For all	∀
∂	∂	Partial differential	∂
∃	∃	There exists	#
∅	∅	Empty set	^
∇	∇	Nabla	ℵ
∈	∈	Element of	∈
∉	∉	Not an element of	∉
∋	∋	Contains as member	∋
∏	∏	n-ary product	∏
∑	∑	n-ary sumation	∑
−	−	Minus sign	-
∗	∗	Asterisk operator	*
√	√	Square root	√
∝	∝	Proportional to	-
∞	∞	Infinit	
∠	∠	Angle	∠
∧	∧	Logical AND	∧
∨	∨	Logical OR	∨
∩	∩	Intersection	∩
∪	∪	Union	∪
∫	∫	Integral	∫

Table 5.8 *Continued*

Character Entity	*Numerical Entity*	*Description*	*What's Displayed*
∴	∴	Therefore	∴
∼	∼	Tilde operator	~
≅	≅	Approximately equal to	≅
≈	≈	Almost equal to	≈
≠	≠	Not equal to	≠
≡	≡	Identical to	≡
≤	≤	Less-than or equal to	≤
≥	≥	Greater-than or equal to	≥
⊂	⊂	Subset of	⊂
⊃	⊃	Superset of	⊃
⊄	⊄	Not a subset of	⊄
⊆	⊆	Subset of or equal to	⊆
⊇	⊇	Superset of or equal to	⊇
⊕	⊕	Circled plus	⊕
⊗	⊗	Circled times	⊗
⊥	⊥	Up tack	⊥
⋅	⋅	Dot operator	⋅

Table 5.9 Miscellaneous Technical Symbols

Character Entity	*Numerical Entity*	*Description*	*What's Displayed*
⌈	⌈	Left ceiling	⌈
⌉	⌉	Right ceiling	⌉
⌊	⌊	Left floor	⌊
⌋	⌋	Right floor	⌋
⟨	〈	Left-pointing angle bracket	〈
⟩	〉	Right-pointing angle bracket	〉

Table5.10 Geometric Symbols

Character Entity	*Numerical Entity*	*Description*	*What's Displayed*
◊	◊	Lozenge	◊

Table 5.11 Miscellaneous Symbols

Character Entity	*Numerical Entity*	*Description*	*What's Displayed*
♠	♠	Black spade suit	♠
♣	♣	Black club suit	♣
♥	♥	Black heart suit	♥
♦	♦	Black diamond suit	♦

Table 5.12 Latin Extended-A

Character Entity	*Numerical Entity*	*Description*	*What's Displayed*
&Oelig;	Œ	Uppercase OE ligature	Œ
œ	œ	Lowercase oe ligature	œ
Š	Š	Uppercase S caron or hacek	Š
š	š	Lowercase s caron or hacek	š
Ÿ	Ÿ	Uppercase Y umlaut	Ÿ

Table 5.13 Spacing Modifiers

Character Entity	*Numerical Entity*	*Description*	*What's Displayed*
ˆ	ˆ	Caret (circumflex)	^
˜	˜	Tilde	~

All of the symbols in Table 5.11 can be seen in Internet Explorer 4.0, but not in Netscape Navigator 4.0.

All of the characters in Table 5.12 can be seen in both Internet Explorer 4.0, but not in Netscape Navigator 4.0.

The characters in Table 5.13 can be viewed within Internet Explorer 4.0. Only the numeric form of these characters can be seen in Netscape Navigator 4.0.

In Table 5.14, everything from the en-dash to the single right-pointing quotation mark can currently be viewed within Internet Explorer 4.0. The exact same char-

Table 5.14 General Punctuation

Character Entity	*Numerical Entity*	*Description*	*What's Displayed*
		En-space	(n-sized space)
		Em-space	(m-sized space)
		Thin space	(Thin space)
‌	‌	Zero-width non-joiner	Nothing is displayed
‍	‍	Zero-width joiner	Nothing is displayed
‎	‎	Left-to-right mark	Nothing is displayed
‏	‏	Right-to-left mark	Nothing is displayed
–	–	En-dash	–
—	—	Em-dash	—
‘	‘	Left single quotation mark	‘
’	’	(High) right single quotation mark	’
‚	‚	Low quote mark	‚
“	“	Left double quotation mark	“
”	”	(High) right double quote mark	”
„	„	Double low quotation mark	„
†	†	Dagger	†
‡	‡	Double dagger	‡
‰	‰	Per thousand (mille) sign	‰
‹	‹	Single left-pointing quotation mark	’
›	›	Single right-pointing quotation mark	‘
€	€	Euro sign	¤

acters can also be seen in Netscape Navigator 4.0, but only when specified using the numeric entity form.

THE FUTURE OF SPECIAL CHARACTERS

As the World Wide Web becomes a truly global phenomenon, it is restricted more and more by its adherence to the alphabets used in the Western Hemisphere.

At the moment, most Web browsers support only the ISO 8859-1 standard, which is capable of supporting the following languages: Afrikaans, Basque, Catalan, Danish, Dutch, English, Faeroese, Finnish, French, Galician, German, Ice-

landic, Irish, Italian, Norwegian, Portuguese, Spanish, and Swedish. This may seem like a lot, but it misses many other European character sets, like Greek and Cyrillic, and does not describe characters in any Asian language.

The World Wide Web Consortium is proposing a new use for the generally under-used <META> tag that would tell the browser which character set it should use to display the characters the Web page contains. It would work by specifying the type of character encoding being used in the Web page by specifying its name—for example the Cyrillic alphabet is contained within the ISO-8859-5 standard, two different Japanese character sets are specified by the SHIFT_JIS and EUC-JP standards, and the current Unicode standard goes under the name UTF-16. Under this scheme, to specify a Web page that used Cyrillic characters, you would use the following code:

```
<META http-equiv="Content-Type" content="text/html;
charset=ISO-8859-5">
```

At the time of this writing there are over 190 different officially recognized names for various character sets. It is unlikely that they will all be adopted for use with the <META> tag, but you can expect that a number of them will. Table 5.15

Table 5.15 ISO Character Sets and the Alphabets They Describe

Name	*Alphabet*
ISO 2022-JP	Japanese
ISO 2022-CN	Chinese (currently at the proposal stage)
ISO 646-IRV	ASCII
ISO 8859-1	Latin 1
ISO 8859-2	East European
ISO 8859-3	Southeast Europe and Miscellaneous (Esperanto, Maltese)
ISO 8859-4	Scandinavian and Baltic
ISO 8859-5	Cyrillic
ISO 8859-6	Arabic
ISO 8859-7	Greek
ISO 8859-8	Hebrew
ISO 8859-9	Turkish
ISO 8859-10	Latin 6 (Inuit and Nordic languages)
ISO 8859-11*	Thai
ISO 8859-12*	Latin7 (Celtic)
ISO 8859-13*	Latin8 (Baltic Rim)
ISO 8859-14*	Latin9 (Sami)

*Proposed, not yet implemented

contains a short listing of some character sets that are thought to be likely candidates for adoption under this scheme.

Expect this particular area of the HTML standard to expand greatly in the short term, as the demand for support of non-European character sets on the World Wide Web grows.

CHAPTER 6

Color, Images, and Imagemaps

Adding images to your Web pages can serve many purposes; images can illustrate and clarify an idea, point out something of particular interest, and be a source of fun and entertainment for your viewers.

Images, depending upon their size and how many colors they contain, can be very large and take a great deal of time to download to a user's browser. Additionally, users who have monitors that display few colors will not get the same image quality as a user whose monitor can display many colors.

THE <IMG> TAG—ADDING IMAGES

Web page images are always one of two kinds: inline or external. Inline images can be displayed on the Web page by the browser, and external images need an external

viewer to be displayed to the user. There are two universally accepted inline image formats: GIF and JPG. The two popular Web browsers, Netscape Navigator and Internet Explorer, also display these file formats as inline images. If you choose to include images that are not in GIF or JPG format (such as TIF, PNG, or BMP), the Web browser may not be able to process and display them, and will ask the user to specify which application should be used to display your images (if it knows what to do with it at all). (More information on image file formats can be found later in this chapter.)

<IMG>

Element Name: Image tag.

Description: Used to insert images into the Web document. The <IMG> tag is an empty element, and does not have an end tag.

Attributes:

ALIGN= *ABSBOTTOM* | *ABSMIDDLE* | *BASELINE* | *BOTTOM* | *LEFT* | *MIDDLE* | *RIGHT* | *TEXTTOP* | *TOP*
Aligns the image according to the value you specify. Aligning an image LEFT or RIGHT causes the image to align with the left or right margin while the text flows around it. Aligning an image TOP, TEXTTOP, MIDDLE, ABSMIDDLE, BASELINE, BOTTOM, and ABSBOTTOM indicates the vertical alignment of the text relative to the image on the same line.

ALT= *text*
Specifies what text to display as an alternative to the image. This text is displayed by browsers who have images disabled and by text-only browsers such as Lynx. The ALT text is also often displayed first, before the image itself is loaded.

BORDER= # *pixels*
Specifies the image border size in pixels. BORDER=0 indicates that the image does not have a border. If the image is a hypertext link, the border color is the same as the LINK color. If the image is not a hypertext link, then the border color is the same as the TEXT color. Both the LINK and TEXT colors are specified in the BODY tag at the top of the hypertext document.

CONTROLS
Specifies the set of video controls to be displayed to control the play of an inline video. Used with the DYNSRC attribute, it is recognized by Internet Explorer only.

DYNSRC= *URL*
Specifies the filename or URL of an inline video. This attribute is recognized in Internet Explorer only.

WIDTH= # *pixels*
Specifies the width of the image in pixels. Specifying the width and height of the image allows the browser to load the image faster because it does not have to measure the image before displaying it. However, if the dimensions you specify are incorrect, your image will be stretched or shrunk to the size you specified, making your image appear distorted.

HEIGHT= # *pixels*
Specifies the height of the image in pixels. Specifying the width and height of the image allows the browser to load the image faster because it does not have to measure the image before displaying it. However, if the dimensions you specify are incorrect, your image will be stretched or shrunk to the size you specified, making your image appear distorted.

HSPACE= # *pixels*
Specifies the amount of space, in pixels, on the left and right sides of the image. Acts as padding between the image and the text or other objects surrounding the image.

ISMAP
Indicates that the image is an image map. This attribute is used alone within the tag, along with a hypertext link to a map file that specifies the sensitive coordinates of the image. The map file specifies what URL to go to when the user clicks on a particular area of the image.

LOOP= *number* | *INFINITE*
Specifies how many times an inline video will play. Specifying INFINITE or –1 will play the video indefinitely. Used with the DYNSRC attribute, it is recognized by the Internet Explorer only.

LOWSRC
Specifies the filename of a low-resolution image to be loaded before the higher resolution defined by the SRC attribute.

SRC= *URL*
Specifies the filename or URL of the image file.

START= *FILEOPEN* | *MOUSEOVER*
Specifies when the inline video will begin playing. FILEOPEN causes the video to play as soon as it is finished loading; MOUSEOVER causes the video to begin playing when the user places the mouse over the video clip. Used with the DYNSRC attribute, it is recognized within Internet Explorer only.

USEMAP= *URL*
Specifies the URL of the client-side image map. This attribute is recognized only by browsers with the ability to interpret client-side image maps. The USEMAP attribute is used with the ISMAP attribute to accommodate both types of image maps.

VRML= *filename* or *URL*
Specifies the filename or URL of an inline VRML world. This attribute launches a VRML viewer to display the VRML file. This attribute is recognized within Internet Explorer only.

VSPACE= # *pixels*
Specifies the amount of space, in pixels, on the top and bottom sides of the image. Acts as padding between the image and the text or other objects surrounding the image.

Sample:

```
<IMG SRC="kscthumb.gif" BORDER=1 ALIGN=RIGHT HEIGHT=40
WIDTH=35 HSPACE=3 VSPACE=3 ALT="Thumbnail picture of Kim">
```

The preceding code appears in a Web browser as shown in Figure 6.1.

The <IMG> tag is very flexible, and is becoming even more so as HTML

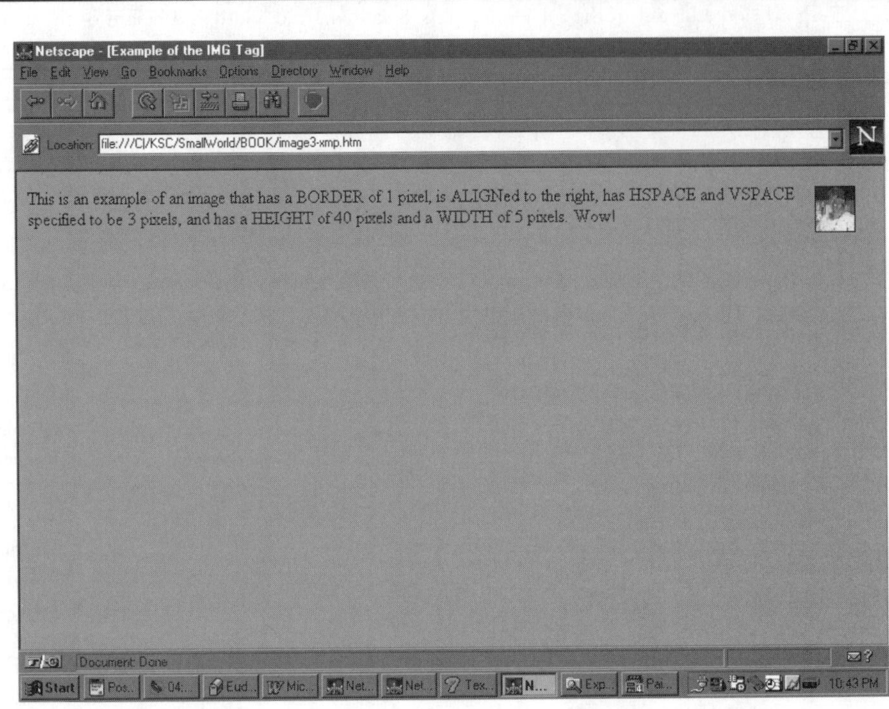

Figure 6.1 Example of the <IMG> Tag Using Several Attributes

develops. Using available <IMG> attributes wisely will produce a better Web page that users will enjoy visiting. Some useful tips to keep in mind are as follows.

- Use thumbnail images wherever possible. If you have a large, high-resolution image that your Web page cannot do without, create a small, low-resolution version to put on your Web page; then, put a hypertext link around that image that takes the user to the larger, higher-resolution image. This way the user is not annoyed by a long download they may not want, and users who want to see the image still can. The sample code for using thumbnails is:

```
<A HREF="ksc.gif"><IMG SRC="kscthumb.gif"></a>
```

- Use images only when they make sense. Covering your Web page with images that do not serve a definite purpose is pointless and annoying to your audience. Users who have to wait too long for useless images to load don't return for a second visit.

- Always specify the ALT attribute. Some users prefer text-only browsers such as Lynx, and there are many users who use graphical browsers and turn image-loading off. If you don't want to annoy users who would end up seeing only a generic indicator that an unexplained image exists, always provide the ALT text to describe the image they would be seeing. And be sensible when describing the image. If you have a banner image that says "Click here for deals," don't describe the image as Ad Banner, but by the message you intend to convey to the viewer.
- Always specify the HEIGHT and WIDTH attributes whenever possible. This allows Web browsers to reserve the correct screen space for the image before the image is downloaded, resulting in the image appearing in the browser window more quickly.
- Specify the BORDER, HSPACE, and VSPACE attributes to improve the layout of your Web document. Adding a border and space around your image will make your Web page look more elegant. Remember that a cluttered page turns users off.

Computers and Color

Before we delve further into the art of creating images for the Web, we need to look at how color is used by computers, and how different computers can interpret the same color in different ways.

Each computer operating system includes extensive routines devoted solely to the production of displaying text and images on-screen. The various types of text displays available to a particular computer is dependent upon the fonts available to that computer. Similarly, the number of colors a computer can display is dependent on the number of colors in its palette. The term *palette* originally referred to the small tray that painters use to hold their paint. Like a painter, the computer has to use the colors from its own palette and then try to "paint" the requested color on-screen. Like a painter, the computer can also mix colors together to get other, completely different colors.

But not all palettes are created equal. To take our painting analogy further, suppose the painter has only a small tray upon which to mix her paints. This means that the range of colors she can place on her painting is effectively limited. If she had a larger palette—and could therefore hold a larger number of color combinations—she could put more color on her canvas. In a similar manner, different computers have different palette sizes, offering more or less color combinations to the user (see Figure 6.2).

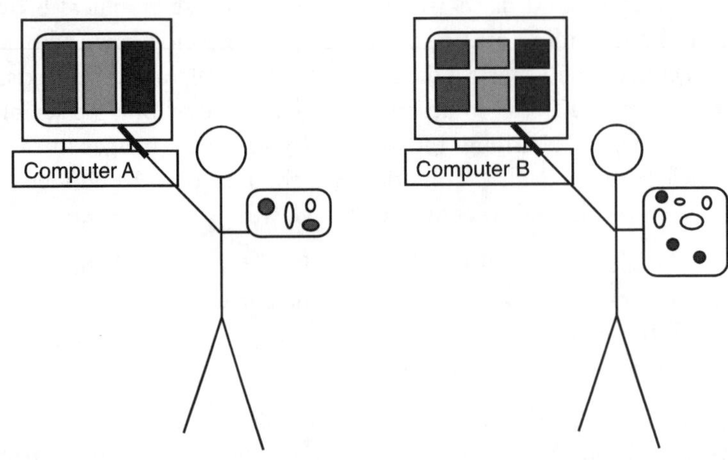

Figure 6.2 A Computer with a Larger Palette of Colors Can Produce More Colors than One with a Smaller Palette

This results in a situation that many experienced Web designers will have run into at least once: a page may look great on one computer, but looks terrible on another. For example, a blue on your system could look blue-green or gray on another computer. A color that appears solid on your screen may look mottled on another. A pair of high-contrast colors on your system may have little or no contrast on another system, or they may be two completely different colors.

You get the picture. The worst scenario is a page that looks perfectly fine on your system looks awful on another—so bad that it renders the page unreadable. So why does this occur?

Palette size is the answer—if your computer can display a larger number of colors than another computer can, then that other system has to come up with a way to approximate the colors that it cannot fully display. Problem is, different operating systems have different ways of displaying color on their systems; in other words, they may have color palettes that are of equal size, but the range of colors they can choose from is different. Also, no two computers display color in exactly the same way. Many people prefer different color, brightness, and contrast settings for their computers—variables that are completely outside of your control. Further, different computers display colors in different ways, and when they can't display a particular requested color, they often choose a poor alternative color to display.

A range of color options are available to computer displays, but most fall into one of three main types: those capable of displaying 256, 65,536, and 16.7 million colors. There are other types as well, particularly in the low-end, such as those displays capable of only 2 or 16 colors. You do not have to worry about designing Web sites that cater to these last two display types—they tend to belong either to obsolete systems incapable of surfing the Web, or to specialized, dedicated systems that would not be suitable for Web surfing either. However, you do have to think about the other display types when designing a Web site that uses color effectively.

Simple color displays and most gray-scale monitors can display up to 256 different colors (or if gray-scale, shades of gray), typical of most VGA and many Super VGA displays. Most Macintosh systems have a palette capable of handling at least 65,536 colors. Increasingly, there are more and more systems capable of displaying up to 16.7 million colors.

Problem is, if you make an image or choose a color attribute for a Web page on a computer that can display up to 16.7 million colors at once, you can count on the fact that it will look completely different on a system with a smaller color palette.

Here's what happens: The computer with the smaller color palette is given a signal to reproduce a particular color that it does not have in its color palette. This color value is then altered or *dithered* to another color that the second computer considers an approximation of the color specified. In a related situation, there are some computers whose graphic cards may have a large palette of colors, but can produce only a small fraction of them on-screen at any one time. As a result, the second computer has little choice but to paint colors that it thinks are close to the original, but in fact look much different to the viewer.

This problem is further complicated by the type of computer that may be used by the viewer. Typically, Unix and Macintosh computers tend to support larger palettes than do most Windows-based PCs. This is fine if you are creating Web pages that will be viewed only on similar systems to your own, but in most cases you can't count on this.

Many PCs are only capable of displaying a much lower palette range than a typical Macintosh or Unix system. Even in cases where PCs are advertised as having "true color" displays, they may in fact only be capable of displaying a small fraction of the total color palette available to them—usually 256 colors—at any one time.

Even among the same Macintosh and Unix machines, colors will be displayed in different ways. If you've ever gone to a store that sells color televisions, you will have noticed that color televisions do not display color the same way. Some can reproduce bright colors more effectively than others, some can produce blacker blacks, and others produce sharper images. The same is true for computer monitors. Even if you have a number of computers equipped in the same manner, you can expect minor idiosyncratic variances in the way they display color. And this doesn't take into account the computer user's own display preferences.

So there is really no way you can effectively guarantee that any color you use on your Web site will look *exactly* like it does on another system. So, what do you do?

You have two main choices: either decide from the outset that how color is displayed on other people's systems does not matter to you, or decide that it does matter and that you should use only those colors that are common to most computer systems. If you choose the first option, then read no further. If you choose the second, read on.

SPECIFYING COLORS

To use color effectively on your Web site so that it will be displayed on other systems with the minimum amount of dithering, design your Web pages to use no more than 256 colors. This is pretty much considered to be the universal palette for the Web.

So which 256 colors do you choose?

Before we can get into that, we have to look at how colors are specified on the Web. Colors can be set by Web authors in one of two ways: either by specifying a color by a name, or by its numerical equivalent.

Color names are the names given to specific color values on a palette. A lot of these are very familiar names for colors, such as black, red, white, and blue. These simple color names describe a specific type of black, red, white, and blue. There is a myriad of other color names for many of the different shades of color, such as olive, fuchsia, cadetblue, or chartreuse. A listing of the most widely-used color names can be found in Appendix D.

The other way colors can be inserted directly into a Web page by a Web author is by specifying a color's numeric value. Each color name has a corresponding numeric value. If you are using the 256-color palette, there is a corresponding color name for every numeric value for a color. But when you move beyond the 256-color palette, there are many, many more numeric values than color names available. Numeric color values therefore give the Web author access to a wider range of colors available on a computer's color palette. These numeric color values are specified in hexadecimal, a numbering system that uses base-16, instead of the more familiar base-10.

In our regular counting system, there are ten individual numbers ranging from 0–9. Numbers higher than 9 are represented by combining number values, for example 42, 491, or 1,298. The hexadecimal numbering system also uses the numbers from 0–9, but where we would normally count 10, instead the letter A is used. 11 is represented by the letter B, 12 by C, and so on up to the letter F, which is 15 in normal base-10. This makes for a base counting system with 16 characters (including 0). Base-10 and Base-16 are compared in Table 6.1.

Table 6.1 Base-10 and Base-16 (Hexadecimal) Values Compared

Base-10	*Base-16 (Hexadecimal)*
1	1
2	2
3	3
4	4
5	5
6	6
7	7
8	8
9	9
10	A
11	B
12	C
13	D
14	E
15	F

Just like base-10, numbers of higher value are achieved by placing numerals together. In hexadecimal, the base-10 number 16 is specified by the hexadecimal number 10. The base-10 number 26 is represented by the hexadecimal number 1A, and the base-10 number 256 is represented by the hexadecimal number FF.

The reason why the hexadecimal counting system was adopted is that it allowed the designers of the original version of Netscape Navigator an easy, convenient, and compact way for encoding 256 color values. The reason the designers of Netscape wanted 256 color values to describe each red, green, and blue elements is because 256^3 equals 16.7 million—the total number of colors used on the largest possible computer color palette.

To convert any hexadecimal value to decimal, multiply the first number by 16, then add the second number (see Table 6.2). For example, the hexadecimal value A has a value of 10 in base-10, so the hexadecimal number AA is 10 x 16 + 10 = 170.

When used to specify numerical color values on the Web, hexadecimal values are used in a triplet format: one hexadecimal number is used to specify the amount of red, green, and blue to be displayed.

A hexadecimal color triplet works like this: The first value describes the amount of red to be shown, the second the amount of green, and the third the amount of blue. A value of 00 means that none of the specified color is used, and FF (256 in base-10) means that the highest amount of a color is used. Here's a sample of the hexadecimal values for red, green, and blue, respectively:

Table 6.2 The 256 Hexadecimal Values Used To Specify Colors on the Web and Their Base-10 Equivalents

00 = 00	20 = 32	40 = 64	60 = 96	80 = 128	A0 = 160	C0 = 192	E0 = 234
01 = 01	21 = 33	41 = 65	61 = 97	81 = 129	A1 = 161	C1 = 193	E1 = 235
02 = 02	22 = 34	42 = 66	62 = 98	82 = 130	A2 = 162	C2 = 194	E2 = 236
03 = 03	23 = 35	43 = 67	63 = 99	83 = 131	A3 = 163	C3 = 195	E3 = 237
04 = 04	24 = 36	44 = 68	64 = 100	84 = 132	A4 = 164	C4 = 196	E4 = 238
05 = 05	25 = 37	45 = 69	65 = 101	85 = 133	A5 = 165	C5 = 197	E5 = 239
06 = 06	26 = 38	46 = 70	66 = 102	86 = 134	A6 = 166	C6 = 198	E6 = 240
07 = 07	27 = 39	47 = 71	67 = 103	87 = 135	A7 = 167	C7 = 199	E7 = 241
08 = 08	28 = 40	48 = 72	68 = 104	88 = 136	A8 = 168	C8 = 200	E8 = 242
09 = 09	29 = 41	49 = 73	69 = 105	89 = 137	A9 = 169	C9 = 211	E9 = 243
0A = 10	2A = 42	4A = 74	6A = 106	8A = 138	AA = 170	CA = 212	EA = 244
0B = 11	2B = 43	4B = 75	6B = 107	8B = 139	AB = 171	CB = 213	EB = 245
0C = 12	2C = 44	4C = 76	6C = 108	8C = 140	AC = 172	CC = 214	EC = 246
0D = 13	2D = 45	4D = 77	6D = 109	8D = 141	AD = 173	CD = 215	ED = 247
0E = 14	2E = 46	4E = 78	6E = 110	8E = 142	AE = 174	CE = 216	EE = 248
0F = 15	2F = 47	4F = 79	6F = 111	8F = 143	AF = 175	CF = 217	EF = 249
10 = 16	30 = 48	50 = 80	70 = 112	90 = 144	B0 = 176	D0 = 218	F0 = 250
11 = 17	31 = 49	51 = 81	71 = 113	91 = 145	B1 = 177	D1 = 219	F1 = 252
12 = 18	32 = 50	52 = 82	72 = 114	92 = 146	B2 = 178	D2 = 220	F2 = 252
13 = 19	33 = 51	53 = 83	73 = 115	93 = 147	B3 = 179	D3 = 221	F3 = 253
14 = 20	34 = 52	54 = 84	74 = 116	94 = 148	B4 = 180	D4 = 222	F4 = 254
15 = 21	35 = 53	55 = 85	75 = 117	95 = 149	B5 = 181	D5 = 223	F5 = 255
16 = 22	36 = 54	56 = 86	76 = 118	96 = 150	B6 = 182	D6 = 224	F6 = 256
17 = 23	37 = 55	57 = 87	77 = 119	97 = 151	B7 = 183	D7 = 225	F7 = 257
18 = 24	38 = 56	58 = 88	78 = 120	98 = 152	B8 = 184	D8 = 226	F8 = 258
19 = 25	39 = 57	59 = 89	79 = 121	99 = 153	B9 = 185	D9 = 227	F9 = 259
1A = 26	3A = 58	5A = 90	7A = 122	9A = 154	BA = 186	DA = 228	FA = 260
1B = 27	3B = 59	5B = 91	7B = 123	9B = 155	BB = 187	DB = 229	FB = 261
1C = 28	3C = 60	5C = 92	7C = 124	9C = 156	BC = 188	DC = 230	FC = 262
1D = 29	3D = 61	5D = 93	7D = 125	9D = 157	BD = 189	DD = 231	FD = 263
1E = 30	3E = 62	5E = 94	7E = 126	9E = 158	BF = 191	DE = 232	FE = 264
1F = 31	3F = 63	5F = 95	7F = 127	9F = 159	BE = 190	DF = 233	FF = 265

- FF0000 - RED
- 00FF00 - GREEN
- 0000FF - BLUE

Other colors can be created by combining different quantities of red, green, and blue. Here are a few other color combinations represented in their hexadecimal form:

- 000000 - Black
- 00FFFF - Aqua
- FF00FF - Fuchsia
- FFFF00 - Yellow
- FFFFF0 - Ivory
- FFFFE0 - Light Yellow
- DDA0DD - Plum
- F08080 - Light Coral
- D2B48C - Chocolate
- 228B22 - Khaki

It may look strange at first, but now that you understand the basics of hexadecimal counting, you won't feel intimidated when you see number combinations like these on a Web page.

There are many graphic programs (like the Color Picker in Photoshop) that express color values in regular base-10. If you need to convert a color from base-10 to hexadecimal, do the following math: divide the first value by 16, then subtract the integer, which becomes the first value of the two hexadecimal characters, and multiply the remainder by 16 for the second hexadecimal value. For example, say you have the base-10 number 99 to convert to hexadecimal. Divide 99 by 16 and you get 6.1875. The 6 is the first of the two characters of the hexadecimal number. Multiply the remainder 0.1875 by 16 and you get 3, which is the same in hexadecimal as in Base-10. So the decimal color value of 99 equals 63 in hexadecimal.

Link: There are easier ways of figuring out the base-10 to hexadecimal for various numeric color values. Here are some convenient Web sites that do the number-crunching for you, or show the equivalent color when a hexadecimal value is entered.

Colorama

http://www.10mb.com/brv/colorama.htm

Type in a hexadecimal color value and click a button to see what it looks like.

JavaScript Example of Hexadecimal to Decimal Conversion

http://cherubino.med.jhu.edu/~raj/MISC/dechexjs.html

A good JavaScript example that calculates between base-10 and hexadecimal values.

Decimal to Hex Converter

http://www.sci.kun.nl/thalia/guide/color/dec-hex.html

A simple base-10 to hexadecimal and vice versa converter program.

Also, if you have a scientific calculator, check its manual. Chances are it has a built-in function that will allow you to convert from one format to the other.

The Safety Palette

As mentioned previously, to ensure that you use colors that appear pretty much the same on all computers, you need to use colors from a range of 256 colors. Right?

Unfortunately, things aren't that straightforward. There are slightly different color palettes used by Macintosh- and MS-Windows-based systems. In fact, only 16 colors are common to both Macintosh and MS-Windows systems. For the record, they are: aqua, black, blue, fuchsia, gray, green, lime, maroon, navy, olive, purple, red, silver, teal, white, and yellow. That's it.

Fortunately, you are not restricted to these colors solely. Netscape Navigator and Internet Explorer improved upon this situation by implementing their own palettes that improve upon those provided by MS Windows-based systems. The color palette they use provides an exact color match for 216 of the colors between the two systems. That means your effective palette of colors is 216.

So what are the color values of this restricted but safe palette? The colors comprising this palette are all of the hexadecimal red/green/blue triplet values containing any combination of the following numbers: 00, 33, 66, 99, CC, and FF. If you use these colors and no others, you can be sure that the colors will look the same across most computing systems. (A full list of these color values can be found in Appendix D.) Try using these colors when specifying color values directly (for such things as fonts or background colors), or when creating images for the Web. Increasingly, many graphic packages offer you a Web palette, which uses the Web-optimized colors described here.

Link: Need some help to choose the colors for use on your Web page? There are also a number of programs designed to help you choose color values interactively for your Web page. Here are just a few of them:

Color Manipulation Device

http://www.meat.com/software/cmd.html (MS Windows 16-bit/32-bit versions available)

Color Scheme Designer

http://www.agt.net/public/bcoppock/software.html (MS Windows 95)

ColorFinder

http://www.acmetech.com/ (Macintosh)

IMAGE FILES FORMATS

For a long time two image file types have reigned supreme on the Web: the Graphic Interchange Format (GIF) and the Joint Picture Experts Group (JPEG or JPG) file format. Both have a number of features that recommend themselves for use on the Web. In addition to JPG and GIF, there are other image file formats vying to be contenders for serious use on the Web. This section looks at all of the major image file formats, their unique features, plus their strengths and weaknesses.

Static-Image File Formats

The original image file formats used on the Web were all static-image file formats; in other words, the formats displayed still pictures only. Moving image or animation file formats was not originally considered for use on the Web. The original HTML 2.0 standard specified four file types for use on the Web: GIF, JPEG/JPG, PICT, and XBM. Of these original four, GIF and JPEG/JPG have become the clear winners for use on the Web. PICT and XBM didn't catch on because they were platform-specific image file formats. PICT is a Macintosh-based image file format known as the Macintosh Picture format. Originally designed to capture the images generated by the native Macintosh program QuickDraw, it stores colors from the full 16.7 million color palette. XBM is a Unix-based image file format known as the X Bitmap format. XBM has a rather limited monochrome palette, and the information is stored as a C language data file, which is then read by a compiler, rather than an image program. Both image file formats are native to their own operating system and have never made successful inroads onto other computing systems. GIF and JPEG/JPG caught on because they were universal.

The GIF and JPEG/JPG image file formats have become dominant on the Web. Of all of the image file formats used on the Web, only the GIF format is understood

by all graphical Web browsers on all of the most commonly used operating systems. This is the preferred format if you want to make your images in your Web pages readable to all. It also has other unique advantages over other image file formats, including the ability to make a specific color transparent, and that they can be used to create simple animations. However, GIF files use a relatively small 256 color palette, making them generally unsuitable for reproducing photographic-quality images. GIF files use compression internally to reduce their overall size, but they do not always produce the smallest possible image when compared to other image file formats.

The JPEG/JPG format is the other main image file format of choice for the Web. Its main advantage is that it uses the full 16.7 million color palette, useful for displaying photographic-quality images. Unlike the GIF format, none of its colors can be rendered transparent. It uses a better compression scheme than does the GIF file format, and will generally produce a better-looking and smaller file size than a GIF file would. Although the smaller file size means it takes less time to download, this advantage can be offset by the fact that it takes the browser longer to read and display the image, due to the larger color palette it must display.

Each image file format has a lot to recommend itself, but each is best suited to particular circumstances. Remember that the color restrictions of the various palettes apply equally to images as well as to other color elements on a Web page. Because of that, you may want to restrict the use of JPG/JPEG image files on your Web site. The 256 colors used by the GIF file format more closely approximate that used by the safety palette, and so is safer to use.

GIF files are also capable of displaying short animation sequences. Though not part of the original GIF specification, most Web browsers (including Internet Explorer and Netscape Navigator) are able to read and display GIFs containing multiple images as a dynamic animation. This has its plus and minuses, all of which are discussed later in this chapter, but it makes for a very convenient way to make small animation sequences without having to invest large sums of money into the equipment needed to produce video or movie files.

It is also possible to specify that a particular color embedded in a GIF file is rendered transparent by the browser, so that the background of the Web page shows through. This is a very handy feature, and enables Web designers to insert images into their Web pages that can appear to float on the Web page. GIF transparency is another feature that is covered in more depth later in this chapter.

Although the JPEG/JPG file format is generally the best file format when small file sizes are required, this is not the case when the original image is in black and white. The compression scheme for JPEG/JPG file format was optimized for color images, and not for black and white images. As a result, if you are using black and white images on your Web site, you may find GIF files to be smaller and better suited to the task.

Both the GIF and JPEG/JPG file formats are capable of progressive or interlaced loading capabilities, though this feature is a relatively recent addition to the JPEG/JPG format. *Progressive loading* means that it is possible to make an image file load piece by piece, so that the whole image does not have to be read by the browser before it begins to start displaying something to the viewer. Though these capabilities are discussed in more depth later in this chapter, as more users get faster connections to the Internet, this feature is being used less and less. In the case of GIF files, this feature can also increase the overall size of a GIF file.

JPEG/JPG image files use a better compression scheme than do GIF files, and as a result JPEG/JPGs tend to be smaller than GIFs. One of the ways it achieves this greater compression is by dropping the occasional pixel value here and there. For example, if an image contains a line made up of five black pixels, then a red pixel, and then four more black pixels, a JPEG/JPG will typically lose the red pixel and encode a line of 10 black pixels. As a result, this "glossy" compression scheme used by JPEG/JPG image files can often make the resulting image appear grainy, and can look a bit rough. This is especially the case for particularly small image files. For this reason you are better off creating small image files as GIFs for such things as customized buttons or tiny pictures.

Table 6.3 summarizes the chief features of each file format.

Other image file formats are beginning to vie for attention on the Web. The standard Windows bitmapped file format (BMP), familiar to many PC users as the image file format used for their Windows background, can be viewed only through Internet Explorer. It offers no file compression so its file size is relatively large compared to either a GIF or JPG/JPEG file. However, it is a very common file format, and is the native saved file format used by Windows Paint and widely compatible with many common business applications. Another file format getting

Table 6.3 The GIF and JPG File Format Features Compared

	GIF	*JPG*
Color Palette	256 colors	16.7 million
Compression Rate	Low	High
Transparency	Yes	No
Animation Capabilities	Yes	No
Photo-Quality Color Reproduction	No	Yes
"Grainy-ness"	Less	More
Progressive Loading Capabilities	Yes	Yes

some attention is the Portable Network Graphics (PNG) file format, which has been devised as a successor to the GIF format. It was designed primarily to replace the GIF image file format, which became instantly unpopular in the Web community when Unisys and CompuServe jointly announced on New Year's Day 1995 that any program that used the GIF file format would now be required to pay them royalties. This was because GIFs use Unisys' patented LZW compression scheme within the file. Understandably, this did not endear the GIF image file format among software developers, and as a result fewer programmers want to support this image file format within their programs. It can support a full 16.7 million color palette, and it can often provide better compression than the equivalent GIF image.

The PNG image file format contains a number of desirable improvements over the GIF format it is designed to replace:

- On average, better compression than GIF, typically 10–30% better
- A nonpatented, lossless compression scheme
- A more efficient interlacing scheme
- An enhanced, true-color palette (higher than 16.7 million colors) and specialized support for grayscale images
- Transparency support

The nonpatented and publicly available specification for PNG, and the fact that it has been officially adopted by the World Wide Web Consortium as a standard image format for the Web are all reasons that are encouraging software developers to include PNG support within their programs.

One feature lacking from the PNG format that may prevent it from replacing GIF entirely on the Web is that it lacks support for storing multiple images to create simple animations.

Link: Interested in learning more about the PNG format?

http://www.boutell.com/boutell/png/

The World Wide Web Consortium's recommended specifications for the format (may be a bit too technical for most people).

http://www.wco.com/~png/

PNG (Portable Network Graphics) Homepage Has anything and everything you might want to know about the PNG image file format.

http://www.wco.com/~png/pngapbr.html

WWW and Online Browsers with PNG Support

A subsection of the previously listed site, but worth pointing out on its own account, it lists the most current information on Web browsers that support the PNG format.

At the time of this writing, only the Internet Explorer 4.0 supports the PNG format—Netscape Navigator does not. Most graphics packages, especially those that are geared towards producing Web-friendly graphics, already support the PNG format, so it is as easy to create PNG files as any other image file format. It remains to be seen whether PNG will succeed the GIF file format, despite the hype it originally aroused when it first came out.

Link: At the time of this writing PNG is supported within Netscape Navigator only by using a graphics plug-in program, and then only when the image is inserted into a Web program by using the <EMBED> or <OBJECT> tag. Here is a quick listing of available PNG plug-ins if you want to try out PNG on a Web page.

http://www.siegelgale.com/

PNG Live plug-in (23-bit MS-Windows operating systems, Macintosh)

http://www.program.com/panacea/index.shtml

PNG Plug-in (OS/2)

http://home.pages.de/~rasca/pngplugin/

PNG Magick plug-in (Unix/X)

Keep in mind that native PNG support within Netscape Navigator has been promised for some time, so you may not need these plug-ins at all by the time you read this.

THE JOY OF GIFS

The GIF image file format contains several features that make it stand out among the other image file formats. These three features are: the ability to create a transparent key color in an image, the ability to create an image that downloaded piece-by-piece in successive lines (interlaced), and the ability to add multiple images within a GIF and then run them so they are animated. Each of these aspects of the GIF image file format will be looked at in this section.

There are in fact two types of GIF files. The original GIF format was set back in 1987, and all it could do was to display a still image in 256 colors. This GIF format was called GIF87a. The successor to the GIF87a format was set in 1989 and is called the GIF89a format, and contains many other features, including animation and transparency. Most graphic programs today automatically create GIF89a format files, and can also save any existing GIF87a format files into the updated GIF89a format for you.

If you find yourself unable to add any of the features described in this section to your GIF file, chances are it is saved to the old GIF87a format, so try saving it as to the GIF89a format. Also, if you are trying to display an animated GIF file, make sure you are using Internet Explorer or Netscape Navigator 2.0 or better, since the ability to display animated GIF files properly was not incorporated until the release of those respective browsers.

Transparent GIFs

The GIF89a format also enables Web designers to specify a particular color (known as a *key* color) to be rendered transparent. This means that wherever that color appears within the GIF, it allows whatever is behind it on the Web page to come through.

There are many programs that allow you to do this. Most professional graphics programs have this feature, as do a number of shareware programs. Many allow you either to specify the color that will be rendered transparent, or use a color-picker tool so that you can select the color instead (see Figure 6.3).

The difference between the use of a transparent GIF and a nontransparent GIF can be striking, as the examples in Figures 6.4 and 6.5 show.

Note how the image in Figure 6.5 merges seamlessly with the Web page, whereas it sticks out like a sore thumb in Figure 6.4.

The decision as to which color should be made transparent should be made well before you get to that point in your graphic program. If you intend to use GIF transparency in an image, make you sure you plan for it. Remember, when you set a color to be transparent, you set it for the entire file, not just a particular part of an image. If you do not take this into account, you can end up with some odd-looking images.

If you are designing a graphic or logo that will be made into a GIF that uses transparency, try to reserve a color that will later become transparent. In the previous example, the background white color was reserved, and deliberately not used within any display elements when designing the logo.

Some people still try to create the same sort of effect by creating an image that will have the same background as that on the Web page. Even if you do get a good color match on your system, chances are it will look completely different on another

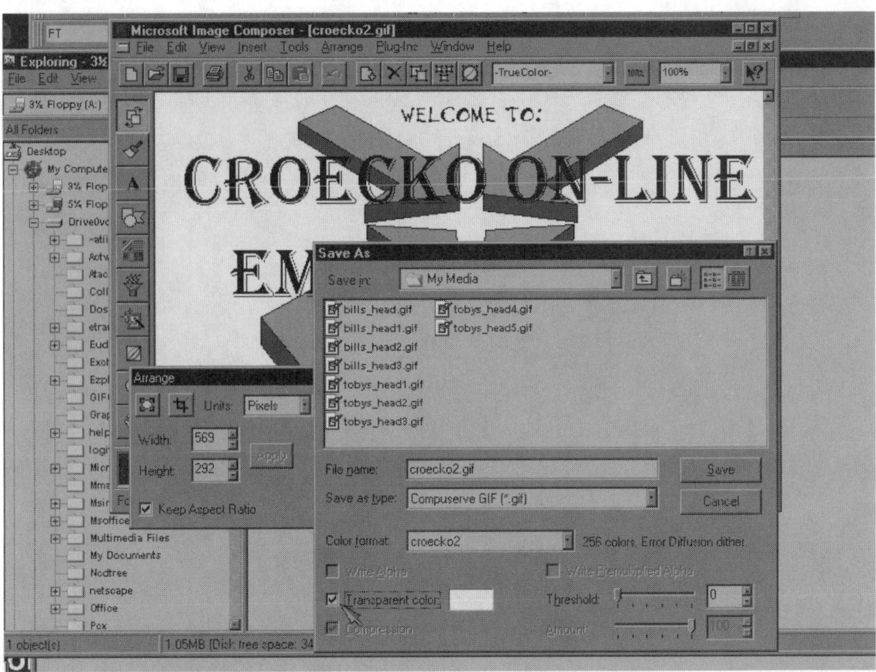

Figure 6.3 Setting the Transparent Color in a GIF File Using Microsoft Image Composer

system, and the image will still stand out like a sore thumb. Creating transparent GIF images are easy, and it is worth investing the time to get the right tools and do things properly.

Link: There are a number of programs and resources that can create transparent images for you, such as the following shareware programs:

WebImage

http://www.group42.com/webimage.htm (MS- Windows 16- and 32-bit)

LView Pro

http://world.std.com/~mmedia/lviewp.html (MS- Windows)

Even if you don't have the tools on your computer, you can add

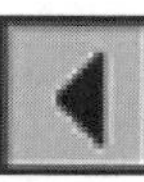

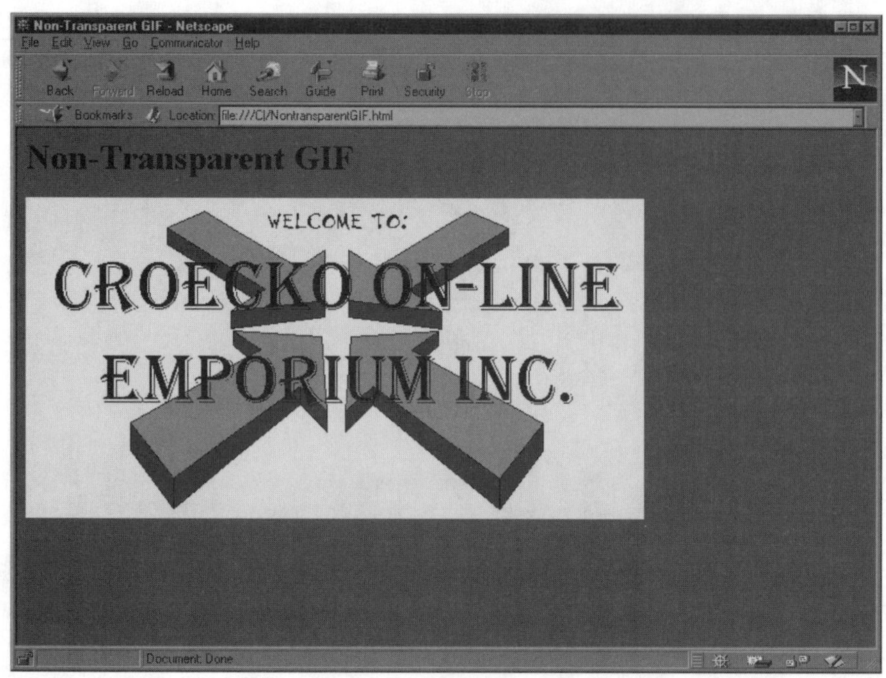

Figure 6.4 An Image Displayed with No Transparency

transparency to your existing GIF files on the Web by using the following online tool:

Fefe's Transparency Apparatus

http://www.inf.fu-berlin.de/~leitner/trans/

Interlaced GIF Files

In the early days of the Web, back when Mosaic was the browser of choice, there was one continual source of annoyance for those early users: you had to wait for the whole page to be transferred to your computer before you could view it. This problem was compounded by the relatively slow links to the Internet many users had at the time. When Netscape Navigator came on the scene, it immediately became a success because it displayed the text and images of a Web page while it was still downloading the Web page.

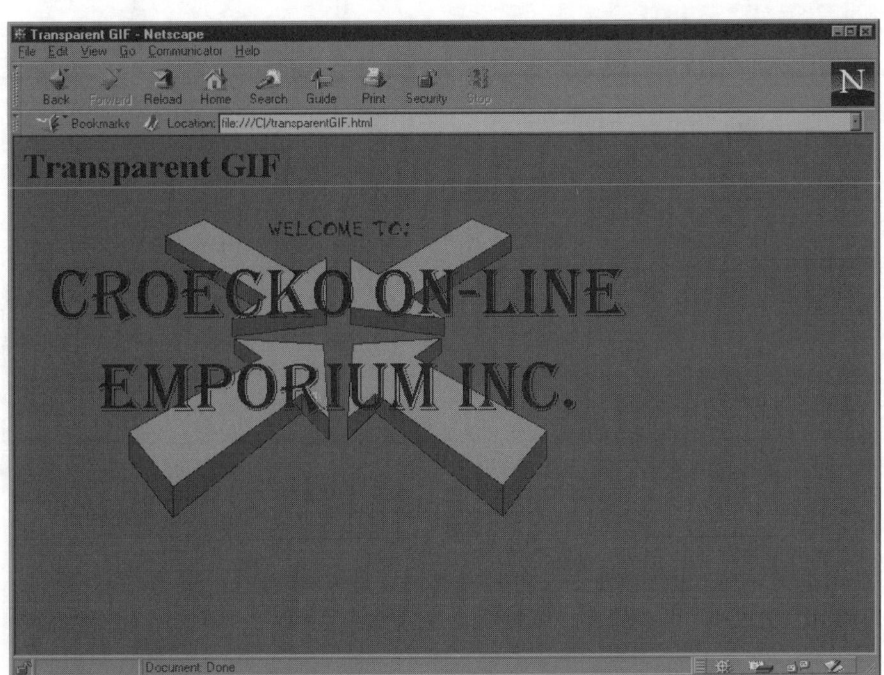

Figure 6.5 The Image from Figure 6.4 Displayed with a Transparent Background

Soon after this, people started using the interlacing feature of GIF files so that the whole picture did not have to be entirely downloaded before the user finally got to see something.

Here's the way interlacing works: As a file is downloaded, one in every three or four lines that comprise the image are displayed in succession. When the bottom of the file is reached, another pass is made, which fills in some of the intervening lines on the page. Over the course of a few passes the entire image is filled in and displayed. The example in Figure 6.6 shows how this is done.

There are a number of programs that can add interlacing to your GIF files. Typically, all you have to do is specify the file to be interlaced, and the program does everything else for you.

This technique is little used these days—the increased bandwidth available to many people, along with the fact that this technique tends to increase the overall size of the file has rendered this technique nearly obsolete.

There are some disadvantages to using this format, however; adding interlacing

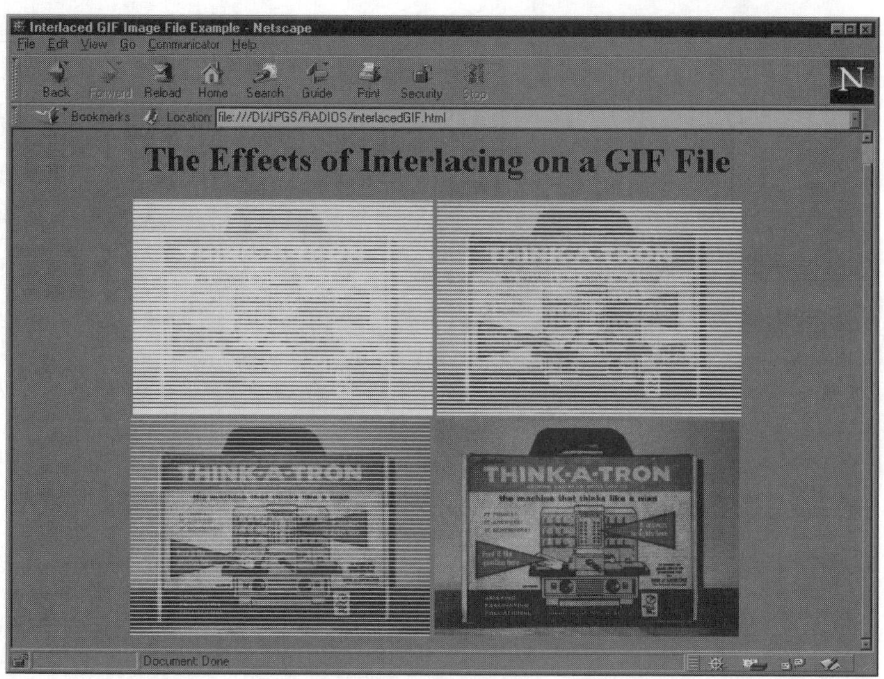

Figure 6.6 Sample of How an Interlaced GIF File is Progressively Loaded by a Web Browser

to a GIF file adds more information to the file, increasing its size. For example, the original GIF file used to illustrate Figure 6.5 was 24,638 bytes in size, but after saving it as an interlaced file, its file size increased to 25,729 bytes. This increase may not seem like much, but it tends to increase relative to the overall size of the GIF, and if you use a lot of them on a Web page the effects will add up.

Link: There are several programs you can download that will add interlacing to your GIF files (among other effects), including the following:

LView Pro

http://world.std.com/~mmedia/lviewp.html (MS- Windows)

GIF Construction Set for Windows

http://www.mindworkshop.com/alchemy/gifcon.html (Windows)

GIFConverter

http://www.kamit.com/gifconverter.html (Macintosh)

WebImage

http://www.group42.com/webimage.htm (MS-Windows 16- and 32-bit)

GIF Animations

A simple way to create effective animation on the Web is to use the animation feature built into the GIF89a image file format. The animation is achieved by inserting multiple GIFs into a single file, then inserting commands so that the images are played in sequence, creating a simple animation.

In effect the GIF animation works like a flip-card cartoon, as each image is displayed for a fraction of a second before the following image in the sequence is displayed.

As is implied by the name of the file format, it has been possible to create animated GIFs since 1989, but they only started appearing on the Web some time after the release of Netscape Navigator 2.0, the first browser that supported this feature of the GIF89a image file specification. It is currently supported within many browsers, including the two most commonly used Web browsers: Netscape Navigator 2.0 and higher, and Microsoft Internet Explorer 3.0 and above. Perhaps the best part of all of this is the fact that no additional plug-ins or software are needed to display these animations, whereas many other animated file types do.

They are easy to create, are relatively small when compared to video or movie files, and can be inserted in a Web page by using the <IMG> tag, just like any other image file. Once the file is downloaded, it resides in the cache of the user's computer, so no further downloads are required.

To have a better understanding of how GIF animation works, it is helpful to know a little bit about how an animated GIF89a file is put together. The header at the beginning of the file describes such things as the type of GIF file format available (either GIF87a or GIF89a), used by graphics programs to identify the type of file. Information that defines the height and width of the GIF image. The header also contains information on the type of color palette used by all of the images in the GIF file—whether it is a 16-bit palette, gray-scale, full 256-color palette or a palette containing a user-defined palette of colors. In most GIF images information detailing the image comes next (the "image block"), but in animated GIFs other information is inserted first.

A control block in the animated GIF file controls the ways in which the image that follows it should be displayed. A control block is inserted before every image

contained in the file, which tells the program displaying such things about the GIF as to whether or not a selected color is transparent. Embedded in this same area of the file is any information pertaining to whether or not the program displaying the image should delay showing the following image in sequence for a set amount of time. At the end of the file is a trailer, which closes off the file.

Before you begin to create an animated GIF file, you need a series of image files to edit (or at the very least, a single image you can manipulate within an animation-creation program) that will become the series of frames in your animation. Figure 6.7 depicts six images of a cat that will be used in an example. The action is as follows: in sequence, the cat is shown blinking, and then sticking out her tongue.

To compile a GIF animation file, use a GIF animation program to create a new GIF file that is set to the dimension of the individual image files. All of the images were then inserted in turn into the program. The control blocks added in the file tell the image program to delay displaying the following image by a certain amount

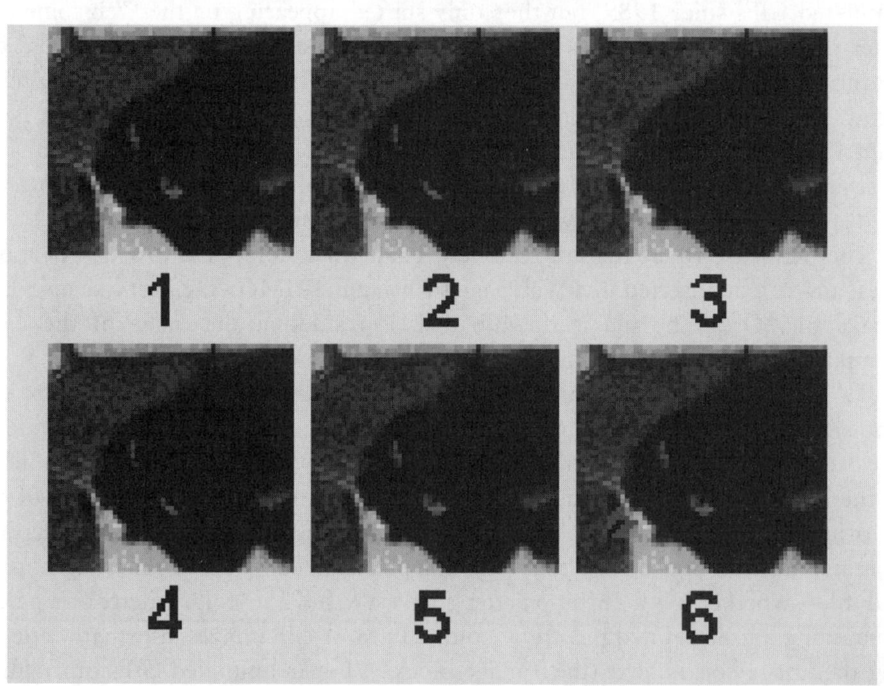

Figure 6.7 Six Individual Images that Will Comprise an Animated GIF File

of time that can be set in the program. A loop element was then added to the beginning of the file so that the animation will display continuously. Figure 6.8 shows how this was done using GIF Construction Set against a Web page displaying the images being used.

Link: A number of programs can help you make animated GIF files, including the following:

GIF ANIMATOR (MS-Windows)

http://www.ulead.com/

GIF Animator for Windows 95

http://www.microsoft.com/sbnmember/download/download.asp

GifBuilder (Macintosh)

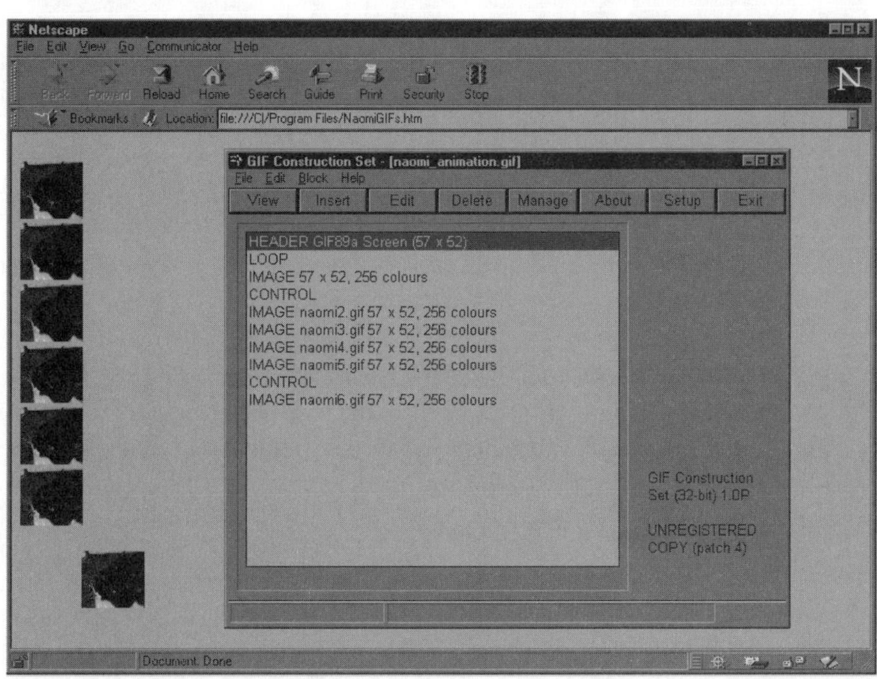

Figure 6.8 Creating an Animated GIF in GIF Construction Set

http://iawww.epfl.ch/Staff/Yves.Piguet/clip2gif-home/GifBuilder.html

GIF Construction Set (Windows)

http://www.mindworkshop.com/alchemy/gifcon.html

Gif.gIf.giF (Macintosh and Windows)

http://www.cafe./net/peda/ggg/

Note that there are a number of limitations on animated GIFs:

- They cannot be used as a background GIF file on a Web page
- The restricted, 256-color palette of GIF files
- There is no way a user can stop the animation once it has begun

In addition to these factors, animated GIF files can become very large very quickly, as more frames and control statements are added to the file.

Some GIF animations are constructed so that when a user's computer comes across them, it is so computing-intensive that it delays the loading of other elements on a Web page. This is most often seen in such things as banner ads, which are deliberately designed this way to draw the user's eyes to it. This is done by adding control statements before each image, and maximizing the amount of time necessary before each image is loaded. Although this technique is arguably effective at getting the user's attention, it detracts from the experience of viewing the Web page. By creating an annoyed viewer, you are not helping your cause much. Finally, keep in mind that too many animated GIFs on a Web page make it appear very busy, and will drive users away.

Link: Why go through all of the bother of creating your own GIF files when you can download one from the Web? There are plenty of online archives on the Web that you can freely download and use on your Web pages. Here are a few of them:

AlDogg's Animated GIF Gallery

http://members.aol.com/drclone/animate.htm

Contains the typical navigational buttons along with such extras as Star Trek, Godzilla, and Beatles animated GIFs.

ddcn's Animated Gif Page

http://206.123.26.2/ddcn/animated.htm

A good collection of basic animated GIFs.

The 1st Internet Gallery of GIF Animation

http://members.aol.com/royalef/gifanim.htm

The first and still one of the best—an extensive selection of animated GIFs and information about the format can be found here.

Stepping Stones Gif Animation Gallery

http://www.ssanimation.com/index.shtml

Contains a number of GIF animations and Web images.

Progressive JPEGs

Progressive JPEGs use an idea similar to that of interlaced GIFs—when downloaded, they display progressively more of the image over several passes. Progressive JPEG files are displayed much more smoothly than an equivalent interlaced GIF file. In many cases you may not even be aware that an image has been loaded piece-by-piece—all of a sudden it just seems sharper.

Though interlaced GIFs are losing favor on the Web, progressive JPGs are gaining ground. The format is supported within Netscape Navigator 2.0 and higher, and Internet Explorer 3.0 and higher. One of the other advantages of this format is that because of the compression scheme used, progressive JPG images can actually be *smaller* than the original, untouched JPG!

The main disadvantage of this format is that while the two most popular browsers understand it, many other browsers do not. Those that do not understand this format generally do not display any image at all. This is expected to change if the format becomes widely adopted in the future.

Link: Want to learn more about progressive JPGs and how to make them? Check out the following sites.

The JPEG Playground

http://www.phlab.missouri.edu/~c675830/jpeg_tests/testgrnd.htm

A good information resource for those who are interested in learning more about the progressive JPG format.

Pegasus Imaging Corporation

http://www.jpg.com/

Produces the PICPress program, an add-on program that works with Adobe Photoshop to produce JPG files that use progressive loading.

JPEG Transmogrifier

ftp://ftp.dev-com/developers/intouch/transmogrifier.sea.hqx

A standalone graphics application for the Macintosh.

Progressive JPEG Information

http://www.in-touch.com/pjpeg2.html

Good resource page for those interested in learning more about progressive JPGs.

Optimizing Your Images

There are many things you can do to reduce the overall size of your image files. This is a good goal to shoot for since smaller file sizes mean an image on your Web site takes less time to download from your Web site than a larger file.

There are a number of programs that will help optimize your GIF, JPEG/JPG, and other file types for you, often without any noticeable difference in picture quality. They achieve this increase by doing a combination of the following:

- Reduce and optimize the number of colors used in the palette of your image
- Remove any interlacing if the image is an interlaced GIF
- Use better compression techniques than those typically used in creating the image format

The results can vary widely, but in some cases you can reduce the file size of an image by up to 75% or more, as Figure 6.9, taken from PhotoImpact GIF Optimizer shows.

If you are trying to optimize an animated GIF, there are other techniques you can do to help reduce the size of the image. Using GIF optimizing programs, you can determine the minimum areas in which the animation actually occurs, and create a bounding box that defines the area of the animated GIF in which the animation occurs, which is almost always smaller than the size of the full image. Once this is known, the program simply computes where the changes in the animation occur, and that is all that is animated.

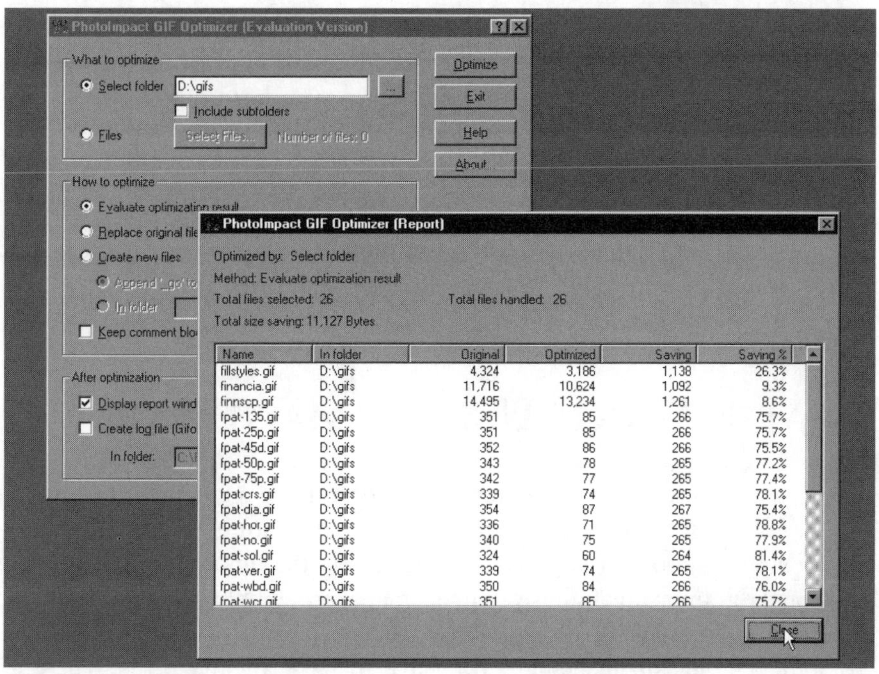

Figure 6.9 Reductions in File Size Achieved by Optimizing a Number of Image Files

Link: A number of good tools are available on the Web to help you optimize the size of your image files. Here's a listing of some of them:

DeBabelizer (Macintosh and MS-Windows)

http://www.equilibrium.com/

A program good at reducing the number of colors used within an image.

HVS ColorGIF (Macintosh and MS-Windows)

http://www.digfrontiers.com/

A program that provides immediate feedback on reduction settings. Also includes fixed palette reduction for images, and has the palettes used by Netscape, Macintosh, and Windows operating systems built in.

GIF Wizard

http://www.gifwizard.com/

A cleverly designed online utility that will help reduce the file size of the GIF files on your Web site, or on your hard drive.

PhotoImpact GIF Optimizer

http://www.ulead.com/

A program that can optimize a number of images in a directory quickly and easily.

Creating and Using Imagemaps

Imagemaps are increasingly an effective way of guiding your users through your Web site. Toolbars, navigational buttons, and other features can greatly aid your users, providing a more visual means of traversing the links that make up a Web site. Though graphically intensive, imagemaps are highly effective at creating professional-looking Web pages.

To start creating an imagemap, you have to have an image file. There are a number of factors to keep in mind when creating a file destined to be an imagemap. Try to keep the following things in mind.

- Keep the number of colors used in the image to a minimum
- If you are using a small file try using a GIF; if a large file, use a JPG
- If possible, try to use the same image file(s) repeatedly through the Web site
- The smaller the overall file size, the better

All of these factors are aimed at keeping the amount of time needed to display the image at a minimum. Essentially, by keeping the file size as small as possible, you reduce the total amount of time needed to download the image. If you use the same image or images repeatedly for imagemaps on your Web pages, once they are downloaded, the images will be subsequently drawn from the user's cache.

The other element needed to create an imagemap is the associated text file containing a number of URLs that are associated with areas contained within the image. A Hotlinks is defined within this file by the Web designer, who specifies certain regions that define a link a user can click on. When the user clicks on it, either the browser or the Web server compares the location of the click to the areas that correspond to a list of URLs. If a match is found, the associated Web page is requested from the Web server and then sent to the user.

Link: There are a number of programs that will create imagemaps for you. Here is a listing of a few of them:

http://weyl.zib-berlin.de/imagemap/Mac-ImageMap.html

A Macintosh program designed for Web servers that also runs the WebSTAR, MacHTTP, or NetPresenz programs.

http://www.mediatec.com

LiveImage

An easy-to-use WYSIWYG program for 32-bit MS- Windows platforms that can be used to generate client-side imagemaps.

http://galadriel.ecaetc.ohio-state.edu/tc/mt/

Map This

A freeware WYSIWYG editor for Windows 95 that creates imagemaps for NCSA, CERN, or CSIM formats.

Mapedit

http://www.boutell.com/mapedit/

A WYSIWYG imagemap program for the MS-Windows and Unix operating systems. Supports both client- and server-side imagemap formats.

There are three types of image map formats the Web author can choose from: server-side imagemaps, client-side imagemaps, and a combination of the two known as client-side imagemaps with server-side support. The following are brief descriptions of each format.

- Client-side imagemaps use map data embedded within the Web page itself. When a user clicks on a mapped region, the information is processed by the Web browser. It does not require any CGI programming, and though not universally supported, it is supported within popular browsers like Netscape Navigator and Internet Explorer.
- Server-side image maps use a separate map data file located on the Web server. When a user clicks on a link, it is processed by the Web server, not

the Web browser. It can be used by all Web browsers and requires a CGI program to work.

- Client-side with server-side support combines the best of both worlds. It processes the image as a client-side imagemap for those browsers that can understand it, and for those that can't it provides server-side support instead.

Though client-side is becoming the norm as more Web browsers are able to support it, the type of imagemap styles recommended is client-side with server-side support for general compatibility across different browsers.

If you intend to create complex imagemaps, the use of an imagemap editor is highly recommended, as it will greatly speed the process of creating the map file. If you cannot get ahold of a good imagemap editor (and there are plenty available for downloading from the Web), use a simple image that will tell you the exact *x, y* coordinates of the various points over the image you want to make into hotlinks.

As stated earlier, if you opt to create a client-side imagemap, the information on where the hotlinks are created for the imagemap is contained within an HTML file. Server-side imagemaps are formatted text files stored on a Web server, and are accessed by sending imagemap coordinates to the server, which interprets and acts upon the information.

<MAP> . . .<MAP>

Element Name: Map tag.

Description: Describes the beginning and end of a client-side image map.

Attributes: None.

Associated Tags: <AREA>

<AREA>

Element Name: Area tag.

Description: Defines the hotspots in a client-side imagemap.

Attributes:

ALT= *text*
Sets the text to appear when the cursor from the user's browser passes over the hotspot.
COORDS= *x,y*
Sets the *x,y* coordinates of the hotspot area.
HREF= *URL*
Sets the link associated with each hotspot.
NOHREF
Sets a region that does not contain a link.
NOTAB (Internet Explorer only)
Describes the tab-able order of a hotspot within an imagemap.
SHAPE= *CIRCLE | POLYGON | RECT*
Specifies the type of hotspot shape. RECT is the default.

- CIRCLE: "center x, center y, radius" values
- POLYGON: the successive x1, y1, x2, y2, etc. points of the polygon
- RECT (default): "left, top, right, bottom" values

TABORDER= *number* (Internet Explorer only)
Sets the tab-able order of a hotspot within an imagemap.

Associated Tag: <MAP>

Sample Code:

```
<MAP>
<AREA SHAPE="RECT" COORD="98,34,23,15"
HREF="http://www.longUnlikelyUrl.net/index.html">
<AREA SHAPE="CIRCLE" COORD="200, 155, 35"
HREF="http://www. longUnlikelyUrl.net/stuff.html">
<AREA SHAPE="POLYGON" COORD="371,235,126,339,190,207"
HREF="http://www.longUnlikelyUrl.net/moreStuff.html">
</MAP>
```

The <MAP> container tag works in conjunction with several <AREA> tags to construct a client-side imagemap. Essentially, the <MAP> tag defines the beginning and end of the imagemap code, and the <AREA> tag describes where the hotspots reside.

The SHAPE and COORD attributes work together: the SHAPE attribute of the <AREA> tag is used to set the type of shape described by the COORD attribute, which describes the point values of the shapes. All of the shapes are closed, so that each shape describes a fixed area that has a definable border. The SHAPE attribute can take three values: RECT, CIRCLE, and POLYGON. CIRCLE describes a circle or ellipse, defined by COORD as: center x, center y, radius. RECT sets a rectangle, defined by COORD in left, top, right, bottom *x,y* coordinates. Finally, POLYGON sets an irregular, multisided shape, and is defined by COORD by several successive *x,y* vertices for the polygon. If the beginning and end coordinates for the polygon do not close automatically, a final link is inferred by the browser that closes the polygon.

The HREF attribute of the <AREA> tag defines the hyperlink associated with the hotspot described by SHAPE and COORD. If no link is used, the NOHREF attribute can be used to specify that a region does not contain a link. NOHREF is handy if you want to have a placeholder in your imagemap—it reserves an area of the imagemap that can be used later when the Web page it is to link to is made. The NOTAB and TABORDER attributes are for Web designers who want to specify a tab-able order for the hotspots. A user pressing the tab key works through the hotspots in the order indicated by the TABORDER attribute. If this is not desired for a hotspot (for example, a hotspot that has not been linked to a valid Web page yet), use the NOTAB attribute so that the area will never be selected in this way. These last two attributes have only recently been introduced within Internet Explorer, and it is the only browser at the present time that understands them. Finally, the ALT attribute sets the text to be displayed by the browser when the mouse hovers over a defined hotspot on the imagemap.

If multiple <AREA> tags specified in a client-side imagemap overlap, the first to be specified in the list takes precedence over any others.

The image in Figure 6.10 depicts a man's face, which has been turned into an imagemap. The hotlinks are contained within the shaded areas that overlap the image, each leading to a specified URL.

The client-side data that is produced within the HTML file looks like this:

```
<HTML>
<HEAD>
<TITLE>
Keith's Profile image map page
</TITLE>
<META NAME="GENERATOR" CONTENT="LiveImage">
</HEAD>
<BODY>
<P>
<!-- Image tags modified by LiveImage for Client Side
Image Map insertion -->
<IMG SRC="Keith's Profile.jpg" USEMAP="#Keith's
Profile" BORDER=0></P>
<!-- Start of Client Side Image Map information -->
<MAP NAME="Keith's Profile">
<!-- #$-:Created by LiveImage available at
http://www.mediatec.com -->
<!-- #$-:Unregistered copy (Kschengi) -->
<!-- #$VERSION:1.26 -->
<!-- #$DATE:Mon Jun 23 22:22:04 1997 -->
<!-- #$GIF:Keith's Profile.jpg -->
<AREA SHAPE=CIRCLE COORDS="164,71,32"
```

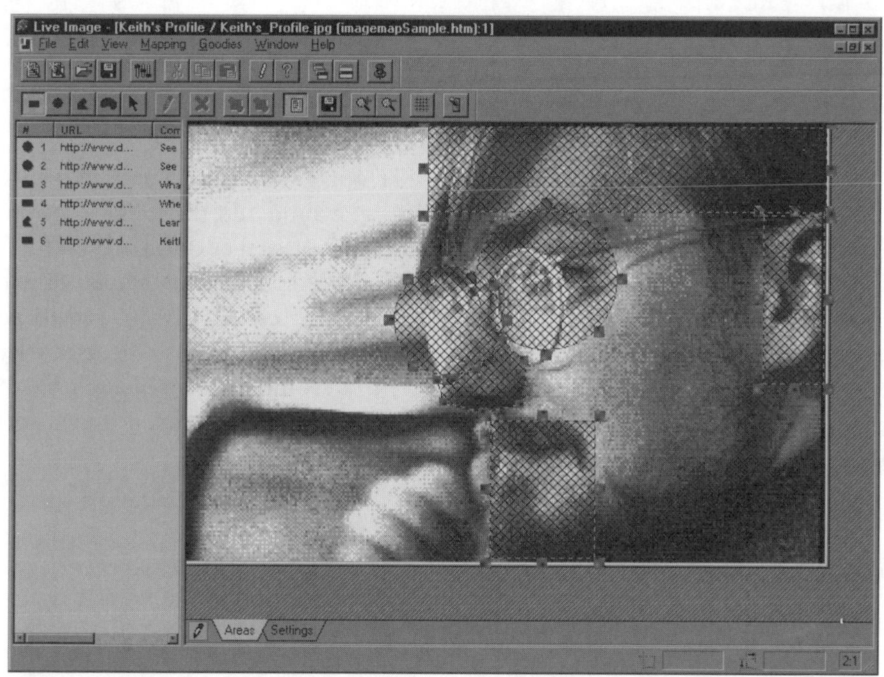

Figure 6.10 Creating an Imagemap within Live Image

```
HREF="http://www.doesNotExist.org/see.html" ALT="See
what Keith sees!">
<AREA SHAPE=CIRCLE COORDS="118,89,25"
HREF="http://www.doesNotExist.org/see.html" ALT="See
what Keith sees!">
<AREA SHAPE=RECT COORDS="264,42,292,118"
HREF="http://www.doesNotExist.org/listen.html"
ALT="What does Keith listen to?">
<AREA SHAPE=RECT COORDS="110,2,293,40"
HREF="http://www.doesNotExist.org/hair.html"
ALT="Where does Keith get his hair done?">
<AREA SHAPE=POLY
COORDS="117,127,135,132,152,128,155,122,154,108,144,99,
132,112,122,116,114,117,117,127"
HREF="http://www.doesNotExist.org/sniff.html"
ALT="Learn more about Keith\'s keen sense of smell!">
<AREA SHAPE=RECT COORDS="139,136,186,198"
```

```
HREF="http://www.doesNotExist.org/munch.html"
ALT="Keith\'s favorite munchies.">
</MAP>
<!-- End of Client Side Image Map information -->
</BODY>
</HTML>
```

The previous example shows a client-side only imagemap. To make this a client-side imagemap with server-side support, we would add the ISMAP attribute of the <IMG> tag, which works in conjunction with the USEMAP="#Keith's Profile" already present in the HTLM code. USEMAP specifies the name of the file on the Web server containing the imagemap coordinates; ISMAP is used to pass along the specific *x,y* coordinates from the browser to the server as the user selects a hotspot. The server-side information file "Keith's Profile" is a simple text file that contains the same information as the client-side HTML file, just in a different form. It looks like this:

```
#Keith's Profile
circle see.html 164,71,32
circle see.html 118,89,25
rect listen.html 264,42,292,118
rect hair.html 110,2,293,40
poly sniff.html
117,127,135,132,152,128,155,122,154,108,144,99,132,112,1
22,116,114,117,117,127
rect munch.html 139,136,186,198
poly contact.html 342,189 444,211 462,166 461,154
370,133 343,189
```

Though it differs from the HTML code in the client-side imagemap, it is not hard to read and understand. Each line begins with the type of shape it describes, followed by the name of the URL it links to, and then the various *x,y* coordinates that make up the hotspot. Typically, this information is held in the */cgi-bin* directory on the Web server, the same directory that normally holds all of the CGI scripts for a Web site.

If you are creating server-side image maps, make sure you know which type of Web server you have, because you have to specify which type you are using in your server-side imagemap. The two formats are CERN and NCSA, and they differ only in the fact that the name of the program that acts upon the information must be contained within the imagemap.

For CERN servers, this program is called htimage, and for NCSA server it is called imagemap. A couple of code examples that demonstrate how they are used follows.

NCSA format:

```
<A HREF="http:// www.doesNotExist.org
/cgi-bin/imagemap/~my website/index.html">
<IMG SRC="Keith's Profile.jpg" ISMAP></A>
```

CERN format:

```
<A
HREF="http://www.doesNotExist.org/cgi-bin/htimage/~my
website/index.html">
<IMG SRC="Keith's Profile.jpg" ISMAP></A>
```

CHAPTER 7

Forms

Most people think of forms—if they think of them at all—in terms of the annoying, paper-based forms that are a necessary nuisance of modern life. Whether you are filling out a job application, doing your taxes, completing a census or filling out a contest ballot, you are filling out a form of one sort or another. Bureaucracy thrives on forms, and so does the Web.

Don't get the wrong idea—forms can be found everywhere on the Web, but they don't have to be the typical, dry forms you find elsewhere. Forms are put to many uses on the Web: If you've filled out a survey, posted some feedback on a Web site or done a keyword search on a search engine like Yahoo! (see Figures 7.1 and 7.2), you have filled out a Web-based form.

Wherever some form of interactive feedback is required, you are likely to find a Web-based form. Without forms, the Web is a one-way medium—forms are a means that allows the Web master a way of getting information for and from the

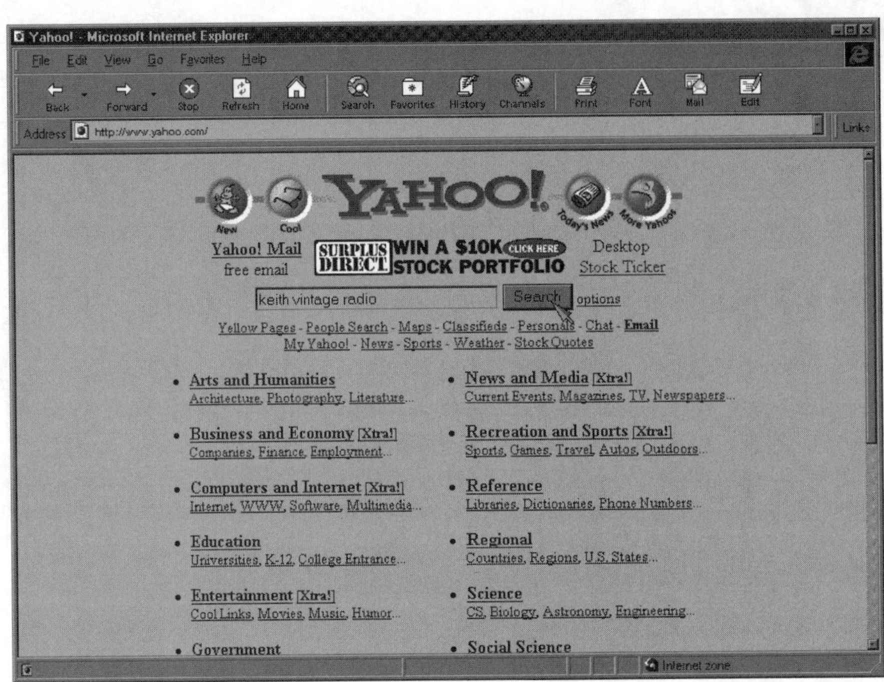

Figure 7.1 Doing a Keyword Search at Yahoo!

user. Forms make the Web truly interactive; without forms there's no convenient way of purchasing goods online, finding Web sites of interest at a search engine, or even telling a Web master how much (or how little) you like their Web site.

Forms have long been a part of the Web, and have been an integral part of it since the HTML 2.0 specification. A well-crafted Web form looks very professional and impressive, but the basic elements necessary for creating a Web form are simple. Creating forms on the Web is easy to do: you simply specify the right HTML codes, and the form appears in the browser.

Using standard HTML tags, you can create forms containing the following features:

- A list of selectable items a user can choose from
- A checkbox list a user can select multiple items from
- A radio button list a user can select a single item from
- Textfields to enable the user to enter text

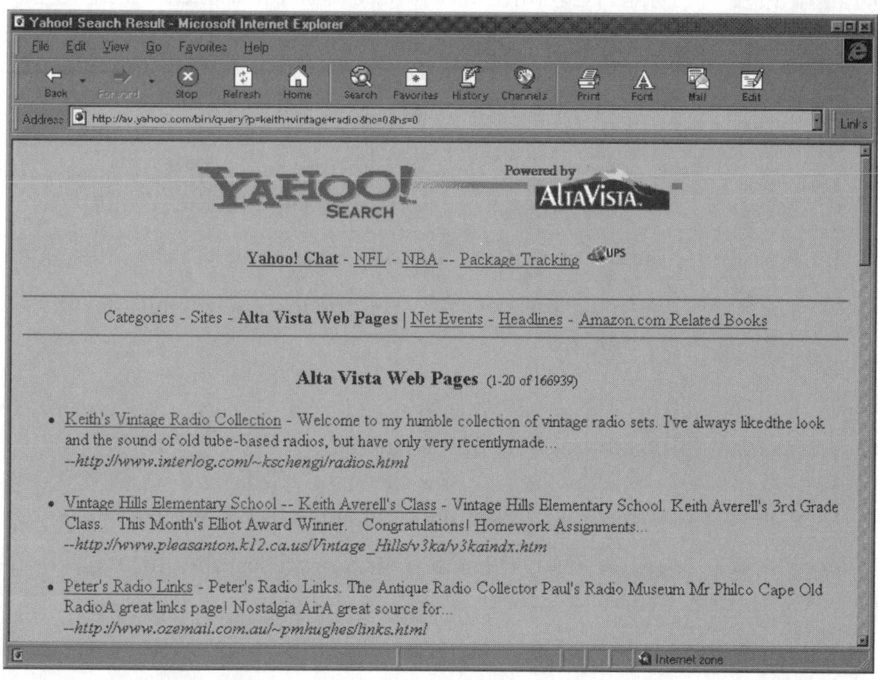

Figure 7.2 The Results of the Search

- Submit, reset, and other buttons allowing the user to send a form, or to alter its contents before submission

There are also a number of features that allow the Webmaster to add additional useful information to the form, including the ability to add fields for entering passwords and identifying fields to distinguish a form to the Webmaster. You can use any or all of these elements on a Web page.

WEB FORM FUNDAMENTALS

Although it is easy to construct the appearance of a Web-based form, a working Web-form is not just a pretty face. Three basic structures go behind the construction of any Web-based form. The first is the Web page containing the form information itself. The second, and probably the most important element is the program that processes the information contained within the form. Finally, there's the actual Web

server that runs the program and processes the information given to it by the program. Figure 7.3 depicts the three pieces necessary for implementing forms on the Web.

Although these three pieces are necessary for processing Web forms, there are several ways in which the information contained within a form is processed. The basic transaction process works like this:

1. A user fills out information in a form, and submits the results.
2. A script on the server receives the form, and processes the information.
3. The script returns a message to the user, acknowledging that the form data has been received.

This is still the most common form process to be found on the Web. Consider a typical transaction process at a Web search engine:

1. You fill in a keyword or two in a field, and click a Submit button.
2. The search engine takes this information and searches through its database for matching keywords.
3. A message is sent back to you, (hopefully) filled with Web sites that match the keywords you submitted.

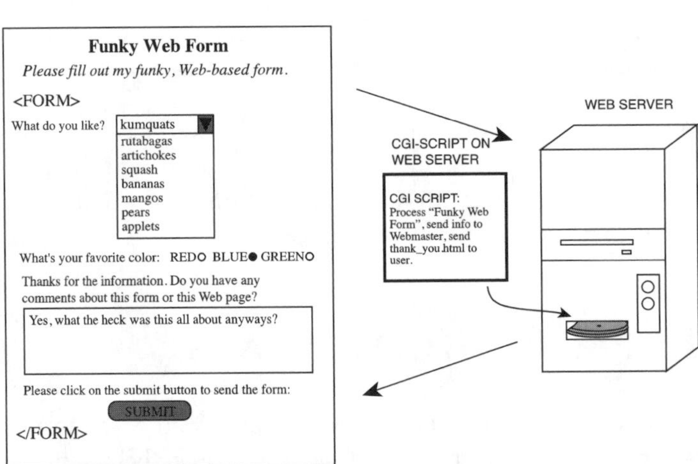

Figure 7.3 The Three Pieces Needed To Process Web Forms

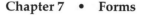

We saw part #1 and part #3 of that process in Figures 7.1 and 7.2 when a couple of keywords are submitted to the Yahoo! search engine, and get the resulting keyword match page back.

It is also quite common for the information from the form to be sent not to the user (who may simply get an acknowledgement page), but to the Web master or another recipient entirely. This transaction process allows for such things as online shopping to simple feedback forms and emails.

Up until quite recently, there was only one way to implement the programming part of this process: through the use of Common Gateway Interface (CGI) scripts. CGI scripts reside on the server, and use a programming language—most typically a language called Perl, though almost any programming language will do—to process the information from the form. More recently, with the introduction of JavaScript, this typical transaction process for forms has been changed, allowing for a greater range of possibilities. JavaScript code is contained within the Web page, and it can do some basic preprocessing before sending the resulting information to either the user or another intended recipient of the form data. Whereas a CGI script means that a person must send information to the server before the information contained in a form is processed, the form can be made to change interactively according to the type of data the user inputs over the course of the form using JavaScript. For example, if a user is entering information about his or her favorite color and selects the color blue, a form element lower down on the same page can be changed so that the form can get further refined information. So, instead of submitting the form to the Web server to begin the next part of the process, an interactive JavaScript form can contain this information internally within the Web page, and can update a list element that further refines the user's choice of color by updating the selectable values (i.e., navy, teal, aquamarine) within the same page.

A whole book can be written on CGI (and many of have already been written) so we will not look at CGI in detail here. For more information on JavaScript, see Chapter 13, "Dynamic Documents." There are also many good sources on the Web where you can obtain preformatted CGI and JavaScripts—once you have the fundamentals of form-construction under your belt, check out these sources so you can tie everything together.

Tip: If you want to implement CGI scripts on your Web pages, make sure you have proper access to your Web server. If you subscribe to an Internet Service Provider, check to see what their policy is regarding running CGI scripts on their Web server. Many ISPs either do not allow their members to run CGI scripts on their Web servers, or only allow them to run a few ready-made scripts. This is because CGI scripts work at a deeper level on the Web server than simple Web pages, and an inexperienced beginner could inadvertently provide a hacker with easy

access and control over a Web server. Check your ISP's policy on CGI scripts before trying to implement any of them.

Note that forms can look quite different depending on the operating system or browser used, as Figures 7.4 and 7.5 show. Figure 7.4 is taken from a Unix-based version of Netscape, and Figure 7.5 is from Internet Explorer.

Don't worry about this too much when designing your forms; though you may not have direct control over the look of the form, the functionality of the form will be the same.

Creating Web Forms

As we previously mentioned, it is very easy to make a Web-based form. All you need is the right HTML code, and your browser takes care of how it is displayed.

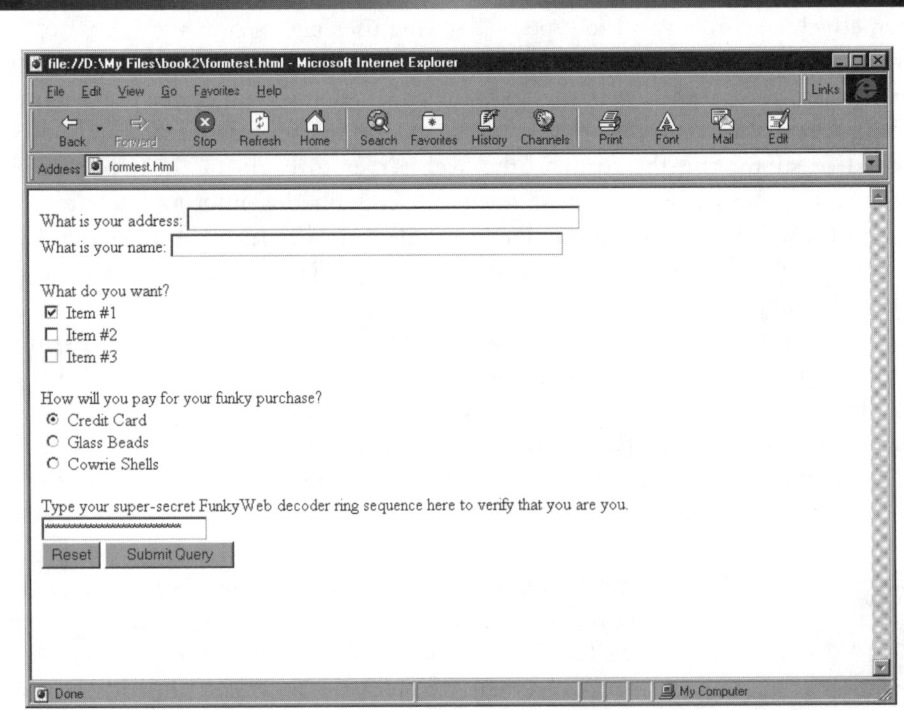

Figure 7.4 Netscape: Different Browsers Running on Different Operating Systems Can Display Very Different-Looking Results

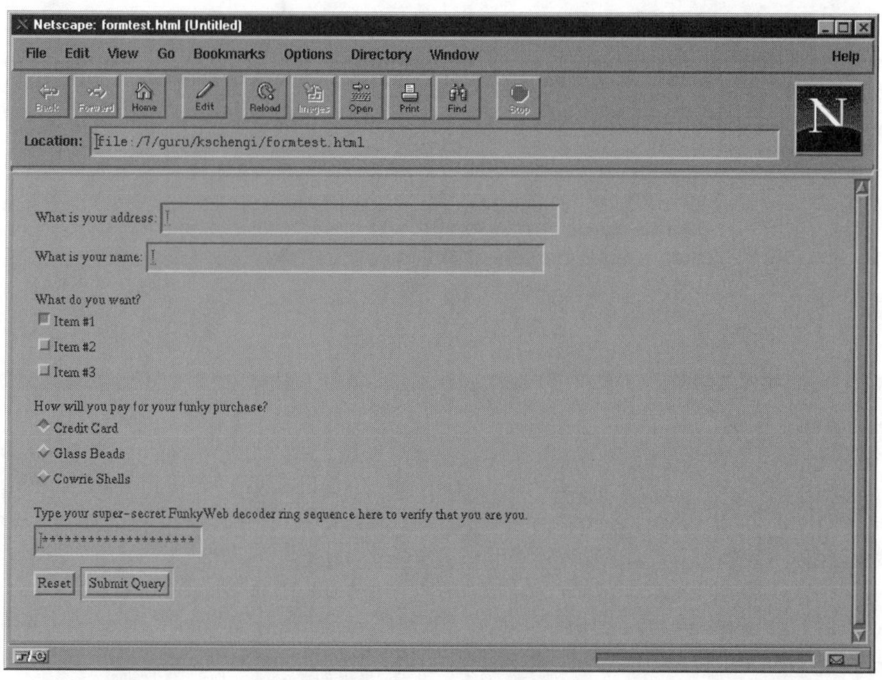

Figure 7.5 Different Browsers Running on Different Operating Systems Can Display Very Different-Looking Results

The tag used to define and encompass an area of a Web page as a form is the <FORM> tag, described in detail next.

<FORM> . . .</FORM>

Element name: Form tag.

Description: Contains and defines the elements that make up an online form.

Attributes:
ACTION= *URL*
Specifies the URL that processes the contents of the form.
ENCTYPE= *MIME type*
Specifies the type of media type used to encode the information contained in the form.
METHOD= *POST | GET*
POST specifies that information from the form is sent to the server as a set of NAME=VALUE pairs separated by ampersand (&) characters. GET specifies that infor-

mation from the form is sent to the server through the environment variable QUERY STRING.
TARGET= *text*
Specifies the name of the frame in which the browser should display the form results after the user submits the information contained in the current form.

Associated with: <INPUT>, <TEXTAREA>, <OPTION> <FIELDSET>, <LEGEND> and <SELECT>.

Sample Code:

```
<FORM METHOD="POST"
ACTION="http://www.myfunkyfunkysite.ca/luv my form">
Please enter the following information: <BR>
Your Full Name: <INPUT TYPE=TEXT>
<INPUT TYPE=RESET> <INPUT TYPE=SUBMIT><BR>
</FORM>
```

The <FORM> tag has four distinct attributes: ACTION, ENCTYPE, METHOD, and TARGET. Of these attributes, only the ACTION and METHOD attributes are required.

The ACTION attribute specifies the destination that the form's information should be sent to. In a nutshell, the ACTION attribute tells the Web server where the data contained in the form should go, and it tells the form to which inbox the form data should go. This inbox typically is located on a local Web server, usually a-URL or an email address. (Information sent to an email address is typically sent using the mailto: format, which does not require any CGI programming to work. Mailto: forms are covered in detail later in this chapter.)

The ENCTYPE attribute specifies the type of media type (i.e., the MIME type) used to encode the information contained within the form. The default filetype for ENCTYPE is application/x-www-form-urlencoded, which sends the data from the form in a URL encoded format. The other possible value for ENCTYPE is multipart/form-data, which enables the form to send additional information, like other files, to provide additional information or instructions to the Web server along with the original data from the form. (For more information on MIME types, see Chapter 2.)

METHOD tells the form how the information in the form should be sent to the Web server. METHOD has two values: POST and GET. POST specifies that information from the form is sent to the server as a set of name/value pairs separated by ampersand (&) characters. GET specifies that information from the form is sent to the server through the environment variable QUERYSTRING. METHOD=GET (the default setting) takes the data from the form and sends this information to the URL specified by the ACTION attribute. The other value of METHOD, POST, instead sends the data from the form as an encoded stream of characters to a Web server. The POST method is generally preferred, since this way is the more flexible of the two, and because some Web servers automatically truncate the data sent to it via the GET method.

The TARGET attribute is used when an acknowledgement Web page is to be posted to a specific Frame within a Framed Web page. It takes a text value that specifies the name of Frame in which the browser should display the form results once the user submits the information contained in the form.

As you can see, the <FORM> tag does more than simply define the area of the Web page that contains form information—it also defines how that information is sent, and even in a few cases, where an acknowledgement should be sent.

In addition to the numerous form elements you can insert within a Web form, you can also use almost all text formatting tags and other such elements within forms. You can even use list tags and tables to better separate form elements, you but note that you *cannot* nest one form within another.

The <FORM> tag is like a canvas, and various elements like checkboxes, radio buttons, and text fields create the picture. Without these elements you would have a blank form, containing all of the means necessary to send data along to the server, but no means to actively enter that data. It would be like having a blank slate without a piece of chalk to write with.

The following HTML tags describe the elements that can define form elements. Note that how these HTML form tags are displayed are entirely dependent on the browser or operating system being used. The same Web form can look very different when viewed under different circumstances. However the form is displayed, rest assured that the functionality of the form and its elements will remain the same across browsers and operating systems.

Individual form element tags are used to create various types of form types when seen through a Web browser. The most commonly used tag is the <INPUT> tag, an empty tag that has a number of attributes that specify the type of form element to be displayed.

<INPUT>

Element name: Input tag.

Description: Specifies the type of form element displayed within a form.

Attributes: INPUT TYPE=BUTTON NAME="*text*" TYPE="*text*" VALUE="*text*"
Creates a button to be used by a JavaScript program.
INPUT TYPE=CHECKBOX (CHECKED) NAME="*text*" TYPE="*text*" VALUE="*text*"

Creates a checkbox that can be enabled or disabled by the user. CHECKED indicates the default selection.

INPUT TYPE=FILE NAME="*text*" TYPE="*text*" VALUE="*text*"

Enables the user to specify a filename that serves as input for the form.

INPUT TYPE=HIDDEN NAME="*text*" TYPE="*text*" VALUE="*text*"

Inserts a value that is not displayed to the user. Usually used to identify the form to the server.

INPUT TYPE=IMAGE (ALIGN) [BUTTON] BORDER URL

Allows an image file to be displayed within a form button.

INPUT TYPE=PASSWORD (MAXLENGTH, SIZE) NAME="*text*" TYPE="*text*" (VALUE="*text*")

Creates a text field for typing in passwords. The SIZE value sets the width of the field in characters.

INPUT TYPE=RADIO (CHECKED) NAME="*text*" TYPE="*text*" VALUE="*text*"

Creates a radio button that can be enabled or disabled by the user. CHECKED indicates the default selection.

INPUT TYPE=RESET

Displays a button displaying the word Reset.

INPUT TYPE=SUBMIT

Displays a button displaying the word Submit.

INPUT TYPE=TEXT (MAXLENGTH, SIZE) NAME="*text*" TYPE="*text*" VALUE= "*text*"

Inserts a text field where users can type information (default).

Associated Tags: <FORM>, <TEXTAREA>, <OPTION> <FIELDSET>, <LEGEND> and <SELECT>.

Sample Code:

```
<FORM METHOD="POST"
ACTION="http://www.myfunkyfunkywebsite.ca">
What is your address: <INPUT TYPE=TEXT SIZE=50 NAME="your
address"> <BR>
What is your name: <INPUT TYPE=TEXT SIZE=50 NAME="your
name"> <BR>
<P>
What do you want? <BR>
<INPUT TYPE=CHECKBOX NAME="buy it" VALUE="item1" CHECKED>
Item #1<BR>
<INPUT TYPE=CHECKBOX NAME="buy it" VALUE="item2"> Item
#2<BR>
<INPUT TYPE=CHECKBOX NAME="buy it" VALUE="item3"> Item
#3<BR>
<INPUT TYPE=HIDDEN VALUE="This is funkyweb's purchasing
form #2">
<P>
How will you pay for your funky purchase? <BR>
<INPUT TYPE=RADIO NAME="pay for it" VALUE="credit"
CHECKED> Credit Card <BR>
<INPUT TYPE=RADIO NAME="pay for it" VALUE="glass"> Glass
Beads<BR>
```

```
<INPUT TYPE=RADIO NAME="pay for it" VALUE="mo"> Cowrie
Shells<BR>
<P>
Type your super-secret FunkyWeb decoder ring sequence
here to verify that you are you.<BR>
<INPUT TYPE=PASSWORD NAME=PASSWORD VALUE="they are buying
our stuff"><BR>
<INPUT TYPE=RESET> <INPUT TYPE=SUBMIT>
</FORM>
```

As you can see, a wide variety of attributes can be added to the <INPUT> tag to modify its behavior. These ten attributes can produce very different form elements with a Web browser, as you can see in Figure 7.6.

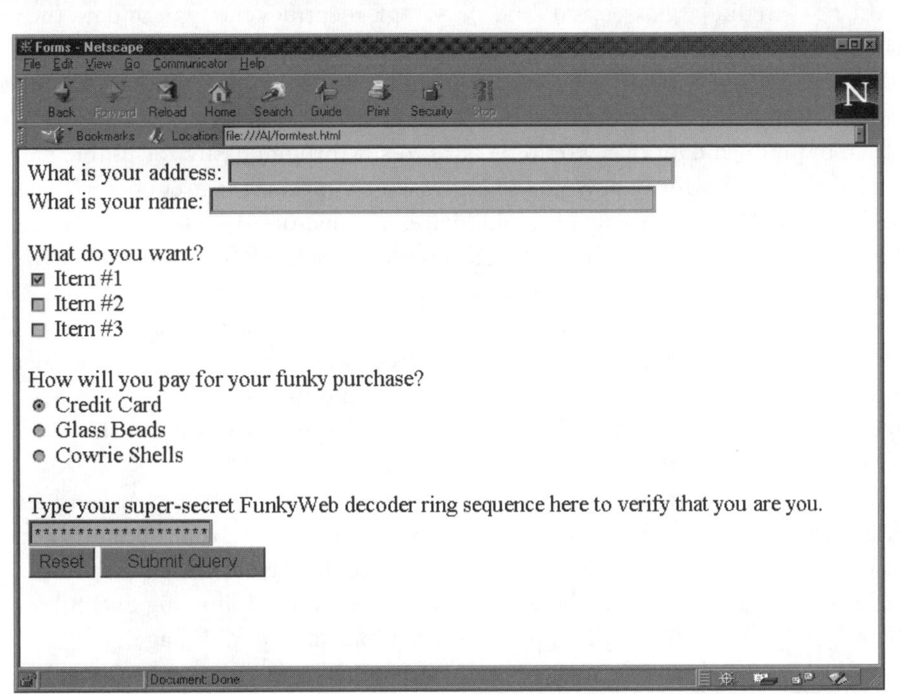

Figure 7.6 The Sample Form Code Displayed in Netscape Navigator

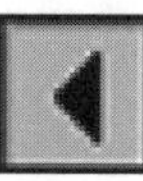

Most of the <INPUT> attributes have three sets of subvalues: NAME, TYPE, and VALUE. The TYPE value always is used to set the form of <INPUT> attribute used (i.e., <INPUT TYPE=CHECKBOX> or <INPUT TYPE=IMAGE>, etc.). NAME and VALUE are a pair of subvalues that work together to identify the fields that have been selected by the user when filling out the form. NAME passes along the "title" of the form element, and VALUE passes along the actual data. Take a look at the following form code fragment:

```
How will you pay for your funky purchase? <BR>
<INPUT TYPE=RADIO NAME="pay for it" VALUE="credit"
CHECKED> Credit Card <BR>
<INPUT TYPE=RADIO NAME="pay for it" VALUE="glass">
Glass Beads<BR>
<INPUT TYPE=RADIO NAME="pay for it" VALUE="mo"> Cowrie
Shells<BR>
```

This code produces three radio buttons, from which a user can choose one value. All three radio buttons share the same NAME ("pay for it"), but have different VALUEs ("credit," "glass," and "mo"). NAME identifies the type of data the user has entered in the form (in this case, how the user intends to pay for the goods being purchased); VALUE tells the recipient of the form data which option was chosen by the user. If there were no NAME attribute, you would simply receive a bunch of jumbled data that would be hard to sift through easily for usable data. If there were no VALUEs, you wouldn't know which options the user chose. Together, NAME and VALUE pairs form the hidden backbone of all Web forms. Note also the CHECKED value, which can be used with either the RADIO or CHECKBOX attributes. CHECKED is used to designate a default value for a list of items. When CHECKED appears beside a particular list of items, it indicates that the particular item (or multiple items, for checkboxes) is chosen. It is always a good idea to specify a default value when using things like radio buttons or checkboxes, so as to ensure a common selection is chosen if a user happens to skim quickly through a Web form and to miss a section accidentally.

The BUTTON attribute is used to create an on-screen button that can be read by a JavaScript program. It is designed to enable JavaScript programmers to create customizable buttons in a Web form. The text displayed within the button is derived from the VALUE attribute that is specified. In the following example code, the words "Java Button" will appear within a button in a Web page.

```
<FORM METHOD="POST"
ACTION="http://www.myfunkyfunkywebsite.ca">
<INPUT TYPE=BUTTON NAME="JavaPortion" VALUE="Java
Button">
</FORM>
```

The CHECKBOX attribute creates a single checkbox that can be enabled or disabled by the user. Checkboxes are usually used in a group, and enable the user to select a number of items simultaneously. The effect of using checkboxes is additive; they are used in situations where you want to offer your user more than one option to choose from. For example, say you sold pizza over the Web. You would want to offer your customers a range of toppings for their pizza orders, not just one. A sample pizza topic list of checkboxes would look something like this:

```
<INPUT TYPE=CHECKBOX NAME="pizza topping"
VALUE="pepperoni" CHECKED> Pepperoni<BR>
<INPUT TYPE=CHECKBOX NAME="pizza topping"
VALUE="cheese"> Extra Cheese<BR>
<INPUT TYPE=CHECKBOX NAME="pizza topping"
VALUE="anchovies"> Anchovies <BR>
```

Using this code, a user could not only select the default setting ("Pepperoni"), but could also choose the "Extra Cheese" and "Anchovies" selections. Checkboxes are used to present multiple options to a user, whereas radio buttons give the user only a single choice from a list of choices. As we noted earlier, the CHECKED value indicates the default selection.

The FILE attribute lets the user add a filename that serves as extra input for the form. Say you were applying for a job online, and wanted to attach a copy of your resume. This field allows you to select the file on your system and send it along with the rest of the form data. When using this attribute, the NAME value must be the destination URL of the inbox for the form information, and the Web author must use the ENCTYPE="multipart/form-data" attribute/value to the <FORM> tag. The following is an example of the FILE attribute used in a code example:

```
<INPUT TYPE=FILE
NAME="http://www.funkyfunkywebsite.com">
```

The latest versions of Internet Explorer and Netscape Navigator add a Browse button next to the field that enables the user to enter the URL. This button allows the user to choose a file contained on their system.

The HIDDEN attribute is used to insert a value into the form that identifies it to the Web server and/or to the Web master. The information contained by the HIDDEN attribute is hidden to the user of the form. Generally it is designed for use in situations where there may be multiple forms at a Web site that may contain similar information. For example, say you run an online candy store that sells all types of candies, and have multiple forms at your Web site. A number of forms on your Web site often contain many of the same candies for sale, because you have different types of gift baskets to offer prospective customers, which often contain

some overlap. To keep the forms distinct you could insert a hidden field, as in the following code example:

```
<INPUT TYPE=HIDDEN NAME="Gift Baskets" VALUE="Candy
Selection 3">
```

The IMAGE attribute enables Web authors to insert buttons of their own creation within a Web form. It has two additional attributes: ALIGN and SRC. ALIGN has a number of values: ASBOTTOM, ABSMIDDLE, BOTTOM, BASELINE, MIDDLE, LEFT, RIGHT, TEXTTOP, and TOP, which specify the alignment of text that appears immediately after this element. TOP aligns the button image in relation to the top of the text that precedes it, MIDDLE aligns the button image to the midline of the text that precedes it, and BOTTOM aligns the button image to the bottom of the text that precedes it. TEXTTOP aligns the button image the top of the text that precedes it, and ABSMIDDLE and ABSBOTTOM align the button image to the absolute (in terms of overall size of the font) midline and bottom of the text that precedes it, respectively. The default value for IMAGE is TOP. The SRC attribute is used to point to the location of the image file. You can use any of the four standard Web image file formats as targets for the SRC attribute: .GIF, .JPG/JPEG, .XBM, or .PICT. (See Chapter 6, "Color, Images, and Imagemaps" for more information on the image file formats that can be used with the SRC attribute.) The BORDER attribute can also be used, and it sets the size of the highlight border around the image button as a pixel value. If BORDER=NONE is specified, no visible border will surround the button. Note that this attribute is supported within Netscape Navigator and Microsoft Internet Explorer.

The following code example specifies a customized button image file.

```
<INPUT TYPE=IMAGE SRC="funkybutton.gif"
NAME="imagebutton1" VALUE="funkybutton" BORDER=NONE>
```

The PASSWORD attribute is used to create a text field for typing in passwords. When a user types a password in this field asterisks (or some other symbol) appear in the field in place of the letters and/or numbers typed. This is to keep any prying eyes from easily guessing the password typed in. It has a couple of additional values: SIZE and MAXLENGTH. SIZE sets the width of the displayed password field in characters. MAXLENGTH sets the maximum number of characters that can be entered in the field—the user will not be allowed to type any more characters than the number allowed by MAXLENGTH. The VALUE value is optional, but if it is used, the value attributed to it is displayed in the field as asterisks. This is useful if you want to prompt the user for certain sets of password characters that always appear. The follow example code shows how the PASSWORD attribute is used:

```
Type in your super-secret password: <INPUT
TYPE=PASSWORD NAME="secret" VALUE="12345" SIZE=8
MAXLENGTH=8>
```

The RADIO attribute is used to create a series a radio buttons on a form. Radio buttons differ from checkboxes in that only one choice can be made from a listing of available options. Use radio buttons when you wish to present only a single option for the user to select. Like the checkbox attribute, it can take the CHECKED attribute to signify a default choice. The NAME value is used to group together a bunch of selectable items, and the VALUE value identifies the individual item. The following code example shows a set of three radio buttons that allow the user to choose only one option:

```
What sort of noun is it? <BR>
A Person <INPUT TYPE=RADIO NAME="nouns"
VALUE="person">,
Place <INPUT TYPE=RADIO NAME="nouns" VALUE="place"> or
Thing <INPUT TYPE=RADIO NAME="nouns" VALUE="thing">?
```

The RESET and SUBMIT buttons display buttons on the form, used for resetting or sending the information contained within the form. The VALUE value is used to override the typical default name for each button, and the value it contains is displayed instead. If the user clicks the RESET button, all of the data fields on the form are set back to their default values. If the user clicks the SUBMIT button, the information contained within the form is sent to the Web server. The following sample code displays how the RESET and SUBMIT elements can be used:

```
<INPUT TYPE=SUBMIT NAME="funkyform1" VALUE="Submit to
this form!"> <INPUT TYPE=RESET NAME="funkyform1">
```

Finally, the TEXT attribute is used to insert a single-line textfield where a user can type in information. It has a couple of additional values: SIZE and MAXLENGTH. SIZE sets the width of the displayed textfield in character. MAXLENGTH sets the maximum number of characters that can be entered in the field—the user will not be allowed to type in any more characters than the number allowed by MAXLENGTH. The VALUE value is optional, but if it is used, the value attributed to it is displayed in the textfield. An example of how the textfield attribute can be used is shown in the following piece of code:

```
Want to add any more info?<BR>
<INPUT TYPE=TEXT NAME="funkyform1" VALUE="This text is
displayed in the form." SIZE=40 MAXLENGTH=40>
```

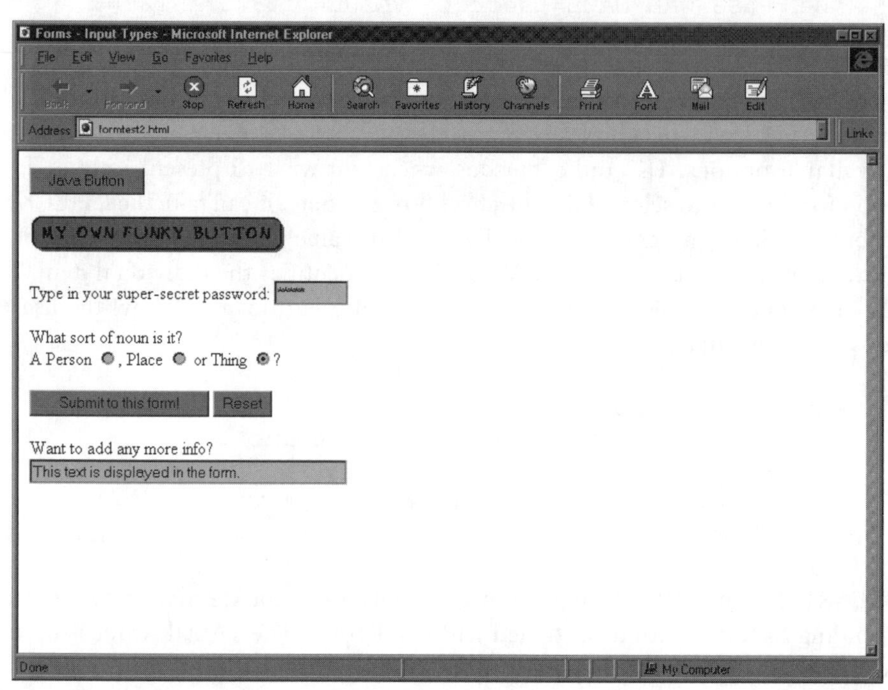

Figure 7.7 All of the <INPUT> Code Examples Displayed

All of the <INPUT> code samples can be seen in Figure 7.7.

Note how formatting elements must be added to the <INPUT> tag in the code examples shown. Since the <INPUT> tag is an empty tag, it can be formatted any number of ways. Things like checkboxes and radio buttons in particular benefit from being formatted in an orderly fashion, making it easier for the user to select from elements of the same groupings. You may wish to use formatting elements like list elements (<LI>), line breaks (<BR>), tables, or other elements to corral groups of <INPUT> tags together. The following code example shows how the same grouping of three radio button elements can be arranged using list elements, line breaks, and a table:

```
What sort of noun is it? <BR>
<UL>
<LI>A Person, <INPUT TYPE=RADIO NAME="nouns"
VALUE="person">
```

```
<LI>Place,       <INPUT
TYPE=RADIO NAME="nouns" VALUE="place">
<LI>or Thing?  <INPUT TYPE=RADIO NAME="nouns"
VALUE="thing">?
</UL>
<P>
<BR>
<P>
What sort of noun is it? <BR>
A Person, <INPUT TYPE=RADIO NAME="nouns"
VALUE="person"><BR>
Place,       <INPUT
TYPE=RADIO NAME="nouns" VALUE="place"><BR> or Thing?
 <INPUT TYPE=RADIO NAME="nouns" VALUE="thing">
<P>
<BR>
<P>
What sort of noun is it?
<TABLE>
<TR>
<TD>A Person,</TD>
<TD><INPUT TYPE=RADIO NAME="nouns" VALUE="person"></TD>
</TR>
<TR>
<TD>Place,</TD>
<TD><INPUT TYPE=RADIO NAME="nouns" VALUE="place"></TD>
</TR>
<TR>
<TD>or Thing?</TD>
<TD><INPUT TYPE=RADIO NAME="nouns" VALUE="thing"></TD>
</TR>
</TABLE>
```

The results of this code example can be seen in Figure 7.8.

Note how some nonbreaking spacing elements ( ) have been added to the code examples that use line breaks and list elements to order the <INPUT> elements. Using nonbreaking space elements is not an exact science—it looks good in the illustration, but because you can never predict the font settings at the user's end, this solution can yield different results on different computers. Other than the table solution used in the code example, you may want to think about using the preformatted tag (<PRE>) to align <INPUT> elements on a Web page. When laying out <INPUT> elements, try to keep both esthetics and functionality in mind.

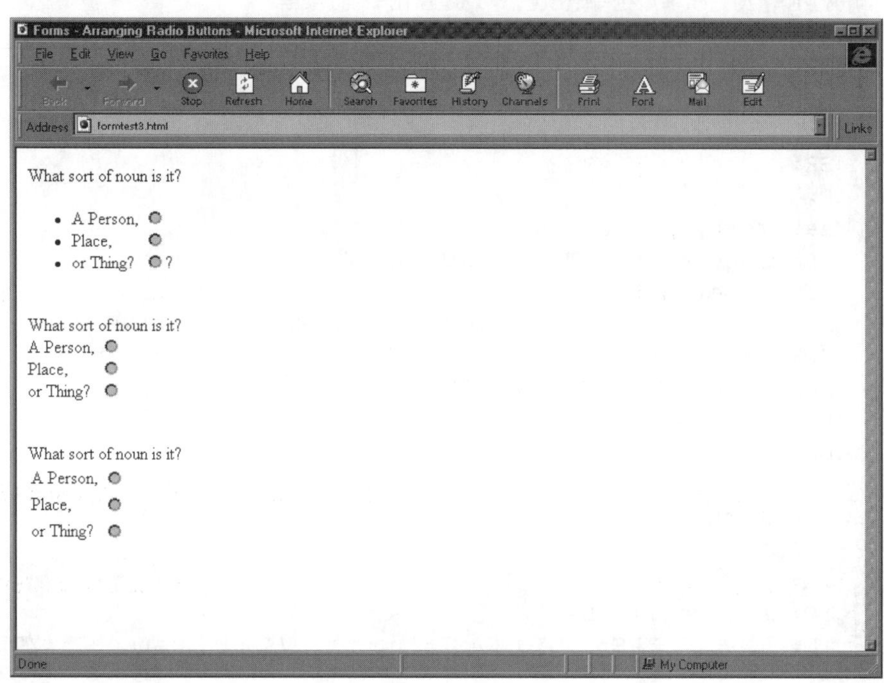

Figure 7.8 Arranged <INPUT> Elements Using List-Elements, Line Breaks, and Tables, Respectively

Creating Selectable Lists

You can use form elements other than the <INPUT> tag on Web-based forms. You can also create drop-down or scrollable option lists within a form by using the <SELECT> and <OPTION> tags. They present lists of options to the user. These option lists are functionally no different than either radio buttons or checkboxes, but they do offer the Web master a different way of presenting optional information within a form. It also can be designed to produce a much more compact way of choosing options on a Web page—would you rather have 30 radio buttons or a drop-down list with 30 items that appears only when the user wants to choose an option? The <SELECT> tag is always used in conjunction with the <OPTION> tag, which behaves like the list element tag (<LI>) within a listing of elements.

<SELECT> . . .</SELECT>

Element name: Select tag.

Description: Specifies an option list within a Web form.

Attributes: NAME= *text*
Specifies the name that is to be submitted as a name/value pair.
SIZE= *text*
Specifies the number of visible items in a drop-down list of items that are initially displayed.
MULTIPLE= *number*
Specifies the amount of options a user can select from the selectable list.

Associated with: <FORM>, <INPUT>, <TEXTAREA>, <FIELDSET>, <LEGEND>, and <OPTION>.

<OPTION>

Element name: Option tag.

Description: Contains the individual elements within the drop-down list. It is always used in conjunction with the <SELECT> tag.

Attributes: SELECTED
Sets the default selection.
VALUE= *text*
Sets a specific value to an option.

Associated with: <FORM>, <INPUT>, <TEXTAREA>, <FIELDSET>, <LEGEND>, and <SELECT>.

Sample Code:

```
<FORM>
<SELECT NAME="JapaneseUkiyo-EArtists">
<OPTION SELECTED VALUE="Hokusai">Hokusai
<OPTION VALUE="Yoshida">Yoshida
<OPTION VALUE="Yoshitoshi">Yoshitoshi
<OPTION VALUE="Hiroshige">Hiroshige
<OPTION VALUE="Eisen">Eisen
</SELECT>
</FORM>
```

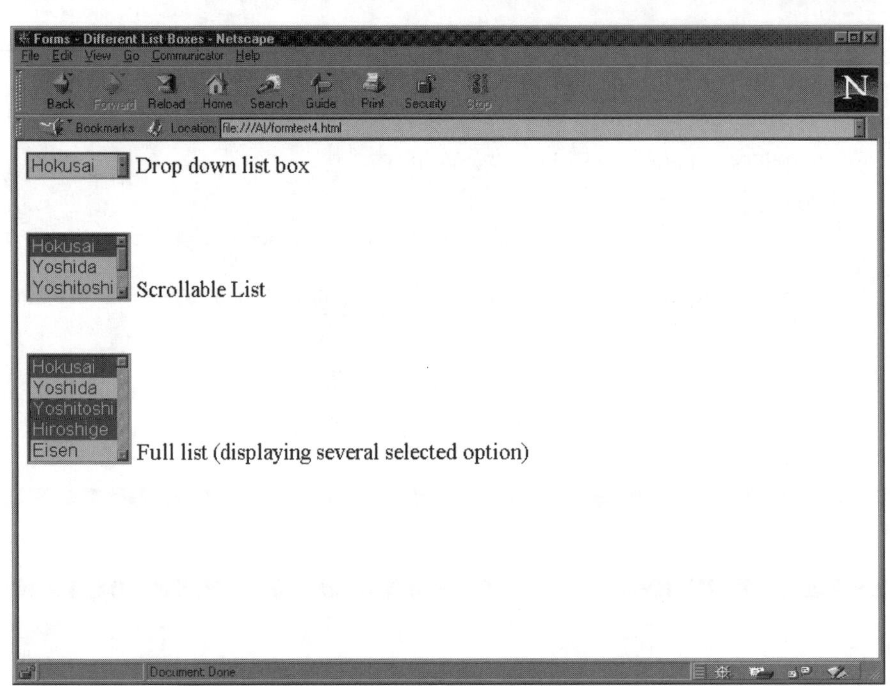

Figure 7.9 The Three Basic Types of Selectable Lists Displayed: A Drop-Down List, a Scrollable List, and a Full List Displaying Multiple Selected Options

Using a combination of <SELECT> and <OPTION> attributes, you can create drop-down lists, and scrollable lists of single or multiple selectable items. The <SELECT> and <OPTION> attributes work much like the ordered or unordered list tags (<OL> and <UL>) and the list element tag <LI>, respectively. The <SELECT> tag encloses the list elements, which are made up of the various <OPTION> tags listed. Note that no other HTML tags are allowed within a pair of <SELECT> container tags.

Unlike the <INPUT> tag, the <SELECT> tag does use NAME/VALUE pairs. Only the NAME attribute is required to specify the title of the selection list, and the value that passed along to the Web server is that specified by each individual <OPTION> tag element. The <SELECT> tag can take two other attributes: MULTIPLE and SIZE. SIZE specifies the number of visible items displayed in the list. The SIZE attribute determines whether or not a selectable list is depicted as a drop-down list, a scrollable list, or full list of items to be selected. By default, if SIZE is not specified, the default value of SIZE=1 is used, and the selectable list appears as a drop-down list of items. The user clicks the down-arrow to the right of the initial element, and the rest of the list appears. If SIZE is greater than 1, but not equal to the total amount of selectable items, a scrollable list appears. Finally, if SIZE equals the total number of selectable items, a full selectable list of the items appears on the Web page. The MULTIPLE value specifies the number of options a user can select from the selectable list. By default, a user can choose a single item from the list, but if you want to allow the user multiple choices from the list (like a series of checkboxes) you can set the maximum number of items to choose from using this value.

Just like you can set a default value for a checkbox or radio button using CHECKED, you can use the SELECTED attribute of the <OPTION> tag to set a default value (or multiple values) for the selectable list. You can also use the VALUE attribute to an alternate text value for an option if you do not want it represented automatically by the value that follows it.

The code example in Figure 7.9 depicts the three basic types of selectable list displays: a drop-down list, a scrollable list, and a full list displaying multiple selected options.

Note that though the SELECTED value generally works within most Web browsers, not all browsers will indicate which of the selections is the default selection to the user.

Multiline Text Entry Areas

There are occasions when you will need to ask your users for lengthy text input that can't be properly contained within a simple <INPUT TYPE=TEXT> tag. In these cases, you will need the flexibility the <TEXTAREA> tag offers. Unlike the <INPUT TYPE=TEXT> tag, <TEXTAREA> is a container tag. The following is a description of its attributes.

<TEXTAREA> . . .</TEXTAREA>

Element name: Textarea tag.

Description: Specifies a multiline field where users can enter several lines of text. It always used in conjunction with the <FORM> tag. The ROWS and COLS attributes determine the dimension of the field in character height and length, respectively.

Attributes: COLS= # *characters*
Sets the width of the field in characters.

NAME= *text*
Sets a name for the data contained within the text field.
ROWS= # *characters*
Sets the height of the field in characters.
WRAP= *OFF | PHYSICAL | VIRTUAL*
Sets how word-wrapping is handled within the field.

Associated tags: <FORM>, <INPUT>, <OPTION>, <FIELDSET>, <LEGEND>, and <SELECT>.

Sample Code:

```
<FORM>
<TEXTAREA NAME="funky text input" ROWS=10 COLS=45>
</TEXTAREA>
</FORM>
```

All you have to do is describe how the textarea should look and behave in the browser using the attributes supplied.

The COLS and ROWS attribute sets the width and the height of the field in characters, respectively. To set a textfield that is 10 characters long and 45 characters in height, you'd use the following code:

```
<TEXTAREA NAME="funky text input" ROWS=10 COLS=45>
</TEXTAREA>
```

The NAME attribute sets a name for the data contained within the text field for the Web server.

The WRAP attribute tells the browser how word wrapping should be handled within the field, and it takes one of three separate values: OFF, PHYSICAL, and VIRTUAL. OFF tells the browser that no word wrapping should be used—any line breaks are those entered by the user. This is the default setting for any textarea. If WRAP is set to VIRTUAL, line breaks are automatically included within the textarea when the text entered hits the boundary specified by the COLS attribute. This line-break information is not included with the rest of the data when the user submits the form. The PHYSICAL value works in the same way as VIRTUAL, but it includes the line-break information when the user submits the form to the Web server.

Like the <INPUT TYPE=TEXT> tag, it is also possible to include some default text to appear within the textarea. The <TEXTAREA> tag is a container tag, and all you have to do to include text within a textarea is to enclose it within the beginning and end <TEXTAREA> tags, as the following code example shows:

```
<TEXTAREA NAME="funky text input" ROWS=5 COLS=25
WRAP=PHYSICAL>
Here is a whole bunch of text that goes on and on and
on and on and so on and so forth and so on and so
```

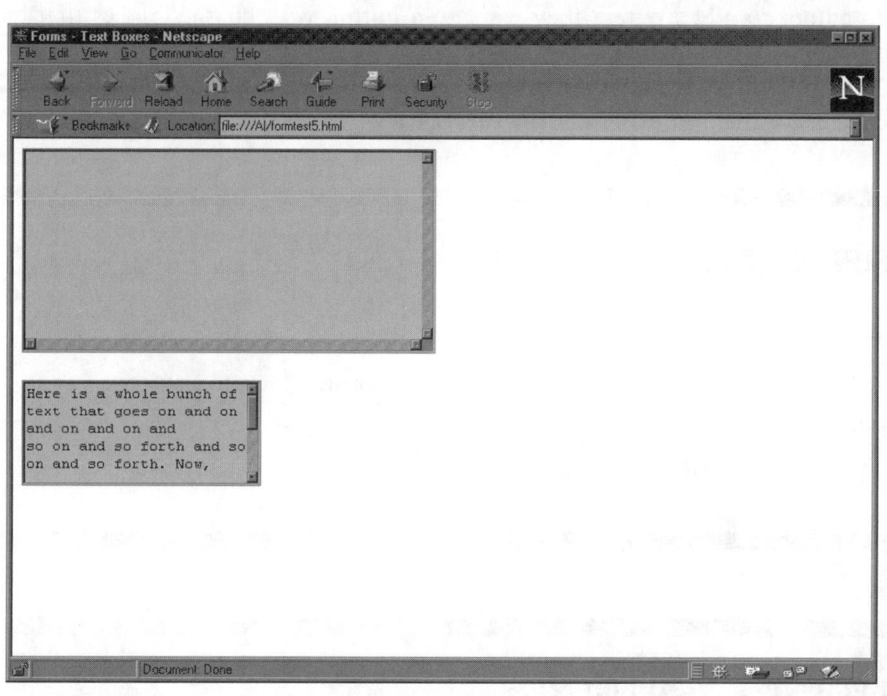

Figure 7.10 The Two <TEXTAREA> Code Examples Displayed

```
forth. Now, notice the scrollbar the magically appears
to the right in this relatively small textarea.
</TEXTAREA>
```

The two code examples used in this section are displayed in Figure 7.10.

Notice how a scrollbar appear to the right of the second textarea. A scrollbar will appear the moment there is more text in the field than can appear at once within it. This allows the user a chance to go back and edit particularly lengthy textual information contained in the textarea.

HTML 4.0 Proposed Form Elements

The recent HTML 4.0 specification includes three new forms-related tags: <FIELD-SET>, <LEGEND>, and <BUTTON>. The first two tags are designed primarily to

add extra formatting components to forms, and the <BUTTON> tag allows the Web author to add any text they want to a button with characteristics that have not previously been defined.

The <FIELDSET> and <LEGEND> tags are always used in conjunction with each other, as the following information shows.

<FIELDSET> . . .</FIELDSET>

Element name: Fieldset tag.

Description: Allows the Web author to group thematically related inputs together.

Attributes: None.

Associated Tags: <FIELDSET>, set of form tags.

<LEGEND> . . .</LEGEND>

Element name: Legend tag.

Description: Used to add a legend to a fieldset.

Attributes: ALIGN = *BOTTOM* | *LEFT* | *RIGHT* | *TOP*
Sets the position of the legend with respect to the fieldset. The ALIGN attribute is deprecated in the HTML 4.0 specification.

Associated Tags: <FIELDSET>, set of form tags.

Sample:

```
<FORM ACTION=" . . " METHOD=POST>
<FIELDSET>
<LEGEND ALIGN="top">Some Info</LEGEND>
Stuff #1: <INPUT TYPE=RADIO NAME="stuff" VALUE="1">
Stuff #2: <INPUT TYPE=RADIO NAME="stuff" VALUE="2">
</FIELDSET>
</FORM>
```

The <FIELDSET> tag is designed to let the Web author group thematically related inputs together, and the <LEGEND> tag is designed to add a title to a fieldset. In the code example listing, note how two <INPUT TYPE=RADIO> buttons are arranged and confined within the fieldset.

<FIELDSET> does not have any attributes, but <LEGEND> does have one: ALIGN. The ALIGN attribute takes one of four possible values: BOTTOM, LEFT, RIGHT, and TOP, which set the position of the legend with respect to the fieldset. The ALIGN attribute is deprecated in the HTML 4.0 specification.

At the time of this writing, neither of these tags are supported within Internet Explorer or Netscape Navigator.

The button tag works in a similar fashion to the basic Submit button, but does not tie the Web author down to a particular function for the button. You can easily change the text of the Submit and Reset buttons, but they have particular predefined functions within the Web form. Similarly, you can use <INPUT TYPE=BUTTON>, but it is tied to use in JavaScript programs. The <BUTTON> tag is designed to overcome the limitations of these other form buttons.

<BUTTON> . . . </BUTTON>

Element name: Button tag.

Description: Displays a button with no predefined function.

Attributes: NAME= *button name*
Assigns a name to the button.
VALUE= *buttonvalue*
Assigns a value to the button.
TYPE= *BUTTON | RESET | SUBMIT*
Specifies the type of button to be displayed.

Associated Tags: The set of form tags.

Sample:

```
<FORM ACTION="http://www.somewhere somehow.ca"
METHOD="post">
<P>
Stuff #1: <INPUT TYPE=CHECKBOX NAME="stuff" VALUE="1"><BR>
Stuff #2: <INPUT TYPE=CHECKBOX NAME="stuff" VALUE="2"><BR>
<BUTTON TYPE=SUBMIT NAME="submit it"
VALUE="submit"></BUTTON>
<BUTTON TYPE=BUTTON NAME="other" VALUE="The Other
Button"></BUTTON>
</FORM>
```

The <BUTTON> tag takes the standard NAME/VALUE pairs typical to most <INPUT> tags, and they have the same functions. The difference is the TYPE attribute, which can take one of three values: BUTTON, RESET, and SUBMIT. RESET and SUBMIT assign those respective button values to the button being specified. The BUTTON value leaves the function of the button open to the Web author.

At the time of this writing, the <BUTTON> tag does not work in Netscape Navigator or in versions of Internet Explorer previous to 4.0 beta 1.

MAILTO: FORMS

There are many occasions where people do not want to set up either CGI or JavaScripts to process the information contained within a simple form. Also, many Internet Service Providers do not allow their users access to the CGI scrips on their systems. If this is the case, you might want to try using a mailto: form instead, which is understood within Internet Explorer and Netscape Navigator.

The mailto: function, like many nonstandard tags, was first instituted within an early version of Netscape Navigator. It is tacked on to a standard anchored hypertext link, as the following example code shows:

```
Tell me how much you like my Web site by sending me <A
HREF=mailto:keith@funkyfunky.ca>email</A>!
```

When a user clicks the hypertext link containing the mailto: value, an email program appears containing the email address of the intended recipient. The mailto: function can be added to the <FORM> tag in the same way it can be added to an anchored hypertext reference tag.

If no preprocessing or action needs to be taken once form information is submitted, you might want to seriously consider using the mailto: function for retrieving information from simple Web forms. The mailto: function uses METHOD=POST and replaces the ACTION attribute with mailto:. Attached to the mailto: value is the email address of the intended recipient of the form data. The following code example shows how to append a mailto: function to the <FORM> tag:

```
<FORM METHOD=POST ACTION="mailto:keith@funkyfunky.ca">
```

Although the mailto: function is recommended primarily for use in simple forms, a mailto: form can contain any form elements used in more standard forms, like checkboxes, text fields, radio buttons, and drop-down lists.

The only problem is that the resulting email received is full of special control characters. However, this output from the form can be decoded for use in other programs. A typical response from a mailto: form containing a simple text field can look like this:

```
Hello%20there%20Keith%2C%20I%20hope%20your%20book%20is%2
0coming%20along%20well%21
```

A more complex form containing information about a user's name, email address, and Web page could look like this:

```
Name=Hortensia+Williams&E-Mail=hortesia@funkyfunky.ca&We
b Page=http%3A%2F%2Fwww.funkyfunky.ca%2F
```

Though this may look daunting, each of these codes has a purpose and can easily be translated. Table 7.1 contains a listing of what the codes in the mailto: output means.

Table 7.1 A Table of the Output Codes and Their Meanings from the mailto: Function

Code	*Meaning*
+	Space
&	Line Break
%OD%OA	Carriage Return
%20	Space
%21	!
%22	"
%23	#
%24	$
%25	%
%26	&
%27	'
%28	(
%29	)
%2B	+
%2C	,
%2F	/
%3A	:
%3D	=
%3F	?
%5C	\
%5E	^
%60	'
%7C	|
%7E	~

Many programs are available that will decode the output from mailto: forms, so if you feel hesitant about including a form on your Web pages because you have no programming experience, there's no longer any excuse.

Link: There are a couple of programs you can download that will help you decode the output you get from a mailto: form. If you are an MS-Windows user, check out WebForms at: http://www.q-d.com/wf.htm, or try inFORMer at: http://www.phoenix.net/~jacobson/hs.html if you are a Macintosh user.

Though mailto: forms are supported in Netscape Navigator and Internet Explorer, keep in mind that not everybody uses them. Browsers that do not recognize mailto: forms may not produce any noticeable reaction to the user; at worst they may produce a completely unexpected result. Typical of this is an error message that can appear after someone clicks the Submit button of a form, and gets an email message back saying that the email program is not properly set up. For this reason, it is always a good idea to insert a prominent notice somewhere in the form saying that it is a mailto: form, and if possible, provide an alternate means for submitting the form information (like a regular email address).

CHAPTER 8

Tables

Tables were first introduced as Netscape extensions; tables proved to be so popular that they were adopted by the W3C for the HTML 3.0 specification. Though originally designed for constructing spreadsheet-like tables of information, they were rapidly adopted for use in Web page layout. With the introduction of tables Web page authors finally had more control over the layout of their pages than ever before.

Tables are so flexible that they can be used to create just about any sort of page layout a Web author desires. The only disadvantage to tables may be their complexity; constructing a table to display correctly can be time-consuming due to the high number of tags and attributes available. Many WYSIWYG (What You See Is What You Get) HTML authoring tools allow authors to arrange text and images on the page in any manner, then generate the appropriate table code in the background.

Viewing this table code in raw HTML reveals just how complicated, and how powerful, tables can be.

It its most basic level, a typical table may contain only three different tags: <TABLE>, <TR>, and <TD>. However, each tag has many attributes, which will give you the power to customize your table to your needs. In addition to these tags are other table-related tags like <CAPTION>, <TH>, and others can further extend a table's capabilities.

The table tag has evolved considerably since it was first introduced by the release of the Netscape 1.1 Web browser. The addition of many handy attributes, such as cell padding, cell spacing, alignment, and column and row spanning, provide Web authors with a great deal of flexibility when designing unique-looking pages.

Tables are now almost universally recognized within most self-respecting browsers. Even text-based browsers are beginning to find ways to ensure that users see what the Web author intends them to see.

The <TABLE> Tag—Creating Tables

The table tag is a container tag, enclosing the whole of your table. As you begin to create your table, keep in mind that both the <TABLE> and </TABLE> tags must be present for your Web browser to display the table. If the end tag is not present, your browser will not display your table.

<TABLE> . . .</TABLE>

Element Name: Table tag.

Description: Used to insert a table into the Web document. The <TABLE> tag is a container tag; the end tag is not optional.

Attributes: ALIGN = LEFT | RIGHT | CENTER
Aligns the table in the browser window according to the value you specify. The default alignment is left. RIGHT aligns the table to the right margin, and CENTER aligns the table in the center of the window.
BACKGROUND = *colorvalue*
Specifies a background image for the table. All table cells and content are displayed over this image. If the image is smaller than the table, the image is tiled to fill the table.
BGCOLOR = *colorvalue*
Specifies a background color for the table. This color can be overridden at the cell level. The color is defined using RBG values.

BORDER = *n pixels*
Specifies the width of the table border in pixels. The default value is 1. Specifying BORDER = O creates a table without visible borders.
BORDERCOLOR = *colorvalue*
Specifies the external border color for the whole table. The color is defined using RBG values. The BORDER attribute must be specified with a value of 1 or greater for the BORDERCOLOR attribute to be effective. This attribute is recognized only within Internet Explorer.
BORDERCOLORDARK = *colorvalue*
Specifies the color of the lower and right-hand borders of the table, creating a 3D effect. The color is defined using RBG values. The BORDER attribute must be specified with a value of 1 or greater for the BORDERCOLOR attribute to be effective. This attribute is recognized only within Internet Explorer.
BORDERCOLORLIGHT = *colorvalue*
Specifies the color of the upper and left-hand borders of the table, creating a 3D effect. The color is defined using RBG values. The BORDER attribute must be specified with a value of 1 or greater for the BORDERCOLOR attribute to be effective. This attribute is recognized only within Internet Explorer.
CELLPADDING = *n pixels*
Specifies the amount of space within cells in pixels.
CELLSPACING = *n pixels*
Specifies the amount of space between cells in pixels.
COLS = *number*
Explicitly defines the number of columns in the table. Specifying this value allows the table to download more quickly, as the browser doesn't have to read the whole table to know the table size.
FRAME = VOID | ABOVE | BELOW | HSIDES | VSIDES | LHS | RHS | BOX | BORDER | FRAME
Allows control over the outer border of the table. The following values indicate what part of the border should be displayed:
VOID - No borders
ABOVE - Top border only
BELOW - Bottom border only
HSIDES - Left- and right-hand side borders only
VSIDES - Top and bottom borders only
LHS - Left border only
RHS - Right border only
BOX - Border on all four sides
BORDER Border on all four sides (same as box); default value
FRAME Border on all four sides
This attribute is recognized only within Internet Explorer, but has recently been adopted within the official HTML 4.0 specification.
HEIGHT = *n pixels/%*
Specifies the height of the table either as a percentage of the window height, or as an absolute value in pixels.
RULES = NONE | ROWS | COLS | ALL
Allows control over the inner cell rules of the table. The following values indicate what part of the border should be displayed:

NONE - No interior borders
ROWS - Horizontal borders are displayed
COLS - Vertical borders are displayed
ALL - All borders are displayed
This attribute is recognized only within Internet Explorer, but has recently been adopted within the official HTML 4.0 specification.
WIDTH = # *of pixels* or % *of browser width*
Specifies the width of the table either as a percentage of the window width, or as an absolute value in pixels.

THE <TH> AND <TD> TAGS—TABLE HEADINGS AND TABLE DATA

The <TH> and <TD> tags contain the text that make up the content for your table. Use the <TH> tag to define the cells that comprise the headings for your table; use the <TD> tag to define all other cells. You can add a heading to your table using the <TH> tag. By default text enclosed by the <TH> tags is centered and in bold font, while the text enclosed by the <TD> tags is left-aligned and in the normal font.

<TH> . . .</TH> and <TD> . . .</TD>

Element Name: Table Heading and Table Data tags.

Description: Both <TH> and <TD> are container tags. Although the end tags are optional, it is good HTML form to use them.

Attributes: ABBR = *text*
Contains the full text of the abbreviated name for a header cell.
ALIGN = LEFT | RIGHT | CENTER
Specifies the horizontal alignment of contents within the cell relative to the cell boundaries. The default alignment is LEFT. RIGHT aligns the content to the right side of the cell, and CENTER aligns the content in the center of the cell.
AXIS = *text*
Specifies a name for a cell, allowing it to be mapped to a tree-like hierarchy. Intended primarily for use in nongraphical browsers.
BACKGROUND = *image filename*
Specifies a background image for the cell. All content in the table cell are displayed over this image. If the image is smaller than the cell, the image is tiled to fill the cell.

BGCOLOR = *colorvalue*
Specifies a background color for the cell. This color overrides any BGCOLOR specified in the <TABLE> element. The color is defined using RBG values.
BORDERCOLOR = *colorvalue*
Specifies the external border color for the whole table. The color is defined using RBG values. The BORDER attribute must be specified with a value of 1 or greater for the BORDERCOLOR attribute to be effective. This attribute is recognized only within Internet Explorer.
BORDERCOLORDARK = *colorvalue*
Specifies the color of the lower and right-hand borders of the table, creating a 3D effect. The color is defined using RBG values. The BORDER attribute must be specified with a value of 1 or greater for the BORDERCOLOR attribute to be effective. This attribute is recognized only within Internet Explorer.
BORDERCOLORLIGHT = *colorvalue*
Specifies the color of the upper and left-hand borders of the table, creating a 3D effect. The color is defined using RBG values. The BORDER attribute must be specified with a value of 1 or greater for the BORDERCOLOR attribute to be effective. This attribute is recognized only within Internet Explorer.
CHAR= *character*
Specifies an alignment character for use with ALIGN=CHAR
CHAROFF= # *of character spaces* or %
Specifies the offset to the first occurrence of the alignment character on each line.
COLSPAN = *number*
Specifies the number of columns spanned by the cell.
HEADERS = *text*
Associates header information for a particular cell in a given column. Designed to make the function of a table clear to users of nongraphical browsers.
HEIGHT = # *of pixels* or % *of browser window height*
Sets the height of the current cell (which in effect sets the height for the row).
NOWRAP
Suppresses word wrap, widening the cell to the width of the cell's contents.
ROWSPAN = *number*
Specifies the number of rows spanned by the cell.
SCOPE = COL | COLGROUP | ROW | ROWGROUP
Designed for nongraphical browsers, this tag provides information on a particular row, column, or group of rows and columns.
VALIGN = BOTTOM | BASELINE | MIDDLE | TOP
Specifies the vertical alignment of contents within the cell relative to the cell boundaries. TOP = aligns the content to the top of the cell, MIDDLE aligns the content to the middle of the cell, BOTTOM aligns the content to the bottom of the cell, and BASELINE aligns the content at the baseline so that all content lines up horizontally.
WIDTH = # *of pixels* or % *of browser window height*
Specifies the width of the cell either as a percentage of the window width, or as an absolute value in pixels. The width of a table column must be consistent, therefore the width of the column will default to the widest cell.

The <TR> Tag—Table Rows

Use the <TR> tag to create rows between table cells created with the <TH> and <TD> tags.

<TR> . . .</TR>

Element Name: Table row tag.

Description: The <TR> tag is a container tag. Although the end tag is optional, it is good HTML form to use it.

Attributes:

ALIGN = LEFT | RIGHT | CENTER
Specifies the horizontal alignment of contents within the cell relative to the cell boundaries. The default alignment is LEFT. RIGHT aligns the content to the right side of the cell, and CENTER aligns the content in the center of the cell.

BGCOLOR = *colorvalue*
Specifies a background color for the cell. This color overrides any BGCOLOR specified in the <TABLE> element. The color is defined using RBG values.

BORDERCOLOR = *colorvalue*
Specifies the external border color for the whole table. The color is defined using RBG values. The BORDER attribute must be specified with a value of 1 or greater for the BORDERCOLOR attribute to be effective. This attribute is recognized only within Internet Explorer.

BORDERCOLORDARK = *colorvalue*
Specifies the color of the lower and right-hand borders of the table, creating a 3D effect. The color is defined using RBG values. The BORDER attribute must be specified with a value of 1 or greater for the BORDERCOLOR attribute to be effective. This attribute is recognized only within Internet Explorer.

BORDERCOLORLIGHT = *colorvalue*
Specifies the color of the upper and left-hand borders of the table, creating a 3D effect. The color is defined using RBG values. The BORDER attribute must be specified with a value of 1 or greater for the BORDERCOLOR attribute to be effective. This attribute is recognized only within Internet Explorer.

CHAR = *character*
Specifies an alignment character for use with ALIGN=CHAR.

CHAROFF = # *of character spaces* or %
Specifies the offset to the first occurrence of the alignment character on each line.

VALIGN = BOTTOM | BASELINE | MIDDLE | TOP
Specifies the vertical alignment of contents within a row of cells relative to the cell's boundaries. TOP aligns the content to the top of the cell, MIDDLE aligns the content to the middle of the cell, BOTTOM aligns the content to the bottom of the cell, and BASELINE aligns the content at the baseline so that all content lines up horizontally.

THE <CAPTION> TAG—TABLE CAPTIONS

The <CAPTION> tag is an optional element that creates a caption for the table. The caption can appear above or below the table.

<CAPTION> . . .</CAPTION>

Element Name: Caption tag.

Description: Used to create a table caption.

Attributes: ALIGN - Specifies the alignment of the caption relative to the table. TOP puts the caption above the table and BOTTOM puts the caption under the table. Microsoft Internet Explorer supports additional values that specify the horizontal alignment of the text within the caption, specifically LEFT, RIGHT, and CENTER.
VALIGN - Specifies the vertical alignment of the caption relative to the table. Values are TOP and BOTTOM. This attribute is recognized only by Microsoft Internet Explorer, and serves the same purpose as ALIGN.

TABLE EXAMPLES

The following examples illustrate how the table elements and their attributes can be applied to construct various tables. Be sure to try these yourself, then tweak them to see what happens when you adjust one or more attributes. The slightest adjustment can make the best improvements to your table's appearance.

A Basic Table

The following table has two columns, a heading row, and two rows below the heading. The only attribute specified is the BORDER, set to the value of 1.

Sample Code:

```
<TABLE BORDER="1">
<TH>Column 1</TH>
```

```
<TH>Column 2</TH>
<TR>
<TD>Cell 1</TD>
<TD>Cell 2</TD>
</TR>
<TR>
<TD>Cell 3</TD>
<TD>Cell 4</TD>
</TR>
<CAPTION>A Basic Table</CAPTION>
</TABLE>
```

The preceding code displays as shown in figure 8.1

The following table (shown in Figure 8.2) has a few more attributes specified. The table has a width of 100% of the window, and COLSPAN and ROWSPAN are used to make larger cells.

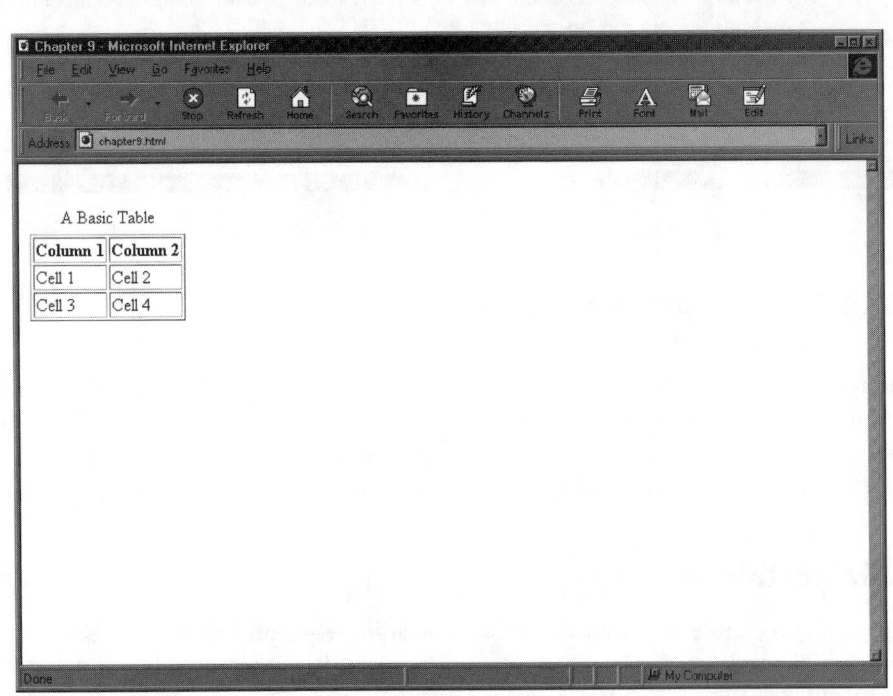

Figure 8.1 A Basic Table

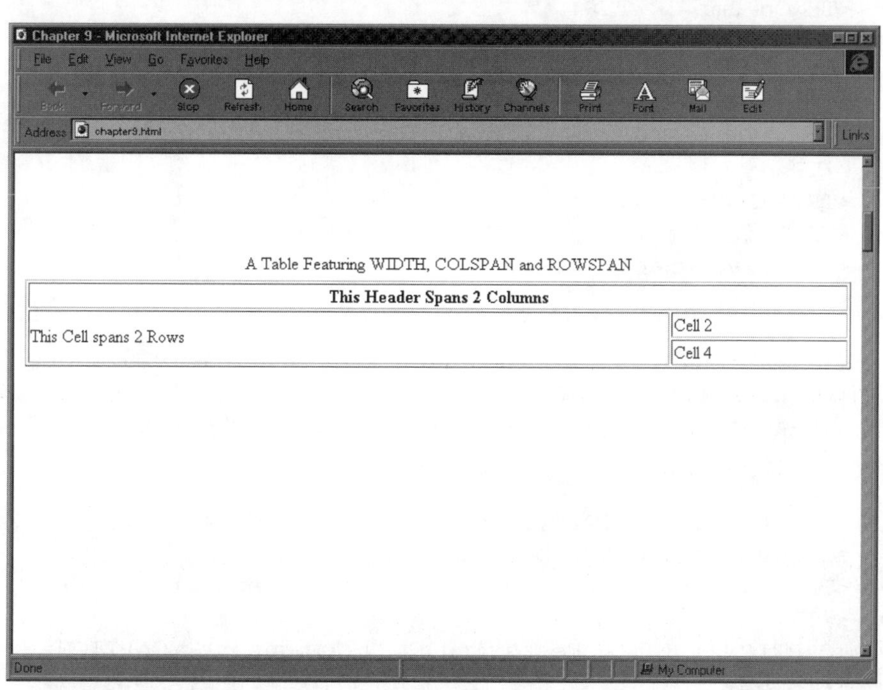

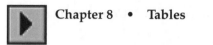

Figure 8.2 A Table Featuring WIDTH, COLSPAN, and ROWSPAN

Sample Code:

```
<TABLE BORDER="1" WIDTH="100%">
<TH COLSPAN=2>This Header Spans 2 Columns</TH>
<TR>
<TD ROWSPAN=2>This Cell spans 2 Rows</TD>
<TD>Cell 2</TD>
</TR>
<TR>
<TD>Cell 4</TD>
</TR>
<CAPTION>A Table Featuring WIDTH, COLSPAN and
ROWSPAN</CAPTION>
</TABLE>
```

The following table demonstrates the cell alignments you can specify by using the ALIGN and VALIGN attributes with the <TH> and <TD> elements.

```
<TABLE BORDER="1" WIDTH="100%">
<TH>Column 1</TH>
<TH>Column 2</TH>
<TR>
<TD>Cells are aligned left by default.</TD>
<TD ALIGN="RIGHT">This cell is aligned right.</TD>
</TR>
<TR ALIGN="CENTER">
<TD>This entire row</TD>
<TD>is aligned center.
</TR>
<TR>
<TD VALIGN="TOP">This cell is <br>vertically aligned
<br>to the top.</TD>
<TD>text<br>text<br>text<br>text<br>text<br>text</TD>
</TR>
<TR>
<TD VALIGN="BOTTOM">This cell is <br>vertically
aligned <br>to the bottom.</TD>
<TD>text<br>text<br>text<br>text<br>text<br>text</TD>
</TR>
<CAPTION>A Table Featuring Cell Alignment</CAPTION>
</TABLE>
```

The preceding code displays as shown in Figure 8.3.

The HTML 4.0 specification introduced two new alignment attributes to the general table specification: CHAR and CHAROFF. CHAR sets the character that the cells should be aligned on, such as a decimal point (.), colon (:), or any other character. This is handy for dealing with tables containing large columns of decimal figures or pricing information, as in the following example:

```
<TABLE border="1">
<TR>
<TH>Menu Items</TH>
<TH>Price</TH>
</TR>
<TR ALIGN="CHAR" CHAR=".">
<TD>Soup du Jour</TD>
<TD>$1.99</TD>
</TR>
<TR ALIGN="CHAR" CHAR=".">
<TD>Square Egg Sandwich</TD>
<TD>$3.50</TD>
</TR>
<TR ALIGN="CHAR" CHAR=".">
```

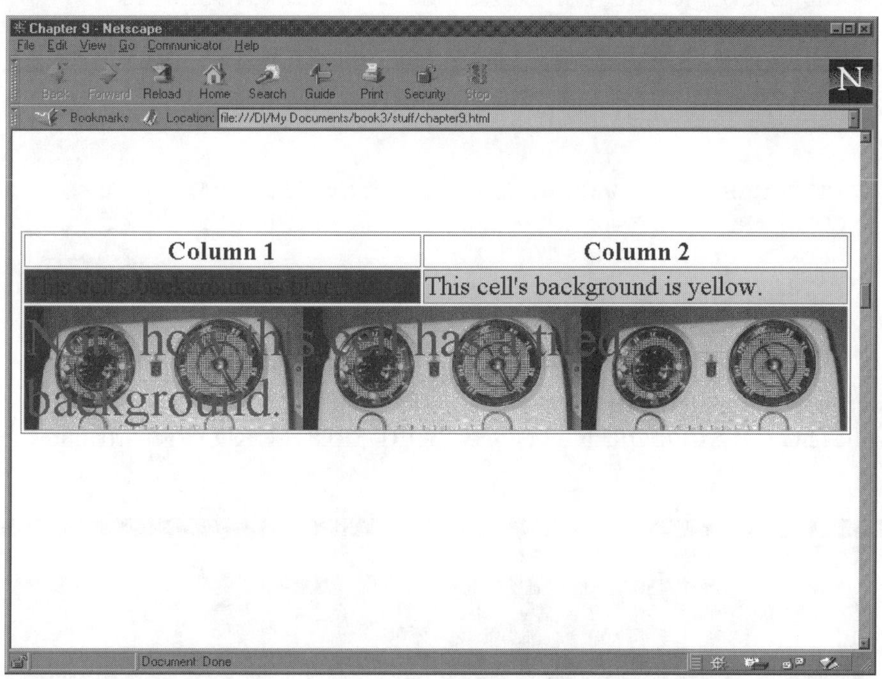

Figure 8.3 A Table Featuring Cell Alignment

```
<TD>Super-Duper Crepe Suzette Supreme with truffles
and caviar</TD>
<TD>$250.75</TD>
</TR>
</TABLE>
```

CHAROFF takes a numerical or percentage setting to space the predefined CHAR character offset from the left margin of the cell. CHAROFF=5 will space the CHAR character five spaces from the left margin of the cell; CHAROFF=50% centers the CHAR character within the cell.

At the moment neither of these two attributes are recognized by either Netscape Navigator or Internet Explorer.

The following table code demonstrates the use of cell background colors and a background image.

```
<TABLE BORDER="1" WIDTH="100%">
<TH>Column 1</TH>
<TH>Column 2</TH>
```

```
<TR>
<TD BGCOLOR="0000FF">This cell's background is
blue.</TD>
<TD BGCOLOR="FFFF00">This cell's background is
yellow.</TD>
</TR>
<TR>
<TD COLSPAN=2 BACKGROUND="crosleyD25.jpg"><FONT
COLOR=RED SIZE=6>Note how this cell has a tiled
background.</FONT></TD>
</TR>
</TABLE>
```

This code will work in both Netscape Navigator and Internet Explorer. The results of this code are displayed in Figure 8.4

The BORDERCOLORLIGHT and BORDERCOLORDARK attributes can

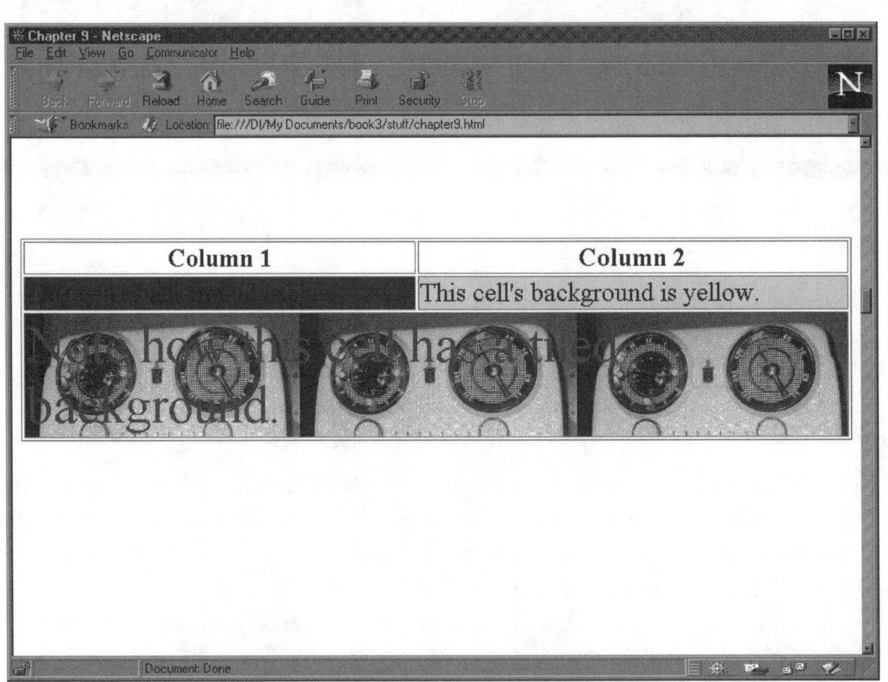

Figure 8.4 A Table Featuring Colored Background and Background Image Attributes

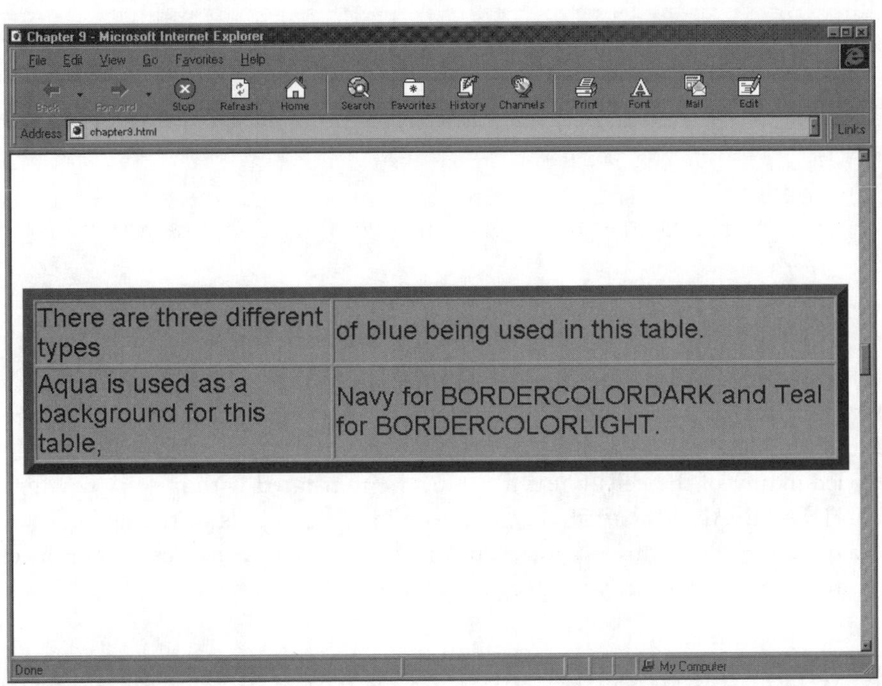

Figure 8.5 A Table Displayed in Internet Explorer Using the BGCOLOR, BORDERCOLORLIGHT, and BORDERCOLORDARK Attributes

make for some very striking-looking tables, but the results can be seen only in Internet Explorer. The following code presents a very eye-catching table (see Figure 8.5) using the BGCOLOR, BORDERCOLORLIGHT, and BORDERCOLORDARK attributes.

```
<TABLE BORDER=10 BGCOLOR="AQUA" BORDERCOLORDARK="NAVY"
BORDERCOLORLIGHT="TEAL">
<TR>
<TD>
<FONT FACE=ARIAL SIZE=5>
There are three different types
</TD>
<TD>
<FONT FACE=ARIAL SIZE=5>
of blue being used in this table.
</TD>
```

```
</TR>
<TR>
<TD>
<FONT FACE=ARIAL SIZE=5>
Aqua is used as a background for this table,
</TD>
<TD>
<FONT FACE=ARIAL SIZE=5>
Navy for BORDERCOLORDARK and Teal for BORDERCOLORLIGHT.
</TD>
</TR>
</TABLE>
```

This table code shows another effect inherent in tables: Font attributes do not carry over into adjoining cells. To make the size of the table larger and easier to see, the font size was set to a value of 5. Despite the fact that there is no end tag specified in any of the cells, the effect must be reinstated within every cell for the <FONT FACE=ARIAL> attribute to be seen in all four cells of the table. There is no easy way of doing this—if you want to add font characteristics within the cells of a table, you must specify it in each and every cell.

Identifying Table Elements to Nongraphical Browsers

The numbers of browsers that are incapable of properly displaying tables is rapidly diminishing, but there are three newly introduced attributes for the <TABLE>, <TD>, and <TH> tags that enable the Web author to identify the table's contents to these viewers.

The HEADER attribute associates header information for a particular cell in a given column, and SCOPE provides information on a particular row, column, or group of rows and columns. These attributes were devised specifically for such devices as speech synthesizers and Braille-based devices, to identify the information in a table more easily.

Use HEADER to clearly identify which table cell belongs to which table header category. For example, in the following code example, HEADER-apples identifies that its cell content (Granny Smith) is associated with Types of Apples rather than with the other column header Types of Oranges.

```
<TABLE>
<TR>
<TH>Types of Apples</TH>
<TH>Types of Oranges</TH>
</TR>
<TR>
```

```
<TD HEADER=apples>Granny Smith</TD>
<TD HEADER=orange>Mandarin</TD>
</TR>
</TABLE>
```

The SCOPE attribute is used in place of the HEADER attribute when you want to identify whole regions of a table rather than identify each cell's contents. When SCOPE is specified it uses the content of the cell it is associated with to identify the type of content held in the row, column, group of rows, or group of columns. The SUMMARY attribute of the <TABLE> tag is used to provide a brief description of the contents of the table as a whole. The following example code illustrates how both attributes can be used.

```
<TABLE BORDER SUMMARY="A listing of some major U.S.
and Canadian radio manufacturers of the 1940s">
<TR>
<TH COLSPAN=2 SCOPE="ROW">U.S. and Canadian Radio
Manufacturers - 1940s</TH>
</TR>
<TR>
<TH SCOPE="COL">Canadian</TH>
<TH SCOPE="COL">U.S.</TH>
</TR>
<TR>
<TD>Addison</TD>
<TD>Zenith</TD>
</TR>
<TR>
<TD>Rogers</TD>
<TD>Philco</TD>
</TR>
</TABLE>
```

These tags were all introduced in the HTML 4.0 specification and are not yet implemented within any browser. However, since they have no visible characteristics, you can include such information into your tables now so that they can be properly read when these attributes are supported at a later date.

THE OTHER TABLE TAGS

Netscape Navigator was the first Web browser to add the ability to create tables in HTML, but another more complex design for creating tables was made official in

the HTML 3.0 specification. Many of these tags duplicate the function of the existing set of Netscape table tags, but there are several that provide better designs for tables, including the ability to format features for groups of rows and columns. Internet Explorer was the first popular browser to widely implement many (though not all) of the tags and their attributes, and many are now recognized within Netscape Navigator as well.

<TBODY> . . .</TBODY>

Element Name: Table body tag.

Description: Defines the body of a table.

Attributes: ALIGN = LEFT | RIGHT | CENTER | JUSTIFY | CHAR
Specifies the horizontal alignment of contents within the cell relative to the cell boundaries. The default alignment is LEFT. RIGHT aligns the content to the right side of the cell, and CENTER aligns the content in the center of the cell.
BGCOLOR = *colorvalue*
Specifies a background color for the cell. This color overrides any BGCOLOR specified in the <TABLE> element. The color is defined using RBG values.
CHAR = *character*
Specifies an alignment character for use with ALIGN=CHAR.
CHAROFF = *# of character spaces* or %
Specifies the offset to the first occurrence of the alignment character on each line.
VALIGN = BOTTOM | BASELINE | MIDDLE | TOP
Specifies the vertical alignment of contents within a row of cells relative to the cell's boundaries. TOP aligns the content to the top of the cell, MIDDLE aligns the content to the middle of the cell, BOTTOM aligns the content to the bottom of the cell, and BASELINE aligns the content at the baseline so that all content lines up horizontally.

Associated Tags: <TABLE>, <THEAD>, <TFOOT>, <TR>, <TD>, <COLGROUP>, <COL>.

<THEAD> . . .</THEAD>

Element Name: Table header tag.

Description: Specifies the header row for a table.

Attributes: ALIGN = LEFT | RIGHT | CENTER | JUSTIFY | CHAR
Specifies the horizontal alignment of contents within the cell relative to the cell bounda-

ries. The default alignment is LEFT. RIGHT aligns the content to the right side of the cell, and CENTER aligns the content in the center of the cell.
BGCOLOR - *colorvalue*
Specifies a background color for the cell. This color overrides any BGCOLOR specified in the <TABLE> element. The color is defined using RBG values.
CHAR - *character*
Specifies an alignment character for use with ALIGN=CHAR.
CHAROFF - # *of character spaces* or %
Specifies the offset to the first occurrence of the alignment character on each line.
VALIGN - BOTTOM | BASELINE | MIDDLE | TOP
Specifies the vertical alignment of contents within a row of cells relative to the cell's boundaries. TOP aligns the content to the top of the cell, MIDDLE aligns the content to the middle of the cell, BOTTOM aligns the content to the bottom of the cell, and BASELINE aligns the content at the baseline so that all content lines up horizontally.

Associated Tags: <TABLE>, <TBODY>, <TFOOT>, <TR>, <TD>, <COLGROUP>, <COL>.

Can contain: <TR>.

<TFOOT>. . .</TFOOT>

Element Name: Table footer tag.

Description: Specifies the footer row for a table.

Attributes: ALIGN = LEFT | RIGHT | CENTER | JUSTIFY | CHAR
Specifies the horizontal alignment of contents within the cell relative to the cell boundaries. The default alignment is LEFT. RIGHT aligns the content to the right side of the cell, and CENTER aligns the content in the center of the cell.
BGCOLOR = *colorvalue*
Specifies a background color for the cell. This color overrides any BGCOLOR specified in the <TABLE> element. The color is defined using RBG values.
CHAR = *character*
Specifies an alignment character for use with ALIGN=CHAR.
CHAROFF= # *of character spaces* or %
Specifies the offset to the first occurrence of the alignment character on each line.
VALIGN = BOTTOM | BASELINE | MIDDLE | TOP
Specifies the vertical alignment of contents within a row of cells relative to the cell's boundaries. TOP aligns the content to the top of the cell, MIDDLE aligns the content to the middle of the cell, BOTTOM aligns the content to the bottom of the cell, and BASELINE aligns the content at the baseline so that all content lines up horizontally.

Associated Tags: <TABLE>, <TBODY>, <THEAD>, <TR>, <TD>, <COLGROUP>, <COL>.

Sample Code:

```
<TABLE BORDER>
```

```
<COLGROUP>
<COL ALIGN=CENTER SPAN=2>
<COLGROUP ALIGN=RIGHT>
<THEAD>
<TR>
<TH>A</TH><TH>B</TH><TH>C</TH>
</TR>
</THEAD>
<TBODY>
<TR>
<TD>1</TD><TD>2</TD><TD>3</TD>
</TR>
<TR>
<TD>3</TD><TD>4</TD><TD>5</TD>
</TR>
</TBODY>
<TFOOT>
<TR>
<TD>6</TD><TD>7</TD><TD>8</TD>
</TR>
</TFOOT>
</TABLE>
```

The results of this code can be seen in Figure 8.6.

The purpose of the <THEAD> container tag is to specify a row designated as the header row, which contains all of the headers for the table. The <TBODY> container tag specifies the main part of the table, and the <TFOOT> container tag specifies rows designated as the footer for the table. Each of these enclose table rows, and are designed to modify the contents of the row or rows it encloses. Both <TBODY> and <TFOOT> do not alter the appearance of the rows they enclose, though the <THEAD> tag bolds all text in the row it contains.

Each of these tags have a number of attributes in the HTML 4.0 specification; however, only the ALIGN, BGCOLOR, and VALIGN attributes are supported within Internet Explorer, and none at all in Netscape Navigator. They are worth investigating though, as they or a revised variant may be adopted within future Web browsers. The ALIGN attribute is already a familiar attribute, specifying the horizontal alignment of cells, and it has five possible values: LEFT, CENTER, RIGHT, JUSTIFY, and CHAR. Of the five, only CHAR is new—it specifies that the contents of the cell should be aligned with a certain character contained in the cell. Internet Explorer recognized LEFT, CENTER, and RIGHT but not JUSTIFY or CHAR. VALIGN is another familiar attribute, which specifies whether the cell contents are aligned with the top, middle, or bottom of the cell.

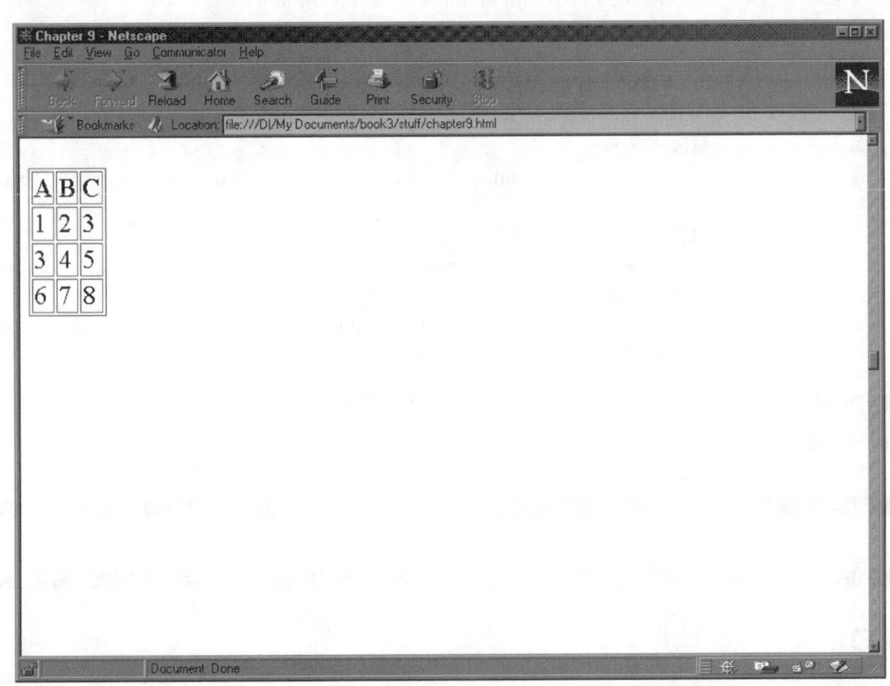

Figure 8.6 The Other Table Tags Displayed in Netscape Navigator

Column Groups and Columns

All of this may lead you to wonder why Microsoft (and later, Netscape) bothered inserting these HTML 3.0 tags in their Web browser when none of their attributes are supported. Where the <TBODY>, <THEAD>, and <TFOOT> tags have real influence is when they are combined in a table that uses the <COLGROUP> and <COL> tags, or with the FRAME or RULE <TABLE> attributes.

<COLGROUP> . . .</COLGROUP>

Element Name: Column group tag.

Description: Specifies settings for a group of columns in a table.

Attributes: ALIGN = LEFT | CENTER | RIGHT
Specifies the horizontal alignment of cell content.
CHAR = *character*
Specifies an alignment character for use with ALIGN=CHAR.
CHAROFF = # *of character spaces* or %
Specifies the offset to the first occurrence of the alignment character on each line.
SPAN = *number*
Specifies how many columns are contained within the current group. Value must be 0 or greater.
VALIGN = TOP | MIDDLE | BASELINE | BOTTOM
Specifies whether the cell contents are aligned with the top, middle, or bottom of the cell
WIDTH = # *of pixel* or % *of browser window*
Specifies the width of the column grouping either as a percentage of the window width, or as an absolute value in pixels.

Associated Tags: <TABLE>, <TBODY>, <THEAD>, <TR>, <TD>, <COL>.

Can contain: <COL>.

<COL>

Element Name: Column tag.

Description: Specifies the default settings for a column or group of columns.

Attributes: ALIGN = LEFT | CENTER | RIGHT
Specifies the horizontal alignment of cell content.
CHAR = *character*
Specifies an alignment character for use with ALIGN=CHAR.
CHAROFF = # *of character spaces* or %
Specifies the offset to the first occurrence of the alignment character on each line.
SPAN = *number*
Specifies how many columns the column specification is to be applied to. Value must be 0 or greater.
VALIGN = TOP | MIDDLE | BASELINE | BOTTOM
Specifies whether the cell contents are aligned with the top, middle, or bottom of the cell.
WIDTH = # *of pixel* or % *of browser window*
Specifies the width of the column either as a percentage of the window width, or as an absolute value in pixels.

Associated Tags: <TABLE>, <TBODY>, <THEAD>, <TR>, <TD>, <COLGROUP>.

Sample Code:

```
<TABLE BORDER>
<COLGROUP>
<COL ALIGN=RIGHT SPAN=2>
```

```
<COLGROUP ALIGN=LEFT>
<THEAD>
<TR>
<TH>APPLES</TH><TH>BANANAS</TH><TH>CHERRIES</TH>
</TR>
</THEAD>
<TBODY>
<TR>
<TD>1</TD><TD>2</TD><TD>3</TD>
</TR>
<TR>
<TD>3</TD><TD>4</TD><TD>5</TD>
</TR>
</TBODY>
</TABLE>
```

If you have a table containing three separate columns, you can use three separate <COLGROUP> tags to set different alignment attributes for each column. This is demonstrated in Figure 8.7, which uses the preceding example code.

Both <COL> and <COLGROUP> control the positioning of elements in the columns they control. Only the ALIGN=LEFT, CENTER, and RIGHT attributes and the SPAN attributes are recognized in the major browsers, but that is enough to demonstrate their effects on a table.

Even though the <COLGROUP> tag is a container tag, it does not have to contain any content to influence the columns in a table—in fact it cannot, because of the way data in HTML tables is structured in rows rather than columns. For this reason the end tag (</COLGROUP>) is usually dropped.

The <COL> tag is an empty tag that can control the layout of elements in multiple columns when used in conjunction with the <COLGROUP> tag. In the following HTML code sample, the elements contained in the first two columns are aligned to the right, and the elements contained in the last column are aligned to the left.

Most of the attributes for <COL> and <COLGROUP> have already been dealt with earlier in the chapter, but there is a new attribute worth mentioning: SPAN. It takes a numerical value and it can be used to group together information about a column. For example, if you wanted to set the width of 10 columns in a table to 20 pixels each, instead of having to add that information to each column, you could apply it all at once through the use of the SPAN attribute, as in the following code sample:

```
<COLGROUP SPAN="10" width="20">
</COLGROUP>
```

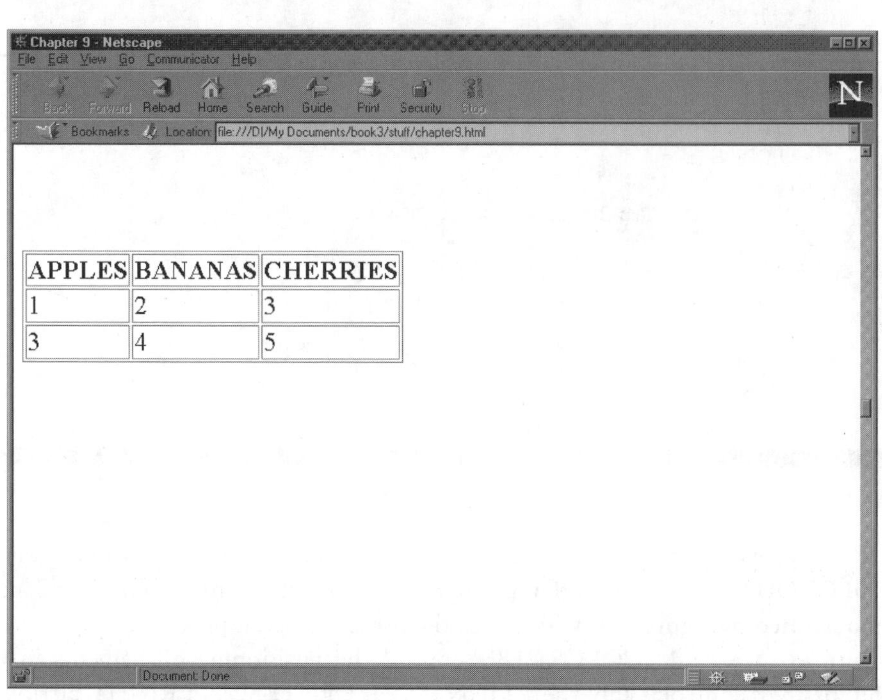

Figure 8.7 The <COL> and <COLGROUP> Tags Used in a Table Displayed within Netscape Navigator

The <COL> and <COLGROUP> tags are powerful tools for the Web designer who wants control over the alignment of the elements contained with the cells of a table, but keep in mind that as of this writing, they are supported only in Internet Explorer.

Frames and Rules

There are two other attributes that can be used when constructing tables to be viewed through Internet Explorer. In Internet Explorer, the <TABLE> tag has two additional attributes: FRAME and RULE. The FRAME attribute controls which sides of cell borders should be displayed. RULES specifies where dividing lines appear within a table.

The FRAME attribute has eight different values: BOX (the default), ABOVE,

BELOW, HSIDES, VSIDES, LHS, RHS, and VOID. BOX draws all four borders around a cell, ABOVE and BELOW draw borders only at the top and bottom of cells, respectively. HSIDES and VSIDES draw horizontal and vertical borders of cells, and LHS and RHS draws the left-hand and right-hand borders of cells, respectively. VOID draws no borders at all. All are used in conjunction with the <TABLE> tag in the following manner: <TABLE BORDER FRAME=BOX>. None of the FRAME values are much use without the BORDER attribute specified. All eight values and the HTML code that produces them are displayed in Figure 8.8.

Similarly, the RULES attribute draws ruled lines for specified parts of the table. RULES has five values: ALL (the default), ROWS, COLS, NONE, and GROUPS. ALL is the same as FRAME=BOX—all cell borders are drawn. ROWS and COLS draws borders between table rows and columns, respectively, and NONE draws no rules within the table at all (though it does draw the table border). The GROUPS attribute works in conjunction with any column groups specified by <COLGROUP>, <COLS>, or spanned rows within a table. All are used in con-

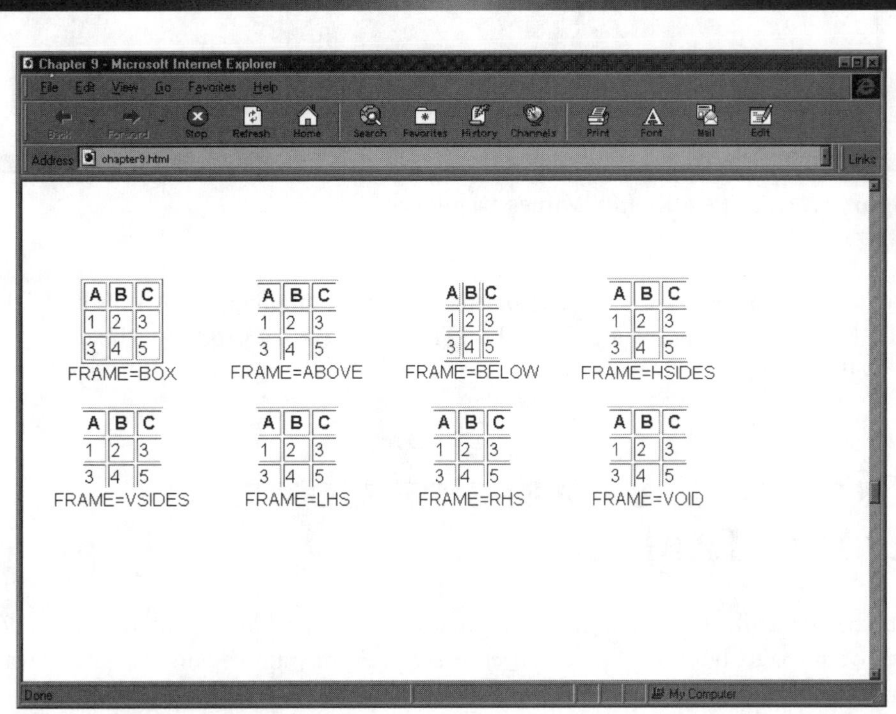

Figure 8.8 All Eight FRAMES Values Displayed

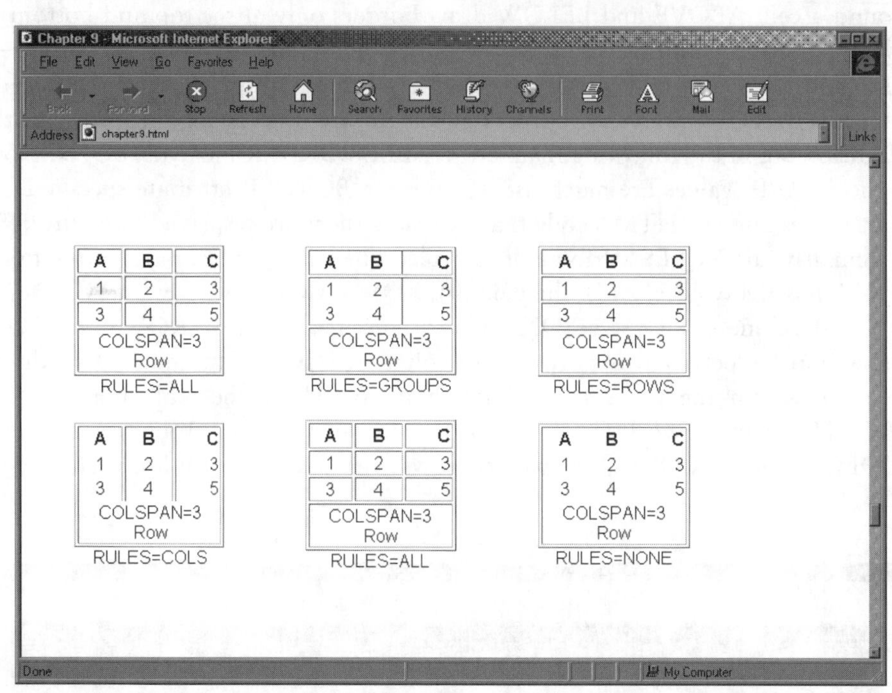

Figure 8.9 All Five RULES Values Displayed

junction with the <TABLE> tag in the following manner: <TABLE BORDER RULE=ALL>. All five values and the HTML code that produces them are displayed in Figure 8.9.

Creating A Table of Contents Using Tables

Maybe you'd like to have a Web page that contains a table of contents on the left side of the page, but don't want to use the set of Frame tags because you don't want to exclude those users who don't use a Frames-capable browser.

Or maybe you'd like to create a Web page containing multiple columns, but don't want to use the <MULTICOL> tag because it only works in Netscape Navigator. Sounds like what you need is a bunch of tables to lay things out on your Web pages.

There are two different approaches to creating a multicolumn display using HTML tables: either create a Web page consisting of two table data cells where all of the contents are arranged in two long columns, or create a table that displays its content in various cells. The second approach is really a variant of the first, and both have their specific uses on a Web page.

The initial table example consists of two columns and two rows. Take away one row and you have a basic table consisting of two table data cells. This may not seem like much of a foundation for a good-looking Web page, but appearances can be deceiving. By using some table tag attributes and a few other tricks, you can divide the content of a page into a columnar format.

Use the WIDTH attribute of the <TD> to help set the dimensions of what will end up being a column in your table, as in the following example.

```
<TABLE>
<TR>
<TD WIDTH=180>
<!-- left-hand table of contents begins -->
<A HREF="intro.html">Introduction</A><BR>
<A HREF="chapter 1.html">Go to Chapter1 </A><BR>
<A HREF="chapter 2.html">Go to Chapter 2</A><BR>
</TD>
<TD>
<!-- right-hand column content begins -->
Welcome to my introductory home page!
</TD>
</TR>
</TABLE>
```

In this case, the WIDTH attribute forces the table column to be 180 pixels wide. The links for this home page appear in the left-hand side of the Web page, and the content appears on the right. As long as the BORDER attribute of the <TABLE> tag is not specified, no actual table borders appear, so the user may not even know that they are looking at a Web page that uses a table as its foundation. In this way you can create a simple table of contents for your Web page that does not rely on the <MULTICOL> tag or set of Frame tags. Add this structure throughout your Web pages to create a stable table of contents.

An alternative method of arranging the table is to further divide the two columns of the previous table into various horizontal cells. This arrangement is ideal if you want to add subject headings within a column on your Web page. The following code example shows a simple table containing two columns divided into three rows:

```
<TABLE>
<TR>
```

```
<TD WIDTH=180>
All About Oranges
</TD>
<TD>
Oranges blah blah blah . . .
</TD>
</TR>
<TR>
<TD WIDTH=180>
All About Apples
</TD>
<TD>
Apples blah blah blah . . .
</TD>
</TR>
<TR>
<TD WIDTH=180>
All About Lemons
</TD>
<TD>
Lemons blah blah blah . . .
</TD>
</TR>
</TABLE>
```

The code may look a bit complicated, but the underlying structure is simple. Essentially the subject heading is contained within the first table data element and the content in the second. Each row contains two table data elements, of which the first cell in each row makes a column that is 180 pixels wide. Using this structure, the subject heading will always appear alongside the content it prefaces. To add some further refinement, add <TR VALIGN=TOP> to force the subject heading (and the content alongside it) to appear at the top of the table cell.

TABLE BINDING

Some more experienced Web authors will immediately see a problem with the <TD WIDTH=180> code used in the previous two examples—it tells the browser to set the width of that cell (and the column it creates) to 180 pixels in width only *as long as the viewer's browser window permits it*. If there are some large images in the right-hand column or if the viewer's browser window is very narrow, you cannot guarantee that the column will be set at 180 pixels.

If you want to fix this column in place, you have to insert something that will force it to the dimension you want. There are two popular options: use an image or use a line of nonbreaking space elements. If you insert an image that is 180 pixels wide in the first column, it will ensure that the contents of the column are never less than 180 pixels wide. You can also use a long line of nonbreaking spaces by using the character entity   that equals the width you desire. This is trickier and less precise, since the size of the nonbreaking space depends on the font size being displayed, so it is always a good idea to set the <FONT SIZE> tag when using this approach.

Want to ensure that your entire Web page cannot be resized by the user, so that *everything* it contains is fixed in place? All you have to do is to force both columns to a specific size, and then contain that table within *another* table of a predetermined size, in effect *binding* the inner table to be displayed at the desired size specified in the larger table. Here is some sample code that demonstrates the effect.

```
<TABLE>
<!-- Beginning of the outer table -->
<TR>
<TD WIDTH=500>
<TABLE>
<!-- Beginning of the inner table -->
<TR>
<TD WIDTH=180>
<1-- Column one -->
<IMG SRC="barney.gif" HEIGHT=100 WIDTH=180>
Here's an image of Barney that sets the width of this
column.
</TD>
<TD>
<!-- Column two -->
<IMG SRC="fred.gif" HEIGHT=100 WIDTH=320>
Here's an image of Fred that sets the width of this
column.
</TD>
</TR>
<!-- End of the inner table -->
</TABLE>
</TD>
</TR>
<!-- End of the outer table -->
</TABLE>
</CENTER>
</BODY>
</HTML>
```

So what you end up with is a table within a table that will appear the same to the viewer, no matter the browser window size. The outer table is set to the sum of the sizes of the two columns: 500 pixels. The outer table is necessary because the images in the column may not be resized in the viewer's browser window, but other elements still can (though to a lesser degree than if the images were not there in the first place). The outer table restricts the overall Web page to the desired size—no amount of resizing the browser display by the user will change the width of the Web page display.

There is a lot more that can be done with some inventive HTML table code—experiment for yourself and you will find HTML tables to be an effective way of laying out the content on your Web pages.

A Final Word about Tables

Tables often prove to be a difficult challenge for Web authors. There are so many attributes available for each element that the coding can appear complex, and become the source of much frustration. But do not despair! Constantly code the table, then check its appearance with your Web browser. Through trial and error, table building will become clear.

An additional snag are the numerous Microsoft Internet Explorer specific attributes—be sure to use that browser when testing those attributes! The good news is that once you have tables figured out, they will seem very easy to construct. As well, there are many WYSIWYG HTML editors that make table construction a snap. Be prepared to edit your table by hand; inevitably, you will want to add attributes that the editor may not yet support. Enjoy!

CHAPTER 9

Frames, Multiple Columns, and Layers

Frames are a relatively recent innovation that allows Web designers essentially to open up a number of different windows that a user can peer through to read the underlying Web page. Perhaps the best way to think of it is that by using Frames, the Web author can display the contents of several pages at once within a space normally reserved for a single page. This capability allows the Web designer greater control over the layout and presentation of material on a Web site, displaying more information within the same space.

Frames are generally not used simply to space and lay things out on a Web page, for reasons that will be made obvious later. As Web page design has evolved, there are two typical uses for Frames:

- Display elements that should always be present on-screen
- Display a table of contents (or something similar)

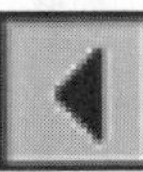

Frames are often used to fix display elements, like toolbars or navigational buttons, on a Web page. This can be accomplished because Frames can be positioned precisely on a Web page by the author, and can be used to Frame a navigational bar in place. What's more, because the bar is contained within a Frame, it can appear as a constant navigational aid that remains in place while the user moves through the Web site. The navigational bar can be made functional by either using imagemaps, or through the use of a JavaScript (or an equivalent script in a different scripting language) (see Figure 9.1).

The other, and perhaps most common reason for using Frames within a Web page is to use it as a table of contents for items that appear within the Web site (see Figure 9.2). Typically, a Frame will appear to one side of the browser window that contains information and links to other portions of the Web site. When a user clicks on a link in the table of contents frame, it changes a page that appears in another Frame. In this way a user can go immediately to the section of the Web site that they are interested in. It is a great way to present the whole of a Web site to the user in a way that makes it easily accessible.

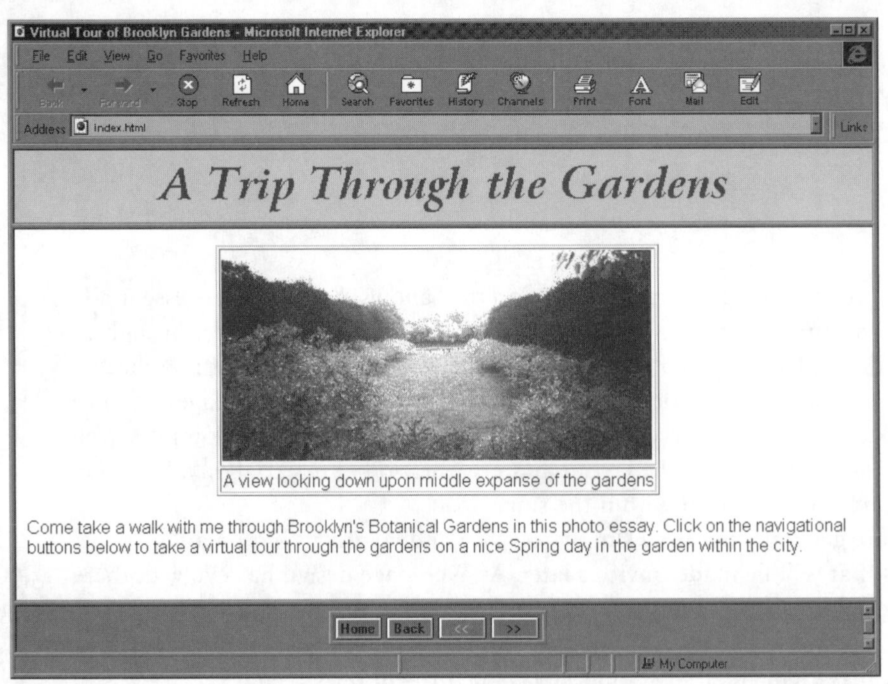

Figure 9.1 Framed Web page Containing a Navigational Bar in a Frame

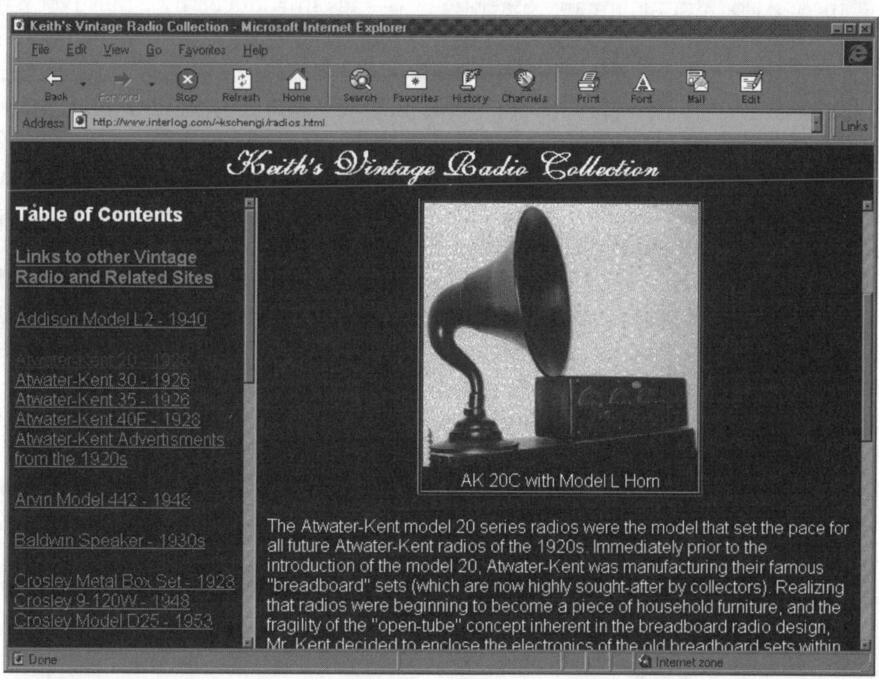

Figure 9.2 Framed Web Page Containing a Table of Contents Frame

It should be noted that these two methods are not mutually exclusive, and can be used in conjunction.

There are other related uses for Frames in addition to those already described. A Frame could also be used to display things like corporate logos, copyright information, or banner ads for other companies. The table of contents scheme can also be used in a similar manner to frame a number of questions and answers. The questions would reside in the table of contents Frame, and when the user clicks on a particular question, the answer appears in a separate Frame.

Frames were a Netscape innovation originally introduced with the launch of Netscape Navigator 2.0. It was later adopted within Microsoft's Internet Explorer 3.0, and then in NCSA Mosaic 3.0. Until very recently, Frames were considered a nonstandard HTML set of elements, but are now recognized as official within the HTML 4.0 specification set by the World Wide Web Consortium (W3C).

Even though Frames are recognized by the most popular browsers, they are not recognized by all, and cannot be viewed through text-based browsers like Lynx. Unlike Netscape's set of table tags, which borrowed heavily from a draft specifica-

tion from the W3C, the implementation of Frames was purely a creation of Netscape's. Also, although many other types of tags introduced by either Netscape or Microsoft that are ignored by other browsers are still able to display the underlying content of a Web page in an adequate (though maybe not as well laid out) manner, as we will see, the architecture behind Frames precludes this. Though there are solutions for even those Web browsers that do recognize Frames, any Web designer who wants to create a Web site using Frames should keep in mind that while the vast majority of Web surfers are viewing Web pages with either Netscape or Internet Explorer, *most* does not mean *everybody*.

There is one other major drawback to Frames worth mentioning: It generally takes longer to load a Framed Web page than any other type of simple Web page. This is because when users load a Framed Web page, they are typically not loading a single Web page and all of its content, but *several* pages and their content all at once. Since each Frame loads an individual page, the more Frames you have, the slowler the download to the user tends to be. There's another related problem as well—if you have misconfigured a Web page of forgot to upload a key page to your Web server, your users will be well-and-truly *stuck*, and possibly unable to navigate their way through your Web site.

It is also impossible for a user to link to a specific point within your Framed Web site. For example, if users only want to add a bookmark or a link to a specific part of your Web page from their own, they are unable to do so. Actually, this is possible, but only if the user wants to wade through your Framed HTML code, find the URL he or she is looking for, and then type it into the browser his or herself. Needless to say most users will rarely go to this extent, and they will simply link to your main Framed Web page, or not at all.

All of this shouldn't scare you off from doing a Framed Web site if it best meets your needs. A well-designed and properly implemented Framed Web site will stand out, and can even make your life as a Web author easier.

Understanding Frames

It is important to understand that when you are designing a Framed Web site, you are dealing with two very different types of HTML pages: the Frame layout page and the content pages. Content pages are basic HTML pages that contain all of the text, graphics, and hyperlinks for the Web site—it is all the material you want your viewers to see. The layout pages contain information about a Framed Web site's structure, setting up where the individual frames appear, and in what frames the various content pages should appear. Figure 9.3 illustrates the difference between the two types of pages that comprise a Framed Web site.

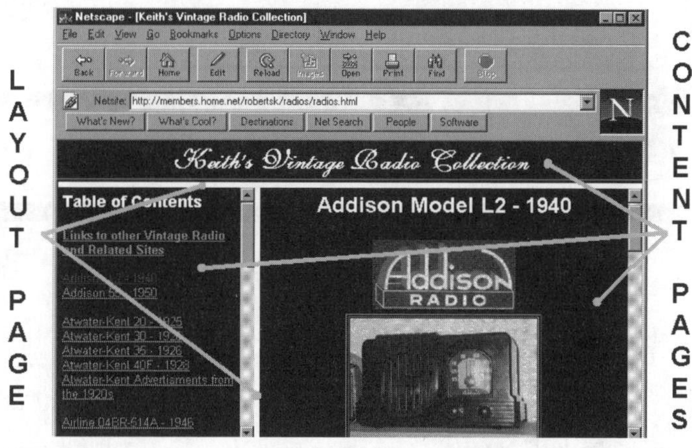

Figure 9.3 Layout Pages and Content Pages in a Framed Web Site

Most of this chapter concentrates on how to create the layout HTML page, as most of the nuts-and-bolts workings behind a Framed Web page take place here.

To understand how a layout page is constructed, you have to know how the tags behind Frames work.

<FRAMESET> . . .</FRAMESET>

Element Name: Frameset tag.

Description: Specifies a set of frames.

Attributes:

BORDER= # *pixels*
Specifies the thickness of the frame border in pixels.
BORDERCOLOR= *colorname or rrggbb*
Sets the color of the frame border (Netscape Navigator 3.0 and higher only).
COLS= # *pixels* | %
Sets the column size for an individual frame in pixels.
FRAMEBORDER= *YES* | *NO* (Netscape Navigator) or *1* | *0* (Internet Explorer)
Sets a global border for all frames.
FRAMESPACING= # *pixels*
Specifies whether or not there is any spacing between frames on a page (Internet Explorer only).

ROWS= # *pixels* | %
Sets the row size for an individual frame in pixels.

Associated Tags: <FRAME>, <NOFRAMES>.

<FRAME>

Element Name: Frame tag.

Description: Specifies the page that contains the content of an individual Frame.

Attributes:
BORDERCOLOR= *colorname* or *rrggbb*
Sets the color of the frame border.
FRAMEBORDER= *YES* | *NO* (Netscape Navigator) or *1* | *0* (Internet Explorer)
Sets a global border for all frames.
LONGDESC= *URL*
Points to a URL that contains more information about the frame.
MARGINHEIGHT= # *pixels*
Sets the vertical margin between the content of a frame and the frame itself.
MARGINWIDTH= # *pixels*
Sets the horizontal margin between the content of a frame and the frame itself.
NAME= *text*
Sets a name for a specific framed space within a Framed Web page.
NORESIZE
Specifies that the dimensions of a frame cannot be changed by the user.
SCROLLING= *AUTO* | *YES* | *NO*
Specifies whether or not a scrollbar should appear within a Frame.
SRC= *URL*
Specifies the URL of the Web page to be displayed within a Frame.

Associated Tags: <FRAMESET>, <NOFRAMES>.

Sample:

```
<HTML>

<HEAD>
<TITLE>Keith's Vintage Radio Collection</TITLE>
</HEAD>
<FRAMESET ROWS="50, *"FRAMEBORDER=0 FRAMESPACING=0>
<FRAME SRC="kvrc.htm"
       MARGINHEIGHT=0
       MARGINWIDTH=0
       NAME="header"
       SCROLLING = "no"
       NORESIZE>
```

```
<FRAMESET COLS="225, *">
<FRAME SRC="toc.htm"
       NAME="toc"
       MARGINHEIGHT=5
       MARGINWIDTH=5
       SCROLLING = "yes"
       NORESIZE>
<FRAME SRC="default.htm"
       NAME="default"
       SCROLLING = "yes"
       NORESIZE>
</FRAMESET>
</FRAMESET>
</HTML>
```

The basic structure behind a Frame page is that the <FRAMESET> tag contains the information for the Framed space, and the <FRAME> tags actually set up and specify how the individual frames are set up. Think of the <FRAMESET> container tag as a type of <BODY> tag for a Framed Web page, and the empty <FRAME> as its content. This analogy is not far from the truth—if you take a look at the preceding example code, you'll notice that there is no <BODY> tag present though the Frames and their content will appear within the browser. Both <FRAMESET> and <FRAME> must be used together to be able to create a Framed Web page.

Both <FRAMESET> and <FRAME> tags share many of the same attributes, though you should note that there are some differences in the ways Netscape Navigator and Internet Explorer handle Frame layout.

BORDER specifies the thickness of the Frame border as a pixel value. Initially implemented under Netscape Navigator 3.0, it has only recently been adopted within Internet Explorer 4.0. Here's how it works: if you want a thick border for all of the Frames to appear on your Web page, you could add a thick five-pixel border by using the following code:

```
<FRAMESET BORDER=5>
. . .
</FRAMESET>
```

BORDERCOLOR can be applied to either a <FRAMESET> or an individual <FRAME>. It is used to set the color of the border of a set of Frames. It can take either a colorname (like black, red, or chartreuse) or a hexadecimal color value (like #FFFFFF). It is worth noting that this attribute has only recently been adopted within Internet Explorer 4.0. For example, to set an individual <FRAME> to the color blue, you could do either of the following:

```
<FRAME BORDERCOLOR=blue>
```

or

```
<FRAME BORDERCOLOR=#0000FF>
```

A full listing of available colornames and hexadecimal color values can be found in Appendix D.

The COLS tag is a <FRAMESET> tag that enables you to set a Frame column. It takes a pixel value, and it specifies that whatever <FRAME> it contains should be displayed as columns (i.e., vertical Frames). In addition to a pixel value, it can also take on a wildcard value, that tells the browser to fill the rest of the space as a column. For example, if we have a Framed Web page that consists of three columns, it could be specified in the following manner:

```
<FRAMESET COLS=75,*,150>
. . .
</FRAMESET>
```

What this tells the browser is that it should reserve one column Frame that is 75 pixels in width, that it should set the third column to 150 pixels in width, and the second, middle column should be whatever space is left over in the browser window. In addition to the pixel and wildcard values, it can also take a percentage value. Since it is impossible to predict the screen resolution that the person is using to view a Web page, a pixel value that has the desired effect on one display may appear completely different on another. In this case, the use of a percentage value is recommended. Although it does not allow for the same precision in laying out the dimensions of various Frames, it generally produces better results across the board. It can be combined with a fixed pixel value and a wildcard value, as in the following example:

```
<FRAMESET COLS=25%,*,90>
. . .
</FRAMESET>
```

The FRAMEBORDER attribute is used by both the <FRAMESET> and <FRAME> and it tells the browser whether or not it should display a global Frame border if appended to <FRAMESET>, or whether an individual Frame should or should not display a border if appended to <FRAME>. FRAMEBORDER is a classic case of how things can go wrong when browser manufacturers disagree on how to specify an attribute. Netscape Navigator uses a simple YES or NO value, whereas Internet Explorer requires either a 1 or 0. By default, a border is always displayed (i.e., YES in Netscape Navigator and 1 in Internet Explorer). If you intend to switch a Frame border off, it is best to use the two different types of attributes together, as shown in the following example:

```
<FRAMESET FRAMEBORDER=NO FRAMEBORDER=0>
. . .
</FRAMESET>
```

It is worth noting that the 1 or 0 approach has been officially endorsed under the W3C's HTML 4.0 specification.

FRAMESPACING is an attribute used by the <FRAMESET> tag, and only within Internet Explorer. It takes a pixel value, and is used to set spacing between frames on a page. This allows some leading or space between individual sets of Frames. It essentially changes the display of the Frame border. The higher the value, the thicker the border of the Frame.

The LONGDESC attribute of the <FRAME> tag is an introduction from the official HTML 4.0 specification, and is used to point to a URL that contains more information about the information contained within the frame. At the time of this writing, this tag is not supported by either Netscape Navigator or Internet Explorer.

The MARGINHEIGHT and MARGINWIDTH are <FRAME> attributes that set the vertical and horizontal margins, respectively, between the content of a Frame and the Frame itself. In other words, they set a margin for the Frame borders, and the text and other elements contained within the individual content pages will appear indented from the sides of the Frame. It takes a numerical pixel value. To set a five pixel wide margin for an individual <FRAME>, you'd use the following code:

```
<FRAME MARGINHEIGHT=5 MARGINWIDTH=5>
```

The NAME attribute is a <FRAME> attribute that is used to distinguish a particular Frame. It takes a text value that generally describes the type of content to appear in the Frame.

For example, a good name for a Frame that will contain a table of contents for a Web site could be:

```
<FRAME NAME="TOC">
```

or

```
<FRAME NAME="TableOfContets">
```

If you have a certain area of the Framed Web site that will always be updated by a link elsewhere, then you might want to name it something appropriate, like the following:

```
<FRAME NAME="Default">
```

or maybe

```
<FRAME NAME="ChangeMe">
```

or something similar. The NAME attribute is an important attribute to use if you intend to have an area of your Framed Web site changed. In a process we describe in detail later in this chapter, a link can change the display within a particular Frame by specifying which Frame should be changed. Make sure you do not use the same name twice within a Framed Web site. The NAME attribute and the SRC attribute (described later in this section) are the only two required attributes of the <FRAME> tag.

The NORESIZE attribute of the <FRAME> tag tells the browser that a particular frame cannot be changed by the user. By default users can change the size of the Frame at will, simply by selecting a Frame and then moving it with their cursor. When NORESIZE is used, it removes this ability, and the Frame is essentially fixed in place.

The ROWS tag is a <FRAMESET> tag that works in exactly the same way as the COLS tag, but produces rows (horizontal Frames) instead of column Frames. It also takes a pixel value, and it can also take on a wildcard value that tells the browser to fill the rest of the space as a column. For example, if we have a Framed Web page that consists of two rows, it could be specified in the following manner:

```
<FRAMESET ROWS=50,*>
. . .
</FRAMESET>
```

In addition to the pixel and wildcard values, it can also take a percentage value. Since it is impossible to predict the screen resolution with which the person is using to view a Web page, a pixel value that has the desired effect on one display may appear completely different on another. In this case, the use of a percentage value is recommended. Although it does not allow for the same precision in laying out the dimensions of various Frames, it generally produces better results across the board. It can be combined with a fixed pixel value and a wildcard value, as in the following example:

```
<FRAMESET ROWS=15%,*,75>
. . .
</FRAMESET>
```

What this tells the browser is that it should reserve one row Frame to be 50 pixels in height, and use the rest of the space left over as another row in the browser window.

The SCROLLING attribute of the <FRAME> tag tells the browser whether or not a scrollbar should or should not appear within a particular Frame. It can take one of three values: AUTO (default), which tells the browser to insert scrollbars when necessary; YES, which tells the browser always to display a scrollbar (even if it is not necessary); and NO, which tells the browser never to display a scrollbar for a Frame. Although there are cases where you may want to use the NO value so that a particular Frame will not contain a scrollbar (like a frame containing a corporate logo, toolbar, or title for the site), there are few cases where you will want to force a Frame to display a scrollbar, even when not needed. Since the AUTO value is there by default, unless you do not want a particular Frame to be displayed, you do not have to worry about specifying this particular attribute in your Frame code.

Finally, the SRC attribute specifies the URL of the content Web page to be displayed within a given Frame. The SRC attribute and the NAME attribute (described earlier in this section) are the only two required attributes of the <FRAME> tag.

Note how the FRAMEBORDER attribute of the <FRAME> tag follows the Internet Explorer convention (either a 1 or 0) rather than Netscape Navigator's. Since Netscape is a member of the W3C, it will someday adopt this strategy for setting the FRAMEBORDER attribute. However, keep in mind that this stripped-down version of the Frame specification as it is currently used by both Internet Explorer and Netscape Navigator does not preclude the possibility that either firm may not add additional tags or functionality to the Frame scheme.

There is an additional Frame tag you must know before proceeding to make any Framed Web pages: the <NOFRAMES> tag. The <NOFRAMES> tag provides the Web author with the opportunity to pass along a message to the viewer using a Web browser that does not recognize the Frame tags. Here is more information on the tag itself:

<NOFRAMES> . . .</NOFRAMES>

Element Name: NOFRAMES tag.

Description: Displays the content it contains only to the user viewing the Web page using Web browsers incapable of reading Frames.

Attributes: None.

Associated Tags: <FRAMESET>, <FRAME>.

Sample Code:

```
<FRAMESET ROWS="75,*">
<FRAME SRC="up.html">
<FRAMESET COLS="35%,65%">
<FRAME SRC="rightside.html">
<FRAME SRC="leftside.html">
</FRAMESET>
</FRAMESET>
```

```
<NOFRAMES><BODY>
If you see text, you are using a Web browser that does
not support Frames. Sorry.
</BODY></NOFRAMES>
```

The <NOFRAMES> container tag is designed for the express purpose of displaying information to those people viewing your Framed Web pages who do have a Frames-capable Web browser. A Frames-capable browser is instructed not to display anything contained within these tags. It is generally considered a good idea to use them in conjunction with the standard <BODY> container tags for those Web browsers that look for a <BODY> tag before they show any displayable content.

TIP: Make sure you use <NOFRAMES>, not <NOFRAME> (without an S). If you are using a Frames-capable browser you will never notice this simple spelling error.

Good frame design should always use the <NOFRAMES> tags; otherwise, people using non-Frame capable browsers will be left in the dark. The best approach (though not always feasible) is to offer the viewer a page that will still look good in a non-Frames capable browser. In some cases it is entirely possible to duplicate an entire Framed Web site within the single layout Framed Web page, contained wholly within the <NOFRAMES> tags. This solution is not always practical, as many Web sites do not easily lend themselves to this change in design, and as new information is added to a Web site, it means that changes have to be made not only to the content page but to the <NOFRAMES> region of the Framed layout page as well. A much better approach, which has been widely adopted, is to present the viewer with an initial home page that allows the user to chose either between a Framed set of Web pages or not. In this manner, the Framed content pages can simply be linked to within the non-Framed Web site. Some minor changes are necessary to accommodate this change in design (like adding links from a main page, or perhaps adding navigational elements within the content pages), but at least you do not have to duplicate the content in more than one place on the Web site.

Tip: It is not a good idea to insert the following kind of sentence within a set of <NOFRAMES> tags:

```
<NOFRAMES>
This Web site uses Frames. Get yourself a real
browser like <A
```

```
HREF="http://home.netscape.com/"Netscape
Navigator</A> or <A
HREF="http://www.microsoft.com/ie/">Internet
Explorer</A> so you can come back and view this
Web site properly.

</NOFRAMES>
```

Nothing is to be gained by insulting a user. There are many users who have no choice but to access the Web through Frames-incapable Web browsers. It is up to you to provide a proper alternative, or at the very least refrain from insulting the users who cannot access your Framed Web site.

Now you have all of the tools you need to starting creating Framed Web pages—static Web pages. To get the most of a Framed Web site, you will have to add links that will dynamically update and change the display of a content Frame in another Frame.

One final note about Frames and layout: Frames are not perfect when it comes to laying out things precisely on a Web page. You may think because you can control the precise dimension of a Frame by using a pixel value that the result is a Frame or a set of Framed pages that will always appear the same. This is simply not the case. Different browsers, different screen-resolutions and other elements out of your control conspire to defeat this idea. For example take the following Framed code example:

```
<HTML>
<HEAD>
<TITLE>JClass Chart</TITLE>
</HEAD>
<FRAMESET ROWS="65, *">
<FRAME SRC="jclasslogo.html"
       MARGINHEIGHT="0"
       MARGINWIDTH="0"
       NAME="header"
       SCROLLING=no
       NORESIZE>
<FRAMESET COLS="300, *">
<FRAME SRC="chart_toc.html"
       NAME="toc"
       MARGINHEIGHT=5
       MARGINWIDTH=5
       SCROLLING=yes>
<FRAME SRC="chart_default.html"
```

```
        NAME="default"
        SCROLLING=yes>
</FRAMESET>
</FRAMESET>
<NOFRAMES>
<BODY BGCOLOR=#FFFFFF>
<P>The JClass Chart HTML documents are designed to be
viewed through a browser that can handle frame tags,
such as <A HREF="http://home.netscape.com/">Netscape
Navigator</A> 3.0 or higher, or <A
HREF="http://www.microsoft.com/ie/">Internet
Explorer</A> 3.0 or higher.
</P>
<P>If you do not have access to such a browser, it is
recommended that you begin at the <A
HREF="chart_default.html">starting page</A> that
explains how the JClass Chart API is arranged, and
then proceed to the <A HREF="chart_toc.html">JClass
Chart Table of Contents</A>.
<P>
</BODY>
</NOFRAMES>
</HTML>
```

Figures 9.4 and 9.5 depict how this same code is interpreted and displayed within two different browsers, Netscape Navigator 3.0 for Unix, and Internet Explorer 4.0 for Windows 95/NT.

The immediate difference between the two images is the amount of each content page that is displayed within each individual Frame of the two different browsers. The user's settings for Internet Explorer use a different default and larger font, so not as much content can be seen within the same space as on Netscape Navigator for the Unix browser. This means that you cannot count on an element on a page always to appear within an initial Framed Web page. The same goes for any other type of Web page too, but this misbelief seems to be more prevalent among Framed Web site designers.

Note also how the spacing for the logo image at the top differs slightly between each browser. In Netscape Navigator, the JClass logo fits nicely, but in Internet Explorer there's a bit of extra spacing for the logo at the bottom. The code is the same, but the display is different. This is the reason why Frames are not recommended as a precise layout tool for creating Web pages. This effect is more pronounced when different screen resolutions or different monitors are used.

In general, be generous using precise pixel values to set a Frame, and go easy on

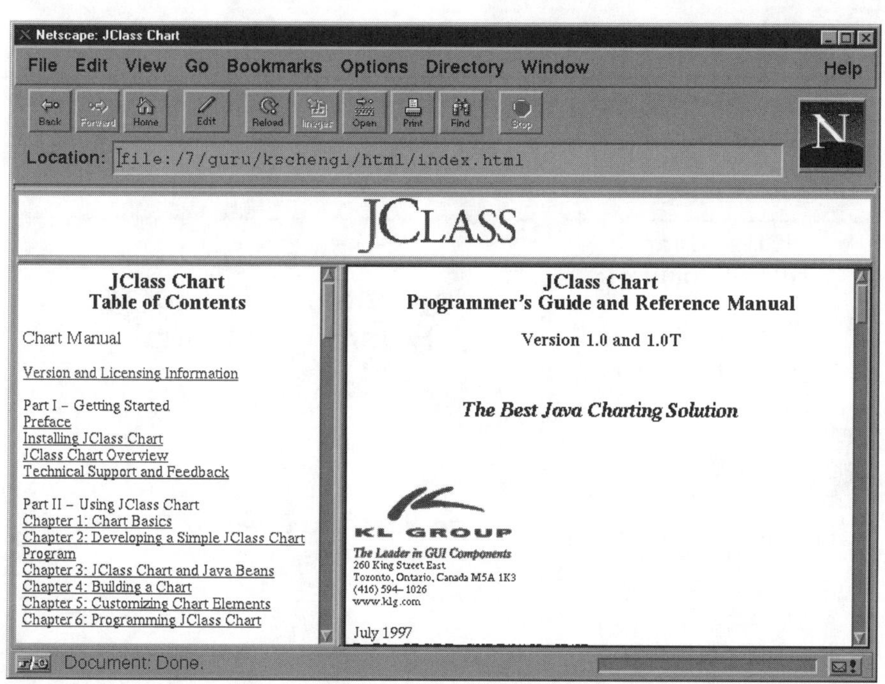

Figure 9.4 Different Browsers Can Display the Same Framed Web Page in Different Ways—Netscape

the SCROLLING=NO attribute, just in case you miscalculated badly and the user cannot see what you want them to see because they cannot readjust the Frame border.

CHANGING FRAME CONTENT

Up until this point we have been talking about the tags to use when creating a layout page for a Framed Web site. Now we get back to content pages.

Content pages are regular HTML pages that contain text, graphics, hyperlinks, and all of the usual elements that can be inserted within a Web page. Things become interesting within a content page when you want to use hypertext links within a Framed Web site. This architecture behind Frames can ease the job of the Web

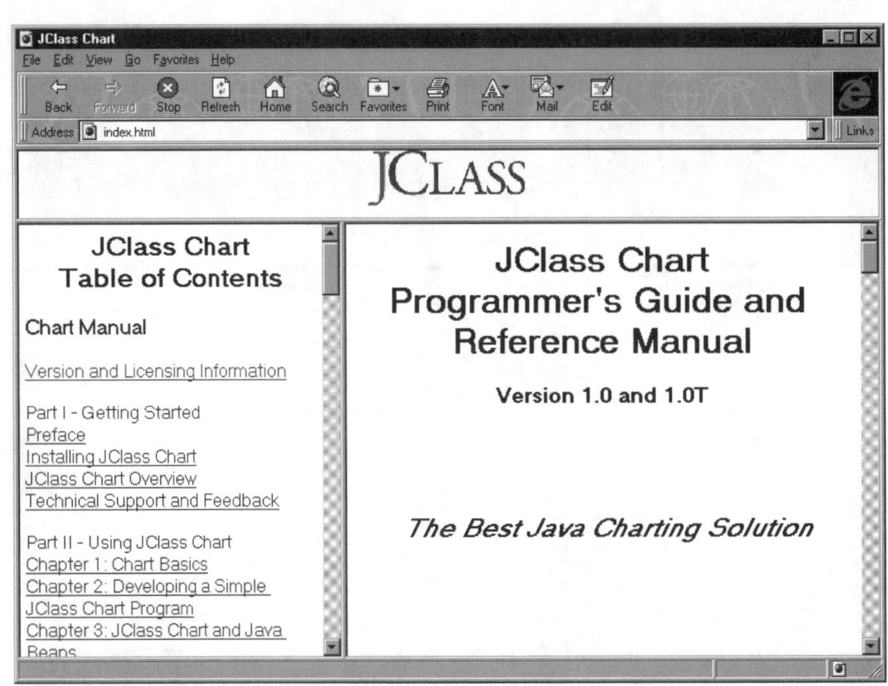

Figure 9.5 Different Browsers Can Display The Same Framed Web Page in Different Ways—Internet Explorer

master—whenever a new content page is created, all that has to be done in most cases is simply to add a link within another, master page (like a table of contents) and *voilà*, an updated Web site.

When you click on a link in a non-Framed Web site, the browser window is cleared, and then proceeds to load the new content contained on the page specified by the link. With Frames, it is possible to have a link update the information portrayed in the frame containing the link, have the link change the contents displayed in *another* frame, or launch a new browser window entirely. All of this can be accomplished by adding the TARGET attribute to a hypertext link, which links either to the NAME of the Frame to be updated, or launches a brand new browser window.

Here's how it works when you want to change the content page within another Frame: a TARGET attribute is added to a URL that points not only to a content page, but also to a target page.

As an example, if you have the following <FRAME> code:

```
<FRAME NAME="CONTENT" SRC="Page1.html">
```

you can update the content of this Frame by making it the TARGET of a link, and then replacing the default page ("Page1.html") with one of your own choosing, as in the following example.

```
<A HREF="Page2.html" TARGET="CONTENT">Turn to Page2</A>
```

Figure 9.6 shows how different links contained within one Frame can update the display in another Frame.

This is the reason why the NAME attribute of the <FRAME> tag is required—the Web browser needs to know which Frame to update. When adding these names, make sure they are descriptive, so you do not easily forget the Frame they belong to.

There is more you can do with the TARGET attribute than simply changing the content of another Frame. TARGET can also take one of five other reserved values:

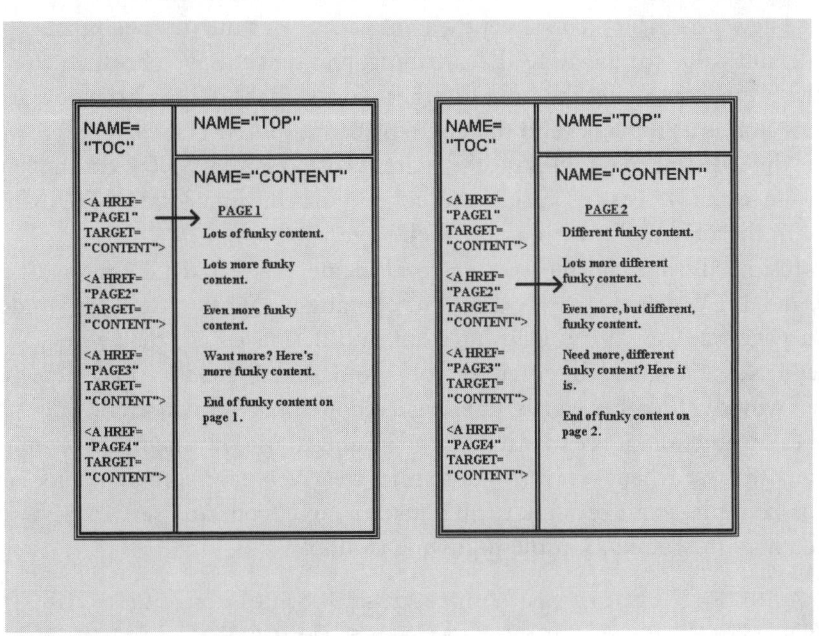

Figure 9.6 Image Displaying the Relationship Between TARGET and NAME

_BLANK
The browser loads the specified URL within a new, unnamed window.

_SELF
The browser loads the specified URL within the same Frame as that in which the TARGETed link resides.

_PARENT
The browser loads the specified within the <FRAMESET> parent of the current Frame.

_TOP
The current frameset is removed and replaced by the contents of the specified URL.

_NEW
The browser loads the specified URL in a new, separate browser window.

All of these reserved functions begin with an underscore (_).

_BLANK tells the browser to load the URL specified within the link to a new browser window. _TOP is now used (in Netscape Navigator 3.0 and up and Internet Explorer 4.0) to break out of the existing frameset and replace it with the specified new page; it is a convenient way of getting out of a framed layout. _SELF is the default value for the TARGET attribute, and tells the Web browser to update only the frame containing the link; in other words, it should load the new page in the same Frame as the link (and thereby replace it). _PARENT tells the browser to update the content based upon the parent of <FRAMESET> of the current Frame—in other words, replacing the content of the immediate <FRAMESET> instead of the <FRAME> with a new Web page.

Confusing? By far the most often used elements of TARGET are _BLANK, _TOP, and_NEW, which provide a way of opening up another browser window to place a page in. The _NEW element is an unofficial element that works in both Netscape Navigator and Internet Explorer and simply loads a page into a new browser window (in other words, opening a second browser window). Since _NEW describes its function, it is easier to remember and to use. It is highly recommended that you use these whenever you want to refer to a Web page contained on a remote site. For example, to make a link to an outside source, you can use TARGET=_TOP within a hypertext link, as in the following example:

```
<A HREF="http://www.FunkyOutsideSite.com/funky.html"
TARGET=_TOP> A Funky Link Outside of This Site</A>.
```

This approach has other benefits, too: By launching a new browser, it ensures you do not accidentally run into an infinite loop of Framed Web pages within a

Framed page. If you link to a page which itself is Framed, you will end up with an entire Framed Web site within a single Frame. If this Web page in turn leads to other Framed Web sites, the user has less and less usable space to play around with. This situation should be avoided at all costs by using the _TOP, _BLANK, or _NEW elements of the TARGET attribute when suitable.

The _TOP element used to work in the same way as _NEW, but in Netscape Navigator 3.0 and up and in Internet Explorer 4.0 it now allows the Web master to break out of the existing frame page layout and replace it with whatever page is specified in the URL.

Tip: You do not have to use the reserved TARGET elements only within a Framed Web page. Though the _TOP, _BLANK, and _NEW elements of the TARGET attribute are most often used within Frames, there is nothing restricting their use elsewhere, and they can be handy when all you want to do is launch some content within a new Frame. Note that this behavior appears only when the user has a Frames-capable browser.

FLOATING FRAMES

Internet Explorer 3.0 introduced an interesting innovation to the field of Frame HTML: inline or *floating frames*. The <IFRAME> tag essentially allows the Web author to embed other Frames within an existing (and otherwise non-Framed) Web page. It is implemented in a very similar fashion to the <OBJECT> tag, in that it allows you to insert one HTML document within another, and they can both be aligned with the surrounding text. (For more information on the <OBJECT> tag, please see Chapter 10.)

Here's a listing of the <IFRAME> container tag's attributes.

<IFRAME> . . .</IFRAME>

Name: Inline (or floating) Frame tag.

Attributes: ALIGN = *LEFT* | *RIGHT* | *TOP* | *MIDDLE* | *BOTTOM*
Sets the alignment of text following the inline Frame.
FRAMEBORDER= *1* | *0*
Determines whether or not a border appears around the Frame.
HEIGHT= # *pixels*

Sets the height of the frame in pixels.
HSPACE= # *pixels*
Sets horizontal spacing around the Frame in pixels.
LONGDESC= *URL*
Points to a URL that contains more information about the floating frame.
MARGINHEIGHT= # *pixels*
Sets a horizontal spacing within the Frame in pixels.
MARGINWIDTH= # *pixels*
Sets the vertical spacing within the frame in pixels.
NAME= *text*
Specifies a title or name for the inline Frame.
SCROLLING= *AUTO* | *YES* | *NO*
Tells the browser whether or not a scrollbar should be displayed within the floating Frame.
SRC= *URL*
Specifies the URL of the Web page to appear within the floating Frame.
VSPACE= # *pixels*
Sets the vertical spacing around the Frame in pixels.
WIDTH= # *pixels*
Sets the width of the Frame in pixels.

Related tags: None.

Sample:

```
<IFRAME ALIGN=RIGHT NAME="FunkyFloatingFrame" WIDTH=400
HEIGHT=250 SRC="frame1.html">
You are looking at a page that contains a floating Frame.
</IFRAME>
```

The ALIGN attribute aligns the floating Frame according to the value specified (see Figure 9.7). Aligning a Frame to the LEFT or RIGHT causes the Frame to align with the left or right margin while the text flows around it. Aligning an image TOP, MIDDLE, BOTTOM, indicates the vertical alignment of the text relative to the image on the same line.

The FRAMEBORDER attribute tells the browser whether or not it should display a global Frame border around the floating Frame. The default value is 1 (always display border).

The HEIGHT attribute specifies the height of the floating Frame in pixels. Similarly, the WIDTH attribute specifies the width of the floating Frame as a pixel value. It is a good idea to specify the HEIGHT and WIDTH of a floating Frame beforehand, as it reduces the overall time the browser needs to display the contents of the floating Frame. If the HEIGHT and WIDTH values are set, the browser simply loads the frame in the browser, and then proceeds to download the rest of the page—both the page containing the floating Frame and the content contained within the Frame itself.

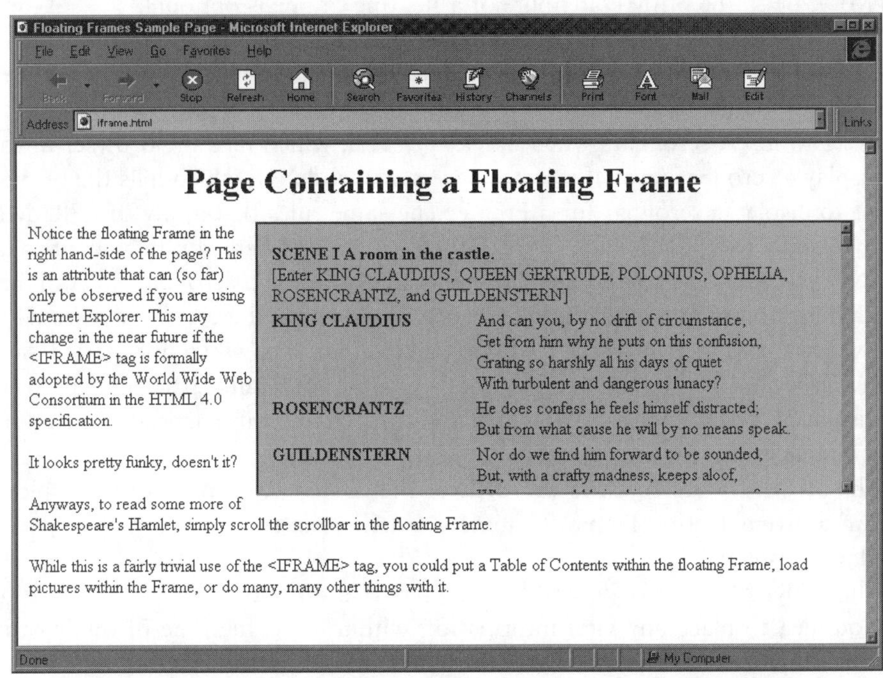

Figure 9.7 Sample Floating Frame Code Displayed in Internet Explorer

The HSPACE attribute specifies the amount of space, in pixels, on the left and right sides of the image. It essentially acts as padding between the floating Frame and the text or other objects surrounding the Frame. Similarly, the VSPACE attribute does the same thing, but instead adds padding to the top and bottom of the floating Frame.

The LONGDESC attribute of the <FRAME> tag is an introduction from the official HTML 4.0, and is used to point to URL that contains more information about the information contained within the floating frame. At the time of this writing, this tag is currently unsupported.

The MARGINHEIGHT and MARGINWIDTH attributes set a margin space for the left and right, top and bottom sides of the floating Frame, respectively. It serves to separate the Frame from its contents.

The NAME attribute serves the same function as it does with a regular Framed Web page—it helps to distinguish one floating Frame from another on a Web page. Similarly, a hyperlink can update the content of the floating Frame by using the

TARGET attribute pointing to the NAME of the Frame. Unlike regular Frame HTML syntax, the NAME attribute of a floating Frame is optional.

The SCROLLING attribute of the <IFRAME> tag tells the browser whether or not a scrollbar should or should not appear within a particular Frame. It takes the same three values as does the <FRAME> tag: AUTO (default), which tells the browser to insert scrollbars when necessary; YES, which tells the browser always to display a scrollbar (even if it is not necessary); and NO, which tells the browser never to display a scrollbar for a Frame. The same rules that apply to <FRAME> apply equally to <IFRAME>: although there are cases where you may want to use the NO value so that a particular Frame will not contain a scrollbar (like a Frame containing a corporate logo, toolbar, or title for the site), there are few cases where you will want to force a Frame to display a scrollbar, even when not needed. Since the AUTO value is there by default, unless you do not want a particular Frame to be displayed, you do not have to worry about specifying this particular attribute in your Frame code.

The SRC attribute specifies the URL of the content Web page to be displayed within a given floating Frame. If no SRC attribute is specified, a blank space is displayed instead.

The <IFRAME> tag is ignored by browsers that do not recognize it, so it is not a good idea to place any vital information within it. At the time of this writing, Internet Explorer is the only browser that currently supports. <IFRAME>; however, it has been officially adopted within the HTML 4.0 specification, so it may appear in other browsers soon.

MULTIPLE COLUMNS

The multicolumn tag is used to create multiple columns of text. It can create striking displays of text, but it is a Netscape Navigator-only tag, which restricts its practical use.

The characteristics of the multicolumn tag follow.

<MULTICOL> . . .</MULTICOL>

Element Name: The multicolumn tag.

Description: Divides text into multiple columns.

Attributes: COLS= # *columns*

Specifies the number of columns to be displayed.
GUTTER= # *pixels*
Sets the amount of pixel spacing between columns.
WIDTH= # *pixels or % of browser window*
Set the total width of the columnar display as either a pixel value or as a percentage of the width of the browser window.

Associated Tags: <BODY>, any other formatting element.

Sample:

```
<MULTICOL COLS=2 GUTTER=5 WIDTH=50%>
This text is displayed within two separate columns. The
&lt;MULTICOL&gt; tag is a relatively recent innovation,
and was first introduced within Netscape Navigator 3.0.
As you can see, the effect can be quite striking, because
it is so different from what you typically see on a Web
page.
</MULTICOL>
```

The COLS attribute sets the number of columns the text should be divided into, and takes a straight numeric value. The GUTTER attribute sets the amount of pixel spacing between the columns, and the WIDTH attribute sets the total width of the columnar display as either a fixed number of pixels, or a percentage of the browser window's width.

Be careful when using this tag: in addition to it being a Netscape Navigator-only tag, it is not very robust and the end result can look shabby under certain circumstances. For example, if you have a long word in a sentence displayed within a column, it may in fact creep into the adjoining column. The following code example, which is displayed in Figure 9.8 (along with the initial sample code) shows this unfortunate effect, as the word <MULTICOL> strays from the first column and enters into the second column.

```
MULTICOL COLS=3 GUTTER=25 WIDTH=350<BR>
<MULTICOL COLS=3 GUTTER=25 WIDTH=350>
This text is displayed within two separate columns.
The &lt;MULTICOL&gt; tag is a relatively recent
innovation, and was first introduced within Netscape
Navigator 3.0. As you can see, the effect can be quite
striking, because it is so different from what you
typically see on a Web page.
</MULTICOL>
```

It is also not a good idea to use the <CENTER> tag with a <MULTICOL> tag—it not only centers the columns, but the text within the columns as well.

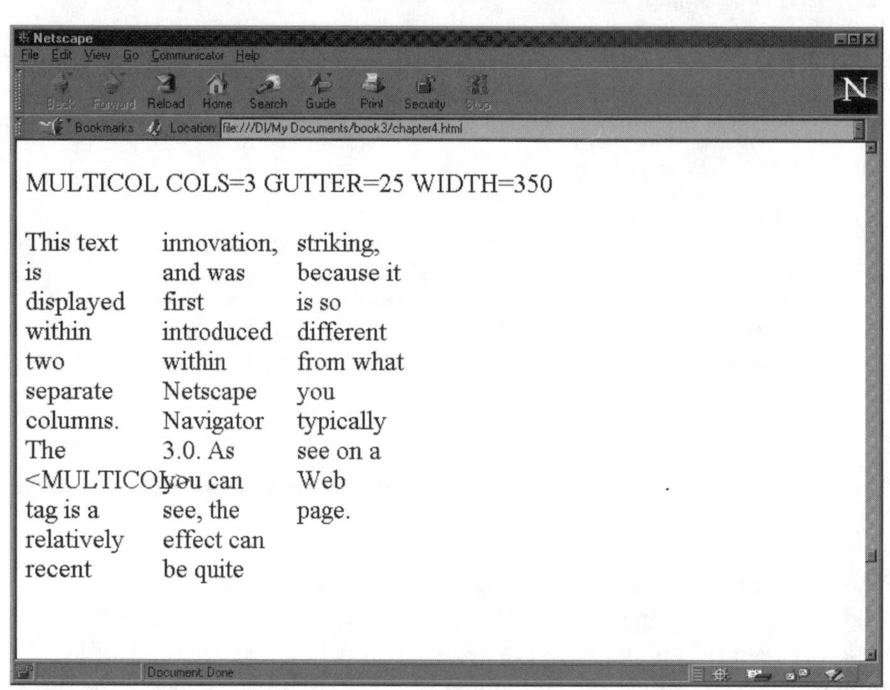

Figure 9.8 Web Page Displaying Two Different Columnar Displays of Text; Note How the Word <MULTICOL> in the Second Example Strays from Its Column

LAYERS

In the initial prerelease version of Netscape Navigator 4.0, Netscape took the opportunity to introduce another set of HTML tags. These new layer tags were designed to provide precisely positioned, overlapping layers on a Web page. These layers can be transparent or solid and can be stacked in a particular order within a Web page. The idea is with a little JavaScript wizardry, you can move around and display different layers to the user. Ideally, a Web user viewing a Web page using the new layer tags should be able to peel away and view the content on the different layers, kind of like a hypertext onion.

The concept needs a bit of explaining, as it is a new one for people within the desktop publishing community, from which many new HTML concepts have been derived. Probably the closest concept familiar to experienced HTML authors is the

idea of having hyperlinks contained within a page, linked to a kind of rolodex that brings new cards into view when you click a link. In a typical Web page that contains local links, you have a larger-than-usual Web page that that takes the viewer to a place further down on the same page they are viewing. This arrangement is handy if you want to limit the number of links to other Web pages, and to keep the total number of Web pages on your site down to a manageable level. Layers add this rolodex function, so that when a user clicks on a link it brings another page forward to the display. In this way you can have many layers of individual pages contained within what is actually a single Web page. In effect, you are flipping through the Web equivalent of a rolodex, all while staying within the single Web page (see Figure 9.9).

To explain Netscape's layer tags further, imagine that this imaginary rolodex held cards that were transparent in some areas, so that you could see the card immediately behind it, or perhaps see several cards immediately behind it through this transparent window. Now imagine that in addition to flipping pages, you could have part of a rolodex card appear in front of another card. So if a small creature sudden ran across your imaginary rolodex, it would seem to appear and reappear as it scurried between the layers (see Figure 9.10).

By now you have a better idea of how layers work. Essentially, they can behave like a standard rolodex, bringing various cards into view—and sometimes multiple

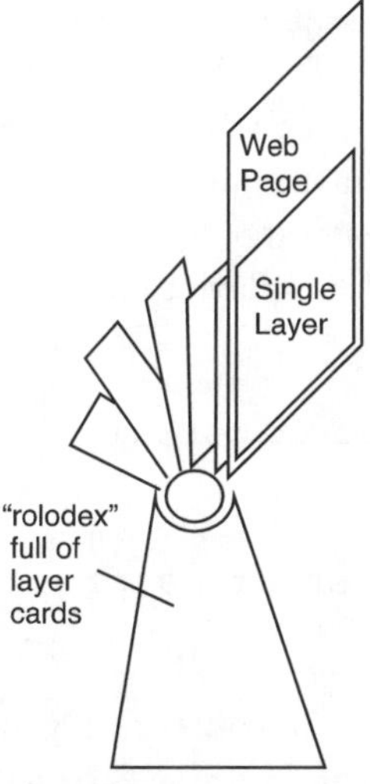

Figure 9.9 Netscape Layers as Rolodex Display

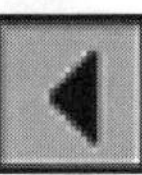

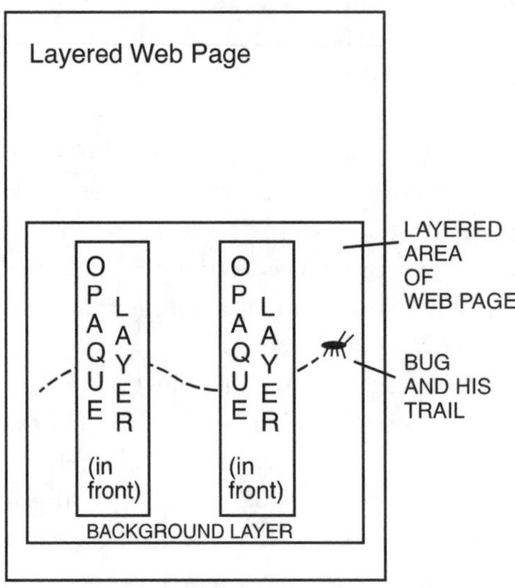

Figure 9.10 Layers That Have Relative Positions on a Web Page

parts of different cards at once—or they can be used for simple animation sequences.

The HTML code for layers is quite simple: the <LAYER> container tag begins and ends a layer on a Web page. The <LAYER> and </LAYER> tags contain all of the content that appears in the layer, which is probably best thought of in terms of separate Web pages. You can have multiple layers by having multiple <LAYER> and </LAYER> tags enclosing separate regions of content within a single Web page. For example, the following code displays two separate layers:

```
<LAYER>
This is one layer of material.
</LAYER>
<LAYER>
This is another layer of material.
</LAYER>
```

Okay, it isn't really this easy. If you try to view the preceding code through Netscape, you won't see much of anything. To make your layers functional, you have to provide a number of other display and ordering characteristics to the <LAYERS> tag.

<LAYER> . . .</LAYER>

Element Name: Layer tag.

Description: The layer tag specifies a layer that can appear on a Web page.

Attributes:

ABOVE = *layername*
Used to specify the stacking order of a layer within a set of layers. If used, the attributes BELOW and Z-INDEX cannot be used—they are mutually exclusive.
BACKGROUND = *filename*
Tiles a background image within a layer.
BELOW = *layername*
Used to specify the stacking order of a layer within a set of layers. If used, the attributes ABOVE and Z-INDEX cannot be used—they are mutually exclusive.
BGCOLOR = *colorname or hexadecimal colorvalue*
Sets the background color of a layer.
CLIP = *x, y, x1, y1*
Specifies the dimensions of a clipping rectangle (a visible layer) that appears within a layer.
HEIGHT = *# pixels or % of browser window*
Specifies the height of the layer in pixels, and sets the reference height for any children layers.
ID = "*layer_name*"
Used to specify the name of the layer. It servers as an identifier to distinguish it from other layers and to JavaScript scripts. Functionally equivalent to the NAME attribute.
LEFT = *# pixels*
Specifies the horizontal positioning of the layer in pixels.
NAME = "*layer_name*"
Used to specify the name of the layer. It serves as an identifier to distinguish it from other layers and to JavaScript scripts. It is functionally equivalent to the ID attribute.
PAGEX = *# pixels*
Specifies the horizontal position of the layer relative to the document window in pixels.
PAGEY = *# pixels*
Specifies the vertical position of the layer relative to the document window in pixels.
SRC = *URL*
Specifies the full pathname of a separate Web page containing HTML-formatted content for the layer.
TOP = *# pixels*
Specifies the vertical positioning of the layer in pixels.
VISIBILITY = *SHOW | HIDE | INHERIT*
Specifies whether or not the layer is visible.
WIDTH = *# pixels or % of browser window*
Specifies the width of the layer in pixels (applies to text only).
Z-INDEX
Used to specify the stacking order of a layer within a set of layers. If used, the attributes ABOVE and BELOW cannot be used—they are mutually exclusive.

Associated Tags: None (however, always used in conjunction with JavaScript).

Sample:

```
<LAYER NAME="Croequo2" LEFT=75 TOP=175 WIDTH=400
VISIBILITY="HIDE">
Yes, we sell funky frogs here!
<P>
<IMG SRC="bullfrog.gif">
</LAYER>
```

One of the parameters you have to add is the NAME attribute, or its alternate, the ID attribute. Both NAME and ID are functionally equivalent. It works much like the NAME attribute within a framed Web page—it specifies the name to be associated with a layer. This is important later, as the JavaScript program uses this attribute to know which layer to manipulate and display.

The LEFT and TOP attributes specify the horizontal and vertical positions at which a layer is to appear as a pixel value. With these attributes it is also possible to position one layer adjacent to another.

The WIDTH attribute determines the horizontal width of the layer in pixels or as a percentage. More correctly, it sets the maximum value for text within a layer before it is wrapped to the next line. Things that cannot be wrapped, such as images, extend beyond the margin. Make sure the width is large enough for both your text and any multimedia or images you may wish to display. HEIGHT behaves in much the same manner in vertical dimension, though its main purpose is to act as a reference height for subsequent children layers specified using percentage values. So if HEIGHT is set initially to 100 pixels, and subsequent layers are set to 90% of that height, they will be set to 90 pixels. If the initial HEIGHT is set to 200 pixels, and subsequent layers are set to 90% of that height, they will be set to 180 pixels.

BGCOLOR and BACKGROUND work just like they do with the <BODY> tag: BGCOLOR sets a background color for an individual layer, and BACKGROUND tiles an image file across the layer. BGCOLOR can take a colorname like red or green, or it can take a hexadecimal color value like #FFFFFF (white) or #000000 (black).

VISIBILITY sets whether a layer is visible or not. VISIBILITY has three values: SHOW, HIDE, and INHERIT. The first two are self-explanatory, and INHERIT means that a layer derives its visibility properties from the parent.

CLIP sets a clipping rectangle for the layer; in other words, it defines the visible layer within a layer. It takes a set of four numbers as a value, which indicate the left, top, right, and bottom value, respectively, in pixels. LEFT and RIGHT take pixel values relative to the sides of the layer, and TOP and BOTTOM specified the number of pixels down from the top of the containing document or layer. The left and top values default to 0, so it is possible to omit these values if the default value is desired. For example, a visible window that is 20 pixels in from the right and 40 pixels down can either be specified as 0, 0, 20, 40, or simply as 20, 40. This is an optional attribute, and if left out, the visible layer takes on the size determined by HEIGHT and WIDTH.

SRC works just like it does for an <IMG> tag: It points to a source file that can contain either layer information, JavaScript code, or both. It is designed to provide a remote resource for the year code on a Web page—instead of having to modify the whole of a Web page every time somebody wants to make a change in it, it can be added to an external Web page pointed to by SRC. This way, it can also draw upon large amounts of data that might otherwise make for an overlarge Web page for the user to download.

PAGEX and PAGEY take an integer value that specifies the horizontal and vertical positions of the top left corner of a layer relative to the enclosing document rather than the enclosing layer. Therefore a setting of PAGEX=200 and PAGEY=100 sets a layer to appear with its top left side beginning 200 pixels in from the left margin, and 100 pixels in from the top margin of the Web page, rather than the space normally set aside for displaying individual layers.

ABOVE, BELOW, and Z-INDEX are used to establish a stacking order for the layers. Their use is mutually exclusive—one of these can be used for a specific layer, though several different values can be used within a stack of layers. Z-INDEX takes an integer value; high-numbered Z-INDEX values are placed above those with lower ones. A layer with a Z-INDEX=3 is higher than that of Z-INDEX=1 or Z-INDEX=–1. At the time of This writing, only positive Z-INDEX values are valid, but the design states that those with negative numbers will automatically be assigned to be *below* the designated parent layer. The ABOVE attribute specifies that a layer is placed on top of a newly created layer, and BELOW identifies the layer immediately beneath a newly created layer.

Though all of this may seem complicated, in fact you need only a few of these attributes to make a layered Web page. For our purposes, the more straightforward examples work best.

The following sample code makes up four different layers for a fictitious firm called Croequo, which sells various flora and fauna.

```
<LAYER NAME = "Croequo0" LEFT = 75 TOP = 175 WIDTH =
400>
Mallards on sale! Drake scott!
<P>
<IMG SRC = "mallard.gift">
</LAYER>

<LAYER NAME="Croequo1" LEFT=75 TOP=175 WIDTH=400
VISIBILITY="HIDE">
Barrel cactus for your prickly needs!
<P>
```

```
<IMG SRC="barrel.gif">
</LAYER>

<LAYER NAME="Croequo2" LEFT=75 TOP=175 WIDTH=400
VISIBILITY="HIDE">
Yes, we sell funky frogs here!
<P>
<IMG SRC="bullfrog.gif">
</LAYER>

<LAYER NAME="Croequo3" LEFT=75 TOP=175 WIDTH=400
VISIBILITY="HIDE">
We got fish de-lish here! Ooops! Don't let them bite
back!
<P>
<IMG SRC="shark.gif">
</LAYER>
```

As you can see, a layer can not only take text, but images as well as text-formatting tags. The only thing to keep in mind is to remember that any images you use are not so big that they extend past the point of the layer.

THE <ILAYER> TAG

In addition to the <LAYER> tag set, Netscape also introduced the <ILAYER> tag set, which has the exact same attributes as the <LAYER> tag set. The only difference between <LAYER> and <ILAYER> is that <ILAYER> denotes an inflow layer; in other words, a layer set within the body of a Web page. Whereas <LAYER> sets the content within a Web page, the <ILAYER> - </ILAYER> tags are used within the regular flow of a Web page containing other HTML elements.

<ILAYER> . . .</ILAYER>

Element Name: Inflow layer tag.

Description: Defines a layer that is set within the body of a Web page.

Attributes: ABOVE = *layername*
Specifies the stacking order of a layer within a set of layers. If used, the attributes BELOW and Z-INDEX cannot be used—they are mutually exclusive.
BACKGROUND = *filename*

Tiles a background image within a layer.
BELOW = *layername*
Specifies the stacking order of a layer within a set of layers. If used, the attributes ABOVE and Z-INDEX cannot be used—they are mutually exclusive.
BGCOLOR = *colorname or hexadecimal colorvalue*
Sets the background color of a layer.
CLIP = *x, y, x1, y1*
Specifies the dimensions of a clipping rectangle (a visible layer) that appears within a layer.
HEIGHT = *# pixels or % of browser window*
Specifies the height of the layer in pixels, and sets the reference height for any children layers.
ID = "*layer_name*"
Specifies the name of the layer. It serves as an identifier to distinguish it from other layers and to JavaScript scripts. It is functionally equivalent to the NAME attribute.
LEFT = *# pixels*
Specifies the horizontal positioning of the layer in pixels. It works differently than the LEFT attribute of the <LAYER> tag; with <ILAYER> it denotes the relative horizontal positioning of the layer.
NAME = "*layer_name*"
Specifies the name of the layer. It serves as an identifier to distinguish it from other layers and to JavaScript scripts. It is functionally equivalent to the ID attribute.
PAGEX = *# pixels*
Specifies the horizontal position of the layer relative to the document window in pixels.
PAGEY = *# pixels*
Specifies the vertical position of the layer relative to the document window in pixels.
SRC = *URL*
Specifies the full pathname of a separate Web page containing HTML-formatted content for the layer.
TOP = *# pixels*
Specifies the vertical positioning of the layer in pixels. It works differently than the TOP attribute of the <LAYER> tag; with <ILAYER> it denotes the relative vertical positioning of the layer.
`VISIBILITY = SHOW | HIDE | INHERIT`
Specifies whether or not the layer is visible.
WIDTH = *# pixels or % of browser window*
Specifies the width of the layer in pixels (applies to text only).
Z-INDEX
Specifies the stacking order of a layer within a set of layers. If used, the attributes ABOVE and BELOW cannot be used—they are mutually exclusive.

Associated Tags: None (however, always used in conjunction with JavaScript).

Sample:

```
While looking for lions in Africa, I remember running
across the Gnu on the great plains. <ILAYER ID="gnu">The
gnu is a large hairy beast with horns, a mean-looking
expression, and an equally-bad temperament if you get too
close</ILAYER>.
```

The only difference between the functionality of the <LAYER> and <ILAYER> attributes is that the TOP and LEFT attributes refer to *relative* vertical and horizontal positioning of the layer, respectively.

The idea behind the <ILAYER> tag is to use it within a regular Web page, and simply add layered functionality to it, or as a source for another layered Web page that uses the SRC attribute to point to the page containing the <ILAYER> tags.

JAVASCRIPT AND LAYERS

Using the sample HTML code from the <LAYER> section, we now have to add a program that will allow us to shuffle the visible order of the cards that appear in the layer.

For each layer in an HTML page there is an equivalent JavaScript layer object. This means essentially that each layer is recognized individually within a program, and has a number of inherent properties that can be manipulated by the JavaScript code.

Table 9.1 contains a listing of available JavaScript objects and properties that apply to Netscape's <LAYER> tag. All of the following layer object properties are essentially the JavaScript equivalents of the many HTML attributes of the <LAYER> tag.

The layer object methods in Table 9.2 allow you to manipulate the appearance of the layers.

For more information on JavaScript in general, see Chapter 13, "Dynamic Documents."

The only JavaScript layers property we will manipulate is the visibility object. Here's what the code looks like:

```
<SCRIPT>
function hideAllCroequoLayers () {
document.layers ["Croequo0"].visibility = "hide";
document.layers ["Croequo1"].visibility = "hide";
document.layers ["Croequo2"].visibility = "hide";
document.layers ["Croequo3"].visibility = "hide";
  }

// the following makes a single layer visible
function changeCroequo (n) {
        hideAllCroequoLayers ();
        document.layers ["Croequo" + n].visibility =
        "inherit";
}
</SCRIPT>
```

Table 9.1 Layer Object Properties

Property Name	*Can it be modifed by end-user?*	*Description*
name	N	Corresponds to the name for the layer as stated in the HTML code by the NAME attribute.
left	Y	The horizontal position of the layer's left edge, stated as a pixel value relative to the origin of the parent layer.
top	Y	The vertical position of the layer's left edge, stated as a pixel value relative to the origin of the parent layer.
pageX	Y	The horizontal position of the layer, stated as a pixel value relative to the page.
pageY	Y	The vertical position of the layer, stated as a pixel value relative to the page.
zIndex	Y	Controls the relative z-order of this layer. Functions in the same way as the HTML Z-INDEX attribute.
visibility	Y	Determines whether or not a layer is visible. Works in the same way as the VISIBILITY HTML attribute, and takes the same three values: show, hide, and inherit.
clip.top clip.left clip.right clip.bottom clip.width clip.height	Y	Defines the clipping rectangle, specifying the part of the layer that is visible.
background	Y	Equivalent to the BACKGROUND HTML tag.
bgColor	Y	Equivalent to the BGCOLOR HTML tag.
siblingAbove	N	Signifies the layer object above this one in z-order, among all layers that share the same parent layer. It is null if the layer has no sibling above it.
siblingBelow	N	Signifies the layer object below this one in z-order, among all layers that share the same parent layer. It is null if the layer has no sibling above it.
above	N	Equivalent to the ABOVE HTML tag. If a stack of layers has a parent layer, then this layer is above it.
below	N	Equivalent to the BELOW HTML tag. If a stack of layers has a below parent layer, then this layer is above it.
parentLayer	N	The parent layer that other layers inherit from—it also sets the base at which a layer can be set above or below this parent layer.
src	Y	Specified the URL for the content for the layer.

Table 9.2 Layer Object Methods

Method Name	*Description*
move By(x, y)	Changes layer position by applying the specified change, and takes a pixel value.
move To (x, y)	Changes the layer position to the specified pixel coordinates. This only takes place within the containing layer.
move To Absolute (x, y)	Changes the layer position to the specified pixel coordinates. This is an absolute positioning within the Web page rather than the containing layer.
resize By (width, height)	Sets the layer to the new height and width values measured in pixels. This does not re-lay-out the HTML contained within the layer, and may in fact clip them.
resize To (width, height)	Resizes the layer to have the specified height and width values measured in pixels. This does not re-lay-out the HTML contained within the layer, and may in fact clip them.
move Above (layer)	Places this layer above another specified layer, without changing either layer's horizontal or vertical position. Both layers will share the same parent layer after restacking.
move Below (layer)	Places this layer below another specified layer, without changing either layer's horizontal or vertical position. Both layers will share the same parent layer after restacking.
load (source string width)	Changes the source of a layer to that indicated by sourcestring while changing the width for which the layer's HTML contents are wrapped. It takes two arguments: the first argument is external file name containing the information for the layer, and the second is the width of the layer as a pixel value.

This code makes the initial layer visible on the Web page, and hides the rest until called for.

The Trigger

We have most of the JavaScript we need to get things rolling. Now all we need is something to trigger the JavaScript so that it will make each layer selectively visible. This can be accomplished through the use of a Java applet, plug-in, or a form.

In this case we will use a simple selection form so that users can choose which layer will be visible. The following code (which also makes up its own layer) does the trick.

```
<LAYER NAME="formlayer" LEFT=500 TOP=225>
<P>
```

```
Make a selection:
<FORM NAME=Croequo>
<SELECT NAME=catalog onChange="changeCroequo
(this.selectedIndex); return false;">
<OPTION>Ducks
<OPTION>Cactus
<OPTION>Frogs
<OPTION>Fish
</SELECT>
</FORM>
</LAYER>
```

The line of JavaScript code added to the <SELECT> tag triggers the rest of the JavaScript program on the Web page to switch the visibility of the layers depending on what has been selected by the user. If no change is made, nothing is done (return false;).

The form in this layer has to be positioned correctly, otherwise it can interfere or be covered by the layers it is meant to manipulate.

Add a bit of extra formatting and text to make things look a bit more interesting, and the resulting code for the Croequo Emporium Inc. Web Catalog looks like this:

```
<HTML>
<HEAD>
<TITLE>Creoquo Catalog</TITLE>
<SCRIPT>
function hideAllCroequoLayers () {
document.layers ["Croequo0"].visibility = "hide";
document.layers ["Croequo1"].visibility = "hide";
document.layers ["Croequo2"].visibility = "hide";
document.layers ["Croequo3"].visibility = "hide";
  }

// the following makes a single layer visible
function changeCroequo (n) {
        hideAllCroequoLayers (); document.layers
        ["Croequo" + n].visibility = "inherit";
}
</SCRIPT>
</HEAD>
<BODY BGCOLOR=#FFFF99>

<H1><FONT FACE=ARIAL>Welcome to Croequo Emporium!
</FONT></H1>
```

```
<P>
<FONT FACE=HELVETICA>
The Croequo Emporium Inc. Web site offers you many
fine critters and plants your needs.
<P>
Click the button to reveal more information from our
funky on-line catalog.</FONT>
<P>
<HR>

<LAYER NAME="Croequo0" LEFT=75 TOP=175 WIDTH=400>
Mallards on sale! Drake scott!
<P>
<IMG SRC="mallard.gif">
</LAYER>

<LAYER NAME="Croequo1" LEFT=75 TOP=175 WIDTH=400
VISIBILITY="HIDE">
Barrel cactus for your prickly needs!
<P>
<IMG SRC="barrel.gif">
</LAYER>

<LAYER NAME="Croequo2" LEFT=75 TOP=175 WIDTH=400
VISIBILITY="HIDE">
Yes, we sell funky frogs here!
<P>
<IMG SRC="bullfrog.gif">
</LAYER>

<LAYER NAME="Croequo3" LEFT=75 TOP=175 WIDTH=400
VISIBILITY="HIDE">
We got fish de-lish here! Ooops! Don't let them bite
back!
<P>
<IMG SRC="shark.gif">
</LAYER>

<LAYER NAME="formlayer" LEFT=500 TOP=225>

<P>
Make a selection:

<FORM NAME=Croequo>
```

```
<SELECT NAME=catalog onChange="changeCroequo
(this.selectedIndex); return false;">
<OPTION>Ducks
<OPTION>Cactus
<OPTION>Frogs
<OPTION>Fish
</SELECT>
</FORM>
</LAYER>

</BODY>
</HTML>
```

When clicked, the selection form brings a different layer into view, as the images in Figures 9.11 and 9.12 attest.

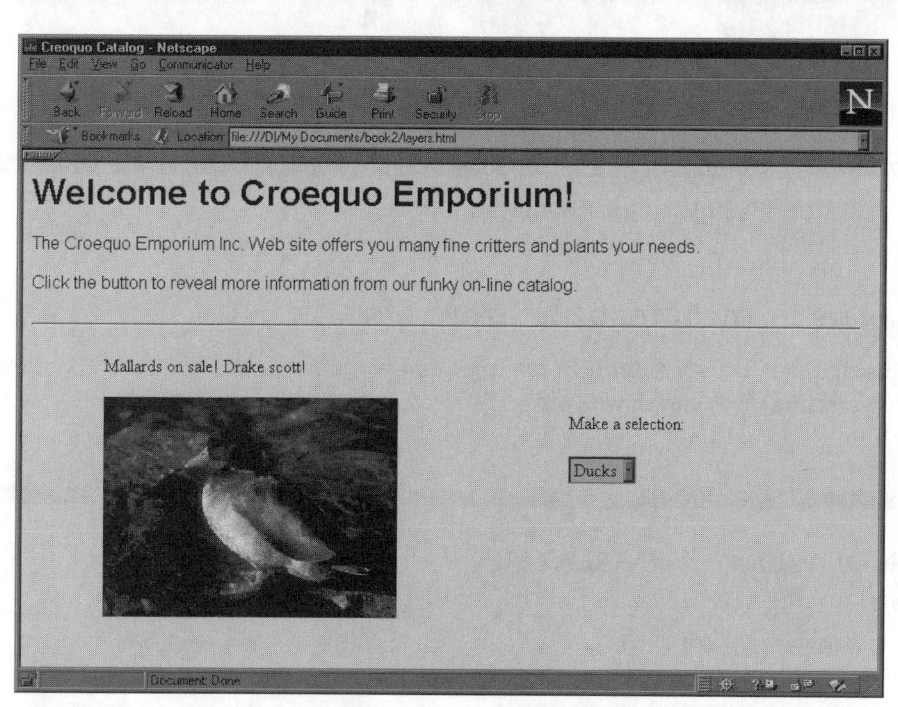

Figure 9.11 Sample Layers Displayed

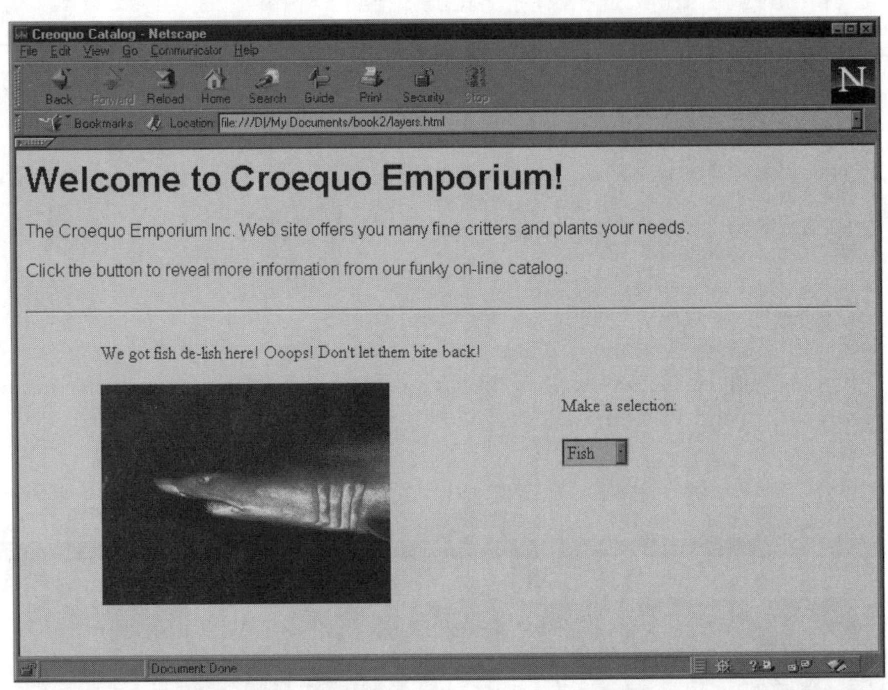

Figure 9.12 Sample Layers Displayed

Layers in Incompatible Browsers

Netscape Navigator is the only browser that supports the <LAYER> tag set. For those browsers unable to view layers properly, Netscape supplies the <NOLAYER> tag.

<NOLAYER> . . .</NOLAYER>

Element Name: Nolayer tag.

Attributes: None.

Associated Tags: <LAYER>

Sample:

```
<NOLAYER>
<P>
```

```
If you were using a layers-compatible browser, you'd be
viewing a layered Web page instead of this statement
</NOLAYER>
```

The <NOLAYER> container tag is designed to be displayed content to Web browsers that cannot display layers, and it is not displayed within layer-compatible browsers. It behaves in exactly the same way as the <NOFRAMES> tag does within a framed Web page.

<NOLAYER> is designed to be placed outside of a layer on a Web page, and can be placed anywhere on the Web page as long as it is outside of a layer.

Anybody who designs a layered Web page should use this tag—it will at least inform people using noncompatible browsers why they cannot view the content correctly.

Figures 9.13 and 9.14 show the effects of the <NOLAYERS> tag inserted into

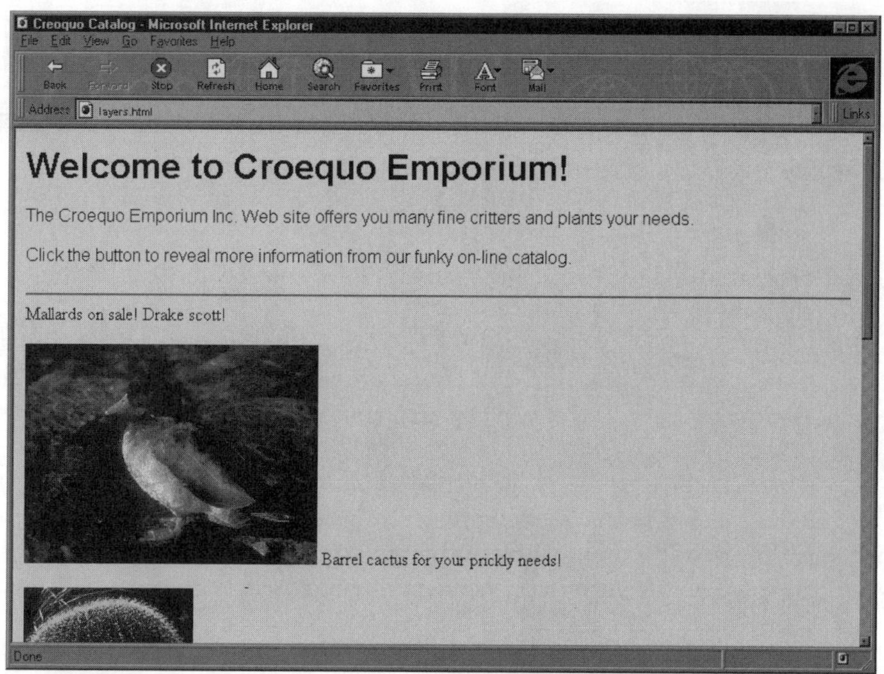

Figure 9.13 A Layered Web Page Seen through an Incompatible Browser

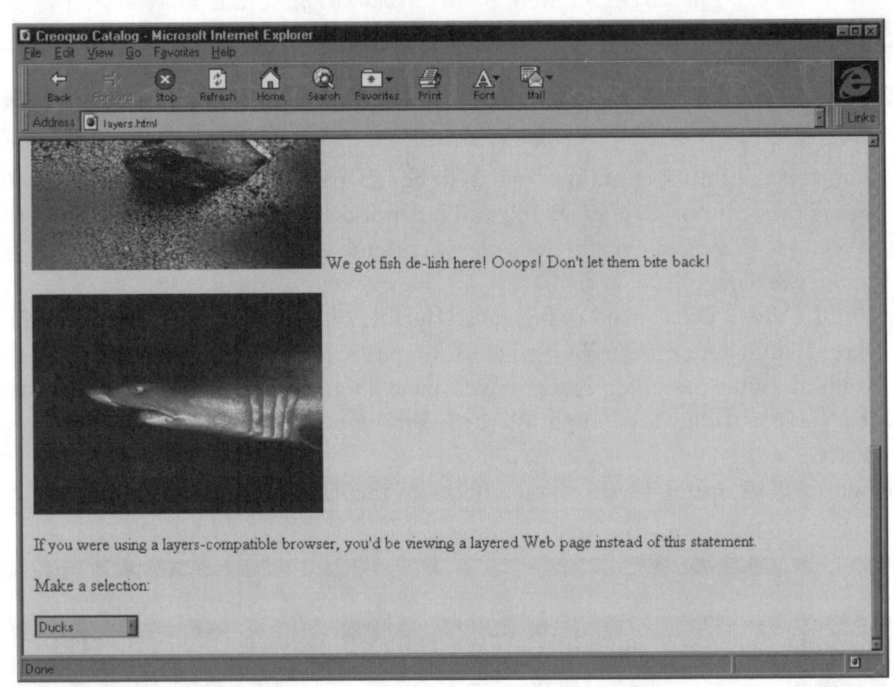

Figure 9.14 A Layered Web Page Seen Through an Incompatible Browser

the test program used earlier in this chapter, and displayed through a non-layer-compatible browser.

Notice how the contents of the layered page are still displayed—they are simply not displayed as a series of layers. The effects of the <NOLAYER> tag can be seen near the bottom of the second screen clip, explaining why the page looks odd to the user.

When you see a layered Web page displayed in this manner, you can see how the <ILAYER> tag would be put to use within Web pages that will likely be viewed in noncompatible as well as compatible Web browsers. The layered aspect will not be as noticeable as seen through the noncompatible browser.

A Future for Layers?

At the time of this writing, very few Web sites have adopted Netscape's <LAYER> tag set. It is unlikely that the <LAYER> tag set will be widely adopted, as it has been superceded by Cascading Style Sheet (CSS) absolute positioning elements, which have been officially adopted under the HTML 4.0 specification, and have been universally adopted. (For more information on CSS, please see Chapter 11). The <LAYER> tag set was never under consideration for adoption under the official HTML 4.0 specification, nor is it likely to be officially adopted anytime soon.

The <LAYER> format may already have several strikes against it from being widely adopted within the HTML authoring community: It requires JavaScript to function, it is a Netscape-only tag set, and much the same effect can be achieved using CSS. The fact that it requires JavaScript to function will keep many HTML authors—especially novices not inclined toward programming—away. As time goes on, compatibility is becoming more of an issue; though Netscape Navigator is still considered the dominant browser, it is not the *only* browser out there. The fact that this is not (as yet) implemented within Microsoft's Internet Explorer will keep many professional authors away. In fact, the only place this author has seen the <LAYER> tag used extensively is in an environment where Netscape Navigator was used exclusively. Unfortunately for Netscape, this situation is rarely the case these days, and if compatibility matters, you are well advised to use the CSS absolute positioning elements (which also work in Netscape Navigator) to achieve similar ends.

CHAPTER 10

Miscellaneous Elements

The World Wide Web is constantly evolving, and it seems a new multimedia application is being introduced every day. Many of these applications are referred to as Netscape plug-ins, since the Netscape browser has the capability to display any media type as an inline application as long as the media's player has been specified in Netscape's list of helper applications. Some common plug-ins include audio, video, and interactive media such as ActiveX and VRML.

Netscape's early solution to including plug-in media in a Web page was the <EMBED> tag. The <EMBED> tag lets Web authors define any media file to be displayed inline on a Web page.

The World Wide Web Consortium recognized that defining new HTML tags for every new media application was not a good solution, and so began to address the problem recently. The W3C solution in the HTML 4.0 specification is the <OBJECT> tag, which can contain any number of attributes to define the media

the Web author is including. Although the <EMBED> tag is still recognized by both Netscape and Microsoft Internet Explorer, it is best to use the <OBJECT> tag as it is now the official HTML standard.

The <EMBED> Tag–Embedding Netscape Plug-in Media

The <EMBED> tag is used to add media supported by Netscape plug-ins to your Web page. This tag was introduced by Netscape and is supported by Netscape 2.0 and later. The <EMBED> tag is also supported by Microsoft Internet Explorer 3.0 and later, but Microsoft recommends the use of the OBJECT tag over the <EMBED> tag. The <EMBED> element is not supported by any version of the W3 HTML specification.

<EMBED> is an empty tag and has three required attributes, HEIGHT, SRC, and WIDTH, but more attributes can be included depending upon the type of plug-in media you are specifying. The browser determines the type of plug-in by reading the file extension of the file specified in the SRC attribute. If the browser does not recognize the file extension, it queries the user for further action.

If the user's browser does not have the correct plug-in application to play your file, the browser displays an error message and the option to download the correct plug-in. Your Web page will appear with a broken image icon where your media file would have been, as shown in Figure 10.1.

A good solution to this is to use the <NOEMBED> tag. <NOEMBED> is a Netscape tag that works in a similar manner to <NOFRAMES>, in that it provides HTML content for browsers that cannot interpret the <EMBED> tag. It's a good idea to use the <NOEMBED> tag to provide the media file as an external link or to display an image that complements the plug-in. An example of using the <EMBED> and <NOEMBED> tags together follows.

```
<EMBED SRC="kim.mov" WIDTH="150" HEIGHT="250"
CONTROLS="TRUE">
<NOEMBED>
<P>
This is a still picture from Kim's Movie.
<IMG SRC=" kim.gif" align=right height=200 width=200>
</NOEMBED>
```

Figure 10.1 Broken Image Icon Displayed

<EMBED>

Element Name: Embed tag.

Description: Embeds Netscape plug-in media into a Web page.

Attributes:
ALIGN= *BOTTOM | LEFT | RIGHT | TOP*
The alignment of the object on the Web page. Values are LEFT, RIGHT, TOP, and BOTTOM. The default value is LEFT.
BORDER= # *pixels*
The size in pixels of the border around the object.
HEIGHT = # *pixels*
The height in pixels of the object. This attribute is required.
SRC= *URL*
The URL of the media file. This attribute is required.

WIDTH= # *pixels*
The width in pixels of the object. This attribute is required.

Sample Code:

```
<EMBED SRC="kim.mov" WIDTH="150" HEIGHT="250"
CONTROLS="TRUE">
```

To list every attribute to address every plug-in would be impossible. Visit the plug-in creators' Web sites for detailed information about valid attributes for that plug-in.

THE <OBJECT> TAG—HTML 4.0 STANDARD FOR EMBEDDING MEDIA

THE OBJECT tag is used to embed multimedia content in a Web page. The OBJECT element is included in the HTML 4.0 specification. The intent of the OBJECT tag is to encompass and replace the IMG tag, and at the same time provide a tag to define new media such as plug-ins and applets. The attributes of the OBJECT tag will depend on the media that is being defined. The OBJECT tag allows for backwards-compatibility with existing browsers, and for future developments.

The OBJECT tag is a container tag requiring both the start and end tags. The IMG tag can be inserted between the start and end tags to have the browser display an image if the media object's plug-in is not available. For example:

```
<OBJECT data=kimvideo.avi type="video/x-msvideo"
alt="A Video of Kim"><img scr=Kimpic. gif alt="A
Picture of Kim"></OBJECT>
```

The <PARAM> tag can also be used within the <OBJECT> tag. The <PARAM> tag is used to pass parameters to the media object itself. For example:

```
<OBJECT CODETYPE="application/java-vm"
CODEBASE="http://somehost/somepath/"
CLASSID="java:program.start" HEIGHT=200 WIDTH=250>
<PARAM NAME="options" VALUE="xyz"> Your browser cannot
display Java. </OBJECT>
```

<OBJECT> . . .</OBJECT>

Element Name: Object tag.

Description: Used to insert media objects into Web pages.

Attributes:

ALIGN= *BASELINE* | *CENTER* | *LEFT* | *MIDDLE* | *RIGHT* | *TEXTBOTTOM* | *TEXTMIDDLE* | *TEXTTOP*
Determines where to place the object on the Web page. Values can be TEXTTOP, MIDDLE, TEXTMIDDLE, BASELINE, TEXTBOTTOM, LEFT, CENTER, or RIGHT. Images use this attribute.
ALT= *text*
Specifies text to display if the user has set their browser not to load images. Images use this attribute.
ARCHIVE= *URL*
Specifies a list of URLs pointing to archives of the media.
BORDER= # *pixels*
Specifies the border size in pixels. If the value is 0, no border is drawn. Images use this attribute.
CLASSID= *URL*
A URL that identifies an implementation for the object. In some object systems this is a class identifier. Java applets use this attribute.
CODEBASE= *directory structure*
Some URLs used to identify media objects require an additional URL to find that object. CODEBASE allows you to specify that URL. CODEBASE defaults to the same base URL as the document if none is specified.
CODETYPE= *text*
Specifies the content type of data expected by the browser or media player.
DATA= *URL*
A URL or filename for the object, such as a GIF file.
DECLARE= *text*
Declares an instance of the object.
HEIGHT= # *pixels*
Specifies the height of the object in pixels.
HSPACE= # *pixels*
Specifies in pixels the amount of space to the left and the right of the object.
NAME= *text*
Allows the object to participate in a FORM.
STANDBY= *text*
Specifies a short text string the browser displays while loading the Object's implementation and data.
TABINDEX= *number*
Specifies the order in which an individual item can be selected from a group of items by using the TAB keyboard key.

TYPE= *MIME type*
This specifies the media type for the file specified by the DATA attribute before the file is retrieved. Specifying the TYPE for a .avi file would look like this: type="application/avi".
VSPACE= *# pixels*
Specifies in pixels the amount of space above and below the object.
USEMAP= *URL*
Specifies a URL or filename for a client-side image map.
WIDTH= *# pixels*
Specifies the width of the object in pixels. Specifying this attribute allows the browser to load the object more quickly than if the attribute was not used.

Sample Code:

```
<OBJECT data=kimshock.dcr type="application/x-director"
width=200 height=225>
<img src=kimshock.gif alt="Best Experienced with
Shockwave">
</OBJECT>
```

Table 10.1 Content Types for Popular Object Media

Type of Media File	*Content-Type*	*File Extension*
Adobe Acrobat	application/pdf	.pdf
AU audio	audio/basic	.au, .snd
AVI video	video/x-msvideo	.avi
Multimedia Director (shockwave)	application/x-director	.dcr, .dir, .dxr
MPEG video	video/mpeg	.mpg, .mpeg
QuickTime video	video/quicktime	.qt, .mov
RealAudio/RealVideo	video/x-pn-realaudio	.ra, .ram, .rm
VRLM Worlds	xworld/x-vrml	.wrl
WAV audio	audio/x-wav	.wav

CHAPTER 11

Cascading Style Sheets

Possibly the most important HTML innovation of recent times is the introduction of Cascading Style Sheets (CSS), a standard first proposed by the World Wide Web Consortium (W3C). It is the first major initiative undertaken by the W3C to introduce some stability to the existing HTML specification and to head off the need for the introduction of even more tags by browser manufacturers by making the need for them unnecessary.

CSS is an effort by the W3C to minimize the need for the introduction of new physical formatting tags by browser manufacturers like Microsoft and Netscape. Much of the drive to provide Web authors with proprietary tags by the browser manufacturers was spurred by the Web authors' desire for better control over the layout of elements on a Web page, similar to what exists in desktop publishing programs. The problem is that over time, these extra tags have increased the overall complexity of Web pages, producing Web pages that can be incompatible between Web browsers.

Web authors must spend an increasing amount of time learning an ever-expanding list of HTML tags and memorizing their functions in order to produce professional-looking Web pages. It is also much harder for disabled people to read pages that contain such recent browser-specific innovations like Frames or Tables. Most translation devices for the vision-impaired (who typically use Braille readers or speech synthesizers) have a hard time reading, navigating, or getting useful information from Web pages using these elements.

With the introduction of many of these new tags, more emphasis has been placed on HTML to adopt layout characteristics, driving HTML far from its original tenant that tags should be designed to display content in a logical fashion. The introduction of CSS retains much of the logical structure in a way that is easy to understand and yet powerful in its effects. Using CSS, you can do the following:

- Specify the point size of text
- Add indentations to text
- Set margins within a Web page
- Add new formatting elements to a Web page, like borders around text
- Use measurement units like inches and centimeters to set precise sizes for display elements
- Set a distinctive style for an individual Web page or a set of Web pages
- Reduce the overall amount of tags needed on a Web page by eliminating the number of container tags used to achieve a specific effect, like <FONT SIZE>
- Much, much more, as the rest of this chapter will reveal

It should be noted that CSS allows the Web author access only to the way in which tags are displayed—it does not affect such fundamental functions as hyperlinks and the way embedded objects behave within a Web page. CSS is a powerful tool designed to address the needs of Web authors who want greater control over the layout characteristics of the elements on a Web page, but not the way in which nonlayout characteristics function.

It must be stressed that at the current time, neither Internet Explorer nor Netscape Navigator apply the whole of the CSS specification to their browsers. Both use only a subset of the complete specification as laid out by the W3C, but since they are both members of the W3C, they will hopefully adopt the full set of CSS elements over time. There are other browsers that do implement the full specification, such as Arena, Amaya, and Emacs-W3, but they are not widely used and are available only for certain operating systems.

Though it is unlikely that the browser manufacturers will stop making up new tags for their browsers, as time goes by and more Web authors become familiar with CSS (and more Web browsers fully implement it), the demand and need for new tags will be significantly diminished.

THE MECHANISMS BEHIND CSS

CSS is not designed specifically to control layout on a Web page; instead it is better thought of as a mechanism for modifying how content is displayed. Despite this, it enables the Web author much finer control over the placement of elements on a Web page than can be achieved using regular HTML tags.

Though the code may look complicated, once you understand style sheet fundamentals, they are relatively easy to implement and it becomes a powerful tool for building professional-looking Web pages.

Here is a very simple example of some HTML code that includes a single CSS element:

```
<HTML>
<HEAD>
<STYLE>H2 {COLOR: GREEN}</STYLE>
</HEAD>
<BODY>
<H1>This Text in this Header is Displayed As
Usual . . .</H1>
<H2>This Text in this Header is Green</H2>
</BODY>
</HTML>
```

The effects of this code, which simply turns all second-level headers green, can be seen in Figure 11.1.

CSS works by specifying the tag you want to modify, and stating how you intend it to be displayed by the Web browser. This is the basics of a CSS rule, which consists of two parts:

- The element to be changed, known as the selector
- A statement that describes how the selector should be displayed, known as the declaration

In the previous code example the selector is the second-level header tag (<H2>) and the declaration assigns the color value green to it: ({COLOR: GREEN}).

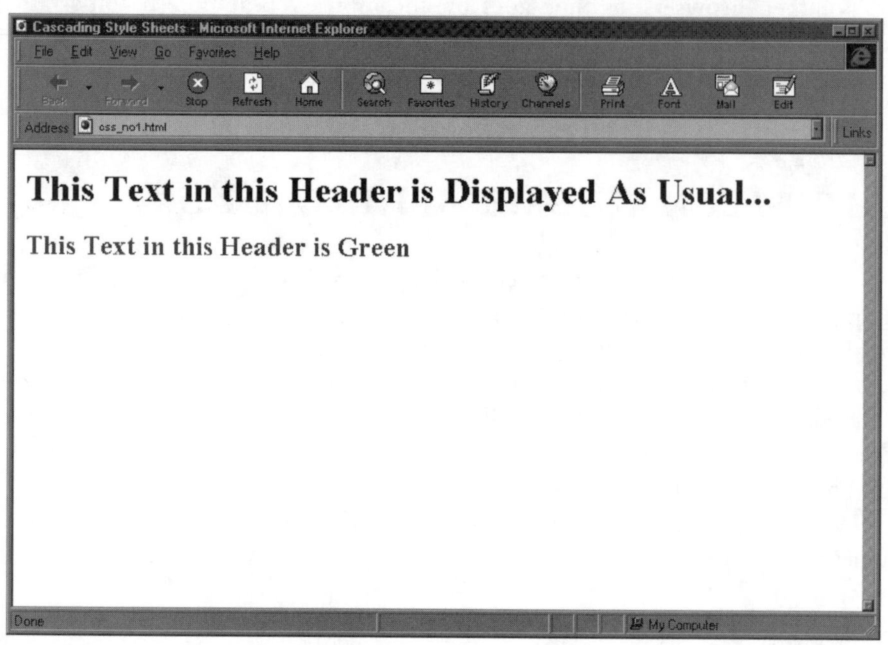

Figure 11.1 Web Page Displaying the Effects of Some Simple CSS Code

There are several ways in which CSS information can be specified within a Web page, but in the previous code example, the CSS information was contained within the <STYLE> tag, and placed within the header of a Web page. There are two new tags you will need to become familiar with if you intend to use a lot of CSS elements in your Web pages: the <STYLE>, <SPAN>, and <DIV> tags.

<STYLE> . . .</STYLE>

Element Name: Style tag.

Description: Adds Cascading Style Sheet information to a Web page.

Attributes: DISABLED
Indicates that the particular CSS function should not be enabled (i.e., displayed).
MEDIA - ALL | BRAILLE | PRINT | PROJECTION | SCREEN | SPEECH
Specifies the type of medium the CSS definitions are designed for.

TITLE - text
Used to name a particular CSS style that a browser can be told to use.
TYPE - MIME type
Specifies the MIME type of the content enclosed by the style tag.

Associated Tags: <SPAN>, <HEAD>

Sample Code:

```
<STYLE>H2 {COLOR: GREEN}</STYLE>
```

The style tag is used to add CSS information to a Web page. It has several optional attributes: DISABLED, MEDIA, TITLE, and TYPE.

DISABLED indicates that the particular CSS function should not be enabled (i.e., meaning it should not be displayed). This is for use in circumstances where you may wish to disable the CSS formatting display in a particular place on the Web page. If used in conjunction with a text-formatting tag, the content is still displayed; it is simply not formatted in the CSS style otherwise indicated. Of the four attributes for <STYLE>, DISABLED is supported in Internet Explorer but is not specified in the HTML 4.0 specification.

MEDIA species which type of medium the CSS formatting is to be used for. At the moment it has five distinct values: ALL, BRAILLE, PRINT, PROJECTION, SCREEN, and SPEECH, all reflecting the different types of media in which the Web page can be viewed. If a device exists to translate the Web page into a different medium, the device will use the CSS elements associated with the particular style used for it. This tag is supported in Internet Explorer and is part of the official HTML 4.0 specification (for more information on its functionality and implications, please see the section on CSS2 at the end of this chapter).

TITLE is used to name a particular CSS style contained within a <STYLE> tag. The idea is to enable a Web author to create a gallery of different formatting styles, which the author can then selectively apply to individual Web pages within a Web site. This attribute is part of the HTML 4.0 specification, but is not currently implemented by the two major browsers.

The TYPE attribute simply specifies the MIME type contained by the <STYLE> tag. There is only one possible value for this at the moment: text/css, which applies directly to CSS. <STYLE> should be used solely within the header (i.e., between the two <HEAD> container tags) of a Web page. This attribute is part of the HTML 4.0 specification, and is recognized in Internet Explorer and Netscape Navigator.

Other HTML tags can be used to apply CSS to a specific section of a Web page, enabling the Web author to set special CSS characteristics for that section, visually differentiating it from the rest of the Web page. This is done by using the <SPAN> and <DIV> tags:

<SPAN> . . .</SPAN>

Element name: Span tag.

Description: Sets CSS information for a specific section within a Web page.

Attributes:

CHARSET = ISO - #
Indicates the international character coding used for the hyperlink.
HREF = URL
Points to a Web page that is viewed when the content contained within the <SPAN> tag is activated.
HREFLANG = text
Specifies the base language of the resource indicated in the HREF attribute.
HREFLANG = MEDIA - ALL | BRAILLE | PRINT | PROJECTION | SCREEN | SPEECH
Specifies the type of medium the CSS definitions are designed for.
REL = URL
Indicates the URL of a subdocument. This attribute is not commonly used.
REV = URL
Indicates the URL of a parent document. This attribute is not commonly used.
TARGET = frame name
Specifies the name of the frame (if any) that the content set by HREF should be viewed within.
TYPE = MIME type
Specifies the MIME type of the content enclosed by the style tag.

Associated Tags: <STYLE>.

Sample Code:

```
<HTML>
<HEAD>
<STYLE>
SPAN {COLOR: RED}
</STYLE>
</HEAD>
<BODY>
<P STYLE="COLOR: GREEN">
Look for the <SPAN>red text</SPAN> that appears within
the green text.
</P>
</BODY>
</HTML>
```

The <SPAN> tag is designed to temporarily override any existing CSS information that may have already been specified. It has a single designated attribute: STYLE. The STYLE attribute can be used to further refine the CSS element displayed. For example, if you wanted to make the red text from the previous code sample 18pt in size-something not covered in the description of how the <SPAN> tag is to be displayed in the header of the Web page-the STYLE attribute can be used to further refine the display of a tag, as in the following code sample:

```
<HTML>
<HEAD>
<STYLE>
SPAN {COLOR: RED}
</STYLE>
</HEAD>
<BODY>
<P STYLE="COLOR: GREEN">
Look for the <SPAN STYLE="FONT-SIZE: 18 PT">18pt-size
red text</SPAN> that appears within the green text.
</P>
</BODY>
</HTML>
```

The <SPAN> tag has many attributes, many of them added in the official HTML 4.0 specification, and none implemented in current browsers. The CHARSET attribute is used to specify the international character coding used for the hyperlink. The default value is the standard Latin-1 ISO standard, which is used by most European languages (including English). Alternate character sets can be specified. The TYPE attribute is used to specify the MIME type of the file type to which the hypertext anchor points (for more information on MIME types, see Chapter 2). The somewhat obscure HREFLANG attribute sets the base language of the resource that is being linked to. The HREF attribute enables the Web author to make the content contained within a set of <SPAN> tags a hypertext link, and the associated TARGET attribute specifies the name of the frame the link should be displayed within, if the content is contained within a framed Web page. For more information on the MEDIA attribute see the <STYLE> section.

CSS can also be implemented within a specific section, or a division of a Web page. The idea is to allow the Web author the ability to add further CSS attributes within part of the Web page. The division (<DIV>) tag contains a CSS divisions in a Web page, which is designed to set the CSS rules for the division it encloses.

<DIV> . . .</DIV>

Element Name: Division tag.

Description: Specifies a section of a Web page in which CSS elements are used.

Attributes: CHARSET - ISO-#

Indicates the international character coding used for the hyperlink.
HREF - URL
Points to a Web page that is viewed when the content contained within the <SPAN> tag is activated.
HREFLANG = text
Specifies the base language of the resource indicated in the HREF attribute.
HREFLANG - MEDIA - ALL | BRAILLE | PRINT | PROJECTION | SCREEN | SPEECH
Specifies the type of medium the CSS definitions are designed for.
REL - URL
Indicates the URL of a subdocument. This attribute is not commonly used.
REV - URL
Indicates the URL of a parent document. This attribute is not commonly used.
TARGET - frame name
Specifies the name of the frame (if any) that the content set by HREF should be viewed within.
TYPE - MIME type
Specifies the MIME type of the content enclosed by the style tag.

Sample:

```
This text is displayed using the default characteristics.
<DIV STYLE="FONT-SIZE: 18 PT; COLOR: TEAL">
Whoa! Big teal-colored text!
<B><I>Still</I></B> big and teal-y.
<P>
</DIV>
Whew! Back to normal text display.
```

Under the HTML 4.0 specification, <DIV> shares all of the same attributes as the <SPAN> tag. Only the ALIGN attribute is currently supported in either Internet Explorer or Netscape Navigator.

The <DIV> tag is used when you want to overrule the existing CSS characteristics that have already been set in place. It will either set specific CSS characteristics where none are set (as in the preceding sample code), or will override any CSS characteristics that have been set elsewhere within a Web page. The effects of the code example can be seen in Figure 11.2.

At this time <DIV> has one usable attribute: ALIGN. This allows the Web author to place the text on a Web page, either to the left of the browser window using the LEFT attribute, to the right with the RIGHT attribute, or centered with the CENTER attribute. A fourth attribute, JUSTIFY, will justify the block of text contained within the <DIV> tag, but it is not supported in either Internet Explorer or Netscape Navigator.

The <DIV> tag also introduces us to the meaning behind the Cascading part of the Cascading Style Sheets, which is: more specific CSS rules tend to override global

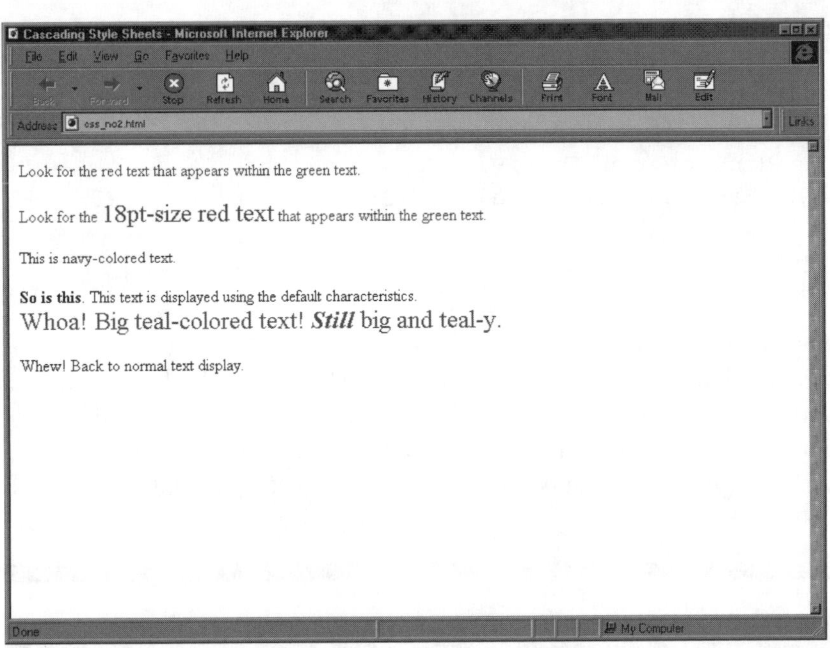

Figure 11.2 The Effect of the <DIV> Tag Code Example Displayed

ones. The designers of CSS realized that there would be situations in which a Web author would want to overrule more global CSS elements with more specific ones—in this case the browser cascades from the more general to the more specific rule. This cascading order is defined by the following rules.

1. General formatting rules apply globally to a Web page.
2. Specific formatting rules within the Web page overrule global ones.
3. If two or more specific formatting elements are specified within a Web page, only the latter reference is applied.

The following code example shows this in action: a specific level-1 header set to the color navy overrules a more global style that sets the level-1 headers to red.

```
<HTML>
<HEAD>
<STYLE>
```

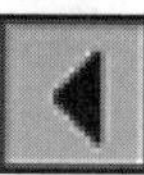

```
H1 {COLOR: RED}
</STYLE>
</HEAD>
<BODY>
<H1>A red level-1 heading</H1>
<H1 STYLE="COLOR: NAVY">Suddenly, a navy level-1
heading overrules!</H1>
<H1>Back to the normal red level-1 heading</H1>
</BODY>
</HTML>
```

The results can be seen in Figure 11.3.

Note how the second level-1 heading is displayed in a navy color, while the first and third level-1 headings are displayed in red. The first level-1 heading inherits the CSS attribute red, which is then specifically overridden by the second navy level-1 heading, and is then restored when we come to the third level-1 heading.

One of the basic implications of the CSS specification is that when you assign

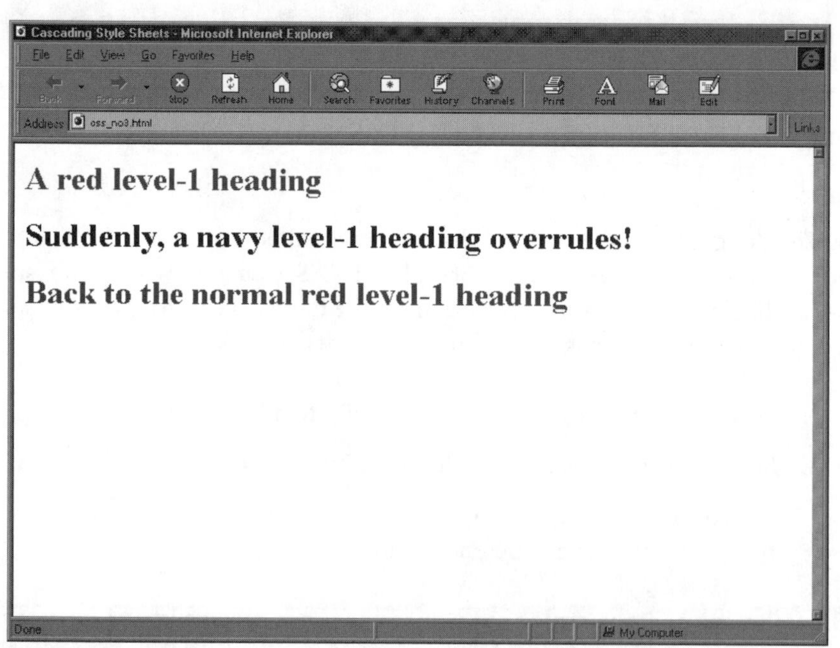

Figure 11.3 Web Page Showing How a More Specific CSS Element Can Override a More General CSS Style

formatting values to a top-level tag type (the <BODY> tag for example) all of the tags underneath it will automatically inherit the same settings as the top-level tag unless specifically overridden elsewhere. If you tack on specific CSS elements to the <BODY> tag, all of the following text, lists, and tables will take on the same properties.

So far, we have shown examples of only a couple of the ways in which CSS information can be specified. There are in fact three different ways in which CSS information can be added to a Web page:

- It can be embedded within the header of a Web page
- It can be embedded within the body of a Web page (usually in certain sections or divisions)
- It can be specified within a separate Web page

We have already seen how <SPAN> is used to embed CSS attributes in the header of a Web page, and how <SPAN> and <DIV> can be used to add CSS elements within the body of a Web page. But the third option, specifying CSS elements in a completely different Web page, is potentially the most appealing for Web authors. By specifying the display and layout attributes in a separate Web page, you can customize the style for a set of Web pages that use ordinary HTML code. To do this, you create a Web page containing nothing but CSS information. Then, you can link another Web page to the CSS page, by using the LINK tag.

For example, the following code example is a part of a Web page that contains nothing but CSS formatting information:

```
A:LINK {
COLOR: BLUE;
TEXT-DECORATION: UNDERLINE;
}
A:VISITED {
COLOR: PURPLE;
TEXT-DECORATION: UNDERLINE;
}
A:ACTIVE {
COLOR: RED;
TEXT-DECORATION: UNDERLINE;
}
P.PREFACE {
TEXT-ALIGN: RIGHT;
TEXT-INDENT: 0.000000PT;
MARGIN-TOP: 0.000000PT;
```

```
MARGIN-BOTTOM: 0.000000PT;
MARGIN-RIGHT: 12.000000PT;
MARGIN-LEFT: 0.000000PT;
FONT-SIZE: 48.000000PT;
FONT-WEIGHT: MEDIUM;
FONT-STYLE: ITALIC;
COLOR: #000000;
TEXT-DECORATION: NONE;
VERTICAL-ALIGN: BASELINE;
TEXT-TRANSFORM: NONE;
FONT-FAMILY: TIMES NEW ROMAN;
}
P.MAPPING TABLE CELL {
TEXT-ALIGN: LEFT;
TEXT-INDENT: 0.000000PT;
MARGIN-TOP: 2.000000PT;
MARGIN-BOTTOM: 2.000000PT;
MARGIN-RIGHT: 0.000000PT;
MARGIN-LEFT: 0.000000PT;
FONT-SIZE: 12.000000PT;
FONT-WEIGHT: MEDIUM;
FONT-STYLE: REGULAR;
COLOR: #000000;
TEXT-DECORATION: NONE;
VERTICAL-ALIGN: BASELINE;
TEXT-TRANSFORM: NONE;
FONT-FAMILY: TIMES;
}
P.COURIERLINE {
TEXT-ALIGN: LEFT;
TEXT-INDENT: 72.000000PT;
MARGIN-TOP: 0.000000PT;
MARGIN-BOTTOM: 0.000000PT;
MARGIN-RIGHT: 0.000000PT;
MARGIN-LEFT: 72.000000PT;
FONT-SIZE: 7.000000PT;
FONT-WEIGHT: MEDIUM;
FONT-STYLE: REGULAR;
COLOR: #000000;
TEXT-DECORATION: NONE;
VERTICAL-ALIGN: BASELINE;
TEXT-TRANSFORM: NONE;
FONT-FAMILY: MONOSPACED;
}
```

```
H1.1SECTION, H2.1SECTION, H3.1SECTION, H4.1SECTION,
H5.1SECTION, H6.1SECTION {
TEXT-ALIGN: RIGHT;
TEXT-INDENT: 0.000000PT;
MARGIN-TOP: 6.000000PT;
MARGIN-BOTTOM: 0.000000PT;
MARGIN-RIGHT: 12.000000PT;
MARGIN-LEFT: 0.000000PT;
FONT-SIZE: 24.000000PT;
FONT-WEIGHT: MEDIUM;
FONT-STYLE: REGULAR;
COLOR: #000000;
TEXT-DECORATION: NONE;
VERTICAL-ALIGN: BASELINE;
TEXT-TRANSFORM: NONE;
FONT-FAMILY: HELVCONDBLK;
}
```

This information is stored in a file called test.css. Note how it changes the display characteristics of a number of regular HTML tags, and further refines some of them into specific classes. The way the CSS information is arranged is much like it is with the <STYLE> tag, but is joined by curly-braces ({ and }). To link this information and thereby apply it to another Web page, you would use the <LINK> tag within the header of that Web page:

```
<HEAD>
<LINK REL=STYLESHEET HREF="test.css" TYPE="text/css">
</HEAD>
```

You may have noticed some of the CSS characteristics specified in the CSS page often applied different display characteristics for the same tag. Some of the code referenced in the CSS page is nonspecific, but in those cases when you want to reference a specific CSS display element, like P.PREFACE (as opposed to P.MAPPING TABLE CELL or P.COURIERLINE), you would reference that information within the Web page by using a special attribute called CLASS, which can be used to specify a CSS style as follows.

```
<P CLASS="PREFACE">
Welcome to the preface of the book!
</P>
```

This same procedure can also be used within a regular Web page, so that particular class CSS elements can be called upon at will within a Web page. The following code example shows this, where three very different forms of the bold

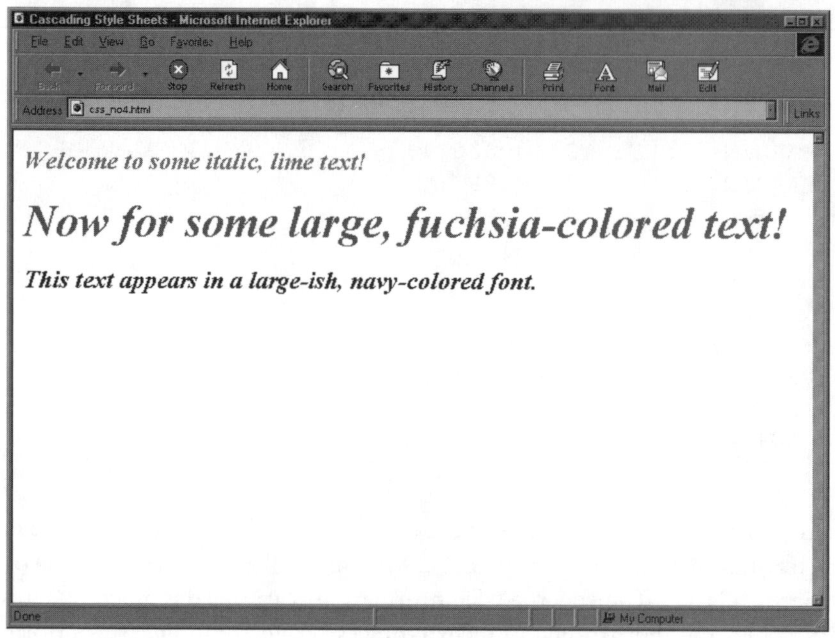

Figure 11.4 The Same Element (a Bold Tag) Displays in Different Ways Depending on the CLASS Specified in the Web Page

(<B>) tag are specified and called upon within a Web page (see the results in Figure 11.4):

```
<HTML>
<HEAD>
<STYLE>
B.FUCHSIA {COLOR: FUCHSIA; FONT-SIZE: 32PT}
B.LIME {COLOR: LIME; FONT-SIZE: 18PT; FONT-STYLE:
ITALIC}
B.NAVY {COLOR: NAVY; FONT-SIZE: 18PT}
</STYLE>
</HEAD>
<BODY>
<B CLASS=LIME>Welcome to some italic, lime text!</B>
<P>
<B CLASS=FUCHSIA>Now for some large, fuchsia-colored
text!</B>
```

```
<P>
<B CLASS=NAVY>This text appears in a large-ish,
navy-colored font.</B>
</BODY>
</HTML>
```

Note how you can join several attributes within a single CSS class by using semicolons (;). There are no limits to the number of attributes you can add in this manner.

In some cases it is desirable to specify several CSS element characteristics together, to be able to reduce the overall amount of code used. For example, say you wanted several headers to be displayed in the same manner. Typically, you would specify them individually, as in the following code snippet:

```
<STYLE>
H1 {FONT-SIZE: 18PT; FONT-FAMILY: "COURIER";
FONT-WEIGHT: ITALIC; COLOR: NAVY}
H2 {FONT-SIZE: 18PT; FONT-FAMILY: "COURIER";
FONT-WEIGHT: ITALIC; COLOR: NAVY}
H3 {FONT-SIZE: 18PT; FONT-FAMILY: "COURIER";
FONT-WEIGHT: ITALIC; COLOR: NAVY}
</STYLE>
```

This code can be condensed by specifying all of these elements at once:

```
<STYLE>
H1 H2 H3 {FONT-SIZE: 18PT; FONT-FAMILY: "COURIER";
FONT-WEIGHT: ITALIC; COLOR: NAVY}
</STYLE>
```

It is also possible to add comments within your CSS so that you can explain the decisions behind the display and layout attributes you chose for a particular tag or class of tags. The comment format for CSS does not follow the format used by HTML (i.e., <! -- commented text -->), but instead it follows the format commonly used for inserting comments in C programming language code. Use /* to begin a comment, and */ to end a comment. The following code displays a comment contained within a CSS part of a Web page:

```
H1 {FONT-SIZE: 18PT; FONT-FAMILY: "COURIER";
FONT-WEIGHT: ITALIC; COLOR: NAVY}
H2 {FONT-SIZE: 18PT; FONT-FAMILY: "COURIER";
FONT-WEIGHT: ITALIC; COLOR: NAVY} /* H2 display
characteristics are the same as H1 for demonstration
purposes only */
```

All of this is a mere sample of what can be done by using CSS within Web pages. The examples shown here have tended to use only a small subset of the available CSS elements to display basic CSS characteristics easily. The CSS-only Web page shown in a previous example uses an expanded set of CSS elements, all of which are explained in the next section.

CASCADING STYLE SHEET ELEMENTS

This section looks at the individual CSS elements that can be specified within a Web page. There are over 50 CSS elements, many of which are recognized within the latest versions of Internet Explorer and Netscape Navigator.

Many CSS elements come in related families, which generally share many of the same attributes and functions, and that is how the following tags will be grouped. Individual CSS elements do not look or behave like HTML tags—therefore they are described in a slightly different fashion than HTML tags. Many of the characteristics are similar, though—for example, CSS elements often have many attributes-but they work in a different fashion from HTML tags. Often many more attributes are available, and they are of a different type than you find with HTML tags.

The information contained within this section can also be found in a more concise fashion in Appendix B.

It should be noted that one of the things keeping CSS back from wide adoption within the Web authoring community is the fact that both Netscape Navigator and Internet Explorer (at least at the time of this writing) support only a subset of the CSS elements listed. The description for the CSS elements that follow tell you how they should work according to the official specification. In many cases CSS elements that are supported in Internet Explorer are not supported in Netscape Navigator, or they are not supported in either browser. In some cases only certain values of the CSS element are supported, or work only when associated with certain HTML tags. There are even cases where a CSS element has been adopted for use within one version of a browser and was later dropped in the next release—presumably an oversight. In general, if a certain feature is already supported within one browser, you can most likely use a CSS element to set it too. For example, the TEXT-DECORATION element has a value called BLINK that flashes the text on and off repeatedly. It is supported within Netscape Navigator—where you could use the <BLINK> tag to do much the same sort of thing—but not in Internet Explorer, which has never supported the <BLINK> tag. It can only be hoped that over time all of these CSS elements will be supported within these two major browsers.

Measurement Units and URLs

There are a number of different types of measurement units that many CSS elements can take. The ability to set specific values for various CSS elements is one of its main strengths. For those CSS values that can take a measurement value, you can use any of the following measurement values: centimeters, inches, millimeters, picas, pixels, and points. To specify a particular type of measurement value, you use a special two-letter contraction, as shown in the following list:

- Centimeter - cm
- Millimeter - mm
- Inches - in
- Picas - pc
- Pixels - px
- Point - pt

To use a value within a CSS element, simply precede the two letter contraction with a numeric value, as in the following example code:

```
<SUB STYLE="BORDER-TOP-WIDTH 5px">Subscript with
border.</SUB>
```

In this example, the top border width is set to a thickness of five pixels.

There are also a number of CSS elements that can take an URL (usually referring to an image file). It is worth noting that specifying URLs in a CSS element differs significantly from how it is typically specified within an HTML tag. An HTML tag typically refers to something like an image file by using the following format:

```
<BODY BACKGROUND="thinkatron.jpg">
```

The equivalent CSS version does not use an equal sign or quotations. Instead it contains the URL within round brackets, immediately preceded by the statement URL without an equal sign, as in the following example:

```
<BODY STYLE="background-image: URL (thinkatron.gif)">
```

Color and Background CSS Elements

The color and background family of CSS elements are used, not surprisingly, to set the color of various HTML tags, and for setting the background characteristics for HTML tags, respectively.

COLOR

Description: Sets the color of text.

Values: colorname or rrggbb color value

Example code: `<B STYLE="COLOR: BLUE">Blue, bold text</B>`

We've already seen several examples of this CSS element in action—it changes the color of the HTML tag attached to it. This CSS element can take either a colorname or a hexadecimal color value (a full listing of valid colornames and color values can be found in Appendix D, "Listing of Common Color Values/Colornames").

BACKGROUND

Description: Sets the background color or image.

Values: colorname or rrggbb color value
URL (name_of_image_file)

Example code: `<BODY STYLE="BACKGROUND: TEAL">`

The background CSS tag is the father of all of the other background CSS tags, all of which share similar characteristics for adding backgrounds to HTML tags. In this case, the code example displays a Web page with a teal background. It works in an equivalent fashion to the HTML tag equivalent <BODY BGCOLOR="TEAL">.

BACKGROUND-COLOR

Description: Sets the background color for an element.

Values: colorname or rrggbb color value
TRANSPARENT - Sets the specified element as transparent.

Example code:

```
<B STYLE="BACKGROUND-COLOR: 00FF00">Bold text with a
difference!</B>
```

This CSS element allows the Web author to add a background to the specified HTML tag. It generally takes either a colorname or a rrggbb hexadecimal color value (a full listing of colornames and color values can be found in Appendix D, "Listing of Common Color Values/Colornames"). In this case, the example code produces a light green background for the words contained within the bold tag. The TRANSPARENT attribute allows whatever background color or image exists to be seen through the background (this is the default value). For example, the following code sample, when added to a Web page, will let the background color or image appear behind the text:

```
<P STYLE="BACKGROUND-COLOR: TRANSPARENT">The teal
background will appear behind this text.
</P>
```

A combination of all of the previous code examples can be seen in Figure 11.5.

BACKGROUND-IMAGE

Description: Specifies a graphic as a background image.
If this element is specified, other CSS elements like BACKGROUND-REPEAT, BACKGROUND-ATTACHMENT, and BACKGROUND-POSITION can also be specified. A color value can also be added.

Values: URL (name_of_image_file)

Example code:

```
<BODY STYLE="background-image: URL(thinkatron.gif)">
```

This CSS element sets a graphic as a background image for an element, and the code example listed behaves much like the HTML equivalent <BODY BACKGROUND="thinkatron.jpg">. If this element is specified, other CSS elements like BACKGROUND-REPEAT, BACKGROUND-ATTACHMENT, and BACKGROUND-POSITION can also be specified, which further modify its behavior. A color value can also be specified, which will cover the areas not covered by the specified image.

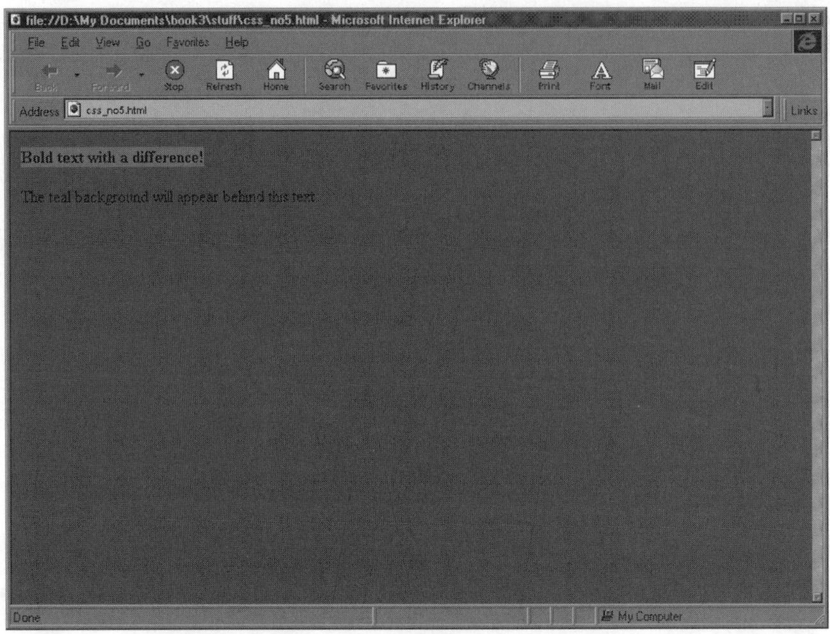

Figure 11.5 The Background and Background-Color Code Examples Displayed

BACKGROUND-REPEAT

Description: If the BACKGROUND-IMAGE element is set, this additional element specifies how the image is repeated on the Web page.

Values:
REPEAT - Image is tiled horizontally and vertically.
REPEAT-X - Image is tiled horizontally.
REPEAT-Y - Image is tiled vertically.
NO-REPEAT - The image is not repeated.

Example code:

```
<BODY STYLE="BACKGROUND-IMAGE: URL(thinkatron.jpg);
BACKGROUND-REPEAT: REPEAT-X">
```

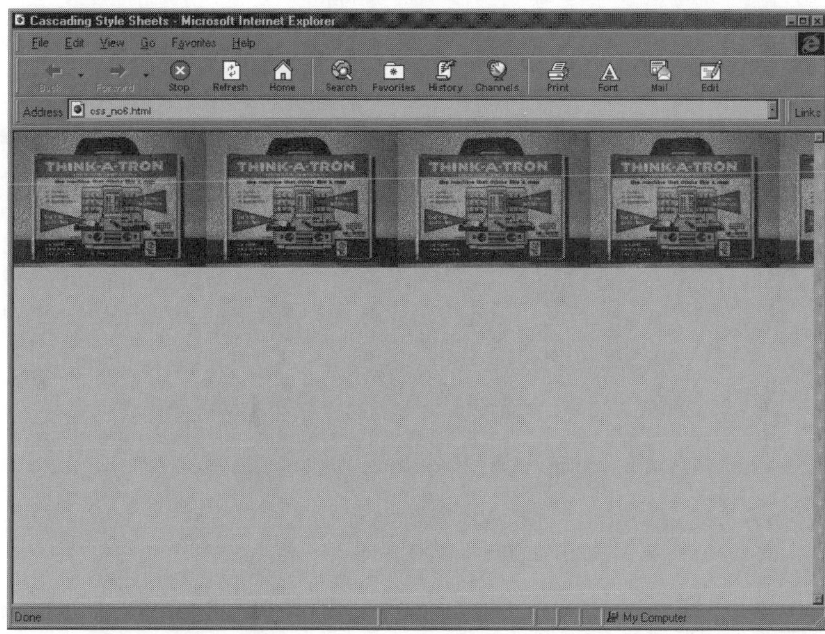

Figure 11.6 A Horizontally Tiled Background Image

This CSS element is always used in combination with the BACKGROUND-IMAGE element, and modifies the way the background image is displayed. It has a number of attributes: REPEAT tiles the image both horizontally and vertically, REPEAT-X tiles the image horizontally, and REPEAT-Y tiles the image vertically. The NO-REPEAT attribute displays the background image only once, in the upper-right corner of the Web page.

Figure 11.6 displays the effects of the sample code previously listed, which uses the attribute REPEAT-X (tile horizontally only):

BACKGROUND-ATTACHMENT

Description: If the BACKGROUND-IMAGE element is set, this additional element specifies whether the background image moves when the browser window is scrolled.

Values: SCROLL - Image moves when the browser window is scrolled.
FIXED - Image does not move when the browser window is scrolled.

Example code:

```
<BODY STYLE="BACKGROUND-IMAGE: URL (thinkatron.jpg);
BACKGROUND-ATTACHMENT: SCROLL">
```

The FIXED attribute of this CSS element behaves much like Internet Explorer's watermark feature, which allows a background image to stay in one place while the text on a Web page scrolls (typically the reverse is true). Internet Explorer achieves this by using the following code:

```
<BODY BACKGROUND="thinkatron.jpg" BGPROPERTIES=FIXED>
```

With CSS, the equivalent code looks like this:

```
<BODY STYLE="BACKGROUND-IMAGE: URL (thinkatron.jpg);
BACKGROUND-ATTACHMENT: FIXED">
```

One of the advantages of the CSS approach is that other modifying CSS elements can be added to modify the background behavior further.

The SCROLL attribute makes the background image scroll when the user scrolls the Web page—this is the default behavior.

BACKGROUND-POSITION

Description: If the BACKGROUND-IMAGE element is set, this additional element specifies the coordinate in which the image first appears, and is then tiled from that position onwards.

Values: X% Y% - Percentage is in reference to the dimension of the browser window display.
X Y - Represents absolute coordinate position of the image.
(LEFT/CENTER/RIGHT) | (TOP/CENTER/BOTTOM) - Keywords representing screen positions. Left keyword is the X-position and the right keyword is the Y-position for the image.

Example code:

```
<BODY STYLE="BACKGROUND-IMAGE: URL(thinkatron.jpg);
BACKGROUND-POSITION: 250 100">
```

This CSS element enables the Web author to set the specific position at which a background image begins to tile on a Web page. It can be set using a percentage value (X% and Y%) of the width and height of the browser window, or a specific coordinate on the Web page (X and Y). In the latter case, pixels is the default measure used, but any measurement value can be specified. In addition, keywords can be used to set the X and Y position as well, such as "left top" or "center bottom" (see Figure 11.7).

Font Properties

A number of CSS elements control the way fonts are displayed on a Web page. There are some difficulties even with using CSS to set font properties, including the fact that there are few truly universal fonts common to all operating systems and browsers. In general, the browser does the best it can to match the requested font with the one specified.

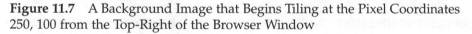

Figure 11.7 A Background Image that Begins Tiling at the Pixel Coordinates 250, 100 from the Top-Right of the Browser Window

FONT-FAMILY

Description: Sets the type of font to be displayed with the specified element.

Values: CURSIVE | FANTASY | MONOSPACE | SANS-SERIF | SERIF - Sets the type of visual characteristics of font family name that can be specified.
font_family - The name of the font to be displayed.

Example code:

```
<H2 STYLE="FONT-FAMILY: ARIAL, SAN-SERIF">Welcome!</H2>
```

This element sets the type of font to be associated with an HTML tag. First, the font_family is specified, such as Arial, Courier, Helvetica, Times New Roman, Lucinda, etc. Then, the type of font desired is specified by one of the following values: cursive, fantasy, monospace, sans-serif, or serif. The second value is used to try to specify the family that the font belongs to, in case the specified font doesn't exist on a user's system. It is designed to be a backup in case the specific font doesn't exist. There are five different font families that can be specified: CURSIVE (e.g., Zapf-Chancery), FANTASY (e.g., Western), MONOSPACE (e.g., Courier), SERIF (e.g., Times-Roman) or SANS-SERIF (e.g., Arial). It is still up to the browser to make the best possible match with the fonts that exist on the user's system.

FONT-SIZE

Description: Sets the display size of text.

Values: LARGE | MEDIUM | SMALL | X-LARGE | X-SMALL | XX-LARGE | XX-SMALL - Specifies the size of the text. Values range from XX-SMALL (smallest) to XX-LARGE (largest).
LARGER | SMALLER - Changes the size of the current specified element relative to a previously specified value.
n value - Specific unit value for the specified element.

Example code:

```
<H3 STYLE="FONT-SIZE: 16pt">Large Heading</H3>
```

The FONT-SIZE CSS element is used to specify the size of the HTML tag it is associated with. It can be specified in several different ways: either by a specific measurement value (e.g., 16pt), by a named value ranging from XX-SMALL to XX-LARGE, or in relative terms using the larger or smaller name values. There are seven named values, roughly corresponding to the same values applied to the <FONT> tag using the SIZE attribute, in the following order:

- <FONT SIZE=1> = XX-SMALL
- <FONT SIZE=2> = X-SMALL
- <FONT SIZE=3> = SMALL
- <FONT SIZE=4> = MEDIUM
- <FONT SIZE=5> = LARGE
- <FONT SIZE=6> = X-LARGE
- <FONT SIZE=7> = XX-LARGE

Similarly, the larger and smaller values work like <FONT SIZE=+1> and <FONT SIZE=-1>, respectively.

FONT-STYLE

Description: Sets whether or not the displayed font is italicized.

Values: ITALIC | NORMAL - Determines whether or not text is italicized
OBLIQUE - Sets an italic-like property if the font used is san-serif.

Example code:

```
<B STYLE="FONT-STYLE: ITALIC">Italicized text</B>
```

The CSS element is used to make the text associated with an HTML tag italic. It has two basic values: ITALIC and NORMAL (the default value). The third, OBLIQUE, is used to set an italic-like property if the font used is a san-serif type font, where an italic reference may not appear much different from its normal appearance.

FONT-WEIGHT

Description: Sets the thickness of the displayed font.

Values: 100 | 200 | 300 | 400 | 500 | 600 | 700 | 800 | 900 - Absolute font weight values.
BOLD | NORMAL - Sets whether or not the specified text element uses a bold face.
BOLDER | LIGHTER - Changes the weight of the current specified element relative to a previously specified value.

Example code:
```
<STRONG STYLE="FONT-WEIGHT: LIGHTER">Not so
strong.</STRONG>
```

FONT-WEIGHT is a CSS element used to specify the thickness (i.e., the boldness) of a displayed font. It can take several different types of values: an absolute, numeric value, ranging from 100-900; a bold or normal (the default) value; or the values lighter or bolder, which decrease and increase the weight of the specified text.

FONT-VARIANT

Description: Specifies whether the identified text is displayed using capital letters.

Values: NORMAL | SMALL-CAPS
These values are toggles to turn the small-caps effect on and off.

Example code:
```
<P STYLE="FONT-VARIANT: SMALL-CAPS">this text is
displayed in all small-caps</P>
```

This CSS element is designed to display the text of an HTML tag either in small-caps, or as normal text. The SMALL-CAPS value is used to display text in capital letters that are set to a smaller-than-normal size. NORMAL uses the browser's default value.

Results from all of the sample CSS code used in this section can be seen in Figure 11.8.

Note that at the time of this writing, all of the FONT CSS elements were supported in Internet Explorer, and FONT-VARIANT is the only FONT-related CSS element not supported within Netscape Navigator.

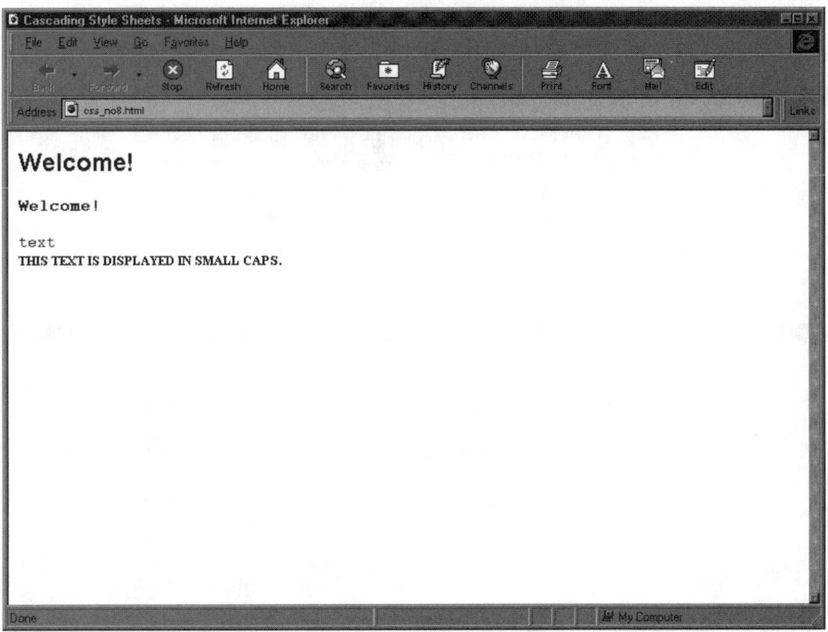

Figure 11.8 All of the Font Element CSS Example Code Displayed within Internet Explorer

FONT

Description: This is a shorthand element that allows the Web author to set fonts quickly in the manner possible under the FONT-FAMILY, FONT-SIZE, FONT-STYLE, and FONT-VARIANT CSS elements.

Values: [FONT-FAMILY shared values:]
CURSIVE | FANTASY | MONOSPACE | SANS-SERIF | SERIF - Sets the type of visual characteristics of font family name that can be specified.
font_family - The name of the font to be displayed.
[FONT-SIZE shared values:]
LARGE | MEDIUM | SMALL | X-LARGE | X-SMALL | XX-LARGE | XX-SMALL - Specifies the size of the text. Values range from XX-SMALL (smallest) to XX-LARGE (largest).
LARGER | SMALLER - Changes the size of the current specified element relative to a previously specified value.

n value - Specific unit value for the specified element.
[FONT-VARIANT shared values:]
ITALIC | NORMAL - Determines whether or not text is italicized.
OBLIQUE - Sets an italic-like property if the font used is san-serif.
[FONT-WEIGHT shared values:]
100 | 200 | 300 | 400 | 500 | 600 | 700 | 800 | 900 - Absolute font weight values.
BOLD | NORMAL - Sets whether or not the specified text element uses a bold face.
BOLDER | LIGHTER - Changes the weight of the current specified element relative to a previously specified value.

Example code:

```
<B STYLE="FONT: MEDIUM ITALIC 16 pt MONOSPACE">Some test
text.</B>
```

For a description of the possible values available to the FONT attribute, see the descriptions for the FONT-FAMILY, FONT-SIZE, FONT-STYLE, and FONT-VARIANT CSS elements.

Text Properties

In addition to font properties, text formatting elements can also be controlled using CSS elements. Using CSS elements, you can specify such things as the spacing between words, the spacing between letters, alignment, indentations, and much more.

WORD-SPACING

Description: Sets the spacing between words.

Values: NORMAL - The browser default word spacing value is used. length_in_units - Sets the length value between words as a unit of measurement.

Example code:

```
<I STYLE="WORD-SPACING: 0.5em">Small word spacing.</I>
```

The WORD-SPACING CSS element is used to set the spacing distance between words on a Web page. The default value is NORMAL, which is the default word spacing value used by the browser. Otherwise, you explicitly set the value of the word spacing. Wide values can make text easier to read (especially if you are using plenty of italic or cursive fonts), or can produce arresting visual effects, but don't space things out too much or too little, or you will make the text on your Web page hard to read.

At the time of this writing, this element was not supported in Netscape Navigator or Internet Explorer.

LETTER-SPACING

Description: Specifies the space between letters.

Values: NORMAL - The browser default letter-spacing value is used. length_in_units - Sets the length value between letters as a unit of measurement.

Example code:

```
<H1 STYLE="LETTER-SPACING: 0.5 in">Wide letter
spacing!</H1>
```

The letter-spacing CSS element enables the Web author to set the amount of space that should appear between the letters in the words on a Web page. The default value is NORMAL, which is the default word-spacing value used by the browser. Otherwise, you can explicitly set the value of the letter-spacing using units of measurement. Be careful about making the values either too high or too small; even though the visual effect can be striking, it can also make your text harder to read.

At the time of this writing, this element was not supported in Netscape Navigator, but is in Internet Explorer, as can be seen in Figure 11.9.

TEXT-DECORATION

Description: Adds a decorative property to the HTML tag specified.

Values:
BLINK - Text blinks.
LINE-THROUGH - Text contains a line through the middle (strikethrough text).
NONE - No decoration is added.
OVERLINE - Text is accompanied by a line running above it.
UNDERLINE - Text is underlined.

Example code:

```
<B STYLE="TEXT-DECORATION: NONE">TEXT-DECORATION:
NONE</B></BR>
<B STYLE="TEXT-DECORATION: OVERLINE">TEXT-DECORATION:
OVERLINE</B></BR>
<B STYLE="TEXT-DECORATION: UNDERLINE">TEXT-DECORATION:
UNDERLINE</B></BR>
```

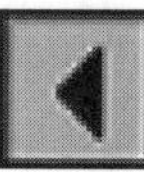

```
<B STYLE="TEXT-DECORATION: LINE-THROUGH">TEXT-DECORATION:
LINE-THROUGH </B></BR>
<B STYLE="TEXT-DECORATION: BLINK">TEXT-DECORATION:
BLINK</B>
```

The TEXT-DECORATION element adds decoration (i.e., a line) to the text of the HTML tag it is associated with. It has five values: NONE, OVERLINE, UNDERLINE, LINE-THROUGH, and BLINK. The value NONE does not add any text decoration, and OVERLINE and UNDERLINE add a line above and below the text, respectively. The LINE-THROUGH value adds a strikethrough line through the text, and BLINK makes the text display turn on and off repeatedly.

Note that the latest version of Internet Explorer at the time of this writing supported all of the values of the TEXT-DECORATION element with the exception of blink, and that the latest version of Netscape Navigator did not support the OVERLINE value.

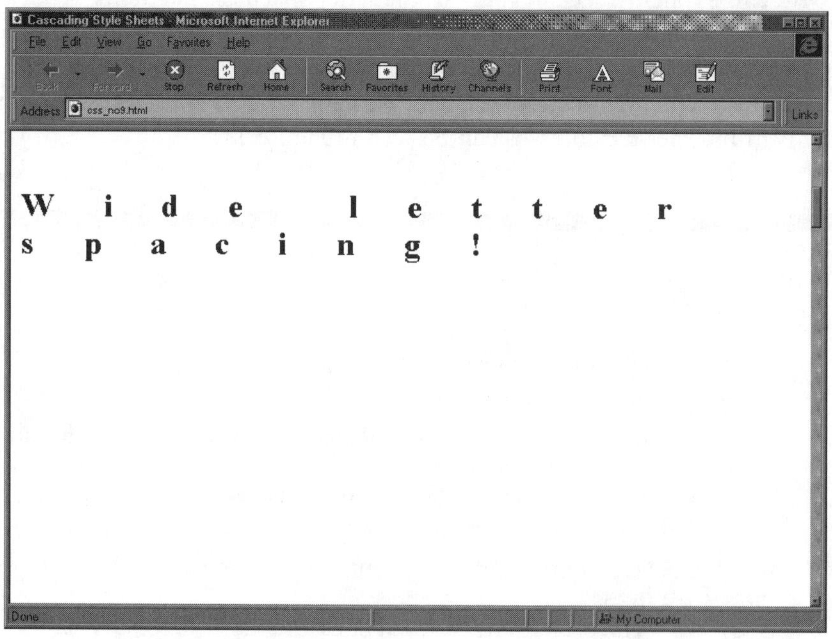

Figure 11.9 The Effects of the Code Examples for the LETTER-SPACING Element as Seen within Internet Explorer

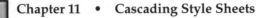

Figure 11.10 depicts Netscape Navigator displaying the example code previously listed (note that the OVERLINE value does not display properly, and that the BLINK value is in the on state).

VERTICAL-ALIGN

Description: Specifies the vertical positioning of the HTML tag it is associated with.

Values: BASELINE | BOTTOM | MIDDLE | SUB | SUPER | TEXT-TOP | TEXT-BOTTOM | TOP - Aligns the on-screen element in relation to the specified value.

Example code:

```
Some text.<B STYLE="VERTICAL-ALIGN: SUPER">Superscript
text.</B> More regular text.
```

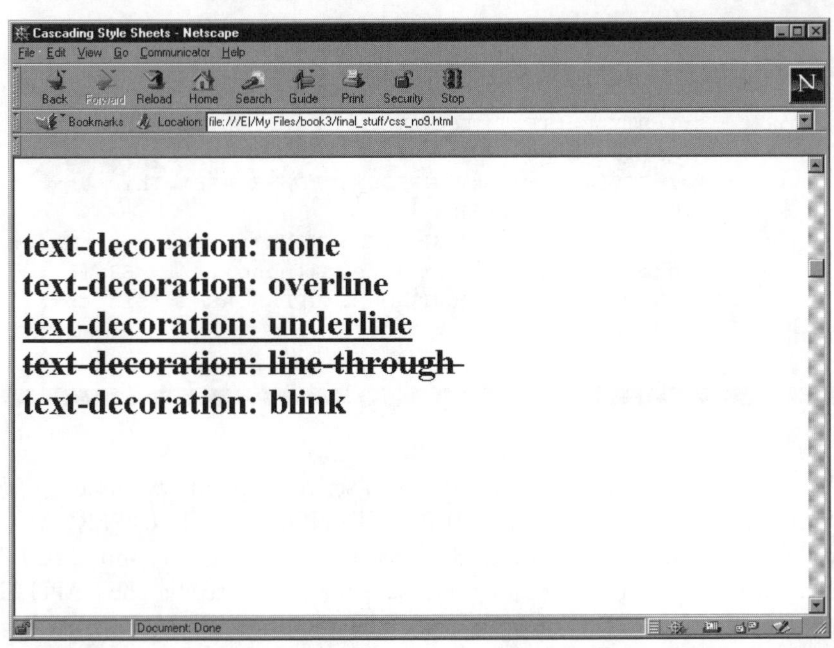

Figure 11.10 All of TEXT-DECORATION's values as Displayed within Netscape Navigator

This CSS element aligns the specified HTML tag (usually text, an image, or an object) relative to the line that it belongs to. The BASELINE value aligns the baseline of the element to that of the parent, and BOTTOM aligns the element relative to the bottom of the line it is contained in. The MIDDLE value aligns the element to the vertical middle-point of the parent (usually an image or object). The SUB and SUPER values are meant to be used for text, and display the text specified as subscript and superscript, respectively (see Figure 11.11). Finally, TEXT-TOP and TEXT-BOTTOM align the element to the top and bottom of the line of text that it is currently associated with.

Note that at the time of this writing, only the SUB and SUPER values of this CSS element appear to be supported within Internet Explorer; none were supported within Netscape Navigator at the time of testing.

TEXT-TRANSFORM

Description: Specifies the type of case to be used on the text.

Values:
CAPITALIZE - Sets the initial letter of a word in uppercase letters.
LOWERCASE - Sets all text to lowercase.
NONE - No transformation is performed.
UPPERCASE - Sets all text to uppercase.

Example code:

```
<I STYLE="TEXT-TRANSFORM: CAPITALIZE">This text is all in
initial caps.</I><BR>
<I STYLE="TEXT-TRANSFORM: LOWERCASE">This text is all in
lowercase.</I><BR>
<I STYLE="TEXT-TRANSFORM: NONE">No text-transformation
takes place with this text (none).</I><BR>
<I STYLE="TEXT-TRANSFORM: UPPERCASE">This text is all in
uppercase.</I>
```

The text-transform CSS element is used to set the type of case used on text. It has four values: CAPITALIZE, LOWERCASE, NONE, AND UPPERCASE. The values LOWERCASE and UPPERCASE force all of the letters the modified HTML tag encloses to all lowercase or all uppercase letters, respectively. The CAPITALIZE value turns the first letter of each word the modified HTML tag encloses to uppercase-known generally as initial caps. Finally, NONE does not transform the text in any way—this value is designed primarily to turn off any previous TEXT-TRANSFORM setting.

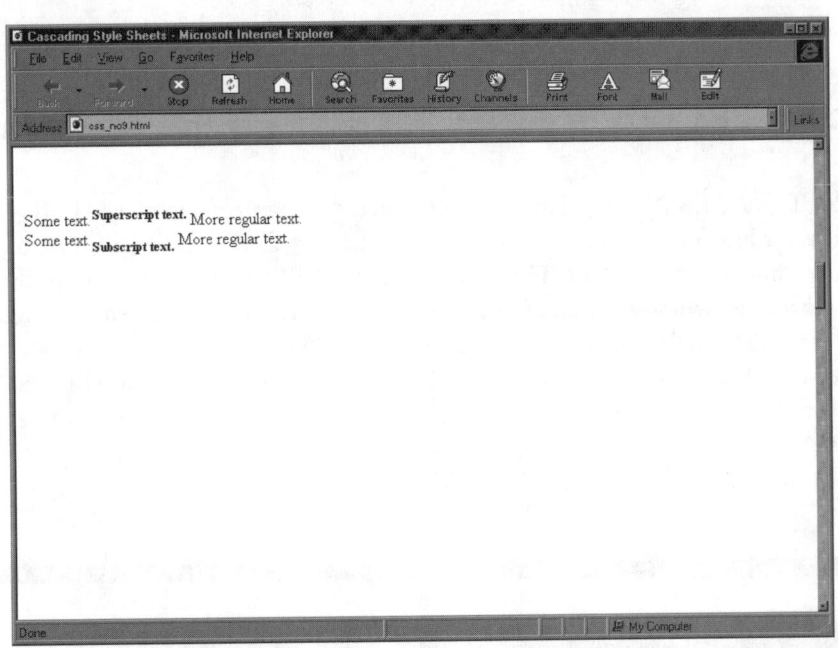

Figure 11.11 The SUB and SUPER Values for VERTICAL-ALIGN as Displayed within Internet Explorer

This CSS element is fully supported by both Internet Explorer and Netscape Navigator. The Figure 11.12 shows the code examples used in this section as displayed within Netscape Navigator.

TEXT-ALIGN

Description: Sets the alignment of the text.

Values: CENTER | JUSTIFY | LEFT | RIGHT - Aligns the text contained by the specified element.

Example code:

```
<TT STYLE="TEXT-ALIGN: CENTER">This text is
centered.</TT><BR>
<TT STYLE="TEXT-ALIGN: JUSTIFY">This text is
justified.</TT><BR>
```

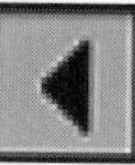

```
<TT STYLE="TEXT-ALIGN: LEFT">This text is
left-aligned.</TT><BR>
<TT STYLE="TEXT-ALIGN: RIGHT">This text is right
aligned.</TT>
```

The TEXT-ALIGN CSS element is designed to align text in the HTML tag it modifies. It has four values: CENTER aligns the text in the middle of the browser window (much like the <CENTER> container tag), LEFT aligns the text to the left of the browser window, RIGHT align aligns the text to the right of the browser window and JUSTIFY justifies the text across the line it is on.

Netscape Navigator recognizes all of these values with the exception of JUSTIFY. Internet Explorer does not recognize any of these values at the time of testing. Figure 11.13 shows how Netscape Navigator deals with all of the code examples used in this section for TEXT-ALIGN.

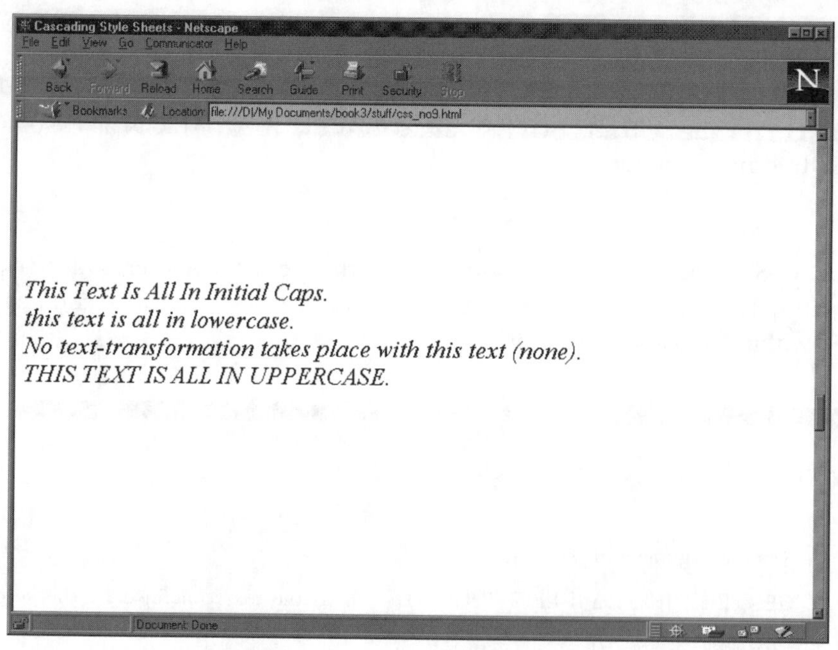

Figure 11.12 The Various Values of the TEXT-TRANSFORM CSS Element Displayed

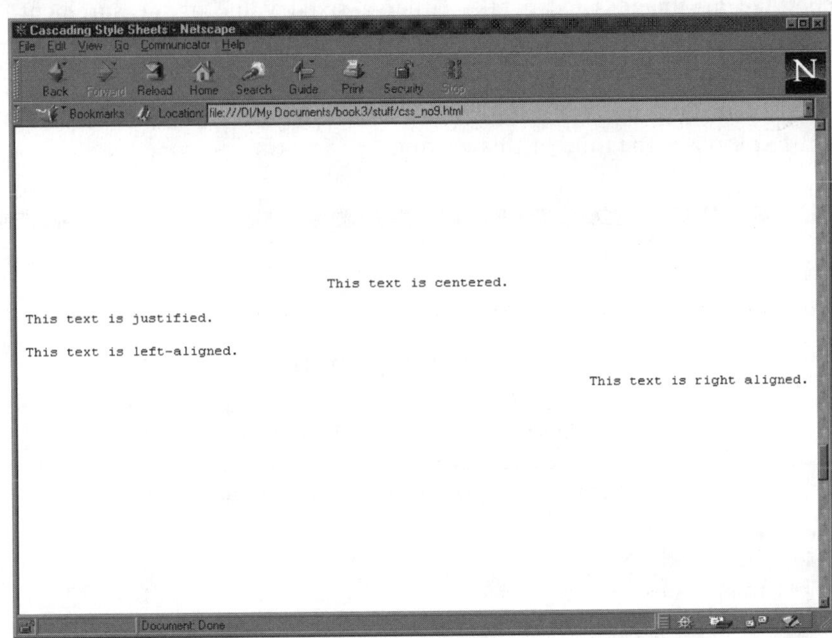

Figure 11.13 The Code Examples for TEXT-ALIGN Displayed in Netscape Navigator

TEXT-INDENT

Description: Sets an indent from the left margin or from a block element.

Values: length_in_units - Specifies the length value as a unit of measurement.
% - Specifies the distance as a percentage of the browser window display.

Example code:

```
<UL>
<LI STYLE="TEXT-INDENT 3.0in">Indented item #1
<LI>Regular item #2
</UL>
<STRONG STYLE="TEXT-INDENT 3.0in">Indented item
#1</STRONG>
```

This CSS element is used to indent items from the left margin, or from a block element (like an image). It can take either a fixed value of measurement, or a percentage value that separates the distance as a percentage of the browser window display.

This element does not work under the latest version of Netscape Navigator or Internet Explorer at the time of this writing.

LINE-HEIGHT

Description: Sets the distance between lines on a Web page.

Values: NORMAL - Sets the line height to the default value used by the browser.
n - Sets a multiple value for the current height of the font in use.
% - Sets a percentage value in relation to the size of the current font in use.
length_in_units - Specifies the length value as a unit of measurement.

Example (The results are shown in Figure 11.14):

```
Baseline<BR>
<H2 STYLE="LINE-HEIGHT: 2in">Hello there!</H2>
```

This CSS element sets the distance between two lines on a Web page. It can take a specific unit of measurement, a multiple value of the current height of the font in use, or a percentage value for the current height of the font in use. It can also take the value NORMAL, which is the default browser value used between the baselines on a Web page—this value is designed primarily to turn off any previous line-height setting. It is supported within both Internet Explorer and Netscape Navigator.

Box Properties

Box properties set the size, circumference, and position of the boxes that represent elements.

MARGIN-TOP

Description: Specifies the distance of an element from the top-edge of the browser window or from the element that appears above it.

Values:

AUTO - Specifies that the browser default value should be used.
% - Sets a percentage value of the element's width.
length_in_units - Specifies the length value as a unit of measurement.

Example code:

```
<I STYLE="MARGIN-TOP: 2 cm">This text is indented 2 cm
from the top margin.</I>
```

The MARGIN-TOP element is used to set the distance of the HTML tag it is associated with to the top-edge of the browser window or the element that appears above it. It can take three types of values: AUTO, which uses the browser's default value, a percentage value that is relative to the element's width, or a specific measured unit value.

This CSS element is fully supported in Netscape Navigator, but not in the latest version of Internet Explorer available at the time of this writing (this is likely a temporary problem since it has worked in previous versions of Internet Explorer).

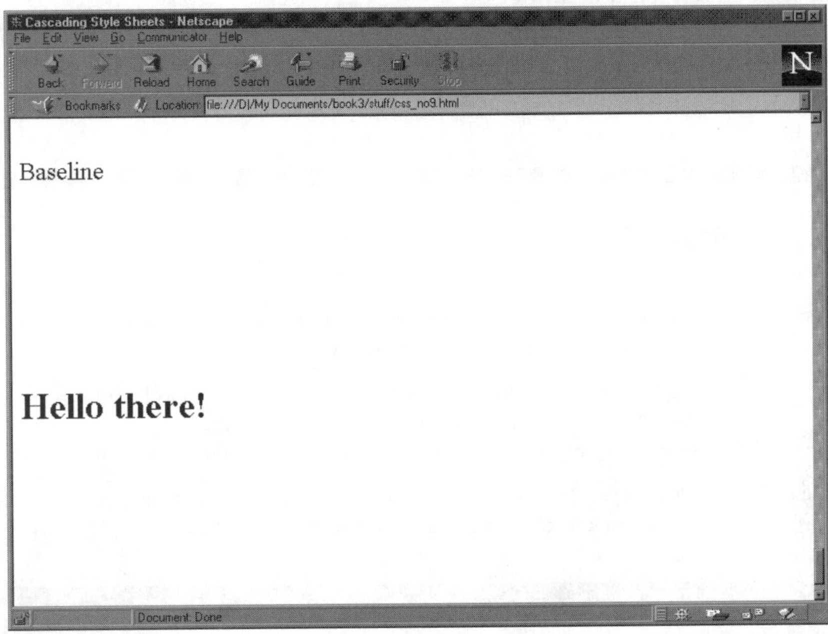

Figure 11.14 The LINE-HEIGHT Example Code Displayed within Netscape Navigator

MARGIN-RIGHT

Description: Specifies the distance of an element from the right-edge of the browser window or from the next element that appears to its right.

Values: AUTO - Specifies that the browser default value should be used.
% - Sets a percentage value of the element's width.
length_in_units - Specifies the length value as a unit of measurement.

Example code:

```
<B STYLE="MARGIN-RIGHT: 500px">This text is indented 500
pixels from the right margin.</B>
```

The MARGIN-RIGHT element is used to set the distance of the HTML tag it is associated with to the right-edge of the browser window or the element that appears to its right. It can take three types of values: AUTO, which uses the browser's default value, a percentage value that is relative to the element's width, or a specific measured unit value.

This CSS element is fully supported in Netscape Navigator, but not in the latest version of Internet Explorer available at the time of this writing (this is likely a temporary problem since it has worked in previous versions of Internet Explorer).

MARGIN-BOTTOM

Description: Specifies the distance of an element from the bottom-edge of the browser window or from the next element that appears below it.

Values: AUTO - Specifies that the browser default value should be used.
% - Sets a percentage value of the element's width.
length_in_units - Specifies the length value as a unit of measurement.

Example code:

```
<TT STYLE="MARGIN-BOTTOM: 1in">This text is indented 1
inch from the element below it.</TT>
```

The MARGIN-BOTTOM element is used to set the distance of the HTML tag it is associated with to the bottom-edge of the browser window or from the next element that appears below it. It can take three types of values: AUTO, which uses the browser's default value, a percentage value that is relative to the element's width, or a specific measured unit value.

This CSS element is fully supported in Netscape Navigator, but not in the latest version of Internet Explorer available at the time of this writing (this is likely a temporary problem since it has worked in previous versions of Internet Explorer).

MARGIN-LEFT

Description: Specifies the distance of an element from the left-edge of the browser window or from the element that appears immediately to the left.

Values: AUTO - Specifies that the browser default value should be used.
% - Sets a percentage value of the element's width.
length_in_units - Specifies the length value as a unit of measurement.

Example code:
```
<ADDRESS STYLE="MARGIN-LEFT: 25pt">This text is indented
25 points from the left margin.</ADDRESS>
```

The MARGIN-LEFT element is used to set the distance of the HTML tag it is associated with to the top-left of the browser window or the element that appears immediately to its left. It can take three types of values: AUTO, which uses the browser's default value, a percentage value that is relative to the element's width, or a specific measured unit value.

This CSS element is fully supported in Netscape Navigator and in Internet Explorer.

MARGIN

Description: This is a shorthand element that enables the Web author to set margin values such as MARGIN-TOP, MARGIN-RIGHT, MARGIN-LEFT, or MARGIN-BOTTOM quickly.

Values: AUTO - Specifies that the browser default value should be used.
% - Sets a percentage value of the element's width.
n[,n,n,n] measurement_units

- If 1 value is present, all borders take the numerical value
- If 2 values are present, the top and bottom borders take the numerical values, respectively
- If 3 values are present, the top, right and left, then bottom take the numerical values, respectively
- If 4 values are present, the top, right, bottom, then left borders take the numerical values, respectively

Example code:

```
<STRONG STYLE="MARGIN: 25px">This text is set off from
all other elements by 25pixels.</STRONG>
```

The MARGIN element is a shorthand element that enables the Web author to set margin values such as MARGIN-TOP, MARGIN-RIGHT, MARGIN-LEFT, OR MARGIN-BOTTOM without having to specify the full value.

Like the other margin CSS properties, this element can take AUTO (the browser's default value) or a percentage value that is relative to the element's width. Unlike the other margin CSS element however, this element can take multiple measured unit values. If a single value is specified, it is applied to all sides equally. If two values are specified, they are applied to the top and bottom sides, respectively. If three are specified, they are applied to the top, right plus left, then the bottom sides, respectively. Four values set the margins for the top, right, left, and bottom sides.

If four length values are specified they apply to top, right, bottom, and left, respectively. If there is only one value, it applies to all sides; if there are two or three, the missing values are taken from the opposite side.

This CSS element is fully supported in Netscape Navigator, but not in the latest version of Internet Explorer available at the time of this writing (this is likely a temporary problem since it has worked in previous versions of Internet Explorer).

All of the margin example code examples from this section can be seen in Figure 11.15.

Padding Properties

In many ways the effects of the padding properties are very similar to those of the margin properties. The idea behind them is different however: they are designed to set the amount of space to insert between the border and the other elements on the Web page. The net effects for each of the padding properties is much the same as those for the margin properties.

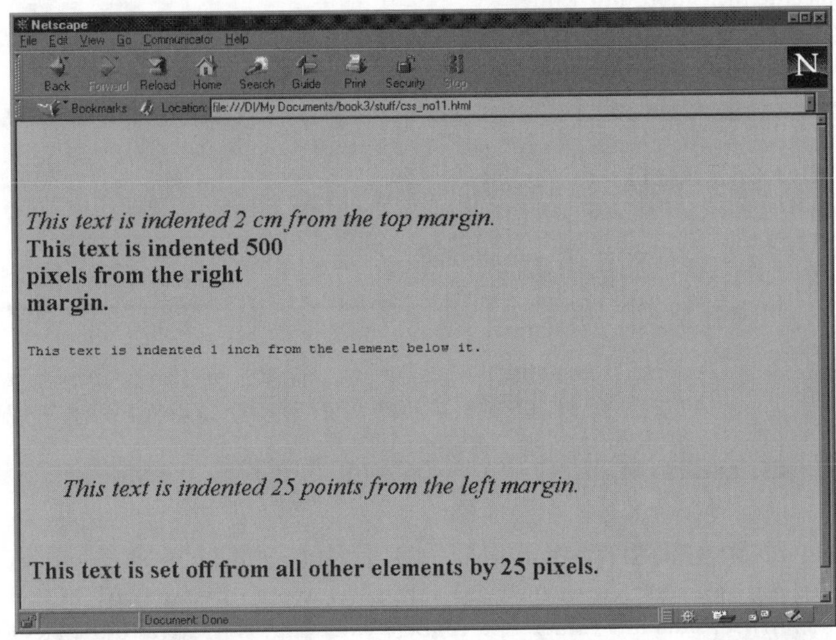

Figure 11.15 All of the MARGIN Code Examples from this Section Displayed within Netscape Navigator

PADDING-TOP

Description: Sets the amount of padding to the top of an element.

Values: % - Sets a percentage value of the element's width. length_in_units - Specifies the length value as a unit of measurement.

Example code:

```
<B STYLE="PADDING-TOP: 1in">This is padded from the top
by 1 inch.</B>
```

The PADDING-TOP element is used to add padding to the top of the HTML tag it is associated with. It can take three types of values: AUTO, which uses the

browser's default value; a percentage value that is relative to the element's width; or a specific measured unit value.

This element works in Netscape Navigator, but does not in Internet Explorer.

PADDING-RIGHT

Description: Sets the amount of padding to the right of an element.

Values: % - Sets a percentage value of the element's width. length_in_units - Specifies the length value as a unit of measurement.

Example code:

```
<I STYLE="PADDING-RIGHT: 10cm">This long, long, long
sentance is padded from the right by 10 centimeters.</I>
```

The PADDING-RIGHT element is used to add padding to the right of the HTML tag it is associated with. It can take three types of values: AUTO, which uses the browser's default value; a percentage value that is relative to the element's width; or a specific measured unit value.

This element works in Netscape Navigator, but not in Internet Explorer.

PADDING-BOTTOM

Description: Sets the amount of padding to the bottom of an element.

Values: % - Sets a percentage value of the element's width. length_in_units - Specifies the length value as a unit of measurement.

Example code:

```
<U STYLE="PADDING-BOTTOM: 2.5cm">This is padded from the
bottom (i.e. from the element below it) by 2.5
centimeters.</U>
```

The PADDING-BOTTOM element is used to add padding to the bottom of the HTML tag it is associated with. It can take three types of values: AUTO, which uses the browser's default value; a percentage value that is relative to the element's width; or a specific measured unit value.

This element works in Netscape Navigator, but not in Internet Explorer.

PADDING-LEFT

Description: Sets the amount of padding to the bottom of an element.

Values: % - Sets a percentage value of the element's width.
length_in_units - Specifies the length value as a unit of measurement.

Example code:

```
<STRONG STYLE="PADDING-LEFT: 15 pt">This is padded from
the left by 15 points.</STRONG>
```

The PADDING-LEFT element is used to add padding to the left of the HTML tag it is associated with. It can take three types of values: AUTO, which uses the browser's default value; a percentage value that is relative to the element's width; or a specific measured unit value.

This element works in Netscape Navigator, but not in Internet Explorer.

PADDING

Description: This is a shorthand element that enables the Web author to set margin values such as PADDING-TOP, PADDING-RIGHT, PADDING-LEFT, or PADDING-BOTTOM quickly.

Values: AUTO - Specifies that the browser default value should be used.
% - Sets a percentage value of the element's width.
n[,n,n,n] measurement_units

- If 1 value is present, all borders take the numerical value
- If 2 values are present, the top and bottom borders take the numerical values, respectively
- If 3 values are present, the top, right and left, then bottom take the numerical values, respectively

- If 4 values are present, the top, right, bottom, then left borders take the numerical values, respectively

Example code:

```
<KBD STYLE="MARGIN: 25 px">This text is padded on all
sides by 25 pixels.</KBD>
```

The PADDING element is a shorthand element that enables the Web author to set padding values such as PADDING-TOP, PADDING-RIGHT, PADDING-LEFT, or PADDING-BOTTOM without having to specify the full value.

Like the other margin CSS properties, this element can take AUTO (the browser's default value) or a percentage value that is relative to the element's width. Unlike the other margin CSS element however, this element can take multiple measured unit values. If a single value is specified, it is applied to all sides equally. If two values are specified, they are applied to the top and bottom sides respectively. If three are specified, they are applied to the top, right plus left, then the bottom sides, respectively. Four values set the margins for the top, right, left, and bottom sides.

If four length values are specified they apply to top, right, bottom, and left, respectively. If there is only one value, it applies to all sides; if there are two or three, the missing values are taken from the opposite side.

All of the margin example code examples from this section can be seen in Figure 11.16.

Border Properties

The border properties set the display of borders around the HTML tag the CSS element is associated with. The properties used by the BORDER-WIDTH, BORDER-COLOR, and BORDER-STYLE properties.

BORDER-WIDTH

Description: Sets the thickness of the border for the specified element. Can set the thickness value for one to four border sides.

Values: n[,n,n,n] measurement_units

Sets the thickness of the border.

- If 1 value is present, all borders take the numerical value
- If 2 values are present, the top and bottom borders take the numerical values, respectively

- If 3 values are present, the top, right and left, then bottom take the numerical values, respectively
- If 4 values are present, the top, right, bottom, then left borders take the numerical values, respectively

THIN | MEDIUM | THICK - Sets the relative thickness of the border.

Example code:

```
<H1 STYLE="BORDER-WIDTH: THICK">A Thick-Border Level-1
Header</H1>
```

The BORDER-WIDTH CSS element sets the thickness of the border for the specified element. It can take three named values that set a thin border (THIN), a thicker border (MEDIUM) and the thickest possible border (THICK). It can also take one to four numeric measurement values: If one value is present, all borders take on the value specified, two values specify the top and bottom and values,

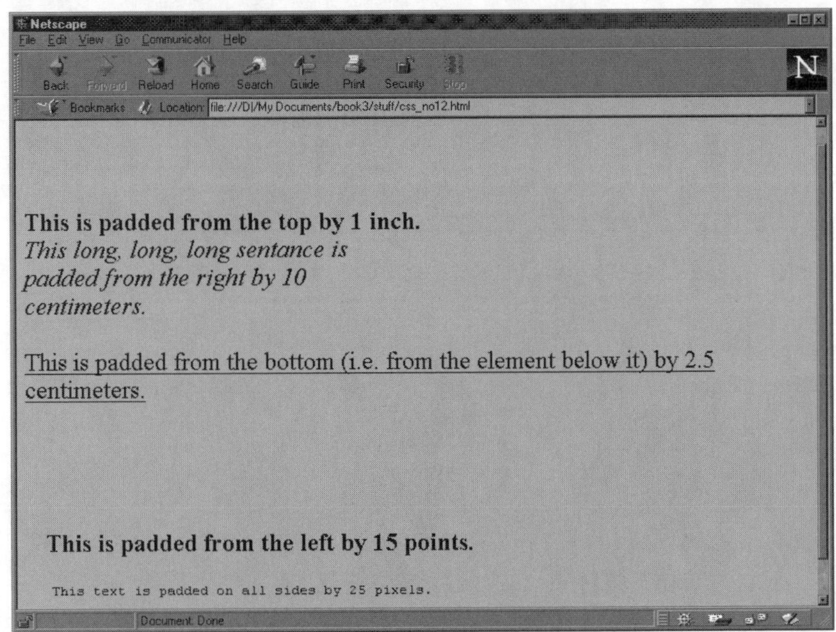

Figure 11.16 All of the Code Examples for the PADDING Section Displayed in Netscape Navigator

respectively, three values sets the top, right and left, then bottom border settings, and four values set the top, right, bottom, then left borders, respectively.

This element works in Netscape Navigator, but not in Internet Explorer. The effect of the previous code sample can be seen in Figure 11.17.

BORDER-COLOR

Description: Sets the color of the specified border sides.

Values: colorname or rrggbb - Sets the color for the border.

Example Code:

```
<H2 STYLE="BRODER-COLOR: MAROON">A Funky Maroon-colored
Border for this Level-2 Header</H2>
```

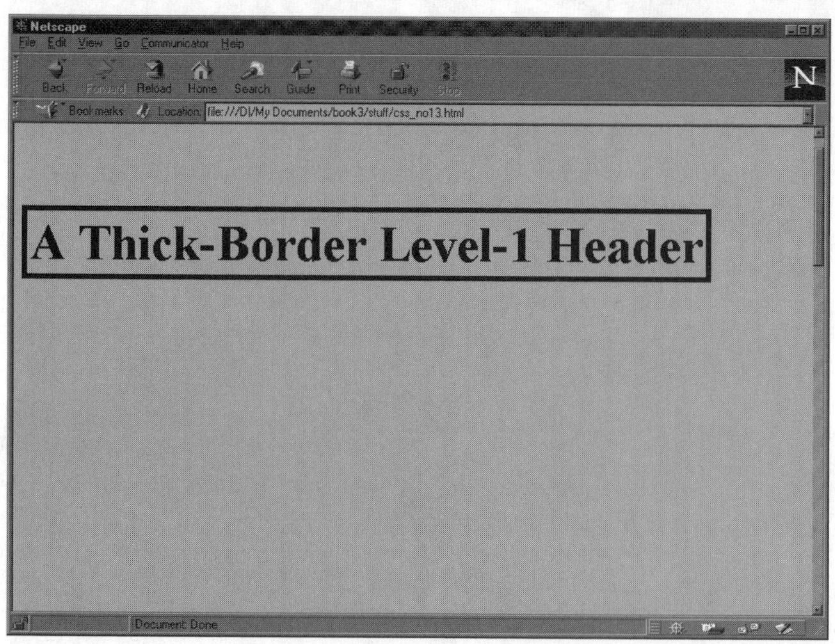

Figure 11.17 The THICK Value of the BORDER-WIDTH CSS Element Associated with a Level-1 Header, as Seen in Netscape Navigator

The BORDER-COLOR element sets the color of the specified border sides. This CSS element can take either a colorname or a hexadecimal color value (a full listing of valid colornames and color values can be found in Appendix D, "Listing of Common Color Values/Colornames").

This element seems to work in IE only when used in conjunction with another border attribute (e.g.,

```
<H3 STYLE="BORDER-STYLE: DOUBLE; BORDER-COLOR:
MAROON">Double bordered maroon-colored header.</H3>
```

works but

```
<H3 STYLE="BORDER-COLOR: MAROON">Maroon-colored
header.</H3>
```

does not). At the time of this writing, it does work at all within Netscape Navigator.

Figure 11.18 displays one of the few code examples

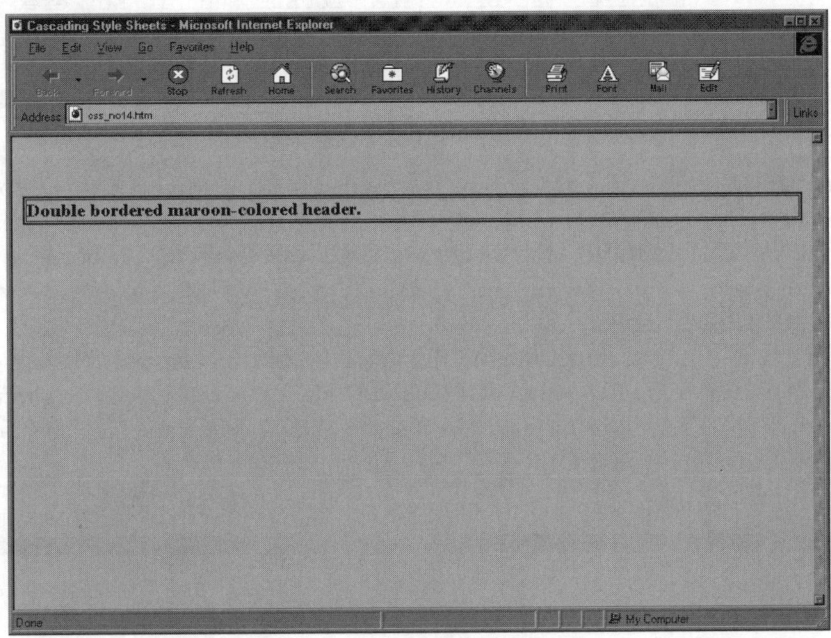

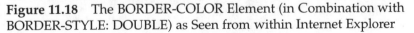

Figure 11.18 The BORDER-COLOR Element (in Combination with BORDER-STYLE: DOUBLE) as Seen from within Internet Explorer

```
(<H3 STYLE="BORDER-STYLE: DOUBLE; BORDER-COLOR:
MAROON">Double bordered maroon-colored header.</H3>)
```

that will work within Internet Explorer.

BORDER-STYLE

Description: Sets the type of border displayed.

Values:
DASHED - A dashed border line is displayed.
DOTTED - A dotted border line is displayed.
DOUBLE - A double line is displayed.
INSET - A 3D inset line is displayed.
GROOVE - A 3D grooved line is displayed.
NONE - No border is displayed, no matter what BORDER-WIDTH value is present.
OUTSET - A 3D outset line is displayed.
RIDGE - A 3D ridged line is displayed.
SOLID - A solid border line is displayed.

Example:

```
<H3 STYLE="BORDER-STYLE: DOUBLE">Double bordered
text.</H3>
```

The BORDER-STYLE CSS element is designed to set a specific type of border display. The DASHED, DOTTED, DOUBLE, and SOLID values are self-explanatory. The INSET, GROOVE, OUTSET, and RIDGE values display 3D border types. NONE displays no border at all, and typically is set to override any previous value set for BORDER-STYLE.

At the time of this writing, Internet Explorer seems capable of displaying only two of BORDER-STYLE's values: SOLID and DOUBLE. Any other value specified (other than NONE) will be displayed as if set to SOLID. Netscape Navigator does not appear to support BORDER-STYLE at all.

BORDER-TOP

Description: Sets the display value for the top border of the specified HTML tag.

Values:
[BORDER-WIDTH shared attributes:]
n [,n,n,n] measurement_units

Sets the thickness of the border.

- If 1 value is present, all borders take the numerical value
- If 2 values are present, the top and bottom borders take the numerical values, respectively
- If 3 values are present, the top, right and left, then bottom take the numerical values, respectively
- If 4 values are present, the top, right, bottom, then left borders take the numerical values, respectively

THIN | MEDIUM | THICK - Sets the relative thickness of the border.
[BORDER-COLOR shared attributes:]
colorname or rrggbb - Sets the color for the border.
[BORDER-STYLE shared attributes:]
DASHED - A dashed border line is displayed.
DOTTED - A dotted border line is displayed.
DOUBLE - A double line is displayed.
INSET - A 3D inset line is displayed.
GROOVE - A 3D grooved line is displayed.
NONE - No border is displayed, no matter what BORDER-WIDTH value is present.
OUTSET - A 3D outset line is displayed.
RIDGE - A 3D ridged line is displayed.
SOLID - A solid border line is displayed.

Example code:

```
<H4 STYLE="BORDER-TOP: THICK DASHED RED">A sassy
fourth-level heading</H4>
```

The BORDER-TOP element is used to set the display value for the top border of the specified HTML tag.

For a description of the possible values available to the BORDER-TOP attribute, see the descriptions for the BORDER-COLOR, BORDER-STYLE, and BORDER-WIDTH elements.

BORDER-RIGHT

Description: Sets the display value for the right border of the specified HTML tag.

Values: [BORDER-WIDTH shared attributes:]
n[,n,n,n] measurement_units
Sets the thickness of the border.

- If 1 value is present, all borders take the numerical value
- If 2 values are present, the top and bottom borders take the numerical values, respectively

- If 3 values are present, the top, right and left, then bottom take the numerical values, respectively
- If 4 values are present, the top, right, bottom, then left borders take the numerical values, respectively

THIN | MEDIUM | THICK - Sets the relative thickness of the border.
[BORDER-COLOR shared attributes:]
colorname or rrggbb - Sets the color for the border.
[BORDER-STYLE shared attributes:]
DASHED - A dashed border line is displayed.
DOTTED - A dotted border line is displayed.
DOUBLE - A double line is displayed.
INSET - A 3D inset line is displayed.
GROOVE - A 3D grooved line is displayed.
NONE - No border is displayed, no matter what BORDER-WIDTH value is present.
OUTSET - A 3D outset line is displayed.
RIDGE - A 3D ridged line is displayed.
SOLID - A solid border line is displayed.

Example code:

```
<H5 STYLE="BORDER-RIGHT: THIN DOTTED BLUE">A thin, blue
dotted fifth-level heading</H5>
```

The BORDER-RIGHT element is used to set the display value for the top border of the specified HTML tag.

For a description of the possible values available to the BORDER-RIGHT attribute, see the descriptions for the BORDER-COLOR, BORDER-STYLE, and BORDER-WIDTH elements.

BORDER-BOTTOM

Description: Sets the display value for the bottom border of the specified HTML tag.

Values: [BORDER-WIDTH shared attributes:]
n[,n,n,n] measurement_units
Sets the thickness of the border.

- If 1 value is present, all borders take the numerical value
- If 2 values are present, the top and bottom borders take the numerical values, respectively
- If 3 values are present, the top, right and left, then bottom take the numerical values, respectively
- If 4 values are present, the top, right, bottom, then left borders take the numerical values, respectively

THIN | MEDIUM | THICK - Sets the relative thickness of the border.

[BORDER-COLOR shared attributes:]
colorname or rrggbb - Sets the color for the border.
[BORDER-STYLE shared attributes:]
DASHED - A dashed border line is displayed.
DOTTED - A dotted border line is displayed.
DOUBLE - A double line is displayed.
INSET - A 3D inset line is displayed.
GROOVE - A 3D grooved line is displayed.
NONE - No border is displayed, no matter what BORDER-WIDTH value is present.
OUTSET - A 3D outset line is displayed.
RIDGE - A 3D ridged line is displayed.
SOLID - A solid border line is displayed.

Example code:

```
<STRONG STYLE="BORDER-BOTTOM: 10px INSET 00FF00">Strong
text, thick like chicken soup.</STRONG>
```

The BORDER-BOTTOM element is used to set the display value for the top border of the specified HTML tag.

For a description of the possible values available to the BORDER-BOTTOM attribute, see the descriptions for the BORDER-COLOR, BORDER-STYLE, and BORDER-WIDTH elements.

BORDER-LEFT

Description: Sets the display value for the left border of the specified HTML tag.

Values: [BORDER-WIDTH shared attributes:]
n[,n,n,n] measurement_units
Sets the thickness of the border.

- If 1 value is present, all borders take the numerical value
- If 2 values are present, the top and bottom borders take the numerical values, respectively
- If 3 values are present, the top, right and left, then bottom take the numerical values, respectively
- If 4 values are present, the top, right, bottom, then left borders take the numerical values, respectively

THIN | MEDIUM | THICK - Sets the relative thickness of the border.
[BORDER-COLOR shared attributes:]
colorname or rrggbb - Sets the color for the border.
[BORDER-STYLE shared attributes:]
DASHED - A dashed border line is displayed.
DOTTED - A dotted border line is displayed.

DOUBLE - A double line is displayed.
INSET - A 3D inset line is displayed.
GROOVE - A 3D grooved line is displayed.
NONE - No border is displayed, no matter what BORDER-WIDTH value is present.
OUTSET - A 3D outset line is displayed.
RIDGE - A 3D ridged line is displayed.
SOLID - A solid border line is displayed.

Example code:

```
<ADDRESS STYLE="BORDER-LEFT: 0.5in RIDGE NAVY">A navy
address.</ADDRESS>
```

The BORDER-LEFT element sets the display value for the left border of the specified HTML tag.

For a description of the possible values available to the BORDER-LEFT attribute, see the descriptions for the BORDER-COLOR, BORDER-STYLE, and BORDER-WIDTH elements.

BORDER

Description: This is a shorthand element that allows the Web author to specify BORDER-TOP, BORDER-RIGHT, BORDER-BOTTOM, and BORDER-LEFT elements easily.

Values:

[BORDER-WIDTH shared attributes:]
n[,n,n,n] measurement_units
Sets the thickness of the border.

- If 1 value is present, all borders take the numerical value
- If 2 values are present, the top and bottom borders take the numerical values, respectively
- If 3 values are present, the top, right and left, then bottom take the numerical values, respectively
- If 4 values are present, the top, right, bottom, then left borders take the numerical values, respectively

THIN | MEDIUM | THICK - Sets the relative thickness of the border.
[BORDER-COLOR shared attributes:]
colorname or rrggbb - Sets the color for the border.
[BORDER-STYLE shared attributes:]
DASHED - A dashed border line is displayed.
DOTTED - A dotted border line is displayed.
DOUBLE - A double line is displayed.
INSET - A 3D inset line is displayed.

GROOVE - A 3D grooved line is displayed.
NONE - No border is displayed, no matter what BORDER-WIDTH value is present.
OUTSET - A 3D outset line is displayed.
RIDGE - A 3D ridged line is displayed.
SOLID - A solid border line is displayed.

Example code:

```
<BIG STYLE="BORDER: THICK GROOVE 3399CC">Groovy
daddy-o.</BIG>
```

The BORDER CSS element is a shorthand element that allows the Web author to specify BORDER-TOP, BORDER-RIGHT, BORDER-BOTTOM, and BORDER-LEFT elements easily. For a description of the possible values available to the BORDER attribute, see the descriptions for the BORDER-COLOR, BORDER-STYLE, and BORDER-WIDTH elements.

BORDER-TOP-WIDTH

Description: Sets the thickness of the top border.

Values: [BORDER-WIDTH shared attributes:]
n[,n,n,n] measurement_units
Sets the thickness of the border.

- If 1 value is present, all borders take the numerical value
- If 2 values are present, the top and bottom borders take the numerical values, respectively
- If 3 values are present, the top, right and left, then bottom take the numerical values, respectively
- If 4 values are present, the top, right, bottom, then left borders take the numerical values, respectively

THIN | MEDIUM | THICK - Sets the relative thickness of the border.

Example code:

```
<SMALL STYLE="BORDER-TOP-WIDTH MEDIUM">Small top-bordered
text.</SMALL>
```

The BORDER-TOP-WIDTH element sets the thickness value of the top border. For a description of the possible values available to the BORDER-LEFT attribute, see the description for the BORDER-WIDTH elements.

BORDER-RIGHT-WIDTH

Description: Sets the thickness of the right border.

Values: [BORDER-WIDTH shared attributes:]
n[,n,n,n] measurement_units
Sets the thickness of the right border.

- If 1 value is present, all borders take the numerical value
- If 2 values are present, the top and bottom borders take the numerical values, respectively
- If 3 values are present, the top, right and left, then bottom take the numerical values, respectively
- If 4 values are present, the top, right, bottom, then left borders take the numerical values, respectively

THIN | MEDIUM | THICK - Sets the relative thickness of the border.

Example code:

```
<SUB STYLE="BORDER-TOP-WIDTH 5 px">Subscript with
border.</SUB>
```

The BORDER-TOP-WIDTH element sets the thickness value of the top border.

For a description of the possible values available to the BORDER-LEFT attribute, see the description for the BORDER-WIDTH elements.

BORDER-BOTTOM-WIDTH

Description: Sets the thickness of the bottom border.

Values: [BORDER-WIDTH shared attributes:]
n[,n,n,n] measurement_units
Sets the thickness of the right border.

- If 1 value is present, all borders take the numerical value
- If 2 values are present, the top and bottom borders take the numerical values, respectively
- If 3 values are present, the top, right and left, then bottom take the numerical values, respectively

- If 4 values are present, the top, right, bottom, then left borders take the numerical values, respectively

THIN | MEDIUM | THICK - Sets the relative thickness of the border.

Example code:

```
<SUP STYLE="BORDER-BOTTOM-WIDTH 10 pt">Superscript with
border.</SUP>
```

The BORDER-BOTTOM-WIDTH element sets the thickness value of the top border.

For a description of the possible values available to the BORDER-LEFT attribute, see the description for the BORDER-WIDTH elements.

BORDER-LEFT-WIDTH

Description: Sets the thickness of the left border.

Values: [BORDER-WIDTH shared attributes:]
n [,n,n,n] measurement_units
Sets the thickness of the right border.

- If 1 value is present, all borders take the numerical value
- If 2 values are present, the top and bottom borders take the numerical values, respectively
- If 3 values are present, the top, right and left, then bottom take the numerical values, respectively
- If 4 values are present, the top, right, bottom, then left borders take the numerical values, respectively

THIN | MEDIUM | THICK - Sets the relative thickness of the border.

Example code:

```
<TT STYLE="BORDER-LEFT-WIDTH THICK">Teletype text with
border.</TT>
```

The BORDER-LEFT-WIDTH element sets the thickness value of the top border.

For a description of the possible values available to the BORDER-LEFT attribute, see the description for the BORDER-WIDTH elements.

WIDTH

Description: This property scales the HTML tag it is associated with to fit the given width dimension.

Values: AUTO - Specifies that the browser default value should be used.
% - Sets a percentage value of the element's width. length_in_units - Specifies the length value as a unit of measurement.

Example code: `<HR STYLE="WIDTH 75px">`

This CSS element is designed to scale the HTML tag it is associated with to fit the specified width dimension. It can take three types of values: AUTO, which uses the browser's default value; a percentage value that is relative to the element's width; or a specific measured unit value.

At the time of this writing, this element is not fully supported in either Netscape Navigator or Internet Explorer.

HEIGHT

Description: This property scales the HTML tag it is associated with to fit the given height dimension.

Values: AUTO - Specifies that the browser default value should be used.
% - Sets a percentage value of the element's height length_in_units - Specifies the length value as a unit of measurement.

Example code: `<HR STYLE="HEIGHT 1in">`

This CSS element is designed to scale the HTML tag it is associated with to fit the specified height dimension. It can take three types of values: AUTO, which uses the browser's default value; a percentage value that is relative to the element's height; or a specific measured unit value.

At the time of this writing, this element is not fully supported in either Netscape Navigator or Internet Explorer.

FLOAT

Description: Sets whether other elements can wrap around the specified element as it floats on a Web page.

Values: NONE - Other elements cannot be displayed to float around the specified element.
LEFT - Other elements can be displayed to the left margin of the specified element.
RIGHT - Other elements can be displayed to the right margin of the specified element.

Example:

```
<IMG SRC="thinkatron.jpg" STYLE="FLOAT: RIGHT">This text
floats to the left of the image.
```

The FLOAT CSS element determines how other elements on a Web page can wrap around the specified element as it floats on a Web page. Typically it is used with images and objects. The value NONE usually is used to override any previously set value for FLOAT, RIGHT displays other elements to the right margin of the specified element, and LEFT displays other elements to the left margin of the specified element.

CLEAR

Description: Specifies whether the identified element will allow other elements to float along its sides.

Values: BOTH - The specified element will be moved below floating elements on either side.
LEFT - The specified element will be moved below floating elements on the left side only.
NONE - Any floating elements are allowed on either side of the specified element.
RIGHT - The specified element will be moved below floating elements on the right side only.

Example:

```
<IMG SRC="thinkatron.jpg">
<I STYLE="CLEAR: BOTH">This text begins below the
previous image file.</I>
```

The CLEAR element determines whether the specified element will allow other elements to float along its sides. The BOTH value moves the specified HTML tag

it is associated with below any floating elements on either side. The LEFT and RIGHT values move the specified HTML tag they are associated with below any floating elements to the left and right side, respectively. The NONE value allows any floating elements to either side of the specified element.

The FLOAT and CLEAR code examples are displayed in Figure 11.19 within Netscape Navigator.

These two elements work in both Internet Explorer and Netscape Navigator.

Classification Properties

These CSS elements allow the author to define the fundamental nature and display of various HTML tags.

It also includes a set of four LIST-STYLE type CSS elements that are designed to be used to describe how list items (i.e., the <LI> tag) are displayed within a Web page.

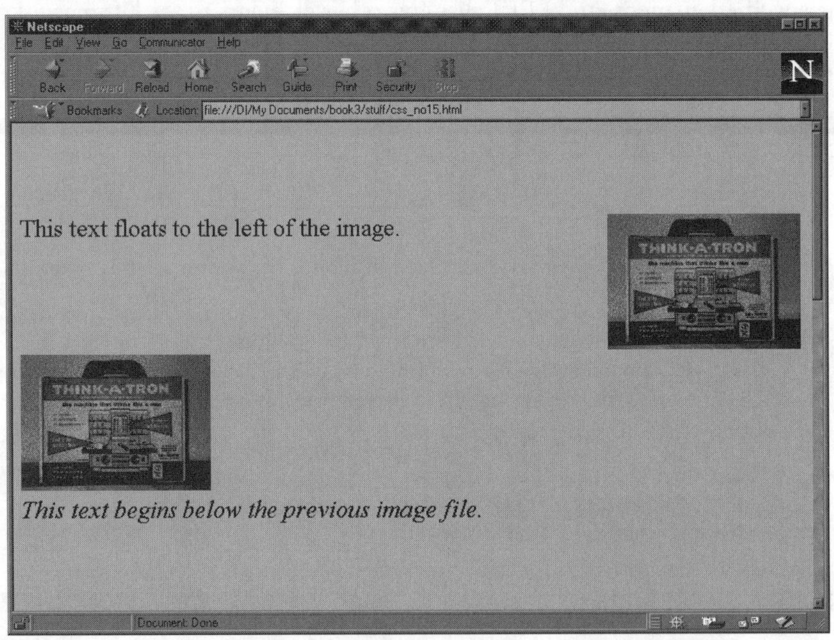

Figure 11.19 The FLOAT and CLEAR Code Examples Displayed within Netscape Navigator

DISPLAY

Description: Controls the underlying HTML nature of the tag. Can be used to fundamentally alter the way a tag is displayed.

Values:
BLOCK - Sets the specified element as a block-type element.
INLINE - Sets the specified element as an inline-type element.
LIST-ITEM - Sets the specified element as a type of list-item.
NONE - Switches off the display of the specified element.

Example code:

```
<B STYLE="DISPLAY: NONE">This text should not be
displayed..</B>

<B STYLE="DISPLAY: LIST-ITEM">This bolded line will be
indented like a list-item would be.</B>

<UL>
<LI STYLE="DISPLAY: BLOCK">This list-item will appear as
a block element
<LI>Here is another list-item to illustrate the point
</UL>

<OL STYLE="DISPLAY: INLINE">
<LI>These list-items will appear as an inline element
<LI>This is contained within an ordered list tag,
<LI>but you will notice that no numbers appear before
<LI>each line.
<LI>(The dots that appear at the beginning of each line
<LI>are typical of the &lt;LI&gt; tag when no &lt;OL&gt;
tag is present).
</OL>
```

The DISPLAY element is used to control the underlying nature of the HTML tag it is associated with, changing the way it is displayed and behaves on a Web page. It has four possible values: BLOCK, INLINE, LIST-ITEM, and NONE. The BLOCK value tells the HTML tag with which this element is associated to behave like a block-type tag (i.e., headers and paragraph tags). The BLOCK value tells the HTML tag with which this element is associated to behave like a character formatting tag (i.e., bold and italic tags). The INLINE value tells the HTML tag with which this element is associated to behave like a list formatting tag (i.e., ordered or unordered list tags). The LIST-ITEM value tells the HTML tag with which this element is associated to behave like a list formatting tag (i.e., ordered or

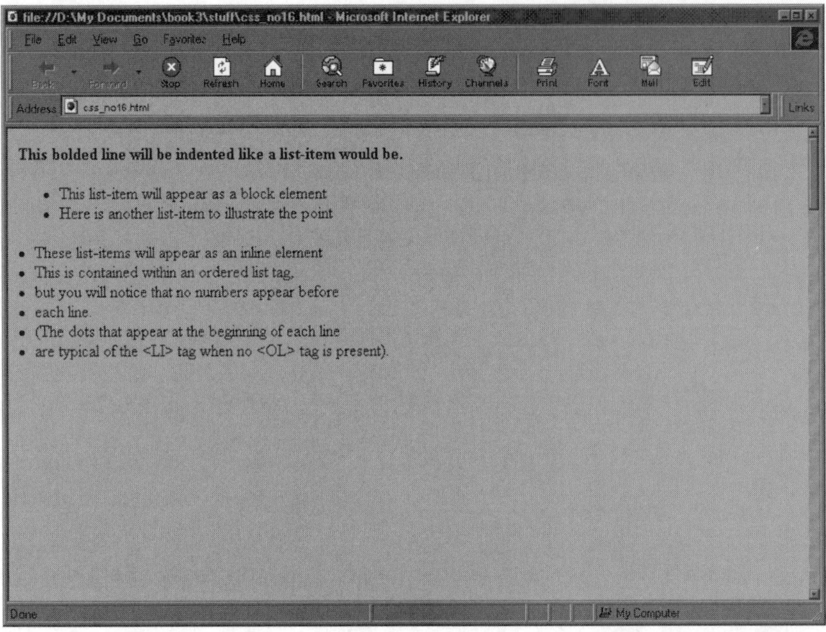

Figure 11.20 DISPLAY Example Code Displayed within Internet Explorer

unordered list tags). Finally, NONE tells the browser to not display the tag with which it is associated, in effect turning the display of that tag off.

Not all of these values appear to be fully supported in Netscape Navigator, as BLOCK and NONE did not work as predicted when viewed through this browser. The BLOCK value does not appear to work in Internet Explorer either, but the other values of DISPLAY are. Figure 11.20 shows how the previous code examples are displayed within Internet Explorer (note that the initial NONE code example does not display—which is what it is supposed to do).

WHITE-SPACE

Description: This element is used to set white space and how carriage returns are handled within a Web page.

Values: NORMAL - The default browser behavior for the HTML tag this element is associated with.
NOWRAP - When this value is set, carriage returns and linefeeds are rendered as single space. However line breaks are not effected.
PRE - When this value is set, all spaces, carriage returns, and linefeeds in the document are displayed as is.

Example code:

```
<P STYLE="WHITE-SPACE: NORMAL">
This text will be displayed
  normally.
</P>

<P STYLE="WHITE-SPACE: PRE">
This text
  should retain
     all
spacing    and      carriage-return
    characteristics.
</P>

<P STYLE="WHITE-SPACE: NOWRAP">
This text
  will not retain
     any of the
spacing    and      carriage-return
    characteristics used here.
</P>
```

The WHITE-SPACE element is a powerful element that controls the way that white space and carriage returns are handled within a Web page when associated with an HTML tag. It takes three possible values: NORMAL, NOWRAP, and PRE. NORMAL tells the browser to use its default behavior for the tag the WHITE-SPACE element is associated with—it is typically used to override any previously set WHITE-SPACE behavior. NOWRAP tells the browser to ignore any carriage returns and linefeeds that are contained in the code, and then render all of the text along a single space. This value does not effect line breaks, so you can use the line break (<BR>) tag to set spacing between lines of text. The PRE value specifies that all spaces, carriage returns, and linefeeds in the document are displayed as is. It essentially allows you to use the display characteristics of the preformatted (<PRE>) tag with another HTML tag.

This CSS element and all of its attributes are supported within Netscape Navigator, but not within Internet Explorer. Figure 11.21 shows how the code examples are displayed within Netscape Navigator.

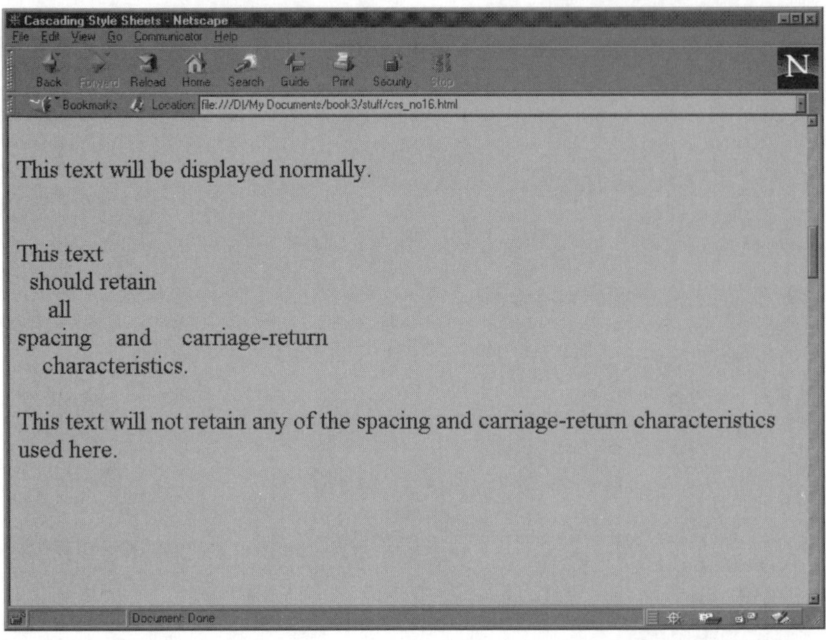

Figure 11.21 The WHITE-SPACE Code Examples as Displayed from within Netscape Navigator

LIST-STYLE-TYPE

Description: Sets the type of list markers that appear before list items.

Values: CIRCLE | DISC | SQUARE - Sets the type of symbol to appear before a list element.
DECIMAL | LOWER-ALPHA | LOWER-ROMAN | UPPER-ALPHA | UPPER-ROMAN - Sets the type of alphanumeric symbol that appears before a list marker.
NONE - No list marker is displayed before a list item.

Example code:

```
<UL>
<LI STYLE="LIST-STYLE-TYPE: DISC">List item preceded by a
disc.
<LI STYLE="LIST-STYLE-TYPE: CIRCLE">List item preceded by
a circle.
<LI STYLE="LIST-STYLE-TYPE: SQUARE">List item preceded by
a square.
<LI STYLE="LIST-STYLE-TYPE: DECIMAL">List item preceded
by a number.
```

```
<LI STYLE="LIST-STYLE-TYPE: LOWER-ALPHA">List item
preceded by a lower-case letter.
<LI STYLE="LIST-STYLE-TYPE: LOWER-ROMAN">List item
preceded by a lower-roman numeral.
<LI STYLE="LIST-STYLE-TYPE: UPPER-ALPHA">List item
preceded by an upper-case letter.
<LI STYLE="LIST-STYLE-TYPE: UPPER-ROMAN">List item
preceded by an upper-roman numeral.
<LI STYLE="LIST-STYLE-TYPE: NONE">List item preceded by
nothing.
</UL>
```

This element sets the type of list markers that appear before list items in a list. The CIRCLE, DISC, and SQUARE values display a solid bullet, hollow bullet, and solid square, respectively before each list item. It is also possible to use another set of values—DECIMAL, LOWER-ALPHA, LOWER-ROMAN, UPPER-ALPHA, UPPER-ROMAN—to set the type of alphanumeric symbol that appears before a list marker as illustrated in the following list:

- Decimal: 1, 2, 3 . . .
- Lower-alpha: a, b, c . . .
- Lower-roman: i, ii, iii . . .
- Upper-alpha: A, B, C . . .
- Upper-roman: I, II, III . . .

At the time of this writing, Netscape Navigator supports only the CIRCLE, DISC, and SQUARE values of LIST-STYLE-TYPE. Internet Explorer supports all of the values of LIST-STYLE-TYPE. Figure 11.22 shows how the code examples used in this section are displayed within Internet Explorer.

LIST-STYLE-IMAGE

Description: Specifies an image to be used as the marker before a list element.

Values: NONE - No list-marker is displayed before a list item.
URL (name_of_image_file) - Specifies the URL of the graphic to be used as a list marker.

Example code:

```
<UL>
<LI STYLE="LIST-STYLE-IMAGE: URL (thinkatron.jpg)">List
item Think-a-Tron #1
```

```
<LI STYLE="LIST-STYLE-IMAGE: URL(thinkatron.jpg)">List
item Think-a-Tron #2
<LI STYLE="LIST-STYLE-IMAGE: URL (thinkatron.jpg)">List
item Think-a-Tron #3
</UL>
```

The LIST-STYLE-IMAGE element allows the Web author to specify an image file to be displayed before a list item. It is used to add a greater visual impact to a set of list items. In addition to the value URL, it can also take the value NONE, which does not display any initial list item image or marker.

This element is not supported in the latest version of Netscape Navigator available at the time of this writing, but it is within Internet Explorer, as Figure 11.23 shows.

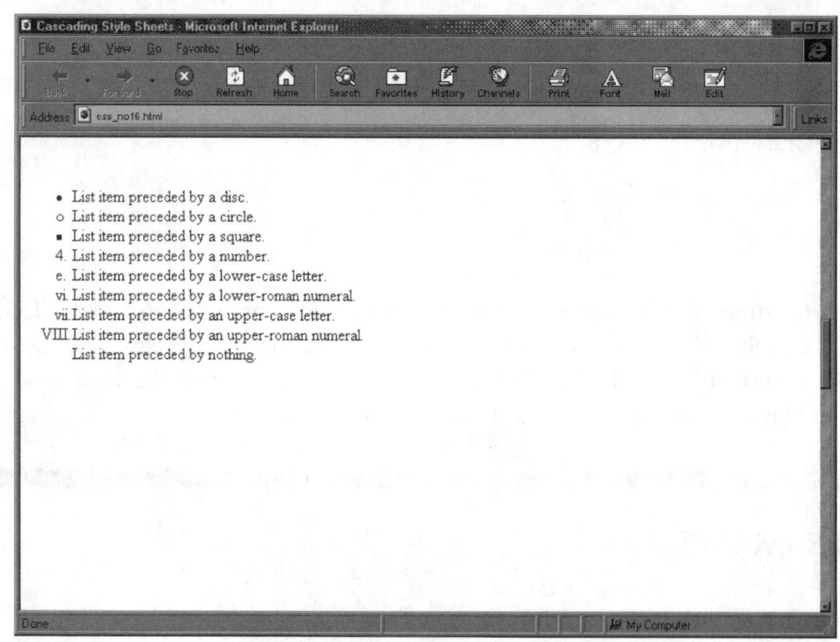

Figure 11.22 The LIST-STYLE-TYPE Code Examples as Displayed within Internet Explorer

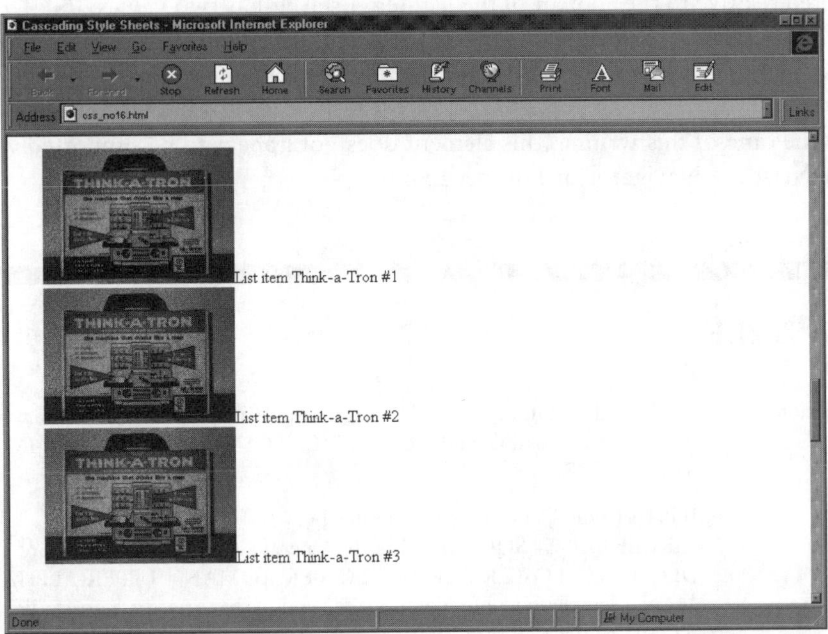

Figure 11.23 The LIST-STYLE-IMAGE Code Example Displayed within Internet Explorer

LIST-STYLE-POSITION

Description: Specifies how a list marker is rendered relative to the content of the list item itself.

Values: INSIDE - Displays the text of a list item at a similar indentation level to the list marker.
OUTSIDE - Displays the text of a list item indented from the list marker.

Example code:

```
<UL>
<LI STYLE="LIST-STYLE-POSITION: INSIDE">Inside value
used.
<LI STYLE="LIST-STYLE-POSITION: OUTSIDE">Outside value
used.
</UL>
```

The LIST-STYLE-POSITION element is used to specify how a list marker is rendered relative to the content of the list item itself. It has two values: INSIDE and OUTSIDE. INSIDE displays the text of a list item at a similar indentation level to the list marker, and OUTSIDE displays the text of a list item indented from the list marker.

At the time of this writing, this element does not appear to be supported within either Netscape Navigator or Internet Explorer.

LIST-STYLE

Description: This is a shorthand element that allows the Web author to set list item markers quickly in the manner possible under LIST-STYLE-POSITION, LIST-STYLE-IMAGE, and LIST-STYLE-TYPE.

Values:
[LIST-STYLE-TYPE shared attributes:]
CIRCLE | DISC | SQUARE - Sets the type of symbol to appear before a list element.
DECIMAL | LOWER-ALPHA | LOWER-ROMAN | UPPER-ALPHA | UPPER-ROMAN - Sets the type of alphanumeric symbol that appears before a list marker.
NONE - No list marker is displayed before a list item.
[LIST-STYLE-IMAGE shared attributes:]
NONE - No list marker is displayed before a list item.
URL (name_of_image_file) - Specifies the URL of the graphic to be used as a list marker.
[LIST-STYLE-POSITION shared attributes:]
INSIDE - Displays the text of a list item at a similar indentation level to the list marker.
OUTSIDE - Displays the text of a list item indented from the list marker.

Example code:

```
<UL>
<LI STYLE="LIST-STYLE: url(thinkatron.jpg) circle
outside">List item
</UL>
```

The LIST-STYLE element is a shorthand element that allows the Web author to set list item markers quickly in the manner possible under LIST-STYLE-POSITION, LIST-STYLE-IMAGE, and LIST-STYLE-TYPE. It shares all of the values of the previously mentioned list style elements.

For a description of the possible values available to the LIST-STYLE element, see the descriptions for the LIST-STYLE-POSITION, LIST-STYLE-IMAGE, and LIST-STYLE-TYPE elements.

Introducing CSS2

Cascading Style Sheets2 (CSS2) is the latest addition by the World Wide Web Consortium to the Cascading Style Sheet specification. It is a new specification designed to work in conjunction with the previous version of CSS (now called CSS1) and add to its capabilities.

At the time of this writing (early December 1997), the CSS2 specification was still very much in a draft state. Not all of the elements had been fully specified in great detail, and none of the elements are supported within any Web browser.

The big picture is that CSS2 adds the following new features:

- Greater ability to specify how CSS items, including XML tags, are selected
- Ability to customize and further refine your Web pages for display on different devices, like Braille readers and television screens
- Enhanced control over such things as margins, borders, and padding
- Greater ability to control the positioning of elements on a Web page
- Ability to make your Web pages more printer friendly
- Ability to change the type of cursor displayed
- Greatly enhanced font selection, including the ability to download specific fonts
- Ability to create tables using Cascading Style Sheets
- Aural style sheets that enable the Web author to specify how a Web page sounds

In many ways the new CSS2 specification not only adds to the existing CSS1 specification, but supercedes many of its elements—in particular the additions to the font, box, and positioning elements are extensive, and if implemented by browser manufacturers will revolutionize the way the Web looks. CSS2 is a surprisingly extensive specification, guiding browser manufacturers on things such as how to display Web pages under very different circumstances, and how it should appear when viewed/read through different devices (like Braille readers, television, or print). There is also an extensive section that deals with how a Web page should sound to anyone who has a computer equipped with a speech synthesis device. Keep in mind that it is a relatively easy process to suggest how things like these should be accomplished within a browser, but it is a very different thing when it

comes to implementing these features. At this early stage it remains to be seen just how much of the CSS2 is eventually adopted (or is even feasible) within the next generation of Web browsers.

This chapter will take a quick overview of some of the more significantly new features contained within the CSS2 specification, and speculate on how these features may be implemented within future browsers.

These new additions to the existing CSS specification are designed to incorporate some of the multimedia elements—particularly those dealing with sound—that were missing from the first CSS specification. With the introduction of paged media, CSS2 also tries to overcome the aspects of the Web that do not lend themselves well to other media types, like printed text. The other aspects of the new specification try to address other issues designed to make Web authors who want to use page-layout techniques happier about using CSS instead of using nonstandard HTML tags.

Aural Style Sheets

The aural style sheet section of the new CSS2 specification is designed not to replace the many ways in which sound is presented on a Web page, but how the text it contains should be read by some sort of speaking device. In large part this aural design is there to aid the blind, but it has other uses too, as the computer reads text to the user under circumstances where using a keyboard may be inconvenient, such as searching the Web for local hotels while you are driving, or when your hands are otherwise occupied with important matters. Many of these new elements can be used in conjunction with standard HTML tags, modifying their aural behavior. Under the aural section of CSS2 you can control such things as the rate at which the text is read, the pitch and brightness of the voice, and even when to spell out acronyms and how to read dates. It is even possible to specify the sex of the voice through the use of the VOICE-FAMILY, as the following valid CSS2 code demonstrates:

```
H1 {voice-family: announcer-guy, male}
P.part.cyrano {voice-family: nasal, male}
P.part.rosalind {voice-family: breathy, female}
```

As this example demonstrates, it will be possible under this scheme to set how your computer will read various types of works in sophisticated ways—the stereotypical monotone computer voice seen in old science fiction movies depicting the future obviously didn't count on CSS2.

Paged Media

The concept of paged media in CSS2 allows the Web author to determine where page breaks occur in different sorts of media, such as computer printers and computer screens. It essentially allows Web authors to determine where they want to set divisions both on the Web (onscreen) and off (printed). This new set of CSS tags allows the Web author to add such things as headers and footers, whether a page should be displayed in landscape or portrait styles, where page breaks should appear, and even where such things as crop marks should be displayed. All of these are great aids to those people who want a Web page to look as good when printed out as it does when it is displayed on a monitor. This control even extends to determining how left and right pages should be printed, allowing the author to set different margins for each side, as in the following code examples.

```
@page :left {
     margin-left: 1.5m;
     margin-right: 1in; }
@page :right {
     margin-left: 1in;
     margin-right: 1.5in; }
```

Note that these ways of dividing things up for the printed page are for the printed page only; the Web page retains all of the special elements (like hyperlinks) that make it distinct, but makes the page itself more print friendly. If you've ever tried to print out anything from the Web and found that your printer didn't understand where the margins of the page were, or if you've tried to print manuals from the Web, you will appreciate this addition to HTML.

There is also support within the CSS2 for dealing with other sorts of media in addition to the printed page. This is a further extension and refinement of the MEDIA attribute used in the <STYLE>, <SPAN>, and <DIV> tags. The new media type portion of the CSS2 specification defines how a Web page should be rendered on completely different forms of media in which the Web could be read. The draft specification of CSS2 calls for types such as BRAILLE so that a Web page can be read on a tactile feedback device for the blind; TV for WebTV devices that display a page using low resolution, color, and limited scrolling capabilities; or HANDHELD for small palmtop computing devices. The possibilities for porting the Web to other media is endless.

Fonts

CSS2 also greatly extends the ways in which font characteristics can be set. Under CSS1 it is possible to set the size, type, and color of a font, but CSS2 goes further by enabling the Web author to specify more precisely the type of font to be displayed. The browser will make a better attempt than is currently possible to find a closer match to the fonts present on the user's system, and if it is not present, download the font type from the Web. This new system allows the Web author

pretty much to specify exactly the type of font to be displayed on a user's screen, opening up the whole typographic family for use on the Web. What's more, the coding scheme that is at the heart of this new mechanism supports Unicode, which allows Web page creators to add support for many non-European font types. Other characteristics can also be specified, such as setting the height of the uppercase letters of a given font, the size of the m-space used in a font, or how low the descending part of a letter (like the tail on the letters p or q) should go.

Selectors

More powerful selectors have been added to CSS2, extending those in the CSS1 specification. Under CSS1, you could specify groupings for different, though similar types of elements. For example if you wanted to display two different types of level-1 headers, you could do it this way:

```
H1.fred     {font-weight: bold;
                  font-size: 12pt;
                  font-family: Helvetica;
                  color: red }
H1.wilma {font-weight: bold;
                  font-size: 12pt;
                  font-family: Helvetica;
                  color: blue }

<H1.fred>Wilma!</H1>
<H1.wilma>What is it Now Fred?</H1>
```

This example displays the first header in a red font, and the second header in blue. CSS2 extends this by adding special operators to the specification, so that whenever a match is found in a document for a specified word, it is displayed differently. By adding an equal sign or an almost equal sign, you could tell the browser to display certain text on a page in a different manner from the rest, as in the following example:

```
A[HREF="trademark"] {color: green}
A[HREF~="copyright, registered, copy"] {color: lime}
```

Under CSS2, any hypertext anchor that contains the word trademark would be rendered in green, whereas a hypertext link containing the word copyright, registered, or copy will be displayed in lime.

There are many other such additions made to CSS2 that have the potential to give Web authors the tools and control that desktop publishers have over printed media while still retaining the underlying structure of HTML. The real question is, will they be implemented? That answer is not so clear, since many of these changes rely on the browser manufacturers to add significant new features to their products. Also, judging by the relatively slow pace the CSS1 specification has been implemented by the major browser manufacturers, this may not happen quickly.

Link: For the very latest information on CSS2, go to the section of the W3C's Web site devoted to the topic at http://www.w3.org/TR/ WD-CSS2/.

CSS and Its Adoption by the Major Browsers

It must be stressed that at the time of this writing (December 1997), neither Internet Explorer nor Netscape Navigator apply the whole of the CSS1 within their respective browsers. Both only use a subset of the complete specification as laid out by the W3C, but since they are both members of the W3C, it is the hope that they will adopt the full set of CSS elements over time. CSS1 (and CSS2) will only be useful to Web authors if they are widely adopted and implemented fully by browser manufacturers. If they are not, CSS will likely disappear, becoming as obsolete as the failed HTML 3.0 specification, which was widely ignored by the browser manufacturers.

It should be noted that one of the things keeping CSS back from wide adoption within the Web authoring community is the fact that both netscape Navigator and Internet Explorer (at least at the time of this writing) support only a subset of the existing CSS elements. In many cases CSS elements that are supported in Internet Explorer are not supported in Netscape Navigator, or they are not supported in either browser. In some cases only certain values of the CSS element are supported, or work only when associated with certain HTML tags. There are even cases where a CSS element has been adopted for use within one version of a browser and was later dropped in the next release—presumably an oversight, but not exactly something that will inspire confidence in CSS for a Web author.

In general, if a certain feature is already supported within one browser, you can most likely use a CSS element to set it too. For example, the TEXT-DECORATION element has a value called BLINK that flashes the text on and off repeatedly. It is supported within Netscape Navigator—where you could use the <BLINK> tag to do much the same sort of thing—but not in Internet Explorer, which has never supported the <BLINK> tag. It can only be hoped that over time all of these CSS elements will be supported within these two major browsers.

The relatively recent introduction of the set of layer tags by Netscape after the initial draft of the CSS1 specification seems to suggest that it is unlikely that we have seen the last of the creation of new, browser-specific tags. But as time goes by and more Web authors become familiar with the details of CSS (and particularly as more Web browsers fully implement and are able to display Web pages that use CSS), the demand and need for new tags will be significantly diminished. Depending on how things turn out, CSS will prove to be either a triumph or a resounding failure for the W3C, ultimately determining the evolution and development of HTML and of the relevancy of the W3C itself.

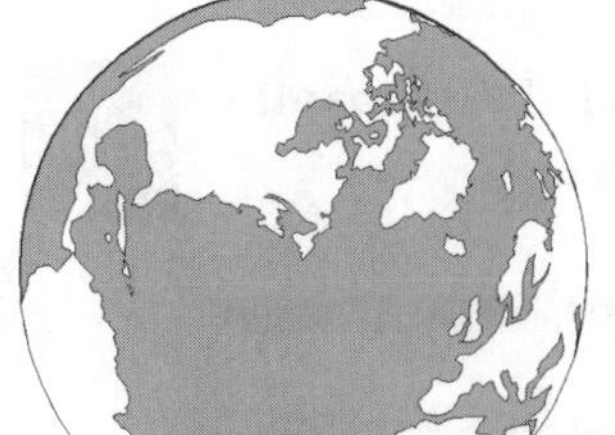

CHAPTER 12

Designing for the WebTV Service

Late in 1996, both Sony and Philips released the WebTV® Internet terminal (see Figure 12.1), a piece of hardware that connects to a television set that provides a way for people who do not have a computer to connect to the Internet. The chief idea behind the WebTV system is to make things as simple as possible for people who do not have a computer to allow them to join the online community. WebTV may seem an esoteric subject, as the current installed base of WebTV units are not extensive when compared to the installed base of Netscape Navigator or Internet Explorer users. Though it still remains to be seen if WebTV is going to take off and claim a sizable share of the Web surfing audience, it does have its own special requirements if you intend to write Web pages for that medium. Besides, given the potential audience (an estimated 95 million homes in the U.S. alone) at the very least this is an audience Web authors should be aware of.

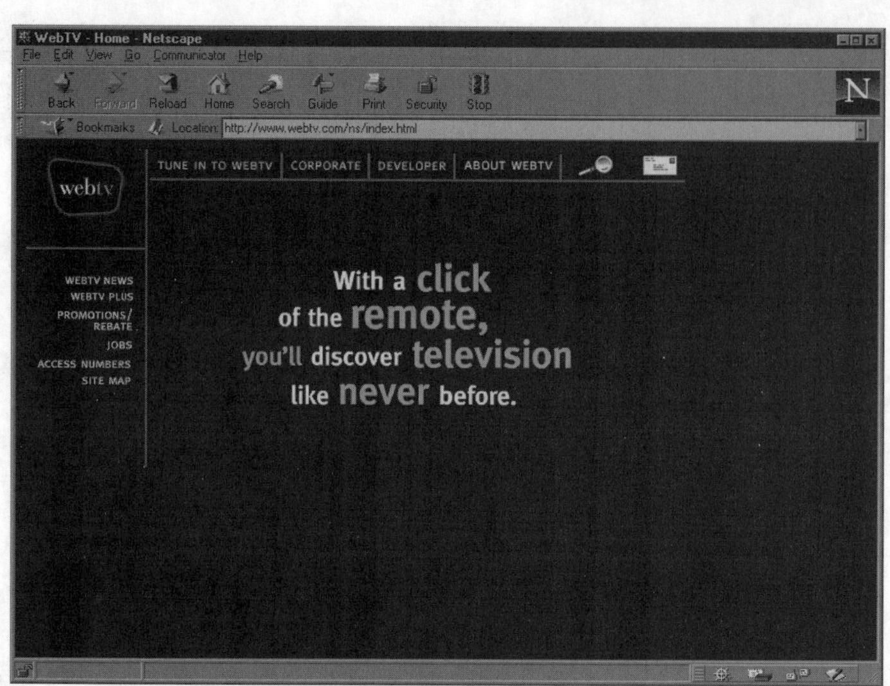

Figure 12.1 The WebTV Home Page
Screen shot(s) reprinted with permission from WebTV Networks, Inc.

What is the WebTV System?

The WebTV Internet terminal can be purchased at the retail level throughout the United States. Users must also subscribe to the WebTV Network service for a nominal monthly fee (see Figure 12.2). Users connect the WebTV box to a standard phone line (as of yet they do not connect to a high-speed cable connection) and another line to their television set. The user then sits back in his or her favorite chair and proceeds to surf the Web on TV using a device similar to a remote control. Users can also send and receive email, but the primary purpose of WebTV is to surf the Web.

At the moment, most Web pages that are written specifically for WebTV are primarily those Web sites that cater to television audiences in some way, such as TV Guide, the Public Broadcast System (PBS), and The Discovery Channel (see

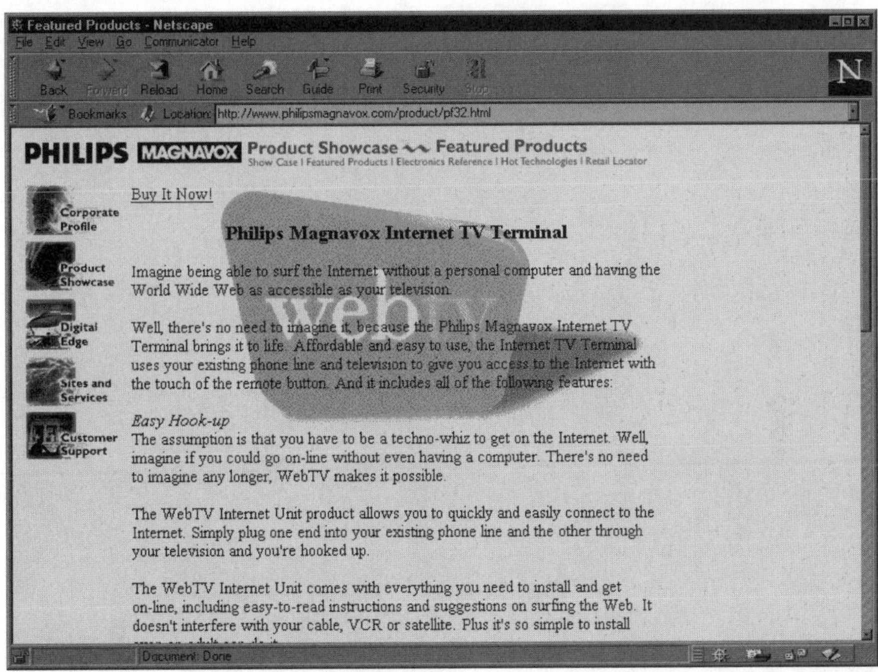

Figure 12.2 The Philips Magnavox WebTV Site

Figure 12.3). The impact of WebTV on the future of HTML should not be underestimated. Recent marketing efforts are strongly positioning WebTV as a consumer electronic device, aiming at a very large segment of the population that still does not have a computer in the home. Now that WebTV is backed by Microsoft, there is a greater possibility that some of the WebTV features embedded in its structure could be up for adoption within more general HTML standards at a later date. No matter how you look at it, learning a little bit about WebTV now may serve you well later.

In addition to the set-top WebTV box, the user gets a remote-control device, which looks very similar to most regular TV remotes. A second, keener glance reveals that it is quite different: The Web button is a dead giveaway that it is not a regular TV remote. However the WebTV remote is designed to function both as a TV remote and as a Web browser interface. The number buttons on the remote

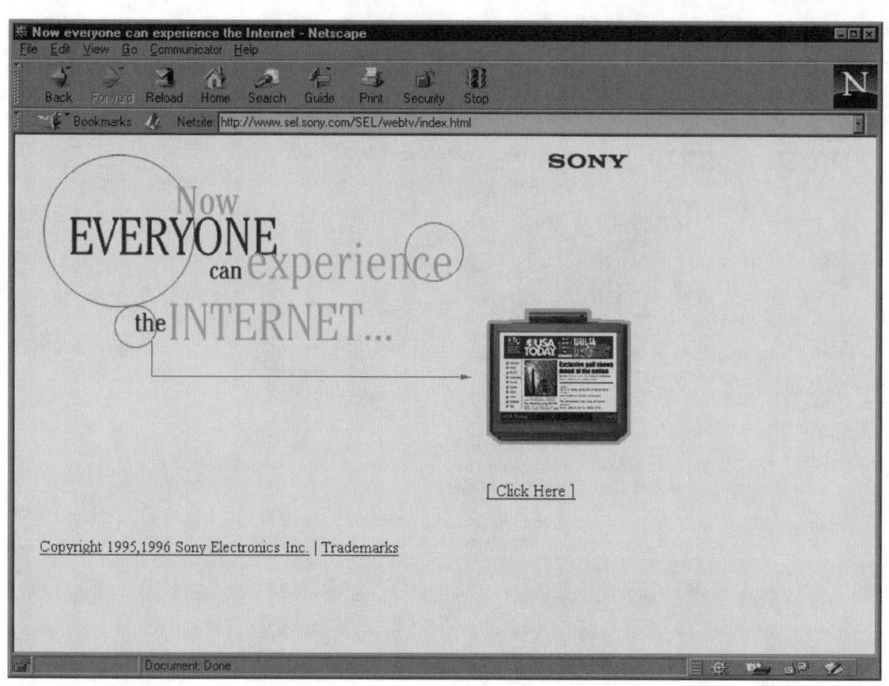

Figure 12.3 The Sony WebTV Site
Courtesy of Sony Electronics, Inc.

work for selecting TV channels in television mode, and for entering numbers when the user selects the WebTV function.

The remote (see Figure 12.4) contains a number of features that work exclusively with WebTV. There are buttons to scroll the page, and back and forward buttons to shuttle between recently viewed Web pages. The Recent button displays information on the last dozen pages visited, and the Home button displays the WebTV default page. There are also four buttons arranged as an oval at the bottom of the control that enable the user to move a cursor around the screen, surrounding a central button (called the Go key) that serves as an Enter key. To move about the screen, a user presses these cursor buttons, and clicks the Go key to select a link. An on-screen keyboard can also be called from the remote when it is necessary to enter information on-screen, or for sending email. The user presses the cursor buttons to choose individual letters—this workable but far from efficient method of typing information can be replaced by a wireless remote keyboard that can be purchased separately. Although some of the features may seem primitive, WebTV is a deliberately simpli-

Figure 12.4 A WebTV Remote Control

fied version of how most computer users traverse the Web. Its design is to bring the Web home for the noncomputer user, and it does this very well.

Differences between WebTV and Computer-Based Browsing

There are a number of features that are significantly different between the WebTV browser and regular computer-based browsers. Here's a short list of some of the major differences.

- Resolution of small items, such as text, is not as crisp as on a computer monitor
- Horizontal screen size is limited to a 544 pixel-wide display
- Frames are not currently supported
- It is possible to scroll vertically, but it is not possible to scroll horizontally
- Many Internet Explorer and Netscape Navigator-specific HTML tags are not supported by WebTV
- It is not possible to download programs as files to a WebTV console

One of the most striking differences between WebTV and a regular browser is the screen size (see Figure 12.5). The WebTV screen is a fixed 420 pixels high by 560 pixels wide. Out of this, the height of an actual Web page displayed on the WebTV set-top box is 378 pixels with a fixed width of 544 pixels. When you are designing Web pages for WebTV, keep this 544 horizontal pixel limit in mind, as there is no horizontal scrolling feature in the WebTV browser—anything over the 544 pixel limit is not displayed. Note that these dimensions apply to the North American version of WebTV; the planned European standard uses a slightly wider screen area to fit with the European PAL TV format, which has better video encoding than the NTSC television standard used in North America.

There are several implications of this relatively small view space. One is that large images (especially those that are over 544 in width) are not recommended. The relatively small viewing space also means that relatively little text is displayed on the screen at once. It is very easy for a user to get lost on a page containing a large amount of text. For this reason, it is recommended that the text used on a Web page be as clear and concise as possible—a good rule to follow in any Web page design. In fact, there are several tips for writing HTML for WebTV that serve

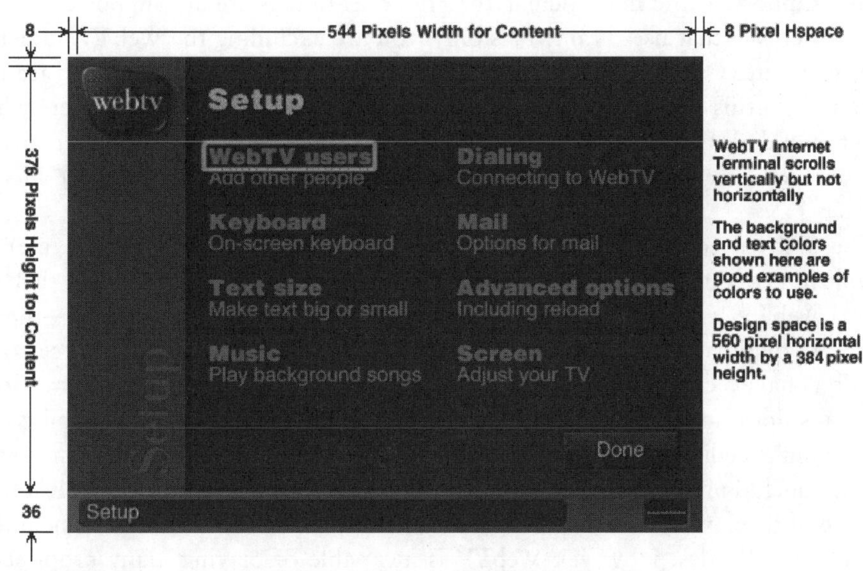

Figure 12.5 The Dimensions of a WebTV Display

as good tips for Web authors in general. It is also recommended that small text sizes be avoided in either HTML or graphics (i.e., an image containing text). This is because small-sized text is difficult to read on a television screen, and because your WebTV user is probably a lot further away from the TV screen than are most people surfing the Web from a computer monitor. Although this does limit Web authors to some extent, it does make Web pages easier to read. By avoiding the use of text that is smaller than the base font size of the browser, you can make Web pages easier to read for both WebTV and non-WebTV surfers.

Tip: If you don't have a WebTV Internet terminal handy, you can get a rough idea of what the viewing experience is like by doing the following:

Increase the default point size of your browser fonts to 18 pts
Narrow the window to match the dimensions of a TV screen
This is only a rough approximation, but it will give you a good idea of what to expect.

WebTV does not recognize all of the Web tags that are considered standard by most Web authors. Many Internet Explorer and Netscape Navigator specific tags are not supported, and in particular, the Frame set of tags are not supported. If you have a Web site that uses Frame tags only, you are excluding the WebTV audience from your site. Other tags that are not recognize by the WebTV browser are not displayed (in this way the WebTV browser is similar to other Web browsers when it comes to displaying tags it does not recognize). WebTV also introduces many of its own exclusive HTML tags. These tags are discussed at length later in this chapter.

The WebTV console is not a computer, so it is not possible for the user to download programs as files down to their set-top box. Since it is assumed that the typical WebTV user does not have a computer, this feature is not missed—there's no point downloading the latest patch for your favorite game or word processor if you don't have a computer to use it on. However, the lack of an ability to download programs does not mean that the WebTV console does not have a capability for playing multimedia files. WebTV consoles are capable of displaying common sound formats, including the .WAV, .AU, MIDI, AIFF, and ShockWave formats. It is also capable of displaying the common graphic file types found on the Web, including JPEG and .GIF files. However, WebTV is incapable of playing many proprietary sound and video file types, such as RealAudio sound files or QuickTime films. WebTV is also incapable of running Java applets, JavaScript, or any other similar programs. Though at the time of this writing WebTV was incapable of playing these file types, expect this to change over time as greater functionality is built into the WebTV browser. Unlike other browsers (with the possible exception of future Java-based browsers), when improvements are made to WebTV, they are automatically added to all WebTV browsers. Since the WebTV browser interface is automatically updated to all users at the same time, HTML authors never have to worry about designing Web pages for users that have not upgraded their browser to those containing the latest features.

There are special color considerations to keep in mind when writing for WebTV. Anybody who looks at a row of televisions for sale at a store will immediately notice that not all TVs are equal when it comes to displaying color. You will find that TVs have a wide range of color hues, so what may appear red on one TV may appear pinkish on another. TVs have a wider variation in displaying color types than computer monitors, so do not expect colors to be displayed in exactly the manner specified (this applies even to the safety palette discussed earlier in this series). In particular, HTML authors creating Web pages for WebTV should not create Web pages using full red (#FF0000) or full white (#FFFFFF), as they both cause distortion on a TV screen, so that the edges of the page will appear to bow. It is instead recommended that HTML authors try substituting a color value that is 90% white, like using the WebTV colornames linen, whitesmoke, or the more universal hexadecimal color value #EFEFEF. This is a good practice for HTML authors to keep in mind, because although black on white text is easier to read than on light gray (the typical background default color for many Web browsers), it is also harsh on the eyes, and can cause eye-strain in the user. Reducing the contrast somewhat between background and text can lead to easier-to-read Web pages.

When it comes to images, there are a lot of sensible suggestions for HTML writers writing for WebTV that apply equally well to other browsers. It is good to consider the order in which the parts of the page are display on-screen. In general, text displays faster than images, and small images load faster than larger images. So try to place any large images you have on a Web page below the initial screen displayed, so the user can read the text while the image finishes loading. When possible, try using JPEG images instead of GIF, as the file size of the former tends to be smaller than the latter. The extra compression involved in the JPEG format does entail some extra number-crunching by the computer or WebTV to process the image, but as CPUs get faster, this is less of an issue. JPGs also provide a much wider palette of colors (numbering in the millions) as opposed to the 256-color palette of GIF images. When possible, try to reuse the same image within your Web pages, so that you can take advantage of automatic caching abilities of most Web browsers and WebTV. In addition, it is always a good idea (WebTV or no) to use the <IMG> tag's WIDTH and HEIGHT attributes with an image file, so that the browser does not have to process the size and width of an image before presenting it on-screen.

WebTV's Special Tags

For those who are interested in crafting Web pages that cater specifically to WebTV viewers, like Netscape and Microsoft, the developers of WebTV have added their own set of HTML tags that work exclusively with their browser. Many of these make a lot of sense when it comes to the WebTV format, while others add functionality that some HTML authors have wished for.

HTML works the same way for WebTV as for other browsers, and in fact WebTV uses the majority of tags in common usage. In summary, it uses most of the HTML specification 2.0 tags, several HTML 3.0 tags, and a few HTML 3.2 tags. In addition, a number of Internet Explorer and Netscape Navigator tags and extensions that are in wide use are also available for use. The following section looks at only those tags that belong wholly to WebTV, or that behave differently through the WebTV browser. A full listing of all recognized WebTV tags can be found in Appendix E.

WebTV Structural Tags

Due to the characteristics of WebTV, several attributes have been added to the standard HTML structural tags (i.e., <BODY> and <HEAD>). An additional tag, <SIDEBAR> has also been added. The other attributes for these tags are discussed in detail in Chapter 2.

<BODY> . . .</BODY>

Element Name: Body tag.

Description: Used to specify the beginning and end of the displayed content of a Web page.

Attributes:

CREDITS = *URL*
Used to specify a Web page signifying the author or authors of the current Web page.
FONTSIZE = *SMALL* | *MEDIUM* | *LARGE*
Used to set the size of text displayed; overrides any values set by the user in their WebTV display.
HSPACE = *number*
Used to set a horizontal fixed space around the content of a Web page in pixels.
INSTRUCTIONS = *URL*
Used to display a Web page that contains additional information.
LOGO = *URL*
Used to display a distinctive logo for a Web page/site in the user's "Favorites" page.
NOHTILEBG
Used to prevent any background image from tiling horizontally.
NOVTILEBG
Used to prevent any background image from tiling vertically.
VSPACE = *number*
Used to set a vertical fixed space around the content of a Web page is pixels.
XSPEED = *number*
Sets the speed for scrolling the background image horizontally.
YSPEED = *number*
Sets the speed for scrolling the background image vertically.

Associated Tags: Other structural tags (i.e., <HTML>, <HEAD>).

Sample:

```
<BODY CREDITS="I did it.html" FONTSIZE=LARGE HSPACE=0
INSTRUCTIONS="neat extra stuff.html NOHTILEBG" LOGO= "my
logo.html" VSPACE=0> . . .</BODY>
```

WebTV adds a number of attributes to the standard <BODY> tag.

The CREDITS attribute is used to set an URL of a page that contains information on the author or authors responsible for designing the Web page. The Web page CREDITS points to is displayed when a user selects the Credits button from within the on-screen Info Panel. Similarly, the INSTRUCTIONS attribute is used to display a Web page containing additional information (such as explaining special features of the page) when the Instructions button from the on-screen Options Panel is selected.

The FONTSIZE attribute is used to set the size of text displayed to either a SMALL, MEDIUM, or LARGE value. This value overrides any default size the viewer may have set in their personal WebTV Setup. The default value for FONTSIZE is MEDIUM.

The HSPACE attribute is used to set a value for the horizontal fixed space around the body content, in effect setting a left and right margin. The default value for HSPACE is eight pixels. It is not recommended that this value be changed, as WebTV uses the margin space for drawing the yellow Highlight rectangle. This value affects only the content of a Web page, and not any sidebars it may contain. HSPACE can be set to zero to make more effective looking splash screens, where no links are displayed. Similarly, the VSPACE attribute is used to set a vertical fixed space around the content of a Web page, in effect setting a top and bottom margin. The default value for VSPACE is six pixels. It is not recommended that this value be changed (for the same reason outlined for HSPACE), though it can also be set to zero to create striking splash-screens.

The LOGO attribute displays another design attribute inherent to WebTV. When a WebTV user saves a Web page to his or her Favorites Web page (essentially a way of bookmarking pages), the standard WebTV logo is displayed. The LOGO attribute points to a Web page that contains a logo signifying the Web page or site. When a WebTV bookmarks a page that uses LOGO, a new image appears in the user's Favorites page. The size of the logo image is 70 x 52 pixels; all other sized images are scaled to fit these dimensions.

The NOHTILEBG attribute prevents any background image from tiling horizontally. Any background image is displayed at the left margin, repeated from the top of the page to the bottom, but does not repeat horizontally. Similarly, the NOVTILEBG attribute prevents a background image from tiling vertically the same way. Note that when either NOHTILEBG or NOVTILEBG is set, the background image does not scroll when the content of the Web page scrolls. In this fashion it is similar in function to Internet Explorer's WATERMARK attribute.

The XSPEED and YSPEED attributes set the speed for scrolling the background image horizontally and vertically, respectively. While the content of a Web page remains in place, the background image moves.

Both XSPEED and YSPEED take a number that reflects a value for the speed of scrolling. By default, XSPEED and YSPEED are set to 0. XSPEED=1 or YSPEED=1

produces a slow scrolling motion, whereas XSPEED=4 or YSPEED=4 produces a much faster scroll.

<SIDEBAR> . . .</SIDEBAR>

Element Name: Sidebar tag.

Description: Defines a sidebar to the left side of the Web page designed to contain items from which the user can choose.

Attributes: ALIGN = CENTER | LEFT | RIGHT
Used to align the content of the sidebar.
WIDTH = # *pixels* | % *of screen width*

Associated Tags: This is a new structural tag similar in form to <HEAD> and <BODY>.

Sample:

```
<SIDEBAR ALIGN=LEFT WIDTH=20%> Content goes here.
</SIDEBAR>
```

The <SIDEBAR> tag is a unique WebTV tag. This structural container tag sets up an area to the left side of the screen that contains selectable items the user can choose from. The sidebar does not scroll with the rest of the content of a Web page. The <SIDEBAR> container tags should be placed after the <HEAD> tags and before the <BODY> tags; it is essentially another structural element introduced to the Web page.

If multiple sidebars are specified, only the first is displayed, and any that follow are displayed as the normal content of the Web page. This is not a safe tag to use if the Web site is not set up exclusively for WebTV users: the <SIDEBAR> tag will be ignored, but its contents will not.

Many times, sidebars in the WebTV interface have a colored background. To provide a colored background for your Web page, create a table the same size as the sidebar and set the BGCOLOR attribute for that table.

The ALIGN attribute is used to align the content that appears in the sidebar. It can take one of three values: CENTER, LEFT, and RIGHT. The default value for ALIGN is LEFT.

The WIDTH attribute is used to specify the total width of the sidebar display. It can take either a numerical pixel value or a percentage value of the total screen width. The default value for width is 0, so if a sidebar is to be created, this attribute must be set.

Sound, Images, and Multimedia Tags for WebTV

<A>. . .</A>

Element Name: Anchor tag.

Description: Creates hypertext links. These tags always need either the HREF or the NAME attribute to define what Web page will be downloaded when the user clicks on the text contained within the anchor tags.

Attributes: NOCOLOR - Used to prevent the text of a link from being drawn in the link color, which is set by <BODY LINK>. The link color is blue by default.
SELECTED - Used to indicate that an anchor should be selected initially with the yellow Highlight rectangle.

Associated Tags: None.

Sample:
```
<A HREF="http://www.webtv.com/" SELECTED NOCOLOR> </A>
```

WebTV adds two additional extensions to the anchor tag. The NOCOLOR attribute is used to stop the browser from displaying the link that has been set. Link color is set by the <BODY LINK> tag. Its default value is blue. The net effect of NOCOLOR in most cases is to hide the link.

The SELECTED attribute is used to set the default link that comes up within a Web page. When a Web page is displayed and there is more than one link on the page, the SELECTED attribute can be set so that the user goes to the next Web page indicated. A yellow rectangle appears over the SELECTED link when the user scrolls to it. The idea is to save the user from having to move the cursor too much on a Web page. The SELECTED attribute works much the same way as it does within a Form. It is recommended that only one SELECTED attribute be used within a single page, but if multiple anchors are selected, the first anchor that appears from the top down will be selected.

<AUDIOSCOPE>

Element Name: Audioscope tag.

Description: Displays a volume control for manipulating sound that appears on a Web page.

Attributes: ALIGN - TOP | MIDDLE | BOTTOM | LEFT | RIGHT | TEXTTOP | ABSMIDDLE | BASELINE | ABSBOTTOM
Used to align the audioscope with the text immediately preceding it.
BORDER - # *pixels*
Used to set the width of the audioscope border in pixels.
GAIN - *number*
Used to set a multiplier for the amplitude display of the audioscope.
HEIGHT - # *pixels*
Used to set the height of the audioscope in pixels.
LEFTCOLOR - *colorvalue*
Used to set the color of the left audio channel in the audioscope.
LEFTOFFSET - # *pixels*
Used to set a vertical offset for the display of the left audio channel in pixels.
MAXLEVEL - *number*
Used to specify the maximum volume at which sound clips should be played.
RIGHTCOLOR - *colorvalue*
Used to set the color of the right audio channel in the audioscope.
RIGHTOFFSET - # *pixels*
Used to set a vertical offset for the display of the right audio channel in pixels.
WIDTH - # *pixels*
Used to set the width of the audioscope in pixels.

Associated Tags: None.

Sample:

```
<AUDIOSCOPE ALIGN=TOP BORDER=5 HEIGHT=100 WIDTH=200
LEFTCOLOR=RED RIGHTCOLOR=BLUE GAIN=2 LEFTOFFSET=2
RIGHTOFFSET=-2 MAXLEVEL=100>
```

The <AUDIOSCOPE> tag is an empty tag used to display an *audioscope*, which is an animated, graphical display reflecting the amplitude of the current sound over time. The audioscope is capable of displaying the amplitude of a sound in stereo, so it displays both the left and right channels. A Web page that uses <AUDIOSCOPE> displays the audioscope, enabling the user some control over the volume of the sound.

The ALIGN attribute is used to align the audioscope with the preceding text. It works in much the same fashion as does the ALIGN attribute with the <IMG> tag. The ALIGN attribute accepts any of nine values: TOP, MIDDLE, BOTTOM,

LEFT, RIGHT, TEXTTOP, ABSMIDDLE, BASELINE, and ABSBOTTOM. TOP aligns the audioscope in relation to the top of the text that precedes it, MIDDLE aligns the audioscope to the midline of the text that precedes it, and BOTTOM aligns the audioscope to the bottom of the text that precedes it. TEXTTOP aligns the audioscope the top of the text that precedes it, and ABSMIDDLE and ABSBOTTOM align the audioscope to the absolute (in terms of overall size of the font) midline and bottom of the text that precedes it, respectively. The default value for ALIGN is BASELINE, which reflects the position at which the text normally appears on a line.

The BORDER attribute is used to set the width of a border that can appear around the audioscope. It takes a numerical value reflecting a border value in pixels. Borders are drawn around an audioscope as antialiased bevels. The default value for BORDER is 1 pixel.

The GAIN attribute is used to set a numerical value for a multiplier for the amplitude display of the audioscope. In other words, it sets the rate at which the user can change the volume level on the audioscope. If set to a value of 2, the user can change the volume level in increments of 2. The default value for gain is 1.

The HEIGHT and WIDTH attributes set the height and width of the audioscope, respectively, as a pixel value. The default value for HEIGHT is 80 pixels, and the default value for WIDTH is 100 pixels. These two attributes work in much the same way as the HEIGHT and WIDTH attributes of the <IMG> tag: They reserve space for drawing the audioscope image on a Web page, making the page, as a whole, load faster.

The audioscope displays stereo sound as separate left and right channels stereo. The color of the line that displays the intensity of the left and right audio channels can be set using the LEFTCOLOR and RIGHTCOLOR attributes, respectively. Both can accept either a colorvalue or colorname. The default value for LEFTCOLOR is #8ECE10 (a yellowy-green color), and the default value for RIGHTCOLOR is #CE8E10 (an orangy-red color).

The positioning of the display of the vertical offset of the left and right audio channels can be set by the LEFTOFFSET and RIGHTOFFSET attributes, respectively. A positive value for these attributes raises the line for of the audio channel above the center of the audioscope display, and a negative value lowers it. The default value for LEFTOFFSET and RIGHTOFFSET is 0 pixels. The purpose of these attributes is to enable the Web author to separate the two channels for a more pleasing visual effect, which can be obtained by specifying a positive value for LEFTOFFSET and a negative value for RIGHTOFFSET.

The MAXLEVEL attribute is used to set the maximum volume level at which a particular sound can be played. When specified, MAXLEVEL takes a numeric value; by default the value for MAXLEVEL is false (i.e., no maximum volume level is imposed).

<IMG>

Element Name: Image tag.

Description: Used to insert images or WebTV animations onto a Web page.

Attributes: RELOAD = *number*
Plays the WebTV animation a specified number of times.
SELECTED
Sets the default area selected when the image is used as an imagemap.
TRANSPARENCY = *number*
Used to set the transparency value of the image displayed.

Associated Tags: None.

Sample:

```
<IMG SRC="IMAGE" RELOAD=5>
```

WebTV adds a number of additional attributes to the <IMG> tag, which controls the behavior of the image to be displayed. Most of the attributes control the behavior of a special type of WebTV-only animation files.

The RELOAD attribute is used to specify how often the WebTV image should be played. It functions in much the same way as the LOOP attribute for <IMG> works in Internet Explorer. By default, the image plays once.

The SELECTED attribute is used together with the USEMAP (server-side imagemap) attribute or the ISMAP (client-side imagemap) attribute to make a WebTV animation into an imagemap. The SELECTED attribute sets the default selection of the imagemap: When the imagemap is selected by the user, the cursor appears over the SELECTED area by default. When used with the ISMAP attribute, an x,y coordinate must be specified that is positioned relative to the top-left corner of the image.

The TRANSPARENCY attribute allows the background image to show through the image. The transparency of the image can range from a value of 0 (fully opaque, the default value) to 100 (fully transparent). Web pages draw fastest when the transparency value is set to 50.

New Text Formatting Tags in WebTV

WebTV provides page designers with many new tags for formatting text and provides additional attributes for familiar tags.

<BLACKFACE> . . .</BLACKFACE>

Element Name: Blackface tag.

Description: The enclosed text is rendered in a double-weight bold font.

Attributes: None.

Associated Tags: None.

Sample:

```
No one knew his <BLACKFACE>deepest, darkest</BLACKFACE>
secrets.
```

The <BLACKFACE> container tag renders the text it encloses in a double-weight bold font. It is typically used for headings or for terms that need extra emphasis. It is perhaps best thought of as double-bolding text.

<FONT> . . .</FONT>

Element Name: Font tag.

Description: Alters the appearance of a particular font on a Web page.

Attributes: EFFECT = RELIEF | EMBOSS | SHADOW
Used to add effects to the text displayed.
TRANSPARENCY = *number*
Used to set the transparency value of the text displayed.

Associated Tags: None.

Sample:

```
<FONT EFFECT=EMBOSS TRANSPARENCY=50>Welcome to Croecko
Industries!</FONT>
```

WebTV introduces two additional attributes to this tag in addition to the SIZE and COLOR attributes used by Netscape Navigator and Internet Explorer.

The EFFECT attribute is used to display the text as either RELIEF (appearing to project from the Web page), EMBOSS (appearing to be set into the Web page), or SHADOW (text appears with a trailing shadow cast down and to the right of the text). By default, EFFECT produces plain text.

The TRANSPARENCY attribute is used to allow the background image to show

through the text. Transparency of text can range from a value of 0 (fully opaque, the default value) to 100 (fully transparent). Web pages draw fastest when the transparency value is set to 50.

<HR>

Element Name: Hard rule tag.

Description: Draws a horizontal rule across the Web page.

Attributes: INVERTBORDER
Draws a horizontal rule that appears raised from the surface of the page.

Associated Tags: None.

Sample: `<HR INVERTBORDER>`

WebTV adds an additional attribute to the commonly used <HR> tag. The INVERTBORDER attribute draws a horizontal rule that seems raised from the surface of the page. By default, when INVERTBORDER attribute is not set, the horizontal rule appears embossed onto the surface of the Web page, as in most other Web browsers.

<LIMITTEXT>

Element Name: Limit text tag.

Description: Sets a maximum width for the text to be displayed.

Attributes: SIZE = *number*
Sets the maximum width of the text to be displayed as a number of characters.
VALUE = *text_string*
Used to set the value attribute of the text string that has the <LIMITTEXT> imposed on it.
WIDTH = *number*
Sets the maximum width of the text to be displayed as a number of pixels.

Associated Tags: None.

Sample: `<LIMITTEXT SIZE=4 WIDTH=45 VALUE="&url;">`

The <LIMITTEXT> is an empty tag wholly unique to WebTV. <LIMITTEXT> sets the maximum width for a specified string of text to be displayed within a given area. It should be used in cases where your text contains special characters, variable text, or expandable text. When the string value is calculated, as in the case of URL text, the WebTV interface will impose the width limits on the text when it is rendered. Since this tag is ignored by browsers that do not support this WebTV-specific tag, it can safely be used within any Web page. Although this tag is not very useful with hard-coded strings, it is recommended when there are text strings that contain special characters or expandable text.

The maximum width of the text displayed by <LIMITTEXT> can be set by either the SIZE or WIDTH attributes, which set the width as a number of characters and pixels, respectively. There is no default size limit imposed by either attribute. If both the SIZE and WIDTH attributes are specified, the WebTV browser uses the smaller of the two sizes.

The VALUE attribute is used to set the text string that will have the <LIMITTEXT> limit imposed on it. In other words, it specifies the text string whose size is to be limited by the SIZE or WIDTH attributes.

<MARQUEE> . . .</MARQUEE>

Element Name: Marquee tag.

Description: Displays a scrolling marquee of text.

Attributes: TRANSPARENCY = *number*

Associated Tags: None.

Sample: `<MARQUEE TRANSPARENCY=50>Hello folks!</MARQUEE>`

The <MARQUEE> is a container tag that displays the text it encloses as a scrolling, horizontal line of text. WebTV implements the <MARQUEE> tag as originally implemented within Internet Explorer, and adds an additional attribute.

WebTV's TRANSPARENCY attribute is used to allow the background image to show through the text as it scrolls across the marquee. Transparency of text can range from a value of 0 (fully opaque, the default value) to 100 (fully transparent). Web pages draw fastest when the transparency value is set to 50.

<NOSMARTQUOTES> . . .</NOSMARTQUOTES>

Element Name: No smart quotes tag.

Description: Used to prevent the substitution of smart quotes within a Web browser.

Attributes: None.

Associated Tags: None.

Sample: Use the following in your code:

```
<NOSMARTQUOTES> printf "Hello world".</NOSMARTQUOTES>
```

By default, the WebTV browser automatically replaces regular quotes (" ") with smart, "66–99" type quote marks (“ ”) and single quotes (' ') within smart, '6–9' single quotes (‘ ’). This isn't always desirable, especially when you are trying to display such things as computer code, where straight quotes are the norm. In cases such as these, use the <NOSMARTQUOTES> container tag to prevent this substitution.

WebTV Form Tags

WebTV introduces a number of attributes to the various types of form tags. For the most part, they are used either to change the form display, or to make it easier for the WebTV viewer to use.

<INPUT> . . .</INPUT>

Element Name: Input tag.

Description: Used to specify a form element type within a Web page.

Attributes: ACTION = *URL*
Used to specify an action when the viewer selects the form control.
NOARGS

Prevents arguments from being sent submitted along with ACTION.
NOHIGHLIGHT
Prevents the highlight cursor from appearing when the user selects the form control.
SUBMITFORM
Used to submit all of the information contained within a form when a particular control is selected.
WIDTH = # *pixels*
Sets the width of the form control in pixels.

Associated Tags: <FORM>.

Sample:

```
<FORM METHOD="POST" ACTION="http://www.croequko inc.com/">
<INPUT TYPE=TEXT SIZE=50 NAME="fred" VALUE="BigBucks"
ACTION="http://www.secret server.org/" NOARGS
NOHIGHLIGHT>
```

The <INPUT> tag is used to specify a form type within a Web page. It is most commonly used to insert such things as checkboxes and radio buttons within a Web page. WebTV adds quite a lot of additional attributes to modify the behavior and add new functions the Web forms.

This ACTION attribute is used to specify a particular action when the user selects the form element it is attached to. It is important to note that this immediately sends whatever value the user enters directly to the server, overriding any action that may have been set by the <FORM> tag.

Use the NOARGS attribute in conjunction with the ACTION attribute to prevent arguments from being submitted along with the action.

The NOHIGHLIGHT attribute prevents the highlight cursor from appearing when the user selects the form element.

The SUBMITFORM attribute is used to submit all of the form's data when the user alters the value of a particular form element. Normally, only the value for the selected form element is sent; with SUBMITFORM, it sends all of the data contained within the form at once.

The WIDTH attribute is used to set explicitly the width of the form control in pixels. By default, the width fits the text content of the input. Any extra text that does not fit in the display is truncated and is displayed with an ellipsis ("...").

Due to the myriad types of <INPUT> tags available, all of the other WebTV <INPUT> specific tags are broken down into the various TYPE attributes they fall under. Other, non-WebTV attributes of the <INPUT> tag are discussed in detail in Chapter 7.

<INPUT TYPE=BUTTON> . . .</INPUT>

Description: Used to create a hidden input field in a form.

Attributes: AUTOSUBMIT
Used to submit the form when the user leaves the page, even if the user has not clicked the Submit button or other control.

<INPUT TYPE=IMAGE> . . .</INPUT>

Description: Adds in images as to form that on act as on input mechanism.

Attributes: LOOP
Used to make the animation play continuously; used in conjunction with ONCLICK.
NOCURSOR
Used to disable the image-map style cursor when a user selects the form.
ONCLICK = *URL*
Used to set the URL of an animation file that plays when it is clicked by the user's cursor.

<INPUT TYPE=RESET>

Description: Used to add a Reset button within a form.

Attributes: BORDERIMAGE = *URL*
Used to set one of the two types of border image files for the button; either file://ROM/Borders/ButtonBorder2.bif (a flat button with rounded corners), or file://ROM/Borders/ButtonBorder3.bif (a convex button with square corners).

<INPUT TYPE=SUBMIT>

Description: Used to add a Submit button to a form.

Attributes:

BORDERIMAGE = *URL*
Used to set one of the two types of border image files for the button; either file://ROM/Borders/ButtonBorder2.bif (a flat button with rounded corners), or file://ROM/Borders/ButtonBorder3.bif (a convex button with square corners).
USEFORM = "*form name*"
Used to specify the name of the form to be submitted when the user clicks the Submit button. By default, the button submits the form that contains the button.
USESTYLE
Used to ensure the text within the button is rendered in the same style as that used on the rest of the Web page.

<INPUT TYPE=TEXT> . . .</INPUT>

Description: Creates a textfield form type.

Attributes:

ALLCAPS
Forces all characters typed to appear in uppercase by default.
AUTOACTIVATE
Used to bring up the on-screen keyboard automatically when the user selects the text form.
AUTOCAPS
Forces the first letter of each word to be uppercase.
BGCOLOR = *colorname* or *colorvalue*
Sets the background color of the text form. Default color is off-white (#EAEAEA).
BORDERIMAGE = *URL*
Used to set one of the two types of border image files for the button; either file://ROM/Borders/ButtonBorder2.bif (a flat button with rounded corners), or file://ROM/Borders/ButtonBorder3.bif (a convex button with square corners).
CURSOR = *colorname* or *colorvalue*
Used to set the color for the cursor in the text entry field. The default value is dark blue (#3333AA).
EXECUTEURL
Treats the text typed in by the user as a URL. The Web browser goes to the specified URL when the user hits Return.
NOSUBMIT

Used to prevent the form from automatically being submitted if the user accidentally hits Return before hitting a Submit button.
NUMBERS
Used to bring up the on-screen keyboard when the user selects the text form; the number 1 is automatically selected on the keyboard.
USESTYLE
Used to ensure the text within the text form is rendered in the same style as that used on the rest of the Web page.

<SELECT> . . .</SELECT>

Element Name: Select tag.

Description: A container tag that provides a list of options to choose from.

Attributes:
AUTOACTIVATE
Used to select the default displayed form list automatically when the user selects it.
BGCOLOR = *colorname* or *colorvalue*
Used to set the background color for the list.
EXCLUSIVE
Used to prevent duplicate entries from appearing within a form list.
SELCOLOR = *colorname* or *colorvalue*
Used to set the background color for the selections in the form list.
SHOWEMPTY
Used to display a form list with an empty string.
TEXT = *colorname* or *colorvalue*
Used to set the text color for items in the form list.
USESTYLE
Used to display the text in the form in the style used on the rest of the Web page.

Associated Tags: <FORM> <OPTION>

Sample:

```
<SELECT SIZE=2 AUTOACTIVATE BGCOLOR=yellow EXCLUSIVE
SELCOLOR=grey TEXT=red USESTYLE MULTIPLE>
<OPTION>Choose me.
<OPTION>No, choose me!
<OPTION>No, choose me instead!
</SELECT>
```

The <SELECT> tag is a container tag that provides a list of options to choose from. WebTV adds a number of attributes to this common type of Form tag. When the user selects a list form, the arrow key is used to move up and down within the list, and the Go button selects the currently highlighted item. For more information on <SELECT> form lists, see Chapter 7.

The AUTOACTIVATE attribute is used to select automatically the default form list displayed. When this attribute is not specified, the user has to press the Go button first to activate the list to be able to select an item from it. In addition, if AUTOACTIVATE is not specified, the arrow buttons on the remote control move the highlight rectangle to the next selectable item on the Web page, rather than within the list itself. It is highly recommended using this tag within a WebTV Web page containing a form list.

The BGCOLOR attribute is used to set the background color for the form list. The default value for BGCOLOR is #AFAFAF (a light gray). Similarly, the SELCOLOR attribute can be used to set the background color for the *selections* appearing within the form list. The default value for SELCOLOR is #EAEAEA (a type of off-white). The TEXT attribute is used to set the color of the text for the items that appear in the form list. A colorname can be used as well as a hexadecimal colorvalue. The BGCOLOR, SELCOLOR, and TEXT attributes work with MULTIPLE attribute or with the SIZE attribute for form lists sizes greater than 1.

The EXCLUSIVE attribute is used to prevent duplicate entries from appearing in a form list. It essentially prunes any accidental multiple entries that appear in a form list.

The SHOWEMPTY attribute displays empty form lists with an empty string. It works with MULTIPLE attribute or with the SIZE attribute for form lists sizes greater than 1.

The USESTYLE attribute is used to display the text that appears in the form list in the current style used within the rest of the Web page.

<TEXTAREA> . . .</TEXTAREA>

Element Name: Text area tag.

Description: Creates a multiline textfield form.

Attributes:

ALLCAPS
Used to capitalize all letters the user types within the text area.

AUTOACTIVATE
Used to select the default displayed text area automatically.

AUTOCAPS
Used to capitalize the first letter of each word the user types within the text area.

BGCOLOR
Used to set the background color of the text area.

CURSOR
Used to change the color of the cursor.

GROWABLE
Used to allow a text area to expand vertically as the viewer types beyond the original boundary of the text area.
NOHARDBREAKS
Disallows a user from entering hard returns within a text area.
NOSOFTBREAKS
Disallows the WebTV browser from inserting soft returns within a text area.
NUMBERS
Automatically brings up the on-screen keyboard and highlights the number 1.
SHOWKEYBOARD
Automatically brings up the on-screen keyboard.
USESTYLE
Used to render the text within the text area to that used within the rest of the page.

Associated Tags: <FORM>.

Sample:

```
<FORM>
<TEXTAREA COLS=60 ROWS-10 ALLCAPS AUTOACTIVATE
BGCOLOR-#AFAFAF CURSOR="yellow" GROWABLE NOHARDBREAKS
SHOWKEYBOARD>
<FORM>
```

WebTV adds a number of additional attributes to the <TEXTAREA> tag, which is most commonly used to add several blanks lines where a user can type in some text within a form.

The ALLCAPS attribute is used to set the on-screen keyboard to uppercase, so that whatever text the viewer types is defaulted to uppercase letters. This makes it easier for most users to see the text being typed. Similarly, the AUTOCAPS attribute capitalizes the first letter of each word the user types within the text area. This is best used for such things as proper names, titles, and addresses.

The AUTOACTIVATE attribute is used to select automatically the default displayed text area that appears on a Web page. When this attribute is not specified, the user first has to press the Go button to activate the list to be able to select an item from it. In addition, if AUTOACTIVATE is not specified, the arrow buttons on the remote control move the highlight rectangle to the next selectable item on the Web page, rather than within the list itself. Its use is highly recommended within a WebTV Web page containing a text area form.

THE BGCOLOR attribute is used to set the background color of a text area. It can take either a colorname or a hexadecimal colorvalue. By default, the colorvalue is set to #EAEAEA (a type of off-white).

The CURSOR attribute is used to set the color for the cursor within the text area. The WebTV HTML interface accepts colornames or hexadecimal colorvalues. The default value for the cursor is #3333AA (a type of dark blue).

The GROWABLE attribute is used to allow a text area to expand vertically as the viewer types beyond the original boundary of the text area.

If you do not want the user to be able to enter hard breaks (i.e., carriage returns) with a text area, use the NOHARDBREAKS attribute. If the user tries to enter a hard break, the selection moves to the next available field. The NOSOFTBREAKS attribute is used to prevent the WebTV browser from sending soft breaks when the form is submitted, which can make the job of interpreting the data from a text area much easier.

The NUMBERS attribute is used to bring up the on-screen keyboard automatically, and highlights the number 1. It is designed to reduce the amount of time the user would otherwise spend activating the on-screen keyboard and then select its number section. This is recommended when numeric input within a text area is expected. Similarly, the SHOWKEYBOARD displays the on-screen keyboard when a user enters a text area. The use of one or the other of these attributes is highly recommended.

The USESTYLE attribute is used to render the text within the text area to that used within the rest of the page.

WebTV Table Tags

WebTV introduces a number of attributes to the various types of table tags. For the most part, they are used either to alter the table display, or to make it easier for the WebTV viewer to use. Although WebTV is currently incapable of displaying Frames, it is capable of displaying Tables. WebTV adds a number of its own tags to the standard set of Table tags, which are discussed in detail in Chapter 8.

<TABLE>...</TABLE>

Element Name: Table tag.

Description: Defines a table display.

Attributes: CELLBORDER = # *pixels*
Used to set the width of the border for table cells as a pixel value.
HREF = *URL*
Used to set the destination URL for the table.
ID = "*table name*"
Used to set a unique name for the table.
NAME = "*table name*"
Used to set a unique name for the table.

TRANSPARENCY = *number*
Used to set the transparency value for the background color for the table.

Associated Tags: <CAPTION>, <TD>, <TH>, <TR>.

Sample:

```
<TABLE CELLBORDER=5 HREF="my table.html" ID="My Funky
Table" TRANSPARENCY=50>
<TR>
<TD>A</TD>
<TD>B</TD>
</TR>
<TR>
<TD>C</TD>
<TD>D</TD>
</TR>
</TABLE>
```

The CELLBORDER attribute is used to set the width of the border for table cells *only* in pixels. By default, the border for table cells is the same as that for the table (set by BORDER).

The HREF attribute is used to set a destination URL for the table. When this attribute is used, it causes the entire table to become an anchor and the HREF attribute defines the URL for that anchor. When the viewer selects the table, the WebTV browser goes to that page.

The ID and NAME attributes are used to set a name for the table. NAME and ID are functionally equivalent attributes used to set a unique name for the table.

The TRANSPARENCY attribute allows the background image to show through the background of the table. The transparency of the image can range from a value of 0 (fully opaque, the default value) to 100 (fully transparent). Web pages draw fastest when the transparency value is set to 50.

<TD> . . .<TD>

Element Name: Table data tag.

Description: Contains the information to be displayed in an individual table cell.

Attributes:

ABSHEIGHT = # *pixels*
Used to set the absolute height of the table cell.
ABSWIDTH = # *pixels*
Used to set the absolute width of the table cell.
MAXLINES = *number*
Used to set the maximum number of lines that can be displayed in the cell.

TRANSPARENCY = *number*
Used to set the rate at which the background image is allowed to show through the background of the cell.

Associated Tags: <CAPTION>, <TABLE>, <TH>, <TR>.

Sample:

```
<TABLE>
<TR>
<TD ABSHEIGHT=50 ABSWIDTH=150 MAXLINES=2
TRANSPARENCY=50>Hello there!</TD>
</TR>
</TABLE>
```

The <TD> tag is used to define the contents of an individual table cell. WebTV adds a number of formatting attributes to this tag.

The ABSHEIGHT and the ABSWIDTH attributes are used to set the absolute height and width of the cell in pixels. There is no default value for either ABSHEIGHT or ABSWIDTH. Anything that does not fit within the table cell is not displayed. Similarly, the MAXLINES attribute is used to set the maximum number of lines that can be displayed within a cell. There is no default value for MAXLINES. Again, anything that does not fit within the cell is not displayed.

The TRANSPARENCY attribute allows the background image to show through the background of the cell. The transparency of the image can range from a value of 0 (fully opaque, the default value) to 100 (fully transparent). Web pages draw fastest when the transparency value is set to 50.

<TH> . . .</TH>

Element Name: Table header tag.

Description: Creates a header for a column whose text is rendered in a bold font.

Attributes:

ABSHEIGHT = # *pixels*
Used to set the absolute height of the table header.
ABSWIDTH = # *pixels*
Used to set the absolute width of the table header.
MAXLINES = *number*
Used to set the maximum number of lines that can be displayed in the header.
TRANSPARENCY = *number*
Used to set that rate at which the background image is allowed to show through the background of the header.

Associated Tags: <CAPTION>, <TABLE>, <TD>, <TR>.

Sample:

```
<TABLE>
<TR>
<TH ABSHEIGHT=25 ABSWIDTH=10 MAXLINES=1 TRANSPARENCY=50>
Hello there!</TH>
</TR>
</TABLE>
```

The <TH> tag is used to define the header for a column of cells in a table. The text contained within a table header cell is centered and rendered in a bold font. WebTV adds a number of formatting attributes to this tag, all of which are shared with the similar <TD> (Table data) tag.

The ABSHEIGHT and the ABSWIDTH attributes are used to set the absolute height and width of the header in pixels. There is no default value for either ABSHEIGHT or ABSWIDTH. Anything that does not fit within the header is not displayed. Similarly, the MAXLINES attribute is used to set the maximum number of lines that can be displayed within a header. There is no default value for MAXLINES. Again, anything that does not fit within the header is not displayed.

The TRANSPARENCY attribute allows the background image to show through the background of the header. The transparency of the image can range from a value of 0 (fully opaque, the default value) to 100 (fully transparent). Web pages draw fastest when the transparency value is set to 50.

<TR> . . .</TR>

Element Name: Table row tag.

Description: Encloses a row of table data.

Attributes: TRANSPARENCY = *number*
Used to set the rate at which the background image is allowed to show through the background of the header.

Associated Tags: <CAPTION>, <TABLE>, <TD>, <TH>.

Sample:

```
<TABLE>
<TR TRANSPARENCY=50>
<TD>Cell 1</TD>
<TD>Cell 2</TD>
</TR>
</TABLE>
```

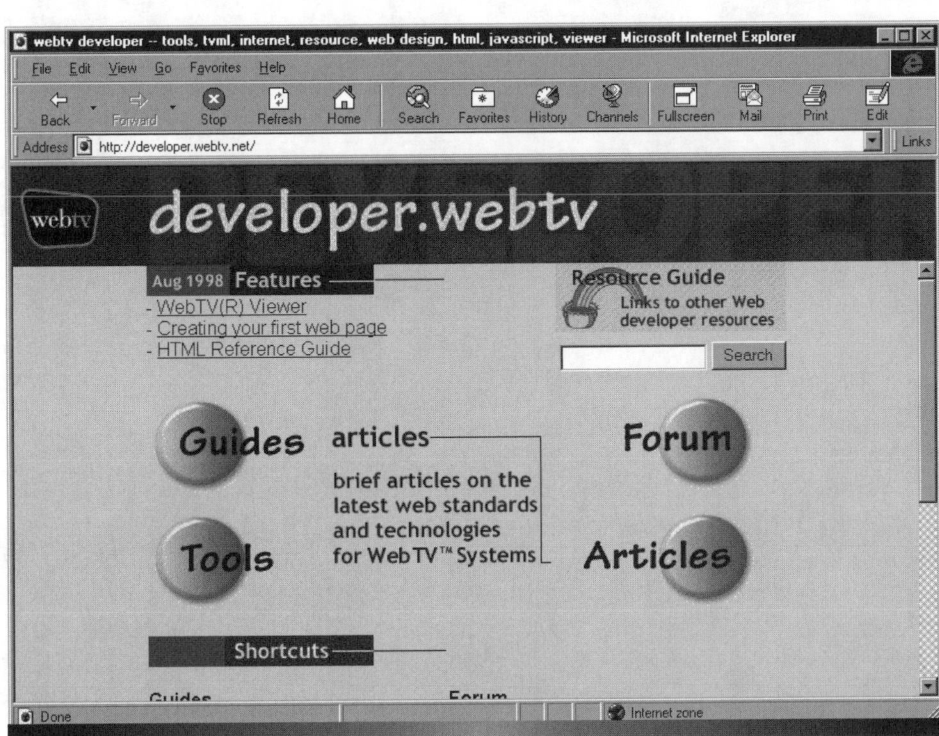

Figure 12.6 WebTV HTML Guide and Reference

WebTV specifies a single additional attribute for the Table row tag: TRANSPARENCY. This attributable allows the background image to show through the row. The transparency of the image can range from a value of 0 (fully opaque, the default value) to 100 (fully transparent). Web pages draw fastest when the transparency value is set to 50.

Link: If you are interested in learning more about crafting pages specifically for WebTV, the canonical reference for WebTV HTML tags and their behavior on WebTV can be found at the WebTV's "HTML Reference" site at: http://www.developer.webtv.net (see Figure 12.6).

CHAPTER 13

Dynamic Documents

Recently there have been new developments in order to make Web pages more exciting. Interactivity is becoming more and more popular and crucial to keeping your audience returning for repeat visits. Since normal HTML produces primarily static content, browser-based scripting languages and programs have been developed to add movement and interactivity to Web pages. The emphasis is on the client, or Web browser, since loading the Web server puts more unneeded stress on computers that already work hard to serve Web pages. The most popular of these new technologies are discussed in this chapter: server push, client pull, JavaScript, JScript, VBScript, ActiveX, and Java applets.

Server Push and Client Pull

A big step towards making Web pages more interesting and eye-catching is to add movement. Before the introduction of animated GIFs, Java, JavaScript, and multi-

media applications such as Shockwave, server push and client pull were two easy, although clumsy, ways of creating movement and animation on Web pages. Server push holds the connection between the Web server and Web client open as the server continually feeds data, such as Web pages or image files, to the client; client pull causes the Web browser to load Web pages automatically over intervals of time. Using server push can create a rudimentary animation; using client pull can create a slide show effect.

Server push is no longer a popular method of creating movement, since other tools such as Java and Shockwave are so much more flexible and powerful. In addition, server push creates a huge load on the Web server and can be very slow and unrewarding from the user's point of view.

Normally a Web client opens a connection when it requests a page, the Web server sends the data to the client, and the connection is closed. With server push, the connection is not closed right away; the server sends the data, waits a period of time, then sends more data. The data can be Web pages that replace each other or images that get replaced, creating an animated image.

Server push requires a CGI (common gateway interface) script to define what data gets served, and at what intervals. Information on creating CGI scripts is not within the scope of this book, as they are specific to what you want to use server push to accomplish, and depend on the type of Web server software you are using to run your Web site.

Client pull is used to make the browser load Web pages automatically at specified time intervals. Unlike server push, the connection between the server and the client is not kept open. Client pull works through the use of the Refresh command in the HTTP-EQUIV attribute of the <META> tag.

The <META> tag occurs inside the <HEAD> element of your Web pages. When a Web browser receives the Refresh command along with a Web page's data, the browser will wait a specified length of time, then reload (or refresh) the page. The amount of time to wait before reloading is defined by the CONTENT attribute of the <META> element.

To reload the same Web page every ten seconds, put the following code within the <HEAD> element:

```
<META HTTP-EQUIV="refresh"
CONTENT=10,http://site.site.com/second.html>
```

Reloading the same Web page every few seconds is useful for automatically updating information that changes, such as Web-based chats or stock quotes. You can also use client pull to reload different Web pages over specified time intervals by adding the URL attribute to the <META> tag. The URL attribute must contain the full Web address of the page to be loaded; relative URLs will

not work. For instance, to load a second Web page after ten seconds, insert the following code:

```
<META HTTP-EQUIV="refresh"
CONTENT="10;URL=http://www.site.com/second.html">
```

To continue loading new pages over time, insert the appropriate URL in the <META> tag. The effect of loading different pages over time is like a slideshow. Many Web sites use client pull to first post a "splash" page that may have a simple design or logo, then load the "main" page where more information is offered. Another use for client pull is when Web sites have moved to a new Web location; the old Web page will contain client pull information in the <META> tag to load the new Web page after a certain period of time. Providing a hypertext link that leads out of the sequence of reloading pages is a good idea; don't force your users to sit through something they don't want to.

JavaScript

JavaScript, created by Netscape Communications, is a scripting language that you can use to write programs to include in your HTML pages. Netscape describes JavaScript as "a compact, object-based scripting language for developing client and server Internet applications. In a client application for Navigator, JavaScript statements embedded in an HTML page can recognize and respond to user events such as mouse clicks, form input, and page navigation." JavaScript originally was recognized only within Netscape, but since version 3.0 it has also worked in Microsoft's Internet Explorer. It should be noted however that due to some variances in the ways that Internet Explorer and Netscape Navigator interpret JavaScript elements, not all JavaScripts will work within both browsers. It is highly recommended that all Web pages containing JavaScripts be tested out on both browsers before being put into practice on a Web site.

There is often confusion regarding the relationship of Sun Microsystems' Java programming language to Netscape's JavaScript. First and most important, Java and JavaScript are two very different programs: Java is a complex, object-oriented programming language, and JavaScript is a powerful yet simple scripting language. Whereas JavaScript can be used only with Web browsers, Java can be used to program just about anything, Internet-related or not.

To insert JavaScript (or any other scripting language) within a Web page, the <SCRIPT> tag should be used.

<SCRIPT> . . .</SCRIPT>

Element Name: Script tag.

Description: Provides information regarding style sheets and client-side scripts.

Attributes:

Language: *language_name*
Specifies the name of the scripting language being used.

Example:

```
<SCRIPT LANGUAGE="JavaScript">
document.write ("Hello World!")
</SCRIPT>
```

JavaScripts are contained in a Web page, and must be surrounded by the <SCRIPT> elements. The LANGUAGE attribute is optional, but it is a good idea to include it to alert the Web browser that the script is JavaScript. Here is an example of a simple JavaScript:

```
<SCRIPT LANGUAGE="JavaScript">
document.write("Hello World!")
</SCRIPT>
```

Which returns the page shown in Figure 13.1.

To cover JavaScript in detail is beyond the scope of this book. For detailed online information and documentation for JavaScript, consult Netscape's JavaScript Web site at http://home.netscape.com/eng/mozilla/Gold/handbook/javascript/index. html.

It is highly recommended that you indicate the presence of scripts on a Web page to those users who may be using a browser incapable of interpreting scripted code. This can be done by using the <NOSCRIPT> tag, which is designed to enclose content intended to be displayed to browsers incapable of utilizing any form of scripting language.

<NOSCRIPT> . . .</NOSCRIPT>

Element Name: No script tag.

Description: Indicates the presence of a scripting language (such as JavaScript or VBScript) to a browser incapable of interpreting scripted code.

Attributes: None.

Example:

```
<NOSCRIPT>
This page makes use of JavaScript for navigational
purposes. Your browser does not support JavaScript
(otherwise you wouldn't be reading this), so please click
<A HREF="alternate.html">here</A> for an alternate
version of our Web site.
</NOSCRIPT>
```

This tag is supported in Internet Explorer and Netscape Navigator 3.0 and higher, and was made official in the final version of the HTML 4.0 specification.

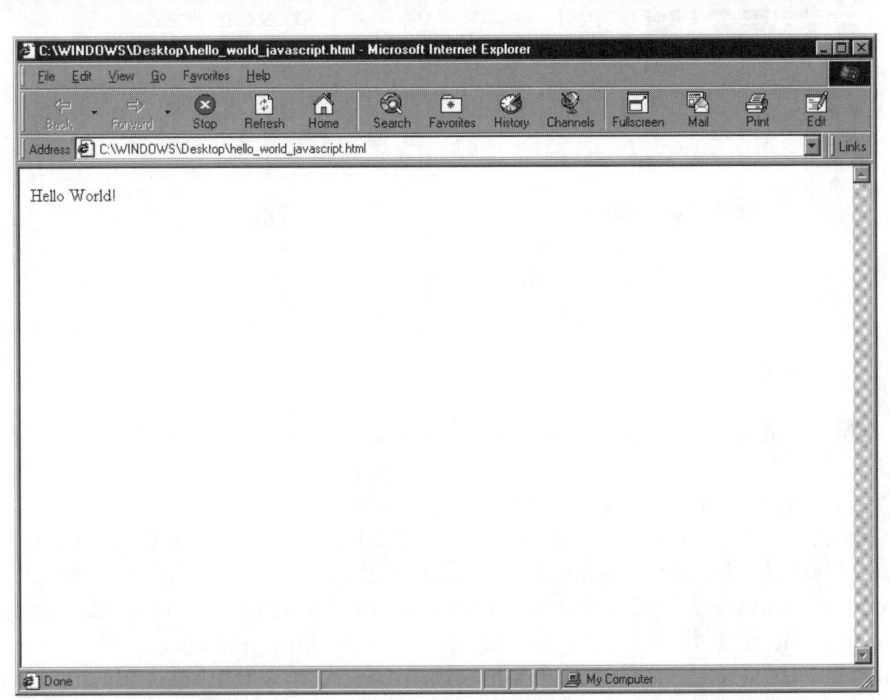

Figure 13.1 A Web Page Displaying the Hello World JavaScript

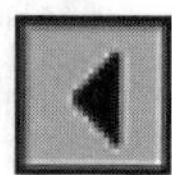

JSCRIPT

JScript, created by Microsoft Corporation, is similar to JavaScript in that it too is a scripting language used to add functionality to your Web pages. As well, JScript is recognized only by the Microsoft Internet Explorer browser, version 3.0 and later. Microsoft describes JScript as "a powerful scripting language targeted specifically at the Internet. It is implemented as a fast, portable, lightweight interpreter for use in World Wide Web browsers and other applications that use ActiveX-Controls, OLE Automation servers, and Java applets."

Like JavaScript, a JScript is enclosed by the <SCRIPT> container elements within the HTML code of the Web page. The LANGUAGE attribute is optional, but it's a good habit to use it to tell the browser the script is JScript.

A simple JScript example follows.

```
<CENTER>
<P>
<H2>Hello, world sample</H2>
<FORM Name="Form1">
<INPUT TYPE=BUTTON VALUE="Click me" NAME="BtnHello"
OnClick="sayhello()">
</FORM>
</CENTER>
<SCRIPT LANGUAGE="JavaScript">
<!--
    function sayhello ()
    {
       alert ("Hello, world!")
    }
//-->
</SCRIPT>
```

This example produces the right-hand frame of the Web page shown in Figure 13.2.

Clicking the button produces Figure 13.3.

To create the button on the page, the <FORM> and <INPUT> elements are used, and the button is named. The JScript itself is defined by the <SCRIPT> elements, and the LANGUAGE attribute is defined to tell the browser the script is JScript. The sayhello function is defined; when the button is clicked, the sayhello function runs, causing an alert window to pop up with the message "Hello, world!" inside it.

To cover JScript in detail is beyond the scope of this book. For detailed online

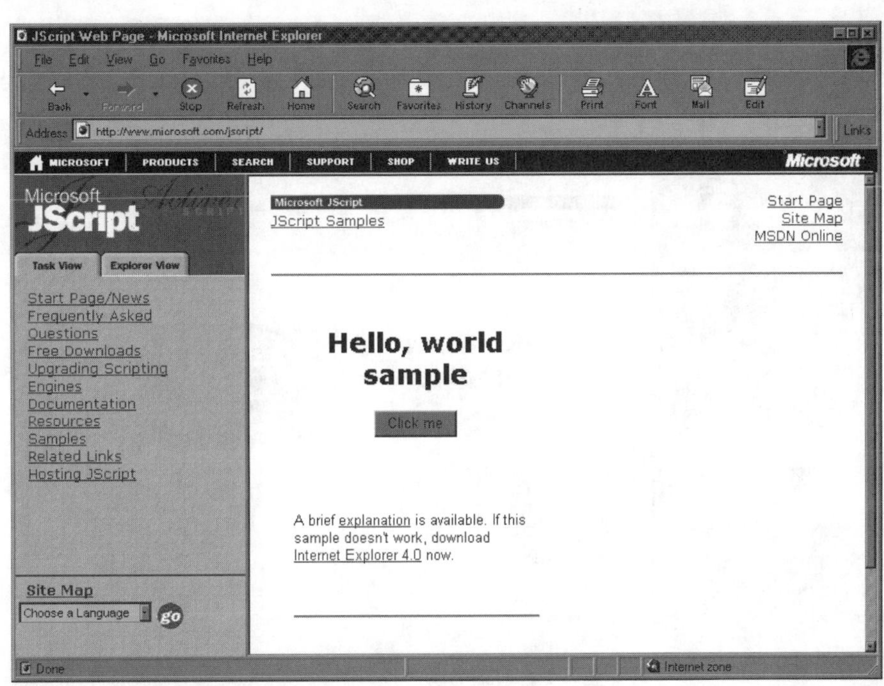

Figure 13.2 A Web Page Displaying the Hello World JavaScript

information and documentation for JScript, consult Microsoft's JScript Web site at hhtp://www.microsoft.com/jscript/.

VISUAL BASIC SCRIPT

Visual Basic Script, also known as VBScript, is a subset of Microsoft's Visual Basic programming language. As described by Microsoft, VBScript "is implemented as a fast, portable, lightweight interpreter for use in World Wide Web browsers and other applications that use ActiveX Controls, OLE Automation servers, and Java applets." In simpler terms, you can create supporting features for an ActiveX or Java application, such as Play and Stop buttons, using VBScript. Only the Microsoft Internet Explorer browser recognizes VBScripts.

Like JavaScript and JScript, a VBScript is enclosed by the <SCRIPT> container

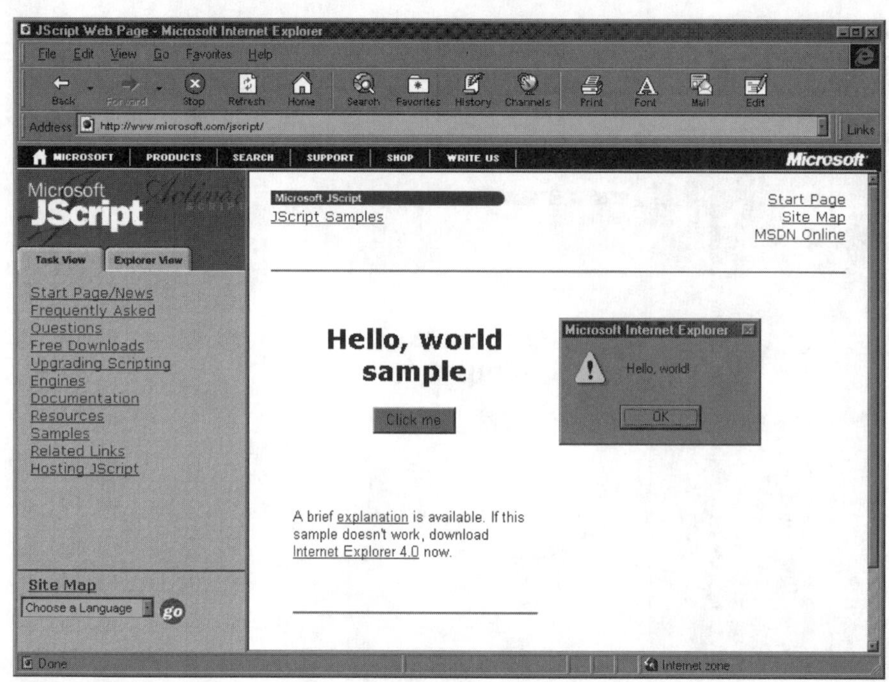

Figure 13.3 A Web Page Displaying the Click Me Button and Its Message Box

elements within the HTML code of the Web page. The LANGUAGE attribute must be used to specify that the script is VBScript, otherwise Microsoft's Internet Explorer browser assumes the script is a JavaScript.

A simple example of VBScript follows. It creates a page with Hello World and a button labeled Click Me. When the user clicks the button, a dialog pops up containing the words Hello World!.

```
<CENTER>
    <P>
    <H2>Hello, world sample</H2>
    <INPUT TYPE=BUTTON VALUE="Click me"
NAME="BtnHello">
</CENTER>
<SCRIPT LANGUAGE="VBScript">
<1--
    Sub BtnHello OnClick
```

```
                    MsgBox "Hello, world!", 0, "My first
active document"
    End Sub
-->
</SCRIPT>
```

This script produces the frame on the right-hand side in the Web page shown in Figure 13.4.

Clicking the button produces Figure 13.5.

To create the button on the page, the <INPUT> element is used, just as it would occur when used in a form. Then, the <SCRIPT> element is declared, and the LANGUAGE attribute is included to tell the browser that the script is a VBScript. The OnClick Event Handler is used to define the BtnHello button declared in the <INPUT> element. The defined procedure for when the user clicks the button is to display a message box containing Hello, World!; the title for the message box is My first active document.

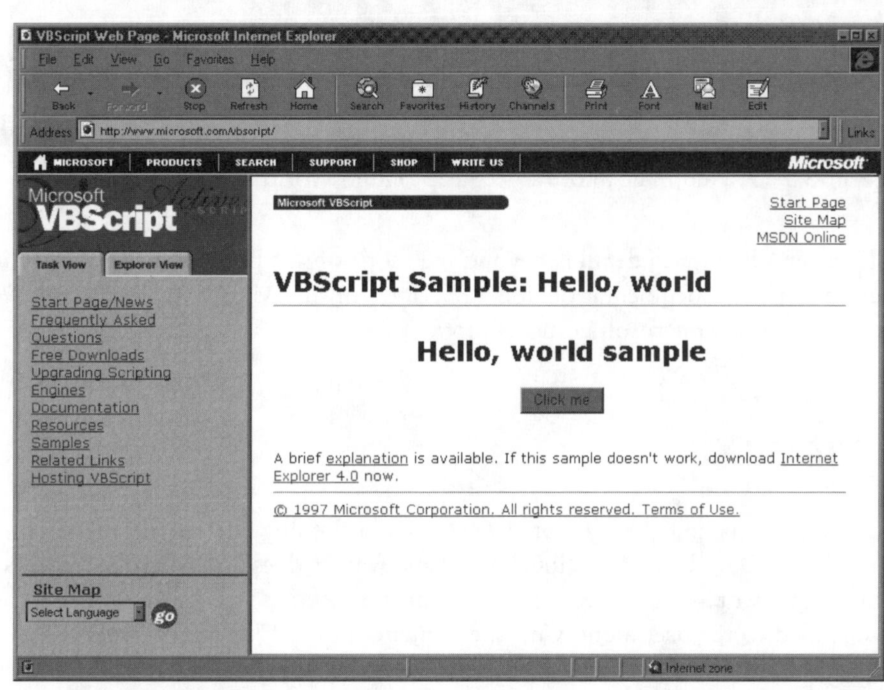

Figure 13.4 A Web Page Displaying the Hello World VBScript

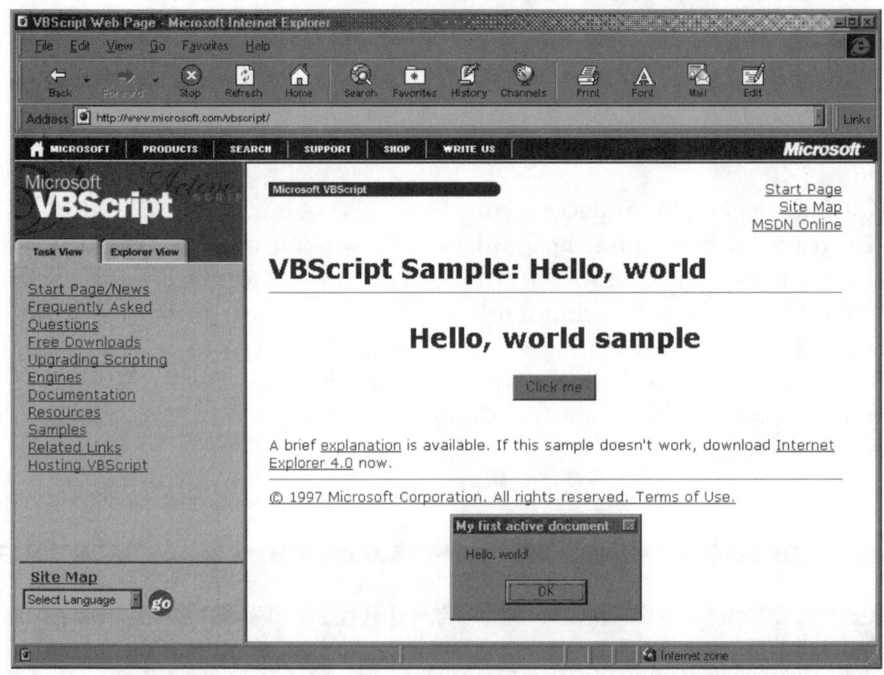

Figure 13.5 A Web Page and the VBScript Hello World Button

To cover VBScript in detail is beyond the scope of this book. For detailed online information and documentation for VBScript, consult Microsoft's VBScript Web site at http://www.microsoft.com/vbscript/.

ACTIVEX

ActiveX is the name for Microsoft's interactive technology designed for use on the Web (Figure 13.6). It works in much the same way as does Sun Microsystem's Java technology or a plug-in—a Web page contains an ActiveX program which is then downloaded to the user along with the contents of the Web page. ActiveX adds a new level of interactivity for the Web, by allowing the Web designer to add full programs to their Web pages, programs that are typically faster than an equivalent Java program.

Unlike Java, ActiveX is not a programming language. When you download a

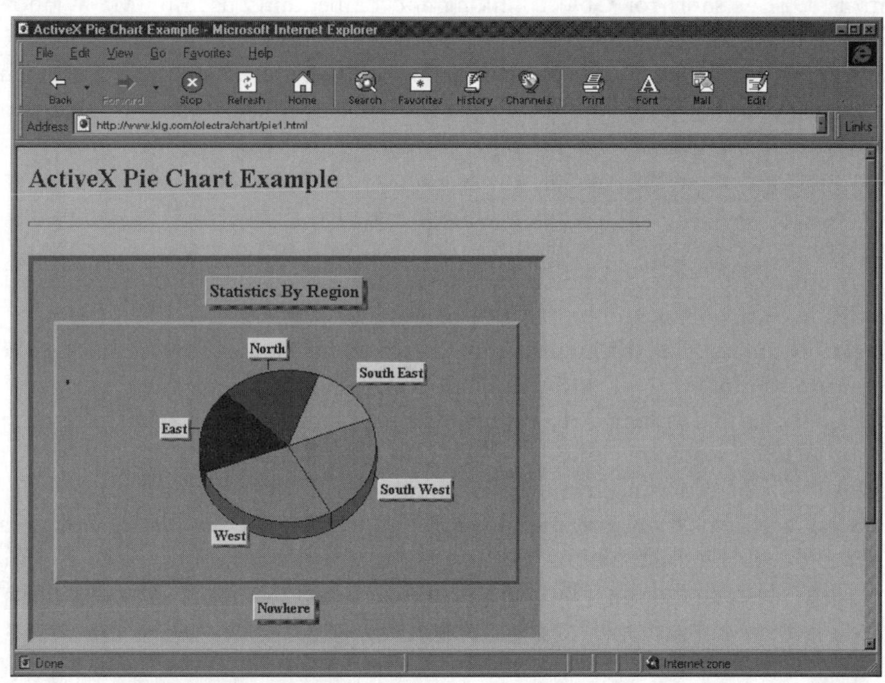

Figure 13.6 A Sample ActiveX Component on a Web Page

Java applet, its code is written in the Java programming language, and its behavior is dictated in part by the constructs of that language. When you download an ActiveX component, you are downloading a component that could have been written in any one of a number of different programming languages, including Visual Basic, C, and C++, the programming languages of choice for MS-Windows programmers. This means that ActiveX programs run as native applications within the browser, and subsequently tend to be much faster than an equivalent Java applet. Unlike a plug-in, ActiveX components are automatically downloaded and are transparently installed on a user's system, subject to the user's approval. This approval adds a level of security when downloading an ActiveX component—a requirement for all ActiveX developers is that they register their components as being safe and noninvasive to the user's system. The user downloading an ActiveX control for the first time is confronted by a Window advising them of the relative security of the program they are about to download, giving the user the choice as to whether to download the control or not.

ActiveX is not a new technology. They are what Microsoft used to call OLE controls. OLE is short for Object Linking and Embedding, used by MS Windows programs to insert an object from one program to another. This means that you can insert an MS Excel spreadsheet within an MS Word or Powerpoint document. To change some figures in the Excel spreadsheet embedded within a Powerpoint document, all the user has to do is to click on the spreadsheet as it appears in Powerpoint, and all of the controls and features of Excel appear *within* Powerpoint. ActiveX/OLE is a tried-and-true technology—many Windows Programmers are interested in ActiveX precisely because it allows them to reuse the code they have already created for other purposes for use on the Web. Nonprogrammers can take preexisting components and paste them onto a Web page.

Probably the most significant difference between Java and ActiveX for most Web designers is the number of different computing platforms they can run on. Java applets can be run on many different operating systems, whereas at the time of this writing, ActiveX components can be run only on systems using Windows 95 or Windows NT. In addition, Java applets can be run on the two most popular Web browsers, Netscape Navigator and Internet Explorer, but ActiveX components can be run only on Internet Explorer 3.0.x. Work is currently under way to bring ActiveX to other computing platforms, including Macintosh and Unix systems.

Java, ActiveX, and plug-ins all have their respective strengths and weaknesses. If you have Web pages that need speed and you have an audience most likely to be using Internet Explorer, then ActiveX is a strong contender. At the moment, the widest audience for Web pages containing ActiveX controls is found within intranets. For firms that have systems that primarily run Windows 95/NT, ActiveX is a wise choice. Many such firms also retain programmers for producing specific programs for use within the firm—many of these programmers are, by necessity, already familiar with programming under MS Windows. By using ActiveX components instead of Java applets, there is a much smaller learning curve for programmers.

Creating and Using ActiveX Controls

You do not have to create your own ActiveX controls to use them within a Web page—you can download tried and tested components that you can modify for your own uses within a Web page. There are several good sites worth checking out if you want to add ActiveX controls to your Web page. If you do a search on the keyword ActiveX on any search engine (like Yahoo! at http://www.yahoo.com/), you will find many such places. A few good places to visit include Microsoft's own set of Web pages on the subject, which can be found at http://www.microsoft.com/activex. Check out The Active Group's Web site at http://www.activex.org/, a consortium of software and systems vendors dedicated to the promotion and widespread adoption of ActiveX, or see c/net's set of Web pages on ActiveX at http://www.activex.com/.

If you are not a would-be ActiveX programmer, you do not need to know the information contained in the rest of this section; however, it reveals of the architecture and design of ActiveX components as used on the Web.

If you intend to develop ActiveX components, you will need a number of tools before you can proceed to create and insert them within a Web page. In addition to having working knowledge of a programming language and an Integrated Development Environment (IDE), you will need to download the Microsoft ActiveX SDK (Software Design Kit). With this SDK you will be able to create the License Pack File (.LPK), which will enable you to create a verifiably secured ActiveX file that users can safely download to their machine. You can obtain the ActiveX SDK package (activex.exe, an 8MB download), from http://www.microsoft.com/msdownload/sbndownload/sbnaxsdk/sbn axsdk.htm.

Link: For more information about the ActiveX SDK, go to http://www.microsoft.com/workshop/prog/sdk/?

Once you have the ActiveX SDK, download the Microsoft Cabinet SDK from http://www.microsoft.com/workshop/prog/cab. This allows you to create the special Cabinet file that stores all the files in the components that need to be downloaded by the user. If you have installed Windows 95/NT, Microsoft Office, or any recent software made by Microsoft, you've already encountered cabinet (or CAB) files; it is the compression scheme used to install all Microsoft software. Downloading the Microsoft Cabinet SDK simply allows you to make and use these types of files yourself.

The idea behind Cabinet files is to reduce the overall time needed to download all of the files necessary for an ActiveX by placing all of the files into a single, compressed file. Much the same idea is used to compress all of the classes within Java applets in a single PKzipped (.ZIP) or a Java Archive (.JAR) file. In fact, Microsoft is extending their Cabinet technology to be used for Java applets as well—they are smaller, and therefore faster to download and execute than the other compressed schemes.

Link: For more information about the CAB SDK, go to http://www.microsoft.com/workshop/prog/cab/ove rview.htm.

Once you created an ActiveX control, you must create a license pack file so that the user's browser can register the control on their computer. To do this, use the lpk_tool.exe program (located in your ActiveX SDK's \bin directory) to create a license pack file for all the ActiveX controls on your page. From the Available Controls list, select and add the ActiveX program you have just created. The reference to the resulting .LPK file is then inserted into your HTML page.

In order for the user's browser to load and run the ActiveX control you have created correctly, you must create an .INF file that lists all of the control's dependencies. Create a text file with the suffix .INF that lists all of the files needed for your component. Here is the content of an example .INF file called OLECTRA.INF.

```
[Add.Code]
olch2x32.ocx=olch2x32.ocx
olch2d32.dll=olch2d32.dll
mfc40.dll=mfc40.dll
msvcrt40.dll=msvcrt40.dll

[olch2x32.ocx]

File=thiscab
Clsid={92D71E93-25A8-11CF-A640-9986B64D9618}
[olch2d32.dll]
File=thiscab

[mfc40.dll]
File=http://www.yoursite.com/yourdemo/mfc40.cab

[msvcrt40.dll]
File=http://www.yoursite.com/yourdemo/
msvcrt40.cab
```

(This and subsequent code examples are derived from KL Group's Olectra Chart program, a demo version of which can be downloaded from their Web site at http://www.klg.com/.)

The CLSID (pronounced Class ID) just specified can be found in many places on your system, including your computer's registry, and it is the same code that will be used later within the HTML of the Web page containing the ActiveX control.

To minimize download time, compress these files contained in your ActiveX component individually using *cabarc.exe* from the Cabinet SDK. To create a corresponding .CAB file that contains Olectra Chart's OCX, DLL, and the .INF files, you'd type the following at the command prompt:

```
cabarc n olectra.cab olch2x32.ocx olch2d32.dll
olectra.inf
```

Once you have created the .LPK and .CAB files, copy them to the server where your Web page is. The .LPK file must be in the same directory as the HTML file that references it. The .CAB file must be in the directory that is specified in the <OBJECT> tag.

Once you have created the ActiveX component, register it with VeriSign, a third-party agency that issues Digital Ids that digitally shrink-wrap the ActiveX component for users. Users are assured that the software was distributed by the genuine provider, and that the software was not tampered with en route to the user. Run the signcode.exe program that comes with ActiveX SDK to begin the process of verifying your new ActiveX component. More information on Digital Ids can be found at VeriSign's Web site at http://www.verisign.com/.

Creating an ActiveX Web Page

The first step to adding an ActiveX control within a Web page is to create the HTML page, and then add the ActiveX control. Any HTML editor will do, but if you use ActiveX extensively in your Web pages, consider getting a copy of Microsoft's ActiveX Control Pad, which can be had from http://www.microsoft.com/workshop/author/cpad/ (note that you must become a Microsoft Site Builder member—a free service—to be able to download the application). The tool that makes the ActiveX Control Pad desirable for Web designers is its Object Editor and Properties Windows, which enables the designer to size and manipulate the properties of the ActiveX control. Once the designer has finished setting the parameters in the program, all of the settings are automatically written to the Web page. This is extremely handy—the number of parameters that often need to be set can be extensive, and ActiveX Control Pad eases this process considerably (Figure 13.7).

Once you have set all of the parameters for the ActiveX control, the ActiveX Control Pad automatically inserts all of the required HTML code, using the <OBJECT> tag. The following example demonstrates this.

```
        <OBJECT ID="Chart2D1" WIDTH=473 HEIGHT=352
        CLASSID="CLSID:92D71E93-25A8-11CF-A640-
9986B64D9618"
        CODEBASE="http://www.yoursite.com/olectra.cab">
        </OBJECT>
```

The one parameter that may not be immediately familiar is the CLASSID (class identifier) attribute, which identifies the control to the computer. When this HTML code is processed by the browser, it checks to see if the ActiveX control is already registered (in other words, checking to see if it already exists on your system) and if not, it then downloads and registers the control. The CODEBASE element in the

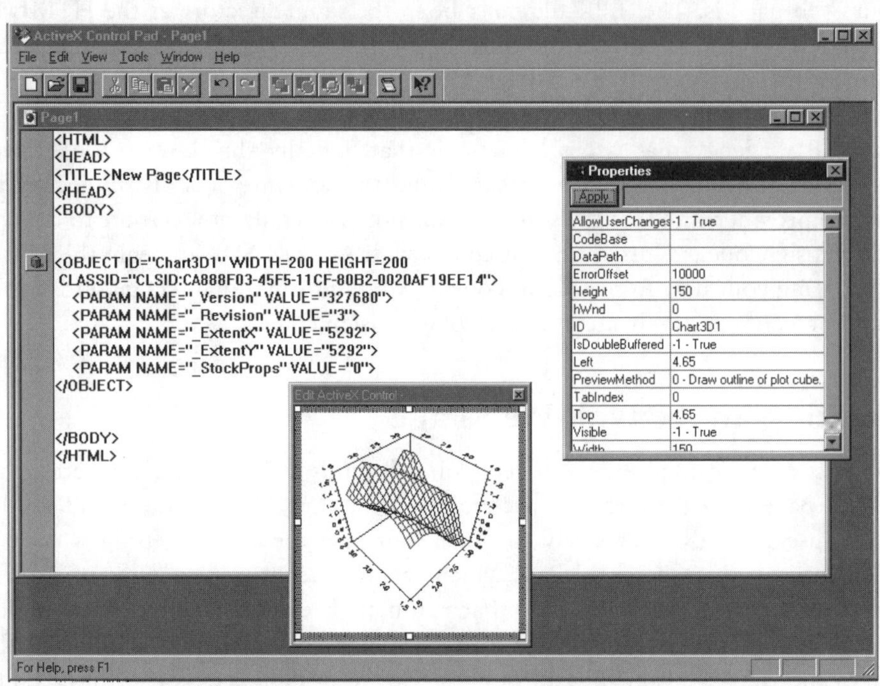

Figure 13.7 The ActiveX Control Pad in Action

previous example points to where the CAB file (which contains all the files users must download to view the control) is located.

You can include VBScript code to access and interactively modify the ActiveX control as it is running. The following code example loads an Olectra Chart ActiveX component, and produces a small form that loads different data into the chart display when the user clicks the appropriate button. This particular component also uses a method (LoadURL) to load data directly from a URL instead of having to add it programmatically.

```
<HTML>

<HEAD>
<TITLE>Loading Data from a URL Example</TITLE>
</HEAD>
<BODY TEXT="#2A0000" BGCOLOR="silver">
```

```
<H2>Loading Data from a URL Example</H2>

<HR WIDTH=75% ALIGN=left SIZE=5><BR>

<OBJECT CLASSID = "clsid:5220cb21-c88d-11cf-b347-
00aa00a28331">
<PARAM NAME="LPKPath" VALUE="olectra.lpk">
</OBJECT>

<OBJECT ID="Chart2D1" WIDTH=473 HEIGHT=352
CLASSID="CLSID:92D71E93-25A8-11CF-A640-9986B64D9618"
CODEBASE="./data/olectra.cab">.
</OBJECT>

<SCRIPT LANGUAGE="VBScript">
Sub Window OnLoad()
                                       'Load an .OC2 file
                                     Chart2D1.loadURL
("http://www.klg.com/olectra/chart/data/profit.oc2")
                                     . 'Load a .DAT file
                  Chart2D1.ChartGroups(1).Data.LoadURL
("http://www.klg.com/olectra/chart/data/1992.dat")
End Sub
.

' Event handler for the first button
Sub Button1OnClick()
                  Chart2D1.ChartGroups(1).Data.LoadURL
("http://www.klg.com/olectra/chart/data/1992.dat")
End Sub

' Event handler for the second button
Sub Button2OnClick() .
                  Chart2D1.ChartGroups(1).Data.LoadURL
("http://www.klg.com/olectra/chart/data/1993.dat")
End Sub

' Event handler for the third button
Sub Button3OnClick()
                  Chart2D1.ChartGroups(1)
.Data.LoadURL("http://www.klg.com/olectra/chart/data/
1994.dat")
End Sub
```

```
</SCRIPT>
<FORM METHOD="POST" NAME="TestForm">
<INPUT TYPE="Button" NAME="Button1" VALUE="1992 Data"
LANGUAGE="VBScript"
ONCLICK="CALL Button1OnClick()">
<INPUT TYPE="Button" NAME="Button2" VALUE="1993 Data"
LANGUAGE="VBScript"
ONCLICK="CALL Button2OnClick()">
<INPUT TYPE="Button" NAME="Button3" VALUE="1994 Data"
LANGUAGE="VBScript"
ONCLICK="CALL Button3OnClick()"><BR>

</FORM>

<HR WIDTH=75% ALIGN=left SIZE=5><BR>

<P>

Here is an ActiveX example embedded and running within
a Web page.<BR>
VBScript was used to create the user interaction in
this demo.<BR>

<P>

<HR WIDTH=75% ALIGN=left SIZE=5><BR>
</BODY>
</HTML>
```

When displayed, this code produces the results in Figures 13.8 and 13.9.

Notice that this HTML code contains not one but two separate components, each referenced by different <OBJECT> tags. The first object points to the license pack (<PARAM NAME="LPKPath" VALUE="olectra.lpk">) that verifies that this is a legitimate, secured ActiveX component. The second sets the working parameters for the component's operation.

Once you have created your Web page containing the ActiveX control embedded in it, you need to test the Web page to ensure that it will load properly on other machines. If you have the ActiveX component on your system already, and you test the Web page containing the component, your system will retrieve the ActiveX component from your system instead of downloading it from the Web server. Run Internet Explorer on a machine that has never come into contact with the new ActiveX control. Navigate to the Web site where your page exists con-

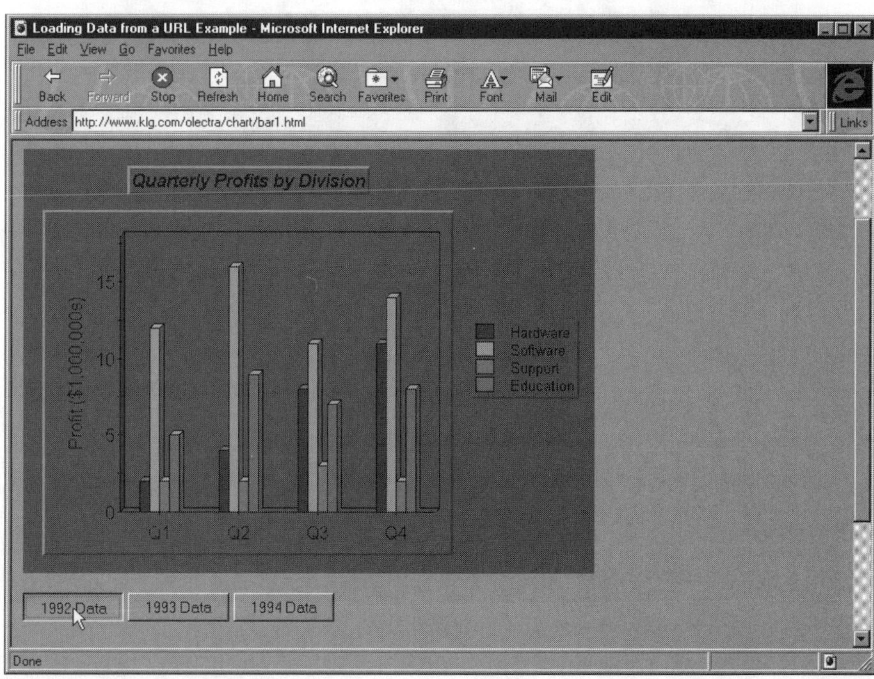

Figure 13.8 A Chart that Shows How ActiveX Can Add Dynamic Elements to a Web Page

taining the ActiveX control—if Internet Explorer displays it, everything has gone well.

You may get a sequence of dialog boxes depending on the security level that your copy of Internet Explorer is set to. You can change these settings by clicking on the View menu, choose Options, and then from the Options dialog, click the Security tab, and then click the Safety Level button. The choices for Security Level are High, Medium, and None. The default for Internet Explorer is High, so controls that have not been digitally signed will not be downloaded.

Keep in mind that ActiveX components will run only under Microsoft's Internet Explorer browser—it will not appear when viewed through Netscape Navigator. Notice how the same ActiveX Web page is rendered by Netscape Navigator 4.0—no ActiveX component. Note also how the browser is unable to interpret the VBScript code imbedded in the Web page, interpreting it as JavaScript (Figure 13.10).

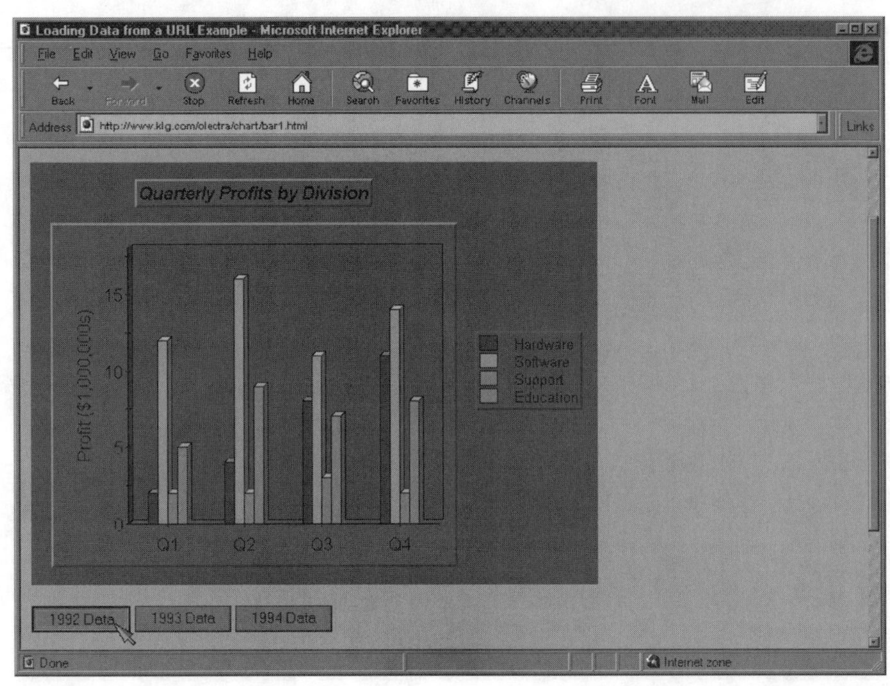

Figure 13.9 Another Chart that Shows How ActiveX Can Add Dynamic Elements to a Web Page

Java and Java Applets

Java is a programming language developed by Sun Microsystems. It has stirred a lot of interest because it is designed to run seamlessly across networks (such as the World Wide Web) and can operate across a variety of different computing platforms. If you write a program using Java, it can be run any computer system or Web browser that can interpret Java code. Java allows for two distinct program types: stand-alone applications and applets. Stand-alone applications can be run directly on a system containing the Java interpreter program, and applets can be inserted and run from Web pages when viewed through a Java-capable browser. This section looks primarily at applets for use on the Web. When you download a Web page containing a Java program, the code is sent to your system and is executed there. Essentially, a program is downloaded to your computer and then run within your Web browser.

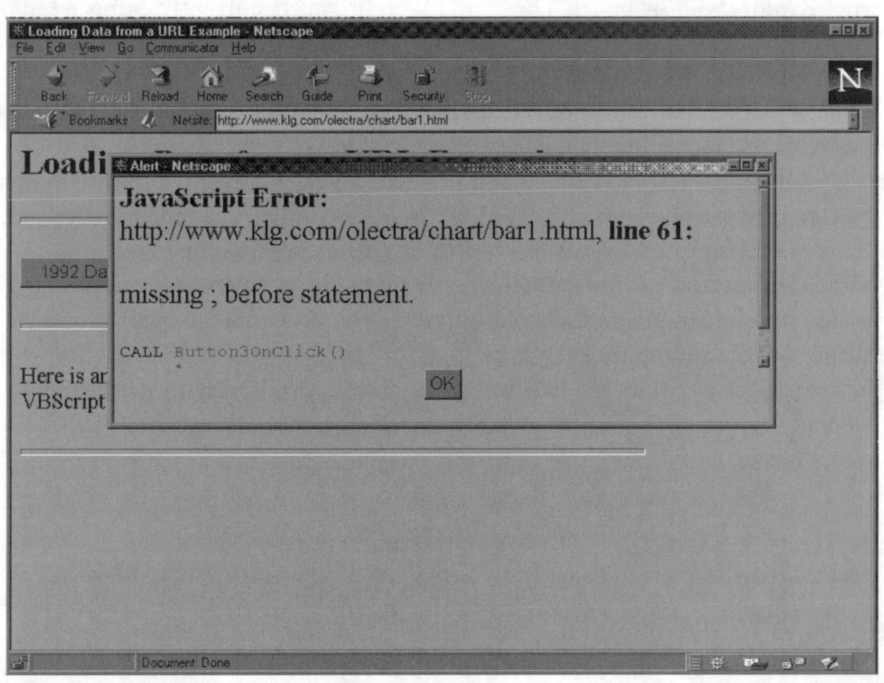

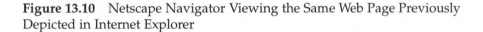

Figure 13.10 Netscape Navigator Viewing the Same Web Page Previously Depicted in Internet Explorer

Java applets are Java programs that can be run and viewed on a Web page through a Java-compatible browser. These Java programs are compiled and ready-to-run—all the Web author has to do is to set the characteristics that tell it how to run. Java applets typically derive its specific operating characteristics from code embedded in the Web page. This allows for a lot of flexibility—you can often use the same Java applet to produce strikingly different displays.

Insert the data and display characteristics into a Web page, then load (or publish) the Web page file and the applet onto your Web server. When a user views your Web page, the Java applet appears, displaying the values and characteristics you have set (if any). The applet and your configuration data are downloaded to the user's Web browser, so the speed of any user-interaction added to the table is limited only by the speed of their system. No further data requests are made to your Web site, as all of the data has been sent to the viewer. This lessens the impact on your Web server, as multiple requests for information are not necessary.

Currently, Java is supported by Netscape Navigator 3.0 or later, and Microsoft's Internet Explorer 3.0 or better. These two Web browsers currently comprise about 90% of the browser market, so the vast majority of the people who view your Web pages are also able to view any Java applets your pages contain.

When it was initially introduced to the Web community, it was the preferred method for producing animated sequences on a Web page. Typical early Java applets found on the Web tended to be "eye-candy"—nice to look at, but you weren't able to do much with it. As Java matures, more and more programmers and corporations are taking an interest in the programming language, and as the Web and the desktop environment begin to merge, it is increasingly being seen as the programming language of choice. Expect Java to become a significant part of the future of computing in general.

Java may well become the programmer's language of choice in the near future. It has many advantages over other popular programming languages, like C, C++, or Visual Basic.

Creating a Simple Java Application

Writing Java programs is not within the scope of this book—whole books have been written on the subject. It is important to understand that Java applets are simply programs that only do what is programmed into them. This section looks at how to create a *very* simple Java program.

Before you can start creating your own Java programs, you have to obtain the necessary tools. The prime source for Java is JavaSoft, a subsidiary of Sun Microsystems, the originators of Java. The JavaSoft Web site (which can be found at http://www.javasoft.com/) is a must-visit for anyone who intends to develop in Java. In addition to the required tools, there is plenty of documentation, sample programs, and other resources the beginning and advanced Java programmer can draw upon.

To develop a Java program, you must obtain the Java compiler (javac), which is contained in the Java Development Kit (better known simply as the JDK). The JDK is available for the following platforms:

- SPARC/Solaris 2.3, 2.4, or 2.5
- X86 Solaris 2.5
- Microsoft Windows NT/95
- MacOS

Go to the JavaSoft Web site and obtain the JDK for your platform. The version used in the following example uses the JDK version 1.0.2, so obtain this version if you intend to follow along.

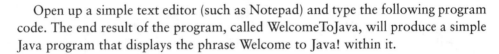

Open up a simple text editor (such as Notepad) and type the following program code. The end result of the program, called WelcomeToJava, will produce a simple Java program that displays the phrase Welcome to Java! within it.

```
import java.applet.Applet;
import java.awt.Graphics;

public class WelcomeToJava extends Applet {
public void paint (Graphics g) {
g. drawString ("Welcome to Java!", 50, 30);
}
```

Here's what's going on in the preceding Java code: The two initial import lines allow the program to draw upon some external Java resources; one for creating applets, the other for drawing graphics on-screen. The next line initiates a public (i.e., openly available) class file called WelcomeToJava. Since it draws upon prewritten Java code (the java.applet.Applet imported earlier) and builds upon it, it extends the java.applet.Applet code. The next line draws upon the graphics routines contained in the imported java.awt.Graphics library of Java code. Since it is used in the same WelcomeToJava program, it does not need to be set up in a separate class file, hence it is void. The next line uses drawString, which is derived from java.awt.Graphics to draw the phrase Welcome to Java to the screen, with a width of 50 pixels and a height of 30 pixels. The final two lines of code contain brackets to close off and contain the program.

Anybody familiar with the C or C++ programming languages will understand what's going on in the code listing. People who are already familiar with these computer languages will have a relatively easy time if they want to learn Java.

Setting Your CLASSPATH

Once you have obtained the JDK from JavaSoft, you have to tell your operating system where to look when a Java program is being run. This is done by setting the CLASSPATH statement. If you do not intend to develop Java program, but simply intend to display and manipulate existing applets in a Web browser, you do not have to go through the following process.

One of the most common problems encountered when trying to run Java-based programs either locally or on the Web is that of an incorrectly set CLASSPATH statement. The CLASSPATH is an environment variable that tells the Web browser and/or operating system where to find the Java classes needed to run a Java pro-

(continued)

gram. The CLASSPATH environment variable consists of the names of directories or the compressed file containing compiled Java classes. The following examples will help you set CLASSPATH properly on your system.

If you are unable to run any Java programs from a Java-capable Web browser, or are getting a number of error messages when trying to view a Web page containing a Java applet, you likely have an incorrectly set CLASSPATH.

The CLASSPATH statement is set either to a directory, or to a specific file. It is possible to have many directories and files specified within the same CLASSPATH statement. Most of the time the CLASSPATH is set to a specific file, usually a compressed PKzip file or a JAR (Java ARchive) file. If you are running a Java applet or program locally on your machine, make sure you know which directory or file the CLASSPATH should be set to.

Windows 95/98

Open your AUTOEXEC.BAT file in a text editor, like Notepad. Add a line that points to the target Java file/directory. If you are trying to point to a file called java_stuff.zip installed in a directory called \foo, you would add something similar to the following to your CLASSPATH:

```
set CLASSPATH=C:\foo\java_stuff.zip
```

Windows NT (3.51 and Higher)

Assuming that java_stuff.zip (the target file) is installed in a directory called \foo, add the CLASSPATH statement to a Windows NT system by doing the following.

1. Double-click Control Panel. The Control Panel window will open.
2. If you are using Windows NT 3.51, double-click System. The System dialog will be displayed.

   If you are using Windows NT 4.0, double-click System. The System Properties dialog will appear. Click Environment.
3. Search the User Environment Variables (or User Variables in Windows NT 4.0) field for an existing CLASSPATH statement. If a CLASSPATH statement exists, select it. In the Value field, add the following to the existing statement:

   C:\foo\java_stuff.zip

   If no CLASSPATH statement exists, in the Variable field, type:

   CLASSPATH

and in the Value field, type:
C:\foo\java_stuff.zip

4. Click OK.

Additional information on CLASSPATH for both these and other operating systems can be found at the JavaSoft Web site at http://www.javasoft.com/.

Once you have correctly set the CLASSPATH on your system, make sure you restart your browser to ensure that it will pick up the new settings.

Compiling and Using the Java Applet

Once you have the code for the preceding example typed out, save it to a file called WelcomeToJava.java. Java is case-sensitive, and it has to match the name specified in the public class line of the program, so make sure that it is spelled WelcomeToJava.java, and not, say welcometojava.java or WELCOMETOJAVA.JAVA.

Open a DOS window and go the directory where the WelcomeToJava.java exists. Type the following at the DOS prompt and press ENTER:

```
javac WelcomeToJava.java
```

If everything goes successfully, you will get a compiled Java program called WelcomeToJava.class. Do a directory listing (dir) to check to see if the WelcomeToJava.class exists. All compiled Java applets use .class as a filename extension. Unlike .exe or .com files, these compiled .class files are not directly executable under any operating system, because they do not contain machine-language code that can be understood directly by the microprocessor. Instead, they are compiled into a byte-code format consisting of machine-language instructions designed for a virtual microprocessor. This virtual microprocessor is the Java Virtual Machine, which interprets the byte-code into a machine-language code that can be understood by your system's microprocessor. As long as the Java Virtual Machine software exists for a computing platform, any Java programs you create will be able to run on that platform.

Congratulations are in order, because you have just written your first Java applet!

To display the new applet, you'll have to embed it within a Web page. To do that you'll have to learn how to use the <APPLET> tag, which is covered in the next section.

The APPLET Tag

On a Web page, Java applets are specified or contained within the <APPLET> tag. To view a Java applet, you have to open a Web browser to open the file that contains the applet—not the compiled Java .class file, but rather the HTML file that contains and specifies how the .class file should be displayed. To view an applet contained in Web page funky_java_applet.html in the directory /applet, type the following in the Location/URL field of your Web browser:

```
file:/applet/funky java applet.html
```

Alternatively, from the File menu of your Web browser, open the /applet directory and select funky_java_applet.html. The Web page and applet appear in the browser.

To view the WelcomeToJava.class in a Web browser, we have to insert the proper parameters into a Web file using the <APPLET> tag.

<APPLET> . . .</APPLET>

Element Name: Apple tag.

Description: Inserts a Java applet within a Web page.

Attributes:

ALIGN= *LEFT* | *RIGHT* | *CENTER* | *TOP* | *MIDDLE* | *BOTTOM* (IE 3.0 and up)
ALIGN= *LEFT* | *RIGHT* | *TOP* | *ABSMIDDLE* | *ABSBOTTOM* | *TEXTTOP* | *MIDDLE* | *BASELINE* | *BOTTOM* (NN 3.0 and up)
Used to specify where the applet appears in the applet window.

ALT= *text*
Used to specify a string of text to be displayed.

ARCHIVE= *filename.zip*
Used to specify the name of a compressed file containing .class files relevant to the applet.

CODE= *filename.class*
Used to specify the name of the Java .class file (a required element).

CODEBASE= *codebaseURL*
Used to specify the full path of the Java applet referenced by CODE, if it is different than that of the Web page used to reference the applet .class file.

HEIGHT= # *pixels*
Used to specify the vertical dimension of the applet window (a required element).

HSPACE= # *pixels*
Used to specify the horizontal distance between the applet window and other elements on the Web page.

MAYSCRIPT (NN 3.0 only)
Used to permit the applet to access JavaScript.

NAME= *appletInstanceName*
Used to specify the name for the applet instance.
VSPACE= # *pixels*
Used to specify the vertical distance between the applet window and other elements on the Web page.
WIDTH= # *pixels*
Used to specify the horizontal dimension of the applet window (a required element).

Associated Tags: <PARAM>

Sample:

```
<APPLET CODE=WelcomeToJava.class CODEBASE="..\.." ALT="My
First Java Applet" WIDTH=200 HEIGHT=200 VSPACE=10
HSPACE=10 ALIGN=RIGHT></APPLET>
```

Most of these attributes are not required to place an applet on a Web page. The minimum required attributes to place a Java applet on a Web page are the CODE, WIDTH, and HEIGHT attributes, as the following example shows:

```
<APPLET CODE=WelcomeToJava.class WIDTH=200
HEIGHT=100></APPLET>
```

This tells the Web browser where to find the .class file, and the width and height of the Java window that will display the applet. For the simplest Java programs, that is often all you have to add to a Web page, as Figure 13.11 shows.

Most of the <APPLET> attributes work within both Internet Explorer and Netscape Navigator, however, there are a few attributes and values specific to each browser. Where there are differences, they are noted later.

There are a number of attributes that modify the display characteristics of the <APPLET> tag: ALIGN, WIDTH, HEIGHT, VSPACE, and HSPACE. Anyone who has used the equivalent attributes of the <IMG> tag will already be familiar with how they work. All of these attributes set the display parameters for the Java window, which is the area within the browser within which the applet appears.

The ALIGN attribute specifies how the applet is aligned in the display window set by WIDTH and HEIGHT. This attribute aligns the applet with respect to the applet window, and can take any of the following values: LEFT, CENTER, and RIGHT. You can also use VSPACE and HSPACE to space an applet away from other elements on a Web page, like text and images, by specifying the number of pixels of space to appear above and below the applet (VSPACE) and to each side of the applet (HSPACE). The LEFT, MIDDLE, and RIGHT attributes are common to both Internet Explorer 3.0 and Netscape Navigator 2.0 and up; the ABSMIDDLE, ABSBOTTOM, TEXTTOP, BASELINE, and BOTTOM are used by Netscape Navigator only, and CENTER is used only by Internet Explorer. ABSMIDDLE and

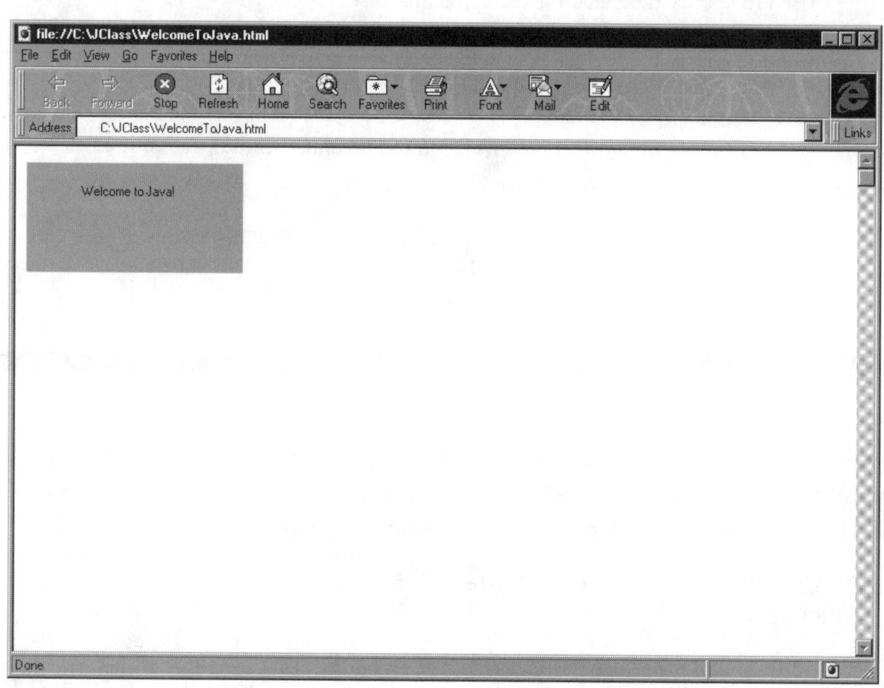

Figure 13.11 The Sample WelcomeToJava Applet Displayed within a Web Page

ABSBOTTOM align the Java window to the absolute midline and bottom of the line of text that precedes it, respectively. TEXTTOP aligns the window to the text that precedes it, BASELINE sets it to the position at which the preceding line of text appears on a line, and BOTTOM aligns the window to the bottom of the line of text that precedes it. CENTER works the same way as MIDDLE.

The ALT attribute is an optional attribute that enables you to insert alternate text in the area where the applet appears. This is useful to insert for those cases where a browser recognizes the <APPLET> tag but is unable to display a functioning applet, or where you want the name or a short description of the applet to appear within the browser.

ARCHIVE is an optional attribute, and is used to decrease the amount of time needed load a Java applet on a Web page. It does this by drawing upon the resources of many different class files at once, contained within a single compressed PKzip file. If the PKzipped archive file and the applet class file reside in a directory on the Web server different from that of the Web page, both must be in a single directory referenced by CODEBASE. This attribute was introduced in Netscape Navigator 3.0 and is not recognized by Internet Explorer.

CODE is a required attribute that specifies the name of the compiled Java file. It always points to the filename of the Java applet, not the full path, which is handled by CODEBASE attribute. CODEBASE is an optional attribute that is used to specify the path of an applet; in other words, the directory containing the applet code referenced by CODE. So if an applet called FunkyApplet.class resides in a directory called java/funky, CODE and CODEBASE would be used in the following way:

```
CODE=FunkyApplet.class CODEBASE=java/funky/
```

CODEBASE is not necessary if the HTML page containing the applet resides in the same directory as the applet itself. Using the preceding example, if the HTML code resided within the java/funky directory, you would not have to specify the CODEBASE.

MAYSCRIPT is an optional attribute that enables the applet to be accessed by JavaScript code running within the Web page. It does not take any specific value. It is recognized only within Netscape Navigator.

The NAME attribute is an optional attribute that specifies the name for the applet instance. This is used only in cases where there are multiple applets on a page that interact with each other.

The WIDTH and HEIGHT attributes are two required attributes that set the display window of the applet display. If you do not know what the explicit size of the applet is supposed to be, expect to tinker with these two settings in order to get the size of the applet window right.

The VSPACE and HSPACE are optional attributes that specify the spacing between the applet window and the rest of the elements on a Web page. VSPACE sets the number of pixels to appear above and below the applet window, and HSPACE sets the spacing to appear to each side of the applet. They work the same way as the <IMG> tag's VSPACE and HSPACE attributes. These attributes gives the applet some room on the Web page, and large values isolate it from other elements on a page.

Note that <APPLET> is a deprecated tag in the official HTML 4.0 specification. The <OBJECT> tag as specified by the World Wide Web Consortium absorbs all of the major functions of the <APPLET> tags. At the time of this writing, support for Java applets using the <OBJECT> tag is limited to Internet Explorer 4.0. Since <APPLET> is still supported in both Netscape and Internet Explorer, it is recommended that <APPLET> be used until <OBJECT> becomes prevalent.

Using the <PARAM> Tag

The more sophisticated Java applets allow the Web author to set the characteristics and values used within the applet. This is done by using the <PARAM> tag, which tells the applet how to operate.

<PARAM>

Element Name: Parameter tag.

Description: Specifies how a Java applet or other program operates.

Attributes: NAME= *parameterName*
Specifies the name of the applet parameter to be used.
VALUE= *parameterValue*
Specifies the value to be associated with applet parameter selected by NAME.

Associated Tags: <APPLET>, <OBJECT>

Sample:

```
<APPLET CODE=NiftyApplet.class CODEBASE="..\.." WIDTH=200
HEIGHT=200>
<PARAM NAME=COLOR VALUE=BLUE>
<PARAM NAME=FONT VALUE=ARIAL>
</APPLET>
```

The <PARAM> tag is an empty tag that has two attributes: NAME and VALUE. NAME specifies the type of the resource to be used, and VALUE sets the value of the resource.

Here's how it works: The Java programmer who creates the applet builds into it a number of methods that can be set external to the applet itself. Each of these methods within the applet can be set by the parameters specified by the <PARAM> tag. Only one NAME/VALUE pair can be used to specify each method used within an applet, but multiple parameters can be specified in an HTML page. This gives the Web author a lot of control over the way that the applet behaves.

For a practical example of this, take a look at the following HTML code. It uses a Java applet called JCTableAppletLite, which produces interactive tables. In this case, one <PARAM> tag inserts the values for a fictitious Top 10 chart. Individual cells in the table are separated by pipe characters (|), and rows are delimited by parentheses ((and)).

```
<HTML>
<HEAD>
<TITLE>Top 10 Chart</TITLE>
</HEAD>
<BODY>
<H1>Top 10 Chart</H1>
<APPLET CODE=jclass/table/JCTableAppletLite.class
CODEBASE=".." HEIGHT=250 WIDTH=600>
<PARAM NAME=cells VALUE="
(1|4|Miscellaneous 'S'|Party Killer|3|Garage|CD-EP|
Unfiled Records)
(2|1|Jolly Tambourine Guy|Lisa
Burger|9|Grunge|Tape|Inverted Reality)
(3|2|Warm Fuzzies|Spacey Tingles|19|New Age|Digital
Cube|Fred)
(4|3|Blantant Pistols|Dirty Coinage Live|10|Punk|CD|
Rip Off Records)
(5|8|The Nihilist Lumber League|Trees Everywhere!|1|
Punk|Tape|Woodchip)
(6|5|Deja Hoodoo|Too Kool 4 U|10|Rap|CD|Yo)
(7|8|Rap Head|Rapped on the Knuckles|6|Rap|Cassette|Yo
Records)
(8|6|Sinister Pete|Melody Fall Down Go Boom|3|Folk
|8-Track|Irish Funk)
(9|10|The Hip Computer 5|Bent, Spindled and Mutilated|
7|Electronic|Punch-cards|HAL)
(10|9|Pop Will Eat Them|Sample-o-rama|8|Electronic|
Diskette|Her Master's Voice)
">
</APPLET>
</BODY>
</HTML>
```

When displayed, the applet produces a simple grid of values (Figure 13.12).

This simple grid does not offer much in the way of advantages over the same information if it was rendered as an HTML grid. The excitement in Java comes from the things it can do that regular HTML cannot. This applet is versatile, and can take a number of additional parameters, such as adding column labels, setting the size and width of cells, adding color, changing fonts, adding images and interactive sorting capabilities. These values have all been added to the basic cell value code seen in the initial Top 10 Chart. As you will see in Figure 13.13, the following code produces a much different table.

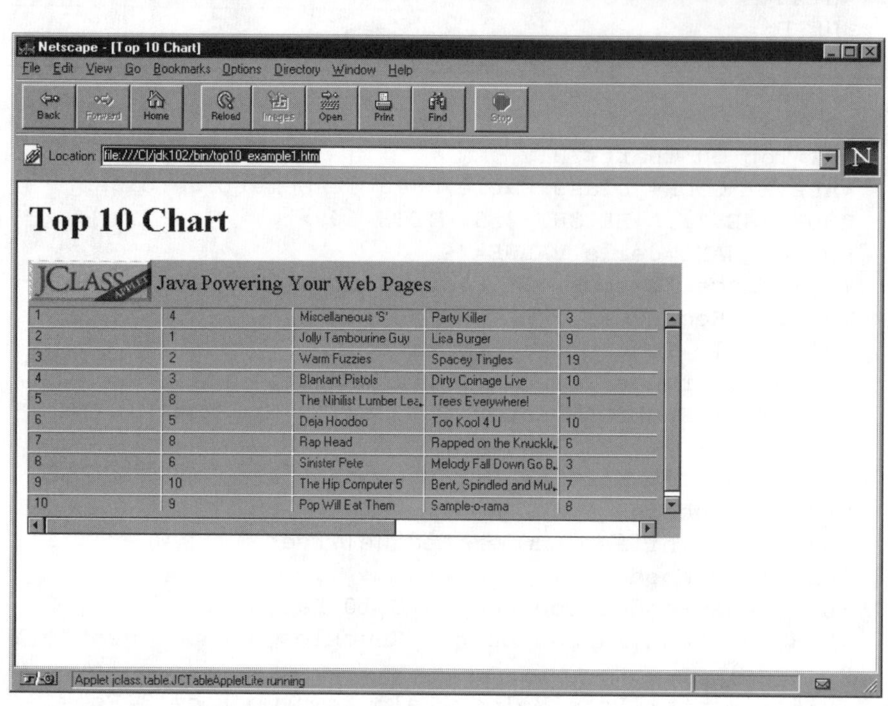

Figure 13.12 The Simple Top 10 Listing Displayed

```
<HTML>
<HEAD>
<TITLE>Top 10 Chart</TITLE>
</HEAD>
<BODY>
<H1>Top 10 Chart</H1>
<APPLET CODE=jclass/table/JCTableAppletLite.class
CODEBASE=".." HEIGHT=340 WIDTH=600>
<PARAM NAME=columnLabels VALUE="This\n Week|Last\n
Week|Artist|Album| Weeks on\n Chart|Type|Format|Label">
<PARAM NAME=pixelWidthList VALUE="(ALL VARIABLE)">
<PARAM NAME=pixelHeightList VALUE="(ALL VARIABLE)">
<PARAM NAME=repeatBackgroundColors VALUE="grey,
lightgrey">
<PARAM NAME=backgroundList VALUE="(ALL ALL REPEAT
COLUMN) (LABEL ALL white)">
```

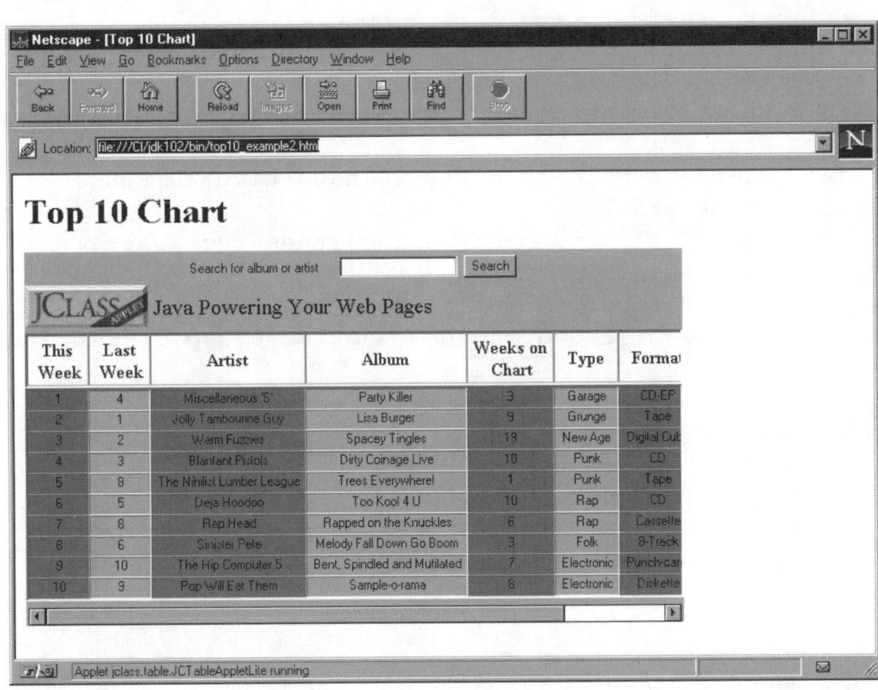

Figure 13.13 The Enhanced Top 10 Listing

```
<PARAM NAME=foregroundList VALUE="(LABEL ALL blue)">
<PARAM NAME=frameShadowThickness VALUE=2>
<PARAM NAME=fontList VALUE="(LABEL ALL
TimesRoman-Bold-16)">
<PARAM NAME=alignmentList VALUE="(ALL ALL
middlecenter)">
<PARAM NAME=trackCursor VALUE=true>
<PARAM NAME=columnLabelSort VALUE=true>
<PARAM NAME=datatypeList VALUE="(all 0 type integer)
(all 1 type integer) (all 4 type integer)">
<PARAM NAME=search VALUE=true>
<PARAM NAME=searchPosition VALUE=place top>
<PARAM NAME=findLabel VALUE="Search for album or
artist">
<PARAM NAME=cells VALUE="
```

```
(1|4|Miscellaneous 'S'|Party Killer|3 |Garage|CD-EP|
Unfiled Records)
(2|1|Jolly Tambourine Guy|Lisa Burger|9|Grunge|Tape|
Inverted Reality)
(3|2|Warm Fuzzies|Spacey Tingles|19|New Age|Digital
Cube|Fred)
(4|3|Blantant Pistols|Dirty Coinage Live|10|Punk|CD|
Rip Off Records)
(5|8|The Nihilist Lumber League|Trees Everywhere!|1|
Punk|Tape|Woodchip)
(6|5|Deja Hoodoo|Too Kool 4 U|10|Rap|CD|Yo)
(7|8|Rap Head|Rapped on the Knuckles|6|Rap|Cassette|Yo
Records)
(8|6|Sinister Pete|Melody Fall Down Go Boom|3|Folk|
8-Track|Irish Funk)
(9|10|The Hip Computer 5|Bent, Spindled and Mutilated|
7|Electronic|Punch-cards|HAL)
(10|9|Pop Will Eat Them|Sample-o-rama|8|Electronic|
Diskette|Her Master's Voice)
">
</APPLET>
</BODY>
</HTML>
```

This example displays just a few of the many features Web authors can define while creating Web pages using the JClass applet. There are over 40 resources that can be used in JClass Applet. They are all specified by using the NAME attribute. The types of VALUE they can take are specific for each NAME resource. In addition to the features explored here, Web authors can also add the following elements:

- Frozen rows and labels
- The ability to resize rows and columns interactively
- The ability to add spanned cells and labels
- The ability to change border styles
- Many other features and functions

You can download an evaluation version of JClass LiveTable Applet at: http://www.klg.com/jclass/table.

Allowing for Browsers that Do Not Support Applets

Not all browsers are capable of displaying Java applets. Any text placed between the <APPLET> and </APPLET> tags is not displayed by Java-capable browsers, but will appear in browsers that cannot handle applets. There is no equivalent to the <NOFRAMES> tag for Java applets. It is good practice to include text within the <APPLET> tags, if only to indicate the fact that an applet exists on the Web page for those people using browsers that cannot view them. Following is an example of how to indicate the presence of an applet to browsers incapable of displaying them.

```
<APPLET CODE=WelcomeToJava.class HEIGHT=150 WIDTH=200>
<B>This page is Java-enhanced.</B><BR>
To view the applet contained within this Web page, you
will need a Java-capable browser.
</APPLET>
```

Using the Java Console

Got everything set up properly and your applet still isn't working as advertised? Maybe there is a problem with the applet itself. Like any other program, Java applets are not immune to programming errors.

You can determine how your applet is executing (or not executing) by using the Java Console. The Java Console is a feature in Netscape Navigator that displays any processing errors that occur while any applet is loading. If there are any errors in running either the HTML code or the applet file when an applet is loaded, corresponding error messages will be displayed in the Java console. Use these error messages to pinpoint and correct the indicated errors, or pass them on to the Java programmer who created the applet.

To display the Java Console in Netscape Navigator 3.0, go the Options menu and click Show Java Console. The Java Console will appear. To display it within Netscape Navigator 4.0, go to the Communicator menu and click Java Console. Rerun the applet to see whether there is a problem with the program.

Microsoft Internet Explorer 3.0 and 4.0 have a feature similar to Netscape's Java Console, which also displays any error messages that occurred while an applet was being loaded. To set this function, launch Internet Explorer, and from the View menu, click Options. Click the Advanced tab, and then check the Enable Java logging setting if you are using Internet Explorer 3.0, or Java Logging Enabled in Internet Explorer 4.0. Click OK. Any errors that occur while Java applets are loading are written to a file called javalog.txt, which can be found in your /WINDOWS directory (or /WINNT40 if you are running Windows NT 4.0).

CHAPTER 14

Future Developments in HTML

One of the biggest challenges involved in writing a book about HTML is that the language is constantly evolving and changing. The HTML language continues to evolve in interesting directions: Microsoft and Netscape have tussled for domination over the browser market, creating Web clients that recognize innovative yet proprietary tags. Web authors experience a great deal of frustration, since the proprietary tag competition between Netscape and Microsoft makes it difficult to design a site that supports both Netscape and Microsoft HTML elements. At the time of this writing, Microsoft seems to be making more headway than Netscape; this is a significant change in the Web climate, considering that at the beginning of 1997, Netscape was inarguably the most popular Web browser on the Internet. Microsoft has recently been working very closely with the W3C to develop and adopt several new technologies, while Netscape is fighting to retain its market share by proposing similar, yet incompatible, tools. Indeed, the more things

change, the more they stay the same. A Web author's only defense is to keep abreast of these new developments, and always to follow the lead of the W3C, since it is that organization that sets the standard for Web technology.

This chapter discusses three of the most recent Web ventures: Extensible Markup Language (XML), Dynamic HTML, and HTML help.

EXTENSIBLE MARKUP LANGUAGE (XML)

Extensible Markup Language, or XML, is a language that lets you use SGML on the World Wide Web. XML is extensible because it does not have a fixed format, whereas HTML does. For instance, HTML has a set of elements and attributes that can be used to create Web pages, and the HTML format is fixed; in other words, authors cannot create their own HTML elements or attributes. XML is different from HTML in that it does not have a fixed format, so authors can create their own XML tags.

Generally speaking, XML is a restricted form of SGML. SGML stands for Standard Generalized Markup Language, and it is the international standard for how to identify and use documents in terms of their content and structure. SGML uses DTDs, or Document Type Definitions, to define the type of document that is marked-up in SGML. Simply put, the DTD tells the browser how to handle each element; for instance, the HTML DTD defines HTML tags, such as headings and lists, so that a Web browser knows what to do with them. An SGML-type document also needs a style sheet to define how each element should be displayed; for instance, text enclosed in head tags display in a larger font size than text enclosed in paragraph tags. HTML is one kind of SGML document type, defined specifically for use on the World Wide Web. Like HTML, XML was introduced by the World Wide Web Consortium.

When HTML was first introduced, many people believed that it was a good alternative to SGML. The HTML element set was well defined and easy to understand and use. However, HTML is fairly limited, and does not allow for obscure kinds of description and formatting. Though the W3C, Netscape, and Microsoft are working hard to expand HTML, it has become clear that continually adding new elements to support diverse intentions is not the answer. Different groups are developing different elements and attributes, and there are many conflicts and very little agreement on what new elements should be developed. In response to this problem, the W3C introduced XML.

XML is important because it has much of the power and flexibility of SGML, but is much simpler to implement. Both authors and programmers can take advantage of XML by using it to mark up documents and develop browsers to read that marked-up document. XML can be used to create new document types to suit the needs of specific audiences. For instance, a music library could use XML to create a DTD to meet the unique needs of music documentation; an engineering library would use XML in a similar way, but would define a DTD to meet their specific needs. In addition browsers would be developed to suit an individual DTD, so that the customized browser could read all the documents using that DTD.

An example of a simple XML document follows.

```
<?XML VERSION="1.0" RMD="NONE"?>
<joke>
<question>What did one strawberry say to the other
strawberry?</question>
<punchline>If you weren't so fresh, we wouldn't be in
this jam!</punchline>
</joke>
```

As you can see, you can use XML to describe and format just about any kind of document; you only have to create the DTD to define whatever tags you need.

Tip: A DTD is not required if you use what is called the well-formed document class. This means that the elements must be balanced and nested properly, and that all start and end tags are present for the elements that contain text. However, if you want to define how the browser displays the document, you must include a style sheet.

XML is growing and continues to be in development. However there are several Internet resources that discuss its background, advantages, and implementation. To find out more about XML, consult these Web sites:

- The XML FAQ (Frequently Asked Questions) is at http://www.ucc.ie/xml/#FAQ-GENERAL.
- The XML Draft Specification is available from the W3C at http://www.w3.org/pub/WWW/TR/WD-xml-lang-970331.html.

Channel Definition Format (CDF)

A good example of the usefulness of XML is in relation to Channel Definition Format, or CDF. CDF is an application of XML, where CDF is a document type created with XML. CDF was developed to mark up documents that will be used with push technology.

Push technology is a recent Internet development where users define what information is of interest to them, and a client program pushes that information to the

user. Push technology is in some ways the opposite of how people use the World Wide Web; on the Web, users browse to the information they want, whereas push technology delivers the information to the user.

Web developers needed a way to format HTML pages so that the pages would be compatible with push clients. XML was used to create the CDF DTD, and in turn Web developers can apply the CDF DTD and CDF elements to their Web pages.

Microsoft Corporation has developed their own push client known as an Active Desktop, available as part of the Internet Explorer 4.0 browser. Simply put, the Active Desktop offers a set of channels to the user; the user chooses what channels they want to receive, allowing information on that channel to be pushed to the desktop. Web authors who want to offer their Web site as a channel create a CDF file that determines what content is pushed to the user's desktop. The Active Desktop client reads the CDF, then pushes the pages specified in the CDF to the Active Desktop client.

A CDF is made up of the following elements:

Channel	Defines the channel
Item	Defines a channel item. An item is a unit of information that is available from the channel
UserSchedule	Defines an update schedule specified by the user
Schedule	Defines a particular update schedule, set by the creator of the CDF
Logo	Defines an image to represent a channel or channel item (this image appears in the channel bar)
Tracking	Defines user tracking parameters of a channel
CategoyDef	Defines a category, and can define a child category of another category

Many of the CDF elements can contain child elements to further define the channel. The elements and their child elements are defined next.

Element: Channel

Child Elements:

Channel	One or more subchannels of this channel. There can be several subchannels, as defined by the creator of the CDF.

Item	One or more article profiles, each providing information on a unit of content. This is usually a Web page.
IntroURI	URI to introductory Web page for channel. Can provide general and setup information. Known as a "welcome" page.
Authorization	Certification of executable content downloadable by this channel ("Authenticode for channels").
MinStorage	Minimum storage size required, in kilobytes.
Tracking	Profile providing information on how channel should perform user tracking.

Element: Item

Child Elements:

HREF	URL of article contents
MIMEType	MIME type of article contents
IsVisible	This item should be visible to the user
Priority	Priority of this item ("HI", "NORMAL", "LOW")
Precache	Publisher recommended download behavior "YES" = do retrieve contents into cache "NO" = do not retrieve contents into cache "DEFAULT" = whatever user has as default

Element: Channel and Item

Child Elements:

LastMod	Last modified date for this Web page.
Title	Title of the Channel or Item.
Abstract	Short description summarizing the article.
Author	Author of the channel.
Publisher	Publisher of the channel.
Copyright	Copyright, usually a name and date.
PublicationDate	Publication date of the channel.

Logo	Logo for channel, usually a small image.
Keywords	Keywords that match this channel, separated by commas.
Category	A category to which this Web page belongs.
Ratings	Rating of the channel by one or more ratings services.
Schedule	Schedule for keeping channel up to date.
UserSchedule	Schedule for updating the channel, specified by the user.

Element: Schedule

Child Elements:

Start	The day the schedule starts to apply.
End	The day the schedule ends; an expiry date.
IntervalTime	The interval of time over which the schedule should repeat.
EarliestTime	Earliest time during the schedule interval that the schedule applies to
LatestTime	Latest time during the schedule interval to which the schedule applied. If it is not equal to EarliestTime, then the time is randomly chosen in range.

Element: Logo

Child Elements:

HREF (Required)	URL to the image for the logo.
Type	String indicating what context image should be used ("BIG", "WIDE", "SMALL", "REGULAR").

Element: CategoryDef

Child Elements:

CategoryName	Name of category.
Description	Textual description of category.
CategoryDef	Subcategories.

A sample CDF file follows.

```
<?XML VERSION="1.0" ENCODING="windows-1252"?>
<CHANNEL HREF="http://www.exn.net/"
BASE="http://www.exn.net"
SELF="http://www.exn.net/ie/exn.cdf">
<TITLE>EXN: Exploration Network</TITLE>
<ABSTRACT>Canada's Source for Science, Nature,
Technology and Adventure.</ABSTRACT>
<LOGO HREF="http://www.exn.net/ie/exn-ie-ico.gif"
STYLE="ICON"/>
<LOGO HREF="http://www.exn.net/ie/exn-ie-small.gif"
STYLE="IMAGE"/>
<LOGO HREF="http://www.exn.net/ie/exn-ie-large.gif"
STYLE="IMAGE-WIDE"/>
<SCHEDULE ENDDATE="1998.01.01">
<INTERVALTIME HOUR="24"/>
</SCHEDULE>
<ITEM HREF="http://www.exn.net/news/"
LASTMOD="1997.09.27T15:58-0500" PRECACHE="NO"
LEVEL="0">
<TITLE>EXN!News Screensaver</TITLE>
<LOGO HREF="http://www.exn.net/ie/exn-ie-ico.gif"
STYLE="ICON"/>
<USAGE VALUE="ScreenSaver"></USAGE>
</ITEM>
<ITEM HREF="http://www.exn.net/news/"
LASTMOD="1997.09.26T11:53-0500" PRECACHE="NO"
LEVEL="0">
<TITLE>EXN!News: News Home Page</TITLE>
<ABSTRACT>EXN!News Home Page</ABSTRACT>
<LOGO HREF="http://www.exn.net/ie/exn-ie-ico-gif"
STYLE="ICON"/>
</ITEM>
</CHANNEL>
```

Microsoft is certainly not the only company making use of CDF, but thus far they have taken its development the furthest. For more information on Microsoft's use of CDF consult the Microsoft Web site at http://www.microsoft.com/standards/cdf.htm. For detailed information about Microsoft's Active Desktop, consult the Internet Explorer 4.0 Web site at http://www.microsoft.com/ie/ie40/. For information on the W3C standard for CDF; which is in agreement with Microsoft's application, see http://www.w3.org/TR/NOTE-CDFsubmit.html.

Dynamic HTML

Dynamic HTML is one of the latest crazes in the development of the HTML language. Both Microsoft and Netscape have jumped on the bandwagon, offering different and competing approaches to making HTML interactive and more interesting.

Simply put, Dynamic HTML allows Web authors to develop interactive Web pages without the need for accessing the Web server. By adding Dynamic HTML attributes to HTML elements, users can control the behavior of scripts (such as JavaScript and VBScript) embedded in the HTML page itself. Groups of HTML elements can be given a name; the scripts then can reference that named element to cause it to react to a user's action. For instance, the color of a hypertext link can change as the user's mouse pointer passes over it.

This section discusses Dynamic HTML from a general point of view; an entire book can be, and has been, written on the subject. To become a Dynamic HTML guru, it is best to start your learning curve here, then move on to a more detailed tome on the subject.

Netscape Dynamic HTML

Netscape's approach to Dynamic HTML is based on Cascading Style Sheets (CSS) and HTML layers. Style sheets provide the ability to control the layout on a page, including margin widths, colors, borders and so on. The concept behind HTML layers is that parts of the HTML page can be moved and modified. In this way, layers give authors the ability to create simple animation.

It is important to note that though Netscape has released a beta version of Navigator 4.0 that can read Dynamic HTML, the World Wide Web Consortium has rejected Netscape's concept of layers as an implementation of Dynamic HTML. As well, the general feeling in the Internet industry is that Microsoft has a firmer handle on developing this new technology. For more information about Netscape's approach to Dynamic HTML, refer to Netscape's Dynamic HTML Web pages at http://developer.netscape.com/one/dynhtml/dynhtml.html.

Microsoft Dynamic HTML

Microsoft's Dynamic HTML is leading the pack, and is being developed in cooperation with the W3C. The Internet Explorer 4.0 browser supports Dynamic HTML. Web authors can dynamically change the structure and style of their Web documents, add multimedia and interactive elements, as well as control the appearance of the Web page.

Microsoft's approach to Dynamic HTML focuses on extending the Cascading Style Sheet (CSS) specification as defined by the W3C. A combination of CSS and JavaScript or VBScript is the engine behind Dynamic HTML's ability to change the appearance of Web pages on the fly in response to user action. Becoming familiar with CSS and either JavaScript or VBScript is an important first step when learning Dynamic HTML.

Tip: For information about Cascading Style Sheets, turn to Chapter 11, "Cascading Style Sheets." For information about JavaScript and VBScript, turn to Chapter 13, "Dynamic Documents."

Microsoft's Internet Explorer 4.0 extends the existing W3C CSS specification in several ways, including the ability of the Web author to specify the absolute positioning of elements on a Web page. As well, it introduces the idea of *data binding*, which enables Web pages to be created on the fly. However, the most important development Internet Explorer 4.0 adds to CSS is that all page elements become objects that can be manipulated directly by a script, such as JavaScript or VBScript, embedded in that Web page. This part of the chapter examines Microsoft's use of objects in Dynamic HTML.

CSS elements are typically used to customize how elements are displayed on the Web page. Style sheet instructions are specified by stating the type of HTML tag to modify, along with a statement telling the browser how to display that tag. The following example demonstrates a simple Web page where all the <H1> elements are blue:

```
<HTML>
<HEAD>
<STYLE>H1 {color: blue}</STYLE>
</HEAD>
<BODY>
<H1>This header is blue.</H1>
</BODY>
</HTML>
```

In this case, the <STYLE> tag sets the color of every <H1> tag in this Web page to blue.

Whereas CSS elements can modify any regular HTML tags in a Web page, Dynamic HMTL works by adding the ID attribute to the CSS elements on a Web page. The ID is essentially the name you are giving to that part of the Web code; the named section can then be referenced by a script in that Web page, which then manipulates the HTML properties on-screen.

The following example illustrates a simple personal Web page using the Dynamic HTML ID attribute to label parts of the HTML code.

```
<BODY BGCOLOR="#FFFFFF" VLINK="#666666" LINK="#000066">
<P>
<TABLE WIDTH = 100%>
<TR>
<TD><B><A HREF="aboutme.html" ID="FirstLink">Learn
about Me!</A></B></TD>
</TR>
<TR>
<TD><B><A HREF="resume.html" ID="SecondLink">Read me
Resume!</A></B></TD>
</TR>
<TR>
<TD><B><A
HREF="mailto:kim@mysite.com"ID="ThirdLink">Email Me!
</A></B></TD>
</TR>
</TABLE>
</BODY>
```

This example doesn't seem very much different from regular HTML, except for the inclusion of the ID attribute in the hypertext link element. Adding the ID attribute to each hypertext link element makes them an object that can be manipulated by a script.

The next step is to insert the script that will change the action or appearance of the HTML objects specified in the rest of the Web document. The following VBScript, when added to a Web page, modifies the appearance of the links on that Web page.

```
<HEAD>
<TITLE>Dynamic HTML Example</TITLE>
<SCRIPT LANGUAGE="VBSCRIPT">
sub FirstLink onMouseOver
document.anchors ("FirstLink").style.color="magenta"
document.anchors ("FirstLink").style.fontsize=18
End sub
sub FirstLink onMouseOut
document.anchors("FirstLink").style.color="black"
document.anchors("FirstLink").style.fontsize=16
End sub
sub Second onMouseOver
document.anchors ("SecondLink").style.color="magenta"
document.anchors ("SecondLink").style.fontsize=18
End sub
```

```
sub SecondLink onMouseOut
document.anchors ("SecondLink").style.color="black"
document.anchors("SecondLink").style.fontsize=16
End sub
sub ThirdLink onMouseOver
document.anchors ("ThirdLink").style.color="magenta"
document.anchors ("ThirdLink").style.fontsize=18
End sub
sub ThirdLink onMouseOut
document.anchors("ThirdLink").style.color="black"
document.anchors("ThirdLink").style.fontsize=16
End sub
</SCRIPT>
</HEAD>
```

When the HTML code and VBScript in the above preceding two examples are both inserted into the same Web page, the font size and color of the hypertext links change as the user passes the mouse pointer over them.

Note in Figure 14.1 that as the user passes his or her mouse pointer over the hypertext links, the font size increases and the color changes from black to magenta.

This makes the hypertext links stand out in a way that regular HTML is not capable of.

The ID attribute in the HREF element is used by the VBScript to modify the behavior of that HTML object:

- The VBScript code uses the onMouseOver and onMouseOut attributes to listen for mouse events
- When a user moves the mouse pointer over the hypertext link containing the ID attribute FirstLink, the onMouseOver attribute associated with the HTML object (FirstLink_onMouseOver) executes the rest of the code
- The code tells the document.anchor attribute to change the link to a different color and font size. In the preceding example, this is done with document.anchors ("FirstLink").style.color="magenta" and document.anchors("FirstLink).fontsize=18
- When a user moves the mouse pointer away from the link, the onMouseOut element in the VBScript responds by changing the link color to black and the link font size to black

This example is just one way to make your Web pages more interesting and interactive. Just about anything is possible, the VBScript or JavaScript is the heart

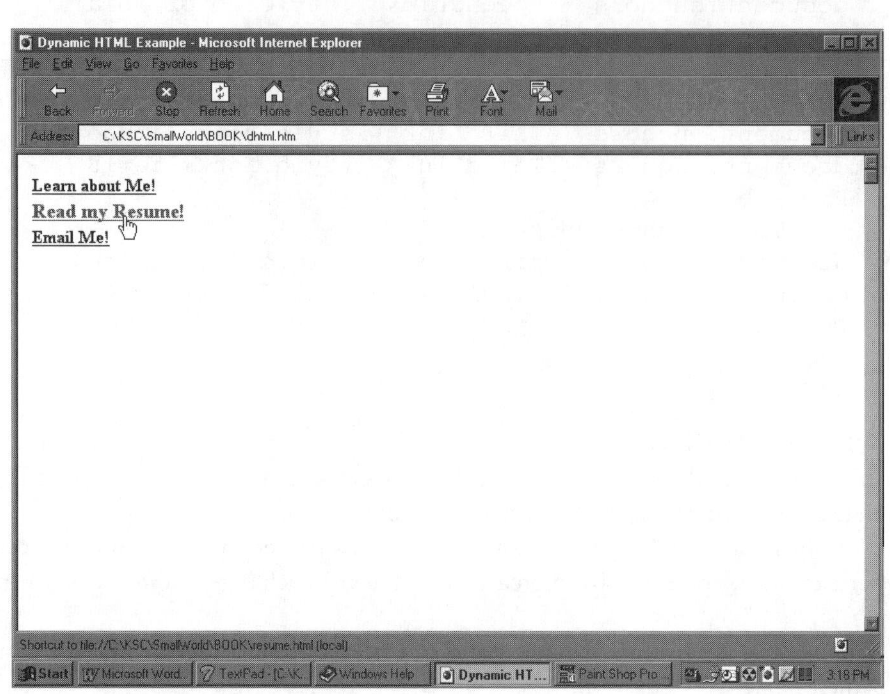

Figure 14.1 The Example Dynamic HTML Code Creates This Effect in the Internet Explorer 4.0 Browser

of the effect you want to create. As always, keep your audience in mind when constructing Dynamic HTML for your pages. Glaring color and font changes may not be appropriate for your Web site or your users. Dynamic HTML is a very large leap forward in Web page development; if Dynamic HTML is widely accepted by the Web community, pages will behave more like CD-ROMs than the traditional, static Web pages we are accustomed to.

Microsoft is actively working with several third-party software vendors, including Macromedia, Inprise, and SoftQuad, to create tools that target Dynamic HTML. Assuming that the Microsoft Dynamic HTML proposal is accepted and adopted by the W3C, Dynamic HTML could be very big indeed.

For more information on the W3C group dedicated to developing the Document Object Model, visit the WC3 Web site at http://www.w3.org/pub/WWW/MarkUp/DOM/. For more information on Microsoft Dynamic HTML, including more sample code like the preceding example, consult Microsoft's Web site at http://www.microsoft.com/sitebuilder/workshop/author/dhtml/.

HTML-Based Online Help Systems

As HTML comes into greater use on the desktop environment as well as on the Web, more uses are being devised for it. As a result, you can expect HTML to crop up in online help systems—the type of information you can get from a program while clicking on the Help menu. Online help typically provides information on how to use the program, points out tips, tricks, and other features of the program, and usually provides an index to enable a user to look up information quickly and easily.

This impending change to HTML-based help systems comes at a time when more and more software manufacturers are trying to reduce costs by eliminating printed manuals for their programs. As a result, online help is expected to carry more of the burden of providing help to end-users of the program.

Initially, HTML seems like an ideal medium for producing online help. HTML is designed to be hyperlinked, and this is a feature used in all online help systems to move from one related topic to another easily. Generally, this also means that links can be located both on the local hard drive and on the Web, where information can be updated continually. It is also able to present information in multiple frames, can display images, and through the use of image-maps can produce a version of context-sensitive help.

However, there are a number of features present in current online help systems that are not easy to reproduce by standard HTML alone. One of these is indexing—how do you easily produce a list of indexable terms and keywords? How do you provide context-sensitive help so that a user can find information on a topic when needed? Many help systems also utilize such things as pop-up windows and click-on "What's This" type help, which cannot be reproduced by HTML alone.

There are plans from several software vendors to meet the challenges of producing an HTML-based online help system that retains as many features as possible that are already present in current help systems, and leverage the benefits inherent in HTML to the best possible effect.

At the time of this writing, the industry's focus is upon two main competing help systems: Microsoft's HTML Help, and Netscape's NetHelp2. This is followed up by some interesting developments by other software manufacturers, especially JavaSoft's JavaHelp.

This section provides a brief glimpse into the challenges facing both the software vendors making these products and the technical writers who will have to write their online documentation to fit the demands of the specific system for which they are writing.

Netscape's NetHelp2

NetHelp2 is Netscape's attempt to create an open standards-based platform for creating and viewing HTML-based online help.

Netscape found itself in a situation where they needed to provide online help for their various products that could work across a wide range of platforms. Since no other solution was available at the time, they developed their own—NetHelp. Originally used within Netscape Navigator 3.0, NetHelp provides a context-sensitive online help solution for any Web-based application or native Macintosh, Unix, or Windows program. Additionally, by the cross-platform nature of HTML and NetHelp, any help system created using this system could be used on any other without recompilation.

The main idea behind NetHelp is that since a majority of Web surfers already have Netscape Navigator, why not use it as the medium to deliver online help to these users as well? By choosing Netscape Navigator (Figure 14.2), the help author does not have to license a help viewer program that would have to be shipped along with their product, and it could access the HTML extensions, Java, JavaScript, and plug-ins used by Navigator.

The chief advantages to NetHelp over other schemes is that, unlike Microsoft's HTML Help, Netscape's NetHelp can be used across different platforms, since Netscape Navigator exists for many more operating systems than does Internet Explorer.

NetHelp2 came about a year after the initial release of the original NetHelp. It includes new features like a URL designator for calling NetHelp2 from HTML, Java, JavaScript, or native applications, a collapsable table of contents, keyword indexing tools, plus support for Dynamic HTML and CSS.

There are two basic models that help authors can choose from when designing online help systems using NetHelp2. NetHelp2 can either be run from within a native application or separately from a Web page. Both formats use a frameset file, which is a Web page that incorporates frame elements and then loads the requested help information and help navigational tools (powered by a JavaScript) within a separate window. The main difference between the two methods is that when launched from within an application, context-sensitive help can be invoked.

To start creating a NetHelp2-based online help system, you will first have to download a copy of the NetHelp Software Development Kit (SDK). Versions of the

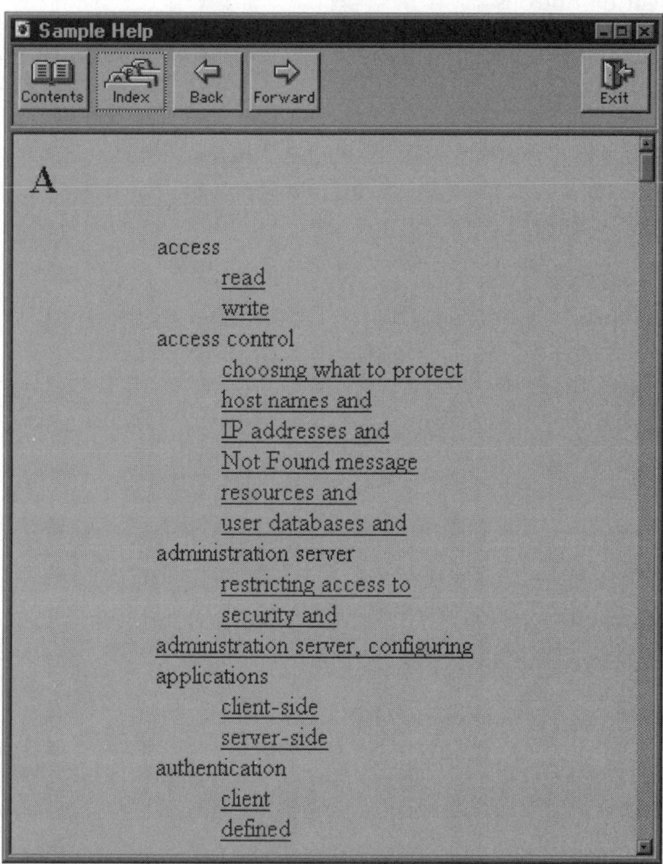

Figure 14.2 Netscape's NetHelp Displayed

NetHelp2 SDK for Unix, Macintosh, and 32-bit MS Windows systems can be found at http://home.netscape.com/eng/help/home/home.htm.

Once you have obtained the NetHelp2 SDK, you have to create the user interface. You can use the simple two-frame example provided in the SDK, as in Figure 14.3.

The two-frame window that appears when the Help button is clicked is created from three separate HTML files:

- help.htm, which is the frameset file that tells navigator to split the window into two named rows, each given a specific size

- navbar.htm, which is the file loaded into the top frame that contains the navigation buttons
- helptopics.htm, which is the file loaded into the bottom frame that contains the Help topic

The help.htm file is the frameset file that holds the files that display the navigation bar and the help topic. It is a very simple frame file consisting of the following code:

```
<FRAMESET ROWS='52,*'>
     <FRAME SRC="navbar.html" SCROLLING=no
MARGINWIDTH=0 MARGINHEIGHT=0 NAME="buttons">
     <FRAME SRC="about:blank" NAME="topic">
</FRAMESET>
```

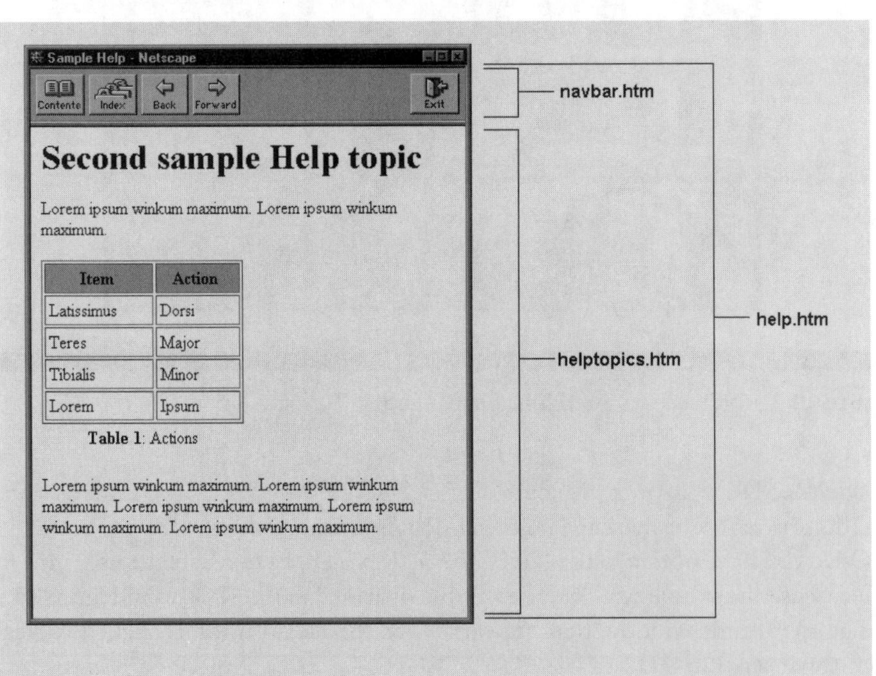

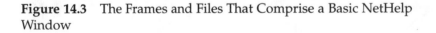

Figure 14.3 The Frames and Files That Comprise a Basic NetHelp Window

It creates two frames and loads their respective content.

The navbar.htm file contains several .GIF images of navigational buttons, and points to JavaScript code to make them functional, as shown in the following example.

```
<TABLE WIDTH=100%>
     <TR><TD ALIGN="left" VALIGN="top">
     <A HREF="contents.html" TARGET="topic">
<IMG SRC="images/content1.gif" BORDER=0 HEIGHT=37
WIDTH=44></A>
     <A HREF="index.html" TARGET="topic">
<IMG SRC="images/index1.gif" BORDER=0 HEIGHT=37
WIDTH=44></A>
     <A
HREF="javascript:parent.frames[1].history.go(-1)">
<IMG SRC="images/back1.gif" BORDER=0 HEIGHT=37
WIDTH=44></A>
     <A
HREF="javascript:parent.frames[1].history.go(1)">
<IMG SRC="images/forward1.gif" BORDER=0 HEIGHT=37
WIDTH=44></A>
     </TD>
<TD ALIGN="right" VALIGN="top">
     <A HREF="javascript:top.close()">
<IMG SRC="images/exit1.gif" BORDER=0></A>
     </TD>
     </TR>
     </TABLE>
```

The interesting aspect of this code is the embedded JavaScript code, which calls a history list when the Back button is clicked (using <A HREF="javascript:parent.frames[1].history.go(-1)">) to be loaded into the lower frame. Similarly, clicking on the Forward button causes the next topic in the history list to get loaded into the lower frame, using the JavaScript code <A HREF="javascript:parent.frames[1].go(1)">. When the user wants to exit the help window, JavaScript is called again (<A HREF="javascript:top.close()">) to close the window.

The helptopics.htm file contains regular HTML and the help content—no new tags or anything out of the ordinary is required. Simply create a separate HTML page for each topic you want to cover, using all of the HTML tags and features available in Netscape Navigator.

If you design the help system to launch from outside of the application, then all you have to specify is the URL of the frameset file, which in turn loads the appropriate help topic. If it is designed to be launched from within an application,

a separate file, called a project file, has to be set up first. The project file is where the operation of the help system is defined, and is a text file that specifies the settings of the help system and maps various topic IDs to the URLs of specific help topic pages. The following is an example of a small project file.

```
                ;       Sample NetHelp Example Project File
                WINDOW-NAME="My NetHelp Example"
                WINDOW-SIZE="400,400"
                <FRAME GROUP SRC = "reference.htm"
    DEFAULT WINDOW="help">

                <ID MAP>
                ;       FILE MENU
                135670 = "helppage1.htm": target="topic"
                135671 = "helppage2.htm": target="topic"
                135672 = "helppage3.htm": target="topic"
                135673 = "helppage4.htm": target="topic"

                ;       TOOLS MENU
                16000 = "helppage5.htm": target="topic"
                16001 = "helppage6.htm": target="topic"
                16002 = "helppage7.htm": target="topic"
                16003 = "helppage8.htm": target="topic"
                </ID MAP>
```

The initial line is a comment describing the contents of the file—all lines that begin with a semicolon (;) are ignored by the browser. It is often useful to include information about the project file in comments such as this. The next few lines describe and define the size of the help window to appear. WINDOW-NAME works in the same manner as does the more familiar <TITLE> tag, and WINDOW-SIZE sets the width and height, respectively, of the window, and the FRAME-GROUP SRC line specifies the URL of the frameset file. The real nuts-and-bolts of the help file begins with the <ID_MAP> container tag, which maps out a help ID to a corresponding URL. Once all of the help Web pages are mapped in this manner, the application developer inserts the project file within the program so that it is launched by an end-user seeking help on the product.

NetHelp2 has a number of features to recommend itself; for those writers already familiar with Netscape's brand of HTML, this help system requires little new knowledge. The improved functions and features in NetHelp2, and the fact that it is freely available make it a good choice for many potential online Help authors. Microsoft has a strong lead in the online Help authoring tools market, and will likely dominate the field, but NetHelp2 is a good alternative.

Microsoft's HTML Help

The odds-on favorite, Microsoft has ambitious plans for its HTML-based online help system, called HTML Help. Microsoft's WinHelp is the current leader and de facto standard for online help systems for 16- and 32-bit MS Windows systems—if you've used an MS Windows program and you've used online help, you've used WinHelp. A whole mini-industry has grown up around WinHelp, and supplies help authors with the tools necessary to create professional-looking online help files quickly and easily. It was therefore something of a shock to this community when Microsoft announced that it would be switching to an HTML-based online help system shortly after setting a recent standard for Windows 95-style online help. However, because of widespread industry support for WinHelp, most people's eyes are on Microsoft's take on their HTML-based online help system.

The current version of WinHelp incorporates many functions not easily reproducible with pure HTML alone. A Windows program using all of the features on WinHelp contains rich context-sensitive help, extensive indexing capabilities, pop-up help tip windows, click-on "What's This" type help, and many other features. Microsoft plans to make HTML Help as feature-rich as WinHelp.

WinHelp relies on a number of interconnecting files. Keywords are contained within a rich text file (.rtf) file, the table of contents are written to WinHelp Contents files (.cnt), and individual project files, which keep track of all of the files contained within an online help system, are written to a WinHelp project file (.hpj). In addition to these files are the bitmapped image files (.bmp and .wmp) referenced by the other files. Considering the complicated procedures behind it, creating effective online documentation using WinHelp is something of an artform, but it is highly versatile and effective. Considerable investment has been made by many software companies to use WinHelp, so Microsoft's alternative HTML Help will have to live up to the expectations of the extensive audience of WinHelp authors.

Similarly, HTML Help consists of many different components that work together, and it relies broadly upon the technologies incorporated into Internet Explorer 3.0. HTML Help consists of five main components: the HTML Help ActiveX control, a layout engine, the HTML Help window, compressed HTML and, for help authors, the Microsoft HTML Help Workshop.

The HTML Help ActiveX Control provides a navigational user interface containing the table of contents, index, and related functions. Not only can this be used for online help systems, but Web authors will also be able to use it on their Web sites to deliver detailed help to the viewer on demand. The layout engine is a tool used to layout the different parts of the help display along with the HTML Help Window, which displays HTML in a customized, resizable window. All of the files ultimately used by HTML Help are compressed to reducing disk space, and processed in such a way that full-text search indexes can be performed on its contents.

Online help authors will need the Microsoft HTML Help Workshop, which is an authoring kit for HTML Help containing the tools necessary for creating and maintaining an HTML Help-based system. It and further information on HTML can be obtained through Microsoft's HTML Help site at http://www.microsoft.com/workshop/author/htmlhelp/.

Web pages (Figure 14.4) follow the standard format—no special tags or attributes need to be added. Using the Microsoft HTML Help Workshop, the help author then needs to create a project file, index, and table of contents files. Constructing these individual files are all handled by wizards from within the Microsoft HTML Help Workshop. It is also used to add ActiveX controls or other functionality to specific topics. The ActiveX control is the heart of the system. It contains all of the extra functionality to make this a robust online help system, including the ability to add pop-up help, indexing capabilities, and many other functions. The resulting HTML files are then compressed, and then can be tested.

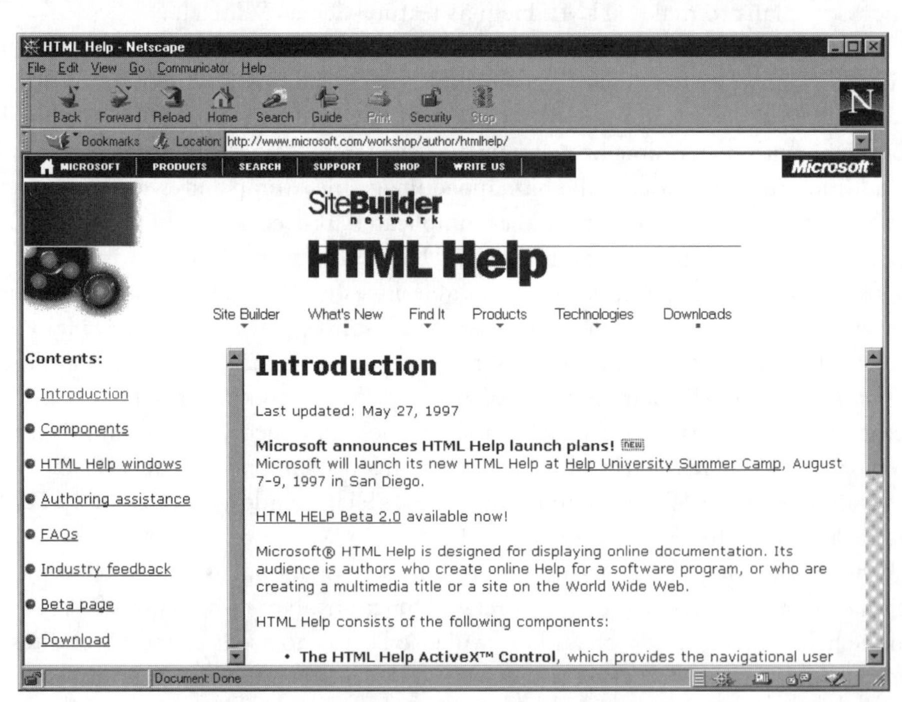

Figure 14.4 The Microsoft HTML Help Web Page

Note: Information on the operating characteristics of HTML Help are still somewhat sketchy at the time of this writing, but Microsoft intends to use standard HTML tags. All the tags you will need to use include the following:

```
<P> . . .</P>
<A> . . .</A>
    HREF=" . . ."
    NAME= . . .
<IMG> . . .</IMG>
    SRC=" . . ."
    BORDER= . . .
    ALIGN= . . .

<B> . . .</B>
<I> . . .</I>
<U> . . .</U>
<BR>
<UL> . . .</UL>
<OL> . . .</OL>
<LI> . . .</LI>
<FONT> . . .</FONT>
    FACE=" . . .:"
    SIZE= . . .
    COLOR= . . .
<HR>
    SIZE= . . .
    COLOR= . . .
    ALIGN= . . .
```

In addition to these tags, you can use any other tag supported by Internet Explorer.

There are a number of pluses and minuses to HTML Help. Since Microsoft has set the standards for online help in the past and is putting a lot of effort into HTML Help, it will likely be widely adopted. Since it is dependent on the technologies first incorporated with Internet Explorer 3.0—and especially ActiveX—it will only be available for computing platforms that can utilize ActiveX files. Microsoft's stated plans are to release HTML Help to Windows 95/NT, and then for the Macintosh, Unix, and Microsoft Windows 3.1 operating systems.

Note: Given the complexity of WinHelp and the time and expense invested in existing online systems that utilize it, there are many firms that aim to provide conversion utilities to take the raw WinHelp files and convert them to the new HTML Help standard.

The following is a list of a few of the companies that either plan on producing utilities that will support HTML Help, or already do so: Note that since HTML Help is still in a prerelease stage at the time of this writing, you will be unable to build full HTML Help systems until the final HTML Help SDK is released.

Help-to-HTML Converter and RoboHELP 4.0 by Blue Sky Software, is at http://www.blue-sky.com/.

HTMhelp, NextHelp and HyperText Suite by HyperAct Inc. is at http://www.hyperact.com/.

IntraWeb by Virtual Media Technology Ltd. is at http://www.virtualmedia.com.au/.

JavaHelp

There is a third possibility for HTML-based online help systems: JavaHelp, a platform/browser-independent online help solution from JavaSoft, the subsidiary of Sun Microsystems in charge of producing the Java programming language (Figure 14.5). JavaHelp is designed to deliver online help for Java-based applications. However, as the use of Java is expected by many to become pervasive in the next few years, JavaHelp has the potential to become a serious contender in the battle for HTML-based online help systems.

You can find more information about JavaHelp at http://www.javasoft.com/products/javahelp/index.html.

One of the main features that makes JavaHelp a potentially desirable option is the fact that Java is a fully cross-platform technology, so a single version of an online help system made using JavaHelp could be used on almost any operating system. Furthermore, the help content and user interface will appear identical in all environments. It is not dependent on a single operating system or browser to operate—as long as Java can be run on a system, then so can JavaHelp.

JavaHelp essentially embeds a browser within the program that it serves. The JavaHelp browser features the controls familiar to most browser users: buttons to go back or forward, an optional URL field, a print feature, and a menu reserved for making bookmarks. The browser and all of its components are all rendered

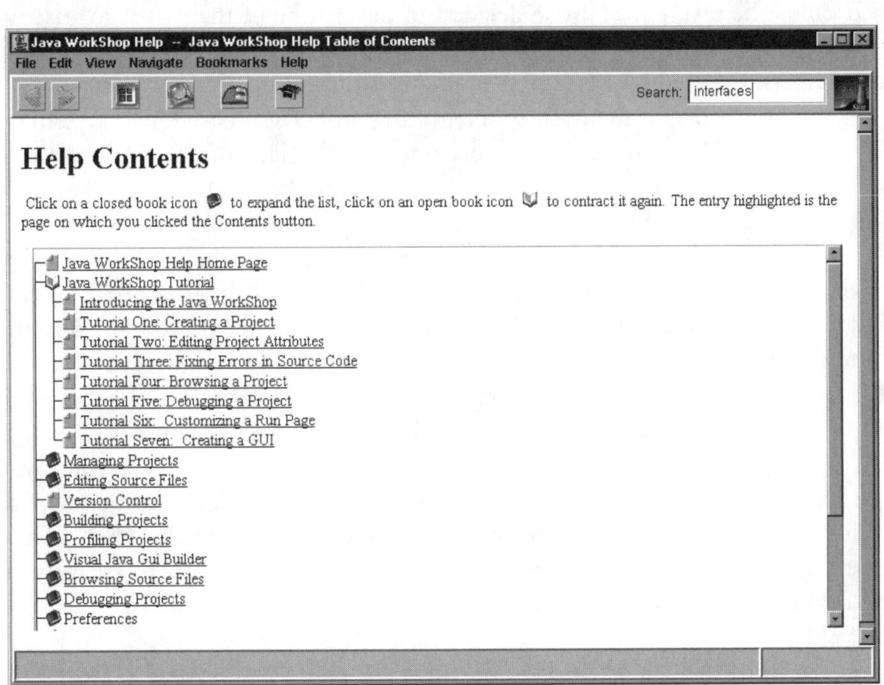

Figure 14.5 The JavaHelp Window Displayed

using Java applets, which enable such functions as a Table of Contents, an Index feature and a Search field. There is also the potential for help authors familiar with the Java programming language to augment the program by adding Java applets either within the body of the help display, or by adding new navigational features. It also implements full text searching capabilities across the HTML files within its documentation set. Since the help-viewer is a full-fledged Web browser in its own right, help authors can use URLs that point to documents contained on the Web. This feature is particularly useful in those cases where a link to ever-changing and topical information is desirable.

Keep in mind that this particular online help system is still in its early stages, and significant changes are likely to occur as it is further refined. Expect it to play a significant role in the online help systems used by Java-based programs and IDEs.

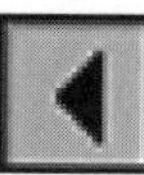

Inprise's JBuilder HTML Help System In the absence of any fully tested HTML-based online help system, Inprise decided to devise one of their own for use with their JBuilder product, an Integrated Development Environment (IDE) for Java programmers.

One likely reason for the push to integrating an HTML-based help system with this product instead of adopting the more traditional Microsoft WinHelp authoring system, is that it would reduce a large amount of duplicate effect on behalf of the programmers creating JBuilder and the technical writers documenting it.

The documentation process for Java programs is unique; the comments inserted into the Java programs by the programmers can be run through a program called javadoc. This program automatically takes all of the comments contained in these files and generates reams of HTML files that document the individual parts that make up a Java program. It is a very efficient process, but to turn the resulting HTML files into another file format containing the same amount of information takes a lot of hand-tooling. Any edits that take place in the meantime by the programmer would mean potentially having to regenerate large amounts of file, which would also then have to be converted by hand. As a result, when javadoc-generated files are necessary in an online help system it is simpler to keep them in their original HTML format.

Link: javadoc comes with the Java Development Kit, which can be found at http://java.sun.com:80/products/jdk/1.1.

A page of Frequently Asked Questions about javadoc can be found at http://java.sun.com:80/products/jdk/faq/javado cfaq.html.

To see an example of javadoc-created information, see the Java API Web pages, which can be found at http://java.sun.com:80/products/jdk/1.1/docs/a pi/packages.html.

The only requirements the JBuilder online HTML docs required was a certain organization of the HTML contained within each Web page, and a modified comment tag that designed to contain indexing information.

Whenever a heading in the documentation is set, two other sets of tags are associated with it. Immediately prior to the heading a unique named anchor tag is added. After the heading comes Borland's modified comment tag, which contains indexing information about the topic being covered. The following example illustrates how this looks.

```
<A NAME="huphalumps and wumphahoozles"> </A>
<H2>Info On Huphalumps and Wumphahoozles</H2>
```

```
<!--BNDX="Huphalumps:information
about"mphahoozles:information about"-->
```

The slightly altered comment tag (<!--BNDX=".."-->) is the indexing tag that JBuilder's indexing program recognizes. It is able to take two separate indexing clauses separated by a semicolon, which can each take a main index entry and a single subindex entry (i.e., "Huphalumps:information about").

When this is run through a program that compiles and assembles an HTML index, the final results can be seen through what is, in effect, a miniature Web browser. When somebody clicks on an index entry, it takes the user to the Web page containing the anchor named (i.e., <A NAME="huphalumps_and_wumphahoozles">, </A>).

The system employed within JBuilder's HTML-based on-line help system is simple to employ and simple to use (see Figures 14.6 and 14.7). It requires minor

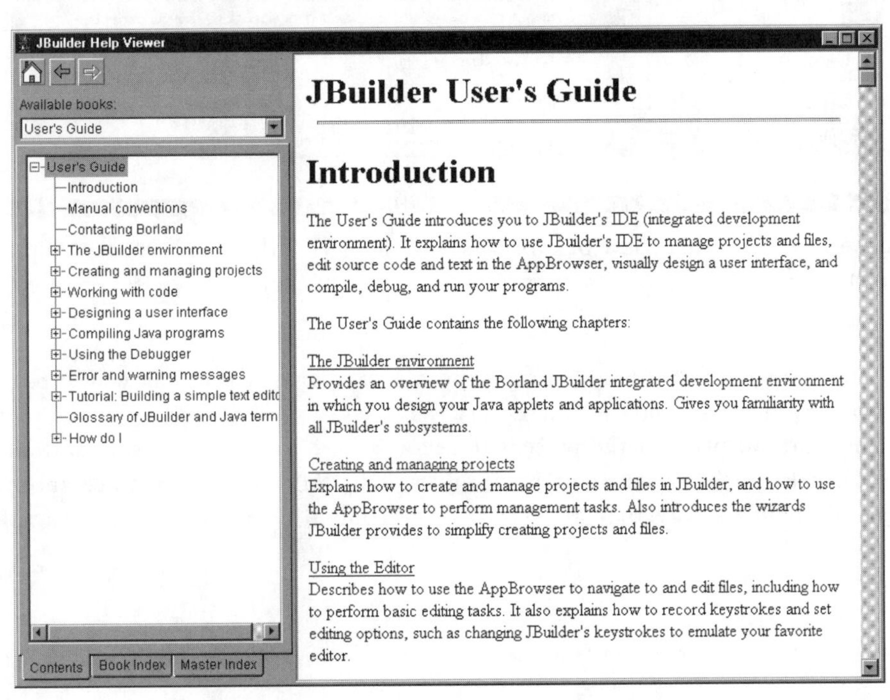

Figure 14.6 A View of Inprise's JBuilder's HTML-Based Online Help System Copyright © 1998. Inprise Corporation. Used with permission.

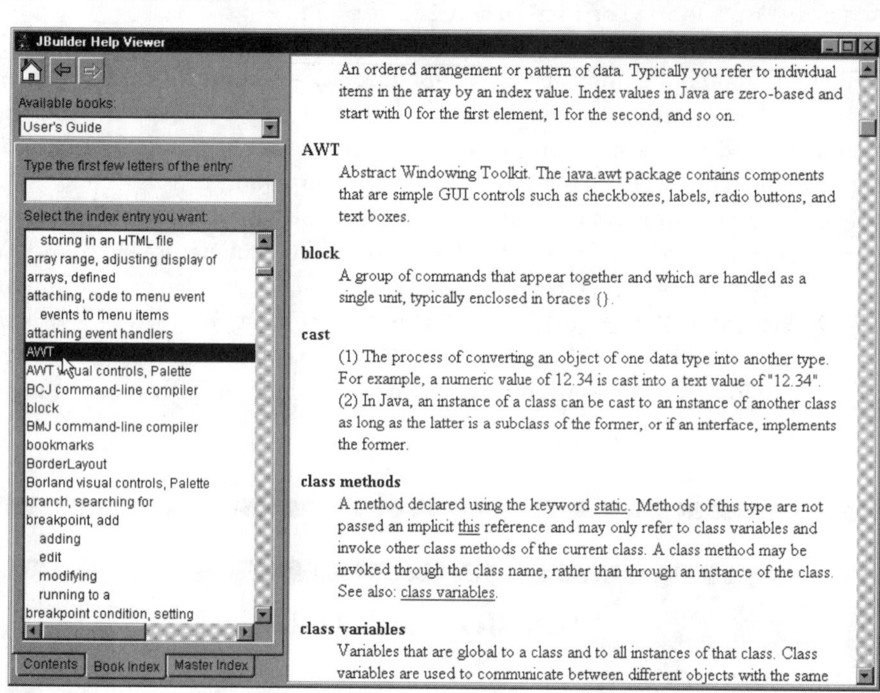

Figure 14.7 Another View of Inprise's JBuilder's HTML-Based Online Help System

modifications to the HTML that typically. already exists within many Web pages, so conversion to Borland's format is relatively easy.

There are no plans at the present time for Inprise to present this as an online HTML help system outside of its JBuilder IDE, but it does illustrate another, relatively painless way that an HTML-based online help system can be implemented.

CHAPTER 15

Sound File Types and Formats

With the development of the first multimedia computers came the first sound file formats. Over the years a myriad of sound file formats have been devised for such things as CD-ROM presentations, music files for digitally based instruments, voice communication, and digital speech synthesis for the blind. The World Wide Web is simply the latest in a long line of computer-based applications to adopt the use of sound.

Unfortunately, there is no consensus on how to "display" sound on the Web, and as a result there is a proliferation of ways and means to insert sound within a Web page. This is further complicated by the fact that the two leading browser manufacturers, Netscape and Microsoft, have adopted ways of playing sound that differ from each other.

To understand how digital audio works on the Web, you have to understand

some basics about digital audio. There are two basic sound file types: recorded and synthesized sound.

In the digital world, all recorded audio data can be defined by the following characteristics:

- Sampling rate in samples per second
- Number of bits used to record each sample
- Number of channels of sound

The sampling rate of a sound is the number of times that a sound is divided up, measured, and recorded. Digitized sounds are typically recorded in the thousands of samples per second, and are often referred to in kiloHertz (kHz), which refers to the thousands of cycles (read: samples) per second that are recorded. We hear sound as an analog waveform: sound is not chopped up into little digital bits, but instead presents itself as a continuous experience to us. To replicate this experience as much as possible, the smaller and more numerous the samples per second, the closer digital sound comes to recreating the natural analog experience of sound.

When you speak to somebody on the telephone, you are listening to a relatively low sample rate of 8,000 samples per second. If you have a Macintosh with a microphone, by default it records at 22,050 samples per second. When you listen to a music CD, you are listening to sound recorded at 44,100 samples per second, twice that of the Macintosh default. If you are one of the few people who acquired a Digital Audio Tape (DAT) machine, you are listening to sound recorded at 48,000. For audio purists, there are new audiophile music CD standards being considered that would sample at roughly twice as many times as the current standard—at over 88,000 samples per second. Audiophiles consider this sampling rate close to the sound reproduction of analog recordings, like the century-old technology behind the production of vinyl records.

There's more to digital sound recording than sampling rates—there's also the number of bits used to record each sample of sound. The bit rate determines how "fine" or "granular" the sound that is being recorded. Typically, most sound formats are recorded at either 8 bits or 16 bits. A 16-bit value for a sound can render a much closer approximation to the original sound than an 8 bit number can. However, more bits means more memory is required to record the resulting number. Though a typical sound recorded with 8 bits at a low sampling rate may not sound terrific, it takes up a lot less memory than the same sound recorded at 16 bits per second at a higher sample rate. In everyday use, there are inevitable tradeoffs when it comes to digitally recording sound—the more samples used per second, the greater the amount of memory needed to record the sound.

Another characteristic of digital sound is the number of channels it uses. A single channel of sound is used for mono sound, and two channels are used for stereo. More channels can be used for such things as surround-sound effects, though for the most part few digital sound file formats you are likely to encounter on the Web are likely to hold more than two channels. This is because the size of the sound file increases dramatically with each channel added.

Much of the same sort of information is contained within synthesized music files. The key difference is that the data stored in the synthesized music file is customized for the device designed to play it back. Information is often handled in a different manner; whereas recorded sound is often played back in a linear fashion, synthesized files may contain information on such musical characteristics as volume, sustain, and attack. Thus, less information is actually needed to reproduce the sound through a synthesized playback machine.

To illustrate this, say you want to reproduce the sound of a high note of a flute for five seconds. If the sound is being digitally recorded, the sound of a flute is digitized over the course of five seconds, and the resulting sound file contains as much information it is capable of in reproducing the sound. A synthesized music file may instead simply instruct to play the flute sound at a certain volume and intensity for five seconds. There are two important consequences of the two different sound file formats used: file size and sound fidelity. Since the synthesized sound file contains only information that is tailor-made for the music playback processor, a lot less data is required to produce the required sound. A synthesized sound file format is typically much smaller in file size than an equivalent, digitally recorded sound file. However, the trade-off is in fidelity—a synthesized flute usually *sounds* like a synthesized flute, because it doesn't contain the rich variances in tonal quality that are captured by the digitally recorded equivalent. Whenever you are choosing a sound file format, the inevitable trade-off you will make will be file size verses fidelity, and this is true not only between digitally recorded and synthetic file types, but between different variations of each.

Ever since the release of Netscape Navigator 3.0, sound is played through a built-in plug-in component called Live-Audio, which can play the following sound file formats: .wav, .au, .mid/.midi, and .aiff/.aif. Similarly, Microsoft built an audio player into Internet Explorer 3.0, which supports the .au, .snd, .mid/.midi, .wav, .aiff/.aif, and .aifc sound file formats. The sound file formats the two have in common are: .aiff, .au, .mid/.midi, and .wav. Most of these sound file formats are digitally recorded sound file formats; the .mid/.midi file format is the only synthesized sound file format available (see Table 15.1).

Here's a quick summary of the sound file formats commonly used on the Web:

Table 15.1 Sound File Formats Supported by Netscape Navigator and Internet Explorer (Versions 3.0 and Higher)

	Netscape Navigator	*Internet Explorer*
.au	X	X
.aif/.aiff	X	X
.aifc		X
.mid/.midi	X	
.snd		X
.wav	X	X

- .aiff/.aif—(Audio Interchange File Format) A popular sound file format common to several operating systems. Digital sound file format.
- .aifc—A sound file format that is essentially the same as .aiff/.aif, but is compressed. Digital sound file format.
- .au—A sound file format first used on SUN/NeXT computers, but has become popular on other, more common operating systems. Digital sound file format.
- .snd—A sound file format used primarily on Macintosh computers. Digital sound file format.
- .midi/.mid—A sound file format readily understood by sound applications for both Macintosh and MS-Windows computers. Synthesized sound file format.
- .wav—A sound format used primarily by MS-Windows computers. Has easily become the most popular sound file formats on the Web.

Of all these sound file formats, the .wav file format has easily become the most popular, if only because of the proliferation of Web surfers using windows-based browsers.

Link: There are plenty of places on the Web devoted to archiving sound files. Here are a few of the larger and more interesting sites you can find:

Eric's MIDI Collection

http://home.hwsys.com/users/erics/midi/midi.htm

A large collection of digitized tunes you can listen to.

Sound America

http://soundamerica.com/

A massive site composed primarily of *.wav* format files, containing such things as animal noises, sounds from TV shows and movies, and much more.

The Daily .WAV

http://www.dailywav.com/

A new .wav file for your listening pleasure every day!

SunSITE Index of Sounds

http://sunsite.sut.ac.jp/multimed/sounds/

Sound effects, commercials, whales, birds, and other miscellaneous sounds are available here. Composed primarily of .au files.

The rest of this chapter looks at the ways that these sound file formats can be incorporated within a Web page.

BACKGROUND SOUND

Sound can augment the graphics and text on a page. It can effectively set a mood for a Web page, or provide an extra cue to users navigating your Web site. Unfortunately, the creators of the two most popular browsers have not been able to come to an agreement on how to implement sound on their Web pages. This section looks at how Internet Explorer has implemented their own sound HTML tag.

There's some interesting background to the development of Microsoft's background sound tag. It is derived largely from the little known (and much less used) <SOUND> tag that was implemented within NCSA Mosaic.

This empty tag was never officially implemented within any HTML specification—it could be found only within NCSA Mosaic. The <SOUND> tag played only .wav sound files, and the Web author could specify that the sounded be played a certain number of times, or that it play continuously. The <SOUND> tag was adopted in a slightly altered format as the <BGSOUND> tag when Microsoft launched Internet Explorer 2.0.

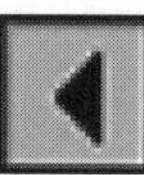

<BGSOUND>

Element name: Background sound tag.

Description: Inserts a background sound into a Web page.

Attributes:

SRC= *filename.wav*
Specifies the path and filename of a sound file (.wav, .au, or .mid format can be used).
LOOP= *number* | *INFINITE*
Specifies the number of times a sound is played.
DELAY= *number*
The number of seconds to delay before playing the sound file.
VOLUME= *number*
The volume level of the sound file. 0 is the loudest, and 10000 produces zero volume output. 0 is the default value.
BALANCE= *number*
Specifies the sound output in a stereo situation. 10000 outputs 100% to the right speaker and 10000 outputs 100% to the left speaker. The default value, 0, balances the output.

Sample:

```
<BGSOUND SRC="honk.wav" LOOP=infinite>
```

Like Mosaic's <SOUND> tag, Internet Explorer's <BGSOUND> tag is an empty tag that enables Web authors to insert a background sound into a Web page.

An addition to being able to play .wav format sound files, <BGSOUND> is also capable of playing the .au and MIDI format (.mid or .midi) sound files. More properly, Internet Explorer is able to interpret and play these sound files to the user; if Microsoft updates Internet Explorer's capabilities, in the future it may be able to play other sound file formats directly.

The LOOP attribute tells the browser how many times it should play the sound file. If LOOP=INFINITE, Internet Explorer continually plays the specified sound file.

Up until the advent of Internet Explorer 4.0, it generally has been recommended that Web authors place any <BGSOUND> tag they use at the bottom of a Web page. If the tag is inserted at or near the top of the document, the browser loads the sound file before processing the rest of the Web page. This may cause a seemingly inexplicable delay to the user viewing your page, who may then be prompted to leave. By placing it at the end of a Web page (just before the end </BODY> tag), the user can read the rest of your Web page while the sound loads. With the advent of Internet Explorer 4.0, it is recommended that any <BGSOUND>

sound tags in a Web page be placed within the <HEAD> container tag—in other words, at the very top of the Web page! They may seem to go against common sense, but Internet Explorer 4.0 seems to load both the sound file and the content of the rest of the Web page without any noticeable delay. It also appears as though Internet Explorer 4.0 will still play sounds contained within a <BGSOUND> tag even if it is not placed within the header of a Web page. Choose where to place the sound file that best suits your audience.

It is recommended that Web authors use background sounds sparingly. When they are implemented within a Web page, try to keep the file size of the sound file small to reduce the amount of time needed for a user to download them. If you are trying to produce a musical background, try using a MIDI file format. As a synthesized file format, MIDI files are inherently small, and pack a lot of information in them. If you have to use a recorded sound file format, try to keep it as small as possible. If you have a large recorded sound file, you can use a sound program to manipulate the file so as to reduce its size; changing a stereo file to mono or reducing its sample rate can bring enormous reductions in file size. (For more information on sound programs, including digital sound recorders, see Chapter 18, "Web Tools: Building a Web Author's Tool Chest").

Try not to use annoying or shocking sounds (unless that is your intent with the Web page). Keep in mind that the <BGSOUND> tag does not give the user any user-interface or other options to control how the sound should be played. Don't make the sound so annoying that you drive users away—something that is very easy to do with sound.

Tip: The HTML 4.0 specification strongly encourages Web authors to use the <OBJECT> tag to add sound and other media features to Web pages. For detailed information about the <OBJECT> tag, please see Chapter 10, "Miscellaneous Elements."

EMBEDDED SOUND

Netscape Navigator takes a very different approach to sound than Internet Explorer. Web designers can insert a sound into a Web page by using the <EMBED> tag. The <EMBED> tag (discussed in detail in Chapter 10, "Miscellaneous Elements") is a general-purpose tag that allows Netscape Navigator to display a plug-in. When Netscape Navigator comes across an <EMBED> tag designed to play a sound file, it does one of two things:

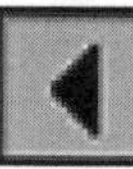

- It launches a program called LiveAudio (included with Netscape Navigator since version 3.0) designed to play sound files using the .aiff, .au, .mid/.midi, or .wav sound file formats.
- It looks for a the plug-in program designed to play the embedded sound file. If it finds it, it plays the file. If it does not find the player, then it asks the user whether or not to download the appropriate player.

Figures 15.1 and 15.2 display the effects of each scenario.

In either case, once the sound file is loaded and appropriate sound player is running, it displays a separate control panel that allows the user to control how the sound is played.

Embedding a sound file format that is recognized by Netscape's LiveAudio player within a Web page is easy. All that is needed to display a simple Web page that will launch LiveAudio is the following:

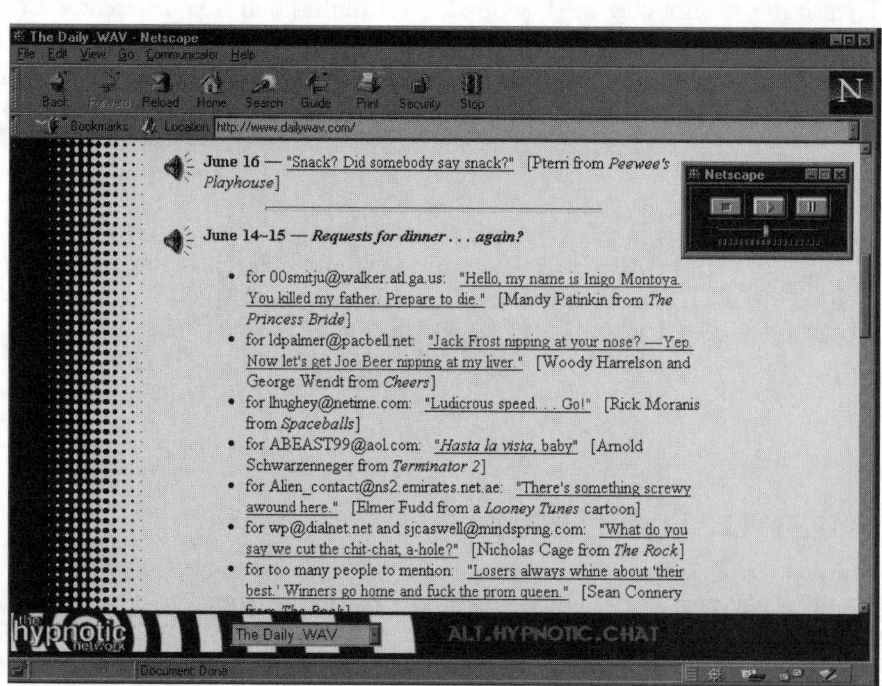

Figure 15.1 The LiveAudio player Is Invoked as a Sound Is Played

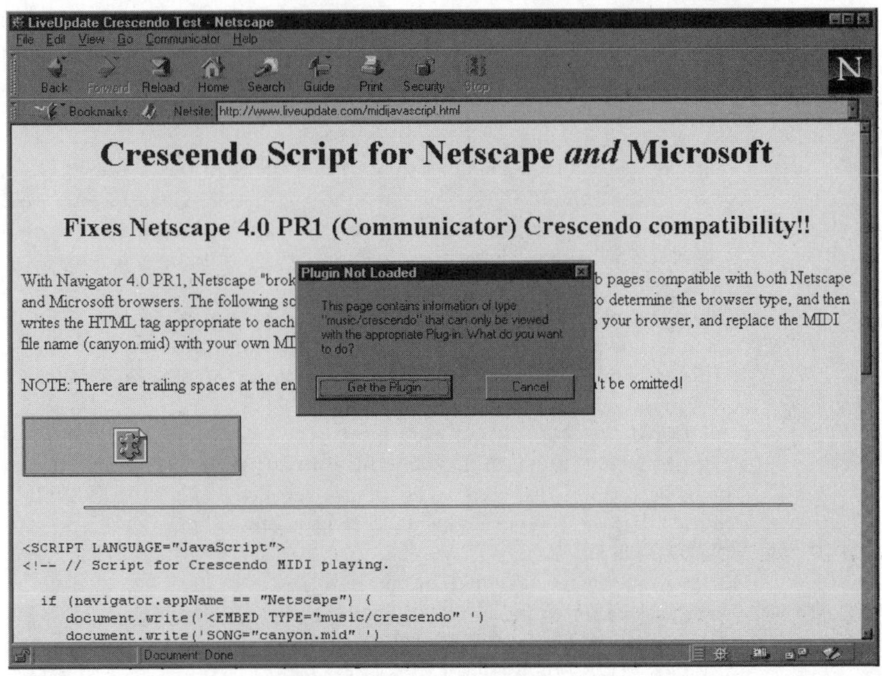

Figure 15.2 The User Is Prompted to Download the Crescendo Sound Player

```
<EMBED SRC=godzilla1.wav WIDTH=144 HEIGHT=60
AUTOSTART=TRUE>
```

This displays the screen shown in Figure 15.3 within a Web page.

Like any other plug-in inserted into a Web page using the <EMBED> tag, there are a number of parameters that can be defined that are specific to the plug-in being inserted. A listing of the attributes that can be used with the LiveAudio player follows.

<EMBED> (LiveAudio Attributes Only)

SRC= *filename.wav*
The filename of the source sound file. Can be .aiff, .au, .mid/.midi, or .wav file formats.
AUTOSTART= *TRUE | FALSE*

When set to TRUE enables the file to play automatically when the Web page is loaded. Default value is FALSE.

LOOP= # | *TRUE* | *FALSE*

When set to TRUE begins to play continuously until the stop button is clicked on the console or the user goes to another page. If a number value is inserted, the sound repeats the number of times indicated.

STARTTIME= *mm:ss*

Sets the time when the sound file should begin playback after loading. If you want to begin the sound at 1 minute 30 seconds after the page has been loaded, you would set the value to 01:30. This attribute works only for Netscape Navigator running on Windows 95, Windows NT, and Macintosh.

ENDTIME= *mm:ss*

Sets the time the sound file should stop playing. If you want to begin the sound at 2 minutes and 35 seconds after the page has been loaded, you would set the value to 02:35. This attribute works only for Netscape Navigator running on Windows 95, Windows NT, and Macintosh.

VOLUME= *0 - 100*

Sets the volume at which the sound file is to be played on a user's computer. This value must be a number between 0 and 100. Is overruled by the MASTERVOLUME attribute if used. Default volume level is the current system volume.

WIDTH= # *pixels*

Used to set the display width of the console.

HEIGHT= # *pixels*

Used to set the display height of the console.

ALIGN= *TOP* | *BOTTOM* | *CENTER* | *BASELINE* | *LEFT* | *RIGHT* | *TEXTTOP* | *MIDDLE* | *ABSMIDDLE* | *ABSBOTTOM*

Tells Netscape Navigator how to align text as it flows around the consoles. Works in a similar fashion to the ALIGN attribute of the <IMG> tag.

CONTROLS= *CONSOLE* | *SMALLCONSOLE* | *PLAYBUTTON* | *PAUSEBUTTON* | *STOPBUTTON* | *VOLUMELEVER*

Sets the type of control to be displayed on a Web page. The default for this field is CONSOLE. The individual height and width for each control type must still be set explicitly by the HEIGHT and WIDTH attributes.

HIDDEN= *TRUE* | *FALSE*

Determines whether or not the console is displayed. By default the value of HIDDEN is set to false, so it is always displayed. Setting HIDDEN=TRUE and AUTOSTART=TRUE effectively makes the embedded sound a background sound.

MASTERSOUND

Used when grouping sounds together using the NAME attribute. It tells Netscape Navigator which file is a genuine sound file and allows it to ignore any stub files. Stub files have a minimum length necessary to activate LiveAudio.

NAME= *text*

Used to set a unique ID for a group of CONTROLS elements, so they all can act on the same sound as it plays.

Example:

```
<EMBED SRC=godzilla1.wav CONTROLS=CONSOLE HIDDEN=FALSE
WIDTH=144 HEIGHT=60 AUTOSTART=TRUE ALIGN=TOP
LOOP=10 VOLUME=20>
```

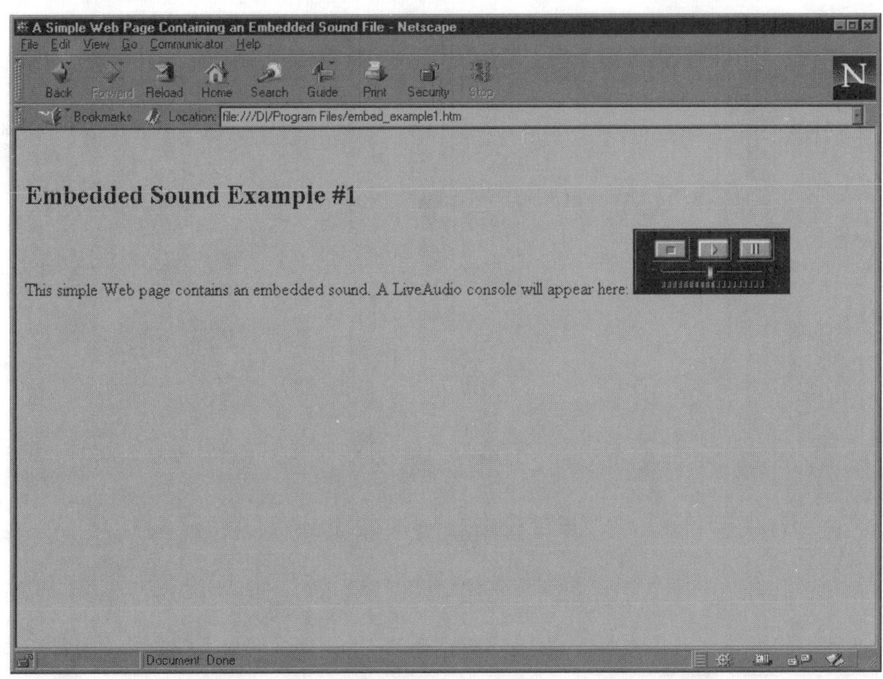

Figure 15.3 A Simple Example of a Sound Embedded in a Web Page

It is possible to have controls of various sizes displayed by setting the CONTROL property along with the proper HEIGHT and WIDTH values. LiveAudio comes with four different main types of controls: a small console, a regular console, a volume level, and three different types of button controls (PLAYBUTTON, PAUSEBUTTON, and STOPBUTTON). The volume level allows the user to adjust the volume level of the sound file as it is being played, whereas the buttons provide the user with some control over the sound being played while taking up as little space on the Web page as possible. The proper HEIGHT and WIDTH settings for each console type are:

- Console - WIDTH=144 HEIGHT=60
- Small Console - WIDTH=144 HEIGHT=15
- Volume Lever - WIDTH=74 HEIGHT=20
- Button - WIDTH=37 HEIGHT=22

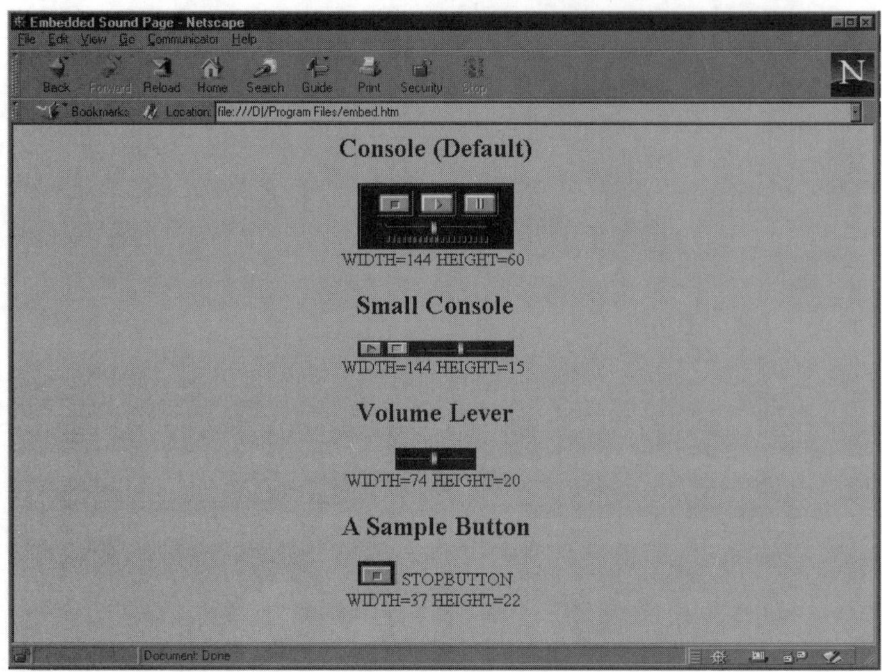

Figure 15.4 The Different LiveAudio Consoles Displayed

The effects of these settings on the display of the various types of console can be seen in Figure 15.4.

You may wish to choose a different type of plug-in to play the sounds on your Web page, either because they are sound file formats not supported by LiveAudio or because the plug-in provides other desirable attributes and features. MIDI files can also be played by a plug-in called Crescendo. Like LiveAudio, Crescendo also uses the <EMBED> tag to control how the sound is played by the plug-in. Both LiveAudio and Crescendo use very similar formats to specify sound files embedded in a Web page.

Link: There are a number of different plug-ins that can be used to play sound within Netscape Navigator. Here are a few of the more popular sound plug-ins:

Crescendo!

http://www.liveupdate.com/midi.html

Enables any Windows PC equipped with an appropriate sound card to play MIDI sound files.

Echo Speech Corporation

http://www.echospeech.com/

Adds high-quality compressed streaming audio to Web pages.

MacZilla

http://maczilla.com/

Plug-in for Macintosh systems so users can listen to .au, .wav, .midi, .aiff, and .mp2 sound file formats in addition to a number of video and movie file formats.

RealAudio

http://www.realaudio.com/

A popular sound file plug-in that delivers high-quality audio.

Talker

http://www.mvpsolutions.com/PlugInSite/Talker. html

A plug-in for Macintosh computers that have the English Text-to-Speech program.

Keep in mind that although most of the manufacturers of these programs offer their sound players for free, the tools needed to create the sound files they use are not. For more information on how to acquire the tools to make sound files for these sound player plug-ins, see the Web sites indicated.

Crescendo has its own set of attributes that can be set by the <EMBED> tag. Many are similar to those attributes recognized by LiveAudio, but offer different services.

<EMBED> (Crescendo Attributes Only)

AUTOSTART= *TRUE | FALSE*
Begins playing the sound file automatically.
BGCOLOR= *colorvalue*
Sets the background color in hexadecimal RRGGBB values.
DELAY= # *seconds*
Delays the start of the sound file after loading by a specified number of seconds.

HEIGHT= # *pixels*
Sets the height of the Crescendo console display in pixels.
LOOP= *TRUE*
Plays the sound file continually.
NOSAVE= *TRUE* | *FALSE*
Disables the "Save As" capability of Crescendo.
TXTCOLOR= *colorvalue*
Sets the text color for the song counter in hexadecimal RRGGBB values.
WIDTH= # *pixels*
Sets the width of the Crescendo console display in pixels.

As you can see, although the names may be different, much of the same functionality is available with Crescendo as with LiveAudio. The Web designer is also able to lay out how much of the Crescendo console appears in Web page simply by setting the HEIGHT and WIDTH characteristics. The following listing shows all of the available options, which are all depicted in Figure 15.5.

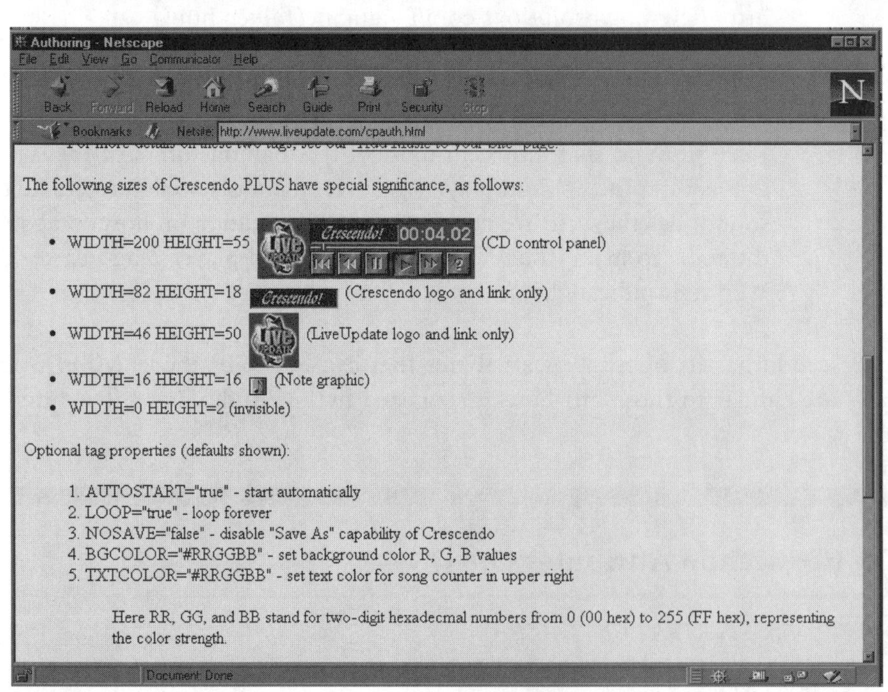

Figure 15.5 The Various Crescendo Consoles Displayed

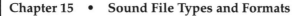

- Full CD-style Control Panel - WIDTH=200 HEIGHT=55
- Crescendo logo and link only - WIDTH=82 HEIGHT=18
- LiveUpdate logo and link only - WIDTH=46 HEIGHT=50
- Single Note graphic - WIDTH=16 HEIGHT=16
- Invisible - WIDTH=0 HEIGHT=2

There are many more sound plug-in applications that can be used and inserted within a Web page. Each plug-in software manufacturer explains all of the ways.

Getting Sound to Co-Exist with Internet Explorer and Netscape Navigator

Despite the differences between Internet Explorer and Netscape Navigator, it is possible to get the two to cooperate to some degree when you want to insert sounds within a Web page.

If you use a sound file format that is common to both platforms (such as .wav), there are several ways to play the sound file so that it gets played within either browser.

To insert a background sound that the user has no direct control over into a Web page that can be read by both Internet Explorer and Netscape Navigator, you could insert the following code into your Web page:

```
<BGSOUND="laughs.wav">
<EMBED SRC="laughs.wav" AUTOSTART=TRUE HIDDEN=TRUE>
```

Since Internet Explorer's <BGSOUND> and Netscape Navigator's <EMBED> tags are not recognized by the other, it is safe to insert this combination of tags into a Web. In each case the sound file will be loaded and played, and will allow the user no control over how it is played.

There are other ways that will provide the end-user ever more control over how the sound file is played.

For example, it is possible to insert a sound within an anchored link. When the user clicks on the link, the user does not go to a new Web page, but instead effectively tells the browser to load and play the sound. It is very easy to implement, and as long as the sound file format can be recognized by both Internet Explorer and Netscape Navigator, it is a simple and elegant way of inserting a sound into a Web page.

```
<A HREF="my_sound.wav">Want to hear a sound?</A>
```

When a user clicks on the link, the browser launches a sound playback program with a console, giving the user some control over how the sound is played. A good example of this in action can be seen in Figure 15.6.

Thanks to the advent of ActiveX and JavaScript, there are increasingly more options available to the Web author who wants to add sound to a Web page, tailor-made to the browser being used to view the page.

For example, the following code uses the <OBJECT> tag (described in detail in Chapter 10, "Miscellaneous Elements") to load the Crescendo control as an ActiveX control when it is viewed from within Internet Explorer, and as a standard plug-in when viewed within Netscape Navigator.

```
<OBJECT ID=Crescendo
     CLASSID="clsid:0FC6BF2B-E16A-11CF-AB2E-
0080AD08A326"
     HEIGHT=55
```

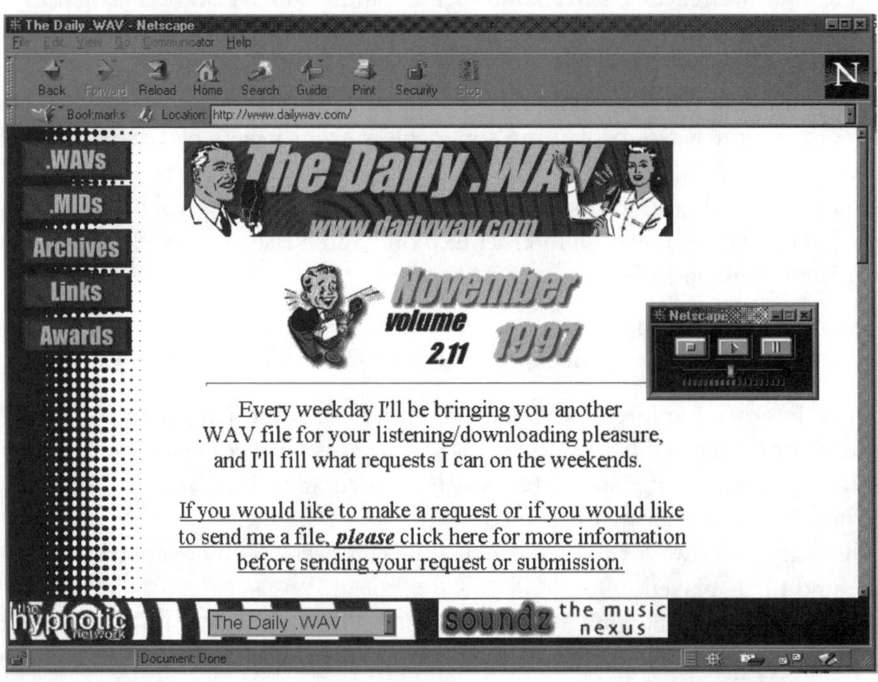

Figure 15.6 The Results of Clicking a "Sound Link" in a Web Page

```
WIDTH=200>
<PARAM NAME="Song" VALUE="funky midifile.mid">
<EMBED TYPE="music/crescendo"
SONG="funky midifile.mid"
PLUGINSPAGE="http://www.liveupdate.com/dl.html"
HEIGHT=55
WIDTH=200>
</OBJECT>
```

In a similar fashion, the following JavaScript code, when used in conjunction with the Crescendo plug-in, first determines which browser is actively viewing the Web page, and then writes the HTML code appropriate to the browser.

```
<SCRIPT LANGUAGE="JavaScript">
<!-- // Script for playing Crescendo MIDI files for
both IE and NN.
  if (navigator.appName == "Netscape") {
     document.write ('<EMBED TYPE="music/crescendo" ')
     document.write ('SONG="funky midifile.mid" ')
     document.write ('PLUGINSPAGE="http://
www.liveupdate.com/dl.html" ')
     document.write ('HEIGHT=55 WIDTH=200></EMBED>') }
  else {if (navigator.appName == "Microsoft Internet
Explorer")
     document.write ('<OBJECT ID=Crescendo')
     document.write ('CLASSID="clsid:OFC6BF2B-E16A-
11CF-AB2E-0080AD08A326" ')
     document.write ('HEIGHT=55 WIDTH=200>')
     document.write ('<PARAM NAME="Song" VALUE="funky
midifile.mid"></OBJECT>')
     }
//--
</SCRIPT>
```

A Final Note About Sound

If you are planning to use sound files that are not of your own creation on a Web page, first get permission to use them.

Keep your audience in mind when you are planning to use sound within a Web page. For example, if you are creating a Web page for a travel agency, placing background sound files reflecting the music of a particular destination helps to set the tone for a page. Playing background string guitar music for a Hawaiian Web

page, bagpipes for a Scottish destination, or the strains of Mozart for a trip to Vienna. Similarly, dark and brooding music can set the tone for a Web page with a scary topic, like a Web page for a Quake-like game or for a Halloween-themed Web page.

As a final word on the topic, try not to make sound the be-all and end-all of a Web site—remember that not all users have sound cards (most business computers still do not have them). Adding some sound to a Web page can enhance the experience of your Web page, but too much sound or a poor selection of sounds will drive people away.

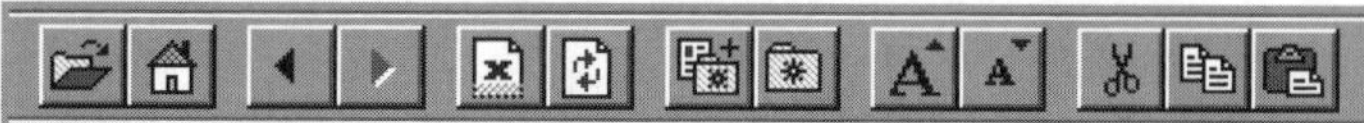

CHAPTER 16

Making Your Web Site Known

By now you know how to write Web pages, and have created your own Web site. Now you want to get the word out so that people know that it is there. After all, what is the point of creating a Web page if nobody knows that it is there?

There are several questions you have to ask yourself: Do you want to target a specific audience, or do you want to get your message out to a more general audience? What are the benefits and the downsides of having a popular Web site? To what lengths will you go to publicize your Web site?

In most cases people will want to make their Web site known to the browsing public at large. The idea is to get your Web page registered so that anybody who is looking for information on the topic covered by your Web page can be found. This is the job of Web search engines and directories like Yahoo! (http://www.yahoo.com/) and Alta Vista (http://www.altavista.digital.com/). If your Web page is targeted

towards a specific viewing audience, you might want to consider exchanging links with other people who have Web pages on the same or similar topic. You also have to consider the benefits and burdens of having a popular Web site—you do not want to get into a situation where you end up with a wildly popular site that results in costing you extra money in external downloading fees from your Internet Service Provider. If you decide to widely publicize your Web site, you have to think of the best way of approaching your potential audience. The last thing you want to do is to annoy the very people whom you want to visit your site, especially if you are trying to sell them something. All of these topics are considered in depth in this chapter.

Registering Your Site with A Search Engine

Most search engines allow users to enter new URLs into their database. This process is usually quite simple: Click on a Submit URL button (or something similar) within the search engine and then type in the URL of your Web page in the form that appears. When you submit your the URL for your Web page, the Web search engine typically checks to ensure that a Web site does exist at the URL you specified, verifying that you spelled the URL to your site correctly.

Most search engines take things from there, and send out a Web robot program a few days later to catalog your site automatically. Other Web directories like Yahoo! ask you to write a brief description of your Web site, and what category (or categories) you think it belongs to (see Figure 16.1). In the case of Yahoo!, a person will check out your site, determine whether or not it meets the criteria (i.e., that you've correctly categorized your Web site, and that it is deemed a useful site to include in the index), and then will add it to their database of Web sites.

It is worthwhile doing some research before submitting a URL. If a search engine uses category listings, check to see which category best fits your Web site. If you find sites similar to your own in a particular category, you've found the right place to register yours. Do not assume a broad category like entertainment means the same thing for every search directory. Also, do not be shy to suggest a new category if you can't find one to match that of your Web page. Although the chances of your Web pages being truly unique diminishes over time as the Web grows, if no other category or subcategory quite fits the topic of your Web page, you may simply be the first to suggest the category to a Web search engine or directory service.

The process of adding URLs to individual search engines and directories worked well when there were only a few of them available, but these days there are dozens and dozens of them. Though the majority of Web surfers tend to limit their searches

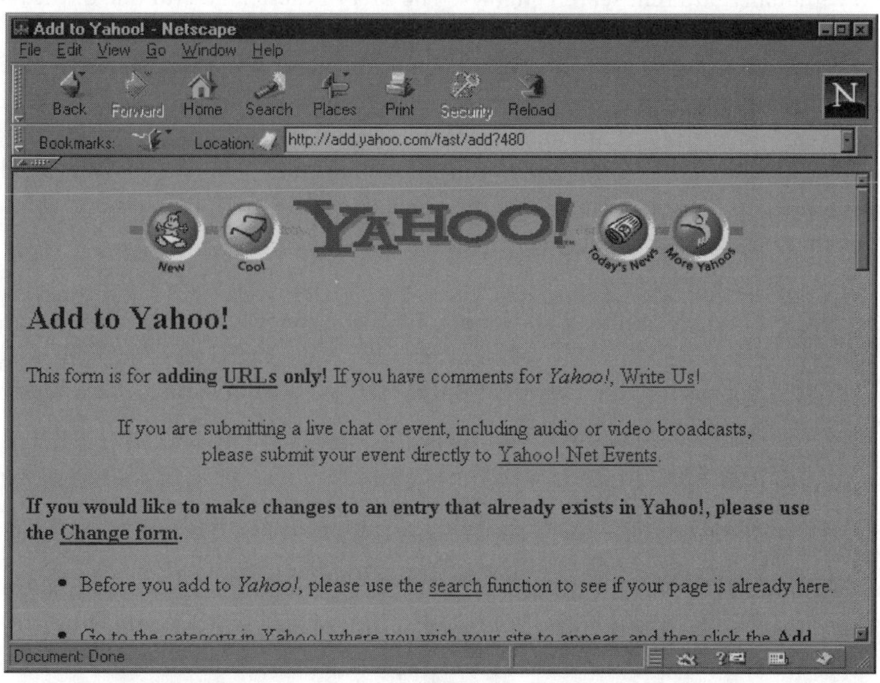

Figure 16.1 The Form to Add a Web Page at Yahoo!

to only a couple of the more popular search engines to draw in as many visitors as possible to your Web site, you want as much coverage as possible. If you target all of the major search engines, you can be sure that you will get some coverage.

Link: The URLs of some of the more popular Web search engines and directories are:

Alta Vista: http://www.altavista.digital.com/

Excite: http://www.excite.com/

Lycos: http://www.lycos.com/

Magellan: http://www.mckinley.com/

Yahoo: http://www.yahoo.com/

Web Crawler: http://www.webcrawler.com/

There are services designed to partially automate the process of registering your URL with many different search engines. The first of these, and still one of the most popular is Submit It! (http://www.submit-it.com/), a service that enables you to register your URL with several search engines at once. You fill in a single master form at the Submit It! Web site, select the search engines to post your URL to, and it takes care of the rest. Like many such services, it now offers professional (i.e., pay for use) services for commercial purposes, but it still offers a free service that enables users to register their URL with as many as 16 search engines and directories at once.

Link: In addition to Submit It! (http://www.submit-it.com/), several other Web sites let you register your Web pages with multiple search engines and directories at once. Here's a partial listing of a few others worth investigating:

Add Me!: http://www.addme.com/

Auto Submit: http://autosubmit.com/promote.html

Easy-Submit: http://www.the-vault.com/easy-submit/

Get the Word Out: http://zeus.worldramp.net/~theword/list.html

As search engines proliferate, many are targeting themselves towards niche audiences, so now there are search engines being devoted exclusively to specific types of Web sites, like music (Music Search: http://musicsearch.com/), Science Fiction (Nebula Search: http:// http://members.aol.com/quaddelta/nebsearch.html), financial services (Money Search: http://www.moneysearch.com), movie reviews (Cinemachine: http://www.cinemachine.com/), even Star Trek sites (James Kirk Search Engine: http://www.webwombat.com.au/trek/), and many, many more. Go to any search engine and type in the keywords "search engine" and a keyword reflecting the topic covered by your Web site. If you find a match, check out the search engine, and make sure you register your URL there.

HTML Search Engine Tricks

Increasingly, search engines obtain the bulk of the URLs for their databases by sending out programs known as *Web robots*, which search the Web for new URLs to add to the database. There is no human intervention—the Web robot finds new Web pages, retrieves them, searches them for keywords, and then automatically

adds them to the database. Knowing how these search engines work can enhance the exposure your Web page can receive within a search engine.

Since most Web robots end up searching for and storing pages by keywords that appear in the page, it makes sense to ensure that keywords reflecting the content of your Web page appear within it. At the very least, try to include an important keyword as the title of your Web page, and within the <TITLE> tags.

Adding a description for the Web page using the <META> tag helps several Web robots to identify and catalog your Web page properly. This is not surprising, since one of the original ideas behind the creation of the <META> tag was for cataloging purposes. Use the NAME attribute of the <META> tag along with the CONTENT attribute and a brief description, such as in the following example:

```
<HEAD>
<META NAME="description" CONTENT="Keith's Budgie
Emporium">
</HEAD>
```

Several tricks have been discovered that can make a listing of a Web more prominent within a Web search engine. For example, the more often a keyword appears within a Web page, the more prominent a listing it often gets when somebody does a search on that topic. When a person searches for a common keyword term, most Web engines place priority on Web pages that contain multiple instances of that keyword. All things being equal, a Web page that uses the word "budgie" ten times within a single page generally appears higher in a user's search for budgie-related Web sites than a Web page that contains less references.

This practice can be taken to extremes; overt repetition of keywords has become known as "search engine spamming." If you have ever seen a Web page with a number of keywords either hidden from view in the header of a Web page, or worse, visible within the body of a Web page, then you've found a case of it. This technique is frowned upon, not only because it creates bulkier Web pages that take longer for the user to download, but because Web robot designers are changing the characteristics of their robots to compensate. Though this technique may have led to a top listing within a search engine in the past, spammed pages are now often passed over by Web robots, proving that Web robot designers have a vested interest in not promoting this technique. However, the judicious use of a few, select keywords within a Web page will aid a Web robot to catalog it properly.

When adding descriptive keywords to your Web site, keep in mind that Web robots are not that smart, so keep things simple and straightforward. For example, do not assume that robots travel the Web with a handy lexicon of rules on common word usage. For example, even though the keywords "Tibetan Buddhism" are derived from the words "Tibet" and "Buddha," most Web robots will not catalog your Web page under such categories. So while somebody looking for Web pages

on "Tibetan" and "Buddhism" are likely to run across your page, they are not as likely to run across it if they enter either "Tibet" or "Buddha." Your best bet is to include all of these keywords within your Web page, to ensure that your Web page comes up in a search on a relevant or related topic a person might make on a search engine. The order of keywords is not always important, either; a person doing a search on a Web engine looking for the words "Earth Mother" are just as likely to find references to Web pages containing the words "Mother Earth" as well. Many search engines let the user get more specific with their searches, but most people don't bother with these advanced search features. Most advanced search operations performed by search engines look for only those Web pages that have keywords in common in a Web page (i.e., "earth" and "mother"), rather than those adjacent to each other (i.e., "earth mother" and "mother earth").

Other things to keep in mind when adding keywords to your Web page is to avoid spelling the keywords with capital letters. Alta Vista has stated that whenever anybody does a search at their site using lowercase letters to spell out a keyword, it will do a case-insensitive match on the keywords (i.e., a search for "cat" will turn up "Cat" and "CAT"). Whenever words are spelled in uppercase letters on a Web page, they are considered distinct from lowercase letters. If a word is found in a Web page, its case is preserved when it is stored in the index. Although the Alta Vista search engine is smart enough to return case-insensitive results to a user, there is no guarantee that all search engines are as sophisticated. Similarly, try not to add keywords containing accented characters, like "café," "noë," or "déjà vu." Accented words used in a query at a search engine typically force it to find an exact match on the entire word. Again, several search engines are sophisticated enough to do some processing on keywords containing accented characters, but it is safer to assume that they do not.

It is a good idea to add keywords to the <META> tag in cases where the top of the Web page is otherwise dominated by code. Most search robots retrieve only the first hundred or so characters on a Web page. If the top of your Web page is composed largely of JavaScript code or is a framed Web page, few keywords describing your Web page will be found by the Web robot.

Since most people do not use the <META> tag for indexing their Web pages, most Web robots are designed simply to get whatever text appears on the page. Processing done at the search engine later removes the tag information, leaving the raw text. If you use keywords in the <META> tag, they will be read and retrieved by the Web spider, even though they will not be visible to the user (unless the user looks at the source for your Web page). Expect any visible words on your Web page to be similarly indexed.

Web robots are rather crude, but they do work well for most search engines. The rules to remember are: use simple keywords, don't use them excessively, and keep things simple.

GETTING LINKED

One of the best ways to get people begin to visit your site is to try to get other people to link to your Web site. One of the most popular approaches is to find other Web sites that are similar in subject or content to yours and then ask the Webmaster of that site for a reciprocal link. Go to a Web search engine and do a search on keywords that closely match those that would describe your site. For example, if you have created a Web site about your pet Chihuahua, do a search for other Web sites that contain keywords like "dog," "canine," "pets," and "Chihuahua." Check out the sites that you find, determine which ones have the most in common to your site, and then ask the Webmasters of the sites you choose whether or not they would add a link to your site in exchange for a link to their site from yours. Most Webmasters are more than willing to add new links to their site in exchange for links to theirs. This type of arrangement is generally beneficial to both parties, as people visiting a site that contains a link back to your site is more likely on average to bring more visitors to your site, and vice versa.

There's a recent Web service that has taken this concept to its logical conclusion—offering banner ads to Web masters that cross-link from your site to another automatically. LinkExchange (http://www.linkexchange.com/) is a free Web service designed to help Web sites advertise each other (Figure 16.2). If you decide to join, you agree to add a banner to your page that will advertise another's Web site. In return, other members display a banner ad for your site on theirs. You get to decide what type of sites you wish to advertise on and to advertise for, so you retain some (though not complete) control over the process.

If you join the service, you are provided with some HTML code to insert into your Web pages. Each time a person views your Web page, a different 400 x 40 banner pixel banner image appears. The HTML code that is inserted into your Web page points to an image that is held at the Exchange's Web site. If a person clicks on the banner, the Exchange's Web server notes the request and redirects the user to the Web page. The Exchange's Web server also keeps track of how often people visit your Web site, and compensates your Web site by portraying your banner ad more often on its member Web sites.

This service has become very popular, and it claims to provide over 100 million collective hits to their banner ads Web-wide every month. This service is not for everybody—a glance at its members list shows that many of its subscribers are commercial or quasi-commercial Web sites. Some people may feel uncomfortable about sponsoring the occasional paid advertisement on their Web site—the Exchange offers a service that enables advertisers to pay for greater access to member sites. However, it does have its benefits as well; you can even check how many times your banner ad has appeared on other member's Web sites, and you can reasonably

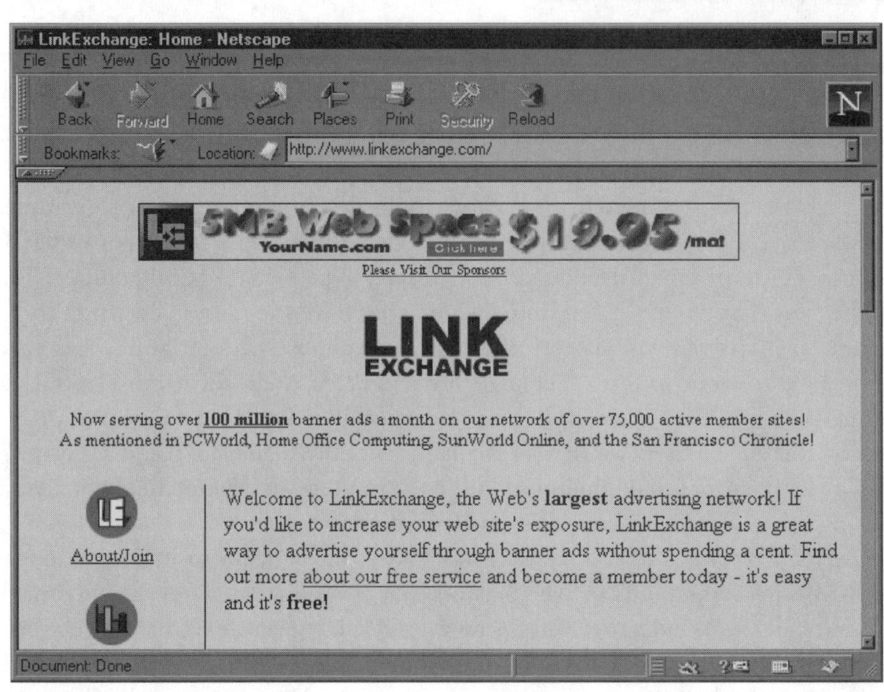

Figure 16.2 Home Page for the LinkExchange

expect to garner more visitors for your Web site through the cross-advertising the Exchange offers. If you are considering making your site into a commercial service, this avenue is worth exploring. Its tracking services will give you a good idea of how useful the service will be to you, and provide you with data on the traffic at your site.

Web Awards

Web awards have become another popular way for Web sites to exchange links effectively. One of the first to come up with and successfully implement the idea of a Web award was the Magellan search engine (McKinley's Internet Directory: http://www.mckinley.com/). Their reviewers evaluate Web sites and award points for things like organization, "Net Appeal," comprehensiveness, and whether or not it is thought-provoking. Based upon the eventual score, award-winning sites are given an award in the form of an image file proudly proclaiming the site as a Magellan award-winning site. Web authors are duly notified and are encouraged to place an image file on their award-winning page (which of course links back to the Magellan Web site). This clever marketing strategy has made the Magellan award symbols ubiquitous on some of the better Web pages on the Web. Problem is, now everybody is trying to copy Magellan and there are so many Web awards available that they have become something of a joke.

Unfortunately, the idea of Web awards has been watered down significantly, as it was realized that anybody could make up his or her own award and hand it over as a prize to other sites. The whole point of many of these awards is to ensure that they get links back to their own, sometimes mediocre, Web pages. Some places even offer you an award just by asking for it (and by adding a link back to their award-giving site). The only way awards actually add any sort of value to the Web is if they come from a well-respected source, so expect to earn some respect for your award before it means anything to seasoned Web masters. By the same token, if someone offers you an award for your Web site, think twice about implementing it. In most cases you will be required to add a graphic of the award and a link back to the parent site. Check out the site and determine if you really want to publicize their site on yours.

Note: The idea that you may receive a dud award for your Web site is not as remote as it may seem. This author has received several such awards, best illustrated by this unsolicited email received some time ago, which read as follows:

Organization: THE JC and JIM awards!!!

To: kschengi@interlog.com

Subject: awards

YOUR WEB PAGE has been selected by the JC and JIM awards as well:___ GREAT ! ! ! Want your award? go to [URL] for a big picture ! ! ! OR if you want a smaller picture go to [another URL] and the pictures must be so that when some one clicks on it the link leads to

[yet another URL] that's also our MAIN OFFICIAL [sic] HOME PAGE if you want to look at it BUT HEY what do I get from this you say? ? ? ?

DON'T WORRY: - } just put the big/small picture on your page email ME [email address] (JC) or [another email address] (JIM) and with in YES WITH IN 24 HOURS ! ! ! you'll be ON OUR MAIN PAGE ! ! ! BE PROUD WE SELECTED ~YOU~ as one of our winners ! ! !

Thank You,

JC and JIM from the JC and JIM awards ! ! !

(Names have been changed and URLs removed from the original message.)

Note that nowhere in the email does it say which Web page had been nominated, or why. Upon investigation, the awarding Web site itself was poorly designed, full of spelling errors and was linked to several other mediocre Web sites. It also contained the following statement: "ALL winners MUST put the JC and JIM banner award on his/her home page." The award graphic was amateurish, and the standard version offered to the "winners" was *huge*—it would easily dominate the Web page of anybody foolish enough to accept this dubious award.

This award scheme was essentially a variation of the classic pyramid scheme, where the people at the top of the pyramid benefit by having many people link to their site. It's a dubious way to seek publicity, and any decent Web author will avoid schemes like these. Although no money changes hands, you have to ask yourself this: who is the real beneficiary of the award? If you come in a distant second, do not accept it.

If you are determined to get an award for your site, and can't wait for a Web service like Magellan to come and offer you one, you can always ask for one. If you want to add some humor to your Web page with a few fake Web awards, try the Fake Web Awards section at Yahoo! at http://www.yahoo.com/ Entertainment/Humor __okes__and_Fun/Int ernet_Humor/ Fake_Awards/.

THE DOWNSIDES OF BEING TOO POPULAR

There is such a thing as being too successful, especially if you have not planned for it. If you are a corporate site, ensure you use fast computers that readily can handle large volumes of visitors at once. A Web system should be robust enough to take surges in usage. For example, people are increasingly using their lunch breaks to surf the Web while at work. Accordingly, there you will find significant peeks at various popular Web sites as it becomes lunch time in time zones where there is a significant population of people connected to the Web (this is especially the case in

North America). Similarly, if your site is given a large amount of Web publicity (for example, the URL is published in a magazine or gets a significant mention at a place that gets a lot of high traffic, like a search engine), you can expect a sudden flood of people to visit your site. One sure way to lose customers at your Web site is to have your Web server refuse them a connection because the Web server can't deal with the number of people visiting. (For an example of this, see the "Keeping on Good Terms with Your ISP" section in Chapter 17.

CHAPTER 17

Working with the Server

When setting out to create a Web page, or any number of Web pages to make up a Web site, designing, authoring, and refining your HTML and image files is more than half the battle. Now, much of the HTML coding is behind you; your pages are rich with content and your images are elegant and relevant to the text. You've checked and double-checked that your hypertext links work perfectly, and you're ready to go public. However, there are a few things you should know about Web servers to get an accurate idea of how a Web server really works.

This chapter discusses issues regarding the Web server itself, including:

- The role of the Web server
- Finding a Web server to host your Web pages
- Uploading your Web files to the Web server

- Basic Unix commands, since many Web servers run on Unix systems
- Setting permissions if your Web server is a Unix system
- Registering your own domain name
- Using firewalls to provide Web server security
- Keeping on good terms with your ISP

By the end of this chapter, you should feel comfortable working with your system administrator in order to get the most out of your Web server.

The Role of the Web Server

A Web server is simply a computer that is connected to the Internet. The Web server responds to requests for files from Web clients. The computer that hosts the Web server software must be accessible to and from the Internet in order to serve Web pages and other Web-based files. The Web server knows how to interpret different kinds of files, then sends information to the Web client, such as Netscape or Internet Explorer, so that the client can display them as appropriate. For instance, HTML files, GIFs, and JPEGs are displayed by the Web client itself. Other files, such as Quicktime movies or Adobe Acrobat PDF files, need helper applications to play or display them.

Web server software can run on most systems; the majority of Web servers on the Internet run on Unix systems, but Windows NT is becoming more and more popular. Web server software is also available for Windows95/98, Apple, and OS/2. Web server software runs the gamut from freeware to shareware to expensive, proprietary programs. For the most part, how much you want to spend will depend on how dependable your Web server needs to be, how much traffic it needs to withstand, and how large your Web site is. For an extensive list of Web server software, consult Yahoo!'s Web server software list at http://www.yahoo.com/Computers_and_Internet/Software/Internet/World_Wide_Web/Servers/.

Finding a Web Server to Host Your Site

Most people purchase their Internet access from an Internet Service Provider, or ISP. ISPs are companies with large Internet-accessible computers that provide Internet service to many, often hundreds or thousands, of people.

Most Internet accounts include a standard amount of Web server space in addition to your email address. Your ISP may place restrictions depending on how much disk space your Web site occupies, and also how much traffic your Web site generates. The best way to get the details about how much space you have and the restrictions involved is to contact your ISP. Very often your ISP's Web site will provide you with much of the information and instructions you will need to create your own corner of the Web on their server.

So how do you choose an ISP for yourself? Probably the best way of getting a feel for what makes an ISP good or bad is to ask any friends you have who are already "connected." Chances are you will hear an equal share of horror stories and hearty recommendations.

Ask your friends whether they have had any trouble connecting to the ISP when they wanted to, how good their technical support is, and the ease of use. Do they feel they are getting their money's worth out of the service, and if not, why not? If you do not know anybody who is already on the Internet, check out the local newspapers for ISP advertisements. Compare the features, benefits, and costs of each, and then call the ones you think offer what you want for more information: If you are able to get through and get sensible answers to your questions, you are doing well. Before subscribing to an ISP, find out if there is an introductory rate. This is a good strategy because if it turns out you are not satisfied with an ISP's services, this gives you the chance to bow out gracefully sooner rather than later. If you are satisfied, nothing is lost, and you also gained the opportunity to assess whether the type of Internet services you thought you needed are adequate.

As with any purchase or leasing arrangement, the phrase *caveat emptor* ("buyer beware") applies when searching for an ISP. There is fierce competition in the marketplace—in large urban centers it is not uncommon to have over a hundred ISPs vying to provide you with their services, in addition to the large national online services for your attentions. As in any industry, there are unscrupulous operators who will gladly take your money while providing the most minimal of services. It is recommended that you call the sales departments of the ISPs you are interested in, ask them detailed questions about the types of services they provide, and find out how they can cater to your needs. In particular, try to determine the level and competence of their technical support staff, and try to get a feel for how service-oriented they are. A good ISP will go the extra mile to please its customer base. If you don't feel comfortable about closing a deal with an ISP, don't do it. Given the sheer numbers of ISPs available in most areas, it is a buyer's market and there is absolutely no reason why you should not get the type of connectivity you want for a reasonable price.

Over time, pricing and usage in the ISP market is becoming more flexible and much more responsive to user's needs. Increasingly there are ISPs offering unlimited access to their systems, often for a flat fee. Most ISPs offer a plethora of pricing options, designed to capture the very occasional user—such as those who simply want to check email—to those hard-core surfers who seem to spend much of their

waking lives connected to the 'Net. Finally, be aware of extra charges when setting up with an ISP. Many ISPs include some form of set-up charge when you join them.

There are more choices than ever before when it comes to choosing an ISP. This is as good a time as any to get connected to the Internet.

Some people do not connect to the Internet through an ISP, and instead gain access to the Internet via their school or company, where they may be able to post their Web site on the school or company Web server. Contact your computer services department to get permission and details on storing your Web site on their server.

Uploading Files to the Web Server

Now that you have created all of your HTML documents and images, you of course want to go public! This section discusses how to upload your Web files to your Web site.

Uploading Files with FTP

A web server is a fairly complex program made up of many files and directories. Where you put your Web files is very important, as they must be in a specific directory so that they can be served to Web clients when the request is made. Before you attempt to move any files to a Web server, consult with your ISP or computer services department to find out where your Web site files should be stored.

The most common way of uploading files is through the use of the File Transfer Protocol, or ftp. You can either use an ftp client, or a simple command line. A popular ftp client for Windows is WS_FTP, and many Macintosh users find Fetch to be the ftp client of choice. By contrast, many Unix users are content with ftp on a command line. These and other ftp clients are usually shareware, and can be found at http://www.shareware.com.

Whichever way you choose to ftp files, the basic steps are the same:

- Open your ftp client, or open a window with a command prompt.
- Change to the local directory on your computer containing your Web site files.
- Connect to your ISP, school, or company Web server. Consult with your ISP or computer services department to get the address to which you should connect.
- Type in your login name and password when prompted.

- Change to the correct directory on the Web server, as directed by your ISP or computer services department; some system administrators require you to create this directory yourself.
- If you have created a directory structure for your Web pages where you have your Web files stored in more than one directory, you must create the same directory structure on your account on the Web server. If you do not mirror the directory structure exactly, your Web site's links and images may not work.
- Be sure to transfer binary files, such as images, in binary mode. Ftp clients usually have a box you can check to do this; for command line FTP, give the Binary command. If you are in doubt, always use binary mode, as your HTML files will not be corrupted if transferred as binary files.
- Transfer your files to your Web account. Be sure to pay close attention to directory structure. With the ftp client, uploading files usually is as simple as clicking the appropriate button. On a command line, use the Put command to upload your files.
- Once your file transfers are complete, you will receive a message similar to "transfer complete."
- Close the ftp client, or if using a command line, type "bye."

Once your files have been uploaded, go to your Web site to be sure all of your links and images are working. If there are errors, it is probably due to a path problem caused by having your files in the wrong directories. You may also have to set the permissions for the files, to allow outside viewers (i.e., those on the Web) to view them. Setting permission is covered in more detail later in this chapter. Also, check that your image and link names are correct. Double check your hypertext links and image tags in your HTML files, then upload the repaired files to the Web server. The previous files on your Web account will be overwritten by the latest files uploaded.

Link: If you have an extensive Web site, or even if you have a small one, you might want to get a program that will automatically check all of the links of your Web pages. These *link validators* operate by working through all of the links on your Web site, and note any problems. The following is a list of such programs and where you can get them.

Astra SiteManager (Windows 95):

http://www.merc-int.com/products/astraguide.html

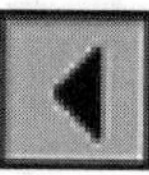

A program that searches for broken links, and visually displays the results.

Linkbot (Windows 95/98):

http://www.tetranetsoftware.com/linkbot- info.htm

A site management tool for Web masters designed to find broken links and many other problems that often befall Web masters.

Linklint

http://www.goldwarp.com/bowlin/linklint/

A program that checks and optionally cross-references all the links on a Web site.

lvrfy

http://www.cs.dartmouth.edu/~crow/lvrfy.html

A script that verifies all the internal links of the HTML pages on your Web server

missinglink

http://www.rsol.com/ml/

A program that runs on your Unix Web servers and verifies the hyperlinks they contain.

NetMechanic

http://www.netmechanic.com/

A free online-based service that searches your Web site and finds broken links, based on the URL you give it.

To help you feel more comfortable with FTP, Figures 17.1 through 17.4 are examples of using an ftp client and a command line to upload files.

Ftp can seem intimidating to users who are new to uploading files; there is no need to worry, as there is very little that can go wrong. The worst that can happen is that you forget to upload every file, and that can be remedied easily by uploading everything again. Keep in mind that files with the same names will be overwritten by the most recently uploaded copy of the file. It will likely be difficult to upload the files to the wrong place, since a responsible systems administrator will ensure you do not have permission to enter directories where you do not belong.

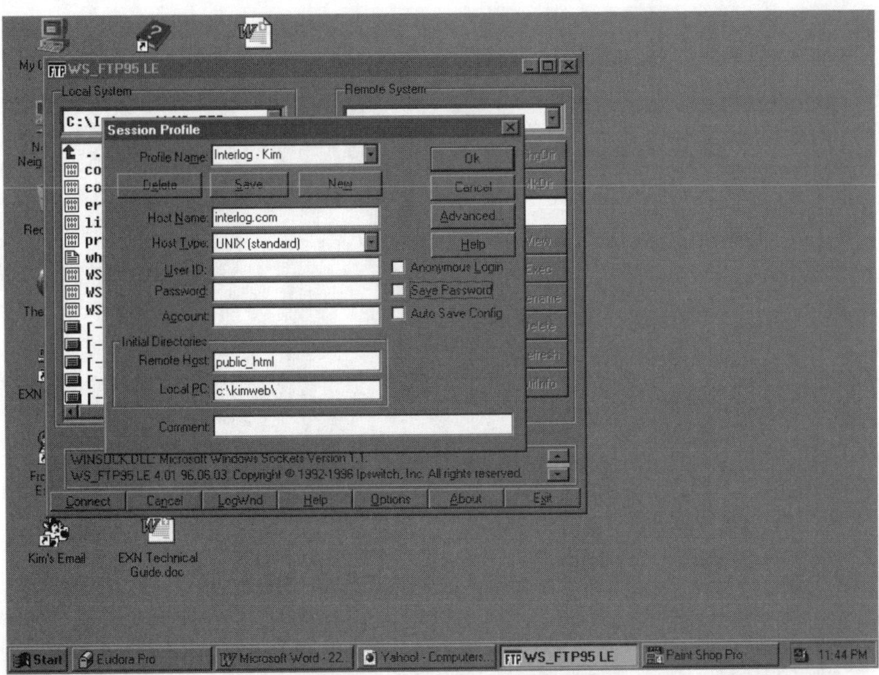

Figure 17.1 The WS_FTP Client for Windows95; the Window in the Foreground Contains the Information Needed to Connect to the Web Server

Basic Unix Commands and Setting Permissions

If your Web server uses the Unix operating system, chances are you will find that knowledge of some basic Unix commands will do you in good stead later. Don't feel you have to learn everything about the Unix operating system—you just need to know enough to get around the system easily and to be able manage the files that comprise your Web site.

If you are familiar with DOS and have used it extensively, you will already have a good idea of how Unix works. Though there are versions of Unix that have much in common with windowing operating systems like MS-Windows and Macintosh, the type of Unix most Web masters are likely to deal with is text-based, where users

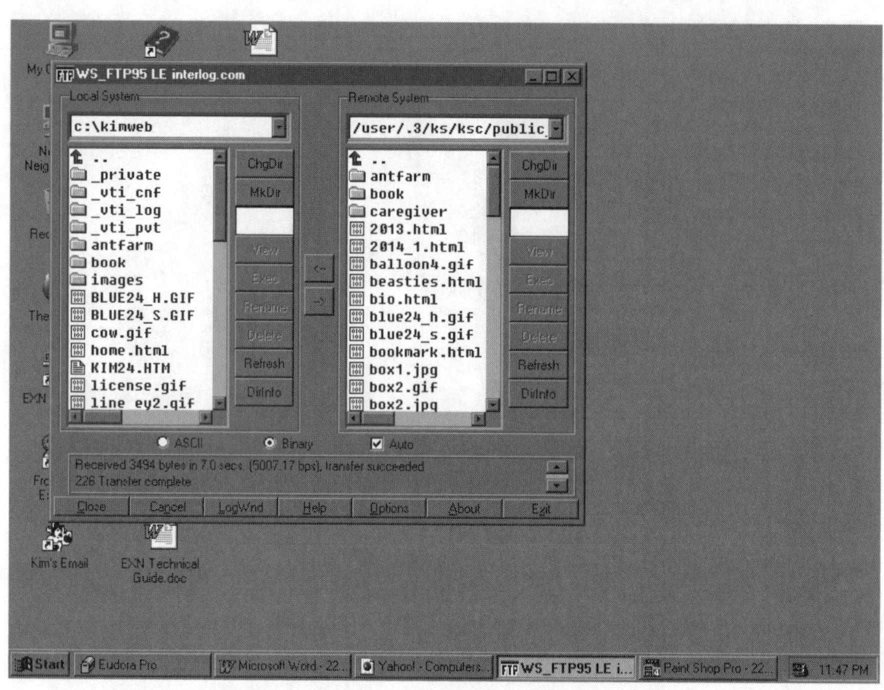

Figure 17.2 The WS_FTP Client Once It Has Connected to the FTP Site

enter commands to be run at the command line. Anybody who knows Unix at all will tell you that the listings in Tables 17.1 and 17.2 are far from being a comprehensive list of Unix commands, but for many people it is all they need to know to get around.

Many ISPs (though not all) provide what is called *shell access,* which allows you to connect directly to your Web server and configure aspects of your Web site while connected to it. In most cases, to log on to the Web server, you will have to use a communications program to connect to it. You can do this with any stand-alone dialing program, like HyperTerminal in 32-bit MS Windows operating systems. The same thing can be also be accomplished by connecting to your ISP in the usual manner (usually through a WinSock program or an Internet Dialing program) and then running a Telnet program (figure 17.5). If you have 32-bit MS Windows operating systems, you've got a copy of it already; from the Start menu click Run, type in "telnet" (without the quotes) and then click OK. A Telnet window appears, at which point you simply type in your username and password (most often the

Figure 17.3 Ftp Using a Command Line; At This Point the User Has Connected to the Web Server, and the Server Is Awaiting Instruction

same name and password used to connect to your ISP in the first place). Once you are logged in, you are set to configure things on the Web server.

First, you need to know how to move around and list the files on your server. There are two commands that do this: ls and cd. The ls command stands for LiSt, and displays all of the files in a directory. To move between directories, use the cd (Change Directory) command. To move to a directory, type the following at the prompt:

```
cd [name_of_directory]
```

To move up a directory, type the following:

```
cd ..
```

If you know the path, you can go to many directory levels at once, as in the following example:

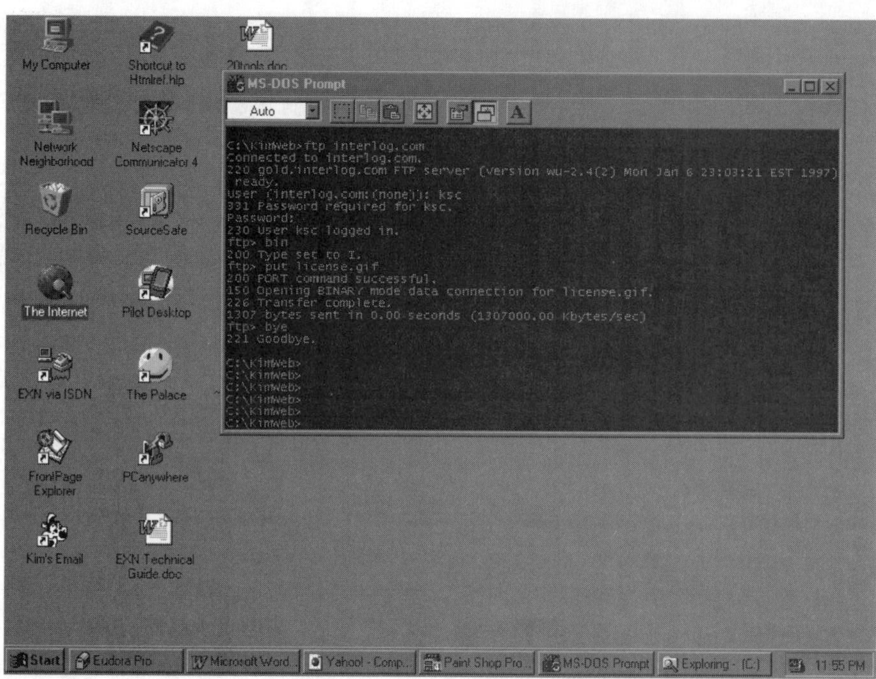

Figure 17.4 Ftp Using a Command Line: Note That the User Switched to Binary Mode, and Transferred a File Using the PUT Command; Once the File Transfer Was Complete, the User Disconnected from the Web Server Using the Bye Command

```
cd [directory1]/[directory2]/[directory3]
```

Most Unix commands have *switches* that allow the user to add extra functions to the command. The cd command does not have many switches that are particularly useful for most users, but the ls command does. A listing and description of some of them follows.

-C Forces multicolumn display of the directory listing

-l Displays the directory listing in a long format

-t Sorts the display by the time it was last modified

-T Displays complete time information for each file listed, including the month, day, hour, minute, second, and year

Table 17.1 Unix Commands

cd	Change Directory. Change to a different directory level.*
chmod	CHange MODe. Set read/write permission for files/directories.
cp	CoPy. Copy files.
ln	LiNk. Make a LiNk to a file.
ls	LiSt. Display a directory listing.*
man	MANual. Display detailed information about a Unix command.
mkdir	MaKe DIRectory. Create a file directory.*
pwd	Return working directory name.*
mv	MoVe. Move files.
rm	ReMove file. Delete files from the server.*
rmdir	ReMove DIRectory. Delete the specified directory from the server.*

*These commands also work under ftp.

Note that the switches, like the Unix commands themselves, are case-sensitive. Unix is a case-sensitive operating system and it is important that you get the case right.

Once you know your way around the Web server, you can begin to do things to the files that comprise your Web site.

To copy and move files, use the cp and mv commands, respectively. If you are familiar with the equivalent MS-DOS copy and move commands, you already know how these commands work. Simply type the command, the file or files to copy or move, and the destination they are to go to, as in the following example:

```
cp [filename] /[destination]
```

and

```
mv [filename] /[destination]
```

Table 17.2 Ftp-Specific Commands

lcd	Local Change Directory. Change the directory at the local machine.
mput	PUT many files to the target location.
put	PUT a single file to the target location.
!ls	Display a local directory LiSting.
!pwd	Return working local directory name.

```
Telnet - interlog.com
Connect  Edit  Terminal  Help
login: kschengi
Password:
Last login: Tue Jun 24 18:24:56 from kschengi
Copyright 1992, 1993, 1994, 1995, 1996 Berkeley Software Design, Inc.
Copyright (c) 1980, 1983, 1986, 1988, 1990, 1991, 1993, 1994
        The Regents of the University of California.  All rights reserved.

BSDI BSD/OS 2.1 Kernel #5: Mon Apr 28 18:44:35 EDT 1997

The following is a non-exclusive list of activities
that are not permitted on this server:
- detaching of 'screen' processes
- execution of IRC bots
- running processes while not logged in

****************************************************
*** Important Information, please read completely ***
****************************************************

Elm users - please run 'relm' to access your mail file. Read and understand
the information presented upon first invocation of it.

When logging in via our dialup pool, you will now be placed on
shell.interlog.com.
gold-kschengi {1}
```

Figure 17.5 Logging On to a Web Server through a Telnet Program

Both cp and mv take a wildcard function, which means you can move a bunch of files at once. To copy all files beginning with the letter s, type in the following:

```
cp s* /[destination]
```

To move all files with the extension .html, type in the following:

```
mv *.html /[destination]
```

Both the cp and mv commands have several switches in common. Here's a brief listing of the more commonly used switches:

-f If there is an existing file with the same name in the target directory, this switch instructs the copy or move command to overwrite it

-i If there is an existing file with the same name in the target directory, this switch instructs the copy or move command to prompt the user whether or not the target file should be overwritten first

Creating and Removing Directories

To keep better track of all of the files on your Web server, it is best to arrange files into directory structures. For example, many Web masters keep such things as images, Java applets, cascading style sheet pages, html files, and related information in separate directories. This arrangement keeps things neat and tidy on your Web server, and you will always be able to track down certain files on the Web server.

To create and remove directories, use the mkdir and rmdir commands (MaKe directory and ReMove directory), respectively. To create or remove a directory simply type the command at the prompt followed by the name of the directory to create or remove, as in the following example:

```
mkdir images
```

or

```
rmdir gifs
```

Here's a brief listing of the more commonly used switches for both mkdir and rmdir:

-d Removes directories and other types of files

-f Removes files without prompting for confirmation, regardless of the file's permissions

-i Prompts the user for confirmation before attempting to remove each file

Similar in function to the rmdir command is the rm (ReMove) command. rm is a very powerful command, and must be used carefully—there are far too many tales of woe by people who accidentally erased more files than they intended to by using this command. For example, if you type in rm * from the root (top-most) directory on your Web server, you are telling the command to remove all files from the system. On some systems this can also remove any directories and the files they contain that lie under the root directory. Try to use this command only for specific files, as in the following cases:

```
rm ugly.html
```

or

```
rm u*.html
```

Another Way of Transferring Files

There is a second way you can add files to a Web site. In many cases it may be possible to use the Unix ftp command, as opposed to a separate ftp program, to shuttle files between a source to the target system that is live on the Web. If this is the case, you can simply transfer files from one machine to the other. All you have to do is to learn how to change directories and learn commands that are applied specifically to either the source or target systems.

For example, we already know that to change to a different directory all you have to do is use the cd command. But say you are on the target machine, and want to change the directory at the source machine so that you can transfer more files—what do you do? Simple—use the lcd command. The lcd (or Local Change Directory) command allows you to change the directory at the source machine, and it works in exactly the same way as cd. If you wanted to go up a local directory level on the machine you are on, you would use cd and type:

```
cd ..
```

Do the same thing with lcd to move up a directory level at the source machine, as in:

```
lcd ..
```

What if you're not sure you've changed to the correct directory? Use the pwd (return working directory name) to find out the name of the target directory you are currently at, and !pwd to find the name of the source directory. In each case, they return the full name of the directory you are working on both on the target drive and the source drive.

Still not sure that the file you are looking for at the source directory is actually there? Use the !ls command, which is the remote source twin of the ls command discussed earlier. To find out what the full directory listing of the remote source directory is when you are currently located on the target drive, you'd type in the following:

```
!ls -1
```

Together, these three sets of commands can be very handy to transfer files between source and target machines quickly and easily (see Table 17.3).

Putting HTML Files in Their Place

So now that you know how to change directories between machines and how to verify that you are in the correct directory and can locate the right files, use the put and mput commands to transfer the files between the source and target. The put

Table 17.3 Local and Remote Unix/ftp File Transfer Commands

Local Commands	*Remote Commands*
cd	lcd
pwd	!pwd
ls	!ls

command will "put" (or transfer) a single file from target to source, as the following example demonstrates:

```
put myfile.html
```

Say you wanted to move all of your HTML files from the source machine to the target—using put to transfer each and every file would get tired awfully fast. Instead use mput, which does a "Many PUT" for you. For example, to move all of your HTML files, you type the following:

```
mput *.html
```

Linking Files

By default, most Web servers are set up so that they default to a particular page filename when somebody enters a Web server. So, if somebody types in the URL http://www.myfunkywebsite.com/, chances are it will actually take the user to a predefined default page, like index.html, so the user actually goes to http://www.myfunkywebsite.com/index.html. However, there are cases where you will not want to automatically use the default name, but you still want to capture the people who may not fill out the full URL to your main home page. In that case, you want to set up a link file.

You can create a link file by using the ln command. You can make two different types of links: a hard link and a symbolic link. A *symbolic link* creates a separate file whose sole job is to point towards the intended target file. A *hard link* works in much the same fashion, but the link file becomes a copy of the target file, and changes whenever the original file is changed. Symbolic links are generally preferred, if only because they are more flexible, allowing the user to specify a filename that can link to a target directory instead of a file, and links can be made across systems.

Say you have a file called welcome.html that is designed as the main entry point for your Web site. To create a symbolic link to this file from a second file called

index.html (a more typical entry filename for many Web sites) you would specify it in the following manner:

```
ln -s welcome.html index.html
```

In this example, welcome.html is the target file, and index.html is the link. Index.html is an actual file on your system, and if you do a full directory listing (ls -l) of the directory it will appear as follows:

```
index.html [filesize] index.html - welcome.html
```

This tells you that the link is active and is working. To create a hard link, simply leave off the -s switch. As a final note, make sure when creating a link file that you do it on your Web server; there's no guarantee it will work if you create it locally on your computer and then move it to the Web server.

Setting Permissions

Permissions are set using the chmod (CHange MODe) command. The permission belonging to a file or directory refers to the type of access you and other people have to a file. For example, you may want other people to read and view the Web pages on your site, but not necessarily to change or write new information to them. In some cases you may not even want a file to be visible to anyone else but yourself. You can set the read/write/visibility settings for a file or directory by using the chmod command.

When you do a full directory listing on a Unix system, you will see a series of nine dashes and letters that appear beside each file. These characters reveal the permission values for that file. These nine characters are arranged in three groups of three. The first set of three characters sets the owner's (i.e., the file creator's) permissions, the next three set the group permissions (i.e., the people who will be viewing the files from the Web), and the final three set the permissions for other (i.e., anybody else). Each of these three characters set the execute, write, and read permissions for owner, group, and other, respectively (Figure 17.6).

To really understand how this works and how to read and set permissions properly, you need to deal with a bit of math you likely didn't learn in high school. First off, all of the initial values of each set of three characters works as a binary, off/on, 0/1 setting—a value is either set or not set. File permissions are specified numerical by using an octal base value, which uses the base 8. Each of the three permission characters take on different octal values. The first character of the three corresponds to the decimal value 4, the second takes the decimal value of 2, and the third equals 1. If all three characters are set to on they equal 7. If the first and third are on, they equal 5, if only the second value is set it equals 2, and so on.

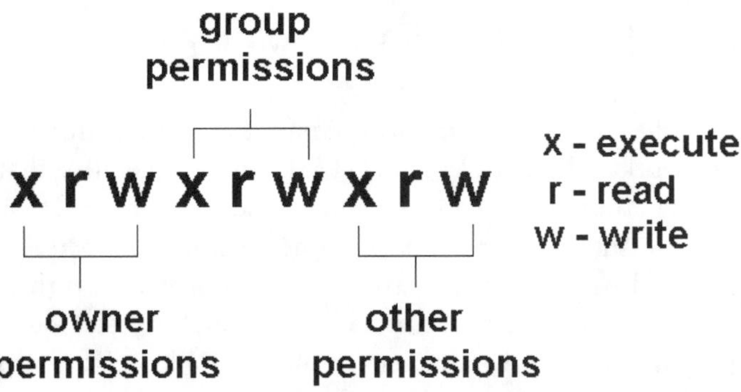

Figure 17.6 The Owner, Group, and Other Permission Settings for chmod

A fairly typical value for chmod is 755, which is specified at the Unix prompt in the following manner:

```
chmod 755 [filename]
```

It sets the following value to the file: rwxr-xr-x. What this says is that the file is readable and executable (if it is a program) by everyone and writeable by the owner only (the sole w value belongs to the owner category). This value typically is used for making programs (like Java applets) on your Web site executable, and allows you to test them out and change them if you need to.

Another typical value is 644, which sets the following value to a file: -rw-r--r--. This says that you have read and write access to the file, and everybody else can only read the file. This value is standard for a typical Web page.

With this information you understand how file permissions work, and you can now configure the permissions to set to your Web files.

Finding Out More Information

If you need any more information on a Unix command, use the man (MANual listing) command. At the prompt, simply type man and the name of the Unix command you want explained further, as in the following example:

```
man mkdir
```

man will also bring up all of the available switches for a given command.

Don't forget when you are done to type "exit" from within your Telnet session to log off your Web server.

Using Internet Firewalls to Provide Server Security

Having a Web site is a terrific way to communicate just about anything to the world. You've worked hard to create HTML and image files that make up a fabulous Web site. Your Web site is live and public to the Internet, and all is right with the world. Or is it? Wouldn't it be a shame if some nasty person could tamper with your files, and perhaps even destroy them? Even worse, if this nasty person has access to Web server files, they may be nasty enough to attempt to compromise the entire computer system. Unfortunately those people exist, and so to protect your files and the computer system as a whole, there are firewalls.

This section discusses firewalls in very broad terms, and is intended to discuss how to come to a decision regarding firewall design, not to provide instructions for building your own firewall. Consult a firewall technology book for detailed information on constructing and maintaining your own Internet security.

A firewall acts as a guarded gateway to your Internet service, in this case a Web site. A firewall is actually a software program that can run on the same computer as the Web server, or on another computer connected to the Web server. A firewall works by examining IP packets traveling between the server and the client. The information is controlled according to IP address and port number in both directions. For instance, a firewall might be configured to block out certain IP numbers, such as everyone from a particular ISP. Firewalls can also be set to keep out requests based on port numbers; for example, the default port for Telnet is 70, so the firewall could block port 70 to disable all attempts to Telnet to and from the protected network.

The firewall must be built according to the needs of the organization using it. You must decide on security policies and a stance for your firewall. A stance is really the philosophy behind your security decisions; are you using the firewall to let everything in except for certain exceptions, or to keep everything out save for certain exceptions? In short, a stance describes the trade-off between ease-of-use and security. A Web site that requires high security will allow only those services required, and all else will be blocked. Conversely, a Web site that values convenience over security will allow all services, and only block those where required.

Before firewall design can begin, you must have very clear policies describing the type and level of security your organization requires. The firewall should directly reflect these security policies. If the policy states that certain actions are prohibited, then you must make sure there are no loopholes, because hackers will find them. Test, test, and test again! Become the worst and most skilled intruder of your worst nightmares, then ensure that this alter ego can be defeated.

Firewalls are not only useful for protecting your network, they can be used to gather statistics on user traffic in both directions and on what services your users are requesting. A firewall can be used to log all activity to and from your network; this information is useful not only to flag suspicious events, but to determine if and when changes to your security policy, and thus to your firewall, are necessary.

Some questions to ask yourself regarding firewalls are:

- Do you have a security policy, and is it accurately reflected by your firewall configuration?
- Are you aware of what protocols and services are required by your users, both internally and externally?
- Who should have access to the service?
- Do you log firewall activity, and scan the logs frequently?
- Have you planned for the inevitable failure, and do you have a plan for repairing the problem, and catching the intruder?

A good resource for further information about firewalls is Yahoo's firewall section at http://www.yahoo.com/Computers_and_Internet/Security_and_Encryption/Firewalls/.

Registering a Domain Name

Are you a company who wants to draw more people more quickly to your Web site? Or are you are an individual who wants to make your Web site something you can truly call your own? Maybe you should think about becoming the (Web)master of your own domain.

Most people who set up a Web site usually have to reference the name of their Internet Service Provider when referring to the name of their home page, i.e., http://www.InternetServiceProvider.com/myname/homepage.html.

This is also true whenever you send email to anybody from your address at myname@InternetServiceProvider.com. This is fine but it is kind of long, not necessarily easy for your friends and associates to remember, and you are inadvertently advertising for your Internet Service Provider whenever you tell anybody else about the location of your home page or send an email. If you are a business, chances are you don't really want to co-advertise your Internet Service Provider or Web hosting service—you are on the Web solely to promote your company, not

somebody else's. As a company, it is also in your best interest to make it as easy as possible for people to remember how to get to your site. If you are an individual and are looking for a way to personalize your Web site or to make it unique, maybe you should consider getting yourself a domain name.

A domain name is the location of your Web site. It is usually made up of three names separated by a period. For instance, EXN: Exploration Network's domain name is http://www.exn.net.

The first part is the name of the host computer, which is the Web server. The second part is the second-level domain name that EXN's system administrator registered with InterNIC. The third part is the top-level domain, which describes what type of organization EXN is. EXN chose to use .net because the site is part of a computer network.

When you store your Web site on your ISP's Web server, your URL will probably be an extension of your ISP's URL. For instance, your home page would have an URL like this:

http://www.yourservice.com/~yourname/

You may prefer to register your own domain name. Your Web files will still be stored in the same place on your Web account, but a domain name and IP number will be aliased to your Web site. So, your URL will look like this:

http://www.yourdomain.com/

Depending on your ISP's domain name registration policy, they may or may not assist you in registering a domain name. Whether your ISP provides guidance or not, it is a good idea to be aware of the process involved in registering your own domain name.

The controlling body for the most common domains is an organization called InterNIC. InterNIC maintains the registration of the .com, net, org, .gov, and .edu top-level domains, shown in Table 17.4.

Country-specific domains, such as .ca for Canada or .mx for Mexico, are maintained by an organization in the host country.

Due to the ever and rapidly increasing number of domain names being snapped

Table 17.4 InterNIC Top-Level Domains

.com	Commercial organization
.net	Network (reserved for major nodes of the Internet)
.org	Nonprofit organization
.gov	Government department
.edu	Educational institution

up for new Web sites, coming up with an unclaimed name is difficult. So before you try registering a site, you have to make sure it hasn't been claimed yet. There are plenty of sites on the Internet that can help you to do this—chances are that if your Internet Service Provider can support your own domain name, it also provides a "whois" search service. The whois search program searches the domain name directory that all Web servers have, and lets you know if there's a match. If there is, you're out of luck because you can't take a name that somebody else has.

If your ISP does not provide this service, there are many others available, such as Domain Name Registration (http://www.domainnameregistry.com/), Domain Name Registration.com (http://www.domainnameregistration.com/), or All domains.com (http://www.alldomains.com/). These sites and many others like it will not only allow you to check to see if a domain name is available, but will help you register it as well. They take care of the paperwork, and you get the name, for a fee. There's also Register.com (http://www.register.com which charges no fee for the service of registering your domain. If you go through one of these third-party domain name providers, make sure you check their fee structure, keeping in mind if you register a U.S. extension that you will have to pay an extra $90 for registering the name on top of whatever they charge. Also, determine whether or not you want to become the sole owner of the name or whether you want the provider for any further administration services. If you are not running your own Web server, expect to pay some sort of additional transfer fee when moving the name and its administration over to your ISP.

In addition, there is some controversy regarding InterNIC's control over the most popular top-level domain names. A competitive organization has recently been set up to develop a more open administration of the global Internet domain-name system, called Generic Top Level Domain. Through the third-party domain-name providers that have signed on with them (which can be found via http://www.gtld-mou.org/docs/reg-results.html), they now offer seven new official top-level domains (listed in Table 17.5) presenting an alternative to the regular names, and offering people a discount from InterNIC's rates.

Keep in mind that even after you register a domain name you may not be able to keep it. If you register a domain name and someone else wants it who can make a reasonable claim to it (i.e., they have a registered trademark or have a legitimate prior claim to the name) they may take you to court. In a few rare cases, people have made money by hoarding names. The classic case here is http://www.television.com/, whose owner was offered $50,000 by C|Net, who turned it down, figuring it was worth more than that (C|Net ended up settling with http://www.tv.com/ instead). It may or may not make you rich, and some people have started calling the many personal domain names "vanity URLs," but registering a domain name is one way to make your Web site truly individual and unique.

Table 17.5 Generic Top-Level Domains

.art	Arts organization
.firm	Commercial firm (an alternative to .com)
.info	Information site
.nom	A name site (designed for the use of individuals)
.rec	Recreational site
.shop	Online shopping site (another possible alternative to .com)
.web	Nonspecific

Registering with InterNIC

If you want to register a domain name using one of the top-level domains controlled by InterNIC, the first step is to connect to the InterNIC Web site at http://www.internic.net. The InterNIC Web site guides you through the stages involved in registering your own domain name (Figure 17.7). Roughly, the process is as follows:

- Search the database for the name you want to use. If it is already being used, then you must choose another name.
- If no one else is using your name, you can go ahead and fill out the form to apply for ownership of that name.

Tip: If the owner of the domain name that you want to use has allowed their ownership of that name to expire, you can apply to InterNIC to take over the name.

There are some costs involved in registering a domain name with InterNIC. At the time of this writing, InterNIC charges $70 to register a domain name and update it in the database for two years. After two years, InterNIC charges $35 to renew the domain name. These charges do not include any changes incurred by transferring the domain name to another party. The InterNIC Web site provides detailed information about their rates and payment options.

It may take several weeks for InterNIC to process and approve your application. You may want to check the InterNIC Web site frequently to monitor the process of your application.

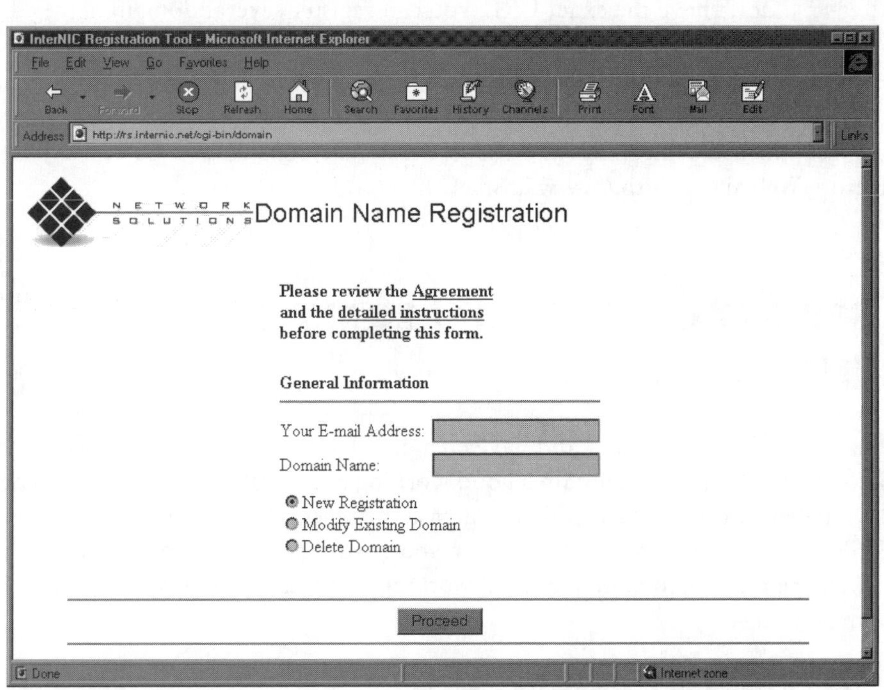

Figure 17.7 A Screen Capture of InterNIC's Second-Level Domain Name Registration Template

See Appendix E for a listing of InterNIC's and Top-Level Domain Organization's domain names plus a listing of all country-level domain names.

The DNS Server

Once you have successfully registered your domain name, you need to advise your service provider of your new URL, and have them alias your Web site account to that domain name. Your service provider will then update their Domain Name System, or DNS, to list your URL with the appropriate IP number. A DNS server is a group of distributed databases containing domain names and their IP numbers. When one DNS server is updated, the others will adopt the change within a day or two. When you request an URL with a Web client, your client consults the DNS server to get the IP number for that URL, then requests the Web page from that Web server.

Tip: If you want to be sure your users will find your Web site even if they don't have the exact URL, you can register several domain names. For instance, EXN has registered exn.ca and exn.net. This way, users who are guessing at EXN's URL will have a better chance of finding it.

To get more technical details about the DNS, consult the DNS Resources Directory Web site at http://www.dns.net.

Keeping on Good Terms with Your ISP

Once you have chosen an ISP and have created a Web site on it, it is in everybody's best interest to keep and maintain a good working relationship with your ISP. There are a number of things you can do to "grease the wheels" with the people who run the ISP, to ensure that you get the service you need when you want it.

To ensure that you maintain a good working relationship with your ISP, aim for two main things:

- Pay your fees and charges promptly
- Make your ISP aware of any significant changes to your Web site

The first point may seem obvious, but it is worth emphasizing. The last thing you want is for your Web site (and Internet access) to disappear overnight. Some ISPs are quicker to erase your Web files than others—most ISPs will send you a warning that your payments are past due, and will give you a certain grace period—but it is generally the best practice to make sure things never get to this point.

The second point comes into play under a number of different circumstances. For example, some ISPs charge a different rate to clients who do commercial business on their Web servers. If you want to place a "for sale" ad for some items you have, or if you are trying to promote a service, you should inform your ISP first. Most ISP operators will make the distinction between what amounts to a small, personal ad on your Web site, and a fully commercial site whose sole purpose is to move product out the door. For another example, you might want to tell your ISP you intend to run a program like an ActiveX component or CGI script on your Web site. Some programs can compromise the security of a Web server; better to tell your ISP of your actions before some hacker takes advantage of some factor of your Web program you haven't thought of, bringing your Web site (and possible your ISP's Web server) to an unhappy end.

(By the way, all of the examples provided so far double as good reasons to keep backup copies of all your Web files and programs.)

By the same token, communication is a two-way street, and a good ISP will provide you with all of the help and information you need to set up a Web site on their server with the least amount of hassle and fuss.

Make sure you get the types of services you require from your ISP, especially when it comes to technical help. Many ISPs have automated the process of providing help for their users by adding extensive information lists of solutions to common problems. Look for these resources on your Web site, but don't be deterred from calling for technical support if you need it. If you're in a position where you can't get on the Web at all, those online resources won't help much. If you find the level of support to be less than desirable, consider jumping to another ISP. Strong competition in the ISP marketplace means that it is a buyer's world, and you can and should get the level of service you need for a reasonable price.

Just as you should take care to ensure that you pay for your ISP services promptly, it is a very good idea to keep track of all of the bills you receive. Many ISPs ranging from small to nationwide operations, have been known to make glaring accounting errors when charging customers. It is fair to state that the traditional strengths of ISPs is getting people connected to the Internet, and not necessarily for their accounting skills. In the vast majority of cases, the ISP is not deliberately out to bilk you, but there are many stories about people being overcharged, and many ISPs have lost large commercial accounts due to poor accounting practices. ISPs will improve in this area only if users bring errors to their attention and force them to do things better in the future.

Also, make sure you know about all of the possible charges you could incur by having a Web site, not just the ones you are being charged for now. For example, take the case of a person who created a Web site that became popular overnight. By the end of the month, he got a whopping bill from his ISP. It turns out that he was being charged for something he had no direct control over—the total amount of downloads from his Web site. His site made use of a lot of pictures and text, so whenever anybody visited the site, they were downloading all of the text and pictures to their system. This person was allotted 100 MB of free downloads from visitors, but after that he was charged on a per megabyte basis for everything above that amount. In this case, because he was on good terms with his ISP, he was able to work things out. The solution in this case was to reduce the graphic content of his Web site in order to reduce the overall size of the downloads made from his site. In addition, he was also able to negotiate with the Internet Service Provider from 100 MB to 500 MB per month. Keep in mind that this was for a noncommercial, fan-based Web site. This example proves that it pays to check with your ISP if there are any hidden charges when you create a Web site.

CHAPTER 18

Web Tools: Building a Web Author's Tool Chest

Most serious HTML authors eventually end up with a tool chest of their favorite Web authoring applications. Despite claims to the contrary by software manufacturers, there is no single HTML editor or tool that handles all types of HTML jobs equally well. Instead, there are a number of individual HTML editors that are exceptional in some areas but lacking in others. Therefore, most Web authors acquire an HTML tool chest over time, containing favorite programs that do particular aspects of HTML very well. A tool chest typically consists of a number of Web editors, some graphic tools, several Web site programs, search and replace tools, and perhaps an HTML-validation program as well.

The following tools and utilities are simply a few of the many tools the authors have found to be useful. Many more are available if you go looking for them. One of the best places to find HTML tools on the Web is TUCOWS at http://

www.tucows.com/. TUCOWS has HTML tools and other goodies for many platforms including Windows 95, Windows 3.1, Macintosh, and OS/2.

HTML Editors

HTML editors are a standard part of any HTML toolkit. There are two basic types of HTML editors: Tag editors and WYSIWYG editors.

Tag editors provides the Web author with direct control over the tags that go into a Web page. Their main advantage is that they are flexible—you can insert a tag anywhere you want within a Web page. Their main disadvantages are that you have to know some HTML basics to get any use out of them, and that creating individual Web pages using this method is slow and labor-intensive.

WYSIWYG editors (actually pseudo-WYSIWYG, as what you see is *not always* what you get, due to the ways different browsers display HTML) present a display that is a rough equivalent of the text and other elements that would be displayed by a Web browser. These types of editors can be add-ons or simple conversion packages to existing word processing programs like Microsoft Word or Corel WordPerfect. Other WYSIWYG editors are stand-alone applications that operate like a word processor; both the SoftQuad's HoTMetaL editor and Microsoft's FrontPage editors work in this way. A WYSIWYG editor's main advantage is speed, because they can produce a lot of HTML pages quickly. This arrangement is perfect if you have a number of already existing documents you want to transform into Web pages. Their main disadvantage is they tend to be inflexible, and may not easily allow you to add new tag types within an HTML document. To choose which type (or types) of HTML editor is suited for you, download a few sample programs and try them out.

The following is a list of popular HTML editors, along with a brief description, and the URL where the editor can be obtained via the Web.

Windows Notepad/Macintosh Simple Text Editors

You can use any basic text editor to write HTML. In the Windows environment, the simple Notepad program is often the HTML editor of choice for many Web authors who like to tinker directly with their HTML code. Macintosh users often start out using the Simpletext editor that is part of the Macintosh operating system. Figure 18.1 shows how to use Notepad to create a Web page.

BBEdit for Macintosh by Bare Bones Software BBEdit is a very simple text-based program, but its simplicity is its beauty. Mac users who are conservative

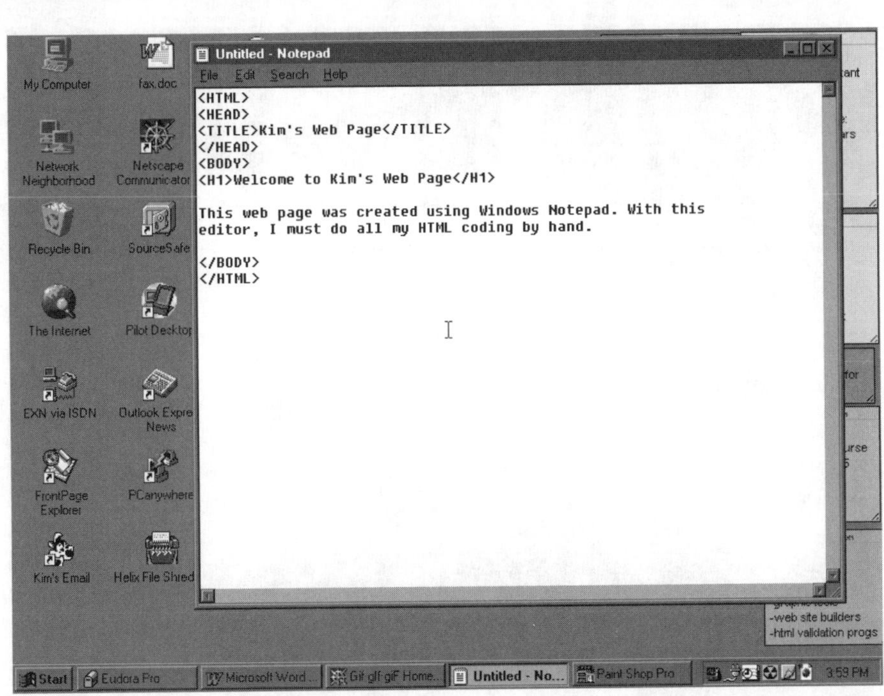

Figure 18.1 Creating a Web Page Using Notepad in Windows95

about disk space will find BBEdit perfect for their needs. Mac users who want a prettier interface will want to look elsewhere. BBEdit can be downloaded from the Bare Bones Software site at http://www.barebones.com/.

HTML Assistant by Brooklyn North Software Works HTML Assistant is a basic text editor, but offers a bit more than a plain text editor such as Notepad or Simpletext. HTML Assistant has a tag toolbar that will insert HTML code for you around the text you have selected. This allows coding to be done slightly faster than coding by hand. Other automated features aid authors in creating tables and frames. HTML Assistant is available in demo and professional versions from Brooklyn North Software Works at http://www.brooknorth.com/. Figure 18.2 shows the HTML Assistant editor in action.

Hot Dog by Sausage Software Hot Dog is very similar to HTML Assistant, in that it is basically a text editor on steroids. Here again Hot Dog allows you to play

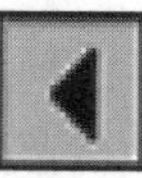

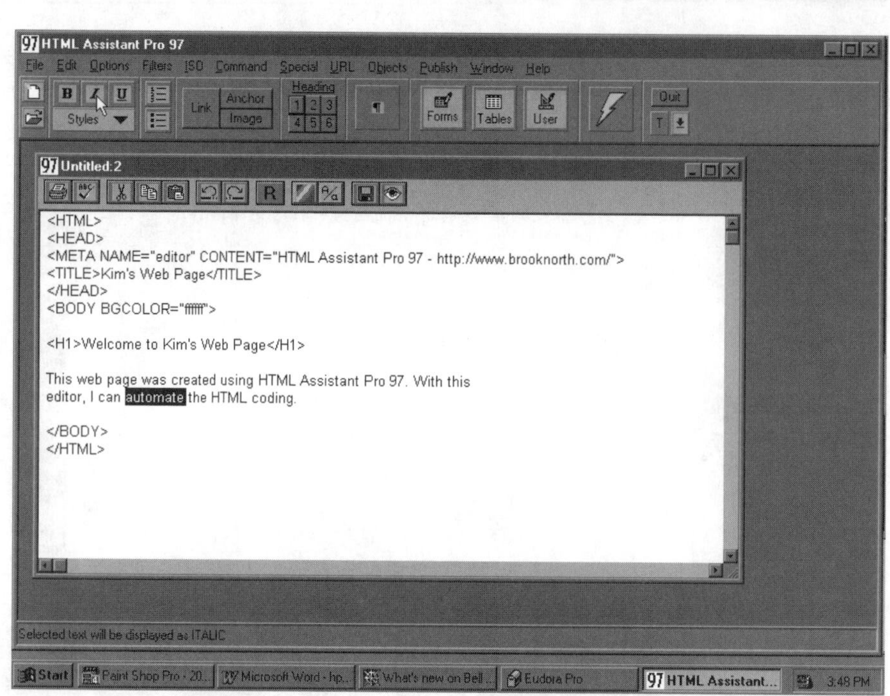

Figure 18.2 Creating a Web Page Using HTML Assistant Pro 97

with individual HTML tags while automating other aspects of tag creation, like creating frames or tables. Hot Dog Express is free, but Hot Dog Professional must be purchased. Both versions are available from Sausage Software at http://www.sausage.com/.

HomeSite by Allaire HomeSite is a powerful HTML editor that also offers some site management tools that can be downloaded and installed separately. HomeSite offers toolbars and buttons to make HTML editing easy, and allows authors to integrate other Web technologies, such as ActiveX controls, Java applets, and JavaScripts. Other features include a global search-and- replace tool and color-coded tags. HomeSite is shareware, and can be downloaded from the Allaire site at http://www.allaire.com/.

HoTMetaL by SoftQuad HoTMetaL is a WYSIWYG editor. The interface works much the same way as a word processor, but with the added features such as tables, frames, and images for creating Web pages. The advantage of editors like HoTMetaL is that the Web page you're editing will look almost exactly as it appears on the Web. As the HTML language develops, SoftQuad makes sure that the editor stays current by offering free HTML extension updates. HoTMetaL comes bundled with site management tools that allow you to manage your entire Web site. HotMetal is available in both evaluation and professional versions from SoftQuad at http://www.softquad.com/.

InContext Spider by InContext Systems InContext Spider, like HoTMetaL, is a WYSIWYG editor. The interface works like a typical word processor, and offers extra goodies such as templates, graphics, backgrounds, Java applets, and a hundred audio clips. This editor supports both Netscape and Microsoft extensions, and the interface is very easy to use. You can get the latest product information about Spider from the InContext Web site at http://www.incontext.com/products/spider1.htm1.

Web Graphic Tools

Having several Web graphics tools at your disposal is an important part of your tool chest. Graphics programs can range from shareware to commercial products; generally the more a tool costs, the more functionality and reliability it offers. Luckily for Web authors who don't want to invest a lot of money in graphic design, both Paint Shop Pro and LView are two graphics programs that are available for downloading from the Internet. They are both shareware, however, and it is important that you register the software if you find you use it regularly. For the Web author who has some cash to spend, Adobe Photoshop is often the graphics package of choice.

The following is a list of popular Web graphic tools, along with a brief description, and the URL where the editor can be obtained via the Web.

Paint Shop Pro by Jasc Inc. Paint Shop Pro is a favorite among Web authors for several reasons: it is freely downloadable shareware, it supports over thirty image formats, it offers many drawing and painting tools including transparency, and it is easy to use. Download the shareware version, but be sure to register it if you use the program beyond the testing phase. Paint Shop Pro is available from Jasc Inc. at htt://www.jasc.com/psp.html.

LView Pro by MMedia Research Corp. LView Pro is another handy tool to keep in your toolbox. Though not as powerful as Paint Shop Pro, LView Pro is useful for viewing graphics and making simple adjustments such as adding transparency, interlacing, and minor editing. LView Pro is shareware, so be sure to register it if you use the program beyond the testing phase. LView Pro is available from MMedia

Research Corp. at http://www.lview.com/. Figure 18.3 is an example of using LView Pro to view a Web graphic.

Adobe Photoshop Adobe Photoshop appears to be the most popular graphic software among Web graphic artists. Though there are no shareware versions of the product, people continue to make the investment because the program is so powerful, and there are so many add-on programs, such as Kai's Power Tools, to create unlimited graphic effects. As well, Photoshop's image creation tools are not restricted to Web use: electronic publishers and graphic artists all over the world have favored this program for several years. The latest product information for Photoshop is available from Adobe Systems at http://www.adobe.com/prodindex/photoshop/main.html.

PhotoImpact GIF Animator by Ulead Systems GIF Animator is a great utility for creating animated GIFs. The interface is simple and easy to use, and allows

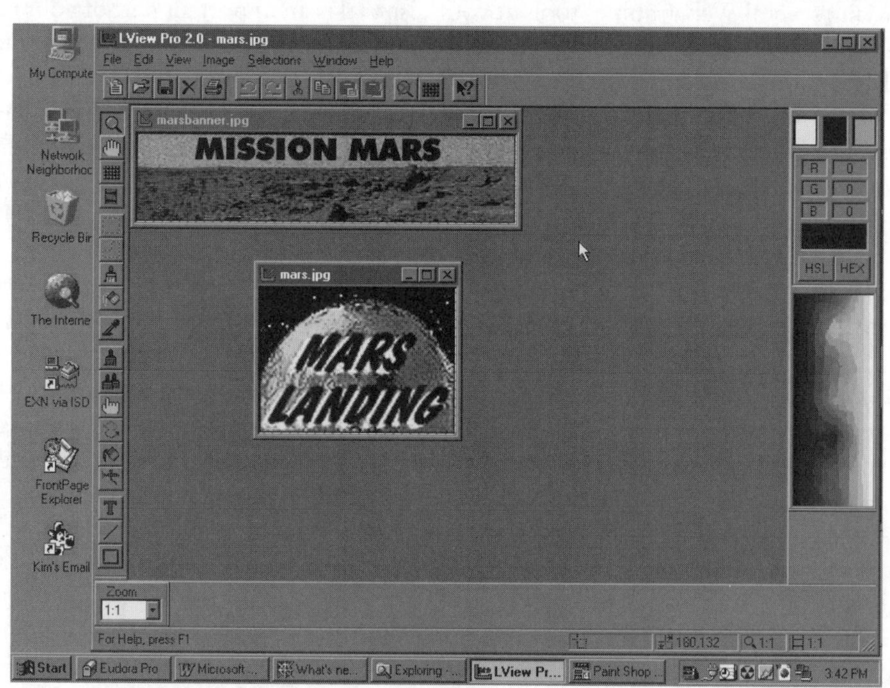

Figure 18.3 Using LView Pro to View a Web Graphic

authors to create GIF animations containing any number of frames and speed rate. GIF Animator is available in a 15-day trial version as well as the commercial version. The latest product information about GIF Animator can be found at the Ulead Web site under PhotoImpact Web Utilities at http://www.ulead.com/.

Gif.gIf.giF by Pedagoguery Software Gif.gIf.giF is another GIF animation utility. It too is simple to use, allowing authors to tweak their animations to include several frames and to control the animation speed. This program is shareware, so be sure to register it if you use it beyond the testing phase. Gif.gIf.giF can be downloaded from the Pedagoguery Web site at http://www.peda.com/ggg/.

LiveImage by LiveImage Corp. LiveImage is a terrific utility for creating client-side image maps. Image maps are images that have "hot spots" that have URLs assigned to them. When a user clicks on a hot spot, the browser loads the specified URL. Using a tool such as LiveImage makes mapping coordinates for URLs easy. Keep in mind, however, that LiveImage only creates a client-side image map. You'll have to do the server-side map on your own. LiveImage offers a free 14-day trial version of their software, available at the LiveImage Web site at http://www.mediatec.com/.

WebMap for the Macintosh WebMap is an image map creation utility for the Macintosh. This tool creates server-side image maps for use with CERN or NCSA compliant Web servers. Creating server-side image maps ensures that all versions of Web browsers will recognize the maps. You can download this shareware utility from http://www.macwiz.com/macwiz/Tricks/Teaching/manuscript/1900-0002.html.

Web Site Management Programs

Up until about two years ago, the only Web creation software that existed were a few HTML editors, graphics programs, and Web server software. Recently, software developers have realized that many Web sites are the effort of a single, or a very few, people. As well, as Web sites become larger they increase in complexity. These two factors have brought about the introduction of a new kind of Web software called Web site builder programs. Web site builder programs often include an HTML editor, a Web site file manager, and often a tool that lets you interface with your Web server. Web site management programs are useful because they can manage the entire Web site, detecting broken hypertext links and incorrect file names before you move your files to the server.

The following is a list of popular Web site management programs, along with a brief description, and the URL where the editor can be obtained via the Web.

NetObjects Fusion by NetObjects NetObjects Fusion is a powerful HTML editor and site management tool rolled into one. Its HTML editor is extremely unique: each part of your Web page, whether it is text or images, is treated as an object. Authors then can drag the objects to anywhere on the page using their mouse; NetObject Fusion dynamically generates a table in the background to accommodate where authors have placed their objects. In this way, Fusion operates much like desktop publishing software. The downside to this editor is that you will never want to edit this HTML by hand, since the tables it has created are so complex that even a small error will throw everything off killer. The Web site management tool is useful for keeping track of all of your Web site files, detecting broken links and displaying your entire site in an easy to read hierarchy. The latest product information for Fusion can be found at the NetObjects Web site at http://www.netobjects.com/netobjects_home.html.

Microsoft FrontPage FrontPage is yet another product offering an HTML editor and site management tool in one product. Again, the interface is very much like a word processor, allowing authors to create tables and frames effortlessly, and insert images and links. FrontPage will also manage your site using a tool called Explorer. Explorer displays your entire Web site as a file listing or hierarchy, keeping an eye on broken links and missing images. If there is a downside to FrontPage, it's that it is biased to creating Internet Explorer custom sites, giving no consideration to Netscape Navigator. Web author beware! FrontPage is available for purchase from Microsoft's Web site at http://www.microsoft.com/frontpage/. Figures 18.4 and 18.5 demonstrate how the FrontPage Explorer displays the structure of a Web site, and how a page is created in the FrontPage editor.

PageMill and SiteMill by Adobe PageMill is similar to NetObjects Fusion in that it too is an HTML editor and site management tool rolled into one package. Fans of Adobe products will like the familiar interface, as creating pages is as simple as using a word processor. SiteMill, the site management tool, is also straightforward and simple to use. The package includes handy extras such as clip art, templates, sounds, and animations. Adobe offers a 15-day trial version of the software as well as the commercial version. The latest product information for PageMill and SiteMill is available at the Adobe Web site at http://www.adobe.com/prodindex/pagemill/main.html.

QuickSite by DeltaPoint Inc. QuickSite combines a WYSIWYG HTML editor with a database-driven Web site management tool. The interface is easy to use, and includes utilities such as an HTML validator to check your code, and an URL checker to find broken links. If the WYSIWYG editor doesn't manage your code as you'd like, you can enter the HTML text editor to hand-code your pages. All Web

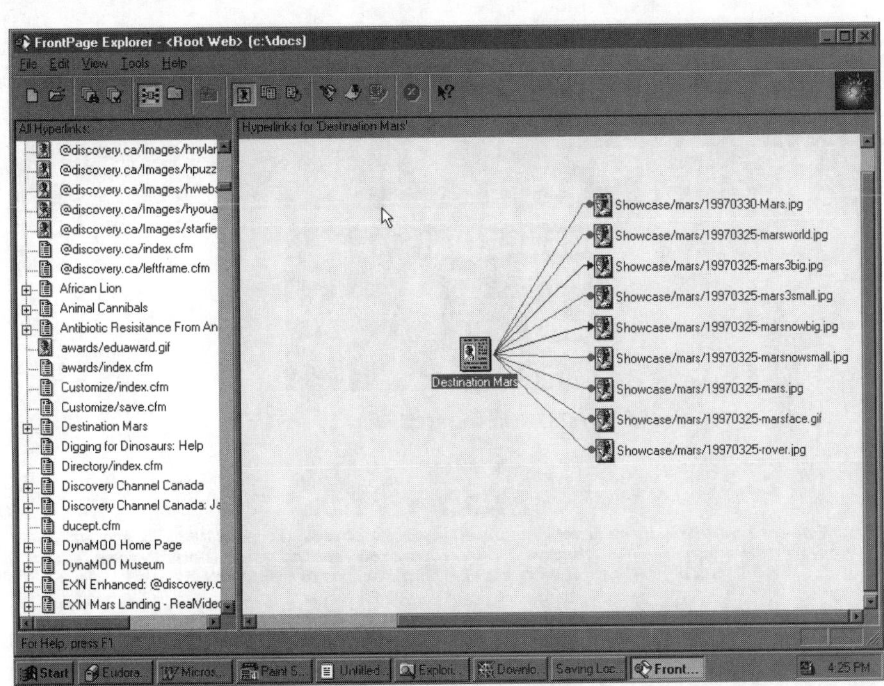

Figure 18.4 Using the FrontPage Explorer to Display the Structure of a Web Site

pages are stored in the QuickSite database; when a change to a page is made, all other pages affected by that change are updated. Creating corporate sites can be done quickly with one of QuickSite's templates. A free 30-day trial version of QuickSite can be downloaded from the DeltaPoint Web site at http://www.deltapoint.com/.

CyberStudio by GoLive Systems Inc. One of the new HTML editor and site management tools for the Mac is CyberStudio. Similar to NetObjects Fusion, CyberStudio offers a grid layout that lets users drag and drop the desired HTML elements into a page. The site management tool allows users to view the hierarchy of their Web site, and offers utilities such as search-and-replace and a spelling checker. Unfortunately, a powerful program such as this demands significant disk space and memory requirements. A 30-day trial version of CyberStudio can be downloaded from the GoLive site at http://www.golive.com.

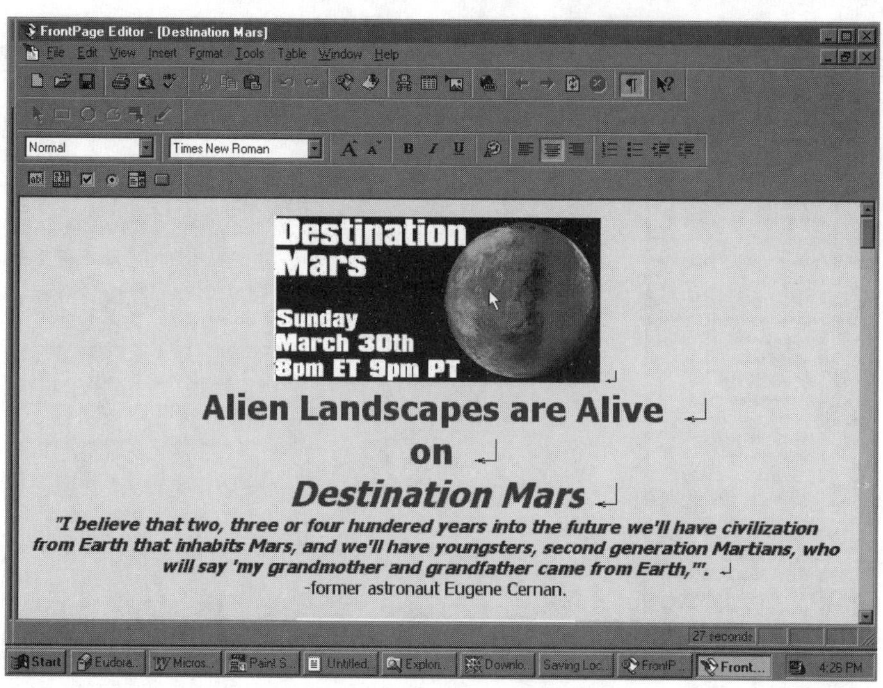

Figure 18.5 Using the FrontPage Editor to Create a Web Page

Search and Replace Tools Every Web author will eventually run into a common problem: the need to change a single item on every single page of your site, for instance a toolbar or graphic. This can be very time consuming, but luckily there are some tools out there that will help make the job a bit less painful. Some search and replace tools are better than others, and new ones are being developed all the time, so keep your eyes open for new programs.

Many Web site management programs now offer search-and-replace utilities. However, if you want to search and replace in one step, there is one tool, Search and Replace by Funduc Software, that will do this for you.

Search and Replace by Funduc Software This simple yet useful utility will change code globally on your Web site. It can add lines of HTML code quickly to all of your Web pages. This program is shareware, and can be downloaded from the Funduc Web site at http://www/funduc.com.

HTML Validation Programs

Several utilities are available that will comb through your Web site to find broken links and missing images. Using programs such as these is a very good idea: it's much better for authors to find and repair their own errors before the public does!

The following is a list of HTML validation programs, along with a brief description, and the URL where the editor can be obtained via the Web.

Doctor HTML by Imagiware, Inc. Doctor HTML is a very useful utility. It is a Web-based utility that retrieves your Web pages to check them for spelling, missing images, and broken hyperlinks. Detailed information on Doctor HTML is available at the Imagiware Web site at http://www2.imagiware.com/RxHTML/.

WebLint WebLint is a Perl script that checks your Web pages for syntax errors and style. Information about WebLint can be found at the WebLint Web site at http://www.cre.canon.co.uk/~neilb/weblint.html.

Web authors with a tool chest full of useful programs and utilities as described earlier will find that they can handle just about any obstacle their Web site throws at them. Expect that as new Web software is developed, your tool chest will evolve and change as well. Many authors find that they need more than one kind of editor, several graphic tools, and several other utilities to meet the diverse needs of their site. It's also a good idea for Web authors to compare their tool chests against those of their peers; if you have a problem that you can't lick, chances are someone else has run into the same problem, and may have a solution he or she is willing to share.

CHAPTER 19

Design Style

Back in version 1.0 of the official HTML specification, there were few ways to change the design of a Web page. Web authors could not control the typeface of a font or its color, tables and frames did not yet exist, and images offered few attributes. Web pages then were very simple, and quite dull. They did excel, however, in displaying information in a clear, no-nonsense fashion.

Now with HTML 4.0, Web authors have more power and flexibility than ever before when designing their pages. But there is always the danger of becoming too zealous in using the new design tags. Web pages that have too many styles quickly become ugly and unwieldy, and difficult to read. The goal of this chapter is to define some style guidelines to keep in mind when authoring Web pages.

Working with Fonts

The <FONT> tag allows authors to define font size and color right down to the individual character. Web authors designing with the Microsoft Internet Explorer

browser in mind can also define the typeface. Using these attributes can produce some handy effects:

- Increasing the font size of the initial character of a paragraph gives the effect of a large initial capital that is common in hardcopy books.
- Putting special text such as footnote numbers in a smaller font size, in addition to using the <SUP> tags, is more attractive than leaving the font size of the footnote the same as the body text.
- Decreasing the font size of a whole body of text can make more information fit in the window of your browser. Keep in mind that small font sizes become difficult to read for users with less than perfect vision.
- Increasing the font size of a whole body of text can make your text more easily read by users who have weak eyesight. If your Web site audience includes senior citizens, increasing your font size is appropriate for your site.
- Defining specific typefaces for your fonts creates the customized look that is otherwise only achievable by creating an image. Remember that users must have the font you specify on their system to see that font; otherwise, their default font, usually Times New Roman, will be used to display the text. Defining a font that is common on most systems, such as Arial, will ensure that more users will see the text as you have designed it. Defining the font typeface is a tag recognized only by the Microsoft Internet Explorer browser.
- Using color to emphasize text is handy when simply bolding or italicizing text isn't appropriate.
- Color can also add an artistic look to your pages. If you design Web pages for artistic endeavors, color can add creativity to your page without having to use graphics, which will take much longer to download than plain colored text.

Figure 19.1 is an example of using fonts for good and for evil.

Remember that the more you vary the text size, color, and typeface of the fonts on your Web page, the more cluttered and messy your pages will appear. Do not use the <FONT> element and its attributes to the point of exhausting your users. Use font tricks for effect; the content of your Web page is always a higher priority than how it looks. For detailed information on the <FONT> element, see Chapter 3, Displayed Elements.

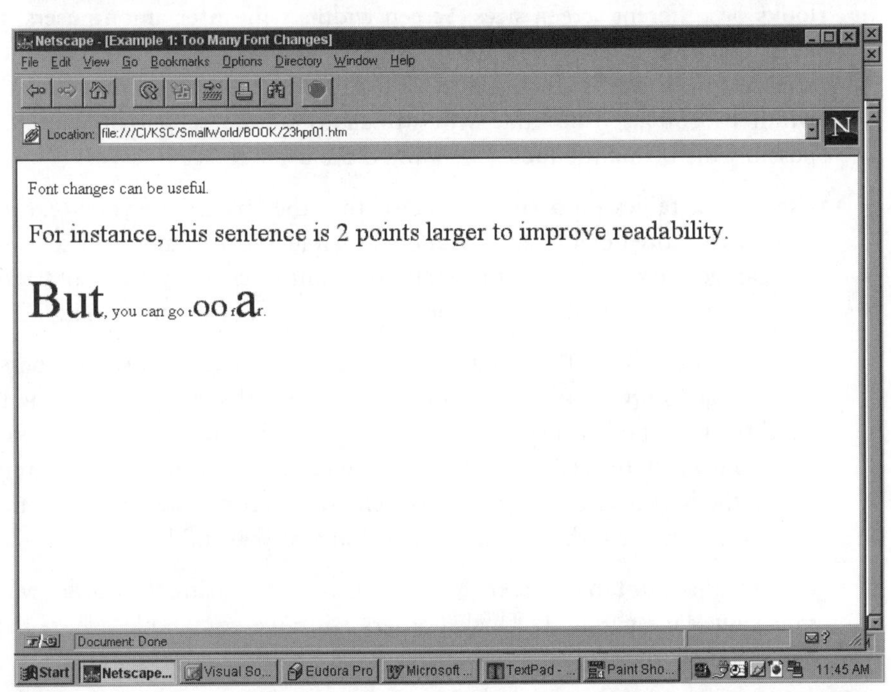

Figure 19.1 Bad and Good Use of Fonts on a Web Page

USING TABLES

The table element is the Web author's best friend. Introduced by the Mosaic version 2.0 browser and supported by Microsoft Internet Explorer version 2.0 and Netscape 1.1 and later, tables can be viewed by the majority of browsers used today.

Tables are a great way to organize lists and charts, but their versatility goes farther than that. Creating several tables on a page gives Web authors the freedom to place text and images in a design not possible with other HTML tags. Setting the border attribute to zero makes your borders invisible, so that your table does not look like a table to the user. The table element allows the author to set very accurate parameters for each table cell, such as width in pixels or by percentage, cell padding and cell spacing, alignment, and so on.

Here are a few tips and tricks for using tables:

- Set your table width to an absolute pixel width to control how your page looks on different screen sizes. Screen widths will differ among users; the most common screen sizes are 640x480 pixels and 800x600 pixels, but screens can be much larger, up to 1280x1024 pixels. If you set your table width to 100%, your table will stretch to fit the screen of your user, possibly distorting the look you wanted the users to see.
- Use several tables on a single page so that the spacing of your text and graphics is more flexible. It is certainly possible to merge and split cells, but this can get messy and frustrating. If you want to create a different layout with the next chunk of information, create a new table to contain it.
- Specify table cell widths using absolute values. If you change the content of your pages often, but want to keep the same table structure, define the width of your table cells. This way, if you remove an image or section of text from a cell, the cell will maintain its width. Unfortunately, you cannot define the height of a cell, so empty cells will become narrow when their content is removed, thus changing the shape of your table.
- If you want your table borders to be visible, try increasing the border width to a value larger than 1. Thick borders will give your table a neat three dimensional effect.
- Many WYSIWYG HTML editors make creating tables very easy. Unfortunately, sometimes these editors aren't able accommodate the many attributes each table tag has. Don't be afraid to go into the raw HTML and do your own fine-tuning to the tables created by your editor.
- If your Web site audience uses the Microsoft Internet Explorer browser, have some fun with the MSIE HTML extensions, such as border color and background color. Keep in mind that users of other browsers will not see these effects.

Figures 19.2 and 19.3 show a page built with tables; Figure 19.2 has borders turned on, and Figure 19.3 has them turned off.

Tables look great when viewed with a browser, but can be a huge mess when viewed in plain HTML. Do not despair: Table code will seem very complex at first, but soon you will become accustomed to it. Using lots of white space in your code to separate rows and columns will make the HTML easier to read and debug. For detailed information on the <TABLE> and related elements, see Chapter 8, "Tables."

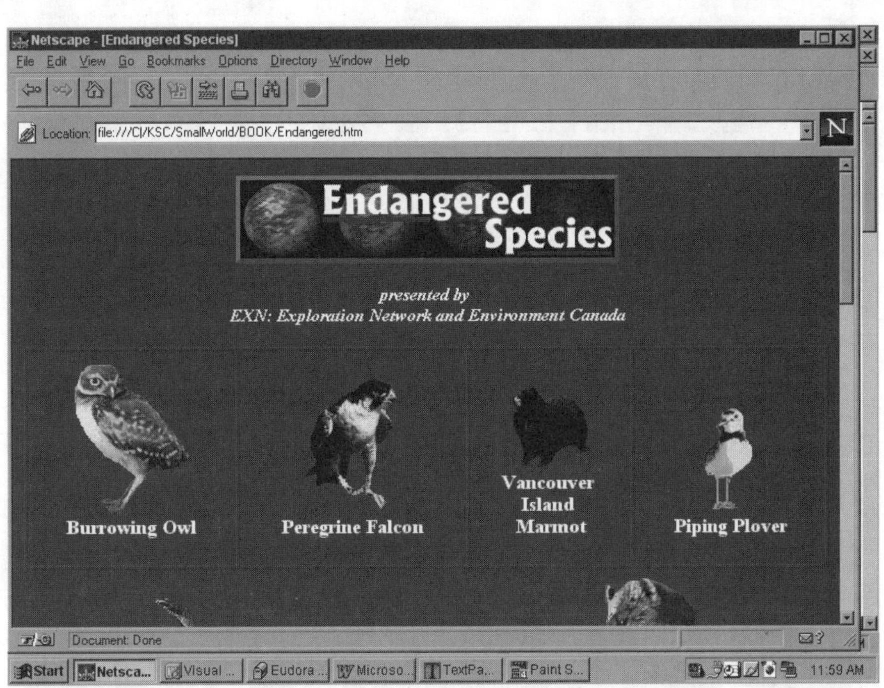

Figure 19.2 Tables with Borders

Using Frames

Frames were first introduced by Netscape version 2.0, and are supported by Mosaic version 3.0 and Microsoft Internet Explorer version 3.0 and later. Earlier versions of browsers will not recognize frames.

Frames continue to be controversial in Web authoring circles. They take tables a step further in that each frame in a given Web browser window is actually an independent Web page. This means that you can essentially display more than one Web page at once, each frame scrolling independently of the others. As cool as this is, it can become a stylistic mess very quickly.

The most important thing to consider when you decide to design with frames is that users with small, 14-inch monitors usually harbor a strong dislike for frames.

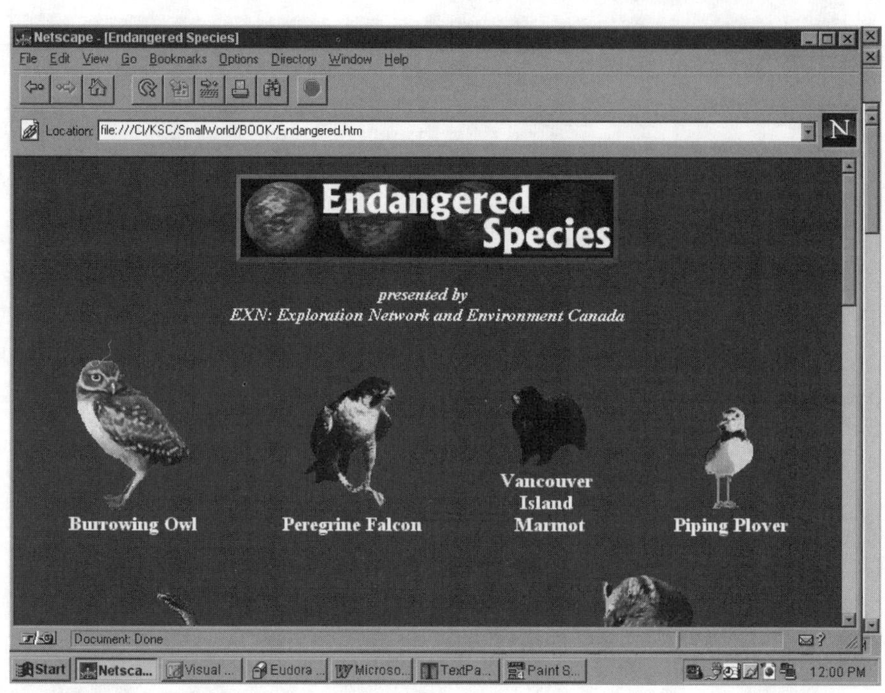

Figure 19.3 Tables without Borders

This is because frames need a large viewing area to look attractive; a Web page containing more than two frames, even on a large monitor, looks crowded and is difficult to navigate.

Here are some things to think about when designing with frames:

- Always, always, always include a page to display to users with browsers that cannot display frames. This page is contained between the <NOFRAMES> tags after the <FRAMESET> tags. Neglecting to include a nonframed version of your Web page is consistent with bad style. Some Web authors go a step further by offering a nonframed version of their entire site.
- Unless you are sure the majority of your audience has large monitors, do not design more than three frames into your Web page. Splitting a screen into more than thirds will only annoy your users.

- Design so that one frame is the dominant frame, with the other frames offering supporting information. For instance, a page with three frames might be designed so that the top frame holds a banner, the middle frame holds the body of information for the page, and the bottom frame holds a toolbar.
- Consider turning off the borders of your frames to give a more seamless effect to your page. Keep in mind that any frame that requires scrolling will have a scrollbar, creating a kind of border.

Figures 19.4 and 19.5 are two examples of pages with frames; Figure 19.4 demonstrates how frames can clutter a page, and Figure 19.5 demonstrates how frames can be used conservatively so as not to distract from the content.

If you can ever use tables where you thought you wanted frames, do so. Frames just aren't that well received, and that may not change until larger monitors become more common.

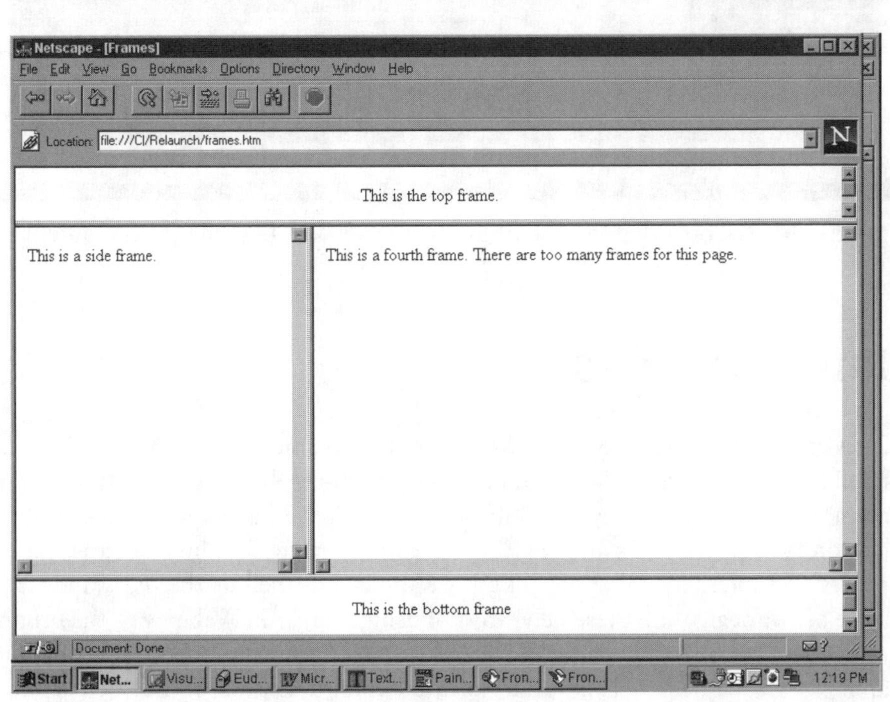

Figure 19.4 Too Many Frames Can Clutter a Page

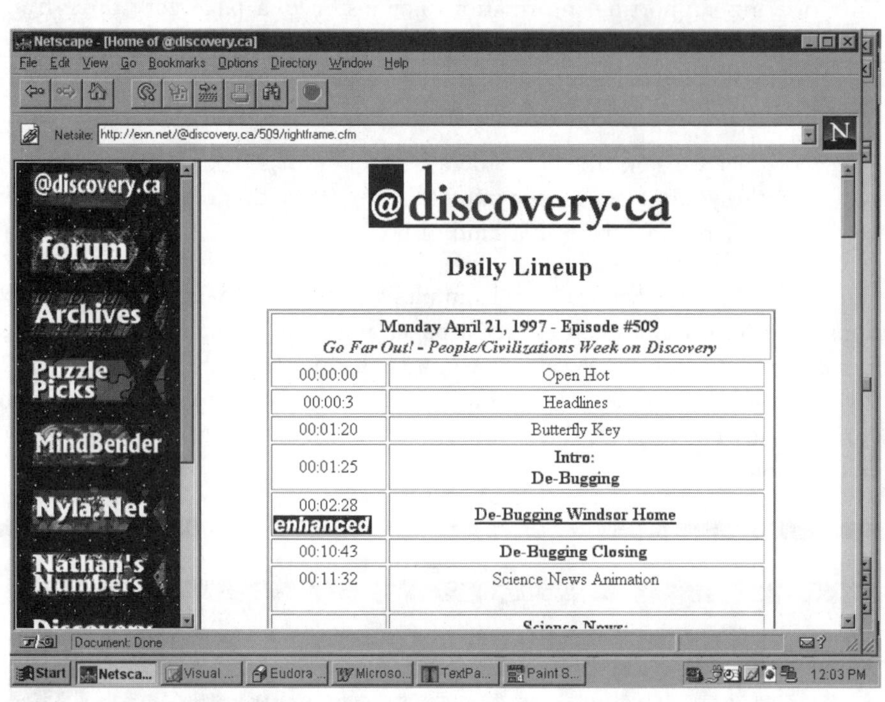

Figure 19.5 A Conservative Use of Frames Does Not Distract from Content

Using Images

Images can really make or break a Web page. Handsome, useful graphics that have a small file size are terrific; large, cumbersome, high-resolution graphics that do not serve a purpose can make your Web page a disaster. Images now come in many forms on Web pages: GIFs and JPGs, background images and image maps, camera captures and interactive graphics like Java applets, as well as the old standby, the picture of your cat. With these new ways of using images in Web pages, the original problem still remains: balancing the urge to shower your users with mind-blowing graphics with the heart-felt desire to keep download time short and your content clear. The following tips will help you find your happy medium.

- Use only the graphics you really need. If plain HTML text is just as appropriate as a graphic, use the text.

- Always use the ALT attribute of the <IMG> tag to provide alternate text for your image. Many users have their images turned off, and Lynx users can see only text; alternate text replaces the image on your page.
- Use the width and height attributes of the <IMG> tag. Specifying the correct dimensions of your image will allow your browser to load graphics faster.
- Do not use image maps for an entire page. Lynx users and people who have set their browsers not to load images will not see your page. Furthermore, large images take too long to download. Use several graphics independently as hypertext links, and be sure to provide a text equivalent.
- Keep your images small, and be sure your GIF images are interlaced. Use as few colors as you feel you can; aiming for no more than 256 colors is a good milestone.
- Watch your file size and choose the lowest when deciding whether to make your images in GIF or JPG format.
- If you are using background images or colors, be sure your foreground text color is not difficult to read against your background. Use contrasting colors whenever possible. Consider enlarging the font size if you think your text might be difficult to read.
- Many users have monitors that display 256 colors or less. If you have your monitor set to more than 256 colors, your users won't have the same viewing experience as you.
- Different computers have different color palettes. An image that displays using one palette on your Macintosh is not going to display exactly the same on a Unix machine or PC.

One of the best ways to test your pages is to ask someone to take a look at them, and give you an honest opinion about your images and color choices. A fresh pair of eyes will give you a clear impression of what you're about to display to the world.

Style Tips and Tricks

Finally, here are some additional guidelines to think about as you design your Web site.

- Be clear about what you want to communicate. Your headings should accurately reflect the content of your pages.

- Design your pages so they are not too dense. Thick fields of text scare users away. Use lots of white space to lighten the load.
- Consider a table of contents. If your page is made up of several important sections, you may want to list your headings at the top of your page, then use hypertext anchors to link to the heading's section.
- Don't waste Web pages. If you have a Web page that does not have a lot of content on it, consider incorporating that information into an existing Web page. Make every Web page a meaningful one.
- Consider putting all your content on one Web page, then use hypertext anchors to link to specific points on your page. This will please users who want to print your information, as it will be contained in one document.
- Use a spell checker and proofread your work! Don't let the whole world know you're not a natural at spelling and grammar.
- Use a consistent design scheme. If you want your Web site to be viewed as a body of work, it's good practice to use similar or at least complimentary color and design strategies to produce a coherent package.
- Give your users a way out. Always have a link returning the user to your home page. Toolbars are terrific here, as you can use the same toolbar on every Web page to direct users to key areas of your site.

These tips are meant only to get you thinking about how you want to design your Web site. There are really no hard and fast rules to Web design, since the intent of your pages must direct your design decisions. For instance, Web pages that are designed to display poetic works will be radically different from a corporate Web site, and so the earlier suggestions must apply to your situation accordingly.

The most important thing to remember is to design for your intended audience. Try to find out what speed of modem they have, what monitor size, their tolerance for slow downloads. If you can define your audience, half the battle is won.

The unfortunate reality is that an author's Web audience is often too wide and varied to be able to cater to so specifically. Most authors must be content with satisfying some of the people some of the time. Some Web authors prefer the grass-roots method, designing for the lowest common denominator; others choose to push the limit, using as much advanced technology as they can, hoping their audience will want to keep up. It is not fair to say what approach is best, only to know what your approach is, and to stick with it.

Link: Many Web sites offer advice on Web site design. Half the fun is finding that they often contradict one another! Take a peek at these sites, then form your own opinion.

Crafting a Nifty Personal Web Site at http://www2.hawaii.edu/jay/styleguide/.

Web Pages that Suck at http://www.webpagesthatsuck.com/.

Dzine at http://www.lcc.gatech.edu/gallery/dzine/.

Bandwidth Conservation Society at http://www.infohiway.com/faster/index.html.

Developer Zone at http://www.projectcool.com/developer/.

Listing of HTML Tags

The following is an alphabetical listing of all of the tags described in detail in this book.

<!-- . . . -->

Element Name: Comment Tag.

Description: Text enclosed between the <!— and —> delimiters is not displayed by graphical Web browsers. Lynx browsers will display the commented text.

Attributes: None.

Sample:

```
<!-- This commented text will not display in a
graphical Web browser-->
```

<!DOCTYPE>

Element Name: Document type definition tag.

Description: Identifies to the Web browser what kind of HTML document it is about to display.

Attributes: None.

Associated Tags: None.

Sample:

```
<!DOCTYPE HTML PUBLIC "-//W3C//DTD HTML 3.2 Final//EN">
```

<A> . . . </A>

Element Name: Anchor tag.

Description: Creates hypertext links. This tag always needs either the HREF or the NAME attribute to define what Web page will be downloaded when the user clicks on the text contained within the anchor tags.

Attributes:

ACCESSKEY = *key*
Specifies the keyboard key associated with the legend.
CHARSET = *ISO-#*
Indicates the international character coding used for the hyperlink.
COORDS = *x, y*
Sets the *x, y* coordinates of the hotspot area.
HREF = *URL*
A hypertext reference that points to the URL of another Web page, or to a specific point within another Web page when used with the NAME attribute. The URL that follows the HREF can be either a path NAME to indicate a link to another Web page on the same Web server, or a full URL to indicate a link to a Web page on an external Web server on the World Wide Web. The URL must be enclosed in quotes.
HREFLANG = *text*
Specifies the base language of the resource indicated in the HREF attribute.
NAME= *text*
Used to NAME a specific part of a Web document so that it can be a TARGET for a hypertext link within the same document, or at a specific point within a Web page.
REL = *URL*
Indicates the URL of a subdocument. This attribute is not commonly used.
REV = *URL*
Indicates the URL of a parent document. This attribute is not commonly used.
SHAPE = CIRCLE | POLYGON | RECT
Specifies the type of hotspot shape. RECT is the default.

- CIRCLE - "center x, center y, radius" values.
- POLYGON - the successive x1, y1, x2, y2, etc. points of the polygon.
- RECT (default) - "left,top,right,bottom" values.

TABINDEX= *number*
Specifies the order in which an individual item can be selected from a group of items by using the TAB keyboard key.

TARGET= *target_name*
Used to specify a specific frame within a Web page. For more information on frames, see Chapter 9, "Frames; Multiple Columns and Layers."
TITLE= *text*
Provides a TITLE for the URL the hypertext link is referencing. Some browsers, such as Microsoft Internet Explorer, display the text specified in the TITLE attribute when the mouse is moved over the hypertext link.
TYPE = *MIME type*
Specifies the MIME type of the file type to which the hypertext anchor points.

Associated Tags: None.

Sample:

```
<A HREF=http://www.exn.net>This hypertext link takes you
to the Exploration Network Web site.</A>
```

<ADDRESS> . . . </ADDRESS>

Element Name: Address tag.

Description: Contains address information.

Attributes: None.

Associated Tags: <BODY>, any other formatting element.

Sample:

```
<ADDRESS>
AP Professional
6277 Sea Harbor Drive
Orlando, FL
32821-9816
</ADDRESS>
```

<APPLET> . . . </APPLET>

Element Name: Applet tag.

Description: Inserts a Java applet within a Web page.

Attributes: ALIGN = *LEFT* | *RIGHT* | *CENTER* | *TOP* | *MIDDLE* | *BOTTOM* (IE 3.0 and up)
ALIGN= *LEFT* | *RIGHT* | *TOP* | *ABSMIDDLE* | *ABSBOTTOM* | *TEXTTOP* | *MIDDLE* | *BASELINE* | *BOTTOM* (NN 3.0 and up)
Specifies where the applet appears in the applet window.
ALT= *text*
Specifies a string of text to be displayed.
ARCHIVE= *filename.zip*
Specifies the name of a compressed file containing .class files relevant to the applet.
CODE= *filename.class*
Specifies the name of the Java .class file. A required element.

CODEBASE= *codebaseURL*
Specifies the full path of the Java applet referenced by CODE, if it is different than that of the Web page used to reference the applet .class file.
HEIGHT= # *pixels*
Specifies the vertical dimension of the applet window. A required element.
HSPACE= # *pixels*
Specifies the horizontal distance between the applet window and other elements on the Web page.
MAYSCRIPT (NN 3.0 only)
Permits the applet to access JavaScript.
NAME= *appletInstanceName*
Specifies the name for the applet instance.
VSPACE= # *pixels*
Specifies the vertical distance between the applet window and other elements on the Web page.
WIDTH= # *pixels*
Specifies the horizontal dimension of the applet window. A required element.

Associated Tags: <PARAM>

Sample:

```
<APPLET CODE=WelcomeToJava.class CODEBASE="..\.." ALT="My
First Java Applet" WIDTH=200 HEIGHT=200 VSPACE=10
HSPACE=10 ALIGN=RIGHT> </APPLET>
```

<AREA>

Element Name: Area tag.

Description: Defines the hotspots in a client-side imagemap.

Attributes:

ALT= *text*
Sets the text to appear when the cursor from the user's browser passes over the hotspot.
COORDS= *x,y*
Sets the *x,y* coordinates of the hotspot area.
HREF= *URL*
Sets the link associated with each hotspot.
NOHREF
Sets a region that does not contain a link.
NOTAB (Internet Explorer only)
Describes the tabable order of a hotspot within an imagemap.
SHAPE= *CIRCLE | POLYGON | RECT*
Specifies the type of hotspot shape. RECT is the default.

- CIRCLE - "center x; center y, radius" values.
- POLYGON - the successive x1, y1, x2, y2, etc. points of the polygon.
- RECT (default) - "left, top, right, bottom" values.

TABORDER= *number* (Internet Explorer only).
Sets the tabable order of a hotspot within an imagemap.

Associated Tags: <MAP>

Sample:

```
<MAP>
<AREA SHAPE="RECT" COORD="98,34,23,15"
HREF="http://www.longUnlikelyUrl.net/index.html">
<AREA SHAPE="CIRCLE" COORD="200, 155, 35"
HREF="http://www. longUnlikelyUrl.net/stuff.html">
<AREA SHAPE="POLYGON" COORD="371,235,126,339,190,207"
HREF="http://www.longUnlikelyUrl.net/moreStuff.html">
</MAP>
```

<B> . . . </B>

Element Name: Bold tag.

Description: Indicates text displayed in bold font.

Attributes: None.

Sample:

```
<B>This text is bold,</B> while this text is more demure.
```

<BASE>

Element Name: Base tag.

Description: Identifies the HTML file's current location.

Attributes: HREF=*URL*
Uses the HREF tag to specify the full Web address of the source Web page.

Sample:

```
<HEAD>
<TITLE>HTML 3.2 Reference Specification</TITLE>
<BASE HREF="http://www.w3.org/pub/WWW/TR/REC-html32.html">
</HEAD>
```

<BASEFONT> . . . </BASEFONT>

Element Name: Basefont tag.

Description: Specifies the base font value(s) for the text to be displayed on a Web page.

Attributes: COLOR= *colorname or colorvalue*
Specifies the color of the font to be displayed.
FACE= *fontname*
Specifies the type of font to be displayed.
SIZE= *number*
Specifies the base font size. Valid ranges are between 1–7 (smallest to largest).

Associated Tags: <FONT>, <BODY>, any other formatting element.

Sample:

```
<BASEFONT=2>
This text is set to a BASEFONT value of 2
<P>
<FONT SIZE=+1>This text has been incremented by
one.</FONT>
<P>
<FONT SIZE=+2>This text has been incremented by two over
the original, &lt;BASEFONT&gt; value.</FONT>
<P>
<FONT FACE=ARIAL COLOR=RED>Other characteristics, such as
color and the font type can also be changed</FONT>
```

<BGSOUND>

Element Name: Background sound tag.

Description: Inserts a background sound into a Web page.

Attributes: SRC= filename.wav
Specifies the path and filename of a sound file (.wav, .au, or .mid format can be used).
LOOP= *number* | *INFINITE*
Specifies the number of times a sound is played.
DELAY= *number*
The number of seconds to delay before playing the sound file.
VOLUME= *number*
The volume level of the sound file. The default value, 0, is the loudest, and 10000 produces zero volume output.
BALANCE= *number*
Specifies the sound output in a stereo situation. 10000 outputs 100% to the right speaker and 10000 outputs 100% to the left speaker. The default value, 0, balances the output.

Sample:

```
<BGSOUND SRC="honk.wav" LOOP=infinite>
```

<BIG> . . . </BIG>

Element Name: Big font tag.

Description: Indicates text displayed in a larger font than regular font size.

Attributes: None.

Sample:

```
<BIG>This text is bigger</BIG> than this text.
```

<BLINK> . . . </BLINK>

Element Name: Blink tag.

Description: Makes the text it encloses flash on and off.

Attributes: None.

Associated Tags: <BODY>, any other formatting element.

Sample:

```
<BLINK>
This text will blink uncontrollably forever! And you have
no control over how it is displayed. Ha ha ha!
</BLINK>
```

<BLOCKQUOTE> . . . </BLOCKQUOTE>

Element Name: Blockquote tag.

Description: Contains a large quotation.

Attributes: CITE= *URL*
Specifies an URL that points to the source of the quotation.

Associated Tags: <BODY>, any other formatting element.

Sample:

```
Sample quotation:
<BLOCKQUOTE>
A cloud lay over Asgaard. Not in the sky, for the sun
shone clear in the soft blue heaven; nor on the earth,
for the flowers starred the meadows with their gay
blossoms and birds sang in the whispering groves.
<P>
The gloom was in the hearts of the &Aelig; and Asynjar,
for Baldur, their darling, the Shining God, was sad.
</BLOCKQUOTE>
```

<BODY> . . . </BODY>

Element Name: Body tag.

Description: Contains all other HTML tags and the entire content of your Web page. The <BODY> tag is mandatory.

Attributes: ALINK= *colorname* or *colorvalue*
Defines the color of a hypertext link as the user clicks on it. The color is defined using RBG values.

BACKGROUND= *colorname* or *colorvalue*
Defines the image for the background of your Web page. This image must be in GIF or JPEG format. See Chapter 6, "Color, Images, and Imagemaps" for more information on images.
BGCOLOR= *colorname* or *colorvalue*
Defines the color of the background of your Web page using RBG values.
LINK= *colorname* or *colorvalue*
Defines the color of a hypertext link before the user clicks on it, using RBG values.
TEXT= *colorname* or *colorvalue*
Defines the default color of the text in your document using RBG values.
VLINK= *colorname* or *colorvalue*
Defines the color of a hypertext link after the user clicks on it, using RBG values.

Associated Tags: All other tags occur within the <BODY> tag.

Sample:

```
<BODY BGCOLOR="#FFFFFF" LINK="#23238E" ALINK="#FF0000"
VLINK="#215E21" TEXT="#000000">
```


Element Name: Break tag.

Description: Adds line breaks at the end of a line of text.

Attributes: CLEAR= *NONE* | *LEFT* | *RIGHT* | *ALL*
Used whenever a floating element exists on a Web page, to break the line and start the text that appears after it in the next clear margin.

Associated Tags: <BODY>, any other formatting element.

Sample:

```
This is a continuous line of text.
<P>
This line of text<BR> is broken up<BR> and spread over
several lines.
```

<BUTTON> . . . </BUTTON>

Element Name: Button tag.

Description: Displays a button with no predefined function.

Attributes: NAME= *button_name*
Assigns a name to the button.
VALUE= *button_value*
Assigns a value to the button.
TYPE= *BUTTON* | *RESET* | *SUBMIT*
Specifies the type of button to be displayed.

Associated Tags: The set of form tags.

Sample:

```
<FORM ACTION="http://www.somewhere somehow.ca"
METHOD="post">
<P>
Stuff #1: <INPUT TYPE=CHECKBOX NAME="stuff" VALUE="1"><BR>
Stuff #2: <INPUT TYPE=CHECKBOX NAME="stuff" VALUE="2"><BR>
<BUTTON TYPE=SUBMIT NAME="submit it" VALUE="submit">
</BUTTON>
<BUTTON TYPE=BUTTON NAME="other" VALUE="The Other
Button"></BUTTON>
</FORM>
```

<CAPTION> . . . </CAPTION>

Element Name: Caption tag.

Description: Creates a table caption.

Attributes: ALIGN = *BOTTOM | LEFT | CENTER | RIGHT | TOP*
Specifies the alignment of the caption relative to the table. TOP puts the caption above the table and BOTTOM puts the caption under the table. Microsoft Internet Explorer supports additional values that specify the horizontal alignment of the text within the caption, specifically LEFT, RIGHT, and CENTER.
VALIGN = *TOP | BOTTOM*
Specifies the vertical alignment of the caption relative to the table. Values are TOP and BOTTOM. This attribute is recognized by Microsoft Internet Explorer only, and serves the same purpose as ALIGN.

Sample:

```
<TABLE BORDER="1">
<TH>Column 1</TH>
<TH>Column 2</TH>
<TR>
<TD>Cell 1</TD>
<TD>Cell 2</TD>
</TR>
<TR>
<TD>Cell 3</TD>
<TD>Cell 4</TD>
</TR>
<CAPTION>A Basic Table</CAPTION>
</TABLE>
```

<CENTER> . . . </CENTER>

Element Name: Center tag.

Description: Horizontally aligns any element of the viewer's browser window.

Attributes: None.

Associated Tags: <BODY>, any other formatting element (other than <BR>).

Sample:

```
<CENTER>This plain text is centered on the Web page.
</CENTER>
<P>
<CENTER><H2>This level-2 header is centered on the Web
page.</H2></CENTER>
<P>
<CENTER>This image<BR> <IMG SRC="philco jnr.jpg"><BR> and
text is centered on the Web page.</CENTER>
```

<CITE> . . . </CITE>

Element Name: Citation tag.

Description: Indicates that the text is a citation. It is usually displayed in italic text.

Attributes: None.

Sample:

```
<CITE>The Last Voyage of Somebody the Sailor</CITE> by
John Barth.
```

<CODE> . . . </CODE>

Element Name: Code tag.

Description: Indicates that the text is a source code sample. It is displayed in a fixed-width font.

Attributes: None.

Sample:

```
To begin the solitaire game, type <CODE>sol.exe</CODE> on
the command line.
```

<COL>

Element Name: Column tag.

Description: Specifies the default settings for a column or group of columns.

Attributes:

ALIGN=*LEFT* | *CENTER* | *RIGHT*
Specifies the horizontal alignment of cell content.
CHAR= *character*
Specifies an alignment character for use with ALIGN=CHAR.
CHAROFF= # *of character spaces* or %
Specifies the offset to the first occurrence of the alignment character on each line.
SPAN= *number*
Specifies how many columns the column specification is to be applied to. Value must be 0 or greater.

VALIGN= *TOP* | *MIDDLE* | *BASELINE* | *BOTTOM*
Specifies whether the cell contents are aligned with the top, middle, or bottom of the cell.
WIDTH= # *of pixel* or % *of browser window*
Specifies the width of the column either as a percentage of the window width, or as an absolute value in pixels.

Associated Tags: <TABLE>, <TBODY>, <THEAD>, <TR>, <TD>, <COLGROUP>

Sample:

```
<TABLE BORDER>
<COLGROUP>
<COL ALIGN=RIGHT SPAN=2>
<COLGROUP ALIGN=LEFT>
<THEAD>
<TR>
<TH>APPLES</TH><TH>BANANAS</TH><TH>CHERRIES</TH>
</TR>
</THEAD>
<TBODY>
<TR>
<TD>1</TD><TD>2</TD><TD>3</TD>
</TR>
<TR>
<TD>3</TD><TD>4</TD><TD>5</TD>
</TR>
</TBODY>
</TABLE>
```

<COLGROUP> . . . </COLGROUP>

Element Name: Column group tag.

Description: Specifies settings for a group of columns in a table.

Attributes:

ALIGN=*LEFT* | *CENTER* | *RIGHT*
Specifies the horizontal alignment of cell content.
CHAR= *character*
Specifies an alignment character for use with ALIGN=CHAR.
CHAROFF= # *of character spaces* or %
Specifies the offset to the first occurrence of the alignment character on each line.
SPAN= *number*
Specifies how many columns are contained within the current group. Value must be 0 or greater.
VALIGN= *TOP* | *MIDDLE* | *BASELINE* | *BOTTOM*
Specifies whether the cell contents are aligned with the top, middle, or bottom of the cell.
WIDTH= # *of pixel* or % *of browser window*
Specifies the width of the column grouping either as a percentage of the window width, or as an absolute value in pixels.

Associated Tags: <TABLE>, <TBODY>, <THEAD>, <TR>, <TD>, <COL>

Can contain: <COL>

Sample:

```
<TABLE BORDER>
<COLGROUP>
<COL ALIGN=RIGHT SPAN=2>
<COLGROUP ALIGN=LEFT>
<THEAD>
<TR>
<TH>APPLES</TH><TH>BANANAS</TH><TH>CHERRIES</TH>
</TR>
</THEAD>
<TBODY>
<TR>
<TD>1</TD><TD>2</TD><TD>3</TD>
</TR>
<TR>
<TD>3</TD><TD>4</TD><TD>5</TD>
</TR>
</TBODY>
</TABLE>
```

<DD> (. . . </DD>)

Element Name: Definition tag.

Description: Defines the definition for the preceding the definition term (<DT>) within a definition list (<DL>). The end tag can be used but is not required.

Attributes: COMPACT
Tells the browser to display the list in a compact form.

Can contain: Text, text markup, <A>, <IMG>

Associated Tags: <DL>, <DD>

Sample:

```
<DL>
<DT>Cardinal<DD>A colorful North American bird. The male
is a deep red.
<DT>Blue Jay<DD>A raucous, intelligent bird.
</DL>
```

<DIR> . . . </DIR>

Element Name: Directory list tag.

Description: Displays a number of directory items in a columnar format. Rarely implemented and little used. Each list item is preceded by a bullet.

Attributes: None.

Can contain: <LI>

Can be contained within: <BLOCKQUOTE>, <BODY>, <DD>, <FORM>, <LI>

Associated Tags: <LI>

Sample:

```
<DIR>
<LI>A
<LI>B
<LI>C
<LI>D
<LI>E
<LI>F
</DIR>
```

<DIV> . . . </DIV>

Element Name: Division tag.

Description: Specifies a section of a Web page in which CSS elements are used.

Attributes:

CHARSET = *ISO-#*
Indicates the international character coding used for the hyperlink.
HREF = *URL*
Points to a Web page that is viewed when the content contained within the <SPAN> tag is activated.
HREFLANG = *text*
Specifies the base language of the resource indicated in the HREF attribute.
MEDIA = *ALL | BRAILLE | PRINT | PROJECTION | SCREEN | SPEECH*
Specifies the type of medium for which the CSS definitions are designed.
REL = *URL*
Indicates the URL of a subdocument. This attribute is not commonly used.
REV = *URL*
Indicates the URL of a parent document. This attribute is not commonly used.
TARGET = *frame name*
Specifies the name of the frame (if any) that the content set by HREF should be viewed within.
TYPE = *MIME type*
Specifies the MIME type of the content enclosed by the style tag.

Sample:

```
This text is displayed using the default characteristics.
<DIV STYLE="FONT-SIZE: 18PT; COLOR: TEAL">
Whoa! Big Teal-colored text!
<B><I>Still</I></B> big and teal-y.
<P>
</DIV>
Whew! Back to normal text display.
```

<DL> . . . </DL>

Element Name: Definition list tag.

Description: Creates a list of definitions, composed of a list of terms and their corresponding definitions.

Attributes: COMPACT
Tells the browser to display the list in a compact form.

Can contain:
, <DD>, <DT>

Can be contained within: <BODY>, <BLOCKQUOTE>, <DD>, <FORM>, <LI>

Associated Tags: <DD>, <DL>

Sample:

```
<DL>
<DT>Cardinal<DD>A colorful North American bird. The male
is a deep red.
<DT>Blue Jay<DD>A raucous, intelligent bird.
</DL>
```

<DFN> . . . </DFN>

Element Name: Definition tag.

Description: Contains a definition of a term.

Attributes: None.

Associated Tags: <BODY>, any other formatting element

Sample:

```
The definition of an isosceles triangle is: <DFN>a
triangle that has two sides of equal length</DFN>.
```

<DT> (. . . </DT>)

Element Name: Definition term tag.

Description: Defines an individual term within a definition list. The end tag can be used but is not required. The <DT> tag is typically followed by a definition (<DD>).

Attributes: COMPACT
Tells the browser to display the list in a compact form.

Can contain: Text, text markup, <A>, <IMG>

Associated Tags: <DL>, <DD>

Sample:

```
<DL>
<DT>Cardinal<DD>A colorful North American bird. The male
is a deep red.
<DT>Blue Jay<DD>A raucous, intelligent bird.
</DL>
```

<EM> . . . </EM>

Element Name: Emphasized text tag.

Description: Indicates that the text is displayed with an emphasized font, usually rendered by Web browsers as italicized text.

Attributes: None.

Sample:

```
<EM>Keep Out!!</EM>
```

<EMBED>

Element Name: Embed tag.

Description: Embeds Netscape plug-in media into a Web page.

Attributes: ALIGN= *BOTTOM | LEFT | RIGHT | TOP*
The alignment of the object on the Web page. Values are LEFT, RIGHT, TOP, and BOTTOM. The default value is LEFT.
BORDER= *# pixels*
The size in pixels of the border around the object.
HEIGHT= *# pixels*
The height in pixels of the object. This attribute is required.
SRC= *URL*
The URL of the media file. This attribute is required.
WIDTH= *# pixels*
The width in pixels of the object. This attribute is required.

Sample:

```
<EMBED SRC="kim.mov" WIDTH="150" HEIGHT="250"
CONTROLS="TRUE">
```

<FIELDSET> . . . </FIELDSET>

Element Name: Fieldset tag.

Description: Allows the Web author to group thematically related inputs together.

Attributes: None.

Associated Tags: <LEGEND>, set of form tags

Sample:

```
<FORM ACTION=".." METHOD=POST>
<FIELDSET>
<LEGEND ALIGN="top">Some Info</LEGEND>
Stuff #1: <INPUT TYPE=RADIO NAME="stuff" VALUE="1">
Stuff #2: <INPUT TYPE=RADIO NAME="stuff" VALUE="2">
</FIELDSET>
</FORM>
```

<FONT> . . . <FONT>

Element Name: Font tag.

Description: Specifies the specific font to be displayed on a Web page.

Attributes:

COLOR= *colorname* or *colorvalue*
Specifies the color of the font to be displayed.
FACE= *fontname*
Specifies the type of font to be displayed.
POINT-SIZE= *number*
Specifies the specific font size to be displayed.
SIZE= *number*
Specifies the base font size. Valid ranges are between 1–7 (smallest to largest).

Associated Tags: <BASEFONT>, <BODY>, any other formatting element

Sample:

```
<BASEFONT=2>
This text is set to a BASEFONT value of 2
<P>
<FONT SIZE=+1>This text has been incremented by
one.</FONT>
<P>
<FONT SIZE=+2>This text has been incremented by two over
the original, &lt;BASEFONT&gt; value.</FONT>
<P>
<FONT FACE=ARIAL COLOR=RED>Other characteristics, such as
color and the font type can also be changed</FONT>
```

<FORM> . . . </FORM>

Element Name: Form tag.

Description: Contains and defines the elements that make up an online form.

Attributes:

ACTION= *URL*
Specifies the URL that processes the contents of the form.
ENCTYPE= *MIME type*
Specifies the media type used to encode the information contained in the form.
METHOD= *POST | GET*
POST specifies that information from the form is sent to the server as a set of NAME=

VALUE pairs separated by ampersand (&) characters. GET specifies that information from the form is sent to the server through the environment variable QUERY_STRING.
TARGET= *text*
Specifies the name of the frame in which the browser should display the form results after the user submits the information contained in the current form.

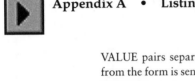

Associated Tags: <INPUT>, <TEXTAREA>, <OPTION> <FIELDSET>, <LEGEND>, and <SELECT>

Sample:

```
<FORM METHOD="POST"
ACTION="http://www.myfunkyfunkysite.ca/luv my form">
Please enter the following information:<BR>
Your Full Name: <INPUT TYPE=TEXT>
<INPUT TYPE=RESET> <INPUT TYPE=SUBMIT><BR>
</FORM>
```

<FRAME>

Element Name: Frame tag.

Description: Specifies the page that contains the content of an individual frame.

Attributes:
BORDERCOLOR= *colorname or rrggbb*
Sets the color of the frame border.
FRAMEBORDER= *YES* | *NO* (Netscape Navigator) or *1* | *0* (Internet Explorer)
Sets a global border for all frames.
LONGDESC= *URL*
Points to a URL that contains more information about the frame.
MARGINHEIGHT= *# pixels*
Sets the vertical margin between the content of a frame and the frame itself.
MARGINWIDTH= *# pixels*
Sets the horizontal margin between the content of a frame and the frame itself.
NAME= *text*
Sets a name for a specific framed space within a framed Web page.
NORESIZE
Specifies that the dimensions of a frame cannot be changed by the user.
SCROLLING= *AUTO* | *YES* | *NO*
Specifies whether or not a scrollbar should appear within a frame.
SRC= *URL*
Specifies the URL of the Web page to be displayed within a frame.

Associated Tags <FRAMESET>, <NOFRAMES>

Sample:

```
<HTML>

<HEAD>
<TITLE>Keith's Vintage Radio Collection</TITLE>
</HEAD>
<FRAMESET ROWS="50, *" FRAMEBORDER=0 FRAMESPACING=0>
<FRAME SRC="kvrc.htm"
       MARGINHEIGHT=0
       MARGINWIDTH=0
```

```
        NAME="header"
        SCROLLING = "no"
        NORESIZE>
<FRAMESET COLS="225, *">
<FRAME SRC="toc.htm"
        NAME="toc"
        MARGINHEIGHT=5
        MARGINWIDTH=5
        SCROLLING = "yes"
        NORESIZE>
<FRAME SRC="default.htm"
        NAME="default"
        SCROLLING = "yes"
        NORESIZE>
</FRAMESET>
</FRAMESET>
</HTML>
```

<FRAMESET> . . . </FRAMESET>

Element Name: Frameset tag.

Description: Specifies a set of frames.

Attributes: BORDER= # *pixels*
Specifies the thickness of the frame border in pixels.
BORDERCOLOR= *colorname* or *rrggbb*
Sets the color of the frame border (Netscape Navigator 3.0 and higher only).
COLS= # *pixels or % of browser width*
Sets the column size for an individual frame in pixels.
FRAMEBORDER= YES | NO (Netscape Navigator) or 1 | 0 (Internet Explorer)
Sets a global border for all frames.
FRAMESPACING= # *pixels*
Specifies whether or not there is any spacing between frames on a page (Internet Explorer only).
ROWS= # *pixels or % of browser width*
Sets the row size for an individual frame in pixels.

Associated Tags: <FRAME>, <NOFRAMES>

Sample:

```
<HTML>

<HEAD>
<TITLE>Keith's Vintage Radio Collection</TITLE>
</HEAD>
<FRAMESET ROWS="50, *" FRAMEBORDER=0 FRAMESPACING=0>
<FRAME SRC="kvrc.htm"
        MARGINHEIGHT=0
        MARGINWIDTH=0
```

```
        NAME="header"
        SCROLLING = "no"
        NORESIZE>
<FRAMESET COLS="225, *">
<FRAME SRC="toc.htm"
        NAME="toc"
        MARGINHEIGHT=5
        MARGINWIDTH=5
        SCROLLING = "yes"
        NORESIZE>
<FRAME SRC="default.htm"
        NAME="default"
        SCROLLING = "yes"
        NORESIZE>
</FRAMESET>
</FRAMESET>
</HTML>
```

<Hn> . . . </Hn>

Element Name: Heading tag.

Description: Specifies a topic heading.

Attributes: ALIGN= *LEFT* | *CENTER* | *RIGHT* | *JUSTIFY* (Netscape 4.0 and Internet Explorer 4.0 only)

Associated Tags: <BODY>, any other formatting element

Sample:

```
<H1>Level-1 Heading</H1>
<H2>Level-2 Heading</H2>
<H3>Level-3 Heading</H3>
<H4>Level-4 Heading</H4>
<H5>Level-5 Heading</H5>
<H6>Level-6 Heading</H6>
```

<HEAD> . . . </HEAD>

Element Name: Header tag.

Description: Contains information about the Web page, and must include the <TITLE> tag.

Attributes: None.

Associated Tags: <BASE>, <ISINDEX>, <LINK>, <META>, <STYLE>, <SCRIPT>, <TITLE>.

Sample:

```
<HEAD>
This text does not display on the Web page.
</HEAD>
```

<HR>

Element Name: Hard rule tag.

Description: Designed to insert a horizontal rule line in a Web page.

Attributes: ALIGN= *LEFT | CENTER | RIGHT*
Aligns the hard rule on the Web page.
COLOR= *colorname* or *colorvalue* (*Internet Explorer only*)
Specifies a particular color for the hard rule line.
NOSHADE
Specifies that the hard rule should be a solid line, with no shade effects.
SIZE= # *pixels* | % *of browser window*
Sets the vertical size of the hard rule line in pixels, or as a percentage of the browser window's width.
WIDTH= # *pixels* | % *of browser window*
Sets the horizontal size of the hard rule in pixels, or as a percentage of the browser window's width.

Associated Tags: <BODY>, any other formatting element

Sample:

```
Here is some text that appears above a horizontal hard
rule.<BR>
<HR>
This text appears beneath the hard rule.<BR>
```

<HTML> . . . </HTML>

Element Name: HTML tag.

Description: Declares the beginning and the end of an HTML document. This is the tag that must appear immediately after the <!DOCTYPE> tag, and its ending tag (</HTML>) must appear at the end of the document.

Attributes: None.

Associated Tags: All other HTML tags.

Sample:

```
<!DOCTYPE HTML PUBLIC "-//W3C//DTD HTML 3.2 Final//EN">
<HTML>
<HEAD>
<TITLE>Kim's Web Page</TITLE>
</HEAD>
<BODY>
All other tags, and the content of your HTML page belong
here.
</BODY>
</HTML>
```

<I> . . . </I>

Element Name: Italic tag.

Description: Indicates text displayed in italic font.

Attributes: None.

Sample:

```
<I>This text is italicized,</I> while this text is not.
```

<IFRAME> . . . </IFRAME>

Element Name: Inline (or "floating") frame tag.

Attributes:

ALIGN = *LEFT* | *RIGHT* | *TOP* | *MIDDLE* | *BOTTOM*
Sets the alignment of text following the inline frame.
FRAMEBORDER= **1** | *0*
Determines whether or not a border appears around the frame.
HEIGHT= # *pixels*
Sets the height of the frame in pixels.
HSPACE= # *pixels*
Sets horizontal spacing around the frame in pixels.
LONGDESC= *URL*
Points to a URL that contains more information about the floating frame.
MARGINHEIGHT= # *pixels*
Sets a horizontal spacing within the frame in pixels.
MARGINWIDTH= # *pixels*
Sets the vertical spacing within the frame in pixels.
NAME= *text*
Specifies a title or "name" for the inline frame.
SCROLLING= *AUTO* | *YES* | *NO*
Tells the browser whether or not a scrollbar should be displayed within the floating frame.
SRC= *URL*
Specifies the URL of the Web page to appear within the floating frame.
VSPACE= # *pixels*
Sets the vertical spacing around the frame in pixels.
WIDTH= # *pixels*
Sets the width of the frame in pixels.

Associated Tags: None.

Sample:

```
<IFRAME ALIGN=RIGHT NAME="FunkyFloatingFrame" WIDTH=400
HEIGHT=250 SRC="frame1.html">
You are looking at a page that contains a floating
Frame.
</IFRAME>
```

<ILAYER> . . . </ILAYER>

Element Name: Inflow Layer tag.

Description: Defines a layer that is set within the body of a Web page.

Attributes:

ABOVE = *layername*
Specifies the stacking order of a layer within a set of layers. If used, the attributes BELOW and Z-INDEX cannot be used—they are mutually exclusive.
BACKGROUND = *filename*
Tiles a background image within a layer.
BELOW = *layername*
Specifies the stacking order of a layer within a set of layers. If used, the attributes ABOVE and Z-INDEX cannot be used—they are mutually exclusive.
BGCOLOR = *colorname or hexadecimal colorvalue*
Sets the background color of a layer.
CLIP = *x, y, x1, y1*
Specifies the dimensions of a clipping rectangle (a visible layer) that appears within a layer.
HEIGHT = *# pixels or % of browser window*
Specifies the height of the layer in pixels, and sets the reference height for any children layers.
ID = "*layer_name*"
Specifies the name of the layer. It serves as an identifier to distinguish it from other layers and to JavaScript scripts. Functionally equivalent to the NAME attribute.
LEFT = *# pixels*
Specifies the horizontal positioning of the layer in pixels. Works differently than the LEFT attribute of the <LAYER> tag in that with <ILAYER> it denotes the relative horizontal positioning of the layer.
NAME = "*layer_name*"
Specifies the name of the layer. It serves as an identifier to distinguish it from other layers and to JavaScript scripts. Functionally equivalent to the ID attribute.
PAGEX = *# pixels*
Specifies the horizontal position of the layer relative to the document window in pixels.
PAGEY = *# pixels*
Specifies the vertical position of the layer relative to the document window in pixels.
SRC = *URL*
Specifies the full pathname of a separate Web page containing HTML-formatted content for the layer.
TOP = *# pixels*
Specifies the vertical positioning of the layer in pixels. Works differently than the TOP attribute of the <LAYER> tag in that with <ILAYER> it denotes the relative vertical positioning of the layer.
VISIBILITY= *SHOW | HIDE | INHERIT*
Specifies whether or not the layer is visible.
WIDTH = *# pixels or % of browser window*

Specifies the width of the layer in pixels (applies to text only).
Z-INDEX
Specifies the stacking order of a layer within a set of layers. If used, the attributes ABOVE and BELOW cannot be used—they are mutually exclusive.

Associated Tags: None (however, always used in conjunction with JavaScript).

Sample:

```
While looking for lions in Africa, I remember running
across the Gnu on the great plains. <ILAYER ID="gnu">The
gnu is a large hairy beast with horns, a mean-looking
expression, and an equally-bad temperament if you get too
close</ILAYER>.
```

<IMG>

Element Name: Image tag.

Description: Inserts images into the Web document. The <IMG> tag is an empty element, and does not have an end tag.

Attributes: ALIGN= *ABSBOTTOM* | *ABSMIDDLE* | *BASELINE* | *BOTTOM* | *LEFT* | *MIDDLE* | *RIGHT* | *TEXTTOP* | *TOP*
Aligns the image according to the value you specify. Aligning an image LEFT or RIGHT causes the image to align with the left or right margin while the text flows around it. Aligning an image TOP, TEXTTOP, MIDDLE, ABSMIDDLE, BASELINE, BOTTOM, and ABSBOTTOM indicates the vertical alignment of the text relative to the image on the same line.
ALT= *text*
Specifies what text to display as an alternative to the image. This text is displayed by browsers who have images disabled and by text-only browsers such as Lynx. The ALT text is also often displayed first, before the image itself is loaded.
BORDER= # *pixels*
Specifies the image border size in pixels. BORDER=0 indicates that the image does not have a border. If the image is a hypertext link, the border color is the same as the LINK color. If the image is not a hypertext link, then the border color is the same as the TEXT color. Both the LINK and TEXT colors are specified in the BODY tag at the top of the hypertext document.
CONTROLS
Specifies the set of video controls to be displayed to control the play of an inline video. Used with the DYNSRC attribute, it is recognized only by Internet Explorer.
DYNSRC= *URL*
Specifies the filename or URL of an inline video. This attribute is recognized only in Internet Explorer.
WIDTH= # *pixels*
Specifies the width of the image in pixels. Specifying the width and height of the image allows the browser to load the image faster because it does not have to measure the

image before displaying it. However, if the dimensions you specify are incorrect, your image will be stretched or shrunk to the size you specified, making your image appear distorted.

HEIGHT= # *pixels*

Specifies the height of the image in pixels. Specifying the width and height of the image allows the browser to load the image faster because it does not have to measure the image before displaying it. However, if the dimensions you specify are incorrect, your image will be stretched or shrunk to the size you specified, making your image appear distorted.

HSPACE= # *pixels*

Specifies the amount of space, in pixels, on the left and right sides of the image. Acts as padding between the image and the text or other objects surrounding the image.

ISMAP

Indicates that the image is an image map. This attribute is used alone within the tag, along with a hypertext link to a map file that specifies the sensitive coordinates of the image. The map file specifies what URL to go to when the user clicks on a particular area of the image.

LOOP= *number | INFINITE*

Specifies how many times an inline video will play. Specifying INFINITE or –1 will play the video indefinitely. Used with the DYNSRC attribute, it is recognized only by the Internet Explorer.

LOWSRC

Specifies the filename of a low-resolution image to be loaded before the higher resolution defined by the SRC attribute.

SRC= *URL*

Specifies the filename or URL of the image file.

START= *FILEOPEN | MOUSEOVER*

Specifies when the inline video will begin playing. FILEOPEN causes the video to play as soon as it is finished loading; MOUSEOVER causes the video to begin playing when the user places the mouse over the video clip. Used with the DYNSRC attribute, it is recognized within Internet Explorer only.

USEMAP= *URL*

Specifies the URL of the client-side image map. This attribute is recognized only by browsers with the ability to interpret client-side image maps. The USEMAP attribute is used with the ISMAP attribute to accommodate both types of image maps.

VRML= *filename or URL*

Specifies the filename or URL of an inline VRML world. This attribute launches a VRML viewer to display the VRML file. This attribute is recognized only within Internet Explorer.

VSPACE= # *pixels*

Specifies the amount of space, in pixels, on the top and bottom sides of the image. Acts as padding between the image and the text or other objects surrounding the image.

Sample:

```
<IMG SRC="kscthumb.gif" BORDER=1 ALIGN=RIGHT HEIGHT=40
WIDTH=35 HSPACE=3 VSPACE=3 ALT="Thumbnail picture of
Kim">
```

<INPUT>

Element Name: Input tag.

Description: Specifies the type of form element displayed within a form.

Attributes:

INPUT TYPE=BUTTON NAME="*text*" TYPE="*text*" VALUE="*text*"
Creates a button to be used by a JavaScript program.
INPUT TYPE=CHECKBOX (CHECKED) NAME="*text*" TYPE="*text*" VALUE="*text*"
Creates a checkbox that can be enabled or disabled by the user. CHECKED indicates the default selection.
INPUT TYPE=FILE NAME="*text*" TYPE="*text*" VALUE="*text*"
Enables the user to specify a filename that serves as input for the form.
INPUT TYPE=HIDDEN NAME="*text*" TYPE="*text*" VALUE="*text*"
Inserts a value that is not displayed to the user. Usually used to identify the form to the server.
INPUT TYPE=IMAGE (ALIGN) [BUTTON] BORDER URL
Allows an image file to be displayed within a form button.
INPUT TYPE=PASSWORD (MAXLENGTH, SIZE) NAME="*text*" TYPE="*text*" (VALUE="*text*")
Creates a text field for typing passwords. The SIZE value sets the width of the field in characters.
INPUT TYPE=RADIO (CHECKED) NAME="*text*" TYPE="*text*" VALUE="*text*"
Creates a radio button that can be enabled or disabled by the user. CHECKED indicates the default selection.
INPUT TYPE=RESET
Displays a button displaying the word Reset.
INPUT TYPE=SUBMIT
Displays a button displaying the word Submit.
INPUT TYPE=TEXT (MAXLENGTH, SIZE) NAME="*text*" TYPE="*text*" value= "*text*"
Inserts a text field where users can type information (default).

Associated Tags: <FORM>, <TEXTAREA>, <OPTION> <FIELDSET>, <LEGEND> and <SELECT>

Sample:

```
<FORM METHOD="POST"
ACTION="http://www.myfunkyfunkywebsite.ca">
What is your address: <INPUT TYPE=TEXT SIZE=50 NAME="your
address"> <BR>
What is your name: <INPUT TYPE=TEXT SIZE=50 NAME="your
name"> <BR>
<P>
What do you want? <BR>
<INPUT TYPE=CHECKBOX NAME="buy it" VALUE="item1" CHECKED>
Item #1<BR>
<INPUT TYPE=CHECKBOX NAME="buy it" VALUE="item2"> Item
#2<BR>
```

```
<INPUT TYPE=CHECKBOX NAME="buy it" VALUE="item3"> Item
#3<BR>
<INPUT TYPE=HIDDEN VALUE="This is funkyweb's purchasing
form #2">
<P>
How will you pay for your funky purchase? <BR>
<INPUT TYPE=RADIO NAME="pay for it" VALUE="credit"
CHECKED> Credit Card <BR>
<INPUT TYPE=RADIO NAME="pay for it" VALUE="glass"> Glass
Beads<BR>
<INPUT TYPE=RADIO NAME="pay for it" VALUE="mo"> Cowrie
Shells<BR>
<P>
Type your super-secret FunkyWeb decoder ring sequence
here to verify that you are you.<BR>
<INPUT TYPE=PASSWORD NAME=PASSWORD VALUE="they are buying
our stuff"><BR>
<INPUT TYPE=RESET> <INPUT TYPE=SUBMIT>
</FORM>
```

<ISINDEX>

Element Name: Is Indexed tag.

Description: Indicates that the HTML document is indexed and part of a searchable directory of Web pages. This tag is no longer commonly used.

Attributes: None.

Sample:

```
<HEAD>
<ISINDEX>
</HEAD>
```

<KBD> . . . </KBD>.

Element Name: Keyboard tag.

Description: Indicates that the text is displayed in typewriter (or fixed-width) font.

Attributes: None.

Sample:

```
<KBD>This is keyboard font,</KBD> and this regular font.
```

<LAYER> . . . </LAYER>

Element Name: Layer Tag.

Description: Specifies a layer that can appear on a Web page.

Attributes:

ABOVE = *layername*
Specifies the stacking order of a layer within a set of layers. If used, the attributes BELOW and Z-INDEX cannot be used—they are mutually exclusive.
BACKGROUND = *filename*
Tiles a background image within a layer.
BELOW = *layername*
Specifies the stacking order of a layer within a set of layers. If used, the attributes ABOVE and Z-INDEX cannot be used—they are mutually exclusive.
BGCOLOR = *colorname .or hexadecimal colorvalue*
Sets the background color of a layer.
CLIP = *x, y, x1, y1*
Specifies the dimensions of a clipping rectangle (a visible layer) that appears within a layer.
HEIGHT = # *pixels or % of browser window*
Specifies the height of the layer in pixels, and sets the reference height for any children layers.
ID = "*layer_name*"
Specifies the name of the layer. It serves as an identifier to distinguish it from other layers and to JavaScript scripts. Functionally equivalent to the NAME attribute.
LEFT = # *pixels*
Specifies the horizontal positioning of the layer in pixels.
NAME = "*layer_name*"
Specifies the name of the layer. It serves as an identifier to distinguish it from other layers and to JavaScript scripts. Functionally equivalent to the ID attribute.
PAGEX = # *pixels*
Specifies the horizontal position of the layer relative to the document window in pixels.
PAGEY = # *pixels*
Specifies the vertical position of the layer relative to the document window in pixels.
SRC = *URL*
Specifies the full pathname of a separate Web page containing HTML-formatted content for the layer.
TOP = *pixels*
Specifies the vertical positioning of the layer in pixels.
VISIBILITY = *SHOW | HIDE | INHERIT*
Specifies whether or not the layer is visible.
WIDTH = # *pixels or % of browser window*
Specifies the width of the layer in pixels (applies to text only).
Z-INDEX
Specifies the stacking order of a layer within a set of layers. If used, the attributes ABOVE and BELOW cannot be used—they are mutually exclusive.

Associated Tags: None (however, always used in conjunction with JavaScript).

Sample:

```
<LAYER NAME="Croequo2" LEFT=75 TOP=175 WIDTH=400
VISIBILITY="HIDE">
Yes, we sell funky frogs here!
<P>
<IMG SRC="bullfrog.gif">
</LAYER>
```

<LEGEND> . . . </LEGEND>

Element Name: Legend tag.

Description: Adds a legend to a fieldset.

Attributes: ALIGN = *BOTTOM* | *LEFT* | *RIGHT* | *TOP*
Sets the position of the legend with respect to the fieldset. The ALIGN attribute is deprecated in the HTML 4.0 specification.

Associated Tags: <FIELDSET>, set of form tags

Sample:

```
<FORM ACTION=".." METHOD=POST>
<FIELDSET>
<LEGEND ALIGN="top">Some Info</LEGEND>
Stuff #1: <INPUT TYPE=RADIO NAME="stuff" VALUE="1">
Stuff #2: <INPUT TYPE=RADIO NAME="stuff" VALUE="2">
</FIELDSET>
</FORM>
```

<LI> (. . . </LI>)

Element Name: List item tag.

Description: Used immediately prior to individual items within directory, menu, ordered, or unordered lists. Some HTML editors add an end tag (</LI>) for each list item, but its use is optional.

Attributes: None.

Associated Tags: <UL>, <OL>, <DIR>, <MENU>

Can contain: text, text markup tag, <A>, <BLOCKQUOTE>, <BR>, <DIR>, <DL>, <FORM>, <IMG>, <MENU>, <P>, <PRE>

Sample:

```
<OL>
<LI>Item #1
<LI>Item #2
<LI>Item #3
</OL>
```

<LINK>

Element Name: Link tag.

Description: Indicates where a Web document fits into the hierarchy of the Web site.

Attributes: REL = *URL*
Indicates the URL of a subdocument.
REV = *URL*
Indicates the URL of a parent document

Sample:

```
<HEAD>
<TITLE>Kim's Web Page</TITLE>
<LINK REL="sub-document"
HREF="http://www.interlog.com/~ksc/burgundy.htm">
<LINK REV="parent docuemnt"
HREF="http://www.interlog.com/~ksc/winegeneral.htm">
</HEAD>
```

<MAP> . . . <MAP>

Element Name: Map tag.

Description: Describes the beginning and end of a client-side image map.

Attributes: None.

Associated Tags: <AREA>

Sample:

```
<MAP>
<AREA SHAPE="RECT" COORD="98,34,23,15"
HREF="http://www.longUnlikelyUrl.net/index.html">
<AREA SHAPE="CIRCLE" COORD="200, 155, 35"
HREF="http://www. longUnlikelyUrl.net/stuff.html">
<AREA SHAPE="POLYGON" COORD="371,235,126,339,190,207"
HREF="http://www.longUnlikelyUrl.net/moreStuff.html">
</MAP>
```

<MARQUEE> . . . </MARQUEE>

Element Name: Marquee tag.

Description: Produces a horizontal line of scrolling text within a Web page.

Attributes: ALIGN= *TOP* | *MIDDLE* | *BOTTOM*
Specifies where the text should appear within the marquee space.
BEHAVIOR= *SCROLL* | *SLIDE* | *ALTERNATE*
Specifies how the text in the marquee should behave.
BGCOLOR= *colorname* or *colorvalue*
Specifies a color for the background of the marquee space.
DIRECTION= *LEFT* | *RIGHT*
Specifies the direction in which the marquee text should scroll.
HEIGHT= # *pixels* | % *of browser window*
Specifies the height of the marquee display as either a fixed pixel value or as a percentage of the browser window.
HSPACE= # *pixels*
Specifies the horizontal (left and right) spacing margins for the outside of the marquee.
LOOP= *number* | *INFINITE*
Specifies the number of times the text in the marquee should cycle.

SCROLLAMOUNT= # *pixels*
Specifies the amount of space in pixels that is between the display of the end of a line and the beginning of the next successive draw of the text.
SCROLLDELAY= # *milliseconds*
Specifies the amount of milliseconds the marquee should wait between drawing successive displays of the text.
VSPACE= # *pixels*
Specifies the vertical (right and left) spacing margins for the outside of the marquee.
WIDTH= # *pixels* | % *of browser window*
Specifies the width of the marquee display as either a fixed pixel value or as a percentage of the browser window.

Associated Tags: <BODY>, any other formatting element

Sample:

```
<MARQUEE>
This text will scroll across the screen.
</MARQUEE>
```

<MENU> . . . </MENU>

Element Name: Menu tag.

Description: Displays lists of items containing no more than a single line per item. Bullets precede each list item.

Attributes: None.

Can contain: <LI>

Can be contained within: <BLOCKQUOTE>, <BODY>, <DD>, <FORM>, <LI>

Sample:

```
<MENU>
<LI>Clam Chowder
<LI>Chicken Soup
<LI>Cream of Mushroom
</MENU>
```

<META>

Element Name: Meta tag.

Description: Provides details about the HTML document that are not covered by the other tags within the <HEAD> tags.

Attributes: NAME= *text*
Indicates a name that a Web search engine would understand.
CONTENT= *text*
Indicates the content of a Web page; a string that will be recorded by a search engine.
HTTP-EQUIV= "refresh"
Used to perform a client pull: The Web browser will refresh to display a specified URL

after a specified number of seconds. These values are specified in the CONTENT attribute.

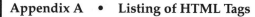

Sample:

```
<HEAD>
<TITLE>Kim's Web Page</TITLE>
<META NAME="description" CONTENT="Kim Silk-Copeland's Web
Page">
<META NAME="keywords" CONTENT="Kim, Silk, Copeland, fun,
HTML, Discovery, EXN">
<META HTTP-EQUIV="refresh" CONTENT="3;
http://www.fis.utoronto.ca/~silk/">
</HEAD>
```

<MULTICOL> . . . </MULTICOL>

Element Name: The multicolumn tag.

Description: Divides text into multiple columns.

Attributes: COLS= # *columns*
Specifies the number of columns to be displayed.
GUTTER= # *pixels*
Sets the amount of pixel spacing between columns.
WIDTH= # *pixels or % of browser window*
Sets the total width of the columnar display as either a pixel value or as a percentage of the width of the browser window.

Associated Tags: <BODY>, any other formatting element

Sample:

```
<MULTICOL COLS=2 GUTTER=5 WIDTH=50%>
This text is displayed within two separate columns. The
&lt;MULTICOL&gt; tag is a relatively recent innovation,
and was first introduced within Netscape Navigator 3.0.
As you can see, the effect can be quite striking, because
it is so different from what you typically see on a Web
page.
</MULTICOL>
```

<NOBR> . . . </NOBR>

Element Name: Nobreak tag.

Description: Prevents the browser from inserting an artificial line break within a long line of text.

Attributes: None.

Associated Tags: <BODY>, any other formatting element (other than <BR>)

Sample:

```
<NOBR>This is a long-ish line of text that will not be
broken up into separate lines by the browser</NOBR>
```

<NOFRAMES> . . . </NOFRAMES>

Element Name: NOFRAMES tag.

Description: Displays the content it contains only to users viewing the Web page with Web browsers incapable of reading frames.

Attributes: None.

Associated Tags: <FRAMESET>, <FRAME>

Sample:

```
<FRAMESET ROWS="75,*">
<FRAME SRC="up.html">
<FRAMESET COLS="35%, 65%">
<FRAME SRC="rightside.html">
<FRAME SRC="leftside.html">
</FRAMESET>
</FRAMESET>
<NOFRAMES><BODY>
If you see text, you are using a Web browser that does
not support Frames. Sorry.
</BODY></NOFRAMES>
```

<NOLAYER> . . . </NOLAYER>

Element Name: Nolayer tag.

Attributes: None.

Associated Tags: <LAYER>

Sample:

```
<NOLAYER>
<P>
If you were using a layers-compatible browser, you'd be
viewing a layered Web page instead of this statement.
</NOLAYER>
```

<NOSCRIPT> . . . </NOSCRIPT>

Element Name: No script tag.

Description: Indicates the presence of a scripting language (such as JavaScript or VBScript) to a browser incapable of interpreting scripted code.

Attributes: None.

Sample:

```
<NOSCRIPT>
This page makes use of JavaScript for navigational
purposes. Your browser does not support JavaScript
```

```
(otherwise you wouldn't be reading this), so please click
<A HREF="alternate.html"> here </A> for an
alternate version of our Web site.
</NOSCRIPT>
```

<OBJECT> . . . </OBJECT>

Element Name: Object tag.

Description: Inserts media objects into Web pages.

Attributes:

ALIGN = *BASELINE | CENTER | LEFT | MIDDLE | RIGHT | TEXTBOTTOM | TEXTMIDDLE | TEXTTOP*
Determines where to place the object on the Web page. Values can be TEXTTOP, MIDDLE, TEXTMIDDLE, BASELINE, TEXTBOTTOM, LEFT, CENTER, or RIGHT. Images use this attribute.
ALT= *text*
Specifies text to display if the user has set his or her browser to not load images. Images use this attribute.
ARCHIVE= *URL*
Specifies a list of URLs pointing to archives of the media.
BORDER= # *pixels*
Specifies the border size in pixels. If the value is 0 no border is drawn. Images use this attribute.
CLASSID= *URL*
A URL that identifies an implementation for the object. In some object systems this is a class identifier. Java applets use this attribute.
CODEBASE= *directory structure*
Some URLs used to identify media objects require an additional URL to find that object. CODEBASE allows you to specify that URL. CODEBASE defaults to the same base URL as the document if none is specified.
CODETYPE= *text*
Specifies the content type of data expected by the browser or media player.
DATA= *URL*
A URL or filename for the object, such as a GIF file.
DECLARE= *text*
Declares an instance of the object.
HEIGHT= # *pixels*
Specifies the height of the object in pixels.
HSPACE= # *pixels*
Specifies in pixels the amount of space to the left and the right of the object.
NAME= *text*
Allows the object to participate in a FORM.
STANDBY= *text*
Specifies a short text string the browser displays while loading the object's implementation and data.
TABINDEX= *number*

Specifies the order in which an individual item can be selected from a group of items by using the TAB keyboard key.
TYPE= *MIME type*
Specifies the media type for the file specified by the DATA attribute before the file is retrieved. Specifying the TYPE for a .avi file would look like this:
type="application/avi".
VSPACE= *# pixels*
Specifies in pixels the amount of space above and below the object.
USEMAP= *URL*
Specifies a URL or filename for a client-side image map.
WIDTH= *# pixels*
Specifies the width of the object in pixels. Specifying this attribute allows the browser to load the object more quickly than if the attribute was not used.

Sample:

```
<OBJECT data=kimshock.dcr type="application/x-director"
width=200 height=225>
<img src=kimshock.gif alt="Best Experienced with
Shockwave">
</OBJECT>
```

<OL> . . . </OL>

Element Name: Ordered list tag.

Description: Displays a number of ordered items in a list.

Attributes:
TYPE= A
List items are preceded by uppercase letters (i.e., A, B, C).
TYPE= a
List items are preceded by lowercase letters (i.e., a, b, c).
TYPE= I
List items are preceded by uppercase Roman numerals (i.e., I, II, III).
TYPE= i
List items are preceded by lowercase Roman numerals (i.e., i, ii, iii).
TYPE= 1
List items are preceded by numbers (i.e., 1, 2, 3).
COMPACT
Tells the browser to display the list in a compact form. The horizontal space between list items is reduced, causing the list to appear more compact.

Can contain: <LI>

Can be contained within: <BLOCKQUOTE>, <BODY>, <DD>, <FORM>, <LI>

Sample:

```
<OL>
<LI>The First item.
<LI>The Second item.
<LI>The Third item.
</OL>
```

<OPTION>

Element Name: Option tag.

Description: The individual elements within the drop-down list. It is always used in conjunction with the <SELECT> tag.

Attributes: SELECTED
Sets the default selection.
VALUE= *text*
Sets a specific value to an option.

Associated Tags: <FORM>, <INPUT>, <TEXTAREA>, <FIELDSET>, <LEGEND>, and <SELECT>

Sample:

```
<FORM>
<SELECT NAME="JapaneseUkiyo-EArtists">
<OPTION SELECTED VALUE="Hokusai">Hokusai
<OPTION VALUE="Yoshida">Yoshida
<OPTION VALUE="Yoshitoshi">Yoshitoshi
<OPTION VALUE="Hiroshige">Hiroshige
<OPTION VALUE="Eisen">Eisen
</SELECT>
</FORM>
```

<P> (. . . </P>)

Element Name: Paragraph tag.

Description: Defines a paragraph of text by inserting a vertical space between lines of text, or other elements on a Web page.

Attributes: ALIGN = *LEFT* | *CENTER* | *RIGHT*
Aligns the text in the browser widow.

Associated Tags: <BODY>, any other formatting element

Sample:

```
<P ALIGN=LEFT>
This paragraph is aligned to the left.
</P>
<P ALIGN=RIGHT>
This paragraph is aligned to the right.
</P>
<P ALIGN=CENTER>
This paragraph is centered.
</P>
```

<PARAM>

Element Name: Parameter tag.

Description: Specifies how a Java applet or other program operates.

Attributes: NAME= *parameterName*
Specifies the name of the applet parameter to be used.
VALUE= *parameterValue*
Specifies the value to be associated with applet parameter selected by NAME.

Associated Tags: <APPLET>, <OBJECT>

Sample:

```
<APPLET CODE=NiftyApplet.class CODEBASE="..\.." WIDTH=200
HEIGHT=200>
<PARAM NAME=COLOR VALUE=BLUE>
<PARAM NAME=FONT VALUE=ARIAL>
</APPLET>
```

<PRE> . . .</PRE>

Element Name: Preformatted tag.

Description: Displays text in a fixed-width font.

Attributes: WIDTH= # *characters*
Specifies the maximum numbers of characters that can appear on a line.

Associated Tags: <BODY>, any other text formatting element

Sample:

```
<PRE>
This text is not quite rendered in an <B>as is</B>
fashion by the browser.
</PRE>
```

<Q> . . . </Q>

Element Name: Quote tag.

Description: Contains a short quotation.

Attributes: CITE= *URL*
Specifies a URL that points to the source of the quotation.

Associated Tags: <BODY>, any other formatting element

Sample:

```
Edmund Burke said that one must <Q>"guard against the
treasure of our liberty, not only from invasion, but from
decay and corruption".</Q>
```

<S> . . . </S>

Element Name: Strike tag.

Description: Indicates a line of text with a horizontal line through it.

Attributes: None.

Sample:

```
<STRIKE>This sentence has a strike through it.</STRIKE>
```

<SAMP> . . . </SAMP>

Element Name: Sample tag.

Description: Indicates that the text is a sample statement, and is displayed in fixed-width font.

Attributes: None.

Sample:

```
<SAMP>This text is enclosed in sample tags.</SAMP> This
text is not.
```

<SCRIPT> . . . </SCRIPT>

Element Name: Script tag.

Description: Provides information regarding style sheets and client-side scripts.

Attributes: Language: *language_name*
Specifies the name of the scripting language being used.

Sample:

```
<SCRIPT LANGUAGE="JavaScript">
document.write("Hello World!")
</SCRIPT>
```

<SELECT> . . . </SELECT>

Element Name: Select tag.

Description: Specifies an option list within a Web form.

Attributes: NAME= *text*
Specifies the name that is to be submitted as a name/value pair.
SIZE= *text*
Specifies the number of visible items in a drop-down list that are initially displayed.
MULTIPLE= *number*
Specifies the amount of options a user can select from the selectable list.

Associated with: <FORM>, <INPUT>, <TEXTAREA>, <FIELDSET>, <LEGEND> and <OPTION>

Sample:

```
<FORM>
<SELECT NAME="JapaneseUkiyo-EArtists">
<OPTION SELECTED VALUE="Hokusai">Hokusai
<OPTION VALUE="Yoshida">Yoshida
<OPTION VALUE="Yoshitoshi">Yoshitoshi
<OPTION VALUE="Hiroshige">Hiroshige
<OPTION VALUE="Eisen">Eisen
</SELECT>
</FORM>
```

<SMALL> . . . </SMALL>

Element Name: Small font tag.

Description: Indicates text displayed in a smaller font than regular font size.

Attributes: None.

Sample:

```
<SMALL>This text is smaller</SMALL> than this text.
```

<SPACER>

Element Name: Spacer tag.

Description: Adds white-space between elements on a Web page. This tag is recognized only by Netscape Navigator, and is not part of the HTML 4.0 specification.

Attributes:

ALIGN= *LEFT* | *RIGHT* | *TOP* | *TEXTTOP* | *MIDDLE* | *ABSMIDDLE* | *BASELINE* | *BOTTOM* | *ABSBOTTOM*
Controls the alignment of text surrounding the spacing block. Can be used only when TYPE=BLOCK.

HEIGHT= # *pixels*
Sets the height of the spacing block as a pixel value. Can be used only when TYPE=BLOCK.

SIZE= # *pixels*
Controls the pixel height or width of a spacing element. Can be used only when TYPE=HORIZONTAL or TYPE=VERTICAL.

TYPE= *HORIZONTAL* | *VERTICAL* | *BLOCK*
Sets the type of white-space area to be defined by the other spacing attributes

WIDTH= # *pixels*
Sets the height of the spacing block as a pixel value. Can be used only when TYPE=BLOCK.

Associated Tags: <BODY>, any other formatting element

Sample:

```
<SPACER TYPE=HORIZONTAL SIZE=100>
This text is indented by a horizontal &lt;SPACER&gt;
tag set to 100 pixels in depth.
<SPACER TYPE=VERTICAL SIZE=100>
This text is separated by the one above it by a
vertical &lt;SPACER&gt; tag set to 100
pixels.
<BR>
This text has a &lt;SPACER&gt; tag in the middle
<SPACER TYPE=BLOCK HEIGHT=100 WIDTH=50> of
it. It contains a discrete white-space block that
is 50 pixels in width and 100 pixels in
height.
```

<SPAN> . . . </SPAN>

Element Name: Span tag.

Description: Sets CSS information for a specific section within a Web page.

Attributes:
CHARSET = *ISO-#*
Indicates the international character coding used for the hyperlink.
HREF = *URL*
Points to a Web page that is viewed when the content contained within the <SPAN> tag is activated.
HREFLANG = *text*
Specifies the base language of the resource indicated in the HREF attribute.
MEDIA = *ALL | BRAILLE | PRINT | PROJECTION | SCREEN | SPEECH*
Specifies the type of medium the CSS definitions are designed for.
REL= URL
Indicates the URL of a subdocument. This attribute is not commonly used.
REV=*URL*
Indicates the URL of a parent document. This attribute is not commonly used.
TARGET = *frame name*
Specifies the name of the frame (if any) that the content set by HREF should be viewed within.
TYPE = *MIME type*
Specifies the MIME type of the content enclosed by the style tag.

Associated Tags: <STYLE>

Sample:

```
<HTML>
<HEAD>
<STYLE>
SPAN {COLOR: RED}
</STYLE>
</HEAD>
<BODY>
<P STYLE="COLOR: GREEN">
Look for the <SPAN>red text</SPAN> that appears within
the green text.
</P>
</BODY>
</HTML>
```

<STRIKE> . . </STRIKE>

Element Name: Strike tag.

Description: Indicates a line of text with a horizontal line through it.

Attributes: None.

Sample:

```
<STRIKE>This sentence has a strike through it.</STRIKE>
```

<STRONG> . . </STRONG>

Element Name: Strong text tag.

Description: Indicates that the text is displayed with a strong font, usually in bold face.

Attributes: None.

Sample:

```
<STRONG>Caution:</STRONG> The Internet can become
addictive!
```

<STYLE> . . </STYLE>

Element Name: Style tag.

Description: Adds Cascading Style Sheet information to a Web page.

Attributes:

DISABLED
Indicates that the particular CSS function should not be enabled (i.e., displayed).
MEDIA = ALL | BRAILLE | PRINT | PROJECTION | SCREEN | SPEECH
Specifies the type of medium for which the CSS definitions are designed.
TITLE = *text*
Used to name a particular CSS style that a browser can be told to use.
TYPE = *MIME type*
Specifies the MIME type of the content enclosed by the style tag.

Associated Tags: <SPAN>, <HEAD>

Sample:

```
<STYLE>H2 {COLOR: GREEN}</STYLE>
```

_{. .}

Element Name: Subscript tag.

Description: Displays enclosed text in subscript font.

Attributes: None.

Sample:

```
Subscript is useful for formulas like H<SUB>2</SUB>0.<BR>
```

^{. . .}

Element Name: Superscript tag.

Description: Displays enclosed text in superscript font.

Attributes: None.

Sample:

```
Superscript is useful for trademarks like
This<SUP>TM</SUP>.
```

<TABLE> . . . </TABLE>

Element Name: Table tag.

Description: Inserts a table into the Web document. The <TABLE> tag is a container tag; the end tag is not optional.

Attributes:

ALIGN=*LEFT | RIGHT | CENTER*
Aligns the table in the browser window according to the value you specify. The default alignment is left. RIGHT aligns the table to the right margin, and CENTER aligns the table in the center of the window.

BACKGROUND=*colorvalue*
Specifies a background image for the table. All table cells and content are displayed over this image. If the image is smaller than the table, the image is tiled to fill the table.

BGCOLOR=*colorvalue*
Specifies a background color for the table. This color can be overridden at the cell level. The color is defined using RBG values.

BORDER=*n pixels*
Specifies the width of the table border in pixels. The default value is 1. Specifying BORDER=0 creates a table without visible borders.

BORDERCOLOR=*colorvalue*
Specifies the external border color for the whole table. The color is defined using RBG values. The BORDER attribute must be specified with a value of 1 or greater for the BORDERCOLOR attribute to be effective. This attribute is recognized within Internet Explorer only.

BORDERCOLORDARK=*colorvalue*
Specifies the color of the lower and right-hand borders of the table, creating a 3D effect. The color is defined using RBG values. The BORDER attribute must be specified with a value of 1 or greater for the BORDERCOLOR attribute to be effective. This attribute is recognized only within Internet Explorer.

BORDERCOLORLIGHT=*colorvalue*
Specifies the color of the upper and left-hand borders of the table, creating a 3D effect. The color is defined using RBG values. The BORDER attribute must be specified with a value of 1 or greater for the BORDERCOLOR attribute to be effective. This attribute is recognized only within Internet Explorer.

CELLPADDING=*n pixels*
Specifies the amount of space within the cells in pixels.

CELLSPACING=*n pixels*
Specifies the amount of space between cells in pixels.

COLS=*number*
Explicitly defines the number of columns in the table. Specifying this value allows the table to download more quickly, as the browser doesn't have to read the whole table to know the table size.

FRAME=*VOID | ABOVE | BELOW | HSIDES | VSIDES | LHS | RHS | BOX | BORDER | FRAME*
Allows control over the outer border of the table. The following values indicate what part of the border should be displayed:

- VOID — No borders
- ABOVE — top border only
- BELOW — Bottom border only

- HSIDES — Left- and right- hand side borders only
- VSIDES — Top and bottom borders only
- LHS — Left border only
- RHS — Right border only
- BOX — Border on all four sides
- BORDER — Border on all four sides (same as box); default value
- FRAME — Border on all four sides

This attribute is recognized only within Internet Explorer, but has recently been adopted within the official HTML 4.0 specification.

HEIGHT = *n pixels/%*

Specifies the height of the table either as a percentage of the window height, or as an absolute value in pixels.

RULES = *NONE | ROWS | COLS | ALL*

Allows control over the inner cell rules of the table. The following values indicate what part of the border should be displayed:

- NONE — No interior borders
- ROWS — Horizontal borders are displayed
- COLS — Vertical borders are displayed
- ALL — All borders are displayed

This attribute is recognized only within Internet Explorer, but has recently been adopted within the official HTML 4.0 specification.

WIDTH = *# of pixels* or *% of browser width*

Specifies the width of the table either as a percentage of the window width, or as an absolute value in pixels.

Sample:

```
<TABLE BORDER="1">
<TH>Column 1</TH>
<TH>Column 2</TH>
<TR>
<TD>Cell 1</TD>
<TD>Cell 2</TD>
</TR>
<TR>
<TD>Cell 3</TD>
<TD>Cell 4</TD>
</TR>
<CAPTION>A Basic Table</CAPTION>
</TABLE>
```

<TBODY> . . . </TBODY>

Element Name: Table body tag.

Description: Defines the body of a table.

Attributes: ALIGN = *LEFT | RIGHT | CENTER | JUSTIFY | CHAR*

Specifies the horizontal alignment of contents within the cell relative to the cell boundaries. The default alignment is LEFT. RIGHT aligns the content to the right side of the cell, and CENTER aligns the content in the center of the cell.

BGCOLOR = *colorvalue*
Specifies a background color for the cell. This color overrides any BGCOLOR specified in the <TABLE> element. The color is defined using RBG values.
CHAR= *character*
Specifies an alignment character for use with ALIGN=CHAR.
CHAROFF= # of character spaces or %
Specifies the offset to the first occurrence of the alignment character on each line.
VALIGN = *BOTTOM | BASELINE | MIDDLE | TOP*
Specifies the vertical alignment of contents within a row of cells relative to the cell's boundaries. TOP aligns the content to the top of the cell, MIDDLE aligns the content to the middle of the cell, BOTTOM aligns the content to the bottom of the cell, and BASELINE aligns the content at the baseline so that all content lines up horizontally.

Associated Tags: <TABLE>, <THEAD>, <TFOOT>, <TR>, <TD>, <COLGROUP>, <COL>

Sample:

```
<TABLE BORDER>
<COLGROUP>
<COL ALIGN=CENTER SPAN=2>
<COLGROUP ALIGN=RIGHT>
<THREAD>
<TR>
<TH>A</TH><TH>B</TH><TH>C</TH>
</TR>
</THEAD>
<TBODY>
<TR>
<TD>1</TD><TD>2</TD><TD>3</TD>
</TR>
<TR>
<TD>3</TD><TD>4</TD><TD>5</TD>
</TR>
</TBODY>
<TFOOTER>
<TR>
<TD>6</TD><TD>7</TD><TD>8</TD>
</TR>
</TFOOTER>
</TABLE>
```

<TD> . . . </TD>

Element Name: Table Data tag.

Description: <TD> is a container tag. Although the end tags are optional, it is good HTML form to use them.

Attributes: ABBR - *text*
Contains the full text of the abbreviated name for a header cell.
ALIGN = *LEFT | RIGHT | CENTER*
Specifies the horizontal alignment of contents within the cell relative to the cell bounda-

ries. The default alignment is LEFT. RIGHT aligns the content to the right side of the cell, and CENTER aligns the content in the center of the cell.

AXIS = *text*

Specifies a name for a cell, allowing it to be mapped to a tree-like hierarchy. Intended primarily for use in nongraphical browsers.

BACKGROUND = *image filename*

Specifies a background image for the cell. All content in the table cell are displayed over this image. If the image is smaller than the cell, the image is tiled to fill the cell.

BGCOLOR = *colorvalue*

Specifies a background color for the cell. This color overrides any BGCOLOR specified in the <TABLE> element. The color is defined using RBG values.

BORDERCOLOR = *colorvalue*

Specifies the external border color for the whole table. The color is defined using RBG values. The BORDER attribute must be specified with a value of 1 or greater for the BORDERCOLOR attribute to be effective. This attribute is recognized only within Internet Explorer.

BORDERCOLORDARK = *colorvalue*

Specifies the color of the lower and right-hand borders of the table, creating a 3D effect. The color is defined using RBG values. The BORDER attribute must be specified with a value of 1 or greater for the BORDERCOLOR attribute to be effective. This attribute is recognized only within Internet Explorer.

BORDERCOLORLIGHT = *colorvalue*

Specifies the color of the upper and left-hand borders of the table, creating a 3D effect. The color is defined using RBG values. The BORDER attribute must be specified with a value of 1 or greater for the BORDERCOLOR attribute to be effective. This attribute is recognized only within Internet Explorer.

CHAR= *character*

Specifies an alignment character for use with ALIGN=CHAR.

CHAROFF= # *of character spaces* or %

Specifies the offset to the first occurrence of the alignment character on each line.

COLSPAN = *number*

Specifies the number of columns spanned by the cell.

HEADERS = *text*

Associates header information for a particular cell in a given column. Designed to make the function of a table clear to users of nongraphical browsers.

HEIGHT = # *of pixels* or % *of browser window height*

Sets the height of the current cell (which in effect sets the height for the row).

NOWRAP

Suppresses word wrap, widening the cell to the width of the cell's contents.

ROWSPAN = *number*

Specifies the number of rows spanned by the cell.

SCOPE = *COL | COLGROUP | ROW | ROWGROUP*

Designed for nongraphical browsers, this tag provides information on a particular row, column, or group of rows and columns.

VALIGN = *BOTTOM | BASELINE | MIDDLE | TOP*

Specifies the vertical alignment of contents within the cell relative to the cell boundaries. TOP aligns the content to the top of the cell, MIDDLE aligns the content to the middle of the cell, BOTTOM aligns the content to the bottom of the cell, and BASELINE aligns the content at the baseline so that all content lines up horizontally.

WIDTH = # *of pixels* or % *of browser window height*
Specifies the width of the cell either as a percentage of the window width, or as an absolute value in pixels. The width of a table column must be consistent, therefore the width of the column will default to the widest cell.

Sample:

```
<TABLE BORDER="1">
<TH>Column 1</TH>
<TH>Column 2</TH>
<TR>
<TD>Cell 1</TD>
<TD>Cell 2</TD>
</TR>
<TR>
<TD>Cell 3</TD>
<TD>Cell 4</TD>
</TR>
<CAPTION>A Basic Table</CAPTION>
</TABLE>
```

<TH> . . . </TH>

Element Name: Table Heading tag.

Description: <TH> is a container tag. Although the end tags are optional, it is good HTML form to use them.

Attributes:

ABBR = *text*
Contains the full text of the abbreviated name for a header cell.
ALIGN=*LEFT | RIGHT | CENTER*
Specifies the horizontal alignment of contents within the cell relative to the cell boundaries. The default alignment is LEFT. RIGHT aligns the content to the right side of the cell, and CENTER aligns the content in the center of the cell.
AXIS = *text*
Specifies a name for a cell, allowing it to be mapped to a tree-like hierarchy. Intended primarily for use in nongraphical browsers.
BACKGROUND=*image filename*
Specifies a background image for the cell. All content in the table cell are displayed over this image. If the image is smaller than the cell, the image is tiled to fill the cell.
BGCOLOR = *colorvalue*
Specifies a background color for the cell. This color overrides any BGCOLOR specified in the <TABLE> element. The color is defined using RBG values.
BORDERCOLOR=*colorvalue*
Specifies the external border color for the whole table. The color is defined using RBG values. The BORDER attribute must be specified with a value of 1 or greater for the BORDERCOLOR attribute to be effective. This attribute is recognized only within Internet Explorer.
BORDERCOLORDARK=*colorvalue*
Specifies the color of the lower and right-hand borders of the table, creating a 3D effect. The color is defined using RBG values. The BORDER attribute must be specified with

a value of 1 or greater for the BORDERCOLOR attribute to be effective. This attribute is recognized only within Internet Explorer.

BORDERCOLORLIGHT=*colorvalue*

Specifies the color of the upper and left-hand borders of the table, creating a 3D effect. The color is defined using RBG values. The BORDER attribute must be specified with a value of 1 or greater for the BORDERCOLOR attribute to be effective. This attribute is recognized only within Internet Explorer.

CHAR= *character*

Specifies an alignment character for use with ALIGN=CHAR.

CHAROFF= # *of character spaces* or %

Specifies the offset to the first occurrence of the alignment character on each line.

COLSPAN=*number*

Specifies the number of columns spanned by the cell.

HEADERS = *text*

The HEADER attribute associates header information for a particular cell in a given column. Designed to make the function of a table clear to users of nongraphical browsers.

HEIGHT = # *of pixels* or % *of browser window height*

Sets the height of the current cell (which in effect sets the height for the row).

NOWRAP

Suppresses word wrap, widening the cell to the width of the cell's contents.

ROWSPAN = *number*

Specifies the number of rows spanned by the cell.

SCOPE = *COL* | *COLGROUP* | *ROW* | *ROWGROUP*

Designed for nongraphical browsers, this tag provides information on a particular row, column, or group of rows and columns.

VALIGN=*BOTTOM* | *BASELINE* | *MIDDLE* | *TOP*

Specifies the vertical alignment of contents within the cell relative to the cell boundaries. TOP aligns the content to the top of the cell, MIDDLE aligns the content to the middle of the cell, BOTTOM aligns the content to the bottom of the cell, and BASELINE aligns the content at the baseline so that all content lines up horizontally.

WIDTH=# *of pixels or % of browser window height*

Specifies the width of the cell either as a percentage of the window width, or as an absolute value in pixels.

The width of a table column must be consistent, therefore the width of the column will default to the widest cell.

Sample:

```
<TABLE BORDER=" 1">
<TH>Column 1</TH>
<TH>Column 2</TH>
<TR>
<TD>Cell 1</TD>
<TD>Cell 2</TD>
</TR>
<TR>
<TD>Cell 3</TD>
<TD>Cell 4</TD>
</TR>
<CAPTION>A Basic Table</CAPTION>
</TABLE>
```

<THEAD> . . . </THEAD>

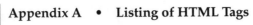

Element Name: Table header tag.

Description: Specifies the header row for a table.

Attributes: ALIGN = *LEFT | RIGHT | CENTER | JUSTIFY | CHAR*
Specifies the horizontal alignment of contents within the cell relative to the cell boundaries. The default alignment is LEFT. RIGHT aligns the content to the right side of the cell, and CENTER aligns the content in the center of the cell.
BGCOLOR = *colorvalue*
Specifies a background color for the cell. This color overrides any BGCOLOR specified in the <TABLE> element. The color is defined using RBG values.
CHAR= *character*
Specifies an alignment character for use with ALIGN-CHAR.
CHAROFF= *# of character spaces* or %
Specifies the offset to the first occurrence of the alignment character on each line.
VALIGN=*BOTTOM | BASELINE | MIDDLE | TOP*
Specifies the vertical alignment of contents within a row of cells relative to the cell's boundaries. TOP aligns the content to the top of the cell, MIDDLE aligns the content to the middle of the cell, BOTTOM aligns the content to the bottom of the cell, and BASELINE aligns the content at the baseline so that all content lines up horizontally.

Associated Tags: <TABLE>, <TBODY>, <TFOOT>, <TR>, <TD>, <COLGROUP>, <COL>

Can contain: <TR>

Sample:

```
<TABLE BORDER>
<COLGROUP>
<COL ALIGN=CENTER SPAN=2>
<COLGROUP ALIGN=RIGHT>
<THREAD>
<TR>
<TH>A</TH><TH>B</TH><TH>C</TH>
</TR>
</THEAD>
<TBODY>
<TR>
<TD>1</TD><TD>2</TD><TD>3</TD>
</TR>
<TR>
<TD>3</TD><TD>4</TD><TD>5</TD>
</TR>
</TBODY>
<TFOOTER>
<TR>
<TD>6</TD><TD>7</TD><TD>8</TD>
</TR>
</TFOOTER>
</TABLE>
```

<TEXTAREA> . . . </TEXTAREA>

Element Name: Textarea tag.

Description: Specifies a multi-line field where users can enter several lines of text. It always used in conjunction with the <FORM> tag. The ROWS and COLS attributes determine the dimension of the field in character height and length, respectively.

Attributes:
COLS= # *characters*
Sets the width of the field in characters.
NAME= *text*
Sets a name for the data contained within the text field.
ROWS= # *characters*
Sets the height of the field in characters.
WRAP= *OFF* | *PHYSICAL* | *VIRTUAL*
Sets how word-wrapping is handled within the field.

Associated Tags: <FORM>, <INPUT>, <OPTION>, <FIELDSET>, <LEGEND>, and <SELECT>

Sample:

```
<FORM>
<TEXTAREA NAME="funky text input" ROWS=10 COLS=45>
</TEXTAREA>
</FORM>
```

<TFOOT> . . . </TFOOT>

Element Name: Table footer tag.

Description: Specifies the footer row for a table.

Attributes:
ALIGN = *LEFT* | *RIGHT* | *CENTER* | *JUSTIFY* | *CHAR*
Specifies the horizontal alignment of contents within the cell relative to the cell boundaries. The default alignment is LEFT. RIGHT aligns the content to the right side of the cell, and CENTER aligns the content in the center of the cell.
BGCOLOR =*colorvalue*
Specifies a background color for the cell. This color overrides any BGCOLOR specified in the <TABLE> element. The color is defined using RBG values.
CHAR= *character*
Specifies an alignment character for use with ALIGN=CHAR.
CHAROFF= # *of character spaces or %*
Specifies the offset to the first occurrence of the alignment character on each line.
VALIGN=*BOTTOM* | *BASELINE* | *MIDDLE* | *TOP*
Specifies the vertical alignment of contents within a row of cells relative to the cell's boundaries. TOP aligns the content to the top of the cell, MIDDLE aligns the content to the middle of the cell, BOTTOM aligns the content to the bottom of the cell, and BASELINE aligns the content at the baseline so that all content lines up horizontally.

Associated Tags: <TABLE>, <TBODY>, <THEAD>, <TR>, <TD>, <COLGROUP>, <COL>

Sample:

```
<TABLE BORDER>
<COLGROUP>
<COL ALIGN=CENTER SPAN=2>
<COLGROUP ALIGN=RIGHT>
<THREAD>
<TR>
<TH>A</TH><TH>B</TH><TH>C</TH>
</TR>
</THEAD>
<TBODY>
<TR>
<TD>1</TD><TD>2</TD><TD>3</TD>
</TR>
<TR>
<TD>3</TD><TD>4</TD><TD>5</TD>
</TR>
</TBODY>
<TFOOTER>
<TR>
<TD>6</TD><TD>7</TD><TD>8</TD>
</TR>
</TFOOTER>
</TABLE>
```

<TITLE> . . . </TITLE>

Element Name: Title tag.

Description: Defines the title of your HTML document.

Attributes: None.

Sample.

```
<HEAD>
<TITLE>Kim's Web Page</TITLE>
</HEAD>
```

<TT> . . . </TT>

Element Name: Teletype tag.

Description: Indicates text that is displayed in fixed-width font.

Attributes: None.

Sample:

```
<TT>This text looks like output from a teletype.</TT>
```

<U> . . . </U>

Element Name: Underline tag.

Description: Indicates text that is underlined by a horizontal line.

Attributes: None.

Sample:

```
<U>This text is underlined.</U>
```

<UL> . . . </UL>

Element Name: Unordered list tag.

Description: Displays a number of unordered items in a list.

Attributes: TYPE= *DISC* | *CIRCLE* | *SQUARE*
Tells the browser to display the bullet as a solid circle, a hollow circle, or a solid square.
COMPACT
Tells the browser to display the list in a compact form. The space between list items is lessened, making the list appear more compact.

Associated Tags: <LI> - Always used with the list element (<LI>) tag, which denotes the individual elements within the list. Each new list item requires its own <LI> tag.

Can be contained within: <BLOCKQUOTE>, <BODY>, <DD>, <FORM>, <LI>

Sample:

```
<UL>
<LI>guitars
<LI>banjos
<LI>ukeleles
<UL TYPE=SQUARE>
<LI>violins
<LI>viols
<LI>double-bass
</UL>
</UL>
```

<VAR> . . </VAR>

Element Name: Variable tag.

Description: Indicates text that is a variable name.

Attributes: None.

Sample:

```
<VAR>a</VAR> plus <VAR>b</VAR> equals <VAR>c</VAR>
```

<WBR>

Element Name: Word break tag.

Description: Tells the browser where a line break can occur in a sentence. It is designed to be used in conjunction with the <NOBR> tag.

Attributes: None.

Associated Tags: <BODY>, <NOBR>, any other formatting element

Sample:

```
<NOBR>
This is a really, really, really, really, really,
really,<WBR> really, really, really, long sentence that
can be broken after the sixth "really". Really.
</NOBR>
```

APPENDIX B

Listing of Style Sheet Elements

BACKGROUND

Description: Sets the background color or image.

Values: colorname or *rrggbb* color value
URL (name_of_image_file)

Example code: `<BODY STYLE="BACKGROUND: TEAL">`

BACKGROUND-ATTACHMENT

Description: If the BACKGROUND-IMAGE element is set, this additional element specifies whether the background image moves when the browser window is scrolled.

Values: SCROLL - Image moves when the browser window is scrolled.

FIXED - Image does not move when the browser window is scrolled.

Example code:

```
<BODY STYLE="BACKGROUND-IMAGE: URL(thinkatron.jpg);
BACKGROUND-ATTACHMENT: SCROLL">
```

BACKGROUND-COLOR

Description: Sets the background color for an element.

Values: colorname or *rrggbb* color value
TRANSPARENT - Sets the specified element as transparent.

Example code:

```
<B STYLE="BACKGROUND-COLOR: OOFFOO">Bold text with a
difference!</B>
```

BACKGROUND-IMAGE

Description: Specifies a graphic as a background image.
If this element is specified, other CSS elements like BACKGROUND-REPEAT, BACKGROUND-ATTACHMENT, and BACKGROUND-POSITION can also be specified. A color value can also be added.
Values:
URL (name_of_image_file)

Example code:

```
<BODY STYLE="background-image: URL(thinkatron.gif)">
```

BACKGROUND-POSITION

Description: If the BACKGROUND-IMAGE element is set, this additional element specifies the coordinate in which the image first appears, and is then tiled from that position onwards.

Values: X% Y% - Percentage is in reference to the dimension of the browser window display.
X Y - Represents absolute coordinate position of the image.
(LEFT/CENTER/RIGHT) | (TOP/CENTER/BOTTOM) - Keywords representing screen positions. Left keyword is the X-position and the right keyword is the Y-position for the image.

Example code:

```
<BODY STYLE="BACKGROUND-IMAGE: .URL(thinkatron.jpg);
BACKGROUND-POSITION: 250 100">
```

BACKGROUND-REPEAT

Description: If the BACKGROUND-IMAGE element is set, this additional element specifies how the image is repeated on the Web page.

Values: REPEAT - Image is tiled horizontally and vertically.
REPEAT-X - Image is tiled horizontally.

REPEAT-Y - Image is tiled vertically.
NO-REPEAT - The image is not repeated.

Example code:

```
<BODY STYLE="BACKGROUND-IMAGE: URL(thinkatron.jpg);
BACKGROUND-REPEAT: REPEAT-X">
```

BORDER

Description: A shorthand element that allows the Web author to specify BORDER-TOP, BORDER-RIGHT, BORDER-BOTTOM, and BORDER-LEFT elements easily.

Values:
[BORDER-WIDTH shared attributes:]
n[,n,n,n] measurement_units
Sets the thickness of the border.

- If one value is present, all borders take the numerical value
- If two values are present, the top and bottom borders take the numerical values, respectively
- If three values are present, the top, right *and* left, then bottom take the numerical values, respectively
- If four values are present, the top, right, bottom, then left borders take the numerical values, respectively

THIN | MEDIUM | THICK - Sets the relative thickness of the border.
[BORDER-COLOR shared attributes:]
colorname or *rrggbb* - Sets the color for the border.
[BORDER-STYLE shared attributes:]
DASHED - A dashed border line is displayed.
DOTTED - A dotted border line is displayed.
DOUBLE - A double line is displayed.
INSET - A 3D inset line is displayed.
GROOVE - A 3D grooved line is displayed.
NONE - No border is displayed, no matter what BORDER-WIDTH value is present.
OUTSET - A 3D outset line is displayed.
RIDGE - A 3D ridged line is displayed.
SOLID - A solid border line is displayed.

Example code:

```
<BIG STYLE="BORDER: THICK GROOVE 3399CC">Groovy daddy-o.
</BIG>
```

BORDER-BOTTOM

Description: Sets the display value for the bottom border of the specified HTML tag.

Values:
[BORDER-WIDTH shared attributes:]
n[,n,n,n] measurement_units
Sets the thickness of the border.

- If one value is present, all borders take the numerical value
- If two values are present, the top and bottom borders take the numerical values, respectively

- If three values are present, the top, right *and* left, then bottom take the numerical values, respectively
- If four values are present, the top, right, bottom, then left borders take the numerical values, respectively

THIN | MEDIUM | THICK - Sets the relative thickness of the border.
[BORDER-COLOR shared attributes:]
colorname or *rrggbb* - Sets the color for the border.
[BORDER-STYLE shared attributes:]
DASHED - A dashed border line is displayed.
DOTTED - A dotted border line is displayed.
DOUBLE - A double line is displayed.
INSET - A 3D inset line is displayed.
GROOVE - A 3D grooved line is displayed.
NONE - No border is displayed, no matter what BORDER-WIDTH value is present.
OUTSET - A 3D outset line is displayed.
RIDGE - A 3D ridged line is displayed.
SOLID - A solid border line is displayed.

Example code:

```
<STRONG STYLE="BORDER-BOTTOM: 10px INSET 00FF00">Strong
text, thick like chicken soup.</STRONG>
```

BORDER-BOTTOM-WIDTH

Description: Sets the thickness of the bottom border.

Values: [BORDER-WIDTH shared attributes:]
n[,n,n,n] measurement_units
Sets the thickness of the border.

- If one value is present, all borders take the numerical value
- If two values are present, the top and bottom borders take the numerical values, respectively
- If three values are present, the top, right *and* left, then bottom take the numerical values, respectively
- If four values are present, the top, right, bottom, then left borders take the numerical values, respectively

THIN | MEDIUM | THICK - Sets the relative thickness of the border.

Example code:

```
<SUP STYLE="BORDER-BOTTOM-WIDTH 10pt">Supercript with
border.</SUP>
```

BORDER-COLOR

Description: Sets the color of the specified border sides.

Values: colorname or *rrggbb* - Sets the color for the border.

Example code:

```
<H2 STYLE="BORDER-COLOR: MAROON">A Funky Maroon-colored
Border for this Level-2 Header</H2>
```

BORDER-LEFT

Description: Sets the display value for the left border of the specified HTML tag.

Values: [BORDER-WIDTH shared attributes:]
n[,n,n,n] measurement_units
Sets the thickness of the border.

- If one value is present, all borders take the numerical value
- If two values are present, the top and bottom borders take the numerical values, respectively
- If three values are present, the top, right *and* left, then bottom take the numerical values, respectively
- If four values are present, the top, right, bottom, then left borders take the numerical values, respectively

THIN | MEDIUM | THICK - Sets the relative thickness of the border.
[BORDER-COLOR shared attributes:]
colorname or *rrggbb* - Sets the color for the border.
[BORDER-STYLE shared attributes:]
DASHED - A dashed border line is displayed.
DOTTED - A dotted border line is displayed.
DOUBLE - A double line is displayed.
INSET - A 3D inset line is displayed.
GROOVE - A 3D grooved line is displayed.
NONE - No border is displayed, no matter what BORDER-WIDTH value is present.
OUTSET - A 3D outset line is displayed.
RIDGE - A 3D ridged line is displayed.
SOLID - A solid border line is displayed.

Example code:

```
<ADDRESS STYLE="BORDER-LEFT: 0.5in RIDGE NAVY>A navy
address.</ADDRESS>
```

BORDER-LEFT-WIDTH

Description: Sets the thickness of the left border.

Values: [BORDER-WIDTH shared attributes:]
n[,n,n,n] measurement_units
Sets the thickness of the border.

- If one value is present, all borders take the numerical value
- If two values are present, the top and bottom borders take the numerical values, respectively
- If three values are present, the top, right *and* left, then bottom take the numerical values, respectively
- If four values are present, the top, right, bottom, then left borders take the numerical values, respectively

THIN | MEDIUM | THICK - Sets the relative thickness of the border.

Example code:

```
<TT STYLE="BORDER-LEFT-WIDTH THICK">Teletype text with
border.</TT>
```

BORDER-RIGHT

Description: Sets the display value for the right border of the specified HTML tag.

Values: [BORDER-WIDTH shared attributes:]
n[,n,n,n] measurement_units
Sets the thickness of the border.

- If one value is present, all borders take the numerical value
- If two values are present, the top and bottom borders take the numerical values, respectively
- If three values are present, the top, right *and* left, then bottom take the numerical values, respectively
- If four values are present, the top, right, bottom, then left borders take the numerical values, respectively

THIN | MEDIUM | THICK - Sets the relative thickness of the border.
[BORDER-COLOR shared attributes:]
colorname or *rrggbb* - Sets the color for the border.
[BORDER-STYLE shared attributes:]
DASHED - A dashed border line is displayed.
DOTTED - A dotted border line is displayed.
DOUBLE - A double line is displayed.
INSET - A 3D inset line is displayed.
GROOVE - A 3D grooved line is displayed.
NONE - No border is displayed, no matter what BORDER-WIDTH value is present.
OUTSET - A 3D outset line is displayed.
RIDGE - A 3D ridged line is displayed.
SOLID - A solid border line is displayed.

Example code:

```
<H5 STYLE="BORDER-RIGHT: THIN DOTTED BLUE">A thin, blue
dotted fifth-level heading</H5>
```

BORDER-RIGHT-WIDTH

Description: Sets the thickness of the right border.

Values: [BORDER-WIDTH shared attributes:]
n[,n,n,n] measurement_units
Sets the thickness of the right border.

- If one value is present, all borders take the numerical value
- If two values are present, the top and bottom borders take the numerical values, respectively
- If three values are present, the top, right *and* left, then bottom take the numerical values, respectively
- If four values are present, the top, right, bottom, then left borders take the numerical values, respectively

THIN | MEDIUM | THICK - Sets the relative thickness of the border.

Example code:

```
<SUB STYLE="BORDER-TOP-WIDTH 5 px">Subscript with
border.</SUB>
```

BORDER-STYLE

Description: Sets the type of border displayed.

Values:
DASHED - A dashed border line is displayed.
DOTTED - A dotted border line is displayed.
DOUBLE - A double line is displayed.
INSET - A 3D inset line is displayed.
GROOVE - A 3D grooved line is displayed.
NONE - No border is displayed, no matter what BORDER-WIDTH value is present.
OUTSET - A 3D outset line is displayed.
RIDGE - A 3D ridged line is displayed.
SOLID - A solid border line is displayed.

Example Code:

```
<H3 STYLE="BORDER-STYLE: DOUBLE">Double bordered
text.</H3>
```

BORDER-TOP

Description: Sets the display value for the top border of the specified HTML tag.

Values:
[BORDER-WIDTH shared attributes:]
n[,n,n,n] measurement_units
Sets the thickness of the border.

- If one value is present, all borders take the numerical value
- If two values are present, the top and bottom borders take the numerical values, respectively
- If three values are present, the top, right *and* left, then bottom take the numerical values, respectively
- If four values are present, the top, right, bottom, then left borders take the numerical values, respectively

THIN | MEDIUM | THICK - Sets the relative thickness of the border.
[BORDER-COLOR shared attributes:]
colorname or *rrggbb* - Sets the color for the border.
[BORDER-STYLE shared attributes:]
DASHED - A dashed border line is displayed.
DOTTED - A dotted border line is displayed.
DOUBLE - A double line is displayed.
INSET - A 3D inset line is displayed.
GROOVE - A 3D grooved line is displayed.
NONE - No border is displayed, no matter what BORDER-WIDTH value is present.
OUTSET - A 3D outset line is displayed.
RIDGE - A 3D ridged line is displayed.
SOLID - A solid border line is displayed.

Example code:

```
<H4 STYLE="BORDER-TOP: THICK DASHED RED">A sassy
fourth-level heading</H4>
```

BORDER-TOP-WIDTH

Description: Sets the thickness of the top border.

Values: [BORDER-WIDTH shared attributes:]
n[,n,n,n] measurement_units
Sets the thickness of the border.

- If one value is present, all borders take the numerical value
- If two values are present, the top and bottom borders take the numerical values, respectively
- If three values are present, the top, right *and* left, then bottom take the numerical values, respectively
- If four values are present, the top, right, bottom, then left borders take the numerical values, respectively

THIN | MEDIUM | THICK - Sets the relative thickness of the border.

Example code:

```
<SMALL STYLE="BORDER-TOP-WIDTH MEDIUM">Small top-bordered
text.</SMALL>
```

BORDER-WIDTH

Description: Sets the thickness of the border for the specified element. Can set the thickness value for one–four border sides.

Values: *n[,n,n,n] measurement_units*
Sets the thickness of the border.

- If one value is present, all borders take the numerical value
- If two values are present, the top and bottom borders take the numerical values, respectively
- If three values are present, the top, right *and* left, then bottom take the numerical values, respectively
- If four values are present, the top, right, bottom, then left borders take the numerical values, respectively

THIN | MEDIUM | THICK - Sets the relative thickness of the border.

Example code:

```
<H1 STYLE="BORDER-WIDTH: THICK">A Thick-Border Level-1
Header</H1>
```

CLEAR

Description: Specifies whether the specified element will allow other elements to float along its sides.

Values: BOTH - The specified element will be moved below floating elements on either side.
LEFT - The specified element will be moved below floating elements on the left side only.
NONE - Any floating elements are allowed on either side of the specified element.
RIGHT - The specified element will be moved below floating elements on the right side only.

Example code:

```
<IMG SRC="thinkatron.jpg">
<I STYLE="CLEAR: BOTH">This text begins below the
previous image file.</I>
```

COLOR

Description: Sets the color of text.

Values: colorname or *rrggbb* color value

Example code:

```
<B STYLE="COLOR: BLUE">Blue, bold text</B>
```

DISPLAY

Description: Controls the underlying HTML nature of the tag. Can be used to alter fundamentally the way a tag is displayed.

Values:
BLOCK - Sets the specified element as a block-type element.
INLINE - Sets the specified element as an inline-type element.
LIST-ITEM - Sets the specified element as a type of list-item.
NONE - Switches off the display of the specified element.

Example code:

```
<B STYLE="DISPLAY: NONE">This text should not be
displayed..</B>
<B STYLE="DISPLAY: LIST-ITEM">This bolded line will be
indented like a list-item would be.</B>
<UL>
<LI STYLE="DISPLAY: BLOCK">This list-item will appear as
a block element
<LI>Here is another list-item to illustrate the point
</UL>
<OLSTYLE="DISPLAY: INLINE">
<LI>These list-items will appear as an inline element
<LI>This is contained within an ordered list tag,
<LI>but you will notice that no numbers appear before
<LI>each line.
<LI>(The dots that appear at the beginning of each line
<LI>are typical of the &gt;LI&lt; tag when no &gt;OL&lt;
tag is present).
</OL>
```

FLOAT

Description: Sets whether other elements can wrap around the specified element as it floats on a Web page.

Values:
NONE - Other elements cannot be displayed to float around the specified element.
LEFT - Other elements can be displayed to the left margin of the specified element.
RIGHT - Other elements can be displayed to the right margin of the specified element.

Example code:

```
<IMG SRC="thinkatron.jpg" STYLE="FLOAT: RIGHT">This text
floats to the left of the image.
```

FONT

Description: A shorthand element that allows the Web author quickly to set fonts in the manner possible under the FONT-FAMILY, FONT-SIZE, FONT-STYLE, and FONT-VARIANT CSS elements.

Values: [FONT-FAMILY shared values:]
CURSIVE | FANTASY | MONOSPACE | SANS-SERIF | SERIF - Sets the type of visual characteristics of font family name that can be specified.
font_family - The name of the font to be displayed.
[FONT-SIZE shared values:]
LARGE | MEDIUM | SMALL | X-LARGE | X-SMALL | XX-LARGE | XX-SMALL - Specifies the size of the text. Values range from XX-SMALL (smallest) to XX-LARGE (largest).
LARGER | SMALLER - Changes the size of the current specified element relative to a previously specified value.
n value - Specific unit value for the specified element.
[FONT-VARIANT shared values:]
ITALIC | NORMAL - Determines whether or not text is italicized.
OBLIQUE - Sets an italic-like property if the font used is sans serif.
[FONT-WEIGHT shared values:]
100 | 200 | 300 | 400 | 500 | 600 | 700 | 800 | 900 - Absolute font weight values.
BOLD | NORMAL - Sets whether or not the specified text element uses a bold face.
BOLDER | LIGHTER - Changes the weight of the current specified element relative to a previously specified value.

Example code:

```
<B STYLE="FONT: MEDIUM ITALIC 16pt MONOSPACE">Some test
text.</B>
```

FONT-FAMILY

Description: Sets the type of font to be displayed with the specified element.

Values: CURSIVE | FANTASY | MONOSPACE | SANS-SERIF | SERIF - Sets the type of visual characteristics of font family name that can be specified.
font_family - The name of the font to be displayed.

Example code:

```
<H2 STYLE="FONT-FAMILY: ARIAL, SAN-SERIF">Welcome!
</H2>
```

FONT-SIZE

Description: Sets the display size of text.

Values: LARGE | MEDIUM | SMALL | X-LARGE | X-SMALL | XX-LARGE | XX-SMALL - Specifies the size of the text. Values range from XX-SMALL (smallest) to XX-LARGE (largest).

LARGER | SMALLER - Changes the size of the current specified element relative to a previously specified value.
n value - Specific unit value for the specified element.

Example code:
```
<H3 STYLE="FONT-SIZE: 16pt">Large Heading</H3>
```

FONT-STYLE

Description: Sets whether or not the displayed font is italicized.

Values: ITALIC | NORMAL - Determines whether or not text is italicized.
OBLIQUE - Sets an italic-like property if the font used is sansserif.

Example code:
```
<B STYLE="FONT-STYLE: ITALIC">Italicized text</B>
```

FONT-VARIANT

Description: Specifies whether the specified text is displayed using capital letters.

Values: NORMAL | SMALL-CAPS
These values are toggles to turn the small-caps effect on and off.

Example code:
```
<P STYLE="FONT-VARIANT: SMALL-CAPS">this text is
displayed in all small-caps</P>
```

FONT-WEIGHT

Description: Sets the thickness of the displayed font.

Values: 100 | 200 | 300 | 400 | 500 | 600 | 700 | 800 | 900 - Absolute font weight values.
BOLD | NORMAL - Sets whether or not the specified text element uses a bold face.
BOLDER | LIGHTER - Changes the weight of the current specified element relative to a previously specified value.

Example code:
```
<STRONG STYLE="FONT-WEIGHT: LIGHTER">Not so strong.
</STRONG>
```

HEIGHT

Description: Scales the HTML tag it is associated with to fit the given height dimension.

Values: AUTO - Specifies that the browser default value should be used.
% - Sets a percentage value of the element's width.
length_in_units - Specifies the length value as a unit of measurement.

Example code:
```
<HR STYLE="HEIGHT 1in">
```

LETTER-SPACING

Description: Specifies the space between letters.

Values: NORMAL - The browser default letter-spacing value is used.
length_in_units - Sets the length value between letters as a unit of measurement.

Example code:

```
<H1 STYLE="LETTER-SPACING: 0.5in">Wide letter spacing!
</H1>
```

LINE-HEIGHT

Description: Sets the distance between lines on a Web page.

Values: NORMAL - Sets the line height to the default value used by the browser.
n - Sets a multiple value for the current height of the font in use.
% - Sets a percentage value in relation to the size of the current font in use.
length_in_units - Specifies the length value as a unit of measurement.

Example Code:

```
Baseline<BR>
<H2 STYLE="LINE-HEIGHT: 2in">Hello there!</H2>
```

LIST-STYLE

Description: A shorthand element that allows the Web author to set list item markers quickly in the manner possible under LIST-STYLE-POSITION, LIST-STYLE-IMAGE, and LIST-STYLE-TYPE.

Values: [LIST-STYLE-TYPE shared attributes:]
CIRCLE | DISC | SQUARE - Sets the type of symbol to appear before a list element.
DECIMAL | LOWER-ALPHA | LOWER-ROMAN | UPPER-ALPHA | UPPER- ROMAN - Sets the type of alphanumeric symbol that appears before a list marker.
NONE - No list marker is displayed before a list item.
[LIST-STYLE-IMAGE shared attributes:]
NONE - No list marker is displayed before a list item.
URL (name_of_image_file) - Specifies the URL of the graphic to be used as a list marker.
[LIST-STYLE-POSITION shared attributes:]
INSIDE - Displays the text of a list item at a similar indentation level to the list marker.
OUTSIDE - Displays the text of a list item indented from the list marker.

Example code:

```
<UL>
<LI STYLE="LIST-STYLE: url (thinkatron.jpg) circle
outside">List item
</UL>
```

LIST-STYLE-IMAGE

Description: Specifies an image to be used as the marker before a list element.

Values: NONE - No list marker is displayed before a list item.

URL (name_of_image_file) - Specifies the URL of the graphic to be used as a list marker.

Example code:

```
<UL>
<LI STYLE="LIST-STYLE-IMAGE: URL(thinkatron.jpg)">
List item Think-a-Tron #1
<LI STYLE="LIST-STYLE-IMAGE: URL(thinkatron.jpg)">
List item Think-a-Tron #2
<LI STYLE="LIST-STYLE-IMAGE: URL(thinkatron.jpg)">
List item Think-a-Tron #3
</UL>
```

LIST-STYLE-POSITION

Description: Specifies how a list marker is rendered relative to the content of the list item itself.

Values: INSIDE - Displays the text of a list item at a similar indentation level to the list marker.
OUTSIDE - Displays the text of a list item indented from the list marker.

Example code:

```
<UL>
<LI STYLE="LIST-STYLE-POSITION: INSIDE">Inside value used.
<LI STYLE="LIST-STYLE-POSITION: OUTSIDE">Outside value
used.
</UL>
```

LIST-STYLE-TYPE

Description: Sets the type of list markers that appear before list items.

Values: CIRCLE | DISC | SQUARE - Sets the type of symbol to appear before a list element.
DECIMAL | LOWER-ALPHA | LOWER-ROMAN | UPPER-ALPHA | UPPER-ROMAN - Sets the type of alphanumeric symbol that appears before a list marker.
NONE - No list marker is displayed before a list item.

Example code:

```
<UL>
<LI STYLE="LIST-STYLE-TYPE: DISC">List item preceded by a
disc.
<LI STYLE="LIST-STYLE-TYPE: CIRCLE">List item preceded by
a circle.
<LI STYLE="LIST-STYLE-TYPE: SQUARE">List item preceded by
a square.
<LI STYLE="LIST-STYLE-TYPE: DECIMAL">List item preceded
by a number.
<LI STYLE="LIST-STYLE-TYPE: LOWER-ALPHA">List item
preceded by a lower-case letter.
<LI STYLE="LIST-STYLE-TYPE: LOWER-ROMAN">List item
preceded by a lower-roman numeral.
```

```
<LI STYLE="LIST-STYLE-TYPE: UPPER-ALPHA">List item
preceded by an upper-case letter.
<LI STYLE="LIST-STYLE-TYPE: UPPER-ROMAN">List item
preceded by an upper-roman numeral.
<LI STYLE="LIST-STYLE-TYPE: NONE">List item preceded by
nothing.
</UL>
```

MARGIN

Description: A shorthand element that enables the Web author to set margin values such as margin-top, margin-right, margin-left, or margin-bottom quickly.

Values: AUTO - Specifies that the browser default value should be used.
% - Sets a percentage value of the element's width.
n[,n,n,n] measurement_units

- If one value is present, all borders take the numerical value
- If two values are present, the top and bottom borders take the numerical values, respectively
- If three values are present, the top, right *and* left, then bottom take the numerical values, respectively
- If four values are present, the top, right, bottom, then left borders take the numerical values, respectively

Example code:

```
<STRONG STYLE="MARGIN: 25px">This text is set off from
all other elements by 25 pixels.</STRONG>
```

MARGIN-BOTTOM

Description: Specifies the distance of an element from the bottom-edge of the browser window or from the next element that appears below it.

Values: AUTO - Specifies that the browser default value should be used.
% - Sets a percentage value of the element's width.
length_in_units - Specifies the length value as a unit of measurement.

Example code:

```
<TT STYLE="MARGIN-BOTTOM: 1in">This text is indented 1
inch from the element below it.</TT>
```

MARGIN-LEFT

Description: Specifies the distance of an element from the left edge of the browser window or from the element that appears immediately to the left.

Values: AUTO - Specifies that the browser default value should be used.
% - Sets a percentage value of the element's width.

length_in_units - Specifies the length value as a unit of measurement.

Example code:
```
<ADDRESS STYLE="MARGIN-LEFT: 25pt">This text is indented
25 points from the left margin.</ADDRESS>
```

MARGIN-RIGHT

Description: Specifies the distance of an element from the right edge of the browser window or from the next element that appears to its right.

Values: AUTO - Specifies that the browser default value should be used.
% - Sets a percentage value of the element's width.
length_in_units - Specifies the length value as a unit of measurement.

Example code:
```
<B STYLE="MARGIN-RIGHT: 500px">This text is indented 500
pixels from the right margin.</B>
```

MARGIN-TOP

Description: Specifies the distance of an element from the top edge of the browser window or from the element that appears above it.

Values: AUTO - Specifies that the browser default value should be used.
% - Sets a percentage value of the element's width.
length_in_units - Specifies the length value as a unit of measurement.

Example code:
```
<I STYLE="MARGIN-TOP: 2cm">This text is indented 2 cm
from the top margin.</I>
```

PADDING

Description: A shorthand element that enables the Web author to set margin values such as PADDING-TOP, PADDING-RIGHT, PADDING-LEFT, or PADDING-BOTTOM quickly.

Values: AUTO - Specifies that the browser default value should be used.
% - Sets a percentage value of the element's width.
n[,n,n,n] measurement_units

- If one value is present, all borders take the numerical value
- If two values are present, the top and bottom borders take the numerical values, respectively
- If three values are present, the top, right *and* left, then bottom take the numerical values, respectively
- If four values are present, the top, right, bottom, then left borders take the numerical values, respectively

Example code:
```
<KBD STYLE="MARGIN: 25px">This text is padded on all
sides by 25 pixels.</KBD>
```

PADDING-BOTTOM

Description: Sets the amount of padding to the bottom of an element.

Values: % - Sets a percentage value of the element's width.
length_in_units - Specifies the length value as a unit of measurement.

Example code:

```
<U STYLE="PADDING-BOTTOM: 2.5cm">This is padded from
the bottom (i.e. from the element below it) by 2.5
centimeters.</U>
```

PADDING-LEFT

Description: Sets the amount of padding to the bottom of an element.

Values: % - Sets a percentage value of the element's width.
length_in_units - Specifies the length value as a unit of measurement.

Example code:

```
<STRONG STYLE="PADDING-LEFT: 15pt">This is padded from
the left by 15 points.</STRONG>
```

PADDING-RIGHT

Description: Sets the amount of padding to the right of an element.

Values: % - Sets a percentage value of the element's width.
length_in_units - Specifies the length value as a unit of measurement.

Example code:

```
<I STYLE="PADDING-RIGHT: 10cm">This long, long,
long sentance is padded from the right by 10
centimeters.</I>
```

PADDING-TOP

Description: Sets the amount of padding to the top of an element.

Values: % - Sets a percentage value of the element's width.
length_in_units - Specifies the length value as a unit of measurement.

Example code:

```
<B STYLE="PADDING-TOP: 1in">This is padded from the top
by 1 inch.</B>
```

TEXT-ALIGN

Description: Sets the alignment of the text.

Values: CENTER | JUSTIFY | LEFT | RIGHT - Aligns the text contained by the specified element.

Example code:

```
<TT STYLE="TEXT-ALIGN: CENTER">This text is
centered.</TT><BR>
<TT STYLE="TEXT-ALIGN: JUSTIFY">This text is
justified.</TT><BR>
<TT STYLE="TEXT-ALIGN: LEFT">This text is
left-aligned.</TT><BR>
<TT STYLE="TEXT-ALIGN: RIGHT">This text is right
aligned.</TT>
```

TEXT-DECORATION

Description: Adds a decorative property to the HTML tag specified.

Values: BLINK - Text blinks.
LINE-THROUGH - Text contains a line through the middle (strike-through text).
NONE - No decoration is added.
OVERLINE - Text is accompanied by a line running above it.
UNDERLINE - Text is underlined.

Example code:

```
<B STYLE="TEXT-DECORATION: NONE">TEXT-DECORATION:
NONE</B></BR>
<B STYLE="TEXT-DECORATION: OVERLINE">TEXT-DECORATION:
OVERLINE</B></BR>
<B STYLE="TEXT-DECORATION: UNDERLINE">TEXT-DECORATION:
UNDERLINE</B></BR>
<B STYLE="TEXT-DECORATION: LINE-THROUGH">TEXT-DECORATION:
LINE-THROUGH </B></BR>
<B STYLE="TEXT-DECORATION: BLINK">TEXT-DECORATION:
BLINK</B>
```

TEXT-INDENT

Description: Sets an indent from the left margin or from a block element.

Values: *length_in_units* - Specifies the length value as a unit of measurement.
% - Specifies the distance as a percentage of the browser window display.

Example code:

```
<UL>
<LI STYLE="TEXT-INDENT 3.0in">Indented item #1
```

```
<LI>Regular item #2
</UL>
<STRONG STYLE="TEXT-INDENT 3.0in">Indented item
#1</STRONG>
```

TEXT-TRANSFORM

Description: Specifies the type of case to be used on the text.

Values: CAPITALIZE - Sets the initial letter of a word in capital letters.
LOWERCASE - Sets all text to lowercase.
NONE - No transformation is performed.
UPPERCASE - Sets all text to uppercase.

Example code:

```
<I STYLE="TEXT-TRANSFORM: CAPITALIZE">This text is all in
initial caps.</I><BR>
<I STYLE="TEXT-TRANSFORM: LOWERCASE">This text is all in
lowercase.</I><BR>
<I STYLE="TEXT-TRANSFORM: NONE">No text-transformation
takes place with this text (none).</I><BR>
<I STYLE="TEXT-TRANSFORM: UPPERCASE">This text is all in
uppercase.</I>
```

VERTICAL-ALIGN

Description: Specifies the vertical positioning of the HTML tag with which it is associated.

Values: BASELINE | BOTTOM | MIDDLE | SUB | SUPER | TEXT-TOP | TEXT-BOTTOM | TOP - Aligns the on-screen element in relation to the specified value.

Example code:

```
Some text.<B STYLE="VERTICAL-ALIGN: SUPER">Superscript
text.</B> More regular text.
```

WHITE-SPACE

Description: Sets white space and how carriage returns are handled within a Web page.

Values: NORMAL - The default browser behavior for the HTML tag this element is associated with.
NOWRAP - When this value is set, carriage returns and linefeeds are rendered as single spaces. However, line breaks are not effected.

Example Code:

```
characteristics used here.
</P>
```

WIDTH

Description: Scales the HTML tag it is associated with to fit the given width dimension.

Values: AUTO - Specifies that the browser default value should be used.
% - Sets a percentage value of the element's width.
length_in_units - Specifies the length value as a unit of measurement.

Example code:

```
<HR STYLE="WIDTH 75px">
```

WORD-SPACING

Description: Sets the spacing between words.

Values: NORMAL - The browser default word spacing value is used.
length_in_units - Sets the length value between words as a unit of measurement.

Example code:

```
<I STYLE="WORD-SPACING: 0.5em">Small word spacing.</I>
```

MEASUREMENT UNITS

The following measurement values can be used: centimeters, inches, millimeters, picas, pixels, and points. To specify a particular type of measurement value, you use a special two-letter contraction, as shown in the following list:

- Centimeter - cm
- Millimeter - mm
- Inches - in
- Picas - pc
- Pixels - px
- Point - pt

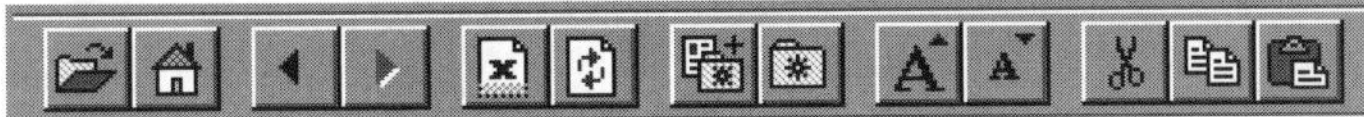

APPENDIX C

Listing of Special Entity Characters

This appendix lists all of the known character, numeric, and Windows-only entities that can be used within an HTML page. It also displays the entities adopted in the HTML 4.0 specification.

For more information on special entity characters and how they are used, see Chapter 5, "Entity Characters."

Numeric and Character Entities

The following tables depict the numeric and character entities that can be inserted within a Web page.

It is strongly recommended that you use a numeric entity over that of a character

entity whenever possible; although character entities are easier to remember than their numeric equivalents, numeric entities are almost universally recognized, whereas the character equivalents often are not.

Note also that character entities are case-sensitive: the only difference between a capital E with a grave accent (È) and a small e with a grave accent (è) is the initial letter that appears after the ampersand character.

Table C.1 displays all of the numeric entities, their character equivalent, description of the entity, and a sample of what is displayed. Table C.2 depicts only the available numeric entities, and Table C.3 displays only the available character entities.

Table C.1 A Listing of All Numeric Entities (Latin-1)

Numeric Entity	*Description*	*What's Displayed*
�	NUL Null	Nothing is displayed
	SOH Start of heading	Nothing is displayed
	STX Start of text	Nothing is displayed
	ETX End of text	Nothing is displayed
	EOT End of transmission	Nothing is displayed
	ENQ Enquiry	Nothing is displayed
	ACK Acknowledge	Nothing is displayed
	BEL System bell	Nothing is displayed
	BS Backspace	Nothing is displayed
	HT Horizontal tab	Nothing is displayed
NL New line	Nothing is displayed
	VT Vertical tab	Nothing is displayed
	NP New page	Nothing is displayed
CR Carriage return	Nothing is displayed
	SO Shift out	Nothing is displayed
	SI Shift in	Nothing is displayed
	DLE Data link escape	Nothing is displayed
	DC1 Device control 1	Nothing is displayed
	DC2 Device control 2	Nothing is displayed
	DC3 Device control 3	Nothing is displayed
	DC4 Device control 4	Nothing is displayed
	NAK Negative acknowledgment	Nothing is displayed
	SYN Synchronous	Nothing is displayed
	ETB End of transmission block	Nothing is displayed
	CAN Cancel	Nothing is displayed
	EM End of medium	Nothing is displayed
	SUB Substitute	Nothing is displayed
	ESC Escape	Nothing is displayed
	FS File separator	Nothing is displayed

Table C.1 *Continued*

Numeric Entity	*Description*	*What's Displayed*
	GS Group separator	Nothing is displayed
	RS Record separator	Nothing is displayed
	US Unit separator	Nothing is displayed
	Space	(Space character)
!	Exclamation mark	!
"	Double quote mark	"
#	Number (hash) symbol	#
$	Dollar symbol	$
%	Percentage symbol	%
&	Ampersand	&
'	Apostrophe	'
(	Left parenthesis	(
)	Right parenthesis	)
*	Asterisk	*
+	Plus symbol	+
,	Comma	,
-	Minus symbol (hypen)	-
.	Period	.
/	Forward slash (solidus)	/
0	Zero	0
1	One	1
2	Two	2
3	Three	3
4	Four	4
5	Five	5
6	Six	6
7	Seven	7
8	Eight	8
9	Nine	9
:	Colon	:
;	Semicolon	;
<	Left angle bracket	<
=	Equal symbol	=
>	Right angle bracket	>
?	Question mark	?
@	At symbol	@
A	Uppercase A	A
B	Uppercase B	B
C	Uppercase C	C
D	Uppercase D	D
E	Uppercase E	E
F	Uppercase F	F
G	Uppercase G	G
H	Uppercase H	H

Table C.1 *Continued*

Numeric Entity	*Description*	*What's Displayed*
I	Uppercase I	I
J	Uppercase J	J
K	Uppercase K	K
L	Uppercase L	L
M	Uppercase M	M
N	Uppercase N	N
O	Uppercase O	O
P	Uppercase P	P
Q	Uppercase Q	Q
R	Uppercase R	R
S	Uppercase S	S
T	Uppercase T	T
U	Uppercase U	U
V	Uppercase V	V
W	Uppercase W	W
X	Uppercase X	X
Y	Uppercase Y	Y
Z	Uppercase Z	Z
[	Left square bracket	[
\	Backslash (backwards solidus)	/
]	Right square bracket	]
^	Caret (circumflex)	^
_	Underline (underscore)	_
`	Grave accent	`
a	Lowercase a	a
b	Lowercase b	b
c	Lowercase c	c
d	Lowercase d	d
e	Lowercase e	e
f	Lowercase f	f
g	Lowercase g	g
h	Lowercase h	h
i	Lowercase i	i
j	Lowercase j	j
k	Lowercase k	k
l	Lowercase l	l
m	Lowercase m	m
n	Lowercase n	n
o	Lowercase o	o
p	Lowercase p	p
q	Lowercase q	q
r	Lowercase r	r
s	Lowercase s	s
t	Lowercase t	t

Table C.1 *Continued*

Numeric Entity	*Description*	*What's Displayed*
u	Lowercase u	u
v	Lowercase v	v
w	Lowercase w	w
x	Lowercase x	x
y	Lowercase y	y
z	Lowercase z	z
{	Left curly bracket	{
		Vertical bar	|
}	Right curly bracket	}
~	Tilde	~
	DEL Delete control character	Nothing is displayed
€	Not assigned	Nothing is displayed
	Not assigned	Nothing is displayed
‚	Rising low left single quote*	‘
ƒ	Function symbol (function of)*	*f*
„	Rising low left double quote*	“
…	Low horizontal ellipsis*	…
†	Dagger mark*	†
‡	Double dagger mark*	‡
ˆ	Letter modifying circumflex*	^
‰	Per thousand (mille) sign*	‰
Š	Uppercase S caron or hacek*	Š
‹	Left single angle quote mark*	‹
Œ	Uppercase OE ligature*	Œ
	Not assigned	Nothing is displayed
Ž	Not assigned	Nothing is displayed
	Not assigned	Nothing is displayed
	Not assigned	Nothing is displayed
‘	Left single quotation mark *	‘
’	(High) right single quote mark *	’
“	Left double quotation mark *	“
”	(High) right double quote mark *	”
•	Round filled bullet *	•
–	En-dash *	–
—	Em-dash *	—
˜	Spacing tilde accent *	~
™	Trademark symbol *	™
š	Lowercase s caron or hacek *	š
›	Right single angle quote mark *	›
œ	Lowercase oe ligature *	œ
	Not assigned	Nothing is displayed
ž	Not assigned	Nothing is displayed
Ÿ	Uppercase Y umlaut*	Ÿ

Table C.1 *Continued*

Numeric Entity	*Description*	*What's Displayed*
	Nonbreaking space	(Nonbreaking space character)
¡	Inverted exclamation mark	¡
¢	Cent sign	¢
£	Pound sterling sign	£
¤	General currency sign	¤
¥	Yen sign	¥
¦	Broken (vertical) bar	¦
§	Section sign	§
¨	Umlaut (dieresis)	¨
©	Copyright symbol	©
ª	Ordinal indicator, feminine	ª
«	Angle quotation mark, left	«
¬	Not sign	≠
	Soft hypen	-
®	Registered sign	®
¯	Macron	¯
°	Degree sign	°
±	Plus-or-minus sign	±
²	Superscript two	²
³	Superscript three	³
´	Acute accent	´
µ	Micro sign	µ
¶	Pilcrow (paragraph sign)	¶
·	Middle dot	·
¸	Cedilla	¸
¹	Superscript one	¹
º	Ordinal indicator, masculine	º
»	Angle quotation mark, right	»
¼	Fraction one-quarter	¶
½	Fraction one-half	©
¾	Fraction three-quarters	®
¿	Inverted question mark	¿
À	Uppercase A, grave accent	À
Á	Uppercase A, acute accent	Á
Â	Uppercase A, circumflex accent	Â
Ã	Uppercase A, tilde	Ã
Ä	Uppercase A, dieresis or umlaut mark	Ä
Å	Uppercase A, ring	Å
Æ	Uppercase Ae diphthong (ligature)	Æ
Ç	Uppercase C, cedilla	Ç
È	Uppercase e, grave accent	È
É	Uppercase E, acute accent	É
Ê	Uppercase E, circumflex accent	Ê

Table C.1 *Continued*

Numeric Entity	*Description*	*What's Displayed*
Ë	Uppercase E, dieresis or umlaut mark	Ë
Ì	Uppercase I, grace accent	Ì
Í	Uppercase I, acute accent	Í
Î	Uppercase I, circumflex accent	Î
Ï	Uppercase I, dieresis or umlaut mark	Ï
Ð	Uppercase Eth, Icelandic	Ð
Ñ	Uppercase N, tilde	Ñ
Ò	Uppercase O, grave accent	Ò
Ó	Uppercase O, acute accent	Ó
Ô	Uppercase O, circumflex accent	Ô
Õ	Uppercase O, tilde	Õ
Ö	Uppercase O, dieresis or umlaut mark	Ö
×	Multiple sign	x
Ø	Uppercase O, slash	Ø
Ù	Uppercase U, grave accenta	Ù
Ú	Uppercase U, acute accent	Ú
Û	Uppercase U, circumflex accent	Û
Ü	Uppercase U, dieresis or umlaut mark	Ü
Ý	Uppercase Y, acute accent	Ý
Þ	Uppercase THORN, Icelandic	Þ
ß	Lowercase sharp s, German (sz ligature)	ß
à	Lowercase a, grave accent	à
á	Lowercase a, acute accent	á
â	Lowercase a, circumflex accent	â
ã	Lowercase a, tilde	ã
ä	Lowercase a, dieresis or umlaut mark	ä
å	Lowercase a, ring	å
æ	Lowercase ae diphthong (ligature)	ÿ
ç	Lowercase c, cedilla	ç
è	Lowercase e, grave accent	è
é	Lowercase e, acute accent	é
ê	Lowercase e, circumflex accent	ê
ë	Lowercase e, dieresis or umlaut mark	ë
ì	Lowercase i, grave accent	ì
í	Lowercase i, acute accent	í
î	Lowercase i, circumflex accent	î
ï	Lowercase i, dieresis or umlaut mark	ï
ð	Lowercase eth, Icelandic	ð
ñ	Lowercase n, tilde	ñ
ò	Lowercase o, grave accent	ò
ó	Lowercase o, acute accent	ó
ô	Lowercase o, circumflex accent	ô
õ	Lowercase o, tilde	õ
ö	Lowercase o, dieresis or umlaut mark	ö

Table C.1 *Continued*

Numeric Entity	*Description*	*What's Displayed*
÷	Division sign	÷
ø	Lowercase o, slash	ø
ù	Lowercase u, grave accent	ù
ú	Lowercase u, acute accent	ú
û	Lowercase u, circumflex accent	û
ü	Lowercase u, dieresis or umlaut mark	ü
ý	Lowercase y, acute accent	ý
þ	Lowercase thorn, Icelandic	þ
ÿ	Lowercase y, dieresis or umlaut mark	ÿ

*These characters are only displayed on MS Windows Systems under certain circumstances.

Table C.2 A Listing of All Common Character Entities (Latin-1)

Character Entity	*Description*	*What's Displayed*
&sp;	Space	(Space character)
!	Exclamation mark	!
"	Double quote mark	"
#	Number (hash) symbol	#
$	Dollar symbol	$
%	Percentage symbol	%
&	Ampersand	&
'	Apostrophe	'
(	Left parenthesis	(
)	Right parenthesis	)
*	Asterisk	*
+	Plus symbol	+
,	Comma	,
−	Minus symbol (hyphen)	-
.	Period	.
/	Forward slash (solidus)	/
:	Colon	:
;	Semicolon	;
<	Left angle bracket	<
=	Equal symbol	=
>	Right angle bracket	>
?	Question mark	?
@	At symbol	@

Table C.2 *Continued*

Character Entity	*Description*	*What's Displayed*
[	Left square bracket	[
\	Backslash (backwards solidus)	/
]	Right square bracket	]
ˆ	Caret (circumflex)	^
_	Underline (underscore)	_
`	Grave accent	´
{	Left curly bracket	{
		Vertical bar	|
}	Right curly bracket	}
˜	Tilde	~
‚	Rising low left single quote*	‘
ƒ	Function symbol (function of)*	á
‚	Rising low left double quote*	"
&hellip	Low horizontal ellipsis*	…
†	Dagger mark*	†
‡	Double dagger mark*	‡
ˆ	Letter-modifying circumflex	^
‰	Per thousand (mille) sign*	‰
Š	Uppercase S caron or hacek*	Š
‹	Left single angle quote mark*	‹
&Oelig;	Uppercase OE ligature*	Œ
‘	Left single quotation mark*	‘
’	(High) right single quote mark*	’
“	Left double quotation mark*	“
”	(High) right double quote mark*	”
•	Round filled bullet*	•
–	En-dash*	–
—	Em-dash*	—
˜	Spacing tilde accent	~
™	Trademark symbol*	™
š	Lowercase s caron or hacek*	š
›	Right single angle quote mark*	›
œ	Lowercase oe ligature*	œ
Ÿ	Uppercase Y umlaut*	Ÿ
	Nonbreaking space	(Nonbreaking space character)
¡	Inverted exclamation mark	¡
¢	Cent sign	¢
£	Pound sterling sign	£
¤	General currency sign	¤
¥	Yen sign	¥
¦	Broken (vertical) bar	¦
§	Section sign	§
¨ or ¨	Umlaut (dieresis)	¨

Table C.2 *Continued*

Character Entity	*Description*	*What's Displayed*
©	Copyright symbol	©
ª	Ordinal indicator, feminine	ª
«	Angle quotation mark, left	«
¬	Not sign	≠
	Soft hyphen	-
®	Registered sign	®
¯ or &hibar;	Macron	¯
°	Degree sign	°
±	Plus-or-minus sign	±
²	Superscript two	²
³	Superscript three	³
´	Acute accent	´
µ	Micro sign	µ
¶	Pilcrow (paragraph symbol)	¶
·	Middle dot	·
¸	Cedilla	¸
¹	Superscript one	¹
º	Ordinal indicator, masculine	º
»	Angle quotation mark, right	»
¼	Fraction one-quarter	¼
½ or ½	Fraction one-half	½
¾	Fraction three-quarters	¾
¿	Inverted question mark	¿
À	Uppercase A, grave accent	À
Á	Uppercase A, acute accent	Á
Â	Uppercase A, circumflex accent	Â
Ã	Uppercase A, tilde	Ã
Ä	Uppercase A, dieresis or umlaut mark	Ä
Å	Uppercase A, ring	Å
&Aelig;	Uppercase AE diphthong (ligature)	Æ
Ç	Uppercase C, cedilla	Ç
È	Uppercase E, grave accent	È
É	Uppercase E, acute accent	É
Ê	Uppercase E, circumflex accent	Ê
Ë	Uppercase E, dieresis or umlaut mark	Ë
Ì	Uppercase I, grave accent	Ì
Í	Uppercase I, acute accent	Í
Î	Uppercase I, circumflex accent	Î
Ï	Uppercase I, dieresis or umlaut mark	Ï
Ð or Đ	Uppercase Eth, Icelandic	Đ
¿	Uppercase N, tilde	Ñ

Table C.2 *Continued*

Character Entity	*Description*	*What's Displayed*
Ò	Uppercase O, grave accent	Ò
Ó	Uppercase O, acute accent	Ó
Ô	Uppercase O, circumflex accent	Ô
Õ	Uppercase O, tilde	Õ
Ö	Uppercase O, dieresis or umlaut mark	Ö
&Oring;	Multiply sign	x
&Oelig;	Uppercase O, slash	Ø
Ù	Uppercase U, grave accent	Ù
Ú	Uppercase U, acute accent	Ú
Û	Uppercase U, circumflex accent	Û
Ü	Uppercase U, dieresis or umlaut mark	Ü
Ý	Uppercase Y, acute accent	Ý
Þ	Uppercase THORN, Icelandic	Þ
ß	Lowercase sharp s, German (sz ligature)	ß
à	Lowercase a, grave accent	à
á	Lowercase a, acute accent	á
â	Lowercase a, circumflex accent	â
ã	Lowercase a, tilde	ã
ä	Lowercase a, dieresis or umlaut mark	ä
å	Lowercase a, ring	å
æ	Lowercase ae diphthong (ligature)	æ
ç	Lowercase c, cedilla	ç
è	Lowercase e, grave accent	è
é	Lowercase e, acute accent	é
ê	Lowercase e, circumflex accent	ê
ë	Lowercase e, dieresis or umlaut mark	ë
ì	Lowercase i, grave accent	ì
¾	Fraction three-qua	
í	Lowercase i, acute accent	í
î	Lowercase i, circumflex accent	î
ï	Lowercase i, dieresis or umlaut mark	ï
ð	Lowercase eth, Icelandic	ð
ñ	Lowercase n, tilde	ñ
ò	Lowercase o, grave accent	ò
ó	Lowercase o, acute accent	ó
ô	Lowercase o, circumflex accent	ô
õ	Lowercase o, tilde	õ
ö	Lowercase o, dieresis or umlaut mark	ö
÷	Division sign	÷
ø	Lowercase o, slash	ø
ù	Lowercase u, grave accent	ù
ú	Lowercase u, acute accent	ú
û	Lowercase u, circumflex accent	û
ü	Lowercase u, dieresis or umlaut mark	ü

Table C.2 *Continued*

Character Entity	*Description*	*What's Displayed*
ý	Lowercase y, acute accent	ý
þ	Lowercase thorn, Icelandic	þ
ÿ	Lowercase y, dieresis or umlaut mark	ÿ

*These characters are only displayed on MS-Windows systems under certain circumstances

Table C.3 A Listing of All Windows-Only Special Characters

Numerical Entity	*Character Entity*	*Description*	*What's Displayed*
‚	‚	Rising low left single quote*	'
ƒ	ƒ	Function symbol (function of)*	*f*
„	‚	Rising low left double quote*	"
…	…	Low horizontal ellipsis*	...
†	†	Dagger mark*	†
‡	‡	Double dagger mark *	‡
ˆ	ˆ	Letter modifying circumflex *	^
‰	‰	Per thousand (mile) sign *	‰
Š	Š	Uppercase S caron or hacek *	Š
‹	‹	Left single angle quote mark *	‹
Œ	&Oelig;	Uppercase OE ligature *	Œ
‘	‘	Left single quotation mark *	'
’	’	(High) right single quote mark *	'
“	“	Left double quotation mark *	"
”	”	(High) right double quote mark *	"
•	•	Round filled bullet *	•
–	–	En-dash *	–
—	—	Em-dash *	—
˜	˜	Spacing tilde accent *	~
™	™	Trademark symbol *	™
š	š	Lowercase s caron or hacek *	š
›	›	Right single angle quote mark *	›
œ	œ	Lowercase oe ligature *	œ
Ÿ	Ÿ	Uppercase Y umlaut*	Ÿ

*These characters are only displayed on MS-Windows systems under certain circumstances.

Table C.4 Greek Characters

Character Entity	*Numerical Entity*	*Description*	*What's Displayed*
Α	Α	Greek capital alpha	Α
Β	Β	Greek capital beta	Β
Γ	Γ	Greek capital gamma	Γ
Δ	Δ	Greek capital delta	Δ
Ε	Ε	Greek capital epsilon	Ε
Ζ	Ζ	Greek capital zeta	Ζ
Η	Η	Greek capital eta	Η
Θ	Θ	Greek capital theta	Θ
Ι	Ι	Greek capital iota	Ι
Κ	Κ	Greek capital kappa	Κ
Λ	Λ	Greek capital lambda	Λ
Μ	Μ	Greek capital mu	Μ
Ν	Ν	Greek capital nu	Ν
Ξ	Ξ	Greek capital xi	Ξ
Ο	Ο	Greek capital omicron	Ο
Π	Π	Greek capital pi	Π
Ρ	Ρ	Greek capital rho	Ρ
Σ	Σ	Greek capital sigma	Σ
Τ	Τ	Greek capital tau	τ
Υ	Υ	Greek capital upsilon	υ
Φ	Φ	Greek capital phi	Φ
Χ	Χ	Greek capital chi	Χ
Ψ	Ψ	Greek capital psi	Ψ
Ω	Ω	Greek capital omega	Ω
α	α	Greek small alpha	α
β	β	Greek small beta	β
γ	γ	Greek small gamma	γ
δ	δ	Greek small delta	δ
Ε	ε	Greek small epsilon	ε
ζ	ζ	Greek small zeta	ζ
η	η	Greek small eta	η
θ	θ	Greek small theta	θ
ι	ι	Greek small iota	ι
κ	κ	Greek small kappa	κ
λ	λ	Greek small lambda	λ
μ	μ	Greek small mu	μ
ν	ν	Greek small nu	ν
ξ	ξ	Greek small xi	ξ
ο	ο	Greek small omicron	ο
π	π	Greek small pi	π
ρ	ρ	Greek small rho	ρ
ς	ς	Greek small final sigma	ς

Table C.4 *Continued*

Character Entity	*Numerical Entity*	*Description*	*What's Displayed*
σ	σ	Greek small sigma	σ
τ	τ	Greek small tau	τ
υ	υ	Greek small upsilon	υ
φ	φ	Greek small phi	φ
χ	χ	Greek small chi	χ
ψ	ψ	Greek small psi	ψ
ω	ω	Greek small omega	ω
ϑ	ϑ	Greek small theta symbol	θ
ϒ	ϒ	Greek upsilon with hook symbol	ϒ
ϖ	ϖ	Greek pi symbol	π

Table C.5 General Symbols

Character Entity	*Numerical Entity*	*Description*	*What's Displayed*
•	•	Bullet	•
…	…	Horizontal ellipsis	…
′	′	Prime	′
″	″	Double prime	″
‾	‾	Overline	‾
⁄	⁄	Fraction slash	/

Table C.6 Letterlike Symbols

Character Entity	*Numerical Entity*	*Description*	*What's Displayed*
℘	℘	Script capital P	𝔓
ℑ	ℑ	Blackletter capital I	ℑ
ℜ	ℜ	Blackletter Capital R	ℜ
™	™	Trademark sign	™
ℵ	ℵ	Alef symbol	ℵ

Table C.7 Arrows

Character Entity	*Numerical Entity*	*Description*	*What's Displayed*
←	←	Leftwards arrow	←
↑	↑	Upwards arrow	↑
→	→	Rightwards arrow	→
↓	↓	Downwards arrow	↓
↔	↔	Left-right arrow	↔
↵	↵	Downwards arrow with corner leftwards	↵
⇐	⇐	Leftwards double arrow	⇐
⇑	⇑	Upwards double arrow	⇑
⇒	⇓	Downwards double arrow	⇒
⇓	⇓	Downwards double arrow	⇓
⇔	⇔	Left-right double arrow	⇔

Table C.8 Mathematical Symbols

Character Entity	*Numerical Entity*	*Description*	*What's Displayed*
∀	∀	For all	∀
∂	∂	Partial differential	∂
∃	∃	There exists	#
∅	∅	Empty set	∅
∇	∇	Nabla	ℵ
∈	∈	Element of	∈
∉	∉	Not an element of	∉
∋	∋	Contains as member	∋
∏	∏	n-ary product	∏
∑	∑	n-ary sumation	∑
−	−	Minus sign	−
∗	∗	Asterisk operator	*
√	√	Square root	√
∝	∝	Proportional to	∝
∞	∞	Infinit	∞
∠	∠	Angle	∠
∧	∧	Logical AND	∧
∨	∨	Logical OR	∨

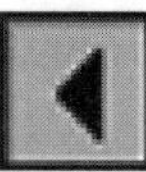

Table C.8 *Continued*

Character Entity	*Numerical Entity*	*Description*	*What's Displayed*
∩	∩	Intersection	∩
∪	∪	Union	∪
∫	∫	Integral	∫
∴	∴	Therefore	∴
∼	∼	Tilde operator	∼
≅	≅	Approximately equal to	≅
≈	≈	Almost equal to	≈
≠	≠	Not equal to	≠
≡	≡	Identical to	≡
≤	≤	Less-than or equal to	≤
≥	≥	Greater-than or equal to	≥
⊂	⊂	Subset of	⊂
⊃	⊃	Superset of	⊃
⊄	⊄	Not a subset of	⊄
⊆	⊆	Subset of or equal to	⊆
⊇	⊇	Superset of or equal to	⊇
⊕	⊕	Circled plus	⊕
⊗	⊗	Circled times	⊗
⊥	⊥	Up tack	⊥
⋅	⋅	Dot operator	⋅

Table C.9 Miscellaneous Technical Symbols

Character Entity	*Numerical Entity*	*Description*	*What's Displayed*
⌈	⌈	Left ceiling	⌈
⌉	⌉	Right ceiling	⌉
⌊	⌊	Left floor	⌊
⌋	⌋	Right floor	⌋
⟨	〈	Left-pointing angle bracket	〈
⟩	〉	Right-pointing angle bracket	〉

Table C.10 Geometric Symbols

Character Entity	*Numerical Entity*	*Description*	*What's Displayed*
◊	◊	Lozenge	◇

Table C.11 Miscellaneous Symbols

Character Entity	*Numerical Entity*	*Description*	*What's Displayed*
♠	♠	Black spade suit	♠
♣	♣	Black club suit	♣
♥	♥	Black heart suit	♥
♦	♦	Black diamond suit	♦

Table C.12 Latin Extended-A

Character Entity	*Numerical Entity*	*Description*	*What's Displayed*
&Oelig;	Œ	Uppercase OE ligature	Œ
œ	œ	Lowercase oe ligature	œ
Š	Š	Uppercase S caron or hacek	Š
š	š	Lowercase s caron or hacek	š
Ÿ	Ÿ	Uppercase Y umlaut	Ÿ

Table C.13 Spacing Modifiers

Character Entity	*Numerical Entity*	*Description*	*What's Displayed*
ˆ	ˆ	Caret (circumflex)	^
˜	˜	Tilde	~

Table C.14 General Punctuation

Character Entity	*Numerical Entity*	*Description*	*What's Displayed*
		En-space	(n-sized space)
		Em-space	(m-sized space)
		Thin space	(Thin space)
‌	‌	Zero-width non-joiner	Nothing is displayed
‍	‍	Zero-width joiner	Nothing is displayed
‎	‎	Left-to-right mark	Nothing is displayed
‏	‏	Right-to-left mark	Nothing is displayed
–	–	En-dash	–
—	—	Em-dash	—
‘	‘	Left single quotation mark	‘
’	’	(High) right single quotation mark	’
‚	‚	Low quote mark	‚
“	“	Left double quotation mark	“
”	”	(High) right double quote mark	”
„	„	Double low quotation mark	„
†	†	Dagger	†
‡	‡	Double dagger	‡
‰	‰	Per thousand (mille) sign	‰
‹	‹	Single left-pointing quotation mark	’
›	›	Single right-pointing quotation mark	‘
€	€	Euro sign	¤

APPENDIX D

Listing of Common Color Values/Colornames

This appendix lists all of the known common color values and colornames that can be used within Web pages. An HTML tag can take any of the rrggbb hexadecimal color values listed here. Many of the colornames are specific to a particular Web browser, and they are listed separately here.

THE SAFE 256-COLOR PALETTE

Most computer displays are capable of displaying only 256 separate colors at a time. Of those colors, only 216 colors can be displayed without being dithered to another color value. The following listing of *safe* color values are those that should

appear uniformly across different computing platforms capable of displaying at least 256 colors.

The safe values are RRGGBB values that contain any combination of the following hexadecimal values:

- 00
- 33
- 66
- 99
- CC
- FF

Note that minor variances in monitor displays make it impossible to achieve perfect color matching across different systems—but Table D.1 Through D.6 will provide a fairly reliable choice of colors that can be used safely when constructing Web pages.

Table D.1 The 36 Hexadecimal Values Beginning with 00

000000	003300	006600	009900	00CC00	00FF00
000033	003333	006633	009933	00CC33	00FF33
000066	003366	006666	009966	00CC66	00FF66
000099	003399	006699	009999	00CC99	00FF99
0000CC	0033CC	0066CC	0099CC	00CCCC	00FFCC
0000FF	0033FF	0066FF	0099FF	00CCFF	00FFFF

Table D.2 The 36 Hexadecimal Values Beginning with 33

330000	333300	336600	33FF00	33CC00	339900
330033	333333	336633	33FF33	33CC33	339933
330066	333366	336666	33FF66	33CC66	339966
330099	333399	336699	33FF99	33CC99	339999
3300CC	3333CC	3366CC	33FFCC	33CCCC	3399CC
3300FF	3333FF	3366FF	33FFFF	33CCFF	3399FF

Table D.3 The 36 Hexadecimal Values Beginning with 66

660000	663300	666600	669900	66CC00	66FF00
660033	663333	666633	669933	66CC33	66FF33
660066	663366	666666	669966	66CC66	66FF66
660099	663399	666699	669999	66CC99	66FF99
6600CC	6633CC	6666CC	6699CC	66CCCC	66FFCC
6600FF	6633FF	6666FF	6699FF	66CCFF	66FFFF

Table D.4 The 36 Hexadecimal Values Beginning with 99

990000	993300	996600	999900	99CC00	99FF00
990033	993333	996633	999933	99CC33	99FF33
990066	993366	996666	999966	99CC66	99FF66
990099	993399	996699	999999	99CC99	99FF99
9900CC	9933CC	9966CC	9999CC	99CCCC	99FFCC
9900FF	9933FF	9966FF	9999FF	99CCFF	99FFFF

Table D.5 The 36 Hexadecimal Values Beginning with CC

CC0000	CC3300	CC6600	CC9900	CCCC00	CCFF00
CC0033	CC3333	CC6633	CC9933	CCCC33	CCFF33
CC0066	CC3366	CC6666	CC9966	CCCC66	CCFF66
CC0099	CC3399	CC6699	CC9999	CCCC99	CCFF99
CC00CC	CC33CC	CC66CC	CC99CC	CCCCCC	CCFFCC
CC00FF	CC33FF	CC66FF	CC99FF	CCCCFF	CCFFFF

Table D.6 The 36 Hexadecimal Values Beginning with "FF"

FF0000	FF3300	FF6600	FF9900	FFCC00	FFFF00
FF0033	FF3333	FF6633	FF9933	FFCC33	FFFF33
FF0066	FF3366	FF6666	FF9966	FFCC66	FFFF66
FF0099	FF3399	FF6699	FF9999	FFCC99	FFFF99
FF00CC	FF33CC	FF66CC	FF99CC	FFCCCC	FFFFCC
FF00FF	FF33FF	FF66FF	FF99FF	FFCCFF	FFFFFF

Table D.7 Hexadecimal Values for Internet Explorer Colornames

Hexadecimal Value	*Colorname*	*Hexadecimal Value*	*Colorname*
00FFFF	Aqua	000080	Navy
000000	Black	808000	Olive
0000FF	Blue	800080	Purple
FF00FF	Fushia	FF0000	Red
808080	Gray	C0C0C0	Silver
008000	Green	008080	Teal
00FF00	Lime	FFFFFF	White
800000	Maroon	FFFF00	Yellow

Internet Explorer Colornames

Table D.7 contains valid colornames and their equivalent hexadecimal values used in Internet Explorer 3.0 and higher. The majority of these colors are safe.

Netscape Navigator 3.0 Colornames

The following is a listing of the 140 colornames that can be used within Netscape Navigator 3.0 and greater. Most (but not all) of these values are described by their hexadecimal equivalents in the following section.

- Aliceblue
- Antiquewhite
- Aqua
- Aquamarine
- Azure
- Beige
- Bisque
- Black
- Blanchedalmond
- Blue
- Blueviolet
- Brown
- Burlywood
- Cadetblue
- Chartreuse
- Chocolate
- Coralcoral
- Cornflowerblue
- Cornsilk
- Crimson
- Cyan
- Darkblue
- Darkcyan
- Darkgoldenrod
- Darkgray
- Darkgreen
- Darkkhaki
- Darkmagenta
- Darkolivegreen
- Darkorange

- Darkorchid
- Darkred
- Darksalmon
- Darkseagreen
- Darkslateblue
- Darkslategray
- Darkturquoise
- Darkviolet
- Deeppink
- Deepskyblue
- Dimgray
- Dodgerblue
- Firebrick
- Floralwhite
- Forestgreen
- Fuchsia
- Gainsboro
- Ghostwhite
- Gold
- Goldenrod
- Gray
- Green
- Greenyellow
- Honeydew
- Hotpink
- **Indianred**
- Indigo
- Ivory
- Khaki
- Lavender
- Lavenderblush
- Lawngreen
- Lemonchiffon
- Lightblue
- Lightcoral
- Lightcyan
- Lightgoldenrodyellow
- Lightgreen
- Lightgrey
- Lightpink
- Lightsalmon
- Lightseagreen
- Lightskyblue
- Lightslategray
- Lightsteelblue
- Lightyellow
- Lime
- Limegreen
- Linen
- Magenta
- Maroon
- Mediumaquamarine
- Mediumblue
- Mediumorchid
- Mediumpurple
- Mediumseagreen
- Mediumslateblue
- Mediumspringgreen
- Mediumturquoise
- Mediumvioletred
- Midnightblue
- Mintcream
- Mistyrose
- Moccasin
- Navajowhite
- Navy
- Oldlace
- Olive
- Olivedrab
- Orange
- Orangered
- Orchid
- Palegoldenrod
- Palegreen
- Paleturquoise
- Palevioletred
- Papayawhip
- Peachpuff
- Peru
- Pink
- Plum
- Powderblue
- Purple
- Red
- Rosybrown

- Royalblue
- Saddlebrown
- Salmon
- Sandybrown
- Seagreen
- Seashell
- Sienna
- Silver
- Skyblue
- Slateblue
- Slategray
- Snow
- Springgreen
- Steelblue
- Tan
- Teal
- Thistle
- Tomato
- Turquoise
- Violet
- Wheatwheat
- Whitewhite
- Whitesmoke
- Yellow

A Spectrum of Hexadecimal Color Values

Table D.8 describes the hexadecimal values matched to the colors they produce. The full range of these colors are available only to those systems capable of displaying a full 16.7 million colors. It is recommended that you test these color values on multiple operating systems before utilizing them.

The table begins with all of the variations of white, then blacks and grays, and then describes the full color spectrum ranging from reds to violets.

Table D.8 Hexadecimal Values and Their Color Equivalents

Hexadecimal Value	*Color*	*Hexadecimal Value*	*Color*
FFFAFA	Snow	37F8DC	Cornsilk
F8F8FF	Ghost White	FFFFF0	Ivory
F5F5F5	White Smoke	FFFACD	Lemon Chiffon
OEDCDC	Gainsboro	FFF5EE	Seashell
FFFAF0	Floral White	F0FFF0	Honeydew
FDF5E6	Old Lace	F5FFFA	Mint Cream
FAF0E6	Linen	F0FFFF	Azure
FAEBD7	Antique White	F0F8FF	Alice Blue
FFEFD5	Papaya Whip	E6E6FA	Lavender
FFEBCD	Blanched Almond	FFF0F5	Lavender Blush
FFE4C4	Bisque	FFE4E1	Misty Rose
FFDAB9	Peach Puff	FFFFFF	White
FFDEAD	Navajo White	000000	Black
FFE4B5	Moccasin	2F4F4F	Dark Slate Gray

Table D.8 *Continued*

Hexadecimal Value	*Color*	*Hexadecimal Value*	*Color*
696969	Dim Gray	00FA9A	Medium Spring Green
708090	Slate Gray	ADFF2F	Green Yellow
778899	Light Slate Gray	32CD32	Lime Green
BEBEBE	Gray	9ACD32	Yellow Green
D3D3D3	Light Gray	228B22	Forest Green
191970	Midnight Blue	6B8E23	Olive Drab
000080	Navy Blue	BDB76B	Dark Khaki
6495ED	Cornflower Blue	F0E68C	Khaki
483D8B	Dark Slate Blue	EEE8AA	Pale Goldenrod
6A5ACD	Slate Blue	FAFAD2	Light Goldenrod Yellow
7B68EE	Medium Slate Blue	FFFFE0	Light Yellow
8470FF	Light Slate Blue	FFFF00	Yellow
0000CD	Medium Blue	FFD700	Gold
4169E1	Royal Blue	EEDD82	Light Goldenrod
0000FF	Blue	DAA520	Goldenrod
1E90FF	Dodger Blue	B8860B	Dark Goldenrod
0013FF	Deep Sky Blue	BC8F8F	Rosy Brown
87CEEB	Sky Blue	CD5C5C	Indian Red
87CEFA	Light Sky Blue	8B4513	Saddle Brown
4682B4	Steel Blue	A0522D	Sienna
B0C4DE	Light Steel Blue	CD853F	Peru
ADD8E6	Light Blue	DEB887	Burlywood
B0E0E6	Powder Blue	F5F5DC	Beige
AFEEEE	Pale Turquoise	F5DEB3	Wheat
00CED1	Dark Turquoise	F4A460	Sandy Brown
48D1CC	Medium Turquoise	D2B48C	Tan
40E0D0	Turquoise	D2691E	Chocolate
00FFFF	Cyan	B22222	Firebrick
E0FFFF	Light Cyan	A52A2A	Brown
5F9EA0	Cadet Blue	E9967A	Dark Salmon
66CDAA	Medium Aquamarine	FA8072	Salmon
7FFFD4	Aquamarine	FFA07A	Light Salmon
006400	Dark Green	FFA500	Orange
556B2F	Dark Olive Green	FF8C00	Dark Orange
8FBC8F	Dark Sea Green	FF7F50	Coral
2E8B57	Sea Green	F08080	Light Coral
3CB371	Medium Sea Green	FF6347	Tomato
20B2AA	Light Sea Green	FF4500	Orange Red
98FB98	Pale Green	FF0000	Red
00FF7F	Spring Green	FF69B4	Hot Pink
7CFC00	Lawn Green	FF0E93	Deep Pink
00FF00	Green	FFC0CB	Pink
7FFF00	Chartreuse	FFB6C1	Light Pink

Table D.8 *Continued*

Hexadecimal Value	*Color*	*Hexadecimal Value*	*Color*
DB7093	Pale Violet Red	BA55D3	Medium Orchid
B03060	Maroon	15332CC	Dark Orchid
C71585	Medium Violet Red	9400D3	Dark Violet
D02090	Violet Red	8A2BE2	Blue Violet
FF00FF	Magenta	A020F0	Purple
EE82EE	Violet	9370DB	Medium Purple
DDA0DD	Plum	D8BFD8	Thistle
DA70D6	Orchid		

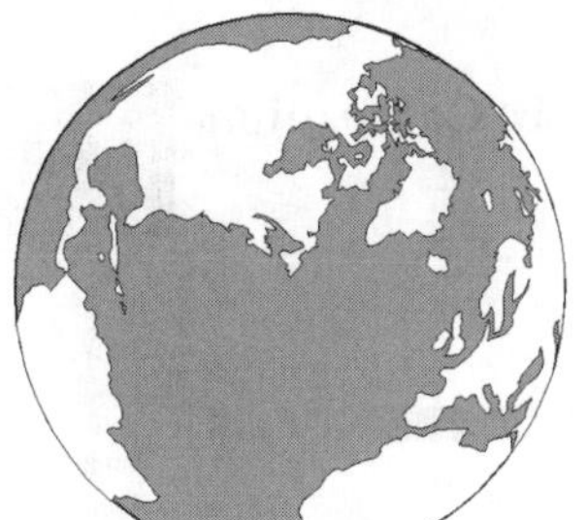

APPENDIX E

Top Level Domains

Top level domain names serve to identify types of organizations on the Internet. The InterNIC organization traditionally has administered the most common top level domain names, and individual countries have administered their own domains.

The following table describe the organization type for the top level domain names in use at the time of writing.

The following is a listing of all country-level domain names.

Table E.1 InterNIC Top Level Domains

.com	Commercial organization
.net	Network (Reserved for major nodes of the Internet)
.org	Nonprofit organization
.gov	Government department
.edu	Education institution

Table E.2 Country Codes for Top Level Domains

Afghanistan	.af	Brunei Darussalam	.bn
Albania	.al	Bulgaria	.bg
Algeria	.dz	Burkina Faso	.bf
American Samoa	.as	Burundi	.bi
Andorra	.ad	Cambodia	.kh
Angola	.ao	Cameroon	.cm
Anguilla	.ai	Canada	.ca
Antarctica	.aq	Cape Verde	.cv
Antigua and Barbuda	.ag	Cayman Islands	.ky
Argentina	.ar	Central African Republic	.cf
Armenia	.am	Chad	.td
Aruba	.aw	Chile	.cl
Australia	.au	China	.cn
Austria	.at	Christmas Island	.cx
Azerbaijan	.az	Cocos (Keeling) Islands	.cc
Bahamas	.bs	Colombia	.co
Bahrain	.bh	Comoros	.km
Bangladesh	.bd	Congo	.cg
Barbados	.bb	Cook Islands	.ck
Belarus	.by	Costa Rica	.cr
Belgium	.be	Cote D'Ivoire	.ci
Belize	.bz	Croatia (Local Name: Hrvatska)	.hr
Benin	.bj	Cuba	.cu
Bermuda	.bm	Cyprus	.cy
Bhutan	.bt	Czech Republic	.cz
Bolivia	.bo	Denmark	.dk
Bosnia and Herzegowina	.ba	Djibouti	.dj
Botswana	.bw	Dominica	.dm
Bouvet Island	.bv	Dominican Republic	.do
Brazil	.br	East Timor	.tp
British Indian Ocean Territory	.io	Ecuador	.ec
		Egypt	.eg

Table E.2 *Continued*

El Salvador	.sv	Kazakhstan	.kz
Equatorial Guinea	.gq	Kenya	.ke
Eritrea	.er	Kiribati	.ki
Estonia	.ee	Korea, Democratic People's Republic of	.kp
Ethiopia	.et	Korea, Republic of	.kr
Falkland Islands (Malvinas)	.fk	Kuwait	.kw
Faroe Islands	.fo	Kyrgyzstan	.kg
Fiji	.fj	Lao People's Democratic Republic	.la
Finland	.fi	Latvia	.lv
France	.fr	Lebanon	.lb
France, Metropolitan	.fx	Lesotho	.ls
French Guiana	.gf	Liberia	.lr
French Polynesia	.pf	Libyan Arab Jamahiriya	.ly
French Southern Territories	.tf	Liechtenstein	.li
Gabon	.ga	Lithuania	.lt
Gambia	.gm	Luxembourg	.lu
Georgia	.ge	Macau	.mo
Germany	.de	Macedonia, the former Yugoslav Republic of	.mk
Ghana	.gh	Madagascar	.mg
Gibraltar	.gi	Malawi	.mw
Greece	.gr	Malaysia	.my
Greenland	.gl	Maldives	.mv
Grenada	.gd	Mali	.ml
Guadeloupe	.gp	Malta	.mt
Guam	.gu	Marshall Islands	.mh
Guatemala	.gt	Martinique	.mq
Guinea	.gn	Mauritania	.mr
Guinea-Bissau	.gw	Mauritius	.mu
Guyana	.gy	Mayotte	.yt
Haiti	.ht	Mexico	.mx
Heard and McDonald Islands	.hm	Micronesia, Federated States of	.fm
Holy See (Vatican City State)	.va	Moldova, Republic of	.md
Honduras	.hn	Monaco	.mc
Hong Kong	.hk	Mongolia	.mn
Hungary	.hu	Montserrat	.ms
Iceland	.is	Morocco	.ma
India	.in	Mozambique	.mz
Indonesia	.id	Myanmar	.mm
Iran (Islamic Republic Of)	.ir	Namibia	.na
Iraq	.iq	Nauru	.nr
Ireland	.ie	Nepal	.np
Israel	.il	Netherlands	.nl
Italy	.it	Netherlands Antilles	.an
Jamaica	.jm	New Caledonia	.nc
Japan	.jp		
Jordan	.jo		

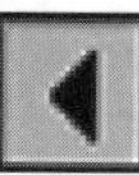

Table E.2 *Continued*

New Zealand	.nz	Sri Lanka	.lk
Nicaragua	.ni	St. Helena	.sh
Niger	.ne	St. Pierre and Miquelon	.pm
Nigeria	.ng	Sudan	.sd
Niue	.nu	Suriname	.sr
Norfolk Island	.nf	Svalbard and Jan Mayen Islands	.sj
Northern Mariana Islands	.mp	Swaziland	.sz
Norway	.no	Sweden	.se
Oman	.om	Switzerland	.ch
Pakistan	.pk	Syrian Arab Republic	.sy
Palau	.pw	Taiwan, Province Of China	.tw
Panama	.pa	Tajikistan	.tj
Papua New Guinea	.pg	Tanzania, United Republic of	.tz
Paraguay	.py	Thailand	.th
Peru	.pe	Togo	.tg
Philippines	.ph	Tokelau	.tk
Pitcairn	.pn	Tonga	.to
Poland	.pl	Trinidad and Tobago	.tt
Portugal	.pt	Tunisia	.tn
Puerto Rico	.pr	Turkey	.tr
Qatar	.qa	Turkmenistan	.tm
Reunion	.re	Turks and Caicos Islands	.tc
Romania	.ro	Tuvalu	.tv
Russian Federation	.ru	Uganda	.ug
Rwanda	.rw	Ukraine	.ua
Saint Kitts and Nevis	.kn	United Arab Emirates	.ae
Saint Lucia	.lc	United Kingdom	.gb
Saint Vincent and the Grenadines	.vc	United States	.us
Samoa	.ws	United States Minor Outlying Islands	.um
San Marino	.sm	Uruguay	.uy
Sao Tome and Principe	.st	Uzbekistan	.uz
Saudi Arabia	.sa	Vanuatu	.vu
Senegal	.sn	Venezuela	.ve
Seychelles	.sc	Viet Nam	.vn
Sierra Leone	.sl	Virgin Islands (British)	.vg
Singapore	.sg	Virgin Islands (U.S.)	.vi
Slovakia (Slovak Republic)	.sk	Wallis and Futuna Islands	.wf
Slovenia	.si	Western Sahara	.eh
Solomon Islands	.sb	Yemen	.ye
Somalia	.so	Yugoslavia	.yu
South Africa	.za	Zaire	.zr
South Georgia and the South Sandwich Islands	.gs	Zambia	.zm
Spain	.es	Zimbabwe	.zw

APPENDIX F

Internet Protocols

The following table lists Internet protocols, their default port numbers, and the hypertext reference used when creating hypertext links.

Table F.1 Internet Protocols

Protocol	*Port*	*Example HREF*
FTP	20	ftp://ftpsite.site.com
Gopher	70	gopher://gophersite.site.com
HTTP (web)	80	http://website.site.com
WAIS (Z39.50)	210	wais://waissite.site.com
Telnet	23	telnet://computer.site.com
Email	N/A	mailto:kim@exn.net

INDEX

A

B

C

D

E

F

G

H

I

J

K

L

M

N

O

P

Q

R

S

T

U

V

W

X

Y